# PERSONAL INJURY AND CLINICAL NEGLIGENCE LITIGATION

Julie Mardell and Kate Serfozo

CLP

Published by

College of Law Publishing,
Braboeuf Manor, Portsmouth Road, St Catherines, Guildford GU3 1HA



British Library Cataloguing-in-Publication Data

A catalogue record for this book is available from the British Library.

ISBN 978 1 905391 90 5

Typeset by Style Photosetting Ltd, Mayfield, East Sussex

Printed in Great Britain by Ashford Colour Press Ltd, Gosport, Hampshire

# Preface

The purpose of this book is to provide an introduction to the large and complex area of personal injury and clinical negligence litigation. It does not set out to cover the subject fully, nor does it purport to include all recent developments in this area of law.

This text has been written as an integrated element of the Legal Practice Course elective 'Personal Injury and Clinical Negligence Litigation', and its aim is to provide a framework upon which the course is built. Students are expected to carry out their own research into some aspects of the course and will receive further tuition in others.

We are grateful to all of our colleagues who have contributed to the book, in particular David Dow and Jeff Lill who wrote and updated previous editions. In addition, we would like to thank Iain Moore at Beachcroft LLP for his assistance.

The Civil Procedure Rules are amended from time to time and it is important that readers make reference to the most up-to-date provisions which can be found on the Ministry of Justice website. This is a fast-changing area of law, and practitioners must update themselves continually.

In the interests of brevity, we have used the masculine pronoun throughout to include the feminine.

The law is generally stated as at 1 September 2009.

JULIE MARDELL and KATE SERFOZO

# PERSONAL INJURY AND CLINICAL NEGLIGENCE LITIGATION

# Contents

# Table of Cases

## A



## B



## C

## D



## E



## F

## L



## M



## N



## O



## P

## Q



## R

## Y

# Table of Statutes

**International legislation**

# Table of Secondary Legislation

**Codes and Agreements**



**EC secondary legislation**

# List of Abbreviations

See **Chapter 2** for commonly used medical abbreviations.

| | |
|---|---|
| ABWOR | assistance by way of representation |
| ACOPs | Approved Codes of Practice |
| ADR | alternative dispute resolution |
| ALP | Accident Line Protect |
| APIL | Association of Personal Injury Lawyers |
| AEI | after the event insurance |
| AvMA | Action against Medical Accidents |
| BEI | before the event insurance |
| CCFA | collective conditional fee agreements |
| CDM 2007 | Construction (Design and Management) Regulations 2007 |
| CFA | conditional fee agreement |
| CHAI | Commission for Healthcare Audit and Inspection |
| CICA | Criminal Injuries Compensation Authority |
| CLS | Community Legal Service |
| CNST | Clinical Negligence Scheme for Trusts |
| CPR 1998 | Civil Procedure Rules 1998 |
| CPS | Crown Prosecution Service |
| CRU | Compensation Recovery Unit |
| CTG | cardiotachograph |
| DPA 1998 | Data Protection Act 1998 |
| DWP | Department for Work and Pensions |
| DSE | display screen equipment |
| ECG | electrocardiogram |
| FAA 1976 | Fatal Accidents Act 1976 |
| FOIL | Forum of Insurance Lawyers |
| GLO | group litigation order |
| GMC | General Medical Council |
| HAVS | hand/arm vibration syndrome |
| HSE | Health and Safety Executive |
| HSOA 2008 | Health and Safety Offences Act 2008 |
| HSWA 1974 | Health and Safety at Work etc Act 1974 |
| ICTA 1988 | Income and Corporation Taxes Act 1988 |
| IRP | independent review panel |
| LA 1980 | Limitation Act 1980 |
| LAA | legal advice and assistance |
| LEI | legal expenses insurance |
| LSC | Legal Services Commission |
| MIB | Motor Insurers' Bureau |
| MID | Motor Insurance Database |
| MPA | multi-party action |
| NHS | National Health Service |
| NHSLA | NHS Litigation Authority |
| NMC | Nursing and Midwifery Council |
| OLA 1957 | Occupiers' Liability Act 1957 |
| PALS | Patient Advice and Liaison Service |
| PAR | police accident report |
| PD | Practice Direction |
| PPE | personal protective equipment |

| | |
|---|---|
| PTSD | post-traumatic stress disorder |
| RIDDOR 1995 | Reporting of Injuries, Diseases and Dangerous Occurrences Regulations 1995 |
| RTA 1988 | Road Traffic Act 1988 |
| SSP | statutory sick pay |
| VWF | vibration white finger |
| WRULD | work-related upper limb disorder |

# Chapter 1

# Introduction to the Work of a Personal Injury and Clinical Negligence Solicitor



## 1.1 Introduction

The aim of this text is to provide an introduction to personal injury and clinical negligence litigation. It is assumed, however, that the basic civil litigation procedure has been studied before. Reference to the Legal Practice Guide, ***Civil Litigation*** and the Civil Procedure Rules 1998 (CPR 1998) may be necessary for those unfamiliar with the essential elements of High Court and county court procedure.

The terms 'personal injury litigation' and 'clinical negligence litigation' are widely used to describe claims for compensation for injuries which a client has suffered. This text will not deal with every type of claim that is encountered in practice, but it should serve as a basic introduction to a fascinating and rapidly developing area of law.

In practice, many personal injury claims will be based on either public liability, where the injury is sustained on property which is open to the public, or product liability, where the injury is caused by products made available to the public. However, in this text, the focus will be on the following:

(a) Road traffic accident and other highway claims. These are usually the most straightforward type of personal injury claim. See **Chapter 3**.

(b) Employers' liability claims. This term is used for personal injury claims where the claimant was injured in the course of his employment and his employer is the defendant. Common examples of this type of personal injury claim arise where workers slip on the factory floor, fall from ladders or are caught in moving machinery. More complex cases arise where workers suffer a disease or injury which manifests itself many years after their exposure to dust, fibres, gases, fumes or noxious substances within the workplace. See **Chapter 4**.

(c) Clinical negligence claims, which arise as a result of the negligence of doctors or other medical professionals, such as nurses, physiotherapists and dentists, or of institutional health providers, such as NHS Trusts or private hospitals. See **Chapter 5**.

(d) Claims for psychiatric injury. These may arise in the context of any of the above types of claim but the law in relation to claims for nervous shock and occupational stress is complex enough to warrant separate treatment in this text. See **Chapter 6**.

While the basic litigation procedures for personal injury and clinical negligence claims and the skills required of the solicitor are similar, there are differences, some of which are significant. Where the procedure for a clinical negligence claim differs notably from that of a personal injury claim, specific reference is made in the text.

Where a fatality arises from an accident in one of the above areas, special considerations arise. These are discussed in **Chapter 17**.

### 1.1.1 Causes of action

In most personal injury and clinical negligence cases, the claim is based on negligence. However, in employers' liability claims and in claims against the highways authority, there may also be a claim arising from breaches of statutory duties. Some of the relevant statutory duties are explored in the text.

In clinical negligence claims against private hospitals and healthcare professionals who have provided advice and treatment on a private basis, there may be a claim in breach of contract. These claims lay beyond the scope of this book.

### 1.1.2 The CPR and the pre-action protocols

In accordance with the overriding objective set out in r 1 of the CPR 1998, personal injury and clinical negligence solicitors and their clients are required to have regard to the costs involved in pursuing the case, and to deal with the matter expeditiously and proportionately. This philosophy is to be adopted from the early days of the dispute, and reference needs to be made to the relevant pre-action protocol, which sets out the steps to be taken by the parties *prior* to the issue of proceedings. The full text of each of the three protocols relevant to personal injury and clinical negligence claims is set out in **Appendices 2 to 4**. The Practice Direction Pre-action Conduct should also be taken into account

## 1.2 Personal injury claims

### 1.2.1 The claimant's perspective

The aim of the claimant's personal injury solicitor is to prove that the defendant was responsible for the client's injuries and to obtain the appropriate amount of compensation. Therefore, there are two essential elements to a personal injury claim: liability and quantum. This may sound obvious, but it is important that these two elements are paramount in the solicitor's mind throughout the case.

Personal injury claims can take time to progress. At the initial interview, it should be explained to the client how it is anticipated the case will proceed and a realistic timescale should be given (although this can be difficult) as to when the matter might be settled or reach trial. The client should be informed of the basic requirements of the relevant pre-action protocol and the time limits imposed on each side. It is important that the client is kept informed as the matter proceeds. Regular letters should be sent, updating the client on the current position. If a proactive approach is taken, this will avoid difficulties in the future.

#### 1.2.1.1 Liability

It is for the claimant to prove his case; the onus will therefore be on the client to persuade the court that the defendant was in breach of a statutory or common law duty owed to the client. The claimant has to prove, on a balance of probabilities, that:

(a) the defendant owed him a duty of care and/or there was a relevant statutory duty;

(b) the defendant was in breach of that duty;

(c) the breach caused injury and consequential losses which were reasonably foreseeable.

This is further explored in the context of the various types of personal injury claim dealt with in this book in **Chapters 3, 4 and 6**.

#### 1.2.1.2 Quantum

The claimant's solicitor should have as his aim the maximisation of damages for his client, and he must take all legitimate steps to achieve that aim. The assessment of damages is dealt with in **Chapter 15** and, where there has been a fatality, in **Chapter 18**. Most solicitors working in this area acknowledge that a weariness on the part of the victim himself can set in if months pass and the claimant perceives that little has been done, or due to anxiety at having to attend trial. This can result in the client accepting inappropriately low offers rather than instructing the solicitor to progress the matter to trial. This should be acknowledged as a factor to be dealt with by the solicitor, and the client's concerns should be anticipated.

Medical evidence is required by the court to prove the injuries suffered by the client. Instructing a doctor may appear to be a simple task, but the choice of the appropriate doctor is significant as the value of the client's injuries will be based on the medical evidence, including the reports of the medical experts. The instruction of experts is dealt with in **Chapter 11** and a list of important medical specialities is contained in **Chapter 2**.

### 1.2.2 The defendant's perspective

In many cases the defendant's personal injury solicitor will be instructed only when proceedings have been issued against the defendant. At all times prior to this, where the defendant is insured, the claimant's solicitor will correspond with the defendant's insurance company. Where the insurance company believes that liability will be established, and in some low value cases where it is not economically viable to defend the claim, it will attempt to reach a settlement. The vast majority of claims are settled before trial and a substantial number of these are settled before proceedings are issued.

Many insurance companies require the insured to sign a letter of authority allowing them to act on the insured's behalf and to dispose of the case in any way that the defendant's solicitor sees fit. This is often a formality, as the terms of the insurance policy will allow the insurance company and its solicitor to have control of the case. The role of insurers is explored further at **3.3**.

## 1.3 Clinical negligence claims

### 1.3.1 The claimant's perspective

The essential aims in a clinical negligence claim are the same as in a personal injury claim, namely, to establish liability and maximise damages. However, these are frequently not the only aims and considerations. The client's trust in a respected profession has been lost, and the client will often lack knowledge and understanding as to what has happened to him. It must be explained to the client that he has to prove his claim, if he is to establish liability. One of the first distinctions which has to be made between personal injury and clinical negligence cases is that the issue of liability is normally far more complicated in the latter, and there is a greater chance that the claimant's claim will fail at trial (see **Chapter 5**). However, the law relating to the quantum of damages is the same in both personal injury and clinical negligence cases.

The costs involved in a clinical negligence case are usually higher than those incurred in a personal injury case. The clinical negligence pre-action protocol will have to be complied with, and the initial investigations prior to commencing the claim will involve the solicitor taking instructions, obtaining the client's medical notes, and then instructing an expert to assess the notes and evidence available. However, it is only then that any preliminary view on liability can be obtained. Unlike a personal injury case, the victim's clinical negligence solicitor will never be able to give a view on liability at the first interview. It will only be when the notes and an expert's view are obtained that any advice on liability can be given to the client.

A common concern expressed by clients is how they will continue to be treated by the doctor/ healthcare professional if there is an ongoing 'doctor/patient' relationship, and advice and support in relation to this may be required. In addition, the solicitor will need to establish whether the client's sole concern is to pursue a damages claim or if he has other objectives, for example to complain to the relevant NHS Trust, to report the alleged misconduct of a healthcare professional to the appropriate regulatory body and to prevent a similar event occurring in the future. In some cases, for example the death of a child, the client may not wish to pursue a claim at all but the other options may be hugely important to him. The options available to the client in such circumstances are set out in **Chapter 5**.

### 1.3.2 The defendant's perspective

The defendant's clinical negligence solicitor will usually be from a firm instructed by the defendant's indemnity insurers. In the case of most NHS bodies, the NHS Litigation Authority (NHSLA) will choose a solicitor from its panel. The defendant's solicitor will have the same basic aims as those of the defendant's personal injury solicitor. If liability can be refuted then the case will be vigorously defended; if liability is established, the case will be settled. However, there are also special factors that the defendant's clinical negligence solicitor must consider. The principal factor is that the defendant is a professional person and, while damages will not be paid by him personally, his reputation, and possibly that of his employer in the case of the NHS, will be brought into question by any admission or finding of negligence on his part. This is one of the reasons why more clinical negligence claims than personal injury claims proceed to trial (although, according to the NHSLA's statistics, fewer than 2% of the claims they deal with actually result in a trial). Establishing liability in a clinical negligence case is not easy. While the patient may complain that the treatment was unsuccessful, it does not follow that the doctor was negligent, and the arguments available to the defendant's solicitor to refute negligence are wider and more complicated than in a personal injury case.

## 1.4 Fraudulent claims

Only the most naive of those acting on behalf of claimants would believe everything every client tells them to be the truth, the whole truth and nothing but the truth. The accounts of even the most honest of people will be tainted by one or more of the following: anger, grief, confusion, a misunderstanding, a sense of indignation, a distorted perspective, an unconscious tendency to exaggerate and, of course, memory loss. Solicitors should always test the evidence of their clients and witnesses, not least of all because a story which does not stack up in the opinion of the solicitor, is likely to be found wanting should the matter be tried in court.

Solicitors acting for claimants may also encounter individuals whose aim is to make an entirely fraudulent claim, or whose conscious exaggeration of their injuries is such as to amount to fraud. Although, as a matter of professional conduct, it is irrelevant whether a solicitor believes his client's version of events to be true or not, where a solicitor *knows* his client is lying, he should take care not to deceive or mislead the court (Solicitors' Code of Conduct 2007, Rule 11.01). Moreover, in circumstances where a reasonably competent lawyer would have realised that the claim was fraudulent and had no reasonable prospect of success, a wasted costs order may be made against the firm (see *Afzal v Chubb Guarding Services Ltd* [2002] EWHC 822, where solicitors were not liable to pay wasted costs).

The Court of Appeal has held that there is no rule of law which allows the court to deprive a claimant of damages to which he is entitled, either where he fraudulently attempted to obtain more than his entitlement or where he lied to support the claim of another claimant (see *Shah v Ul-Haq and Others* [2009] EWCA Civ 542). However, such claimants may be punished in costs (see *Booth v Britannia Hotels Ltd* [2002] EWCA Civ 529) and/or be prosecuted for perjury or deception offences.

Defendants, and particularly their insurers, are becoming increasingly wise to such matters, and they are showing a greater inclination to investigate potentially fraudulent claims thoroughly, including using covert surveillance, and to challenge them in court. An allegation of fraud must be pleaded, the burden of proof resting with the defendant.

## 1.5 Conclusion

Personal injury and clinical negligence litigation is a diverse and expanding area. At its least complex, it may involve a claim for compensation for minor injuries suffered as a result of a road traffic accident, or, at the other extreme, it may involve representing a child who is severely disabled, allegedly as a result of being starved of oxygen at birth.

This text aims to provide an introduction to personal injury and clinical negligence litigation, but reference should also be made to practitioners' works and original sources. Where appropriate, reference must be made to the CPR 1998 and pre-action protocols.

## 1.6 Overviews of personal injury and clinical negligence claims

### 1.6.1 Main steps in typical personal injury claim

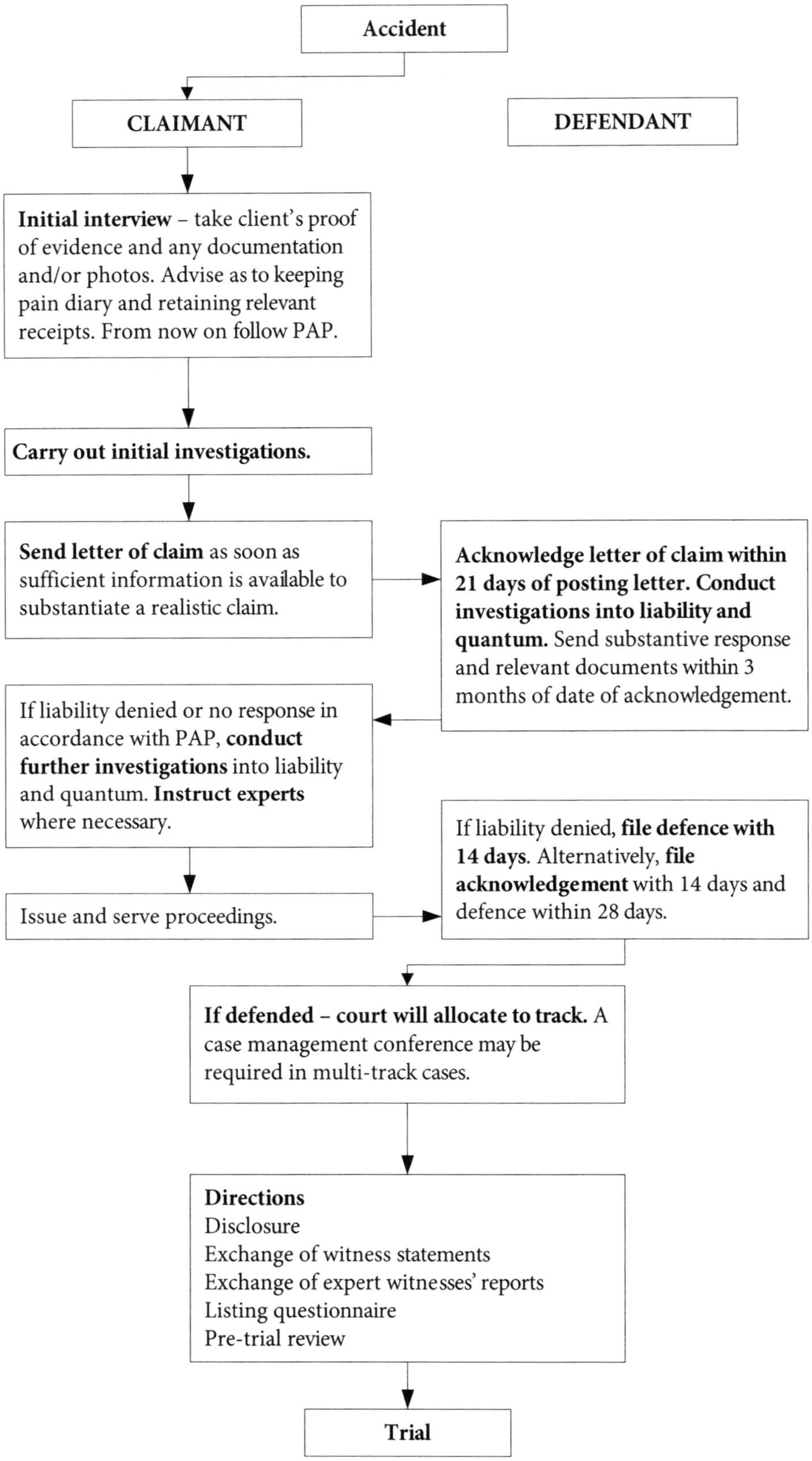

### 1.6.2 Main steps in typical clinical negligence claim against an NHS Trust

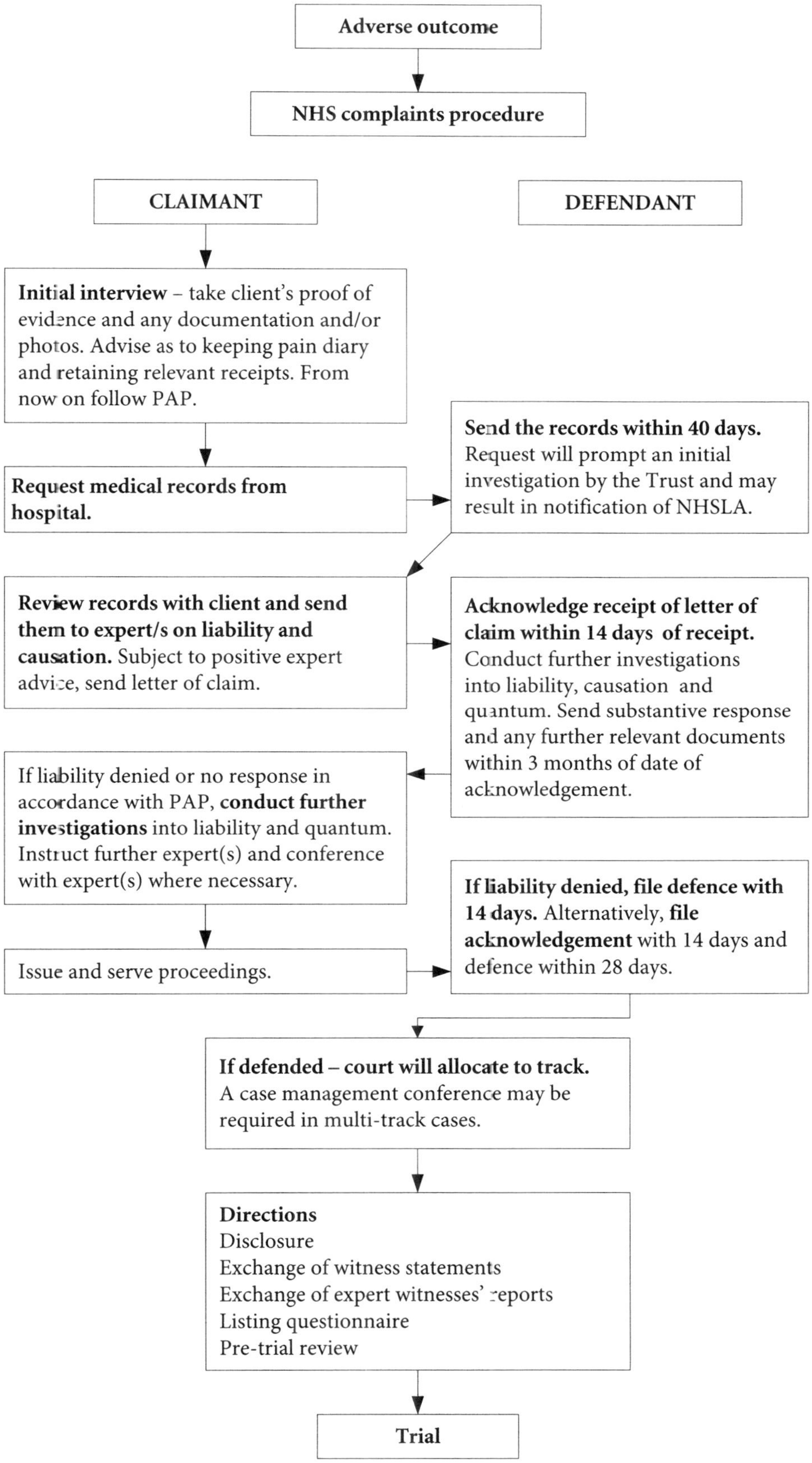

# Chapter 2

# Personal Injury and Clinical Negligence Terminology



## 2.1 Introduction

A trainee solicitor who enters the personal injury/clinical negligence department of a legal firm has to cope not only with the pressures of being able to understand fully and advise accurately on the law, but also with a barrage of unfamiliar medical terms. If a trainee is faced on his first day with his colleagues referring to claims dealing with work-related upper limb disorders (WRULD), vibration white finger (VWF), post-traumatic stress disorder (PTSD), etc, and he is unfamiliar with the terminology, he will obviously be at a disadvantage.

There can be no doubt that proficient solicitors who practise in this area have extensive medical knowledge and a detailed understanding of the terms used. This knowledge enables them to comprehend fully clients' complaints, experts' reports and medical notes, and also enables them to explain matters thoroughly to clients. For example, upon receipt of a medical report obtained following a simple road traffic accident, the solicitor must read the report carefully and then send it to the client. If the client subsequently contacts his solicitor stating that he does not understand the terms used in the medical report, it is not acceptable for the solicitor to say, 'Neither do I'!

In addition, it is important for the trainee solicitor to have some knowledge of the areas of medical specialisation, so that appropriate experts can be instructed.

The purpose of this chapter is to assist in the understanding of the terms and abbreviations commonly found in personal injury/clinical negligence work, and of the main areas of specialisation. It should be noted, however, that a medical dictionary is an essential requirement for the personal injury solicitor, and more detailed medical texts may also be of use.

## 2.2 Common injuries, conditions and medical terms

### 2.2.1 Orthopaedic injuries

Orthopaedic (bone) injuries are the most common injuries encountered in a personal injury claim. They are normally incurred as a result of falling, or from being involved in a road traffic accident.

The most common terms found in orthopaedic medical reports are as follows:

(a) *Arthrodesis* – means a joint that has been fused, either because of pre-existing joint disease or because of injury as a result of trauma to the joint.

(b) *Arthroplasty* – means that the joint has been reconstructed, often by the use of a joint implant to replace one or more parts of the components of a joint.

(c) *Contusion* – means an injury to the skin and the deeper tissues in the surrounding area which is accompanied by bleeding from damaged blood vessels. The skin, however, is not broken. The simplest form of contusion is a bruise, developing through to a contusion accompanied by a large haematoma, which is a collection of blood under the surface of the skin.

(d) *Dislocation* – means an injury which results in the bones of a joint being out of alignment or connection with one another. There is usually associated ligament and soft tissue damage.

(e) *Fracture* – means a break in the continuity of a bone.

(f) *Sprain* – means an injury in the region of a joint with associated ligament and soft tissue damage.

(g) *Subluxation* – a joint which has subluxed has undergone a partial dislocation, and subluxation is a term which is sometimes used to describe a sprain.

A client who has an orthopaedic injury may also undergo *traction*, ie a system of weights and pulleys is used to pull muscle groups, so as to reduce/immobilise fractures and put the bones back into alignment.

In general, the most common fractures occur to:

(a) *The clavicle (collar bone)* – these fractures are especially common in children and young adults, and are almost always due to falls or direct trauma to the point of the shoulder. Treatment involves wearing a sling until the pain has subsided. Surgical intervention is very rarely required and is usually indicated only if there is a risk to nearby nerves or blood vessels.

(b) *The surgical neck of the humerus (the long bone stretching from the shoulder to the elbow)* – these fractures are usually treated with a sling; but if badly displaced, are surgically treated and fixed with metal pins.

(c) *The shaft of the humerus* – these fractures can occur at any point along the humerus and are usually treated by immobilising the fracture in a plaster of Paris cast for six to eight weeks.

(d) *The radius (the bone running from the elbow to the base of the thumb)* – there are many different types of radial fracture but the most common is the Colles fracture.

(e) *The femur (the thigh bone)* – these fractures can occur at any point along the length of the femur. The most common sites are the neck or the shaft of the femur. Treatment tends to be surgical. Clients with fractures of the shaft of the femur will be placed in a Thomas splint, which immobilises the fracture.

(f) *The tibia and fibula* – these two bones make up the part of the leg from beneath the knee to the ankle. Fracture of these two bones can result from direct or indirect trauma.

(g) *The pelvis* – a number of bones which together form a ring-like structure at the base of the spine. The pelvis contains the vertebrae of the sacral spine and the hip joints, and fractures can occur at any point. Fractures to the pelvis are of two main types: first, isolated fractures of one of the bones which make up the pelvis; and, secondly, double fractures of the bones which make up the pelvic rim.

### 2.2.2 Hand injuries

In interpreting medical reports regarding hand injuries, a basic understanding of the anatomical position of the hand is required.

The functional parts of the hand are the wrist and the fingers. If the wrist is flexed, the hand is brought forward; if the hand is positioned as if to push someone away, it is said to be extended. The wrist is described as being 'pronated' if the palm of the hand is pointing towards the floor, and is described as being 'supinated' if the hand is positioned to receive something.

If the hand is made into a fist, the fingers are described as flexed; if the hand is opened out as if to receive something, the fingers are described as extended.

The fingers are described as the distal half of the hand, and are made up of three joints. Working from the palm of the hand out towards the end of the fingers, the three joints are the metacarpo-phalangeal joint (the knuckles), the proximal interphalangeal joint, and the distal interphalangeal joint, which is the joint nearest to the finger nails. The thumb has the same number of joints, but appears shorter because it attaches to the hand lower down; 70% of the function of the hand is provided by the thumb.

### 2.2.3 Head injuries

The following terms are used in relation to head injuries:

(a) *aphasia* – the loss of power of speech;

(b) *anosmia* – the loss of the sense of smell;

(c) *cerebral oedema* – a swelling of the brain;

(d) *closed head injury* – a head injury in which there is no open skull fracture;

(e) *concussion* – instantaneous loss of consciousness due to a blow on the head;

(f) *diffuse axonal injury* – a brain injury which involves shearing of the brain tissue itself;

(g) *dysphasia* – a difficulty in understanding language and in self-expression;

(h) *extradural haematoma* – a blood clot which lies immediately above the brain and its protective membranes and below the surface of the skull;

(i) *Glasgow Coma Scale* – a system of assessing neurological function;

(j) *hydrocephalus* – a condition which arises due to an increase in the amount of cerebro-spinal fluid within the cranial cavity;

(k) *hemiplegia* – paralysis of one side of the body;

(l) *intracerebral* – within the substance of the brain itself;

(m) *monoplegia* – a paralysis of one limb;

(n) *open head injury* – a head injury with an associated depressed skull fracture;

(o) *subdural haematoma* – a blood clot lying in-between the brain and its protective membranes.

### 2.2.4 Injuries to the skin

The following terms are used to describe injuries to the skin:

(a) *abrasion* – occurs when the surface of the skin is rubbed off due to a mechanical injury;

(b) *hypertrophy* – the overgranulation of scar tissue which can lead to disfigurement;

(c) *laceration* – a wound to the skin which has jagged, irregular edges.

### 2.2.5 Whiplash injuries

The term 'whiplash injury' is not a medical term at all, but it is one which is used by lawyers and the general public to describe a whole range of symptoms suffered, in the main, by someone whose head is thrown forward in a sudden forceful jerk – literally whipped forward – and back. Medical practitioners may prefer to use the terms 'cervical sprain' or 'hyperextension injuries of the neck'. This type of injury is commonly associated with road traffic accidents, but it can also result from other accidents (such as tripping and slipping), sporting activities (such as biking and diving), and assaults.

The cause of the injuries associated with whiplash is the stretching and straining of the soft tissues – the tendons, ligaments and muscles – supporting the cervical spine (ie in the neck region). Symptoms can be of widely varying severity, and may include pain and stiffness in the neck, backache, tingling and numbness in the arms and possibly in the hands, headaches, dizziness, ringing in the ears, tiredness, inability to concentrate, memory loss, blurred vision, nausea and reduced libido. Typically, symptoms will not be present immediately after the accident but will develop over one or two days, and may gradually get worse before they start to improve. Most people make a full recovery within days or weeks, but where symptoms are severe, it may take months or even years for them to subside.

As these injuries are to the soft tissues, they cannot be detected by means of an MRI scan, CT scan or an x-ray, and they are otherwise difficult to diagnose accurately. This means that it is sometimes difficult to assess whether a claim is spurious or not.

### 2.2.6 Work-related upper limb disorders

The term 'repetitive strain injury' is commonly used by the general public to describe musculoskeletal problems of the arm and hand associated with repetitive activity, such as typing or assembly work. However, this term does not accurately reflect the fact that the condition may not be due to repetitive work and may not be the result of a strain. Consequently, the term 'work-related upper limb disorder' (WRULD) is to be preferred.

WRULDs, which are common across a wide range of occupations, may be caused by repetitive or forceful activities, including lifting or carrying heavy objects, poor posture and/or carrying out activities for long periods without adequate breaks. In some cases, a WRULD may be caused by a single strain or trauma resulting, for example, from carrying a heavy load. In other cases, problems are caused by vibration, due to the use of tools such as chainsaws, grinders or drills.

Symptoms include aches, pain, weakness, numbness, tingling, stiffness, swelling and cramp in the arm and hand, including the fingers, wrist, forearm, elbow, shoulder and neck. In many instances, rest or adjustments to the working environment (the desk layout or assembly line) or the way that work is managed will alleviate the symptoms, but in some cases the condition is permanent.

It may be possible for a precise medical diagnosis to be made, for example, carpal tunnel syndrome, tenosynovitis or vibration white finger.

Controversy surrounds claims for WRULDs due to the fact that some specific conditions, such as carpal tunnel syndrome, may be caused by factors not related to the workplace and because some WRULDs are non-specific (ie, a medical diagnosis is not possible).

### 2.2.7 Industrial deafness

Industrial deafness claims are brought by those who have suffered hearing loss due to exposure at work to a high level of noise for a long period of time. For example, employees working in the steel industry, shipbuilding or other manufacturing industry may suffer from industrial deafness. Expert medical evidence is required to prove the loss of hearing, and evidence relating to the employees' working conditions is also required. Employers should, for example, have a system of assessing the risk from noise, provide ear protectors and have clearly marked zones where ear protection must be worn.

### 2.2.8 Asbestos related conditions

Where people are exposed to asbestos, dust or fibres may be inhaled which can move to the lungs or to the pleura, which is the membrane surrounding the lungs. Where this occurs, a number of conditions of varying severity may arise.

Asbestosis is a form of *pneumoconiosis*, which is a general term applied to any chronic form of inflammation of the lungs affecting people who are liable to inhale irritating substances or particles at work. Asbestosis occurs due to the inhalation of mainly blue or brown asbestos dust, which leads to the development of widespread scarring of the lung tissue and causes severe breathing difficulties. The main hazard, however, is the potential for the development of a type of cancer called mesothelioma, which affects the lungs, the pleura or, more rarely, the ovaries.

Pleural plaques are areas of fibrosis, sometimes partly calcified, on the pleura. Typically, there are no symptoms, but there is evidence to conclude that individuals who have pleural plaques have an increased risk of developing mesothelioma.

Where these areas of fibrosis are more widespread, they can prevent the lungs from working properly and thereby cause difficulties with breathing. This is known as pleural thickening

### 2.2.9 Occupational asthma

Occupational asthma may develop following exposure to a precipitating factor in the workplace, for example flour.

Asthma is a breathing disorder characterised by a narrowing of the airways within the lungs. The main symptom is breathlessness and an associated cough. It is an extremely distressing condition and, if left untreated, can be fatal.

### 2.2.10 Occupational dermatitis

Dermatitis is an inflammation of the skin, which is usually caused by direct contact with some irritating substance.

Occupational dermatitis is the most common of all the occupational diseases.

### 2.2.11 Occupational stress

Following the case of *Walker v Northumberland County Council* [1995] 1 All ER 737, in which a social services officer received compensation for stress induced by his employment (he suffered a nervous breakdown), a number of occupational stress claims have been brought before the courts. Careful consideration needs to be given as to whether the particular client will satisfy the necessary criteria to persuade the court to award damages in these circumstances. Occupational stress is considered in more detail in **Chapter 6**.

### 2.2.12 Post-traumatic stress disorder

Post-traumatic stress disorder (PTSD) has become more prominent in recent years. This expression refers to a psychological illness in which the claimant suffers from a variety of symptoms, which may include flashbacks, panic attacks, palpitations, chest pain, nausea, constipation, diarrhoea, insomnia, eating disorders, extreme fatigue and loss of libido.

It is important that medical evidence is obtained to support the injury, so that the defendants cannot make the allegation that the claimant has simply been 'shaken up'. This type of injury must be considered by the claimant's solicitor, even if the client concentrates only on his physical injuries when he is asked at the first interview what injuries he has suffered as a result of the accident. Post-traumatic stress is considered in more detail in **Chapter 6**.

### 2.2.13 Obstetrics

A normal labour and delivery take place in three stages. The first stage refers to the period of time it takes the cervix to dilate fully to 10 cms, and this is the longest stage of labour. The full dilation of the cervix is also associated with the rupture of the amnion, which is the tough fibrous membrane lining the cavity of the womb during pregnancy, containing amniotic fluid which supports the foetus. The rupture of the amnion is often referred to as 'the breaking of the waters'. The second stage of labour is the actual birth of the baby. The third stage is the delivery of the placenta.

If a baby is deprived of oxygen, it is said to have become 'hypoxic'. Hypoxia refers to a state where there is an inadequate supply of oxygen to maintain normal tissue function. If a baby is deemed to be in danger, it will be intubated and ventilated. This involves the insertion of an endotracheal tube into the baby's trachea to facilitate the maintenance of the baby's airway.

Once a baby is born, it is assessed using the Apgar score. This is a method of assessing a baby's condition by giving a score of 0, 1 or 2 to each of five signs: colour, heart rate, muscle tone, respiratory effort, and response to stimulation. A total score of 10 is the best Apgar score. If a baby is described as 'apnoeic', it means that it is not breathing; 'bradycardia' refers to the fact that the baby's heart is beating too slowly.

Perinatal mortality refers to the death of a foetus after the 28th week of pregnancy and to the death of the newborn child during the first week of life.

### 2.2.14 Cerebral palsy

Cerebral palsy is a general term used by medical practitioners to refer to a set of neurological conditions occurring in infancy or early childhood which affect movement and coordination. There are several different types of varying severity, the main ones being:

(a) *Spastic cerebral palsy* – some of the muscles in the body are tight, stiff and weak, making control of movement of the affected arm or leg difficult. The degree of spasticity can vary significantly from case to case, but in the most severe cases the muscles in the affected limb may become permanently contracted.

(b) *Athetoid (dyskinetic) cerebral palsy* – characterised by involuntary slow, writhing movements of the limbs and sometimes sudden muscle spasms. Sufferers have difficulty holding items or staying in one position.

(c) *Ataxic cerebral palsy* – problems include difficulty with balance, causing unsteadinesss when walking, shaky movements of the hands, making writing difficult, and speech difficulties.

(d) *Mixed cerebral palsy* – a combination of two or more of the above.

In addition to the above symptoms, there may a lack of coordination of the muscles of the mouth, causing speech and feeding problems, visual and hearing problems, and epilepsy. The symptoms often lead others to conclude that the sufferer has learning difficulties, but the condition does not, of itself, affect intelligence.

In a minority of cases (thought to be about 1:10) cerebral palsy is caused by problems during labour and birth, such as lack of oxygen or trauma. In the majority of the remaining cases, the damage arises while the baby is developing in the womb, as a result of genetic problems, malformations of the brain or maternal infection, such as rubella or toxoplasmosis. Infantile infections (especially encephalitis or meningitis) can also be causative.

Cerebral palsy is not a progressive condition, but the strains it places upon the body can lead to further problems in later life. There is no cure, but sufferers can benefit greatly from physiotherapy, occupational therapy, speech therapy and conductive education.

## 2.3 Areas of medical speciality

In dealing with his caseload, the personal injury and clinical negligence lawyer may require expert evidence to be given by a wide range of medical specialists. The following are amongst the most common areas of expertise. In order to avoid offending medical experts, it is useful to remember that consultant surgeons are known as 'Mr' 'Mrs' or 'Ms', rather than 'Dr'.

(a) *Anaesthesia* – either renders the patient unconscious (general anaesthesia) or removes sensation in a specific area (local anaesthesia), thereby enabling surgery or other procedures to be performed without the patient incurring pain and distress. An anaesthetist assesses the patient's fitness to undergo anaesthesia, chooses and administers the appropriate drugs, monitors the patient during the operation or procedure, and supervises the recovery period. He also plays a major role in pain management. A consultant anaesthetist will usually have 'FRCA' (Fellow of the Royal College of Anaesthetists) after his name.

(b) *Cardiology* – the study of the diseases of the heart. A cardiologist is a physician who specialises in this branch of medicine. A cardiac surgeon carries out surgical procedures in relation to the heart. If a cardiac surgeon has also been trained in the field of vascular surgery (relating to diseases affecting the arteries and veins) and/or thoracic surgery (relating to diseases inside the thorax – the chest – including the oesophagus and the diaphragm), he will be a cardiovascular, cardiothoracic or cardiovascular thoracic surgeon. A consultant cardiologist will usually have 'MRCP' or 'FRCP' (Membership or Fellowship of one of the Royal Colleges of Physicians) after his name. A cardiac surgeon will have 'FRCS' (Fellow of the Royal College of Surgeons) after his name.

(c) *Dermatology* – deals with the diagnosis and treatment of disorders of the skin, such as eczema, psoriasis, dermatitis and skin infections, and those affecting the hair and nails. A consultant dermatologist will usually have 'MRCP' or 'FRCP' after his name.

(d) *Geriatric medicine* – relates to disorders and diseases associated with old age (usually over 65) and their social consequences. A consultant geriatrician will usually have 'MRCP' or 'FRCP' after his name.

(e) *Gynaecology* – deals with the female pelvic and urogenital organs in both the normal and diseased state. It encompasses aspects of contraception, abortion and in vitro fertilisation (IVF). Practitioners may also specialise in obstetrics (see below). A consultant gynaecologist will have 'MRCOG' or 'FRCOG' (Membership or Fellowship of the Royal College of Obstetricians and Gynaecologists) after his name.

(f) *Haematology* – the study and treatment of blood and blood disorders, such as blood clotting deficiencies, leukaemia, myeloma, lymphoma, and Hodgkin's Disease. A haematologist also deals with blood transfusions and treatments involving warfarin and heparin. A consultant haematologist will have FRCPath' (Fellowship of one of the Royal Colleges of Pathologists) after his name.

(g) *Medical oncology* – the treatment of cancer. Clinical oncologists are largely concerned with radiotherapy, whilst medical oncologists deal with the medical management of those suffering from the disease. They liaise with primary care providers, clinical oncologists and other health professionals, and providers of palliative care. The consultant oncologist may have 'MRCP' or 'FRCP', or 'FRCR' (Fellow of the Royal College of Radiologists) or 'FRCS' after his name.

(h) *Neurology* – the study of the nervous system and its disorders, ie the patient's nerves, sensory and motor functions and reflexes, and will cover injuries to the brain, neck and back, neurodegenerative disorders, epilepsy and multiple sclerosis. A consultant neurologist will have 'MRCP' or 'FRCP' after his name. A neurosurgeon operates on the brain and spine, and deals with trauma and injuries to both, with brain tumours and haemorrhages, and with spinal nerve problems. A consultant neurosurgeon will have 'FRCS' after his name.

(i) *Obstetrics* – covers pregnancy and birth, and is concerned with the health of the mother and of the foetus from conception to delivery. The obstetrician will also deal with sterilisations and infertility, cervical cancer, tumours of the ovaries and endometriosis. Both doctors and nurses can specialise in obstetrics. A consultant obstetrician will have 'MRCOG' or 'FRCOG' after his name.

(j) *Occupational health* – this deals with the effect of work on the individual's health, both mental and physical, and the effect of ill-health on the individual's work. Specialists identify and treat specific occupational illnesses and diseases, and deal with the prevention of ill-health caused by chemical, biological, physical and psychological factors arising in the workplace. The term 'occupational health' covers a number of areas, and therefore there are various specialists, including occupational physicians, occupational psychologists, occupational health nurses, occupational hygienists, disability managers, workplace counsellors, health and safety practitioners, and workplace physiotherapists. The consultant occupational physician will usually have 'FFOM' (Fellow of the Faculty of Occupational Medicine) after his name. Others specialising in this area may have a Diploma in Occupational Medicine (DOccMED).

(k) *Ophthalmology* – the diagnosis and treatment of disorders of the eye. The consultant ophthalmologist will usually have 'FRCOphth' (Fellow of the Royal College of Ophthalmologists) after his name.

(l) *Orthopaedics* – this is concerned with injuries to and disorders of the bones and muscles. Surgeons who work in this area may specialise in certain parts of the body – the knee, the hip, the spine etc. The orthopaedic surgeon will have FRCS after his name, possibly followed by (Orth) and/or (Tr & Orth) signifying his specialism in orthopaedics and trauma.

(m) *Paediatrics* – diseases and illness affecting children. A paediatrician may have a sub-speciality, eg a paediatric neurologist, a paediatric surgeon, etc. The consultant paediatrician will normally have 'MRCP' or 'FRCP' after his name, and may have 'FRCPCH' (Fellow of the Royal College of Paediatrics and Child Health).

(n) *Palliative care* – the care of patients suffering from a terminal illness, including pain control and psychological and spiritual care, and the provision of services either at home or in a hospital, hospice or day centre. It also encompasses support for the family of the patient, which continues into the bereavement period.

(o) *Pathology* – the science of the changes which the body goes through as a result of disease. A pathologist examines body samples in order to diagnose disease and undertakes post-mortem examinations in order to determine the cause of death. The consultant pathologist will have 'FRCPath' after his name.

(p) *Physiotherapy* – the use of exercise, manipulation, and heat in the treatment of disease or injury, which is often essential in the rehabilitation process. All physiotherapists will have either 'MCSP' (Member of the Chartered Society of Physiotherapy) or 'FCSP' (Fellow of the Chartered Society of Physiotherapy) after their names, and must be registered with the Health Professions Council, the regulatory body for physiotherapists.

(q) *Psychiatry* – the branch of medical science which treats mental disorder and disease, and which helps with the management of individuals with learning disabilities. A psychiatrist deals with depression, PTSD, drug and substance abuse, schizophrenia, etc. A consultant psychiatrist will have 'MRCPsych' or 'FRCPsych' (Member or Fellow of the Royal Colleges of Psychiatrists) after his name.

(r) *Psychology* – the scientific study of how people think, how and why they act, react and interact as they do. It covers memory, rational/irrational thought, intelligence, learning, personality, perception and emotions. Psychology is used in promoting rehabilitation and assessing rehabilitation needs following an accident. There are a number of different branches, including educational psychology (concerned with children's learning and development), clinical psychology (concerned with reducing psychological stress in those suffering from depression, mental illness, brain injuries and the after effects of trauma), health psychology (concerned with behaviour relating to health, illness and care) and occupational psychology (relating to how people perform at work). Psychologists are not medically qualified but rather have a graduate degree in psychology plus an accredited postgraduate qualification leading to chartered status.

(s) *Rheumatology* – medical speciality concerned with the study and management of diseases of the joints and connective tissue, including rheumatoid arthritis, osteoarthritis, osteoporosis, whiplash and repetitive strain injury. A consultant rheumatologist will have 'MRCP' or 'FRCP' after his name.

## 2.4 Common abbreviations used in medical records

| | |
|---|---|
| AAL | Anterior axillary line |
| ACTH | Adrenocorticotrophic hormone |
| ADH | Antidiuretic hormone |
| AE | Air entry |
| AF | Atrial fibrillation |
| AFB | Acid fast bacillus (TB) |
| AFP | Alpha-fetoprotein |
| AJ | Ankle jerk (reflex) |
| Alk | Alkaline (phos = phosphatase) |
| An | Anaemia |
| ANF | Antinuclear factor |
| Anti-D | This gamma globulin must be given by injection to Rhesus negative mother who delivers/aborts Rhesus positive child/foetus to prevent mother developing antibodies which could damage a subsequent Rhesus positive baby |
| Apgar | Apgar score: means of recording baby's condition at and shortly after birth by observing and 'scoring' (0, 1 or 2) 5 parameters |
| AP | Anteroposterior |
| APH | Antepartum haemorrhage |
| ARM | Artificial rupture of membranes (labour) |
| ASO | Antistreptolysin O |
| ATN | Acute tubular necrosis |
| A/V | (a) Anteverted<br>(b) Arterio venous |
| AXR | Abdominal x-ray (plain) |
| Ba | Barium |
| BD | To be given/taken twice a day |
| BJ | Biceps jerk (reflex, see AJ) |
| BMJ | British Medical Journal |
| BMR | Basal metabolic rate |
| BO | Bowels open |
| BP | British Pharmacopoeia |
| BP | Blood pressure |
| BS | (a) Breath sounds<br>(b) Bowel sounds<br>(c) Blood sugar |
| $C_2H_5OH$ | Alcohol |
| ca | Carcinoma/cancer |
| Ca | Calcium |
| Caps | Capsules |
| CAT scan | Computed axial tomograph scan |
| CBD | Common bile duct |
| cc | (a) Carcinoma (cancer)<br>(b) Cubic centimetre |
| CCF | Congestive cardiac failure |
| Ch VS | Chorionic villus sampling |
| CI | Contraindications |
| Cl | Clubbing (of finger or toe nails) |
| CLL | Chronic lymphocytic leukaemia |
| CML | Chronic myeloid leukaemia |

| | |
|---|---|
| CMV | Cytomegalovirus |
| CN I-XII | Cranial nerves 1 – 12 |
| CNS | Central nervous system |
| C/O | Complaining of |
| $CO_2$ | Carbon dioxide |
| COETT | Cuffed oral endotracheal tube |
| COT | Cuffed oral tube (an endotracheal tube used for ventilating a patient who cannot breathe unaided) |
| CPD | Cephalo-pelvic disproportion (baby too large to fit through pelvis) |
| CSF | Cerebro-spinal fluid |
| CT | Computerised tomography |
| CTG | Cardiotocograph (trace during labour of baby's heart and mother's contractions) |
| CVA | Cardiovascular accident (stroke) |
| CVP | Central venous pressure |
| CVS | Cardiovascular system |
| Cx | Cervix |
| CXR | Chest x-ray |
| Cy | Cyanosis |
| DB | Decibel |
| D&C | Dilation (cervical) and curettage |
| DM | Diabetes mellitus |
| DNA | Deoxyribonucleic acid (also 'did not attend') |
| DOA | Dead on arrival |
| D&V | Diarrhoea and vomiting |
| DVT | Deep venous thrombosis |
| D/W | Discussed with |
| Dx | Diagnosis |
| ECG | Electrocardiography |
| ECT | Electroconvulsive therapy |
| EDC | Expected date of confinement |
| EDD | Expected date of delivery |
| EEG | Electroencephalogram/graph (brain scan) |
| ENT | Ear, nose and throat |
| ERCP | Endoscopic retrograde choledochopancreatico/graphy/scope |
| ERPC | Evacuation of retained products of conception |
| ESR | Erythrocyte sedimentation rate (blood) |
| ETR | Examined through clothes |
| EtoH | Alcohol |
| ET(T) | Endotracheal (tube) |
| EUA | Examined under anaesthesia |
| FB | (a) Finger's breadth<br>(b) Foreign body |
| FBC | Full blood count |
| FBS | Foetal blood sampling (a procedure which is carried out during labour to check on the baby's condition) |
| FH | Family history |
| FHH | Foetal heart heard |
| FHHR | Foetal heart heard regular |
| FHR | Foetal heart rate |
| FMF | Foetal movements felt |
| FSE | Foetal scalp electrode |
| FSH | Follicle-stimulating hormone |
| G | gram |

| | |
|---|---|
| GA | General anaesthesia |
| GB | Gall bladder |
| GFR | Glomerular filtration rate |
| GI | Gastro-intestinal |
| GIT | Gastro-intestinal tract |
| G6PD | Glucose 6 phosphate dehydrogenase |
| GP | General practitioner |
| GTT | Glucose tolerance test (for diabetes) |
| GU | Genito-urinary |
| GUT | Genito-urinary tract |
| h | Hour |
| Hb | Haemoglobin |
| Hct | Haemocrit |
| HOCM | Hypertrophic obstructive cardiomyopathy |
| HPC | History of presenting complaint |
| HRT | Hormone replacement therapy |
| HS | Heart sounds |
| HVS | High vaginal swab |
| Hx | History |
| ICP | Intracranial pressure |
| ICS | Intercostal space |
| IDA | Iron deficiency anaemia |
| IDDM | Insulin dependent diabetes mellitus |
| Ig | Immunoglobulin |
| IJ | Internal jugular vein |
| IM | Intramuscular |
| ISQ | In status quo |
| IT | Intrathecal |
| ITP | Idiopathic thrombocytopenic purpura |
| ITU | Intensive therapy unit |
| iu | International unit |
| IUCD | Intrauterine contraceptive device |
| IV | Intravenous |
| IVC | Inferior vena cava |
| IVI | Intravenous infusion (drip) |
| IVU | Intravenous urography |
| Ix | Investigations |
| J | Jaundice |
| °JACCO | No jaundice, anaemia, cyanosis, clubbing or oedema |
| JVP | Jugular venous pressure |
| $K^+$ | Potassium |
| kg | Kilogram |
| KJ | Knee jerk (reflex, see AJ) |
| kPa | Kilopascal, approximately 7.5 mmHg |
| L | (a) Litre<br>(b) Left |
| LA | Local anaesthesia |
| LBBB | Left bundle branch block |
| LFTs | Liver function tests |
| LH | Luteinising hormone |
| LIF | Left iliac fossa |
| LIH | Left inguinal hernia |
| LMN | Lower motor neurone |

| | |
|---|---|
| LMP | First day of the last menstrual period |
| LN | Lymph node |
| LOA | Left occiput anterior (position of baby's head at delivery, see also LOP, ROA, ROP, LOL, ROL, OA, OP) |
| LOC | Loss of consciousness |
| LOL | Left occipitolateral (see LOA) |
| LOP | Left occiput posterior (see LOA above) |
| LP | Lumbar puncture |
| LS | Letter sent |
| LSCS | Lower segment caesarean section (the 'normal' type of caesarean section) |
| LSKK | Liver, spleen and kidneys |
| LUQ | Left upper quadrant |
| LVF | Left ventricular failure |
| LVH | Left ventricular hypertrophy |
| mane | In the morning |
| mcg | Microgram |
| MCL | Mid clavicular line |
| MCV | Mean cell volume |
| µg | Microgram |
| mg | Milligram |
| mist | mixture |
| mitte 1/12 | Supply/give/send/provide |
| ml | Millilitres |
| mmHg | Millimetres of mercury (pressure) |
| mMol | Millimol |
| MRI | Magnetic resonance imaging (=NMRI) |
| MS | Multiple sclerosis |
| MSU | Mid stream urine |
| N&V | Nausea and vomiting |
| Na | Sodium |
| $NaHCO_3$ | Sodium bicarbonate |
| NAD | Nothing abnormal diagnosed/detected |
| NBM | Nil by mouth |
| ND | Notifiable disease |
| ng | Nanogram |
| NG | (a) Naso-gastric<br>(b) Carcinoma/cancer (neoplastic growth) |
| NMCS | No malignant cells seen |
| NMR | Nuclear magnetic resonance (scan) |
| noct/nocte | At night |
| NOF | Neck of femur |
| N/S | Normal size |
| NSAID | Non-steroidal anti-inflammatory drugs |
| $O_2$ | Oxygen |
| OA | (a) Occipito-anterior (see LOA)<br>(b) Osteoarthritis |
| OCP | Oral contraceptive pill |
| OE | On examination |
| OP | Occipito-posterior (see LOA) |
| Orthop. | Orthopnoea (breathlessness on lying flat) |
| P | Pulse |
| P or $\pi$ | Period |
| PA | Posteroanterior |

| | |
|---|---|
| PAN | Polyarteritis nodosa |
| PC | Post cibum (after food) |
| $pCO_2$ | Partial pressure of carbon dioxide (normally in blood) |
| PCV | Packed cell volume |
| PERLA | Pupils are equal and react to light and accommodation |
| PE | (a) Pulmonary embolism |
| | (b) Pre eclampsia |
| PEFR | Peak expiratory flow rate |
| PET | Pre-eclamptic toxaemia |
| pg | Picogram |
| pH | Acidity and alkalinity scale. Low is acidic. High is alkaline. pH7 is about neutral |
| PH | Past/previous history |
| PID | (a) Pelvic inflammatory disease |
| | (b) Prolapsed intervertebral disc |
| PIP | Proximal interphalangeal |
| PL | Prolactin |
| PMH | Past/previous medical history |
| PND | Paroxysmal nocturnal dyspnoea |
| PN (R) | Percussion note (resonant) |
| po | Per os (by mouth) |
| $pO_2$ | Partial pressure of oxygen (normally in blood) |
| POH | Past/previous obstetric history |
| POP | Plaster of Paris |
| PoP | Progesterone only pill |
| PPH | Post-partum haemorrhage |
| pr | Per rectum (by the rectum) |
| prn | As required – of eg, pain killers |
| PRV | Polycythaemia rubra vera |
| PTH | Parathyroid hormone |
| PTT | Prothrombin time |
| PU | Peptic ulcer |
| PV | Per vaginam (by the vagina) |
| QDS | To be given/taken 4 times a day |
| R | Right *or* respiration |
| RA | Rheumatoid arthritis |
| RBBB | Right bundle branch block |
| RBC | Red blood cell (erythrocyte) |
| RE | Rectal examination |
| Rh | Rhesus factor |
| RIC | Raised intracranial pressure |
| RIF | Right iliac fossa |
| RIH | Right inguinal hernia |
| ROA | Right occiput anterior (see LOA) |
| ROL | Right occipito-lateral (see LOA) |
| ROM | Range of movement |
| ROP | Right occiput posterior (see LOA) |
| RS | Respiratory system |
| RT | Radiotherapy |
| RTA | Road traffic accident |
| RTI | Respiratory tract infection |
| RUQ | Right upper quadrant |
| SB | Serum bilirubin |
| S/B | Seen by |

| | |
|---|---|
| SBE | Subacute bacterial endocarditis |
| SC | Subcutaneous |
| S/D | Systolic/diastolic (heart and circulation) |
| SE | Side effects |
| SH | Social history |
| SJ | Supinator jerk (reflex: see AJ) |
| SL | Sub linguinal (under the tongue) |
| SLE | Systemic lupus erythematosus |
| SOA | Swelling of ankles |
| SOB (OE) | Shortness of breath |
| SOS | (a) if necessary |
| | (b) see other sheet |
| SROM | Spontaneous rupture of membranes |
| stat | Immediately |
| Supp | Suppositories |
| SVC | Superior vena cava |
| SVD | Spontaneous vaginal delivery |
| SVT | Supraventricular tachycardia |
| SXR | Skull x-ray |
| Ts and As | Tonsils and Adenoids |
| TCI 2/52 | To come in (to be admitted to hospital), in 2 weeks' time |
| tds | To be given/taken 3 times a day |
| TGH | To go home |
| THR | Total hip replacement |
| TIA | Transient ischaemic attack |
| TJ | Triceps jerk (reflex: see AJ) |
| TPR | Temperature, pulse and respiration |
| TSH | Thyroid stimulating hormone |
| TTA | To take away |
| TVF | Tactile vocal fremitus |
| TX | Transfusion |
| UC | Ulcerative colitis |
| U&E | Urea and electrolytes (biochemical tests) |
| UG | Urogenital |
| UMN | Upper motor neurone |
| URTI | Upper respiratory tract infection |
| USS | Ultra sound scan |
| UTI | Urinary tract infection |
| VA | Visual acuity |
| VE | Vaginal examination |
| VF | Ventricular fibrillation |
| VT | Ventricular tachycardia |
| V/V | Vulva and vagina |
| VVs | Varicose veins |
| WBC | White blood corpuscle/white blood cell count |
| WCC | White blood cell count |
| WR | Wasserman reaction |
| wt | Weight |
| XR | X-ray |

## 2.5 Diagrammatic representation of the human skeleton

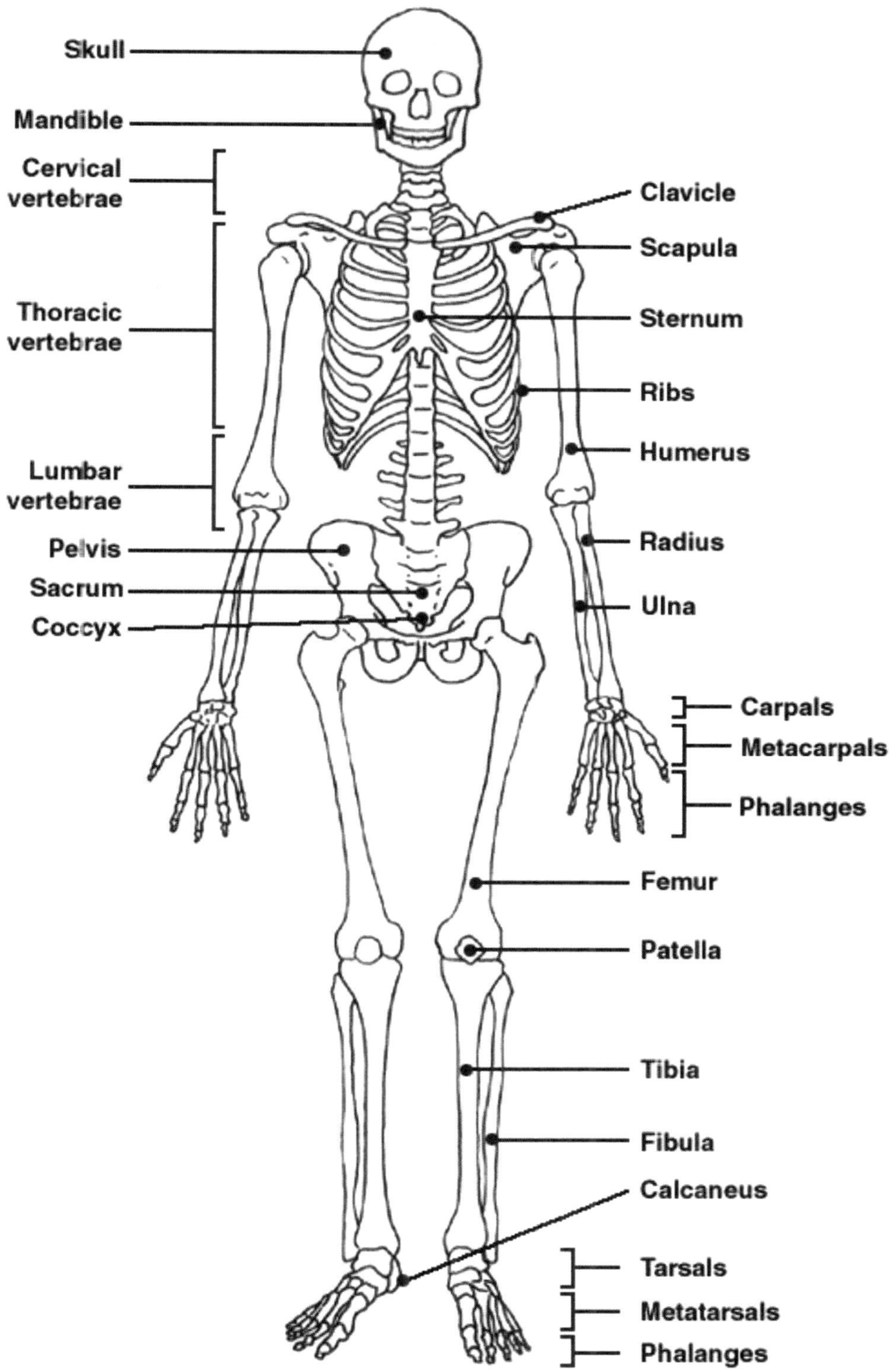

## 2.6 Conclusion

A basic understanding of the medical terms involved in personal injury and clinical negligence cases can assist the trainee when reading medical reports, and also provides an insight into the client's problems which can often be useful in the negotiation of any settlement.

## 2.7 Further reading

Kemp and Kemp, *The Quantum of Damages* (Sweet & Maxwell)

*Black's Medical Dictionary* (A & C Black Publishers Ltd)

*Dorland's Medical Abbreviations* (W B Saunders Company)

Other appropriate medical textbooks.

# Chapter 3
# Road Traffic and Other Highway Claims: The Law



## 3.1 Introduction

According to the Department of Transport's statistics bulletin, *Road Casualties Great Britain; 2007 – Main Results*, there were 247,780 road casualties in Great Britain in 2007, and 30,720 people were either killed or seriously injured. Not surprisingly therefore, road traffic accidents form a large part of the personal injury lawyer's casework.

A road user may be liable to an injured person, or to the estate or dependants of a deceased person, on the basis of common law negligence. A highways authority may be liable to such people on the basis of negligence and/or breach of statutory duty.

## 3.2 Establishing liability for road traffic accidents

### 3.2.1 The duty of one road user to another

All road users have a duty of care to avoid causing injury to others who it may reasonably be anticipated may be injured by their actions or failure to act. The term 'road user' includes not only those driving motor vehicles or riding motorbikes or bicycles, but also their passengers, pedestrians and owners of roadside property, such as signs and bollards, and the highway itself, which in most cases will be the local highway authority.

Clearly, a driver has a duty to drive carefully so as not to cause injury to his passengers or other road users, but other examples include the duty of a driver to not park his vehicle where it might constitute a danger, the duty of a pedestrian not to step into the path of a vehicle, and the duty of the highway authority to keep the highway in good repair.

This duty of care is well established and, in the majority of cases, will not be in dispute between the parties.

### 3.2.2 The standard of care

The standard of care is that of the ordinary skilful driver, and it is not lowered to take account of the fact that the driver is a learner driver (see *Nettleship v Weston* [1971] 2 QB 691).

A driver is not entitled to assume that other road users will always exercise reasonable care and skill, but he is not 'bound to anticipate folly in all its forms' (*London Passenger Transport Board v Upson* [1949] AC 1555). Neither is the duty so high that it equates to a guarantee of the claimant's safety. In *Ahanonu v South East Kent Bus Company Limited* [2008] EWCA Civ 274, where the claimant had been trapped between the defendant's double-decker bus and a metal bollard, the Court of Appeal reversed the finding that a driver of the bus had been negligent. Lord Justice Laws said that the judge had imposed a counsel of perfection on the bus driver, thereby distorting the nature of the driver's duty, which was no more or less than a duty to take care.

This view was reiterated in *Stewart v Glaze* [2009] EWHC 704 (QB), where a driver was found not liable for injuries incurred by the claimant, who had stepped into the path of his car without warning. The judge commented that it was important to ensure the court was not guided by '20:20 hindsight'.

### 3.2.3 Breach of duty

Each case must turn on its own facts. It is for the court to decide whether there has been any breach of the duty to take reasonable care in relation to other road users. When trying to answer this vital question, personal injury lawyers should consider legislation designed to regulate the conduct of road users and the Highway Code.

#### 3.2.3.1 Are there any breaches of statutory provisions?

You should consider whether the condition of any of the vehicles or the behaviour of any of the individuals involved in the accident constitutes a breach of statutory provisions. Evidence of the defendant being found guilty of a relevant criminal offence is of particular importance to the claimant's solicitor in order to establish breach of duty, but a relevant conviction of the claimant may assist the defendant's solicitor in negating liability or establishing contributory negligence. The following issues are some, but by no means all, of the matters for which you should look out:

(a) *Vehicle maintenance*:

(i) Under s 40 of the Road Traffic Act 1988 (RTA 1988), it is an offence to use, cause or permit another to use a motor vehicle on a road when its condition is such that its use involves a danger of injury to any person.

(ii) Under s 41A of the RTA 1988, a person who uses a motor vehicle, or causes or permits such a vehicle to be used on a road when the vehicle does not comply with regulations governing the construction and use of brakes, steering-gear or tyres, is guilty of an offence. Current regulations relating to tyres specify a minimum tread depth, prohibit the mix of radial and cross-ply tyres, and require tyres to be inflated to the correct pressure for the vehicle.

(b) *Poor driving*. The most important issues of relevance are as follows:

(i) Speeding – many speeding offences will be prosecuted under s 89(1) of the Road Traffic Regulations Act 1984, although other sections of the Act deal with speed restrictions on special roads and those subject to temporary restrictions. Driving at a speed in excess of the limit is not necessarily in itself sufficient evidence of negligence (*Quinn v Scott* [1965] 2 All ER 588). Neither will driving below the speed limit automatically negate liability. Under the Highway Code, drivers should adjust their driving to the prevailing conditions and circumstances. So they must take account of the weather, available light, road layout, weight of traffic, parked vehicles or other obstructions, the presence of cyclists and motorcyclists, and the likelihood of pedestrians, particularly children, crossing the road. A driver who fails to adjust his speed in appropriate circumstances risks prosecution for dangerous or careless driving.

(ii) Dangerous driving – under s 2 of the RTA 1988, it is an offence to drive dangerously on a road or other public place. For the purposes of this section, a person drives dangerously if the way he drives falls far below what would be expected of a competent and careful driver, and it would be obvious to a competent and careful driver that driving in that way, or driving the vehicle in its current state, would be dangerous. (For causing death by dangerous driving, careless driving or whilst under the influence of alcohol, see **17.3.1**.)

(iii) Careless driving – under s 3 of the RTA 1988, it is an offence to drive without due care and attention. A person will drive in this way if the way he drives falls below what would be expected of a competent and careful driver.

(c) *The influence of alcohol or drugs.* Under ss 4 and 5 of the RTA 1988, a person commits an offence if he drives, attempts to drive, or is in charge of a motor vehicle on the public highway or a public place, when he is unfit to do so through drink or drugs (s 4), or after consuming so much alcohol that the proportion of it in his breath, blood or urine exceeds the prescribed limit (s 5). The current prescribed limits for alcohol are 35 microgrammes of alcohol in 100 millilitres of breath; 80 milligrammes of alcohol in 100 millilitres of blood; and 107 milligrammes of alcohol in 100 millilitres of urine.

(d) *The use of mobile phones.* Under s 41D of the RTA 1988, it is an offence to drive or supervise the driving of a motor vehicle whilst holding a hand-held mobile telephone contrary to the relevant regulations. Although it is currently not an offence to use a hands-free telephone, should an accident occur whilst the driver is using such equipment, a prosecution for careless or dangerous driving might arise.

(e) *The wearing of seat belts and child restraints.* Under s 14 of the RTA 1988, it is an offence to drive or ride in a motor vehicle on a road without wearing a seat belt as prescribed by regulations made by the Secretary of State. In accordance with the Motor Vehicles (Wearing of Seat Belts) Regulations 1993 (SI 1993/176) (as amended), the driver must ensure that seat belts are worn, where they are available, by all passengers under the age of 14. Under s 15 of the RTA 1988, the driver must ensure that children are strapped into an appropriate child restraint. The current regulations apply only to children who are both under 1.35 metres in height and under 12 years old.

(f) *The wearing of safety helmets.* Under s 16 of the RTA 1988, it is an offence to ride on a motor cycle without a safety helmet in accordance with the relevant regulations. Followers of the Sikh religion who are wearing a turban are exempt from this requirement.

### 3.2.3.2 Are there any breaches of the Highway Code?

A failure on the part of any road user to observe a provision of the Highway Code does not of itself render that person liable to criminal proceedings. Some of the rules set out in the Code, identified by the use of the words 'must' or 'must not', reflect statutory requirements, the breach of which amounts to a criminal offence, whilst others, which are in the nature of guidance, do not. In accordance with s 38(7) of the RTA 1988, all breaches of the Code may be relied upon in the civil courts to establish breach of duty. However, a breach of the Highway Code does not create a presumption of negligence but is merely one of the circumstances which the court will consider when establishing whether a breach of duty has occurred (*Powell v Phillips* [1972] 3 All ER 864, CA).

The personal injury solicitor requires a good knowledge of the Code. Although the printed version must be used for all legal proceedings, you can access an adapted on-line version at www.direct.gov.uk/en/TravelAndTransport/Highwaycode/index.htm.

### 3.2.3.3 *Res ipsa loquitur*

The maxim *res ipsa loquitur* is sometimes thought of as a rule of law whereby the burden of proof shifts from the claimant to the defendant. This is a misunderstanding: it is, in fact, a rule of evidence, and the burden of proof remains on the claimant throughout. Roughly translated as 'the thing speaks for itself', the maxim means that the facts of the case are sufficient proof in themselves. It may be applied in circumstances where the claimant is unable to adduce any evidence as to how or why the accident happened, but is able to show that:

(a) the accident is such that, in the ordinary course of events, it would not have occurred without negligence; and

(b) whatever inflicted or caused the damage was under the sole management and control of the defendant.

In such circumstances, where it appears to be more likely than not that the defendant's breach of duty led to the accident, the maxim enables the court to conclude that the claimant has established a prima facie case against the defendant. It is therefore sometimes said that the evidential burden shifts to the defendant. In order to avoid liability, the defendant must either give an explanation of what happened which is inconsistent with negligence or, where he is unable to give such an explanation, demonstrate that he exercised all reasonable care.

In *Ng Chun Pui & Others v Le Chuen Tat & Another* [1988] RTR 298, a coach driven by the first defendant and owned by the second defendant left the carriageway, crossed a grass verge and collided with a public bus travelling in the opposite direction. One passenger in the bus was killed and its driver and other passengers were injured. In the absence of any evidence of any mechanical defect within the defendant's coach, the claimants did not offer any evidence as to how the accident arose but relied on the maxim *res ipsa loquitur*. However, the court accepted evidence put on behalf of the defendants that the driver had been obliged to react to another, untraced vehicle, which had cut in front of him, causing him to brake and swerve, and that this reaction did not constitute a breach of duty. (Reading the full text of the judgment in this case may prove useful for furthering comprehension of *res ipsa loquitur*.)

It is not common for liability in road traffic accidents to be established on the basis of the maxim *res ipsa loquitur*, as there will usually be evidence from the claimant, in the form of eye-witness testimony and/or expert opinion, as to how and why the accident occurred. One case in which it was successfully used is *Widdowson v Newgate Meat Corporation & Others* (1997) *The Times*, 4 December. The claimant, who was suffering from mental disorder, had been walking at the side of a dual carriageway just before midnight, when he was hit by a van driven by an employee of the respondent company. Neither the claimant, who could not be considered a reliable witness, nor the driver of the van gave evidence. Having heard evidence from a psychiatrist on behalf of the claimant, the Court of Appeal held that despite the claimant's mental illness, he was aware of road safety issues, was not a risk-taker and did not have any suicidal tendencies. Moreover, it was 'pure surmise' that he fell into the van's path as a result of losing his balance. Consequently, the defendants had failed to put forward a plausible explanation.

### 3.2.4 Vicarious liability

Under the doctrine of vicarious liability, an employer is liable for damage caused by the negligence of an employee whilst acting in the course of his employment. So, if an employee is driving whilst carrying out work for his employer and causes a road traffic accident due to his negligence, the employer will be liable for any resulting personal injury or damage to property.

You will find a more detailed analysis of vicarious liability in **4.5**.

### 3.2.5 Causation

The claimant will have to prove that the breach of duty caused the loss and damage complained of. He will have to show that 'but for' the defendant's breach, the injuries would not have arisen. Causation will be disputed where the defendant argues:

(a) that the cause of the injury was not the defendant's breach of duty but the claimant's own negligence. In *Whittle v Bennett* [2006] EWCA 1538, a car driven by the defendant in excess of the speed limit and too close to the car in front, was involved in a collision with the claimant's car. Although the defendant's actions were negligent, the court held that the accident was caused by the gross negligence of the claimant, who had been attempting a U-turn manoeuvre on a busy single-carriage 'A' road. Courts frequently find that the negligence of the defendant and the claimant have played a part in causation, and apportion damages accordingly (see **3.2.6**).

(b) that the accident could not have caused the injuries complained of. In recent years, it has become increasingly common for insurers to defend on this basis in low-velocity impact claims. This type of accident, where damage to the vehicles may be no more than a scratch, typically results in whiplash, where there are no visible signs of injury. In some instances, defendants are going further than disputing the severity of the injuries; they are making positive allegations that the claimant has fabricated the claim. The Court of Appeal considered these types of cases in *Kearsley v Klarfeld* [2005] EWCA Civ 1510 and *Casey v Cartwright* [2006] EWCA Civ 1280, and gave guidelines as to how they should be dealt with. These guidelines are beyond the scope of this book.

## 3.2.6 Contributory negligence

The claimant has a duty to take care of his own safety and to take reasonable precautions against risks of injury of which he was aware or ought to have been aware. His actions or failure to act might amount to a breach of this duty, and the court may conclude that the claimant was partly responsible for the accident itself and/or the injury suffered. Section 1(1) of the Law Reform (Contributory Negligence) Act 1945 states:

> Where any person who suffers damage as a result partly of his own fault and partly of the fault of any other person or persons, ... the damages recoverable in respect thereof shall be reduced to such an extent as the court thinks just and equitable having regard to the claimant's share in the responsibility for the damage.

Therefore, the court will reduce the amount of damages payable by the defendant to the claimant only where the defendant is able to prove, on the balance of probabilities:

(a) that the claimant was at fault;

(b) that the fault was causative of the injury suffered; and

(c) that it would be just and equitable for the claimant's damages to be reduced.

When determining the extent to which damages will be reduced, the court will apportion responsibility between the parties by looking at the relative causative potency of what each of the parties has done and their respective blameworthiness. (You may find it useful to read the full judgment in *Eagle v Chambers* [2003] EWCA Civ 1107.)

It would be rare for a court to find a pedestrian more responsible than a driver of a vehicle (and therefore reduce damages by more than 50%), unless the pedestrian suddenly moved into the path of the vehicle. The court will consider all the relevant circumstances, including whether the driver was driving in a manner appropriate for the prevailing conditions, whether he was aware that pedestrians were about and might step into the road, and the age of the pedestrian. Children are not expected to exercise the degree of care reasonably expected of an adult. Very young children will never be held to have been negligent, and those under the age of 12 are seldom held to be so. However, in the case of *Enrari v Curry & Another* [2006] EWCA Civ 120, the claimant, who was 13 years old at the time of the accident, was held to be 70% to blame for the accident which had left her brain-damaged. The defendant driver had been travelling at no more than 20 miles per hour when the claimant stepped into the road without looking.

In the following types of cases, the courts will follow the precedents set in the cases cited:

(a) Where a driver or passenger fails to wear a seat belt, damages will be reduced by 25% in cases where the injury would not have happened at all, or by 15% where the injuries would have been less severe (*Froom v Butcher* [1976] QB 268).

(b) Where a motor cyclist fails to wear a crash helmet, damages will be reduced by 15% (*O'Connell v Jackson* [1972] 1 QB 270) or, where the helmet's chin strap is not fastened, by 10% (*Capps v Miller* [1989] 1 WLR 839).

(c) Where a passenger allows himself to be carried in a vehicle when he knows the driver is drunk and should not be driving, damages will be reduced by 20% (*Owens v Brimmel* [1977] QB 859).

(d) Although there is no legal compulsion for a cyclist to wear a helmet, and there has not been a case where damages have been reduced as a result of a cyclist's failure to wear a helmet, in *Smith v Finch* [2009] EWHC 53 (QB) the judge appeared to suggest that such a failure would amount to contributory negligence. On the facts of this case, however, the wearing of a helmet would have made no difference to the injuries sustained by the claimant.

If the claimant has contributed to his own injuries in more than one way, the court will not necessarily calculate the overall reduction simply by adding the normal percentage reductions together. So, in *Gleeson v Court* [2007] EWHC 2397 (QB), where the claimant had allowed herself to be driven in a car when she was aware that the driver was drunk (20% reduction) and had sat in the boot of the hatchback car (25% reduction), the overall reduction was 30%.

The reduction of damages as a result of contributory negligence will be a theoretical, rather than an actual, disadvantage to the motorist who has the benefit of fully comprehensive insurance, as his own insurer, being bound to indemnify him for his own injuries irrespective of blame, will cover any shortfall in damages recovered from the defendant. However, few pedestrians, particularly children, will have relevant insurance cover, and therefore they will suffer a loss in real terms from any finding of contributory negligence.

## 3.3 Insurance

### 3.3.1 Statutory provisions and types of policy

Under s 143(1) of the RTA 1988, any person who drives, or causes or permits another person to drive a motor vehicle on a road or other public place, must have a policy of insurance which, at the very least, covers third party risks. The minimum protection afforded by what is commonly known as a Road Traffic Act policy or third party insurance covers:

(a) the death or bodily injury of a third party;

(b) damage to property belonging to a third party up to £1,000,000; and

(c) any emergency treatment, ie medical or surgical examination or treatment which is required by those suffering an injury (including a fatal injury) immediately following the accident.

A common type of policy, known as Third Party Fire & Theft, provides this minimum cover, plus cover for the policyholder's own vehicle should it be damaged or destroyed by fire or stolen. Neither of these types of policies indemnifies the policyholder where his own vehicle is otherwise damaged due to his own negligence, or where nobody was at fault. More importantly, neither do they cover the policyholder for injuries that he might himself suffer in such circumstances. It is perhaps little understood by the public at large how common road traffic accidents are, how devastating the resulting injuries can be, and just how important adequate financial compensation is for someone suffering long-term disability.

Policies which are commonly known as 'fully comprehensive' cover the minimum risks and damage to the policyholder's property. They might also cover the injury or death of the policyholder and legal expenses arising from taking or defending proceedings following an accident, but terms do vary and should be checked carefully.

### 3.3.2 Road Traffic Act 1988, ss 151–152

Sometimes, a situation will arise where the defendant was driving a vehicle which was covered by a policy of insurance at the time of the accident, but the insurer may have grounds to avoid paying damages to the claimant. This may arise where:

(a) the driver of the vehicle who was responsible for the accident was insured to drive that vehicle under the terms of the policy, but the insurance company was entitled to cancel the policy due to a breach of its terms, eg driving whilst under the influence of alcohol, or failure to disclose a material fact, eg the existence of previous driving convictions or a medical condition, such as diabetes or epilepsy; or

(b) the driver of the vehicle was not insured to drive the vehicle, eg where a family member or friend of the policyholder drove the vehicle, with or without the policyholder's permission, or a thief drove the vehicle.

In any of the above situations, the claimant should not be dissuaded from issuing a claim against the driver on the grounds that damages will not be recovered even if judgment is obtained. Under s 151 of the RTA 1988, the insurance company will be obliged to pay out on the judgment to the claimant, provided notice of the proceedings is given to the insurer, under s 152 of the Act, before or within seven days of commencement of the proceedings. Because it is not always clear at the start of proceedings whether or not any of the above situations applies, those acting for claimants in road traffic accident cases should always send out the required notice to the insurer of the vehicle (see **12.3.4**).

Under s 151(4), there is an exception in relation to third parties who were willing passengers in a vehicle they knew or had reason to believe had been stolen.

### 3.3.3 The insurer's role in civil proceedings

Although a claimant is able to issue proceedings directly against the negligent driver's insurers instead of or in addition to the driver (see **10.3.1.2**), many solicitors acting for claimants will proceed only against the driver. If the claimant succeeds in obtaining judgment against the defendant driver, the insurer is obliged to pay out. Consequently, in order to protect their own position, insurers insert a clause into their policies which enables them to initiate or defend proceedings in the name of the insured. This means that the insurer will chose which firm of solicitors to use and will give instructions as to how the matter should be dealt with, including the making and accepting of any offers to settle.

### 3.3.4 Obtaining insurance details

Where an accident has resulted in personal injury, under s 154 of the RTA 1988, all drivers involved must supply details of their insurance to others involved in the accident. It is a criminal offence either to refuse to supply this information, or to supply false information.

In addition, the Motor Insurers' Bureau (see **3.4**) maintains the Motor Insurance Database (MID), a centralised database of motor insurance policy information of all insured UK vehicles. Insurers who underwrite motor insurance for vehicles on UK roads are obliged to be members of the MIB and to submit the policy details of all vehicles to the MID. For a small fee, those who have suffered injury and/or loss due to a motor accident, or their representatives, may make an on-line enquiry to obtain information regarding the insurance details of other vehicles involved (www.askmid.com).

## 3.4 The Motor Insurers' Bureau

It is not uncommon for individuals to suffer personal injury as the result of the negligence of an uninsured driver or a driver who cannot be traced. The Motor Insurers' Bureau (MIB) was founded in 1946 with the specific purpose of entering into agreements with the Government to compensate victims of negligent and uninsured drivers. All motor insurers are obliged under the RTA 1988 to be a member of the MIB and to contribute to the fund from which compensation is paid. These contributions are funded by the premiums paid by their policyholders.

The relevant agreements, explanatory notes and application forms may be found on the MIB's website at www.mib.org.uk.

### 3.4.1 The Uninsured Drivers Agreement 1999

The Uninsured Drivers Agreement 1999 ('the 1999 Agreement') relates to claims arising from the negligence or intentional assaults of uninsured drivers who can be identified, where the incident occurred on or after 1 October 1999. Under the 1999 Agreement, the MIB is obliged to satisfy any judgment obtained against the defendant which remains unsatisfied, provided the claimant complies with the requirements of the Agreement. Accordingly, the claimant must take all reasonable steps to obtain judgment against every person who may be liable, including any person who may be vicariously liable (clause 14.1(a)).

However, the MIB does not have to wait until judgment is obtained before compensating victims, and it therefore makes sense to make an application to the MIB prior to the commencement of proceedings. The application should be made by completing and returning the MIB's standard form to the MIB or its nominated solicitors, together with documents in support (clause 7.1). It is important to note that the application must be signed by the claimant or his solicitor. If this is not complied with, the MIB can refuse to accept the application (clause 7.2 of the 1999 Agreement).

Where the MIB accepts that the uninsured driver was negligent, it will try to settle the matter in order to avoid civil proceedings. Where the MIB declines responsibility to pay compensation, the injured party has the option of commencing proceedings against the uninsured driver. The claimant's solicitors should name the MIB as second defendant, but if this is not done, the MIB will usually seek to be joined as a party to the proceedings.

The 1999 Agreement sets out a far more complicated set of procedural steps than its predecessors, and it is widely thought to be in need of amendment. A summary of the main points is set out below, but those acting for claimants should be aware that this is a minefield for the unwary. The MIB is more than willing to use minor breaches of the procedural steps to reject claims, and therefore reference must be made to the detail of the 1999 Agreement itself and to the associated guidance notes. Where the MIB is a party to the proceedings, it will receive notification of various stages of the proceedings, court hearings, etc directly from the court, and the claimant's solicitor should ask the MIB to waive compliance with some of the notice requirements. Copies of the relevant documentation and the application form may be obtained from the MIB website at www.mib.org.uk.

#### 3.4.1.1 Obtaining information regarding insurance details

As mentioned in **3.3.4**, in accordance with s 154 of the RTA 1988, all drivers involved must supply details of their insurance to others involved in the accident. Clause 13 of the 1999 Agreement places a requirement on all would-be claimants to make full and timely use of their rights under s 154. The MIB can avoid its obligations unless the claimant, as soon as reasonably practicable:

(a) demanded the particulars specified in s 154; and

(b) where there was a refusal to supply the information, complained to a police officer in respect of the failure; and

(c) used all reasonable endeavours to obtain the name, address and registered keeper of the vehicle.

#### 3.4.1.2 Notice requirements

Where civil proceedings are issued, the claimant must give the MIB notice in writing that he has commenced proceedings. This notice must be received by the MIB no later than 14 days after commencement of proceedings (clause 9.1), together with the following documents (in so far as they have not already been supplied to the MIB):

(a) the completed application form and supporting documents as required by clause 7.1;

(b) a copy of the sealed claim form;

(c) a copy of any relevant insurance policy covering the claimant;

(d) copies of all relevant correspondence in the possession of the claimant or his solicitor;

(e) a copy of the particulars of claim;

(f) a copy of all other documents required by the rules of procedure to be served on the defendant (although it is not necessary to enclose the response pack); and

(g) such other information relevant to the proceedings as the MIB may reasonably require.

The notice and supporting documentation must be served either by facsimile transmission, or by registered or recorded delivery post to the MIB's registered office (clause 8.1). Service by ordinary post and Document Exchange is not allowed.

Clauses 10 and 11 require notification to the MIB in writing within seven days of the occurrence of the following:

(a) service of proceedings;

(b) filing of a defence;

(c) amendment of particulars of claim;

(d) setting down for trial;

(e) notification of trial date received.

In the event that the claimant intends to enter judgment, the claimant must, not less than 35 days before applying for judgment, give notice in writing to the MIB of his intention so to do (clause 12).

#### 3.4.1.3 Assignment of judgment and undertakings

In accordance with clause 15 of the 1999 Agreement, the MIB is not obliged to settle the judgment unless the claimant:

(a) assigns the unsatisfied judgment to the MIB or its nominee. This enables the MIB to pursue the uninsured driver for the amount paid to the claimant;

(b) undertakes to repay to the MIB any part of the judgment which is set aside, or any compensation received by the claimant from other sources in respect of the same incident (clause 17.1).

### 3.4.2 The Untraced Drivers Agreement 2003

The Untraced Drivers Agreement 2003 ('the 2003 Agreement') relates to accidents occurring on or after 14 February 2003 and requires the MIB to consider applications for compensation for victims of 'hit and run' cases where the owner or driver cannot be traced.

The 2003 Agreement applies where:

(a) the death of, or bodily injury to, a person or damage to property of a person has been caused by, or arisen out of, the use of a motor vehicle on a road or other public place in Great Britain; and

(b) the event giving rise to the death, bodily injury or damage to property occurred on or after 14 February 2003; and

(c) the death, bodily injury or damage to property occurred in circumstances giving rise to liability of a kind which is required to be covered by a policy of insurance.

Clearly, in this type of incident, where the identity of the person responsible for the accident is not known, it is not possible to commence civil proceedings. Where a person who has suffered injury and loss wishes to claim under the 2003 Agreement, he must make an application in writing to the MIB. If the application is signed by a person who is neither the applicant nor a solicitor acting on behalf of the applicant, the MIB may refuse to accept the application (clause 4(2)).

#### 3.4.2.1 Exclusions from the Agreement

The 2003 Agreement does not apply (inter alia) where:

(a) the person suffering death, injury or damage was voluntarily allowing himself to be carried in the vehicle and before the commencement of his journey in the vehicle (or after such commencement if he could reasonably be expected to have alighted from the vehicle) he knew or ought to have known that the vehicle:
  (i) had been stolen or unlawfully taken, or
  (ii) was being used without insurance, or
  (iii) was being used in the course or furtherance of crime, or
  (iv) was being used as a means of escape from or avoidance of lawful apprehension;

(b) the property which has been damaged was insured and the applicant has recovered the full amount of his loss from the insurer;

(c) the claim is for damages to a vehicle and at the time of the incident that vehicle was uninsured. This prevents an applicant benefitting from the 2003 Agreement when his own vehicle was being driven unlawfully.

#### 3.4.2.2 Time limit for making an application

As a result of the Supplementary Agreement, which came into force on 1 February 2009, the normal periods of limitation, as set out in the Limitation Act 1980, now apply (see **Chapter 7**).

#### 3.4.2.3 Requirements

The applicant, or person acting on behalf of the applicant, must have reported the event to the police (clause 4(3)(c)):

(a) in the case of claims for death or bodily injury alone, not later than 14 days after the event occurred; and

(b) in the case of claims for property damage, not later than five days after the event occurred.

Evidence of the report must be supplied in the form of the crime or incident number, and the applicant must have co-operated with the police in any investigation they conducted.

#### 3.4.2.4 Investigation of claims

The MIB is under an obligation to make an award only if it is satisfied, on the balance of probabilities, that the death, bodily injury or damage was caused in such circumstances that the unidentified person would (had he been identified) have been held liable to pay damages to the applicant in respect of it.

The MIB shall investigate the claim and reach a decision as to whether it must make an award to the applicant, and where it decides to make an award, it will determine the amount. Where the MIB gives notice to the applicant that it has decided to make him an award, it shall pay the award within 14 days of a written confirmation from the applicant that he accepts the award.

#### 3.4.2.5 Compensation

The MIB shall award a sum equivalent to the amount which it would have awarded to the applicant for general and special damages if the applicant had brought successful proceedings to enforce a claim for damages against the unidentified person. In calculating the sum payable, the MIB shall adopt the same method of calculation as the court would adopt in calculating damages (clause 8).

It will include in the award a sum representing interest on the compensation payable at a rate equal to that which a court would award a successful litigant (clause 9).

#### 3.4.2.6 Contribution towards legal costs

In accordance with clause 10, the MIB will make a contribution to the claimant's costs. In practice, it will usually include in the award a sum towards the cost of obtaining legal advice, subject to a minimum of £500 and a maximum of £3,000 (plus VAT and reasonable disbursements).

## 3.5 Duties of the highway authority

Claims against highway authorities range from those made by pedestrians who have tripped or slipped on pavements or pathways, to those made by motorists who have been injured in accidents caused by the poor state of roads. Solicitors acting for claimants injured in road traffic accidents should always consider the possibility that a highways authority may be liable to their client in addition to or instead of another road user.

### 3.5.1 Who is the relevant highway authority?

The local highway authority will be the local county council, metropolitan district council, unitary authority or, in London, either Transport for London or the relevant London borough council. The Secretary of State for Transport or, for roads in Wales, the Secretary of State for Wales, is the highway authority for most motorways and trunk roads.

Section 36(6) of the Highways Act 1980 (HA 1980) requires every council to keep an up-to-date list of all roads and traffic routes within its area for which it is responsible. Section 36(7) states that any person may consult the list at the council offices free of charge. Consequently, if there is any doubt as to whether it is the council who has responsibility or whether the road is in private ownership and privately maintainable, recourse can be made to the records.

It is common for neighbouring councils to enter into agency agreements, whereby one council undertakes maintenance of certain highways on behalf of the other. Ultimate responsibility remains with the statutory highway authority, and legal proceedings should be issued accordingly.

### 3.5.2 Duty to maintain the highway

#### 3.5.2.1 Duty under statute and common law

Under s 41(1) of the HA 1980, a highway authority has a duty to maintain (which includes a duty to repair) any highway which is maintainable at the public expense. Section 36(2) defines a highway 'maintainable at public expense' as:

(a) a highway constructed by a highway authority;

(b) a highway constructed by a council within its own area, or a highway constructed outside of its area for which it has agreed to be responsible;

(c) a trunk road;

(d) a footpath or bridleway created or diverted by the local authority.

Highway authorities have a similar duty to maintain highways under common law (see *Dabinett v Somerset County Council* [2006] LTL 20/4/2007), and breaches of both statutory and common law duties are commonly pleaded in particulars of claim. Highway authorities also have duties in common law nuisance and under s 150(1) of the HA 1980 to remove obstructions from the highway, but these are outside the ambit of this text.

### 3.5.2.2 Flooding and snow and ice

Is the duty to maintain the highway limited to the surface of the road itself? In *Department of Transport, Environment and the Regions v Mott Macdonald Ltd & Others* [2006] EWCA Civ 1089, the Court of Appeal considered whether the highway authority was liable to the claimants, who had all been injured in road accidents caused by a dangerous accumulation of water on the surface of the highway, due to the longstanding blockage of the drains serving the road. In overturning the judge's decision, the Court concluded that the duties of a highway authority are not confined to the repair and the keeping in repair of the surface of the highway, and that it is obliged to maintain the drains in good repair. This duty is not limited to the repair of physical damage to the drains, but extends to the clearance of blockages. However, you should note that where a statutory authority, such as Thames Water or Severn Trent, has adopted responsibility for the drains in accordance with an agreement under the Water Industry Act 1991, it will be that authority, rather than the highway authority, which will be responsible for any accident resulting from a failure to maintain the drains.

Does the highway authority have a duty to prevent or remove the accumulation of snow or ice on the highway? It appears that there is no such duty under common law (*Sandhar v The Department of Transport, Environment and the Regions* [2004] EWHC 28 (QB)), but in 2003 an amendment was made to the HA 1980 to impose such a duty. Section 41(1A) requires highway authorities to ensure 'so far as is reasonably practicable, that safe passage along a highway is not endangered by snow and ice', and this would appear to include the need to undertake preventative gritting as well as clearing away accumulations of snow and ice. What is reasonably practicable is ultimately a matter for the courts, but one would expect highway authorities to be able to demonstrate that they have, at the very least, planned and implemented a winter maintenance plan in accordance with guidance published by the Department of Transport.

### 3.5.2.3 The role of contractors

Although the general rule is that employers are not liable for the torts of their independent contractors, statutory duties are non-delegable. Consequently, a highway authority which delegates responsibility for the repair and maintenance of a highway, does not escape liability to a claimant who is injured due to the negligent failure of the contractor to discharge its responsibilities.

### 3.5.2.4 The role of statutory undertakers

There are organisations, such as those dealing with gas, electricity, water, cable TV and telephones, which have apparatus on or under the highway. Such statutory undertakers are entitled to break up the highway under licences granted by the highway authority. They are, of course, required to take measures to ensure the highway is safe whilst the works are being carried out and to make good the highway following the completion of the works. Nevertheless, the responsibility to ensure that the highway does not pose a danger to road users remains with the highway authority and, subject to a successful defence under s 58 of the HA 1980, a claim against it for injuries caused by the dangerous condition of the highway will be successful. Where there is a possibility that a s 58 defence may be successful, claimants should commence proceedings against both the highway authority and the statutory undertaker. Where proceedings are commenced against the highway authority only, those acting for the authority should consider whether it is appropriate to issue an additional claim under CPR 20, in order to pass all or part of the blame to the statutory undertaker (see **12.12**).

### 3.5.3 Breach of duty

In order to succeed in a claim against the highways authority, a claimant will have to prove:

(a) that the condition of the highway made it a foreseeable danger to road users; and

(b) the condition of the highway was due to the failure of the highways authority to maintain it; and

(c) that the damage was caused by the dangerous condition of the highway.

In applying the forseeability test, the danger must be foreseeable to a road user having reasonable care for his own safety. In *Rider v Rider* [1973] 1 All ER 294, Sachs LJ concluded that:

> The highway authority must provide not merely for model drivers, but for the normal run of drivers to be found on their highways, and that includes those who make the mistakes which experience and common sense teach us are likely to occur.

#### 3.5.3.1 The statutory defence

Under s 58 of the HA 1980, a highway authority may, in its defence, prove that it had taken such care as in all the circumstances was reasonably required to ensure that the highway was not dangerous for traffic. For the purposes of such a defence, the court will attempt to balance the public and private interests, and will have regard to the following matters:

(a) the character of the highway, and the traffic which was reasonably to be expected to use it;

(b) the standard of maintenance appropriate for a highway of that character and used by such traffic;

(c) the state of repair in which a reasonable person would have expected to find the highway;

(d) whether the highway authority knew, or could reasonably have been expected to know, that the condition of the part of the highway to which the action relates was likely to cause danger to users of the highway;

(e) where the highway authority could not reasonably have been expected to repair that part of the highway before the cause of action arose, what warning notices of its condition had been displayed.

A highway authority will not necessarily be liable for injuries resulting from an accident which occurred shortly after a defect in the highway arose, but it will need to provide evidence that systems of regular inspection and maintenance were in place in order to detect each defect and repair it within a reasonable time. If it is able to show that the frequency of inspections was appropriate for the nature and character of that particular highway and that, at the time of the last inspection before the accident, the defect was not present or not considered to be dangerous, it is likely to be successful in its defence. If, however, it had been aware of the defect but had taken an unreasonable time to effect the necessary repairs, the defence will not succeed. What is a 'reasonable time' will depend on the nature of the defect and the potential consequences to road users of failing to repair it.

### 3.5.4 Tripping and slipping cases

Tripping and slipping claims against highway authorities (and other land owners) are very common, and they have increased in recent years. They may arise, for example, as a result of uneven or unstable paving stones, broken or missing kerbstones, potholes, protruding tree roots, missing manhole covers and highway surfaces which have become slippery, such as where there is an abundance of moss or wet leaves, or an accumulation of snow or ice.

As with other claims regarding the highway, the courts have been at pains to point out that each case should turn on its own facts and that the trial judge should determine whether the highway is in a dangerous condition. The court in *Littler v Liverpool Corporation* [1968] 2 All ER 343 gave the following guidance:

> The test ... is reasonable foreseeability of danger. A length of pavement is only dangerous if, in the ordinary course of human affairs, danger may reasonably be anticipated from its continued use by the public who usually pass over it. It is a mistake to isolate and emphasise a particular difference in levels between flagstones unless that difference is such that a reasonable person who noticed and considered it would regard it as presenting a real source of danger. Uneven surfaces and differences in level between flagstones of about an inch may cause a pedestrian ... to trip and stumble, but such characteristics have to be accepted.

When considering the point at which differing levels in a highway become dangerous to pedestrians, practitioners sometimes do refer to one inch as being the appropriate measurement. However, claimants have been successful where the difference has been as little as one-eighth of an inch (*Pitman v Southern Electricity Board* [1978] 3 All ER 901).

## 3.6 Conclusion

Road traffic accident claims are the most common type of personal injury claims, and they are, in the main, fairly straightforward. This means that the trainee solicitor or junior solicitor is likely to be dealing with this type of case when he is first introduced to personal injury work. It is useful to be aware that many low value claims will be handled, on behalf of claimants and defendants, by individuals who have no legal qualifications, sometimes with minimal training and supervision. If the solicitor has a thorough understanding of the legal principles which govern RTA claims, he will bring clarity to the procedure and will be better able to bring about the optimum conclusion for his client.

## 3.7 Further reading

Whalan, M, *Road Traffic Accident Claims* (CLT Professional Publishing)

# Chapter 4
# Employers' Liability Claims: The Law



## 4.1 Introduction

An employer may be personally liable to an injured employee on the basis of:

(a) common law negligence; and/or

(b) breach of statutory duty, for example under the Health and Safety at Work, etc Act 1974 (HSWA 1974), the Occupiers' Liability Act 1957 (OLA), or European Directives covering safety by way of regulations under the HSWA 1974.

The heads of liability are not mutually exclusive. For example, in certain circumstances the employer may be liable to the injured employee under both heads, while in other circumstances the employer may be liable only in common law negligence but not otherwise. The employer may also be vicariously liable to the injured employee where the injury was caused by a tort (eg, negligence) of another employee who was acting in the course of his employment.

## 4.2 The employer's common law duty of care

An employer is under a duty to take reasonable care of his employees' health and safety in the course of their employment. This includes providing health checks (especially if employees are engaged in hazardous work), equipment to protect employees from injury, and medical equipment in order to mitigate the effects of any injury.

This duty to take 'reasonable care' was explained by Lord Wright in *Wilsons and Clyde Coal Co v English* [1938] AC 57 as requiring an employer to exercise due care and skill in four particular areas, ie to provide:

(a) competent staff;

(b) adequate plant and equipment;

(c) a safe system of work; and

(d) safe premises.

Many of the common law duties are confirmed or strengthened by statute and regulations, but common law rules are an important indication of how courts are likely to interpret new regulations (see **4.3.2.3** below). Each of the four areas identified by Lord Wright is discussed in further detail below.

### 4.2.1 Competent staff

In many cases the employer will be vicariously liable for the negligence of an employee which results in injury to a fellow worker. An employer can also be personally liable under its common law duty. The duty is on the employer to take reasonable care to provide competent fellow workers. Whether the employer has failed to take reasonable care may depend upon the knowledge that he has (or ought to have) of the workmate's incompetence or inexperience, etc. In *Hudson v Ridge Manufacturing Co* [1957] 2 QB 348, the employers were held liable for continuing to employ a man who over a space of four years had habitually engaged in horseplay such as tripping people up. On the day in question he tripped the claimant, as a result of which the claimant injured his wrist. The court held that as this potentially dangerous misbehaviour had been known to the employers for a long time, and as they had failed to prevent it or remove the source of it, they were liable to the claimant for failing to take proper care of his safety.

However, in other cases involving practical jokes by fellow workers the employers have been held not liable on the basis that they could not reasonably have foreseen the behaviour that caused the injury (*Smith v Crossley Bros* (1951) 95 Sol Jo 655; *Coddington v International Harvester Co of Great Britain* (1969) 113 SJ 265).

### 4.2.2 Adequate plant and equipment

Accidents may also occur either because no plant or equipment is provided, or because inadequate equipment is provided. For example, if an employee suffers injuries falling from a makeshift means of gaining access to high shelves, the employer will be liable if no ladder has been provided for this purpose.

'Plant' simply means anything used in the course of work. It will include everything from large and complicated machinery (eg, a paper mill) to the most basic equipment (eg, an office chair). The duty rests on the employer to take reasonable steps to provide adequate equipment and materials to do the job, and then to maintain that equipment. For example, if an office swivel chair gives way under an employee, the employer may be liable for failing to maintain the chair, or for having inadequate provision for maintenance or renewal. The employer will also be vicariously liable if employees fail to maintain or repair such plant or equipment.

The duty to maintain plant and equipment in good order is now supplemented by the Provision and Use of Work Equipment Regulations 1998 (SI 1998/2306) (see **4.3.2.3**). When considering whether plant has been adequately maintained, the court will look to current practice, which will be different according to the type of equipment involved. Depending on the type of equipment, all or any of the following matters may be relevant, and evidence should be looked for, both when using the pre-action protocol and at the disclosure stage of litigation:

(a) inspection and servicing records;

(b) reports of defects, breakdown or poor running;

(c) replacing worn-out parts or equipment;

(d) steps taken to repair or replace equipment shown to be defective.

The frequency and method of inspection or testing that employers should adopt will depend on the nature of the equipment in question. Items which are subject to stress, such as ropes, should be inspected and, if necessary, replaced more regularly (see Provision and Use of Work Equipment Regulations 1998, reg 6) than items which are subject simply to ordinary wear and tear, such as floor coverings.

The requirement to provide adequate plant also extends to a duty to make reasonable provision of safety and protective equipment, eg goggles, safety gloves and shoes. This duty at common law is now supplemented by the Personal Protective Equipment at Work Regulations 1992 (SI 1992/2966) (see **4.3.2.4**).

If an employee is injured as a result of a latent defect in the equipment he is using, he may also be able to rely on the Employer's Liability (Defective Equipment) Act 1969, which imposes a form of strict liability on the employer. Section 1(1) provides:

> Where … an employee suffers personal injury in the course of his employment in consequence of a defect in equipment provided by his employer for the purposes of the employer's business and the defect is attributable wholly or partly to the fault of a third party (whether identified or not) the injury shall be deemed to be also attributable to negligence on the part of the employer.

### 4.2.3 Safe system of work

The duty to provide a safe system of work is very wide and will be a question of fact to be considered in each case. It covers such things as:

(a) the physical layout of the plant;
(b) the method by which work is carried out;
(c) the sequence in which work is to be carried out;
(d) the provision of instructions;
(e) the taking of any safety precautions;
(f) the provision of proper warnings and notices (*Speed v Thomas Swift & Co* [1943] KB 557).

The employer must take care to see that the system is complied with, bearing in mind the fact that an employee may become careless after a time, especially if the work is of a repetitive nature (*General Cleaning Contractors Ltd v Christmas* [1953] AC 180).

**Examples**

In *General Cleaning Contractors v Christmas* [1953] AC 180, the claimant window cleaner was instructed by his employers in the sill method of cleaning windows. He was to hold on to the window sash whilst cleaning. A window closed on his fingers and he fell to the ground. It was held that the employers were in breach of their duty to provide a safe system of work, as they should have told the claimant to test the sashes to see if they were loose, and should have provided him with wedges.

In *Morgan v Lucas Aerospace Ltd* [1997] JPIL 4/97, 280–1, the claimant was employed in the defendants' factory to clean waste swarf (oil contaminated with metal waste) from trays underneath machinery. He had been given no formal training. Swarf caught in the machine cut through his heavy-duty glove, causing a gash to the claimant's hand. The claimant alleged this injury was caused by the defendants' failure to provide and maintain a safe system of work. In the first instance, it was held that the defendants were not absolved from the duty to provide a safe glove merely because it was difficult or expensive to obtain. If no better glove could be obtained at a reasonable price, the whole system was unsafe. The defendants appealed. On appeal, it was held that it was not necessary for the claimant to prove what alternative system of work could be adopted and which would have been safer. The claimant proved that the defendants allowed an unsafe practice to be adopted which they ought to have known to be unsafe and which they could have altered. If the gloves provided were the best available, the obligation of the defendants was to devise a system which would remove or reduce the risk of injury.

### 4.2.4 Safe premises

It is accepted that the duty of care extends to the provision of safe premises. The duty applies not only to premises occupied by the employer, but also to premises occupied by a third party where the employee is working temporarily (*General Cleaning Contractors Ltd v Christmas* [1953] AC 180; *Wilson v Tyneside Window Cleaning Co* [1958] 2 QB 110). The duty is supplemented by the Workplace (Health, Safety and Welfare) Regulations 1992 (SI 1992/3004) (see **4.3.2.5**).

Slipping and tripping cases are frequent causes of negligence claims at work, as is shown by the amount of advice and preventative information available to employers from the Health & Safety Executive (HSE). The employer must act reasonably to ensure that floors and means of access are reasonably safe.

### 4.2.5 The requirement of 'reasonableness'

It should be remembered that the duty on the employer is not absolute but merely a duty to take reasonable care. Generally a high standard will be required, but it will vary according to the circumstances.

The standard of care demanded of an employer was summarised by Swanwick J in *Stokes v Guest Keen and Nettlefold Bolts & Nuts Ltd* [1968] 1 WLR 1776:

> The overall test is still the conduct of the reasonable and prudent employer, taking positive thought for the safety of his workers in the light of what he knows or ought to know; where there is a recognised and general practice which has been followed for a substantial period in similar circumstances without mishap, he is entitled to follow it, unless in the light of common sense or newer knowledge it is clearly bad; but where there is developing knowledge, he must keep abreast of it and not be too slow to apply it …

Section 16 of the HSWA 1974 authorises Approved Codes of Practice (ACOPs), which set out guidance as to what is good practice in a particular trade and, as such, are a reflection of current informed thinking in the health and safety industry. Similarly, Guidance Notes issued by the HSE, although not binding, will be indicative of whether good working practices were being followed. It will be difficult for an employer to argue that a risk could not be foreseen where information was available in documents published by the HSE.

In *Stokes*, Swanwick J went on to say that an employer:

> … must weigh up the risk in terms of the likelihood of injury occurring and the potential consequences if it does; and he must balance against this the probable effectiveness of the precautions that can be taken to meet it and the expense and inconvenience they involve.

The employer must take into account the likelihood and potential gravity of an injury. It must then consider the measures necessary, and the cost involved in taking those measures, to avert the risk of injury. In *Latimer v AEC Ltd* [1953] AC 643, the claimant was one of 4,000 employees at the defendant's factory. During a night shift, the claimant slipped on the factory floor, the surface of which had become oily following recent flooding after a thunderstorm. The House of Lords held that it was reasonable for the defendant to put on the night shift rather than close the factory until the oily surface had been rendered safe.

The duty of care is owed to each employee individually, and so all the circumstances relevant to each employee must be taken into account. A good illustration of this is the case of *Paris v Stepney Borough Council* [1951] AC 367, in which the employers were held to be negligent for failing to supply goggles to a one-eyed workman, even though it was not necessary to provide goggles to fully-sighted workers.

### 4.2.6 Personal nature of duty

The employer will escape liability only if he shows that both he and the person to whom he delegated the duty exercised reasonable care in the discharge of that duty (*Davie v New Merton Board Mills Ltd* [1959] AC 604). Therefore, the duty is not discharged, for example, merely by delegating it to an apparently competent manager, if that manager in fact fails to act competently (*Sumner v William Henderson & Sons Ltd* [1964] 1 QB 450; *McDermid v Nash Dredging & Reclamation Co Ltd* [1987] 2 All ER 878).

An employer can remain liable for the safety of an employee, even while the employee is under the control of someone else. For example, where a worker on a building site is injured whilst working on a different building site under the control and instruction of different contractors, because he had been sent to work for the contractors by his own employer, his employer can be found liable for failing to ensure that he was properly trained and for failing to maintain a safe system of work even though the employer had no control over management of that site (*Morris v Breaveglen* [1993] ICR 766, CA).

In certain circumstances both an independent contractor and an occupier of a building can also owe a duty of care to the employee of one of its subcontractors. See *E H Humphries (Norton) Ltd, Thistle Hotels v Fire Alarm Fabrication Services Ltd* [2006] EWCA Civ 1496. The judge was entitled to find in the circumstances that the defendant's right to supervise the work so as to ensure that it was carried out safely, imposed on it a duty of care which extended to the employees of the subcontractor who actually carried out the work. The defendant had been negligent in failing to obtain from the subcontractor a proper method statement of the work to be carried out, or a proper risk assessment.

## 4.3 Breach of statutory duty

The relationship between an employer and employee is usually closely regulated by statute. The basic principles are set out below.

Legislation generally falls into one of the following categories:

(a) The HSWA, ss 2 and 3 impose obligations on employers and the self-employed to ensure, so far as reasonably practicable, the health and safety of their employees and members of the public who might be affected by their activities.

(b) Regulations (made under the HSWA 1974, s 15, to comply with EU Directives).

In addition, s 16 of the HSWA 1974 authorises Approved Codes of Practice (ACOPs), which set out what is good practice in a particular trade. Unlike a breach of the 1974 Act or regulations, a failure to observe an ACOP will not give rise to criminal liability, but it will be admissible in evidence in criminal proceedings. These Codes will also be admissible in civil proceedings as evidence of good practice in the trade and, as such, are a reflection of current informed thinking in the health and safety industry. Similarly, Guidance Notes issued by the HSE, although not binding, will be indicative of whether good working practices were being followed.

### 4.3.1 Civil liability for breach of statutory duty

To be successful in a civil claim based on a breach of statutory duty, the injured employee must show that:

(a) the breach is actionable in a civil court;

(b) the duty is owed to the claimant by the defendant;

(c) the claimant's loss is within the mischief of the Act;

(d) the defendant is in breach of the duty;

(e) the breach caused the loss.

#### 4.3.1.1 Is the breach of duty actionable in a civil court?

A breach of statutory duty is primarily a crime, but it can also give rise to civil liability except where the statute expressly provides otherwise. For example, there is express exclusion of civil liability for breaches of general duties under the HSWA 1974 (s 47(1)).

The Management of Health and Safety at Work and Fire Precautions (Workplace) (Amendment) Regulations 2003 (SI 2003/2457) amend the Management of Health and Safety at Work Regulations 1999 (SI 1999/3242) ('the Management Regulations') so that employees may bring civil claims against their employers where they are in breach of duties imposed by the Management Regulations. This is of particular significance, as the Management Regulations include an obligation on employers to perform an adequate risk assessment (reg 3; see **4.3.2.1**). However, claims by non-employees are excluded.

#### 4.3.1.2 Has the defendant breached his statutory duty?

The standard required of the employer to fulfil his statutory duty is a question of construction of the statute. The common formulae are as follows:

(a) *'Absolute' (or strict) duty*: where a state of affairs is required to exist and that state does not exist, the employer is in breach (even if he has not been negligent).

(b) *'So far as reasonably practicable'*: when judging whether there has been a breach, the court will balance the risk against any sacrifice (eg, in terms of time, trouble or money) required to avoid the risk. In *Davies v Health & Safety Executive* [2002] EWCA Crim 2949, [2003] IRLR 170, the court considered s 40 of the Health and Safety at Work, etc Act 1974, which deals with the interpretation of 'reasonably practicable'. Section 40 imposes on the defendant the burden of proving to the court that it was not reasonably practicable to do more than was in fact done to satisfy the duty (the reverse burden of proof). This was attacked by the defendant as being incompatible with the presumption of innocence in Article 6(2) of the European Convention for the Protection of Human Rights and Fundamental Freedoms 1950. On appeal, the Court found that Article 6(2) was not breached, and confirmed that a defendant who wishes to raise a defence of reasonable practicability does have the legal burden of calling positive evidence to prove that it was not possible to have done more to prevent the death or injury. The Court justified this stance by observing that the defence should not be difficult for a defendant to prove, as he will have this information to hand, whereas it would be unreasonable to place this burden on the prosecution.

(c) *'As far as practicable'*: this is a duty stricter than 'reasonably practicable'. For example, current knowledge of the risk of injury will be relevant in judging whether a safety precaution was 'practicable'. The onus is on the person on whom the duty is imposed to show that compliance was not 'practicable'.

### 4.3.2 Health and safety legislation

It is not possible to set out here all the legislation currently in force; what follows is a summary of some of the regulations which are most frequently relied on in claims for personal injury.

#### 4.3.2.1 Management of Health and Safety at Work Regulations 1999

The revised Management of Health and Safety at Work Regulations 1999 (SI 1999/3242) came into force on 29 December 1999 and replaced the Management of Health and Safety at Work Regulations 1992. These Regulations implement European Health and Safety Directives relating to the employer's obligations in respect of health and safety for workers, and in relation to minimum health and safety requirements for the workplace as to fire safety.

The main provisions regarding employer's duties are as follows:

**Risk assessment (reg 3)**

All employers are required to make a suitable and sufficient assessment of the risks to health and safety of their employees and persons who are not in their employment but who are affected by the conduct of their undertaking. Having made an assessment of the health and safety risks, it is incumbent upon the employer to try to diminish the risks that have been identified. If the employer has five or more employees, there is a duty to record the risk assessment (reg 3(6)), and to note any significant findings of the assessment and whether any group of employees is identified as being especially at risk. The assessment should be made by asking employees how they carry out their functions, together with taking advice from a relevant health and safety expert and ergonomists. The assessment should be updated and reviewed regularly.

The duty on employers to carry out a risk assessment is likely to be one of the areas highlighted by personal injury lawyers to substantiate whether or not the employer has acted reasonably to provide a safe system of work and to establish the question of foreseeability of harm in negligence claims. In *Allison v London Underground Ltd* [2008] EWCA Civ 71, the Court of Appeal held that the employers were held liable when the claimant, a tube train driver, suffered an injury as a result of prolonged use of a traction brake controller. In his judgment Smith LJ asked:

> How is the court to approach the question of what the employer ought to have known about the risks inherent in his own operations? In my view, what he ought to have known is (or should be) closely linked with the risk assessment which he is obliged to carry out under regulation 3 of the 1999 Regulations. That requires the employer to carry out a suitable and sufficient risk assessment for the purposes of identifying the measures he needs to take … what the employer *ought* to have known will be what he *would* have known if he had carried out a suitable and sufficient risk assessment.

Smith LJ went on to say:

> Plainly, a suitable and sufficient risk assessment will identify those risks in respect of which the employee needs training. Such a risk assessment will provide the basis not only for the training which the employer must give but also for other aspects of his duty, such as, for example, whether the place of work is safe or whether work equipment is safe.

Clearly the question of whether an employer has carried out a suitable and sufficient risk assessment will be a central issue in establishing liability in many cases.

**Principles of prevention (reg 4)**

According to reg 4, the principles of prevention of risk to be applied are to:

(a) avoid risks;

(b) evaluate the risks which cannot be avoided;

(c) combat the risks at source;

(d) adapt the work to the individual, especially as regards the design of workplaces, choice of work equipment, and choice of working and production methods, with a view to alleviating monotonous work and work at a pre-determined rate to reduce their effects on health;

(e) adapt to technical progress;

(f) replace the dangerous by the non-dangerous or less dangerous;

(g) develop a coherent overall prevention policy which covers technology, organisation of work, working conditions, social relationships and the influence of factors relating to the working environment;

(h) give collective protective measures priority over individual protective measures; and

(i) give appropriate instruction to employees.

**Review of health and safety arrangements (reg 5)**

Employers must make appropriate arrangements for planning, organisation, control, monitoring and review of preventative and protective measures.

**Health surveillance (reg 6)**

Employers are required to have an appropriate policy on risk surveillance, having regard to the findings of risks identified by the risk assessment. For example, if the risk assessment of employees showed that there were risks to health from airborne dust, that identified risk should be kept under review by regular health checks for rises in respiratory problems in employees.

**Health and safety assistance (reg 7)**

Employers must appoint competent persons to assist the employer in carrying out compliance with statutory safety provisions. The Regulations require a safety audit to be carried out by accredited auditors who are suitably qualified. The audit will identify potential hazards in the workplace.

**Information for employees (reg 10)**

Employers must give information which is comprehensible to employees on health and safety risks and protective measures that should be adopted.

**Employers' duties to 'outside workers' (reg 12)**

Employers must provide information to 'outside workers' relating to hazards and the protective and preventative measures being taken.

**Employee capabilities and health and safety training (reg 13)**

Employers must provide adequate health and safety training to employees when first recruited and subsequently on being exposed to new risks. Such training should be repeated periodically.

**Risk assessment for new or expectant mothers (reg 16)**

For the purpose of reg 16, 'new or expectant mother' means an employee who is pregnant, who has given birth within the previous six months or who is breastfeeding. Where the workforce includes women of child-bearing age and the work is of a kind which could involve risk to the health and safety of a new or an expectant mother, or of the baby, the risk assessment required by reg 3 must include an assessment of that risk. If at all possible, the employee's working conditions or hours of work should be altered so as to avoid the risk. If it is not reasonable or possible to avoid the risk by these means, the employer may suspend the employee from work for so long as is necessary to avoid the risk.

Where a new or an expectant mother works at night and obtains a certificate from a registered medical practitioner or registered midwife showing it is necessary for her health and safety that she should not work for any period identified in the certificate, the employer shall suspend her from work for so long as is necessary for her health and safety.

**Protection of young employees (reg 19)**

A 'young person' means any person who has not attained the age of 18. In relation to young persons, reg 19 states that employers are under a duty to ensure that young persons are protected from risks which arise as a consequence of the young persons' lack of experience, or absence of awareness of existing or potential risks, or the fact that young persons have not yet fully matured. Subject to this, employers are not allowed to employ young persons for work which is beyond their physical or psychological capacity, or involves harmful exposure to agents which are toxic, carcinogenic, cause heritable genetic damage or harm to an unborn child, or which in any other way may chronically affect human health. Employers must not allow young persons to work where they may be involved in harmful exposure to radiation; nor involve the risk of accidents which it may reasonably be assumed cannot be recognised or avoided by young persons owing to their insufficient attention to safety, or lack of experience or training.

**Duties of employees (reg 14)**

Although the main thrust of the Regulations is to confirm the obligations on employers in relation to health and safety, there are also obligations on employees, who have a duty to:

(a) use machinery, equipment, dangerous substances or other equipment in accordance with the training and instructions which have been given to them by their employer; and

(b) inform the employer of anything which the employee considers to represent a danger to health and safety, or any shortcomings in the employer's arrangements for health and safety.

### 4.3.2.2 Health and Safety (Display Screen Equipment) Regulations 1992 (as amended)

The Health and Safety (Display Screen Equipment) Regulations 1992 (SI 1992/2792) are applicable to new display screen equipment (DSE) as from 1 January 1993, and to existing DSE from 1 January 1996. However, the requirement of ongoing risk assessment applies to both old and new DSE as from 1 January 1993.

The main provisions are as follows:

(a) Employers must make a risk assessment of workstations used by display screen workers and reduce risks identified (reg 2).

(b) Employers must ensure that display screen workers take adequate breaks, and must ensure that an appropriate eyesight test is carried out by a competent person (reg 5).

(c) Employers must provide users with adequate health and safety training in the use of any workstation upon which they may be required to work (reg 6).

(d) Employers must also provide adequate health and safety information to DSE operators, which should cover such things as information and reminders of how to reduce risks, such as early reporting of problems and provision of adjustable furniture (reg 7).

The main health problems associated with DSE operation are:

(a) general fatigue caused by poor workstation design;

(b) upper limb disorders, such as peritendonitis or carpal tunnel syndrome. Repetitive strain injury (RSI) is the most common problem experienced by keyboard users;

(c) eyesight problems, such as temporary fatigue, sore eyes and headaches.

Employers should have, and be able to show that they have, an adequate policy designed to reduce risks associated with DSE work. The policy should identify hazards, such as visual fatigue, and action to be taken to reduce risk, such as provision of eyesight tests, screen filters and training in workstation adjustment.

### 4.3.2.3 Provision and Use of Work Equipment Regulations 1998 (as amended)

The Provision and Use of Work Equipment Regulations 1998 (SI 1998/2306) replace the Provision of Work Equipment Regulations 1992. The Regulations apply to all types of machine, appliance, apparatus, tool or installation for use at work (reg 2) in all types of workplaces. The Regulations are intended to ensure the provision of safe work equipment and its safe use. The main provisions are as follows:

(a) The employer shall ensure the suitability of work equipment for the purpose for which it is provided. The equipment must be suitable, by design and construction, for the place in which it will be used and for the intended purpose (reg 4).

(b) The employer must ensure that the equipment is maintained in an efficient state (reg 5(1)) and, if machinery has a maintenance log, that the log is kept up to date (reg 5(2)).

The wording of reg 5(1) was considered by the Court of Appeal in *Stark v Post Office* [2000] ICR 1013. The claim concerned an accident at work, where a postman was thrown from a bicycle provided by his employer when part of the front brake snapped in two. It was accepted that the defect to the bicycle would not have been detected by a rigorous inspection. Nevertheless, the Court found that the form of words used in the regulation gave rise to a finding of strict liability in relation to the provision of work equipment.

In *Ball v Street* [2005] EWCA Civ 76, the Court of Appeal reinforced the view that reg 5(1) gives rise to liability where injury is caused by machinery that is not in an efficient state of repair. The claimant was a farmer who was injured when part of a hay bailing machine fractured and ricocheted into his left eye. The Court found that notwithstanding that this was a 'freak accident', it was only necessary for the claimant to prove that the equipment failed to work efficiently and that that failure caused the accident. The Court found that the machine was no longer in good repair, neither was it in an efficient state, and such failure caused the accident. The imposition of an absolute duty by the Regulations was designed to render the task of an injured workman easier by simply requiring him to prove that the mechanism of the machine, that is the significant part of the machine, failed to work efficiently or was not in good repair and that such failure caused the accident. In this context 'efficient' refers to its state of repair from a health and safety standpoint and not from that of productivity.

Despite this apparent strict line taken by the courts, there have been examples where defendants have escaped liability. In *Smith v Northamptonshire County Council* [2008] EWCA Civ 181, the appellant local authority appealed against a decision that it was strictly liable under the Provision and Use of Work Equipment Regulations 1998, reg 5(1), for failure to maintain an access ramp used by the respondent employee (S) at a person's home. S was employed by the local authority as a carer/driver. As part of her duties she was required to collect a person (C) from her home and take her by minibus to a day centre. As S was pushing C in a wheelchair down a ramp which led out from C's house, S stepped on the edge of the ramp which gave way, causing her to stumble and injure herself. The ramp had been installed by the NHS some years previously. The Court of Appeal allowed the appeal on the basis that the duty to maintain could not normally apply to something which was part of someone else's property. It could furthermore not normally apply to something in relation to which access was limited, and in relation to which, if some maintenance was necessary, consent to carry out the work was required. S's appeal to the House of Lords was dismissed. Their Lordships confirmed that control over the use of equipment is not enough. Control over the equipment must be demonstrated. This could not be achieved simply from the fact that an employer has assessed and inspected the piece of equipment in question.

(c) If the work equipment must be assembled and installed correctly in order for it to be safe to use, the employer must ensure that:

(i) it is inspected after installation and prior to being put into service; or

(ii) it is inspected after assembly at its new location (reg 6(1)).

(d) The employer must ensure that employees have adequate health and safety information, and, if appropriate, instruction in the use of equipment (reg 8).

(e) The employer must ensure that anyone using the equipment has had adequate training, including as to any risks which use may entail and precautions to be adopted (reg 9). In particular, the ACOP attached to these Regulations states that induction training is particularly important when young people first enter the workplace.

(f) Employers must ensure the protection of persons from dangerous parts of machinery in the following order of precedence (reg 11):

(i) by fixed guards if practicable; but if not

(ii) by other guards or other protection devices if practicable; but if not

(iii) by use of jigs, holders, push-sticks or similar protective devices where practicable; but if not

(iv) by providing information, instruction, training and supervision as is necessary.

(g) Employers must ensure that where equipment or the substances produced are at a very high or low temperature, there must be protection to prevent injury to any person (reg 13).

(h) Employers must ensure that, where appropriate, equipment is provided with one or more easily accessible stop controls, and, where appropriate, emergency stop controls, and that they are clearly visible and identifiable (regs 15, 16 and 17 respectively).

(i) Employers must ensure that, where appropriate, the equipment is provided with suitable means to isolate it from all sources of energy. This must be clearly identifiable and readily accessible. Appropriate measures must be taken to ensure that reconnection of the energy source to the equipment does not expose any person using the equipment to any risk (reg 19).

(j) The equipment must be suitably stabilised and suitably lit (regs 20 and 21 respectively).

(k) When maintenance is being carried out, equipment must be shut down if reasonably practicable (reg 22).

(l) The equipment must be suitably marked with appropriate health and safety information and warning devices as appropriate (regs 23 and 24).

(m) Due to the rising number of accidents arising out of the use and misuse of forklift trucks, there are comprehensive regulations relating to the use of mobile work equipment. The Regulations require employers to ensure that employees are not carried on mobile equipment unless it is both suitable and incorporates reasonably practicable safety features (reg 25). They also seek to reduce the risk of equipment rolling over or overturning by placing on the employer an obligation to increase the stability of the equipment by making structural alterations if necessary (regs 26–28).

#### 4.3.2.4 Personal Protective Equipment at Work Regulations 1992 (as amended)

The Personal Protective Equipment at Work Regulations 1992 (SI 1992/2966) make provision for the supply of protective and safety equipment, for example: eye-protectors, respirators, gloves, clothing for adverse weather conditions, safety footwear, safety hats, high-visibility jackets, etc.

The main provisions are as follows:

(a) Employers must ensure that suitable personal protective equipment (PPE) is provided to employees at risk to their health and safety while at work. Such PPE is not suitable unless (reg 4(4)):

   (i) it is appropriate to the risk involved, the conditions at the place where the exposure to the risk may occur, and the period for which it is worn;

   (ii) it takes account of ergonomic requirements and the health of persons who may wear it, and of the characteristics of the workstation of each such person.

(b) Before choosing PPE the employer should make an assessment to ensure that it is suitable and compatible with other work equipment used at the same time (reg 6).

(c) Employers must ensure that PPE is maintained in efficient working order and good repair (reg 7). The obligation to supply protective equipment relates to identified risks. The Regulations will not be concerned with risks other than those necessitating protective equipment, and no absolute duty was intended to be imposed by reg 7(1) in relation to other risks (see *Fytche v Wincanton Logistics* [2003] EWCA Civ 874). In *Fytche*, the claimant suffered frostbite in the little toe of his right foot because there was a small hole in his boot where the steel cap met the sole. The steel-capped boots were PPE within the 1992 Regulations. The Court found that the boots were provided for the purpose of protecting the employee's foot from falling objects, and therefore his claim must fail.

(d) Employers must ensure that where PPE is provided, employees obtain such information, instruction and training as is adequate to ensure that they know what risks the PPE will avoid or limit, the purpose of the PPE, and any action they must take to ensure efficient working of the PPE, and must ensure that this information is available to employees (reg 9).

### 4.3.2.5 Manual Handling Operations Regulations 1992 (as amended)

The Manual Handling Operations Regulations 1992 (SI 1992/2793), reg 2(1), provides a definition of 'manual handling operations' as any transporting of a load (including the lifting, carrying and moving thereof) by hand or bodily force. Over one-quarter of accidents reported to the HSE involve manual handling. Despite moves toward mechanisation in industry, there are still many jobs, such as packaging and warehouse work, requiring the day-to-day lifting of heavy objects. Many claims are brought by health service staff, who may have to lift and carry heavy patients as part of their everyday duties.

The Regulations make provision as follows:

(a) So far as reasonably practicable, employers must avoid the need for employees to undertake any manual handling involving risk of injury (reg 4(1)(a)).

(b) If avoidance is not reasonably practicable, employers must make an assessment of manual handling risks, and try to reduce risk of injury. The assessment should address the task, the load, the working environment and the individual's capability (reg 4(1)(b)).

In *Brazier v Dolphin Fairway Ltd* [2005] EWCA Civ 84, at the time of the alleged injury the claimant was trying to lift down a wooden 6-feet by 6-feet pallet from a stack of pallets which was about 6-feet high. That was the system of work at C's place of employment and was known to his employers. There was a witness statement on behalf of the employers so indicating, and also using words to the effect that the pallets were 'fairly lightweight'.

The judge dismissed the claim on the basis that there was no evidence as to the weight of the pallet that was being lifted down. He said: 'I have no means of knowing how heavy it was or whether it was heavy enough to give rise to a foreseeable risk of injury.' He then went on to say that there was evidence that the pallet was roughly 6-feet by 6-feet: '... but I am completely at sea as to the forces and the strains which the claimant had to undergo. I have no expert engineering evidence which tells me anything about the forces of the strains.' The judge took the view that there was no evidence that the system of work that was being employed was unsafe.

On appeal (granting leave to appeal) the Court of Appeal found that it was arguable that the judge made an error of principle. Smith LJ put it like this:

> There comes a point when one does not need detailed evidence or expert evidence. The judge had evidence of a man being required to lift down a 6-feet by 6-feet wooden pallet; a pallet which when in use had to be strong enough to take considerable weight and be used with a fork lift truck. It seems to me to be arguable that no further evidence was needed to decide that a system which required someone to bring down such an object from a height of 6-feet would place that person at risk of injury.

(c) If it is not reasonably practicable to avoid manual handling operations which involve risk of injury, employers must take steps to reduce manual handling to the lowest level reasonably practicable (reg 4(1)(b)(ii)). In the context of assessing manual handling risks for the purpose of complying with reg 4, the correct approach is for the employer to consider the particular task in the context of the particular place of work and the particular employee who has to perform that task: see *O'Neill v DSG Retail Ltd* [2002] EWCA Civ 1139. In this case the employer conceded that it had failed to give adequate training once it had recognised it was necessary to increase awareness of the risks in manual handling, and therefore it had failed to reduce the risk of injury 'to the lowest level reasonably practicable' (as required by reg 4(1)(b)(ii)).

(d) Employees must be provided with information on the weight of each load, and the heaviest side of any load (reg 4(1)(b)(iii)).

Regulation 4 was amended by the Health and Safety (Miscellaneous Amendments) Regulations 2002 (SI 2002/2174) by the addition of the following paragraph:

> (3) In determining for the purposes of this regulation whether manual handling operations at work involve a risk of injury and in determining the appropriate steps to reduce that risk regard shall be had in particular to—
>
> (a) the physical suitability of the employee to carry out the operations;
>
> (b) the clothing, footwear or other personal effects he is wearing;
>
> (c) his knowledge and training;
>
> (d) the results of any risk assessment carried out pursuant to regulation 3 of the Management of Health and Safety at Work Regulations 1999;
>
> (e) whether the employee is within a group of employees identified by that assessment as being especially at risk; and
>
> (f) the results of any health surveillance provided pursuant to regulation 6 of the Management of Health and Safety at Work Regulations 1999.

Employees have a duty to make full use of any system of work provided by the employer to reduce manual handling risks (reg 5). As to the meaning of 'so far as reasonably practicable' in reg 4(1), see *Hawkes v Southwark LBC* [1998] EWCA Civ 310. In this case, it was found that the defendant had not carried out any risk assessment as required under the Regulations. The judge made it clear that the burden of proving what was 'reasonably practicable' lay on the defendant, and that failure to carry out an assessment did not by itself prove liability, rather it was the failure to take appropriate steps to reduce risk of injury to the lowest level reasonably practicable that was at issue. See also the Lifting Operations and Lifting Equipment Regulations 1998 (SI 1998/2307), which deal with health and safety requirements with respect to lifting equipment.

### 4.3.2.6 Workplace (Health, Safety and Welfare) Regulations 1992

The Workplace (Health, Safety and Welfare) Regulations 1992 (SI 1992/3004) apply to all workplaces except ships, construction sites and mining operations (reg 3). The Regulations are concerned with the way in which the building and the facilities within it may affect employees.

The main provisions are as follows:

(a) Workplace equipment, devices and systems must be maintained in efficient working order and good repair (reg 5).

(b) There must be adequate ventilation (reg 6).

(c) The indoor temperature during working hours must be reasonable, and thermometers must be provided to enable employees to determine the temperature (reg 7).

(d) Workplaces must have suitable lighting, which, if reasonably practicable, should be natural light (reg 8).

(e) Workplaces, including furniture, fittings, floors, walls and ceilings, must be kept sufficiently clean, and waste materials must not be allowed to accumulate (reg 9).

(f) Every workstation must be arranged so that it is suitable for any person likely to work there (reg 11).

(g) Every floor or traffic route surface must be suitable for the purpose for which it is used. In particular, it must have no hole or slope, or be uneven or slippery so as to expose any person to a risk to his health or safety. So far as reasonably practicable, every floor or traffic route must be kept free of obstructions or articles which may cause a person to slip, trip or fall (reg 12). The claim in *Coates v Jaguar Cars Ltd* [2004] EWCA Civ 337 concerned an accident that occurred as the claimant was going up a number of steps at the defendant's factory. The claimant tripped on the third stair, causing him to fall and break his arm. The claimant contended that this amounted to a breach of reg 12 as, if there had been a handrail, he would not have fallen. The Court of Appeal held that there had been no reason to find that the steps posed any real risk provided that those who had used them used a sufficient degree of care, as had been the case for any other steps of this nature. The judge at first instance was correct to have dismissed the claim.

(h) So far as reasonably practicable, effective measures must be taken to avoid injury to persons caused by falling or being struck by a falling object (reg 13).

(i) Suitable and sufficient sanitary conveniences must be provided at readily accessible places. They must be adequately lit and ventilated, and kept in a clean and tidy condition (reg 20).

(j) Suitable and sufficient washing facilities must be provided, including showers if required by the nature of the work for health reasons (reg 21).

(k) An adequate supply of wholesome drinking water must be provided at the workplace, which should be readily accessible and conspicuously marked where necessary.

### 4.3.2.7 Work at Height Regulations 2005

The Work at Height Regulations 2005 (SI 2005/735) impose health and safety requirements with respect to work at height where there is a risk of a fall liable to cause personal injury. They contain minimum safety and health requirements for the workplace, including minimum health and safety requirements at temporary or mobile construction sites.

**Meaning of work at height**

Working at height is defined in reg 2(1) as:

> (a) work in any place, including a place at or below ground level;
>
> (b) obtaining access to or egress from such place while at work, except by a staircase in a permanent workplace,
>
> where, if measures required by these Regulations were not taken, a person could fall a distance liable to cause personal injury.

**To whom do the Regulations apply?**

The Regulations apply to employers, to the self-employed, and to any person under an employer's control. This means that the Regulations apply not only to employees working under their employer's control, but also to contractors to the extent that they are under the control of building owners.

**Duties relating to the organising and planning of work at height**

Every employer is under a duty to ensure that work at height is properly planned, supervised and carried out in a safe manner, subject to it being reasonably practicable to do so. This duty includes the selection of work equipment in accordance with reg 7 (reg 4).

Persons undertaking work at height must be competent, or, if being trained, supervised by a competent person (reg 5).

**Requirement for Management Regulations risk assessment**

There are prescribed steps to be taken to avoid risk from work at height, including provision of a risk assessment under reg 3 of the Management Regulations (see **4.3.2.1**), which should:

(a) identify whether it is reasonably practicable to carry out the work safely otherwise than at height; and if not

(b) provide sufficient work equipment for preventing, so far as is reasonably practicable, a fall occurring and to minimise the distance or consequences should a fall occur (reg 6 and Sch 1).

**Duties relating to the selection of work equipment**

When selecting work equipment for use in work at height, the person concerned must give collective protection measures priority over personal protection measures; and must also take account of

(a) the working conditions and the risks to the safety of persons at the place where the work equipment is to be used;

(b) in the case of work equipment for access and egress, the distance to be negotiated;

(c) the distance and consequences of a potential fall;

(d) the duration and frequency of use;

(e) the need for easy and timely evacuation and rescue in an emergency;

(f) any additional risk posed by the use, installation or removal of that work equipment, or by evacuation and rescue from it (reg 7).

The Regulations also impose duties for the avoidance of risks from fragile surfaces, falling objects and danger areas, requiring that such areas are clearly indicated (regs 9–11); and require the inspection of certain work equipment and of places of work at height (regs 12 and 13 and Sch 7).

### 4.3.2.8 Control of Substances Hazardous to Health Regulations 2002

The Control of Substances Hazardous to Health Regulations 2002 (SI 2002/2677) came into force on 21 November 2002 and revoke and replace the 1994 Regulations. They provide a comprehensive and systematic approach to the control of hazardous substances at work, which include chemicals, airborne dusts, micro-organisms, biological agents and respiratory sensitisers.

The main duties on employers are as follows.

**(a) To carry out a formal risk assessment**

Regulation 6 provides that 'an employer shall not carry on any work which is liable to expose any employees to any substance hazardous to health unless he has made a suitable and sufficient assessment of the risks created by that work to the health of those employees and of the steps that need to be taken to meet the requirements of these Regulations.' The assessment should be reviewed if circumstances change. In *Naylor v Volex Group Plc* [2003] EWCA Civ 222, the claimant was exposed to a hazardous substance during her employment with the defendant, and as a result suffered from industrial asthma. The defendant had carried out a risk assessment based on standards provided by the HSE which were subsequently withdrawn. The Court of Appeal held that in those circumstances a new risk assessment should have been carried out, and that the defendant was therefore in breach of reg 6.

**(b) To prevent or control exposure to risks**

Regulation 7 sets out the duty that the employer must ensure that the exposure of employees to hazardous substances is either prevented or, where this is not reasonably practicable, adequately controlled.

In *Dugmore v Swansea NHS Trust* [2003] 1 All ER 333, the claimant developed a severe allergy to latex as a result of wearing surgical gloves. The Court of Appeal held that the defendant should have provided vinyl gloves and was in breach of its duty to control the claimant's exposure to latex under reg 7.

The prevention or adequate control of the exposure to hazardous substances must be secured by measures other than the provision of personal protective equipment so far as is reasonably practicable. This means that the employer's first act should be to control the process or substance hazardous to health by, for example, closing off the process or machine, or by providing suitable exhaust ventilation.

**(c) To ensure proper use of and to maintain personal protective equipment**

Regulation 8 provides that employers must take reasonable steps to ensure that any control measure or personal protective equipment is used or applied properly.

There is also a duty on every employee to make full and proper use of such equipment, and to report any defect in it to his employer.

Regulation 9 provides that employers must ensure that any control measure is maintained in an efficient state, in efficient working order and in good repair. For example, where respiratory equipment is provided, the employer must ensure that thorough examinations and tests of that equipment are carried out at suitable intervals.

**(d) To monitor exposure of employees**

Regulation 10 requires monitoring to ensure the maintenance of adequate control to substances hazardous to health, or to protect the health of employees. Certain substances and processes require monitoring at specified intervals, and the results of all monitoring must be recorded and kept for at least five years. Where the monitoring relates to the personal exposure of individual employees, the records must be kept for at least 40 years.

**(e) To provide health surveillance of employees where necessary**

Regulation 11 requires suitable health surveillance where it is appropriate (ie, where a particular task is known to make employees susceptible to a particular injury or disease). Medical surveillance is required for certain substances or processes, and a health record must be kept in respect of each employee under surveillance for at least 40 years.

**(f) To provide information and training to employees regarding hazardous substances**

Regulation 12 requires an employer to provide its employee with such information, instruction and training as is suitable and sufficient for the employee to know the risks to health created by such exposure, and the precautions which should be taken.

### 4.3.3 Statutory duty and common law negligence

The claimant employee will frequently make a claim both in common law negligence and for breach of statutory duty. Although the two are distinct causes of action, they are inevitably linked. It is usually difficult, but not impossible, to show that, if the employer has complied with regulations, he has nevertheless been negligent. In *Bux v Slough Metals Ltd* [1974] 1 All ER 262, the employer was found to have complied with regulations which required the provision of goggles to its employees and so had complied with its statutory duty, but it had failed to instruct the employee to wear the goggles and so was in breach of its common law duty. (See also *Franklin v Gramophone Co Ltd* [1948] 1 KB 542; *Close v Steel Co of Wales* [1962] AC 367.)

Equally, the employer may be liable for breach of statutory duty even though he has not been negligent. The onus of proof may also be different in the two causes: in negligence the onus is upon the claimant to show a breach; for breach of statutory duty the onus is often on the defendant to show that he acted 'as far as (reasonably) practicable' (see **4.3.1.2**).

## 4.4 Vicarious liability

### 4.4.1 Definition

An employer will be vicariously liable for his employee's torts if committed in the course of his employment. Therefore, it falls to be established:

(a) whether the tort was committed by an employee; and

(b) whether that employee was acting in the course of (ie, within the scope of) his employment.

### 4.4.2 'Course of employment'

The employee must have committed the tort 'in the course of his employment', which is less clear than may first appear. There are many cases on the point, but the nearest to a formulation of a rule is that the employer will be liable for acts of employees if they perform an authorised act in an unauthorised way, but will not be liable for acts not sufficiently connected with authorised acts. This is examined in further detail at **4.4.3** below.

### 4.4.3 Disobedience of orders by employees

Having established that an employer will be liable for acts of his employees if they are acting within the course of their employment, it is necessary to examine the situation where the employee disobeys the orders of his employer in relation to the way he carries out his work. In *Rose v Plenty* [1976] 1 All ER 97, a milkman had been told by his employers not to allow children to help him on his rounds. Subsequently he allowed a child to assist him, and the child was injured while riding on the milk float due to the milkman's negligent driving. On appeal to the Court of Appeal, the employer was found to be vicariously liable. The Court held that the employee was doing his job but was using a method that his employers had prohibited. Nonetheless, he was still found to be working within the scope of his employment as it was performed for the benefit of the defendant's business.

Contrast the above with *Lister and Others v Hesley Hall Ltd* [2001] 2 All ER 769. The facts of the case were that the warden of the school abused boys while they were resident at the school. The House of Lords held the defendant vicariously liable for the acts of its employee. The Lords said that the court should not concentrate on the nature of the actual act complained of (abuse) but on the closeness of the connection between the nature of the employment and the tort complained of. They found that the defendant employed the warden to care for the claimants. The abuse took place while he was carrying out the duties required by his employment. On that basis, the proximity between the employment and the tort complained of was very close, and therefore the defendant ought to be liable.

The Court of Appeal applied the reasoning in *Lister and Others v Hesley Hall Ltd* in the subsequent case of *Mattis v Pollock* [2003] EWCA Civ 887. There, the claimant was stabbed by a doorman of a nightclub who was employed by the defendant nightclub owner. The Court found that the defendant expected the doorman to carry out his duties in an aggressive manner; and where an employee was expected to use violence while carrying out his duties, the likelihood of establishing that an act of violence fell within the scope of his employment was greater.

## 4.5 Occupiers' liability

### 4.5.1 Occupiers' liability to lawful visitors

The OLA 1957 replaces common law rules concerning the duty owed by an occupier to a lawful visitor.

Under s 1(1), 'occupier' is given the same meaning as at common law (s 1(2)), the test for which was said by Lord Denning in *Wheat v E Lacon & Co Ltd* [1966] AC 522 to be, 'who is in sufficient control?'.

A 'visitor' is a person who would be treated as an invitee or licensee at common law (s 1(2)) and who therefore is a lawful visitor (as opposed to a trespasser). The duty of care extends not only to the visitor's person, but also to his property (s 1(3)).

### 4.5.2 The nature of the duty of care

The common duty of care is a duty to take such care as in all the circumstances of the case is reasonable to see that the visitor will be reasonably safe in using the premises for the purposes for which he is invited or permitted by the occupier to be there (s 2(2)).

The common duty of care does not impose on an occupier any obligation to a visitor in respect of risks willingly accepted as his by the visitor (s 2(5)).

### 4.5.3 Discharging the duty of care

The duty is to take 'such care as … in all the circumstances … is reasonable', taking into account the degree of care, and of want of care, which would ordinarily be looked for in such a visitor (s 2(3)). A warning may discharge the duty of care if it is enough to enable the visitor to be reasonably safe (s 2(4)).

In *Tomlinson v Congleton Borough Council and Another* [2002] EWCA Civ 309, [2003] 2 WLR 1120, the claimant was injured when diving into a lake despite signs prohibiting swimming and warning that to do so was dangerous. The defendants argued that the risk of danger was an obvious one which the claimant had willingly accepted; that they owed the claimant no duty of care; or if they did, that it had been discharged by the display of warning notices.

The Court of Appeal agreed with the court of first instance and found in favour of the claimant. The House of Lords overturned the Court of Appeal decision on the basis that it would be unreasonable to impose a duty to protect people from self-inflicted injuries that they sustained when voluntarily taking risks in the face of obvious warnings. Even if the local authority had owed the claimant a duty of care, that duty would not extend to preventing the claimant from diving or warning him against dangers that were obvious. Their Lordships took the view that it was not appropriate to find in favour of the claimant and thereby impose a duty on local authorities to protect those foolish enough to ignore clear warnings. This would be at the expense of the vast majority of people who might find that they were barred from all manner of recreational activities on public land, for fear that they might injure themselves and decide to sue the local authority.

### 4.5.4 Employing an independent contractor

Where injury is caused to a visitor by a danger due to the faulty execution of any work of construction, maintenance or repair by an independent contractor employed by the occupier, the occupier will not be treated by this reason alone as answerable for the danger if in all the circumstances (s 2(4)(b)):

(a) he had acted reasonably in entrusting the work to an independent contractor; and

(b) he had taken such steps (if any) as he reasonably ought in order to satisfy himself that:

  (i) the contractor was competent, and

  (ii) that the work had been properly done.

The duty of care under the Act is therefore delegable to an independent contractor. This should be contrasted with the personal nature of the common duty of care owed to an employee, which is non-delegable (see *Wilsons & Clyde Coal v English* [1938] AC 57).

### 4.5.5 Exclusion or modification of duty of care

By s 2(1) of the OLA 1957, an occupier may extend, restrict, modify or exclude his duty to any visitor. However, this must be read subject to s 2 of the Unfair Contract Terms Act 1977, under which, in the case of business liability:

(a) a person cannot by reference to any contract term, or to a notice given to persons generally or to particular persons, exclude or restrict his liability for death or personal injury resulting from negligence;

(b) in the case of other loss or damage, a person cannot so exclude or restrict his liability for negligence except in so far as the term or notice satisfies the requirement of reasonableness.

## 4.6 Remoteness of damage

The defendant will be liable to the claimant only if it can be proved that it was foreseeable that the claimant would suffer damage of the kind that the claimant did in fact suffer. The claimant will generally recover for:

(a) damage which was reasonably foreseeable; or

(b) damage which can be shown to flow as a direct consequence of the breach.

Once damage is established as foreseeable (no matter how small), the claimant can recover for the full extent of the injury even if this was unforeseeable (*Smith v Leech Brain & Co Ltd* [1962] 2 QB 405).

## 4.7 Causation

Whether the claimant can establish causation is a question of fact to be decided by the judge in each case. The basic test both for common law negligence and breach of statutory duty is the 'but for' test . In *Clough v First Choice Holidays and Flights Ltd* [2006] EWCA Civ 15, Phillips LJ said that the term 'but for'

> encapsulates a principle understood by lawyers but applied literally or as if the words embody the entire principle the words can mislead. The claimant is required to establish a causal link between the negligence of the defendant and his injuries, or in short, that his injuries were indeed consequent on the negligence.

The claimant is not required to show that the breach is the sole cause of the loss; it is sufficient if the breach materially contributed to the loss (*Bonnington Castings Ltd v Wardlaw* [1956] AC 613). To determine who caused the accident, the courts apply common sense to the facts of the case. If a number of people can be shown to have been at fault, that does not necessarily mean that they all caused the accident; it is a question of looking at the facts and deciding which factors are too remote and which are not (*Stapley v Gypsum Mines Ltd* [1953] AC 663).

In most straightforward personal injury claims the issue of causation will be clear. However, this may not be so in occupational disease cases, where two or more defendants have negligently exposed an employee to work practices that may prove injurious to health. This was the situation in the House of Lords' ruling in *Fairchild v Glenhaven Funeral Services Ltd and Others; Fox v Spousal (Midlands) Ltd; Matthews v Associated Portland Cement Manufacturers (1978) Ltd and Others* [2002] UKHL 22, [2002] 3 All ER 305. Here, during the course of his career with more than one employer, the claimant had been exposed to asbestos dust which in later years manifested itself as mesothelioma, for which there is no cure. The House of Lords found that where there had been employment with more than one employer and:

(a) both employers had a duty to take reasonable care to prevent the claimant from inhaling asbestos dust; and

(b) both were in breach of that duty; and

(c) the claimant did subsequently suffer from mesothelioma,

then the claimant could recover damages from both former employers. In these circumstances it was not necessary to satisfy the 'but for' causation test. It was enough that the claimant was able to prove that a defendant had materially increased his risk of injury. In his speech to the House, Lord Bingham of Cornhill put it like this: '... such injustice as may be involved in imposing liability on a duty breaking employer is heavily outweighed by the injustice of denying redress to a victim'.

The case of *Barker v Corus (UK) plc & Others* [2006] UKHL 20 is another House of Lords decision following hot on the heels of *Fairchild v Glenhaven Funeral Services*. In *Barker v Corus*, the House of Lords concluded that where it was established that a number of employers were liable, on the basis that they had negligently exposed an employee to asbestos and thereby created a risk of mesothelioma which did in fact occur, those employers should be liable to the claimant only to the extent of the share of the risk created by their breach of duty. To understand this case it is necessary to take a step back to the previous state of the law. Prior to this judgment, if there were a number of employers all of whom were negligent to some degree, the claimant would simply sue all of them and claim joint and several liability (ie sue all potential defendants for 100% of the loss and let them apportion the blame between them). This allowed the claimant to gain damages in full from one defendant in circumstances where the others might be insolvent or uninsured. Not surprisingly, defendants and their insurers were keen to resist this.

The facts of the case are as follows. The employer (Corus) appealed against a decision of the Court of Appeal in respect of its liability for damages for negligently exposing Mr Barker to asbestos dust, from which he ultimately died, having contracted mesothelioma. During his career he had worked at three stages where he was exposed to asbestos dust. The first two episodes were due to breaches of duty by his then employers. However, the third instance occurred when he was self-employed, and arose due to his failure to take reasonable care for his own safety.

The Court of Appeal held that the defendant was jointly and severally liable with the first employer, but subject to a 20% reduction for B's contributory negligence while he was self-employed.

The defendant submitted that it should not be liable at all as a matter of causation, since there had been a period when B, and no one else, had been responsible for his exposure to asbestos dust; and submitted, amongst other things, that it should be severally liable only according to the share of the risk created by its breach of duty.

By a majority decision the House of Lords held that a defendant who is found liable under the *Fairchild* exception to the usual rule of causation, will be liable only to the extent that it contributed to the risk.

*Fairchild* constitutes an exception to the normal principles of causation. In the House of Lords judgment it was accepted that there may well be instances when the same principle should be applied to other circumstances. However, those circumstances are likely to be strictly controlled by the courts.

In *Sanderson v Hull* [2008] All ER (D) 39 (Nov), the claimant alleged that she had been infected by the campylobacter bacterium as a result of her employer's breach of duty during the course of her employment as a turkey plucker. At first instance the judge held that her case fell within the *Fairchild* exception. However, the Court of Appeal disagreed. The Court did not accept that this was a case where it was impossible for the claimant to show that 'but for' negligence on the part of her employer there would have been no injury. The appeal judges stated that the conditions set out in *Fairchild* in respect of mesothelioma cases, which might justify a relaxation of the test, were not intended to exclude the application of the exception to other diseases, but an essential element is the impossibility of the claimant satisfying the 'but for' test: mere difficulty of proof is not enough.

### 4.7.1 The Compensation Act 2006

Because of the implications of the House of Lords' ruling in *Barker v Corus*, Parliament acted quickly to negate its effect in the form of s 3 of the Compensation Act 2006, which came into force on 26 July 2006. The effect of s 3 is that where mesothelioma is contracted as a result of negligent exposure to asbestos in the course of employment with more than one employer, the employers will be jointly and severally liable for the damage caused. This means that the employee can claim compensation in full from any one of the negligent employers, who may in turn claim against the remaining employers for a contribution according to their share of the blame.

## 4.8 Defences

### 4.8.1 *Volenti non fit injuria*

Where the defence of *volenti non fit injuria* applies, if a person engages in an event, being aware of and accepting the risks inherent in that event, he cannot later complain of, or seek compensation for, an injury suffered during the event. In order to establish the defence, the claimant must be shown not only to have perceived the existence of danger, but also to have appreciated it fully and voluntarily accepted the risk.

In *ICI v Shatwell* [1965] AC 656, two brothers, both experienced shotfirers, agreed to test detonators without obeying safety regulations imposed by their employers. Both were injured when one of the detonators exploded. One of the brothers sued his employer on the basis that ICI were vicariously liable for injuries caused to him by the negligence of his fellow worker. The Court held that ICI were not liable. Shatwell had voluntarily consented to a risk of which he was well aware. The Court went on to say that the defence of *volenti non fit injuria* should be available where the employer is not himself in breach of statutory duty and is not vicariously in breach of any statutory duty through neglect of some person of superior rank to the claimant and whose commands the claimant is bound to obey, or who has some special and different duty of care.

It is important to note that in *ICI v Shatwell* there was no breach of statutory duty by the employers. The defence is not available to an employer on whom a statutory obligation is imposed as against liability for his own breach of that obligation.

While *volenti non fit injuria* may be a defence in theory, in practice it is rarely successful; an employee will not often consent freely to run the risk of injury with full knowledge of that risk. The only real defence to a work-based claim will therefore be contributory negligence.

### 4.8.2 Claimant's contributory negligence

The contributory negligence of the claimant may sometimes reduce the damages to be awarded against the defendant. It is for the judge to decide the proportion of responsibility of the claimant and to reduce the amount of damages accordingly.

The Law Reform (Contributory Negligence) Act 1945, s 1 provides that:

> [If] any person suffers damage as a result partly of his own fault and partly of the fault of any other person ... damages recoverable in respect thereof shall be reduced by such extent as the court thinks just and equitable having regard to the claimant's share in responsibility for the damage.

'Fault' is defined by s 4 as 'negligence, breach of statutory duty, or other act or omission which gives rise to a liability in tort or, apart from this Act, gives rise to the defence of contributory negligence'.

The question for the court, when considering contributory negligence, is whether the claimant acted reasonably in taking the risk (*AC Billings & Son Ltd v Riden* [1968] AC 240). Whether the claim is in negligence or for breach of statutory duty, there cannot be a finding of 100%

contributory negligence (see *Anderson v Newham College of Further Education* [2002] EWCA Civ 505).

In assessing the claimant's conduct, allowance will be made for his working conditions. Mere inadvertence by the employee will generally not be sufficient for contributory negligence, for example where the employee is engrossed in his work or is in a hurry to get on with his job. The relative age and experience of the claimant will also be a relevant consideration for the court when deciding questions of contributory negligence. Disobedience or reckless disregard for the employer's orders are far more likely to give rise to a finding of contributory negligence.

In *Eyres v Atkinsons Kitchens & Bathrooms* [2007] EWCA Civ 365, the defendant was the claimant's employer. The claimant asserted that the defendant was liable in negligence and/or for breach of statutory duty because it caused or permitted him to drive when he was too tired after having worked excessively long hours without a proper break.

At the time of the accident, the claimant was a 20-year-old kitchen fitter employed by the defendant. Long hours, resulting in good money, were accepted by all the defendant's employees to be normal. If the work took them far from their factory base, the fitters, including the claimant, tended to prefer a long drive back to Bradford and getting home late rather than staying away overnight. The claimant was held to be 25% to blame for his injuries because he had not been wearing a seat belt. The court was asked to consider the degree of culpability of the claimant, as he had, whilst driving, become tired and liable to fall asleep.

The court concluded that the claimant had to bear some further responsibility for the accident, but went on to say that the claimant was in that predicament because his employer had put him there. His employer was next to him, fast asleep. His employer was doing nothing to guard against the very risk of injury from which he ought to have been saving his employee. Bearing in mind the relative blameworthiness of the parties' respective faults and their degrees of responsibility, the judge assessed the claimant's overall contributory negligence at 33%.

In *Sherlock v Chester City Council* [2004] EWCA Civ 201, the claimant was a joiner who lost his thumb and index finger in an accident when using a circular saw provided by his employer. He claimed that his employer was both negligent, for failing to carry out an appropriate risk assessment, and in breach of statutory duty in relation to breaches of reg 3 of the Management of Health and Safety at Work Regulations 1999, reg 20 of the Provision and Use of Work Equipment Regulations 1998, and reg 4 of the Manual Handling Operations Regulations 1992. On appeal to the Court of Appeal, Arden LJ considered whether it was appropriate for there to be findings of contributory negligence in a breach of statutory duty case:

> There may be some justification for the view [that the findings of contributory negligence are not appropriate] in cases of momentary inattention by an employee. But where a risk has been consciously accepted by an employee, it seems to me that different considerations may arise. That is particularly so where the employee is skilled and the precaution in question is neither esoteric nor one which he could not take himself ... In those circumstances it seems to me that the appellant can properly be required to bear the greater responsibility. I would assess his responsibility for the accident at 60 per cent.

When considering contributory negligence, it should be remembered that many statutory duties apply to employees and not employers. For example, the Management of Health and Safety at Work Regulations 1999, reg 14 places a duty on employees to use equipment in accordance with training and instructions.

## 4.9 Enforcement of health and safety at work

The function of enforcement is carried out by:

(a) the HSE, which deals broadly with industrial working environments;

(b) various specialist agencies appointed on behalf of the HSE (eg, the Hazardous Installations Directorate);

(c) local authorities, which deal broadly with non-industrial working environments such as the retail, office, leisure and catering sectors.

### 4.9.1 Health and safety inspectors

Health and safety inspectors have wide powers to enter premises and carry out investigations. As a result of an investigation revealing a contravention, an inspector may:

(a) issue an improvement notice requiring any contravention to be remedied;

(b) serve a prohibition notice requiring the contravention to be remedied and fixing a time after which the activity is prohibited unless remedied;

(c) commence a criminal prosecution (which may give rise to a relevant conviction that can be used against the employer by the employee in subsequent civil proceedings).

### 4.9.2 The employer's duty to report, maintain and implement safety provisions

The following are the principal requirements imposed on an employer:

(a) An employer who employs five or more persons must have written details of his policy in regard to the organisation, control, monitoring and review of health and safety measures.

(b) An employer is under a duty to report certain accidents, diseases and dangerous occurrences to the HSE on Form F2508. Employers are also able to report accidents to the HSE by posting information direct to their Internet site at www.riddor.gov.uk. This enables the HSE to consider an investigation of the incident. All occurrences which are required to be reported must be recorded and details of the injuries must be kept in an accident book. The records must be kept for at least three years.

(c) The employer may (and in certain circumstances must) have a safety representative to represent the health and safety interests of the employees. Such a representative has wide powers to investigate potential hazards and dangerous occurrences, and to follow up complaints made by employees.

(d) In addition to the safety representative, the employer may (and in certain circumstances must) have a safety committee, the function of which includes:

    (i) the studying of accidents and notifiable diseases in order to recommend corrective measures to management;

    (ii) making recommendations on safety training;

    (iii) examining reports of the HSE and safety representatives;

    (iv) making recommendations on developing/changing safety rules.

(e) Where an employee is injured at work and claims benefit, in certain circumstances the employer is obliged to complete Form B176 to be sent to the Department of Work and Pensions.

(f) Subject to certain exceptions, an employer is required by the Employers' Liability (Compulsory Insurance) Act 1969 to take out insurance against liability to his own employees.

### 4.9.3 Employers' liability – enforcement through criminal proceedings

Criminal prosecutions can be brought against both the company and individual directors for breaches of the HSWA 1974.

Section 2(1) is the key provision of the HSWA 1974. It states that 'it shall be the duty of every employer to ensure, so far as is reasonably practicable, the health, safety and welfare at work of all his employees'.

The Court of Appeal established in *R v Gateway Foodmarkets Ltd* [1997] 3 All ER 78 that s 2(1) of the HSWA 1974 imposed a duty of strict liability. This is qualified only by the defence that the employer has done everything reasonably practicable to ensure that no person's health and safety is put at risk. The defendants appealed against their conviction for failing to do everything reasonable to ensure the safety of their employees. The facts of the case were that a supermarket manager died after falling down an open lift shaft which he had been trying to repair. He had entered the room to free the lift, which had become jammed, by hand – a regular though unauthorised practice of which head office was unaware – but failed to notice that the trap door had been left open by contractors. The Court dismissed the company's appeal and held that s 2(1) of the Act was to be interpreted so as to impose liability in the event of a failure to ensure safety unless all reasonable precautions had been taken not only by the company itself, but also by its servants and agents on its behalf.

In *R v HTM Ltd* [2006] EWCA Crim 1156, the Court re-affirmed that a defendant to a charge under the ss 2, 3 or 4 of the HSWA 1974, could adduce evidence in support of its case that it had taken all reasonable steps to eliminate the likelihood of the relevant risk occurring. In a preparatory hearing, the judge ruled that evidence of foreseeability was admissible as it was relevant to the case alleged against the defendant, particularly with regard to the reasonable practicability of its ensuring the health, safety and welfare of its employees, and that the Management of Health and Safety at Work Regulations 1999, reg 21 did not preclude the defendant from relying upon any act or default of its employees in its defence. The defendant was entitled to put before the jury evidence to show that what had happened was purely the fault of one or both of its employees. If the jury were persuaded that everything had been done by or on behalf of the defendant to prevent the accident from happening, the defendant would be entitled to be acquitted: *R v Gateway Foodmarkets Ltd* applied.

Following concern at the low level of fines being imposed for offences under the HSWA 1974, the Court of Appeal has given guidance on the factors to be taken into account by courts when considering the appropriate penalty for this type of offence. In *R v Howe & Son (Engineers) Ltd* [1999] 2 All ER 249, the Court stated that the aim of the Act was to ensure safety for employees and the public, and therefore fines needed to be large enough to convey that message. In general, they should not be so large as to put the employer out of business. In determining seriousness, the court should consider:

(a) how far short of the appropriate standard the defendant had been;
(b) that the standard of care was the same for small organisations as for large;
(c) the degree of risk and extent of danger involved; and
(d) the defendant's resources and the effect of a fine on its business.

Aggravating factors could include:

(a) failure to heed warnings;
(b) deliberate breach of regulations in pursuit of profit or saving money; and
(c) loss of life.

Mitigating factors could include:

(a) early admission of responsibility;
(b) a plea of guilty;
(c) taking action to remedy any breach brought to the company's notice; and
(d) a good safety record.

The Court further held that it was incumbent upon a defendant seeking to make representations about its financial position to provide copies of accounts to the court and the prosecution in good time.

The above guidelines were considered by the Court of Appeal in *R v Rollco Screw & Rivet Co Ltd* [1999] 2 Cr App R (S) 436. The defendant company and two of its directors protested that the length of time given for payment of fines was inappropriate, and that no distinction should be made between personal and corporate defendants (as there was a risk of double penalty if directors and shareholders were the same people). On appeal, the Court agreed that a personal defendant's period of punishment had to remain within acceptable boundaries; this was not true of a corporate defendant, as the same sense of anxiety was unlikely and a fine could be ordered to be payable over a longer period. The level of fines must make it clear that directors had a personal responsibility; there was a risk of double penalty in smaller companies where directors were also shareholders and would be the principal losers.

The Health and Safety Offences Act 2008 (HSOA 2008), which came into force on 16 January 2009, was introduced as a result of concern that sentences under the HSWA 1974 were too lenient. The HSOA 2008 does not create any new offences, but it raises the maximum penalties available to the courts in respect of many health and safety offences. Previously such offences were punishable only by fines (maximum £5,000 in the magistrates' court). Under the HSOA 2008, most offences under the HSWA 1974 (and regulations made under it) will also carry a sentence of imprisonment for 12 months following prosecution in the magistrates' court, and for two years following prosecution in the Crown Court. The maximum fine that may be imposed in the magistrates' court increases to £20,000; fines imposed by the Crown Court are unlimited.

Where an accident results in death and the evidence indicates that a serious criminal offence other than a health and safety offence may have been committed, the HSE is required to liaise with the CPS in deciding whether to prosecute. This is dealt with in more detail in **Chapter 17**.

## 4.10 Conclusion

As stated at the beginning of this chapter, the possible heads of liability of an employer are not mutually exclusive. When acting for a claimant, it is important for the solicitor to consider all heads of claim in order to maximise the client's chances of success. It is necessary to succeed under only one head for the claimant to be successful overall. Defendant's solicitors need to be alert to possible arguments of contributory negligence on the part of the claimant, although there is generally less scope for substantial reductions for contributory negligence in work-based claims than in road traffic accident claims. It is important that the solicitors for both sides regularly review the evidence available, including all relevant health and safety documentation which can often hold the key to establishing liability and which it is essential to obtain at an early stage .

## 4.11 Further reading

The above is merely an overview of the law as it relates to liability in employer's liability claims. For a more detailed consideration of the subject, reference should be made to the following sources of information:

Redgrave, Hendy and Ford, *Redgrave's Health and Safety* (Butterworths).

Munkman, *Employer's Liability* (Butterworths).

*Tolley's Health and Safety at Work Handbook* (Tolley).

www.hse.gov.uk

# Chapter 5
# Clinical Negligence: The Law



## 5.1 Introduction

Clinical negligence claims arise when a medical practitioner, such as a doctor, nurse, midwife or dentist, or an institutional health provider, such as an NHS Trust or a private hospital, breaches his or its duty of care to the claimant, who is injured as a result of the breach. The claimant may seek legal advice following an adverse outcome from medical treatment, for example an unexpected injury or condition, a worsening of the original condition, an increased length of stay in hospital, a subsequent unplanned re-admission, a transfer to the intensive care unit, or perhaps even the death of the patient. However, whereas in the case of an accident on the highway or in the workplace it is generally a straightforward matter to establish breach and causation, this is not so in clinical negligence claims. The fact that the claimant has had an unexpected or disappointing outcome from the medical treatment he received does not necessarily mean that the healthcare provider failed to act with reasonable care and skill. Even where a breach can be established, it may not be possible to show that the breach caused the injury, as the underlying medical condition may have led to the same outcome for the patient in any event.

From the outset, the claimant's solicitor will need to manage his client's expectations with sympathetic tact and diplomacy. His client may struggle to understand why the case is not as clear-cut as he had imagined and, in the absence of a very careful explanation, may feel that the solicitor is simply incompetent. The client may have objectives other than compensation, such as an explanation as to what went wrong, an apology, the punishment of those responsible and the assurance that similar mistakes will not happen in the future. These options should be explored with him and the shortcomings of each option highlighted. For instance, the NHS complaints procedure will not lead to the payment of compensation. The NHS complaints procedure and the disciplinary procedures followed by the General Medical Council and the Nursing and Midwifery Council are dealt with in **5.9** and **5.11** below.

Clinical negligence claims are, in the main, more complex than personal injury claims, and should therefore be handled only by those solicitors who have the required specialist skills. For a number of reasons, including the implicit allegations of professional incompetence, the high levels of compensation awards and the need for NHS Trusts in particular to maintain the confidence and support of the public, claims are frequently defended.

Where a patient has been treated privately and a certain outcome had been anticipated, such as in the case of cosmetic surgery or dentistry, a claim may be brought for breach of contract. However, most claims against NHS Trusts and private doctors and hospitals are brought under the tort of negligence. If the claim is to be successful, the claimant must show, on a balance of probabilities, that the essential elements are proved, ie:

(a) that the medical practitioner or institutional health provider owed him a duty of care;

(b) that the medical practitioner or institutional health provider breached that duty;

(c) that he suffered injury and losses as a result of that breach of duty, which were reasonably foreseeable.

Each of these three elements is examined in detail below.

## 5.2 The duty of care

### 5.2.1 The medical practitioner

It is clear that a doctor, nurse, midwife or other medical practitioner owes a duty of care to his patients. This is unlikely to be a matter in dispute between the parties. The duty of care owed by a doctor is wide-ranging but would encompass, for example:

(a) properly assessing the patient's condition by taking account of the symptoms, the patient's views and an examination, where necessary;

(b) working within the limits of personal competence;

(c) keeping professional knowledge and skills up to date;

(d) prescribing drugs or administering treatment only where in possession of adequate knowledge of the patient's health and where satisfied that the drugs or treatment are appropriate for the patient's needs;

(e) keeping clear, accurate and legible records;

(f) being readily accessible when on duty;

(g) consulting and taking advice from colleagues, where necessary; and

(h) referring a patient to another practitioner, where this in the patient's best interests.

### 5.2.2 The institutional health provider

Where a medical practitioner is an employee of an NHS Trust, the institutional health provider will be vicariously liable for its employees' breaches of duty. However, the NHS Trust itself owes a duty of care to the patient, and can be sued for negligence without the claimant having to prove negligence on the part of an individual medical practitioner. The leading case in this area is *Wilsher v Essex Area Health Authority* [1988] AC 1074, in which it was held that an institutional health provider has a duty to provide services of doctors of sufficient skill and that there was no reason why a health authority could not be liable for a failure to provide such services.

The duty of care owed by an institutional health provider encompasses, for example:

(a) the provision of staff with the appropriate levels of knowledge, experience and ability;

(b) the provision of adequate instruction, training and supervision of staff;

(c) the provision of equipment which is reasonably suitable for the patient's needs and is maintained in good working order;

(d) ensuring that the working conditions within the hospital are not such that they lead to levels of fatigue or stress which pose a risk to the patient; and

(e) ensuring that appropriate systems are in place for the storage and retrieval of patients' records.

In respect of private treatment, the doctors and some other healthcare providers will usually be independent contractors. Where it is their breach of duty which has led to the claim, vicarious liability is not applicable. A private hospital is vicariously liable for the breaches of duty of its own employees, such as nurses, and it will also owe a duty to provide appropriate services and equipment.

## 5.3 Breach of the duty of care

### 5.3.1 The *Bolam* test

Some errors made by doctors are clearly in breach of their duty of care, for example where a swab is left in the patient during an operation, where the wrong limb is amputated or where an incorrect drug is administered. However, difficulty arises in cases where a medical practitioner exercises his professional judgement and decides to take one course of action rather than another, or perhaps decides not to act at all. In the realms of diagnosis and treatment, there is scope for genuine differences of opinion, and a doctor will not necessarily be negligent because the decisions he took did not result in the outcome the patient was hoping for.

Consequently, in clinical negligence claims, the normal 'reasonable man' test is modified. In order to show a breach of duty, the claimant must show that the doctor has followed a course of action which is not supported by any reasonable body of medical opinion. This has become known as the *Bolam* test after the case of *Bolam v Friern Hospital Management Committee* [1957] 1 WLR 582, in which it was held that:

> The test as to whether there has been negligence or not is not the test of the man on top of the Clapham omnibus because he has a special skill. The test is the standard of the ordinary skilled man exercising and professing to have that special skill. A man need not possess the highest expert skill; it is well established law that it is sufficient if he exercises the ordinary skill of an ordinary competent man exercising that particular art … A doctor is not guilty of negligence if he has acted in accordance with a practice accepted as proper by a reasonable body of medical men skilled in that particular art … a doctor is not negligent, if he is acting in accordance with such a practice, merely because there is a body of opinion which takes the contrary view.

Thus, if the defendant NHS Trust can show that the doctor it employed acted in accordance with a reasonable body of opinion, it will have a defence to the claim. The word 'reasonable' is important, because it is possible that a sizeable group of doctors might hold firm and honest beliefs which are rejected by their peers, for example because they are outdated or have been disproved.

This point was addressed when the House of Lords considered the *Bolam* test in *Bolitho v City and Hackney Health Authority* [1997] 3 WLR 1151 (see **5.5.4** for the facts of this case). It held:

> The court is not bound to hold that a defendant doctor escapes liability for negligent treatment or diagnosis just because he leads evidence from a number of medical experts who are genuinely of the opinion that the defendant's treatment or diagnosis accorded with sound medical practice. … The court has to be satisfied that the exponents of the body of opinion relied upon can demonstrate that such opinion has a logical basis.

Practitioners sometimes refer to the *Bolam* test as the 10% rule. It is said that if 10% of the doctors in the country would have taken the same course of action, and that action has a logical basis, then it will not be a negligent act.

A number of further clarifications should be noted:

(a) A medical practitioner will be judged in accordance with the reasonable body of opinion which existed at the time of the alleged negligent act. It would, of course, be inequitable to consider medical practice which exists at the time of trial, as advances in knowledge and practice are almost inevitable.

(b) A medical practitioner will normally be judged in accordance with the opinion of practitioners of the same rank and experience. So the standard of an obstetric senior registrar is assessed by reference to the opinion of other obstetric senior registrars rather than that of a consultant obstetrician. However, a doctor has a responsibility to ensure that he practises within the confines of his own knowledge and experience, and where he fills a more demanding role, a higher standard of care may be applied. The position of an inexperienced doctor was considered in *Wilsher v Essex Area Health Authority* [1988] AC 1074. The facts of this case were that Dr Wiles, a senior house officer (a junior rank in the medical hierarchy), was attending to a premature baby in an intensive care neo-natal unit when he made the mistake of inserting a catheter into a vein instead of an artery. Dr Wiles asked Dr Kawa, the senior registrar, to check to see that what he had done was correct, but Dr Kawa failed to notice the mistake. As a result the child was given excess oxygen which the claimant alleged caused near blindness.

It was held that the standard of care required of those who worked in the intensive care neo-natal unit was that of the ordinary skilled person exercising and professing to have that special skill, but that the standard was not to be to be determined by reference to the rank and status of an individual filling a particular post, but rather to the nature of the post itself. Because Dr Wiles had elected to perform the duties of a specialised role, inexperience was no defence to an allegation of negligence.

Glidewell LJ said that an inexperienced doctor who exercised a specialist skill and who made a mistake would satisfy the necessary standard of care if he had sought the advice and help of his superior when necessary. In this particular case, Dr Wiles had sought the advice of Dr Kawa and therefore was not in breach of duty. Although Dr Kawa *was* in breach of duty, the claimant was unable to establish causation and the claim failed.

## 5.4 *Res ipsa loquitur*

The maxim *res ipsa loquitur* may be applied in clinical negligence cases in circumstances where the claimant is unable to adduce any evidence as to how or why the injury has occurred but asserts that it would not have occurred in the absence of the defendant's negligence (see **3.2.3.3**).

In *Cassidy v Ministry of Health* [1951] 2 KB 343, the claimant attended a hospital due to a problem affecting two fingers on one hand, but following an operation and post-operative treatment, the whole hand was affected. The court held that he was entitled to rely on the maxim *res ipsa loquitur* and that the defendant had failed to explain how the injury could have occurred without negligence.

The approach to *res ipsa loquitur* in clinical negligence litigation was reviewed by the Court of Appeal in *Ratcliffe v Plymouth and Torbay Health Authority* [1998] PIQR P170. Dismissing the claimant's appeal, the Court expressed surprise at the suggestion that courts were having difficulty in assessing the applicability of the doctrine to cases involving allegations of clinical negligence, and reviewed the relevant principles in detail.

Lord Justice Brooke made the following points:

(a) The maxim applies where the claimant relies on the happening of the thing itself to raise the inference of negligence, which is supported by ordinary human experience, and with no need for expert evidence.

(b) The maxim can be applied in that form to simple situations in the clinical negligence field (a surgeon cutting off a right foot instead of the left; a swab left in the operation site; a patient who wakes up in the course of a surgical operation despite a general anaesthetic).

(c) In practice, in contested clinical negligence cases the evidence of a claimant which establishes the *res* is likely to be buttressed by expert evidence to the effect that the matter complained of does not ordinarily occur in the absence of negligence.

(d) The position may then be reached at the close of the claimant's case that the judge would be entitled to infer negligence on the defendant's part unless the defendant can then adduce some evidence which discharges the inference.

(e) This evidence may be to the effect that there is a plausible explanation of what may have happened which does not rely on negligence on the defendant's part.

(f) Alternatively, the defendant's evidence may satisfy the judge on the balance of probabilities that he did exercise proper care. If the untoward outcome is extremely rare, or is impossible to explain in the light of the current state of medical knowledge, the judge will be bound to exercise great care in evaluating the evidence before making such a finding.

The judgment goes some way in explaining why *res ipsa loquitur* is not commonly pleaded in such cases. Whilst it is commonplace for a claimant not to have full knowledge of what had occurred, particularly if the procedure was an operation carried out under anaesthetic, in practical terms, few cases are brought to trial without full disclosure of relevant information being supplied by the defendant, and both sides will rely on expert evidence. Consequently, by the time the matter comes to trial, most claimants will be able to particularise allegations of negligence and the trial opens 'not in the vacuum of available evidence and explanation' as sometimes occurs in road traffic accident cases. The court will be able to decide the case on the evidence which is presented.

## 5.5 Causation

In a clinical negligence claim, the claimant will argue that, as a result of the negligent treatment by the doctor or hospital, he suffered an unexpected injury or condition, his pre-existing injury or condition became worse, he failed to recover from that condition, or the chances of him recovering diminished. Where a patient has died, his estate or dependants may argue that the death was caused by negligent treatment.

However, the issue of causation which is likely to be admitted (subject to liability) in personal injury cases, is likely to be hotly disputed by the defendant in clinical negligence cases. In personal injury cases, the claimant is normally fit and well prior to the accident, and it is clearly the accident which caused the injury. In contrast, in clinical negligence cases, the adverse outcome complained of can arise as a result of many different variables, and it may be difficult to show that 'but for' the breach, this outcome would not have arisen.

Also in contrast with personal injury cases, in clinical negligence cases, the term 'liability' is usually confined to matters relating to breach of duty. 'Causation' is dealt with separately and the evidence of a further medical expert may be required. Consequently, where the defendant admits liability prior to trial, the claimant's solicitor should seek confirmation that the defendant also admits causation.

### 5.5.1 The 'but for' test

The claimant has to satisfy the court, on a balance of probabilities, that, but for the defendant's breach of duty, he would not have suffered the injury complained of. If, for example, a failure to treat a patient has made no difference because he would have died in any event, his death will not have been caused by negligence.

In *Barnett v Chelsea and Kensington Hospital Management Committee* [1969] 1 QB 428, three night-watchmen attended a casualty department complaining of vomiting after drinking tea three hours previously. The men were sent home with instructions to go to bed, and if necessary to call their own doctors. They went away but one of them died later that night, and the cause of death was subsequently found to be arsenic poisoning. In an action brought by the widow, the defendant was found to be in breach of duty. However, the court found that the deceased would have died of the poisoning even if he had been treated with all the necessary care. Therefore, the claimant had failed to establish on the balance of probabilities that the defendant's negligence caused the deceased's death.

The claimant does not have to prove that the defendant's breach of duty was the sole cause of the injury. It is enough for him to show that the breach made a material (ie something more than minimal) contribution towards the injury.

It is possible for the court to hold more than one type of healthcare professional jointly responsible for personal injuries that result from negligence. This is well illustrated in the case of *Prendergast v Sam and Dee Ltd* (1989) *The Times*, 14 March, in which a pharmacist misread a prescription and gave the claimant a drug which resulted in irreversible brain damage. The pharmacist was held to be 75% responsible, and the doctor who wrote the prescription was held to be 25% at fault because his handwriting was illegible.

### 5.5.2 Causation and loss of a chance

As the claimant must prove causation on a balance of probabilities, the courts have held that a claimant cannot claim for the loss of a prospect of recovery where the chance of recovery is less than probable. In *Hotson v East Berkshire Health Authority* [1987] AC 750, a 13-year-old boy, was climbing a tree to which a rope was attached when he lost his grip and fell 12 feet to the ground. He was subsequently taken to hospital, where the staff failed to diagnose a fracture and sent him home to rest. When he returned to the hospital, the correct diagnosis was made. As a result of the initial failure to give a correct diagnosis, he was left with a disability of the hip and a risk of future osteoarthritis. At first instance, the trial judge found that if the health authority had correctly diagnosed and treated the claimant when he first attended hospital, there was a high probability (which he assessed at a 75% risk) that his injury would have followed the same course it had followed. In other words, the doctor's delay in making the correct diagnosis had denied the claimant a 25% chance that, if given immediate treatment, he would have made a complete recovery. Accordingly, the claimant was awarded 25% of the appropriate damages. The defendant's appeal to the Court of Appeal was dismissed, but the House of Lords overturned the decision. The claimant had failed to prove causation as the lost chances of recovery, being less than 50%, were less than probable.

This approach was confirmed in the case of *Gregg v Scott* [2005] UKHL 2. The claimant, Mr Gregg, visited his GP, Dr Scott, because he had discovered a lump under his left arm. Dr Scott negligently misdiagnosed the lump as a lipoma or benign fatty tumour and therefore as non-cancerous. Nine months later, the claimant went to a new GP who was more cautious and referred him on to a specialist. It was then that he discovered that he had cancer of a lymph gland. By that time the tumour had spread and he had to undergo painful chemotherapy. The claimant sued Dr Scott, alleging that he should have referred the claimant to hospital and that, if he had done so, the condition would have been diagnosed earlier and there would have been a significant likelihood of a cure. Although the claimant could claim for the extra pain and suffering caused by the defendant, the claimant tried to sue on the basis that he had suffered a loss due to diminished chances of surviving the cancer. On appeal to the House of Lords, their Lordships found in favour of the defendant on the basis that the claimant was unable to prove that his negligence had caused or materially contributed to the injury. It had not been shown that, on the balance of probabilities, the delay in commencing the claimant's treatment had affected the course of his illness or his prospects of survival, which had never been as good as even. Further, liability for the loss of a chance of a more favourable outcome should not be introduced into personal injury claims.

### 5.5.3 Causation and failure to warn

As informed consent is required before any type of medical procedure is performed, it is essential that a doctor advises his patient of any risk inherent in that procedure (see **5.6.4** below). If the doctor fails to do so and the risk materialises, the court will consider whether or not the patient would have consented to the operation anyway. If the patient, aware of the risk, would have so consented, causation cannot be established. However, if the patient would not have consented, clearly the breach of duty in failing to warn him of the risk caused the loss, and he will be entitled to damages representing the difference in his current condition and the condition he would have been in had the operation not been performed.

In *Chester v Afshar* [2004] UKHL 41, the House of Lords modified conventional causation principles on policy grounds. Miss Chester suffered from back pain and was referred to Mr Afsar, a consultant neurosurgeon. He advised surgery but failed to warn her of a small (1–2%) inherent risk that the operation, no matter how expertly performed, could result in a serious complication, causing partial paralysis. The operation was performed three days later and the risk materialised. The operation itself was not performed negligently. The difficulty in this case was that the claimant was unable to say that she would never have had the operation had she known of the risk; merely that she would not have had it as soon as she did, as she would have explored other options first. Moreover, the failure to warn had not increased the risk. Consequently, the 'but for' test could not be satisfied. The House of Lords found in the claimant's favour and, in so doing, veered away from conventional causation principles. Their Lordships justified their ruling on policy grounds, on the basis that the loss arose from the violation of the patient's right to make an informed choice due to the failure to warn. Lord Steyn said:

> I have come to the conclusion that, as a result of the surgeon's failure to warn the patient, she cannot be said to have given informed consent to the surgery in the full legal sense. Her right of autonomy and dignity can and ought to be vindicated by a narrow and modest departure from traditional causation principles. On a broader basis I am glad to have arrived at the conclusion that the claimant is entitled in law to succeed. This result is in accord with one of the most basic aspirations of the law, namely to right wrongs. Moreover, the decision announced by the House today reflects the reasonable expectations of the public in contemporary society.

### 5.5.4 Causation and failure to attend

In *Bolitho v City and Hackney Health Authority* [1997] 3 WLR 1151, the House of Lords considered causation in the context of a doctor's breach of duty in failing to attend a child. The child claimant (aged 2 years) who had been treated for croup at St Bartholomew's Hospital, was discharged but then readmitted. He suffered episodes of extreme breathing difficulties and, during one such episode, the nurse called for a doctor to attend. The senior registrar was dealing with a clinic and was unable to attend, and the senior house officer did not attend either because the batteries of her pager were flat. The child subsequently suffered cardiac arrest which led to brain damage. The defendant accepted that the failure to attend the child was in breach of duty, but it disputed that the failure was causative of any damage. It was agreed that if the child had been intubated (to create an airway), the child would not have suffered the cardiac arrest and consequently would not have incurred brain damage. The senior registrar gave evidence to the effect that she would not have intubated had she attended. There was a dispute between experts called by the parties as to whether intubation would have been the appropriate course of action to take in those circumstances, bearing in mind the risks associated with that procedure. The House of Lords dealt with the case by taking a two-stage approach:

(a) The court first considered what the doctor would have done if she had attended the child. This was a fact-finding exercise and the *Bolam* test was not relevant at this stage. From the senior registrar's evidence, it was accepted by the court that she would not have intubated the child and that the senior house officer would not have done so without her permission.

(b) The court went on to consider whether the failure to intubate would have been negligent. At this point the *Bolam* test was relevant, and the court found that a reasonable body of medical opinion would support the registrar's decision not to intubate.

Consequently, their Lordships found in favour of the defendant.

## 5.6 Consent

The patient's consent is required by the medical practitioner before any sort of operation is performed or treatment (such as an injection of drugs or manipulation of a limb) administered. The consent must be freely given and informed. It need not be in writing, although, in relation to surgical procedures, it invariably will be, and the patient will be asked to sign a consent form. The standard NHS consent forms are drafted widely so as to allow a surgeon to deal with any procedure that he deems to be necessary, in the patient's best interests, during the course of the operation. However, the surgeon would be justified in carrying out such additional measures only where they were closely related to the initial procedure, or where they became necessary due to an emergency.

In *Williamson v East London and City Health Authority* [1998] Lloyd's Rep Med 6, the claimant agreed to an operation to replace a leaking silicone breast implant. Immediately prior to the operation, the surgeon noted that the situation was worse than had originally been thought, but did not tell the claimant that she intended to carry out a more extensive procedure than she had initially planned, and no further consent form was signed. A mastectomy was performed without the patient's consent and the patient sued the health authority. The court found that the clinician did not properly or sufficiently inform the claimant of her intention to increase the scope of the operation, the claimant had not consented to the operation, and accordingly damages were awarded in respect of the claimant's pain and suffering.

Where treatment is less risky, oral consent is common. It may also be implied by the very fact that the patient has consulted the doctor.

If the medical practitioner acts without consent, this may lead to a criminal prosecution for battery and to civil proceedings under the tort of trespass to the person (or battery in particular). The basis of these actions is that the interference with the physical integrity of the patient was intentional. (A consideration of the tort of battery lies beyond the scope of this book.)

However, where the medical practitioner seeks the consent of the patient and advises him, in broad terms, of the nature of the operation or treatment, but fails to advise him of all the associated risks, the consent may not be fully 'informed' but it will not be invalidated (see *Chatterton v Gerson* [1981] QB 432). This failure to advise fully may lead to civil proceedings in negligence (see **5.6.4**).

Where the patient suffers from a mental incapacity and thereby falls under Pt IV of the Mental Health Act 1983, his consent is not required for any medical treatment necessary for the management of his mental disorder. (A consideration of the treatment of those who are mentally incapacitated also falls outside the scope of this book.)

### 5.6.1 Emergency treatment

In some instances, for example in emergencies, consent may not be possible. Where treatment is necessary to save the life or preserve the health of the patient in such circumstances, a failure to obtain consent will not render the doctor liable in civil or criminal proceedings. There is no English case specifically on this point, but in *Wilson v Pringle* [1986] 3 WLR 1, CA (which was about two boys fighting in a school playground), Croom-Johnson LJ speculated as to what sort of physical contact would be acceptable in the conduct of daily life and would therefore provide a defence to an action for trespass. He considered the actions of a surgeon who performs an urgent operation on an unconscious patient brought into hospital, when that patient could not give consent himself and there were no next of kin to give consent on his behalf, and held that such action was acceptable in the ordinary conduct of everyday life and therefore not a battery. Similar thoughts have been expressed *obiter* in a number of subsequent cases.

### 5.6.2 Consent by children

Section 8(1) of the Family Law Reform Act 1969 provides a presumption that a child may give valid consent for medical treatment at the age of 16. This area of the law was examined closely in *Gillick v West Norfolk and Wisbech Area Health Authority and Department of Health and Social Security* [1986] AC 112, in which it was held that the important point is the degree of understanding by the child of what is going to happen.

### 5.6.3 Refusal of consent

The basic proposition is that an adult of sound mind has the right to autonomy and self-determination, and therefore can refuse to consent to medical treatment, even where this may lead to his death. Many of the reported cases deal with women who are in the later stages of pregnancy, and where the medical practitioners, concerned to protect the foetus as well as the mother, apply for a declaration from the court that it would be lawful to carry out the required medical procedure without the mother's consent. These cases show that the court is not able to take the interests of a foetus into account. In *St George's Hospital NHS Trust v S; R v Collins and others, ex p S* [1998] 3 All ER 673, the Court of Appeal said:

> In our judgment while pregnancy increases the personal responsibilities of a woman it does not diminish her entitlement to decide whether or not to undergo medical treatment. Although human, and protected by the law in a number of different ways ... an unborn child is not a separate person from its mother. Its need for medical assistance does not prevail over her rights. She is entitled not to be forced to submit to an invasion of her body against her will, whether her own life or that of her unborn child depends on it. Her right is not reduced or diminished merely because her decision to exercise it may appear morally repugnant. The declaration in this case involved the removal of the baby from within the body of her mother under physical compulsion. Unless lawfully justified, this constituted an infringement of the mother's autonomy. Of themselves, the perceived needs of the foetus did not provide the necessary justification.

In the case of *Re MB (An Adult: Medical Treatment)* (1997) 38 BMLR 175, a woman who was 40 weeks pregnant and in labour refused to consent to a caesarean section because she had a phobia about needles and therefore could not consent to anaesthesia. Her life and that of her unborn child were therefore at risk. The Court of Appeal held that a competent woman could chose to reject medical intervention, even on irrational grounds, ie where the decision was so outrageous in its defiance of logic or of morally accepted standards that no sensible person could have arrived at it. However, in this case, the appellant's fear of needles had made her incapable of making a decision in relation to anaesthesia and had therefore rendered her temporarily incompetent.

### 5.6.4 Failure to advise of risk

In order that consent to the proposed treatment may be fully informed, the medical practitioner must, so far as is possible, advise the patient as to the risks involved in treatment and the likelihood and nature of any side-effects. Where a patient asks a question, the medical practitioner must answer the question honestly. Clearly, a failure to advise a patient about sizeable risks will be negligent, whether or not the patient asks a specific question, but what about where the risks are very small and there is no specific question?

The case of *Sidaway v Board of Governors of the Bethlem Royal Hospital and Maudsley Hospital* [1985] AC 871, governs the nature of the obligation placed upon the doctor to tell the patient about the risks of the proposed operation. The claimant complained of persistent pain in the right shoulder and left arm. The claimant was admitted to hospital and an operation was carried out on her back to attempt to free her from pain and discomfort. During the operation the spinal cord was damaged, which left the claimant severely disabled. The claimant sued the hospital and the surgeon's estate. It was not claimed that the operation had been negligently performed; rather, the claim was based on the failure to warn the claimant of the risk of damage to a nerve root and the spinal cord.

It was held that if there was a significant risk which would affect the judgement of a reasonable patient, it was the duty of the doctor to inform the patient of that risk to enable him to decide which course to adopt. What constitutes a 'significant risk' was not precisely defined, but Lord Bridge referred to a significant risk of grave consequences, for example one greater than 10%, and Lord Templeman said that a doctor should tell the patient about a danger which may be 'special in kind or magnitude or special to the parties'.

The expert evidence produced at trial showed that there was 1% to 2% risk of damage to either the nerve root or the spinal cord, and that the risk of damage to the spinal cord of the severity suffered by the claimant was less than 1%. The experts also stated that the judgement of a surgeon not to frighten his patient by talking about the risk of death or paralysis would be in accordance with a practice accepted as proper by a responsible body of competent neurosurgeons.

The House of Lords held that the *Bolam* test should be applied to disclosure as well as to treatment and diagnosis (Lord Diplock dissenting; he believed that the patient should be informed of the risks as a matter of law), and found for the defendant. It is important to note, however, that the *Bolam* test has since been modified by *Bolitho*. The court will consider the facts of each particular case and, where there is a body of medical opinion which agrees with the decision not to reveal a slight risk to the patient, will consider whether there is a logical basis for that decision.

In *Newbury v Bath DHA* (1999) 47 BMLR 138, it was held that if the claimant was led to believe that the operation was trivial and risk free, and such was not the case, that advice would be wrong and negligent within the terms of *Sidaway*. The judge went on to give examples of circumstances where the patient was entitled to be told when surgery was not in the mainstream of treatment:

(a) if it involved a method which was entirely new or relatively untried;
(b) if the method had fallen out of use because it has been shown to be defective and was not accepted by a responsible body of medical opinion.

It should be noted that in *Chester v Afshar* (see **5.5.3**) the House of Lords found that the surgeon *had* been negligent in accordance with the *Bolam* test. The claimant had specifically asked about the risks involved in the operation and had not been given a full and honest answer. Although the House of Lords used the lack of consent to justify a finding in favour of the claimant, this case is predominantly about the issue of causation and the decision was based on policy grounds.

In relation to the warning of such risks, see *Lybert v Warrington HA* (1996) 7 Med LR 71 for guidance as to the form such warnings should take. In this case, the claimant claimed damages for failure to advise on the risk of the possibility of failure of a sterilisation operation. The court held that it was the duty of those running the sterilisation unit to ensure that there was a proper and effective system for warning patients at some stage. Ideally, the warning should be given orally and in writing, and could have been given on admission, or before the patient agreed to sterilisation or before discharge. There was evidence that no warning at all had in fact been given.

## 5.7 The role of the NHS Litigation Authority

The NHS Litigation Authority (NHSLA) handles clinical negligence claims against NHS bodies and administers a risk-pooling scheme, the Clinical Negligence Scheme for Trusts (CNST), which provides unlimited cover for members of the scheme and their employees against such claims. (Health professionals who provide advice and treatment on a private basis and self-employed health professionals, such as GPs, are not covered by the scheme and must carry their own indemnity insurance.) Membership of the CNST is voluntary, but all Foundation Trusts, NHS Trusts and Primary Care Trusts (PCTs) are currently members of the scheme. Members contribute to the scheme in accordance with the level of risk they pose. For example, hospitals that perform high-risk procedures, such as obstetrics, have higher levels of contributions than those which do not.

The NHSLA relies on a panel of solicitors' firms which are specialised in clinical negligence litigation to handle defence work on their behalf. Fewer than 2% of cases referred to the NHSLA are concluded at trial.

The *NHSLA Clinical Negligence Reporting Guidelines* (4th edn, January 2007) set out a framework within which claims managers working for Trusts report cases of alleged clinical negligence to the NHSLA. In every case where medical records are requested, the Trust should make a preliminary analysis on the available evidence to assess whether there is a reasonable prospect of a claim being made. Where there has been a serious adverse event, or where there is a potential claim of a value of over £250,000, the NHSLA should be informed as soon as possible, usually before a claim has been issued. The receipt of a letter of claim should be reported within 24 hours.

## 5.8 The structure of the NHS

The clinical negligence solicitor should have an understanding of the basic structure of the NHS. The following is an outline of the structure of the NHS in England. The systems in the rest of the UK are similar, but there are differences which lie outside the scope of this book. A diagrammatical structure is provided at **5.14**.

(a) The Department of Health is responsible for standards of health and social care and is accountable to Parliament. It provides strategic leadership to the NHS.

(b) Regional management of the NHS is devolved to 10 Strategic Health Authorities (SHAs), which are responsible for setting, managing and monitoring performance strategies at a local level.

(c) Special Health Authorities provide specialist services across England, eg the NHS Litigation Authority (see **5.7**) and the NHS Blood and Transport, which is responsible for providing supplies of blood, organs and associated services to the NHS.

(d) Primary Care Trusts (PCTs) are responsible for the provision of health services to the local communities they serve. This includes the delivery of front-line services (known as primary care services), which are provided by general practitioners, dentists, opticians, pharmacists, walk-in centres and NHS Direct, and which are usually the first point of contact for those having a health problem. It also includes the planning and purchasing of secondary care from secondary care service providers. Primary Care Trusts control approximately 80% of the NHS budget.

(e) NHS Trusts (also known as acute trusts) are responsible for running many of the country's hospitals. Some are regional or national centres for more specialised care, and some are attached to hospitals and provide training for health professionals. They may also provide services in the community, through health centres, clinics or in the patient's own home.

(f) Ambulance Trusts are responsible for responding to 999 calls and transporting patients to and from hospital for treatment.

(g) Mental Health Trusts oversee the specialist care required by those with mental health problems, such as severe anxiety or psychotic illness. They do this in partnership with other primary care and secondary care providers and local council services departments.

(h) Care Trusts manage integrated services between health and social care which arise from joint working agreements between the NHS and local authorities.

(i) Foundation Trusts were introduced in April 2004 with the aim of de-centralising the provision of health services in England and tailoring them to meet the needs of the local population. They have more financial and operational freedom than other NHS Trusts and are accountable to local people, who may become members and governors, but they remain part of the NHS. There are now 103 such trusts, and a large number of applicants are currently awaiting authorisation.

## 5.9 The NHS complaints procedure

In April 2009, the Government introduced a simplified two-stage process for handling complaints about NHS services in accordance with the Local Authority Social Services and National Health Service Complaints (England) Regulations 2009 (SI 2009/309) ('the Regulations'). The procedure applies to complaints concerning all NHS staff, whether they are GPs, hospital doctors, nursing staff, ambulance crew, administrators or cleaners. The procedure is not relevant where treatment has not been funded by the NHS, even where that treatment was provided in an NHS hospital. A complaint by a patient may encompass any expression of dissatisfaction, from a complaint about the food or politeness of staff, to one about diagnosis or treatment (ie a clinical complaint), and may be made orally, in writing or electronically.

The purpose of the complaints procedure is to enable complaints to be dealt with simply and swiftly, at a local level if at all possible. The Government recognises that speedy resolution of the complaint to the complainant's satisfaction may avoid the instigation of civil proceedings, especially where the adverse outcome has not resulted in particularly serious consequences for a patient. In May 2009, in a letter written to the Chief Executives and Finance Directors of all NHS bodies by the Chief Executive of the NHS Litigation Authority, and endorsed by the Chief Executives of various medical bodies, such as the Medical Defence Union, the British Medical Association and the Royal College of Nursing, the importance of providing apologies and explanations to patients and their relatives was clearly set out. The letter stresses the importance of staff being open when dealing with complaints, and being properly trained and supported in order to facilitate transparency. However, human nature being as it is, practice may fall short of these aims.

When advising a client about the right to complain in relation to NHS care, and how to go about it, there are a number of matters for the solicitor to explain:

(a) The complaints procedure does not provide for the payment of compensation to the complainant, although some NHS Trusts operate a policy of offering limited compensation, and the proposed NHS Redress Scheme will, if and when it comes into operation, provide a formal basis for such payments (see **5.10**). Therefore, particularly in relation to those who have suffered severe injury and consequential financial loss, the complaints procedure is unlikely to provide a complete solution in itself.

(b) In addition to ensuring that the complainant's voice does not go unheard, the complaints procedure will ensure that the matter is investigated quickly by the relevant

NHS body, while events are still fresh in the minds of those involved. This may provide the claimant's solicitor with valuable information for civil proceedings, should they become necessary.

(c) An apology, an offer of treatment or other redress is not an admission of negligence (Compensation Act 2006, s 2).

(d) In the past, it was common for the complaints procedure to be suspended as soon as legal proceedings were commenced, or even when the complainant communicated an intention to commence proceedings. The Department of Health has stated that this should no longer happen, and it has undertaken to write to all NHS bodies reminding them of this. Generally, it is advisable to exhaust the complaints procedure before commencing proceedings.

(e) The purpose of the procedure is to satisfy complaints, rather than apportion blame amongst staff, and it is separate from disciplinary procedures. A complaint may bring the shortcomings of individual members of staff to the notice of the management of an NHS body, which may then consider taking action in accordance with its internal disciplinary procedures. Negligence amounting to gross misconduct may lead to dismissal and/or a referral of the matter by the NHS body to an individual's professional body. However, a complainant should not assume that this will happen, and he may wish to seize the initiative and bring the matter to the attention of the appropriate professional body himself (see **5.11**).

(f) There are various sources of information and bodies that will provide assistance regarding the complaints procedure:

   (i) Basic information as to how to complain and how the complaint will be dealt with may be found on the NHS website (www.nhs.uk).

   (ii) Each NHS Trust has its own complaints policy, and this is normally found on the Trust's own website. For example, the Surrey and Sussex Healthcare NHS Trust's 'Patient Complaints Management Policy and Procedure' may be found at www.surreyandsussex.nhs.uk/about_us/documents/ppg/0106complaints.pdf.

   (iii) There is a Patient Advice and Liaison Service (PALS) within each Trust, which is staffed by NHS employees and volunteers. Its role is to provide confidential advice and assistance to patients, their relatives, visitors to the hospital and staff members, with the aim of resolving problems and concerns quickly, wherever possible. It does not investigate formal complaints but it can provide advice as to the complaints procedure, and it will refer complainants on to the Independent Complaints Advocacy Service. The website of the National Network of NHS Patient Advice and Liaison Services may be found at www.pals.nhs.uk, although some individual PALS have their own websites.

   (iv) The Independent Complaints Advocacy Service (ICAS) is an organisation which is independent of the NHS. Its staff, known as advocates, can assist with all stages of the complaints procedure, for example writing letters of complaint, contacting third parties on the complainant's behalf and attending meetings with him. Its website may be found at www.seap.org.uk/icas.

   (v) The Citizens Advice Bureau and NHS Direct can also provide help and assistance.

The complaints procedure involves two stages, local resolution and, if the complainant remains dissatisfied, referral to the Health Service Commissioner.

## 5.9.1 Local resolution

Local resolution is seen by the Government and the NHS Executive as the main thrust of the complaints procedure. Complaints are most likely to be voiced to staff on the spot, and it is these front-line staff or their departmental managers who are the people best placed to make the initial response. The aim is to resolve problems and answer concerns of patients and their families immediately and informally if possible, thereby reducing the need for legal proceedings and the associated cost to the public purse.

Regulation 3 requires each NHS body, which includes Strategic Health Authorities, Primary Care Trusts and NHS Trusts, to make arrangements for the handling and consideration of complaints. These arrangements must be such as to ensure that

(a) complaints are dealt with efficiently;
(b) complaints are properly investigated;
(c) complainants are treated with respect and courtesy;
(d) complainants receive, so far as is reasonably practicable—
    (i) assistance to enable them to understand the procedure in relation to complaints; or
    (ii) advice on where they may obtain such assistance;
(e) complainants receive a timely and appropriate response;
(f) complainants are told the outcome of the investigation of their complaint; and
(g) action is taken if necessary in the light of the outcome of a complaint.

Each NHS body must designate a person, known as a 'responsible person' to be responsible for ensuring compliance with the arrangements and, in particular, ensuring that action is taken if necessary in the light of the outcome of the complaint. This will be the Chief Executive Officer, although he may authorise others to act on his behalf. Each NHS body must also designate a person as a 'complaints manager', to be responsible for managing the procedures for handling and considering complaints. The responsible person and the complaints manager may be the same person.

A complaint should be made within 12 months of the date the matter complained of occurred or, if later, the date when it came to the notice of the complainant. However, the time limit shall not apply where the NHS body is satisfied that the complainant had good reasons for not making the complaint within the time limit and, notwithstanding the delay, it is still possible to investigate the complaint effectively and fairly.

Unless a complaint is made orally and is resolved to the complainant's satisfaction not later than the next working day after the day on which the complaint was made, a complaint must be dealt with in accordance with the procedures set out in the Regulations. This means that the NHS body should:

(a) acknowledge the complaint not later than three working days after the day on which it receives the complaint;
(b) investigate the complaint in a manner appropriate to resolve it speedily and efficiently, and, during the investigation, keep the complainant informed, as far as reasonably practicable, as to the progress of the investigation;
(c) as soon as reasonably practicable after completing the investigation, send a response to the complainant setting out how the complaint has been considered, its conclusions, a confirmation that it is satisfied that any necessary action has been taken or is proposed to be taken, and details of the complainant's right to take his complaint to the Health Service Commissioner;
(d) provide the response within six months commencing on the day on which the complaint was received, or such longer period as may be agreed by the NHS body and the complainant, or set out in writing to the complainant the reasons why this has not been possible and provide a response as soon as possible thereafter.

Each NHS body must maintain systems for monitoring complaints, and must prepare an annual report which is made available to any person on request.

### 5.9.2 The Parliamentary and Health Service Ombudsman and the Public Service Ombudsman for Wales

The Parliamentary and Health Service Ombudsman ('the Ombudsman') deals with complaints arising in England (www.ombudsman.org); the Public Service Ombudsman for Wales (www.ombudsman-wales.org.uk) deals with complaints arising in Wales. There are separate ombudsmen for Scotland and Northern Ireland.

The Ombudsman, who is independent of the NHS and the Government, will investigate complaints where the NHS body has refused to investigate the complaint on the basis that it is outside the time limit, or where the complaint has been dealt with by NHS complaints procedure and the complainant is still dissatisfied. Complaints which have not been through the local resolution and independent review process are unlikely to be considered by the Ombudsman. The complaint should generally be made within one year of the event complained of, although there is discretion to extend this limit in cases where there is good reason for the delay.

Where the Ombudsman finds in favour of the complainant, in accordance with the Principles of Remedy (see www.ombudsman.org.uk/improving_services/principles/remedy/index.html), she will recommend that the health authority offers a remedy which will return the complainant to the position he would have been in had the service provided to him been of the proper standard, or compensate him appropriately where this is not possible.

The remedies which may be recommended by the Ombudsman include:

(a) an apology, an explanation, and acknowledgment of responsibility;

(b) remedial action, such as reviewing or changing a decision on the service given to the complainant, revising published material, revising procedures to prevent recurrence of that particular problem, training or supervising staff, or any combination of these;

(c) financial compensation.

Although the Ombudsman has no power to enforce her recommendations, they are generally followed.

The Ombudsman publishes reports regarding her investigations. The Annual Report 2007–08 may be found at www.ombudsman.org.uk/pdfs/ar_08.pdf.

## 5.10 The NHS Redress Scheme

In June 2003, the Chief Medical Officer (CMO) published his recommendations for reform of the system for handling and responding to clinical negligence claims in a Consultation Paper entitled *Making Amends*. The NHS Redress Act 2006, which received Royal Assent on 8 November 2006, gives effect to the proposal set out in recommendation 1 of *Making Amends*, namely, to introduce an NHS Redress Scheme to initiate investigations when things go wrong, to provide remedial treatment, rehabilitation and care where needed, and to offer appropriate explanations and apologies and financial compensation in certain circumstances.

The purpose of the Scheme is to provide an alternative to seeking redress through the courts, as the latter is seen as slow, expensive and a drain on NHS resources. If the Scheme is brought into being, it is believed that it will initially be targeted at straightforward, lower-value claims (up to £20,000). If an offer is not made, or is rejected, the person's right at common law to sue for negligence will remain unaffected by the Scheme.

No precise time frame for commencement of the Scheme has been provided. It appears the Government intends to monitor the success of a similar system in Wales (the NHS Redress (Wales) Measure), which is due to commence in autumn 2010, and the new NHS complaints procedure, before making further decisions about the Scheme.

## 5.11 Disciplinary proceedings

Those who have been injured or who have lost a loved one as a result of a clinical error may be keen to see those responsible punished, and the solicitor will need to give advice regarding the appropriate disciplinary procedures. A detailed consideration of the conduct of the proceedings lies beyond the scope of this book.

### 5.11.1 Disciplinary proceedings against doctors

Doctors must be registered with the General Medical Council (GMC) in order to practise medicine in the UK. The GMC has responsibility for investigating complaints about doctors, and it can take action if the doctor's fitness to practise is impaired due to any of the following grounds:

(a) misconduct;
(b) poor performance;
(c) receipt of a criminal conviction or caution;
(d) physical or mental ill-health;
(e) determination by a regulatory body either in the British Isles or overseas.

The GMC's procedures are divided into two separate stages: 'investigation' and 'adjudication'. At the investigation stage, cases are investigated to assess whether the matter is sufficiently serious to warrant referral for adjudication. The adjudication stage consists of a hearing of those cases which have been referred to a Fitness to Practise Panel.

A Fitness to Practise Panel may come to any of the following conclusions:

(a) the doctor's fitness to practise is not impaired and no further action should be taken;
(b) the doctor's fitness to practise is not impaired but he is required to give an undertaking, eg to have further training or to work only under supervision;
(b) the doctor's fitness to practise is not impaired but a warning should be issued;
(c) the doctor's fitness to practise is impaired and –
  (i) conditions should be placed on the doctor's registration (for example, restricting the doctor to certain areas of practise or stating that he must be supervised), or
  (ii) the doctor's name should be suspended from the medical register, or
  (iii) the doctor's name should be erased from the medical register.

An appeal may be made by either side within 28 days.

### 5.11.2 Disciplinary proceedings against nurses and midwives

The Nursing and Midwifery Council (NMC) is the regulatory body for nurses and midwives. The NMC has a duty to investigate once an allegation has been made against a member to the effect that his fitness to practise is impaired due to:

(a) misconduct;
(b) lack of competence;
(c) a conviction or caution;
(d) physical or mental ill-health; or
(e) where a different healthcare profession has already determined that he is unfit to practise,

The sanctions which may be imposed at the end of the procedure are as follows:

(a) the issue of a caution;
(b) the removal of the practitioner from the register for a specified period, after which he may apply for his name to be restored; or

(c) the removal of the practitioner from the register indefinitely;

## 5.12 Criminal proceedings

The CPS may bring a prosecution for manslaughter against a medical practitioner following an incidence of gross clinical negligence which results in the death of a patient (see **17.3.3**).

## 5.13 Further reading

Balen (ed), *APIL Clinical Negligence* (Jordans)

Lewis, *Clinical Negligence – a practical guide* (Tottel Publishing)

www.gmc-uk.org

www.healthcarecommission.org.uk

## 5.14 Diagram – Structure of the NHS

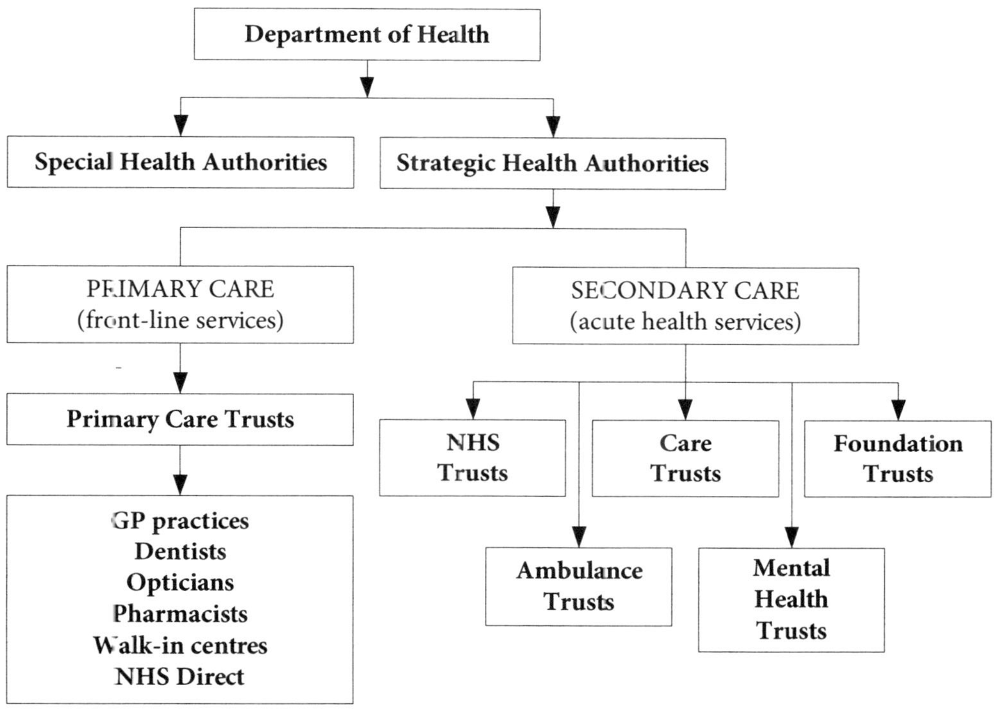

# Chapter 6
# Claims for Psychiatric Injury



## 6.1 Introduction

Not all accidents result in physical injury. Claims for psychiatric injury or illness have risen markedly in recent years, and are usually awarded in a claim arising from an accident (so-called 'nervous shock 'claims) or as a consequence of occupational stress. The purpose of this chapter is to examine some particular issues that arise when dealing with these types of claim.

## 6.2 Claims for nervous shock

There have been a number of high-profile nervous shock cases arising out of disasters such as Hillsborough, which involved a crush at the Sheffield Wednesday FC stadium in 1989. In the Hillsborough case, a number of claims were brought against the police by spectators and relatives of the victims who were present at the stadium or who had seen the disaster unfolding on the television (*Alcock v Chief Constable of South Yorkshire Police* [1992] 1 AC 310). Other claims were brought by police officers who had been on duty in the stadium and who were traumatised by what they saw (*White v Chief Constable of South Yorkshire* [1999] 2 AC 455). These cases establish certain 'control mechanisms' that limit liability for psychiatric injury.

### 6.2.1 What is nervous shock?

In order to claim for psychiatric injury there must be expert medical evidence that the claimant has suffered a recognised psychiatric illness which is more than temporary grief, fright or emotional distress. In recent years the courts have recognised a wide range of psychiatric injuries, including chronic fatigue syndrome (*Page v Smith* [1996] AC 155), pathological grief disorder (*Vernon v Bosley* [1997] 1 All ER 577) and post-traumatic stress disorder (PTSD) (*Alcock v Chief Constable of South Yorkshire* Police [1992] 1 AC 310). In establishing whether a claimant has suffered a recognisable psychiatric illness, a medical expert is likely to refer to two main systems of classification of psychiatric illnesses currently used in the UK:

(a) the *Diagnostic and Statistical Manual of Mental Disorders of the American Psychiatric Association*, 4th edn (DSM IV); and

(b) *The World Health Organisation International Classification of Mental and Behavioural Disorders*, 10th edn (ICD-10).

The most common psychiatric illness that arises is PTSD following a life-threatening experience or exposure to the sudden death of a close relative, the symptoms of which are listed at **2.2.12**.

### 6.2.2 Primary and secondary victims

In order to bring a claim for negligently inflicted psychiatric illness, a person must fall into one of two categories established by the House of Lords in *Alcock v Chief Constable of South Yorkshire Police* [1992] 1 AC 310. Primary victims will normally be involved in the events as participants, but it will be relatively rare for a primary victim directly involved in the events not to suffer any physical injury as well. Secondary victims are normally witnesses of injury caused to primary victims, and have not suffered physical injury themselves but have suffered psychologically from what they saw or heard. The key importance of this classification between primary and secondary victims is that if the claimant can show that he is a primary victim then he is likely to be treated more favourably by the courts.

#### 6.2.2.1 Primary victims

A primary victim must show that some personal injury (ie, physical injury or psychiatric injury) was reasonably foreseeable as a result of the defendant's negligence so as to bring him within the scope of the defendant's duty of care. No distinction should be made between a physical or a psychiatric injury.

The case of *Page v Smith* [1996] AC 155 was the first time that the House of Lords had considered a claim brought by a primary victim. The claimant's car was involved in a collision with a car driven by the defendant. The collision was not severe and the claimant suffered no physical injuries, but he claimed damages on the basis that shortly after the accident he suffered a recurrence of chronic fatigue syndrome from which he had suffered 20 years before. The House of Lords held that as a participant in the accident he was a primary victim, and therefore it was not necessary for him to show that the psychiatric harm he suffered was foreseeable in a person of normal fortitude. It made no difference that the claimant was predisposed to psychiatric illness – the normal 'egg-shell skull' rule applied so that the defendant had to take his victim as he found him.

In *Corr v IBC Vehicles* [2006] EWCA Civ 331, the claimant brought proceedings under the Fatal Accidents Act following the suicide of her husband, who had been badly injured in a factory accident whilst employed by the defendant. He suffered PTSD which resulted in deep depression, and some six years after the accident he committed suicide by jumping off the roof of a multi-storey car park. The Court of Appeal held that the claimant did not need to establish that at the time of the accident the deceased's suicide had been reasonably foreseeable, as the suicide flowed from the psychiatric illness for which the defendant was admittedly responsible.

In *Johnstone v NEI International Combustion Limited* [2007] UKHL 39, the House of Lords rejected claims by workers who had been negligently exposed to asbestos by the defendants and who had developed clinical depression as a consequence of being told that they had pleural plaques which indicated a risk of future illness. It was argued on behalf of the claimants that they should be regarded as primary victims and should therefore be entitled to recover damages regardless of whether or not psychiatric injury was a foreseeable consequence of the defendants' negligence. The House of Lords rejected this argument on the basis that the illness had been caused by the fear of the possibility of an unfavourable event which had not actually happened and was therefore not actionable.

#### 6.2.2.2 Secondary victims

A secondary victim must show that it was reasonably foreseeable that a person of reasonable fortitude would have suffered some psychiatric injury. Foreseeability of psychiatric injury is of critical importance to secondary victims, as they will normally be outside the scope of persons who might suffer foreseeable physical injury.

In addition to the test of reasonable fortitude, *Alcock v Chief Constable of South Yorkshire Police* [1992] 1 AC 310 established that a secondary victim must satisfy three further control mechanisms if he is to succeed in a claim for damages for psychiatric injury:

(a) *A close tie of love and affection to the immediate victim.* In *Alcock*, the claimants were various relations of the immediate victims, some of whom had been present at the Hillsborough football stadium and some of whom had watched the disaster unfold on television. The House of Lords held that there is a rebuttable presumption of sufficiently close ties between spouses, parents and children, but that in all other cases the closeness of the tie had to be proved. One claimant had been present at the ground and witnessed the incident in which his two brothers were killed, but his claim failed because he did not produce evidence of a close tie of love and affection to his brothers. However, in a subsequent case, damages were awarded to the half-brother of one of the Hillsborough victims because the judge found evidence that he was particularly close to his half brother.

(b) *Closeness in time and space to the incident or its aftermath.* In *Alcock*, several claimants were not present at the ground but went there subsequently to identify the bodies of their relatives. The earliest had arrived between eight and nine hours after the accident, which was held by the House of Lords not to be part of the immediate aftermath.

Subsequent decisions have seen a relaxation in the courts' approach to what constitutes the immediate aftermath. In *Walters v North Glamorgan NHS Trust* [2002] EWHC 321 (QB), [2002] All ER (D) 65, the mother of a baby claimed psychiatric injury as a result of witnessing her child's decline and death due to misdiagnosis at the treating hospital. The period from first onset of injury to death was 36 hours. The claimant issued proceedings against the hospital for damages. The court found that although clearly not a primary victim, she could succeed as a secondary victim if her psychiatric injury was induced by shock as a result of the sudden appreciation by sight or sound of a horrifying event or its immediate aftermath. The court found that the whole period of 36 hours could be seen in law as a horrifying event, and the claimant was therefore entitled to recover damages. In *Galli-Atkinson v Seghal* [2003] EWCA Civ 697, the claimant appealed to the Court of Appeal following a decision dismissing her claim for nervous shock. The facts of the case were such that the claimant was present at the immediate aftermath of a road traffic accident at which her daughter had died. At that time she was told of the death of her daughter, but did not see the body until some hours later in the mortuary. It was only when she viewed the body that the claimant broke down and suffered the psychiatric condition that formed the basis of her claim. On appeal, the Court found that, provided events retained sufficient proximity, the subsequent viewing of the body could be seen as part of the aftermath of the incident, and on that basis the claim could succeed.

(c) *The claimant must suffer 'nervous shock' through his own unaided senses.* In *Alcock*, the House of Lords confirmed that the secondary victim must establish that his illness was induced by a shock or, in the words of Lord Ackner, 'the sudden appreciation by sight or sound of a horrifying event, which violently agitates the mind'. Some of the claimants in *Alcock* had watched the events at Hillsborough unfold via live television broadcasts. This was held to be insufficient to satisfy the test of proximity, because watching the events on television was not felt to be equivalent to witnessing the events at first hand.

### 6.2.2.3 Employee victims

In *White v Chief Constable of South Yorkshire* [1999] 2 AC 455, the claimants were police officers who were severely traumatised by their duties at the aftermath of the Hillsborough Stadium disaster. They claimed compensation for their psychiatric injury against the police service. It was conceded that none of the claimants had been exposed to any personal physical danger, but their case was that the Chief Constable was vicariously liable for the negligence of the police officer who caused the catastrophe by admitting the crowd in to the pens. The claimants argued that by the negligent creation of the horrific situation, the Chief Constable was in breach of his duty not to expose the claimants to unnecessary risk of injury and was consequently liable for their injuries. The House of Lords rejected their claims and confirmed that, unless employees can show a risk of physical injury (and therefore fall into the category of primary victims), they will be treated as secondary victims and subject to the control tests established in *Alcock* (see **6.2.2.2**). Part of the reason for this was undoubtedly public policy – since all the claims for compensation by relatives of the victims had already been rejected, it could – and did – cause a public furore if police officers were compensated in less deserving cases. The effect of this decision is that the *Alcock* test applies to all psychiatric injury claims where personal injury is not reasonably foreseeable; employees do not get special consideration.

In *Young v Charles Church (Southern) Ltd* (1997) 39 BMLR 146, it was established that an employee who suffered psychiatric illness after seeing a workmate electrocuted close to him could recover damages against his employer as a primary victim because of the risk to himself of physical injury. The court decided that the ambit of the regulations was not limited to physical electrocution. The statute gave protection to employees from kinds of injury which could be foreseen as likely to occur when the electrical cable or equipment was allowed to become a source of danger to them. This included mental illness caused to the claimant by the shock of seeing his workmate electrocuted in circumstances where he was fortunate to escape electrocution himself.

Contrast the above case with *Hunter v British Coal* [1999] QB 89, CA. The claimant was a driver in a coalmine. His vehicle struck a hydrant, causing it to leak. With the help of a workmate, he tried to stop the flow but failed. He left the scene in search of help. When the claimant was 30 metres away, the hydrant burst, and he was told that someone was injured. On his way back to the scene, he was told that the workmate who had been helping him had died. The claimant thought he was responsible and suffered nervous shock and depression. He brought proceedings for damages against his employers. It was held that a claimant who believes he has been the cause of another's death in an accident caused by the defendant's negligence could recover damages as a primary victim if he was directly involved as a participant in the incident. However, a claimant who was not at the scene could not recover damages as a primary victim merely because he felt responsible for the incident. In this case, the claimant was not involved in the incident in which the workmate died as he was 30 metres away and suffered psychiatric injury only on being told of the death some 15 minutes later. Therefore, there was not sufficient proximity in time and space with the incident. Also, the illness triggered by the death was not a foreseeable consequence of the defendant's breach of duty of care, as it was an abnormal reaction to being told of the workmate's death, triggered by an irrational feeling that the claimant was responsible.

### 6.2.2.4 Professional rescuers

Before *White v Chief Constable of South Yorkshire and Others* [1999] 2 AC 455 it had been thought that rescuers were automatically to be treated as primary victims. However, in *White* the House of Lords rejected the police officers' claims for psychiatric injury, stating that there was no authority for placing rescuers in a special position. The decision was based on two factors:

(a) the problem of applying a definition to delineate the class of rescuers that could claim; and

(b) the fact that, if the law did allow the claims to succeed, the result would be unacceptable to the ordinary person, who would think it wrong that police officers should have the right to compensation for psychiatric injury out of public funds when bereaved relatives did not. Fairness demanded that the appeal be allowed, and the claims were therefore dismissed.

A rescuer who is not exposed to danger of physical injury, or who does not believe himself to have been so exposed, is therefore classified as a secondary victim who must satisfy the control mechanisms set out in *Alcock* before he can recover damages for pure psychiatric injury.

In *Stephen John Monk v (1) PC Harrington Ltd (2) HTC Plant Ltd (3) Multiplex Constructions Ltd* [2008] EWHC 1879 (QB), the claimant had been working as a self-employed foreman on site during the construction of Wembley Stadium. While he was working, a temporary platform fell 60 feet onto two fellow workers. One of the men died from his injuries shortly after the accident, the other suffered a broken leg. Having arrived at the scene of the accident, the claimant tried to help both men and, specifically, to comfort the man with the broken leg. Thereafter, as a result of the accident, he began to suffer from symptoms of PTSD, which ultimately caused him to stop work. The defendant admitted liability for the accident, and the claimant claimed damages for psychiatric injury on the grounds that his involvement in the accident was such that he fulfilled the necessary conditions to recover compensation as a rescuer; and even if he was unable to bring himself within the rescuer category of primary victim, he could nevertheless establish the necessary proximity to the accident, which he believed he had caused, in order that he could be regarded as an unwilling participant.

While it was accepted by the court that the claimant had provided significant help and comfort to the injured men, and that this assistance entitled him to be regarded as a rescuer, the claimant could not show on the evidence that he had reasonably believed that he was putting his own safety at risk. He could not therefore establish himself as a primary victim on the basis of his acts as a rescuer. As for the second ground advanced by the claimant – that he was a primary victim as an unwilling participant – it was held that he had to show that his injuries were induced by a genuine belief that he had caused another person's injury or death, and there was no reasonable basis for such a belief in this case. Therefore, it was not reasonably foreseeable that someone in his position would suffer psychiatric injury as a result of such a belief.

#### 6.2.2.5 Bystanders as victims

A 'mere bystander' will be unable to claim damages for pure psychiatric injury as he will be unable to satisfy control mechanisms for a secondary victim outlined at **6.2.2.2** above. This is well illustrated by the case of *McFarlane v EE Caledonia Ltd* [1994] 2 All ER 1, which arose out of the Piper Alpha oil rig disaster. The claimant had been off duty on a support vessel some 550 metres away when he witnessed the explosions and consequent destruction of the oil rig, which resulted in the death of 164 men. His claim failed as he was not himself in any danger, and it had not been shown that it was reasonably foreseeable that a man of ordinary fortitude would have suffered a psychiatric injury as a result of what he saw.

## 6.3 Occupational stress

### 6.3.1 The meaning of occupational stress

Stress is a feature of nearly every workplace, and indeed is often seen as desirable to motivate and encourage people. However, too much pressure can lead to psychological problems and physical ill-health.

In trying to come to some workable definition of 'occupational stress', Hale LJ, in *Hatton v Sutherland; Barber v Somerset County Council; Jones v Sandwell Metropolitan Borough Council; Bishop v Baker Refractories Ltd* [2002] EWCA Civ 76, [2002] 2 All ER 1, referred to three documents which she said the Court had found particularly helpful:

(a) *Stress in the Public Sector – Nurses, Police, Social Workers and Teachers* (1988) defines stress as 'an excess of demands upon an individual in excess of their ability to cope'.

(b) *Managing Occupational Stress: a Guide for Managers and Teachers in the School Sector* (Education Service Advisory Committee of the Health and Safety Commission, 1990) defines stress as 'a process that can occur when there is an unresolved mismatch between the perceived pressures of the work situation and an individual's ability to "cope"'.

(c) The HSE booklet *Stress at Work* (1995) defines stress as:

> The reaction people have to excessive pressures or other types of demand placed upon them. It arises when they worry that they can't cope ...
>
> Stress is not the same as ill health. But in some cases, particularly where pressures are intense and continue for some time, the effect of stress can be more sustained and far more damaging, leading to longer term psychological problems and physical ill health.

In *Hatton v Sutherland*, the judge concluded that harmful levels of stress are more likely to occur in situations where people feel powerless or trapped, and are therefore much more likely to affect people at junior levels; and, secondly, stress is a psychological phenomenon which can lead to either physical or mental ill-health, or both.

### 6.3.2 Duty of care

In *Petch v Commissioners of Customs and Excise* [1993] ICR 789, it was accepted that the ordinary principles of employers' liability applied to claims for psychiatric illness arising from employment. Although the claim in *Petch* failed, Colman J, in *Walker v Northumberland County Council* [1995] 1 All ER 737, applied the same principles in upholding the claim. In this case, Mr Walker was a conscientious but overworked manager of a social work area office, with a heavy and emotionally demanding work-load of child abuse cases. Although he complained and asked for help and for extra leave, the judge held that his first mental breakdown was not foreseeable. There was liability, however, when he returned to work with a promise of extra help, which did not materialise, and he experienced a second breakdown only a few months later.

*Petch* and *Walker* have both been cited with approval by the Court of Appeal in *Garrett v Camden LBC* [2001] EWCA Civ 395.

### 6.3.3 Reasonable foreseeability and breach of duty

In *Hatton v Sutherland* [2002] EWCA Civ 76, the Court of Appeal set out guidance for courts to follow in occupational stress cases which was approved by the House of Lords in *Barber v Somerset* [2004] UKHL 13. Hale LJ set out the guidance as follows:

(1) There are no special control mechanisms applying to claims for psychiatric (or physical) illness or injury arising from the stress of doing the work the employee is required to do. The ordinary principles of employer's liability apply.

(2) The threshold question is whether this kind of harm to this particular employee was reasonably foreseeable: this has two components (a) an injury to health (as distinct from occupational stress) which (b) is attributable to stress at work (as distinct from other factors).

(3) Foreseeability depends upon what the employer knows (or ought reasonably to know) about the individual employee. Because of the nature of mental disorder, it is harder to foresee than physical injury, but may be easier to foresee in a known individual than in the population at large. An employer is usually entitled to assume that the employee can withstand the normal pressures of the job unless he knows of some particular problem or vulnerability.

(4) The test is the same whatever the employment: there are no occupations which should be regarded as intrinsically dangerous to mental health.

(5) Factors likely to be relevant in answering the threshold question include:

(a) The nature and extent of the work done by the employee. Is the workload much more than is normal for the particular job? Is the work particularly intellectually or emotionally demanding for this employee? Are demands being made of this employee unreasonable when compared with the demands made of others in the same or comparable jobs? Or are there signs that others doing this job are suffering harmful levels of stress? Is there an abnormal level of sickness or absenteeism in the same job or the same department?

(b) Signs from the employee of impending harm to health. Has he a particular problem or vulnerability? Has he already suffered from illness attributable to stress at work? Have there recently been frequent or prolonged absences which are uncharacteristic of him? Is there reason to think that these are attributable to stress at work, for example because of complaints or warnings from him or others?

(6) The employer is generally entitled to take what he is told by his employee at face value, unless he has good reason to think to the contrary. He does not generally have to make searching enquiries of the employee or seek permission to make further enquiries of his medical advisers.

(7) To trigger a duty to take steps, the indications of impending harm to health arising from stress at work must be plain enough for any reasonable employer to realise that he should do something about it.

(8) The employer is only in breach of duty if he has failed to take the steps which are reasonable in the circumstances, bearing in mind the magnitude of the risk of harm occurring, the gravity of the harm which may occur, the costs and practicability of preventing it, and the justifications for running the risk.

(9) The size and scope of the employer's operation, its resources and the demands it faces are relevant in deciding what is reasonable; these include the interests of other employees and the need to treat them fairly, for example, in any redistribution of duties.

(10) An employer can only reasonably be expected to take steps which are likely to do some good: the court is likely to need expert evidence on this.

(11) An employer who offers a confidential advice service, with referral to appropriate counselling or treatment services, is unlikely to be found in breach of duty.

(12) If the only reasonable and effective step would have been to dismiss or demote the employee, the employer will not be in breach of duty in allowing a willing employee to continue in the job.

(13) In all cases, therefore, it is necessary to identify the steps which the employer both could and should have taken before finding him in breach of his duty of care.

(14) The claimant must show that that breach of duty has caused or materially contributed to the harm suffered. It is not enough to show that occupational stress has caused the harm.

(15) Where the harm suffered has more than one cause, the employer should only pay for that proportion of the harm suffered which is attributable to his wrongdoing, unless the harm is truly indivisible. It is for the defendant to raise the question of apportionment.

(16) The assessment of damages will take account of any pre-existing disorder or vulnerability and of the chance that the claimant would have succumbed to a stress related disorder in any event.

*Young v Post Office* [2002] EWCA Civ 661 was decided after *Hatton v Sutherland* and considered whether it is the responsibility of the claimant to inform the employer if he is unable to cope, and whether the claimant will be contributorily negligent if he fails to do so. The claimant had worked for the Post Office for a number of years and had been promoted to workshop manager. He had no direct line manager, and when a new computer system was introduced he was expected to familiarise himself with it without formal training. The claimant began to show signs of stress and eventually suffered a nervous breakdown, and subsequently took four months off work to recover. Arrangements were made to allow the claimant to return to work gradually and on a flexible basis. When the claimant returned to work he quickly shouldered the burden of the management position that had led to his breakdown. Seven weeks later the claimant was again unable to continue due to stress and left. The defendants contended that they had done all that they could in offering a less stressful work pattern for the claimant. On appeal, the Court found for the claimant, as it was plainly foreseeable that there might be a recurrence if appropriate steps were not taken when the claimant returned to work, and the employer owed a duty to take such steps. Although the employer had told the claimant that he could adopt a flexible approach to his work, the reality was that he was a hardworking and conscientious employee, and it was foreseeable that he would quickly revert to overworking, and the employer had a duty to ensure that help was on hand. Regarding the allegation of contributory negligence, the Court found that this was not relevant in this case and would be unusual but was 'theoretically possible'.

The High Court decision in *Barlow v Broxbourne Borough Council* [2003] EWHC 50 (QB), [2003] All ER (D) 208 (Jan), provides an example of the application of the principles set out by the Court of Appeal in *Hatton v Sutherland*. B had initially been employed as a gardener and had obtained several promotions to become senior operations manager in 1993. B's claim was based on two broad grounds: systematic victimisation and 'general' bullying. He alleged that from approximately 1997 he had been deliberately victimised and bullied by senior members of the council's staff, which had caused him to suffer emotional distress and psychological injury. The alleged 'victimisation' and 'bullying' had included receipt of lengthy letters detailing B's non-performance, threats of disciplinary action and, at times, abusive language. Medical experts for each party were agreed that B had suffered a moderately severe depressive episode. Consequently, B had been unable to continue working for the council. B argued that he had been exposed to such stress at work that he had developed a stress-related illness which had prevented him from remaining in the council's employ. However, B's claim failed on the following grounds:

(a) The actions of the council and its employees did not give rise to a foreseeable risk of injury. Hale LJ's guidelines in *Hatton v Sutherland* applied. In the circumstances, it was not necessary for the court to consider causation issues.

(b) The council could not have reasonably known or foreseen that the conduct complained of by B would have caused him harm.

(c) Nothing in B's behaviour, at the time, had given any cause for concern about the risk of psychiatric illness.

This judgment assists the defendant by confirming that the alleged incidents of bullying and/or harassment must be considered in context. In the context of the claimant's working environment, the use of bad language (which was not disputed at trial) and the actions of his line managers in highlighting areas of non-performance, did not amount to victimisation or bullying.

In *Intel Corporation (UK) Limited v Daw* [2007] EWCA Civ 70, Pill LJ approved of the guidance in *Hatton* but warned courts against following it too slavishly:

> A very considerable amount of helpful guidance is given in *Hatton*. That does not preclude or excuse the trial judge either from conducting a vigorous fact-finding exercise, as the trial judge in this case did, or deciding which parts of the guidance are relevant to the particular circumstances. The reference to counselling services in *Hatton* does not make such services a panacea by which employers can discharge their duty of care in all cases. The respondent, a loyal and capable employee, pointed out the serious management failings which were causing her stress and the failure to take action was that of management. The consequences of that failure are not avoided by the provision of counsellors who might have brought home to management that action was required. On the judge's findings, the managers knew it was required.

This approach was endorsed by the Court of Appeal in *Dickins v O2 plc* [2008] EWCA Civ 1144, when the Court upheld the trial judge's decision to award the claimant damages for injury caused by occupational stress.

Ms Dickins' job involved the preparation of management and regulatory accounts. She found one particular audit in February 2002 'extremely stressful'. She had a short holiday but returned to work exhausted, and on 11 March 2002 she asked her line manager for a different and less stressful job. As there were no vacancies available at the time, Ms Dickins was told that the matter would be reviewed in three months. On 23 April 2002 she requested a six-month sabbatical. She said she was stressed out, was having a real struggle to get out of bed in the mornings and to get to work on time because she felt so drained of physical and mental energy, and she did not know how long she could carry on before being off sick. She was advised to access O2's confidential counselling helpline, and was told that her request for a sabbatical would be considered. On 30 May 2002 Ms Dickins repeated her concerns during her appraisal and was referred to occupational health, albeit with some delay. Before any appointment was fixed she suffered a breakdown and never returned to work.

The Court of Appeal upheld the judge's finding that psychiatric injury was reasonably foreseeable from 23 April 2002 onwards. There was sufficient indication of impending harm to health, given the claimant's description of the seriousness of her symptoms and the important background context that these problems had not come 'out of the blue'. The fact that the claimant had been mentioning difficulties over a period of time was significant, given that she was usually a conscientious employee.

The Court of Appeal also agreed with the trial judge that the defendant employer was in breach of duty in not sending her home and in not making an immediate referral to occupational health.

More recently, in *Connor v Surrey County Council* (High Court, 19 March 2009), the claimant, a head teacher in a primary school, was awarded damages against the defendant local education authority for its failure to have regard to the effect of its conduct on her health or to give her the support she needed, which resulted in her suffering severe depression. The defendant raised in its defence the issue of foreseeability of injury, and argued that there were no signs of impending harm to the claimant's health, particularly as she had not been absent from work prior to her breakdown. However, the judge held that the fact that the claimant had not been absent from work was irrelevant; the risk was apparent from comments made by the claimant and others, and action should have been taken to respond to it.

It seems clear from these recent decisions that, in an appropriate case, it may not be necessary to show that the claimant has previously suffered a breakdown if his words and actions in the recent past would alert a reasonable employer to the risk of illness. Furthermore, whereas *Hatton* had indicated that an employer who offered a confidential counselling service was unlikely to be found in breach of duty, the recent cases cast doubt over whether the provision of such a service will exonerate an employer.

### 6.3.4 Causation

Having established a breach of duty, it is still necessary to prove that the particular breach of duty caused the harm. Where there are several different possible causes (as will often be the case with stress-related illness), the claimant may have difficulty proving that the employer's breach of duty was one of them. This will be a particular problem if, as in *Garrett v Camden LBC* [2001] EWCA Civ 395, the main cause was a vulnerable personality which the employer knew nothing about. However, the employee does not have to prove that the breach of duty was the sole cause of his ill-health: it is enough to show that it made a material contribution (see *Bonnington Castings Ltd v Wardlaw* [1956] AC 613). Expert medical evidence will be crucial in determining causation.

### 6.3.5 Damages

The *Hatton* guidelines (see **6.3.3**) suggested that an employer found liable for psychiatric injury caused by occupational stress should pay only for that proportion of the injury caused by his wrongdoing and not for any part of the injury caused by other factors. However, in *Dickins v O2*, the Court of Appeal was critical of the trial judge's decision to reduce the total damages by 50% for the other non-tortious factors which had contributed to the claimant's illness. In the Court's view, albeit *obiter*, the injury was indivisible, and so an employer should be liable for the whole injury if it is proved that the tort has made more than a minimal contribution to the injury.

Although further guidance by the Court of Appeal on the whole issue of apportionment can be expected, for the time being it seems that no reduction should be made for the other stresses which contributed to a claimant's illness. A more appropriate route may be for defendants to argue that particular heads of damage (eg loss of future earnings) should be discounted to reflect the fact that a claimant might in any event have suffered a breakdown at some time in the future.

## 6.4 Conclusion

In 1998 the Law Commission presented its report on *Liability for Psychiatric Illness*, which made a number of recommendations for reform of this area of the law, but so far the Government has not acted on those recommendations. The report is useful reading to understand what is undoubtedly a complex area of the law.

The increase in the number of occupational stress claims has prompted the HSE to publish a guide to provide a step-by-step approach to tackling the causes of stress at work and to provide management standards, and this is also useful starting point when considering a claim of this type.

## 6.5 Further reading

Butterworths Personal Injury Litigation Service

Law Commission Consultation Paper, *Liability for Psychiatric Illness* 1995 (Law Com No 137)

www.hse.gov.uk

# Chapter 7
# Limitation of Actions



## 7.1 Introduction

The law relating to limitation is fairly complex and can cause difficulties for the unwary. Each year, there is a steady flow of case law relevant to this area, partly because clients seek legal advice far too late, but also because an embarrassing number of solicitors breach the duty of care owed to their clients by failing to ensure that proceedings are issued within the limitation period. Consequently, one of the first priorities for the claimant's solicitor will be to identify when the limitation period ends and, having established this, to mark the file with that date and enter it into the diary system.

The principal statute dealing with limitation issues is the Limitation Act 1980 (LA 1980).

For the purpose of limitation in a personal injury claim, 'personal injury' includes any disease and any impairment of a person's physical or mental condition (s 38).

## 7.2 The limitation period

Under ss 11 and 12 of the LA 1980, where a claimant claims damages for negligence, nuisance or breach of duty, and that claim consists of or includes a claim for personal injuries, the claimant must normally commence his claim (ie the claim form must be issued, or received by the court in order to be issued) within three years from:

(a) the date on which the cause of action accrued; or

(b) the date of knowledge (if later) of the person injured (s 11(4); see **7.3** below).

When calculating the three-year period (generally referred to as the 'primary' limitation period), the day on which the cause of action accrued is excluded (s 2). Therefore, in a simple road traffic accident case, generally the claimant has three years from the incident (excluding the date of the incident) in which to commence the claim. If the last date of this period is a Saturday, Sunday or Bank Holiday, the time is extended until the next day when the courts are open and the claim can be issued.

Where the three-year period has expired, the claimant is not prohibited from commencing proceedings, although if he does so, the defendant may seek to have the claim struck out on the grounds that it is statute barred. However, the claimant may apply to the court for the limitation to be disapplied under s 33 of the LA 1980 (see **7.8**).

## 7.3 Date of knowledge

A claimant may work in an environment which exposes him to injurious dust particles such as asbestos dust or coal dust. It may be many years before an illness or disease manifests itself, and it may be some time later before the claimant realises what the cause of his illness is. Similarly, in a clinical negligence context, a patient may be fully aware of his pain and suffering but assumes that it is entirely due to an underlying illness, rather than due to negligent advice from or treatment by a doctor. In such circumstances, it is not unusual for a claimant to issue proceedings many years after the expiry of the three-year limitation period and to seek to rely on a later date of knowledge under s 14 of the LA 1980. Where he seeks to do so, the burden of proof rests with the claimant.

### 7.3.1 Section 14 of the Limitation Act 1980

Section 14 of the LA 1980 defines 'date of knowledge' for the purpose of ss 11 and 12 as follows:

> (1) In sections 11 and 12 of this Act references to a person's date of knowledge are references to the date on which he first had knowledge of the following facts—
>
> (a) that the injury in question was significant; and
>
> (b) that the injury was attributable in whole or in part to the act or omission which is alleged to constitute negligence, nuisance or breach of duty; and
>
> (c) the identity of the defendant; and
>
> (d) if it is alleged that the act or omission was that of a person other than the defendant, the identity of that person and the additional facts supporting the bringing of an action against the defendant;
>
> and knowledge that any acts or omissions did or did not, as a matter of law, involve negligence, nuisance or breach of duty is irrelevant.

need to have C who knew action was attributable to d but not know this gives them a right to claim

> (2) For the purposes of this section an injury is significant if the person whose date of knowledge is in question would reasonably have considered it sufficiently serious to justify his instituting proceedings for damages against a defendant who did not dispute liability and was able to satisfy a judgment.
>
> (3) For the purposes of this section a person's knowledge includes knowledge which he might reasonably have been expected to acquire—
>
> (a) from facts observable or ascertainable by him; or
>
> (b) from facts ascertainable by him with the help of medical or other appropriate expert advice which it is reasonable for him to seek;
>
> but a person shall not be fixed under this subsection with knowledge of a fact ascertainable only with the help of expert advice so long as he has taken all reasonable steps to obtain (and, where appropriate, to act on) that advice.

### 7.3.2 The meaning of knowledge and the starting of the clock

In *Halford v Brookes* [1991] 3 All ER 559, it was stated that knowledge does not mean 'know for certain and beyond the possibility of contradiction', but rather 'know with sufficient confidence to justify embarking on the preliminaries to issue of proceedings, such as submitting a claim to the proposed defendant, taking legal advice and other advice and collecting evidence'.

Consequently, the date of a claimant's knowledge is the date on which the claimant first knew enough of the various matters set out in s 14(1) to begin to investigate whether he has a claim against the defendant. For example, where a specialist told the claimant that he had an inhaled disease or industrial injury and the only source for this could be his work for the defendants (*Corbin v Penfold Metalizing* [2000] Lloyd's Rep Med 247), or where the claimant was told by a community worker that his deafness could have been caused by his work in a mill (*Ali v Courtaulds Textiles Limited* [1999] Lloyd's Rep Med 301).

It should be noted that knowledge will be present even though the claimant's psychological condition leads to a state of denial. In *TCD v (1) Harrow Council (2) Worcester County Council (3) Birmingham City Council* [2008] EWHC 3048 (QB), the clamant sought damages in relation to child abuse suffered from 1975 and 1981. The fact that her psychological or mental state 'may have meant that she was in denial and/or could not face reliving her abuse for the purposes of the claim', was not relevant for the purposes of determining her knowledge (although it was relevant in relation to the exercise of discretion under s 33 – see **7.8**).

Although it may be possible to identify a specific date when it is clear that the claimant had the requisite knowledge, the court may determine that the claimant should have acquired this knowledge at an earlier date.

## 7.3.3 Actual and constructive knowledge

Where a claimant wishes to rely on a later date of knowledge, he will seek to fix that date as being the date when he actually acquired the requisite knowledge. This is known as 'actual knowledge'. The defendant, though, may argue that the claimant had actual knowledge of these matters at an earlier date and/or *should* have obtained knowledge at an earlier date, and that the claimant is thereby fixed with 'constructive knowledge'.

### 7.3.3.1 Actual knowledge

When considering the question of actual knowledge, claimants will often seek to rely on a date when they were told that their injury or illness was caused by the defendant's actions, usually by a doctor or a solicitor. However, the court may determine that a claimant had actual knowledge at an earlier date.

In *Spargo v North Essex District Health Authority* [1997] 8 Med LR 125, the court held that a subjective test was to be applied, namely 'What did the claimant know?' and not 'What would a reasonable layman realise?' The facts of the case were that the claimant had been diagnosed as suffering from selective brain damage and was compulsorily detained in hospital from 1975 until 1981. The proceedings were not issued until 1993, although the claimant had first consulted solicitors in 1986. At this time she did not know whether she had a case but felt clear in her own mind that her suffering was attributable to a mistaken diagnosis. It was held on appeal that because the claimant was clear in her own mind that a connection existed between her suffering and the misdiagnosis when she first sought legal advice in 1986, it was not necessary for the court to enquire further whether a rational lay person would have been willing to say that he knew of a connection between the suffering and the misdiagnosis without first obtaining a medical confirmation.

In *AB and Others v Ministry of Defence* [2009] EWHC 1225 (QB), the court looked at limitation as a preliminary issue in the context of 10 conjoined test cases. The claimants, all veteran servicemen, sought damages in respect of numerous illnesses suffered by them as a result of exposure to ionising radiation following nuclear tests by the British Government in the 1950s. It was held that actual and constructive knowledge could arise only when a veteran had been made aware of the Rowland study in 2007, which was the first credible scientific evidence that the exposure could cause the illnesses complained of. Consequently, applying that test, none of the 10 cases was statute barred. However, five of the veterans had already formed a strong belief that exposure to radiation had caused their illnesses, and this was sufficient to amount to actual knowledge. These cases would have been statute barred had the court not exercised its discretion under s 33 to dis-apply the limitation period (see **7.8**).

It is possible that a claimant may be fixed with actual knowledge of certain facts even if a medical expert has advised him that this was not the case. In *Sniezek v Bundy (Letchworth) Ltd* (2000) LTL, 7 July, the Court of Appeal ruled that the claimant had the knowledge from the date when he went to complain to his doctor of severe symptoms but was assured that there was no link between the illness and his work. The Court decided that the claimant knew that his severe throat symptoms, which had persisted for five years, were a significant injury, and that he had always attributed them to his work. The fact that a doctor subsequently advised him that this was not the case, did not change the fact that he had actual knowledge.

#### 7.3.3.2 Constructive knowledge

In accordance with s 14(3) (see **7.3.1**), a claimant cannot argue that he did not have the requisite knowledge due to his ignorance of the law, or because he failed to make further enquiries or seek appropriate advice. The test is an objective one: knowledge which would have been obtained by a reasonable man in the same circumstances as the claimant will be imputed to the claimant.

In *Forbes v Wandsworth Health Authority* [1997] QB 402, the claimant, who suffered from poor circulation, underwent surgery for a by-pass operation. This was not a success and a further by-pass was performed the next day. Unfortunately, the second operation was too late to be successful and the claimant was told that it was necessary to amputate his leg to prevent gangrene, to which he agreed. The sole allegation was that the authority had been negligent not to perform the second operation sooner. The claimant did not seek advice until seven years after the limitation period had expired. The Court of Appeal held by a majority that the claimant was deemed to have constructive knowledge as soon as he had time to overcome the shock of the injury, take stock of his disability and seek advice.

In *Kew v Bettamix Ltd (formerly Tarmac Roadstone Southern Ltd) & Others* [2006] EWCA Civ 1535, the claimant issued proceedings in respect of injuries suffered from his exposure to vibrating equipment during his employment with the defendants. As early as 1991 the claimant had experienced numbness in his fingers, but had thought this was due to his age. On 29 March 2000, following a routine occupational health care assessment, he was informed by means of a letter from an occupational physician that his symptoms might be attributable to his exposure to vibration at work. The Court held that it was necessary for the claimant to have sufficient knowledge to make it reasonable for him to seek to acquire further knowledge of the link between his injury and his prior working conditions. He did not have such knowledge until 29 March 2000, when he received the physician's letter. Although he was not told about the causative link at that time, he knew that there was a real possibility that his working conditions had caused his symptoms, and a reasonable man would have investigated further. He was therefore fixed with constructive knowledge at that date.

In *Pearce v Doncaster MBC* [2008] EWCA Civ 1416, the Court of Appeal considered the knowledge of a man who claimed damages from the local authority for its failure to take him into care when he was a child. The claimant's actual knowledge arose when he saw his care records, shortly before issuing proceedings. However, constructive knowledge took place several years earlier, when he had requested his files but had failed to take up the appointment to view them, even though the authority had offered to pay his train fare.

It is not necessary for the court to specify an exact date when constructive knowledge took place. In *White v EON and Others* [2008] EWCA Civ 1436, the claimant claimed damages for vibration white finger (VWF) caused whilst working for the defendant between 1962 and 1996. He argued that he first had the requisite knowledge in the summer of 2003, when he saw an advert from a claims company describing the symptoms of VWF. At first instance, the judge dismissed his claim on the basis that he knew he had a significant injury and it was reasonable for him to have obtained medical advice which would have led to his linking that injury to his employment. Consequently, he had constructive knowledge at the end of 1996. On appeal, the claimant's argument that it was illogical for the judge to have plucked the end of 1996 as the date of constructive knowledge, because nothing significant happened at that point to have led to that knowledge, was dismissed by the Court of Appeal. The Court held that the end of 1996 was the *latest time* at which the claimant could be fixed with constructive knowledge, as the claimant's symptoms had reached a plateau by that time.

The issue of constructive knowledge of the identity of the defendant was considered in *Henderson v Temple Pier Co Ltd* [1998] 1 WLR 1540. In this case, it was held that, where a claimant instructed solicitors to bring a claim for damages, on the proper construction of s 14(3) of the LA 1980 the claimant was fixed with constructive knowledge of facts which the solicitor ought to have acquired.

### 7.3.4 The injury was 'significant'

In order to determine whether the claimant was aware that the injury was significant, further guidance is provided in s 14(2). This states that an injury is significant if the claimant would reasonably have considered it sufficiently serious to justify instituting proceedings against a defendant who did not dispute liability and was able to satisfy a judgment.

In *McCoubrey v Ministry of Defence* [2007] EWCA Civ 17, the Court of Appeal considered the case of a soldier who, during a training exercise in 1993, had been deafened by a thunderflash which had been thrown negligently into his trench. The claimant had known almost immediately that he had suffered the injury, and this had been confirmed by medical examinations. However, he had continued working in the army without complaint until 2003, when he was told that he could not accompany his unit to Iraq because of his disability. At that stage, he became aware of the consequences of the injury, consulted solicitors and issued proceedings. It was held that time had started to run in 1993, as soon as the claimant had become aware of his deafness. When determining whether an injury is 'significant', the court should consider the gravity of the injury and not its effect, or perceived effect, on the personal life or career of the claimant.

Moreover, if an injury is significant, the fact that the symptoms attributable to it subsequently became worse is irrelevant for purpose of determining when knowledge took place (see *Brooks v J & P Coates (UK) Ltd* [1984] 1 All ER 702). The date of knowledge is not affected by the fact that the consequences turned out to be more serious than was initially thought.

This principle should be distinguished from that which applies to a case involving multiple but separate illnesses. In *AB and Others v Ministry of Defence* (see **7.3.3.1**), the defendant argued that in cases of multiple illnesses arising from the same course of events, time starts to run as soon as the claimant has knowledge of the first injury that could be said to be significant, irrespective of the fact that he might learn of other injuries much later. This would mean that a serviceman who suffered from a skin complaint immediately following the nuclear tests, and who had the requisite knowledge regarding this injury, would not be able to pursue a more substantial claim for cancer which arose many years later, unless the court exercised the s 33 discretion (see **7.8**). The court rejected this argument, preferring the approach that the later injury was the injury 'in question', and that a claim in respect of the former injury could proceed only if the s 33 discretion was exercised.

In *R v Hoare* [2008] UKHL 6, the House of Lords gave valuable insight as to whether the test to be applied in relation to knowledge that the injury was significant is an objective or a subjective one. Lord Hoffmann said:

> Section 14(2) is a test for what counts as a significant injury. The material to which that test applies is generally 'subjective' in the sense that it is applied to what the claimant knows of his injury rather than the injury as it actually was. Even then, his knowledge may have to be supplemented with imputed 'objective' knowledge under section 14(3). But the test itself is an entirely impersonal standard: not whether the claimant himself would have considered the injury sufficiently serious to justify proceedings but whether he would 'reasonably' have done so. You ask what the claimant knew about the injury he had suffered, you add any knowledge about the injury which may be imputed to him under section 14(3) and you then ask whether a reasonable person with that knowledge would have considered the injury sufficiently serious to justify his instituting proceedings for damages against a defendant who did not dispute liability and was able to satisfy a judgment.

### 7.3.5 Attributable to the act or omission

'Attributable' means 'capable of being attributable to' and not necessarily 'caused by'. The knowledge of the 'act or omission' does not necessarily include knowledge that the act or omission is actionable in law. For example, if the claimant has asthma but does not know that this is due to his working conditions, time does not start to run. However, if he is aware that his asthma is capable of being attributed to those working conditions, time starts to run even though he may not know that his employer may have been to blame.

In *Dobbie v Medway Health Authority* [1994] 1 WLR 1234, CA, Mrs Dobbie had surgery to remove a lump in her breast. It was only during the operation that the surgeon took the decision to perform a mastectomy (removal of the breast), as he believed the lump was cancerous. In fact, the lump was not cancerous and the mastectomy had been unnecessary. Mrs Dobbie accepted at the time that the surgeon had acted reasonably and it was her good fortune that the lump was not cancerous. It was only several years later, when she heard about a similar case, that Mrs Dobbie took legal advice and commenced proceedings. The Court of Appeal held that she knew of the removal of her breast and the psychological and physical harm which followed within months of the operation, and she knew it to be significant. She also knew that her injury was the result of an act or omission of the health authority and, therefore, time began to run even though she did not appreciate until later that this act or omission may have been negligent.

### 7.3.6 The identity of the defendant

In most cases the claimant will know who is responsible for his injuries, but s 14(1)(c) will assist a claimant where there is a delay in identifying the defendant, eg in the case of a hit and run motor accident (assuming an application is not made to the Motor Insurers' Bureau – see **3.4**).

The identity of the defendant may prove problematic in cases involving corporate groups. In *Simpson v Norwest Holst Southern Ltd* [1980] 2 All ER 471, the claimant worked on a building site, and his contract of employment stated that he was employed by Norwest Holst Group. However, this did not identify his employer because at least four companies made up Norwest Holst Group, including Norwest Holst Ltd and Norwest Construction Co Ltd, and the claimant's payslips stated simply that his employer was 'Norwest Holst'. In the circumstances, the Court of Appeal found for the claimant, on the basis that neither the contract nor the payslips identified the employer, and it was not reasonable to expect the claimant to request further particulars of the identity of his employer prior to the expiry of his primary limitation period. For a case on similar facts, see *Rush v JNR (SMD) Ltd* (CA, 11 October 1999), where it was held that knowledge of a number of potential defendants was not sufficient knowledge for the purpose of s 14.

## 7.4 Persons under a disability

Under s 38(2) of the LA 1980, a person is under a disability while he is an infant (a person who has not attained the age of 18) or lacks capacity (within the meaning of the Mental Capacity Act 2005) to conduct legal proceedings.

Under s 28(6), while a person is under a disability, he may bring a claim at any time up to three years from the date when he ceased to be under a disability. Consequently, where a child is injured, limitation does not start to run until he reaches his 18th birthday and it expires on his 21st birthday.

Where a person is disabled within the meaning of the Mental Capacity Act 2005, the start of the limitation period is delayed only if he was so disabled when the cause of action first accrued. If the disability comes into existence after that date, time continues to run. However, under s 33(3) of the LA 1980 (see **7.8**) the court will have regard to any period or periods of disability when it considers its discretion to disapply the limitation period.

## 7.5 Limitation in assault cases

Until January 2008, the limitation period in relation to acts of deliberate assault, including indecent assault, followed the House of Lords' decision in the case of *Stubbings v Webb* [1993] AC 498, which involved child abuse at a children's home. The House of Lords held that deliberate assault did not fall under s 11(1) actions for 'negligence, nuisance or breach of duty' but under s 2, and therefore the correct limitation period was six years from the date of the cause of action (or the age of 18 in the case of a child) rather than three years. However, there was no discretion to disapply the period under s 33, which led to unfairness in cases where the victim had been a child or otherwise vulnerable at the time of the assault and, as a result, lacked the psychological capacity to bring a claim.

The House of Lords departed from this approach in *R v Hoare* [2008] UKHL 6, the facts of which were as follows. In 1988, the claimant had been subjected to a serious sexual assault by Hoare, who was subsequently convicted of attempted rape and sentenced to life imprisonment. The claimant had not brought civil proceedings against him within the six-year limitation period as Hoare did not have the financial means to pay any damages that the court might award. However, in 2004, whilst on day release from prison, Hoare purchased a lottery ticket and won over £7 million. When the claimant heard of the defendant's windfall, she commenced proceedings against him, seeking to rely on the court's discretion to disapply the limitation period under s 33. The House of Lords heard the claimant's appeal against the decision that her claim was statute barred, together with four other cases, all relating to the abuse of children in children's homes.

Their Lordships held that *Stubbings* had been wrongly decided, and they extended the meaning of claims under 'negligence, nuisance or breach of duty' to include deliberate assault. Consequently, the limitation period in assault cases was three years. They remitted the matter to the judge, for him to reconsider whether the court was able to exercise its discretion under s 33 to disapply this limitation period (see **7.8**).

## 7.6 Claims following fatal accidents

### 7.6.1 Claims under the Law Reform (Miscellaneous Provisions) Act 1934

Where a claim is brought on behalf of the deceased's estate, s 11(5) of the LA 1980 provides that if the injured person dies before expiration of the limitation period of three years as set out in s 11(4), the limitation period shall be three years from:

(a) the date of death; or

(b) the date of the personal representative's knowledge,

ignore date of accident

whichever is the later. If there is more than one personal representative and they have differing dates of knowledge, time runs from the earliest date of knowledge (s 11(7)).

If the injured person dies after the expiry of the primary limitation period under s 11(4) without commencing proceedings, the claim is statute-barred. However, the court does have a general discretion to override the above provisions and disapply the limitation period under s 33 of the LA 1980 (see **7.8**).

### 7.6.2 Claims under the Fatal Accidents Act 1976

Section 12(1) of the LA 1980 provides that a claim under the FAA 1976 cannot be brought if death occurred when the person injured could no longer maintain a claim and recover damages in respect of the injury, whether because of a limitation problem or for any other reason. In other words, the dependants of the deceased are not in a better position than the deceased would have been, and if the deceased's claim would have been statute-barred under s 11 of the LA 1980, the dependants' claim is similarly barred. When considering whether a claim brought by the deceased person would have been time-barred, no account may be made of the possibility that the court would have exercised its discretion under s 33 to disapply the limitation period.

If the claim is not already statute-barred due to the expiry of the primary limitation period, s 12(2) provides that the limitation period for the dependants under the FAA 1976 is three years from:

(a) the date of death; or

(b) the date of knowledge of the person for whose benefit the claim is brought,

whichever is the later.

If the dependants fail to commence their claim within this limitation period, an application can be made under s 33 to disapply the limitation period.

## 7.7 Other periods of limitation

Although in the vast majority of personal injury cases the three-year rule will apply, it is possible that a special rule applies, for example in regard to claims relating to aircraft under the Carriage by Air Act 1961 or the Warsaw Convention, or relating to vessels used for navigation under the Maritime Conventions Act 1911 or the Merchant Shipping Act 1995. In these cases, the limitation period is generally two years.

The most common form of special rule is in respect of contributions between tortfeasors under the Civil Liability (Contribution) Act 1978, where no claim to recover a contribution may be brought after the expiration of two years from the date on which the right accrued. This is generally the date on which judgment was given against the person who is seeking the contribution, or the date when he pays or agrees to pay compensation.

## 7.8 The court's discretion to override the limitation period

Section 33 of the LA 1980 gives the court a wide and unfettered discretion to disapply the three-year limitation period. Section 33(1) provides that:

> If it appears to the court that it would be equitable to allow an action to proceed having regard to the degree to which—
>
> (a) the provisions of section 11 or 11A or 12 of this Act prejudice the plaintiff or any person whom he represents; and
>
> (b) any decision of the court under this subsection would prejudice the defendant or any person whom he represents;
>
> the court may direct that those provisions shall not apply to the action, or shall not apply to any specified cause of action to which the action relates.

The onus rests upon the claimant to show why the limitation period should be disapplied (*Halford v Brookes* [1991] 3 All ER 559).

Under s 33(3), the court is required to have regard to all the circumstances of the case, and it will attempt to balance the needs of the parties by seeking to avoid prejudice caused to the claimant by depriving him of the right to continue with the claim, or prejudice caused to the defendant by allowing the matter to continue when he has been deprived of the ability to defend himself.

The court is specifically directed to six factors, which are outlined below:

(a) the length and reasons for the delay on the part of the claimant;

(b) the effect of any delay on the cogency of the evidence;

(c) the conduct of the defendant following the date of the cause of action;

(d) the duration of any disability (within the meaning of the Mental Capacity Act 2005) suffered by the claimant after the cause of action arose;

(e) the conduct of the claimant after he became aware that he might have a claim against the defendant;

(f) the steps taken by the claimant to obtain medical, legal or other expert advice, and the nature of any advice received.

Guidance in relation to s 33(3)(a) was provided by the Court of Appeal in *Coad v Cornwall and Isles of Scilly Health Authority* [1997] 1 WLR 189, CA. The Court held that it must apply a subjective test when determining why the claimant had delayed, the length of the delay and whether the reason was good or bad. There was no requirement for the claimant to provide a 'reasonable' explanation.

When considering s 33(3)(b), the extent to which evidence is less cogent, the Court of Appeal highlighted the importance of written evidence when memories of witnesses are unreliable due to the lapse of time (see *Farthing v North East Essex Health Authority* [1998] Lloyd's Rep Med 37, CA). In 1981, the claimant had had a hysterectomy which was negligently performed, but proceedings were not issued until 1995. When considering her application under s 33, the court found that due to the lapse of time a number of the witnesses had died, or had moved abroad and could recall little of the events in question. However, the Court of Appeal further found that because there was considerable evidence available in the form of the medical records and a letter from the surgeon to the claimant's GP written shortly after the operation, there would be little need for reliance on memory alone and consequently the appeal should be allowed.

In *TCD v Harrow Council and Others* (see **7.3.2**), it was argued on behalf of the claimant that she had been unable to confront some aspects of the abuse to the extent that would be necessary for the purposes of litigation, and that she had delayed proceedings until her children were older. Nevertheless, the judge repeated what was said in *Hoare* (see **7.5**), that not everyone who brings a late claim for damages for sexual abuse, however genuine his or her complaint, can expect the court to exercise the s 33 discretion favourably. He refused to exercise his discretion in relation to the claims against two of the authorities on the grounds that the long delay meant that evidence was not forthcoming and the defendants were therefore severely prejudiced. (Discretion was not exercised in relation to the third claim due to the weakness of the claim.)

In relation to s 33(3)(c), where the court is satisfied that the defendants have brought upon themselves the prejudice that they claim to suffer, that should be taken into account and the prejudice should be significantly discounted. In the case of *Hammond v West Lancashire Health Authority* [1998] Lloyd's Rep Med 146, CA, the defendants claimed prejudice to their case as they had destroyed the deceased's x-rays after three years had elapsed. The Court held that the destruction of the x-rays was a policy implemented by the defendants, and which had no regard for the time limits of the LA 1980. Consequently, although the prejudice caused to their case should still be taken into account, it would be significantly discounted.

These factors are guidelines only, and the court is entitled to take into account any other matter which it considers to be relevant. For example, the time of notification of the claim to the defendant is of extreme importance in ascertaining prejudice, although there is no specific reference to this in s 33. In addition, the court is entitled to consider the ultimate prospects of the claim being successful. In *TCD v Harrow Council and Others* (see above), the judge refused to grant discretion in relation to the case against Worcester County Council on the grounds that the claim had no realistic prospects of success. (Also see *Forbes v Wandsworth Health Authority* at **7.3.3.2**).

In the case of *Hoare* (see **7.5**), the House of Lords remitted the matter to the judge to reconsider the application of s 33 in accordance with the opinions of their Lordships. In *A v Hoare* [2008] EWHC 1573 (QB), the parties agreed that the main reason why the claimant had not commenced proceedings within the limitation period was because the defendant had been impecunious and, because he had been serving a life sentence, this was unlikely to change. She had commenced proceedings in 2004, almost 14 years after expiry of the three-year limitation period, principally because she had learned that the defendant had won £7 million on the lottery. It was also agreed that there was no reported authority on the court being asked to exercise its discretion under s 33 on the grounds that the defendant was impecunious. However, the judge determined that this was a relevant factor when considering the exercise of the discretion to disapply the limitation period. In doing so, he took into account the fact that the defendant's own actions were the cause of his impecuniosity. The judge found in favour of the claimant and exercised his discretion under s 33. (The full judgment in this case may aid understanding of the application of s 33.)

Where the proceedings are brought against the defendant outside the limitation period as a result of the negligence of the claimant's solicitor, and the claim is not allowed to proceed, the claimant may have a claim against his own solicitor. It has been argued by defendants that the fact that the claimant has a cast-iron claim against his own solicitor provides an overwhelming reason why the limitation period should not be disapplied; the claimant will not be prejudiced because he can pursue an alternative claim against his solicitor (rather than the defendant). However, although the ability to claim against the solicitor is a factor for the court to bear in mind, it is not an absolute bar against disapplying the limitation period.

The court considered this issue in *Steeds v Peverel Management Services Ltd* [2001] EWCA Civ 419. In this case, solicitors issued proceedings 49 days outside of the limitation period. On appeal, the court found that the district judge at first instance was wrong to treat the claimant's good claim against his own solicitors as justification for refusing to exercise a discretion under s 33. The better view was that the existence of a claim against his own solicitors was a relevant factor in weighing the degree of prejudice suffered by the defendant in not being able to rely on the limitation period as a defence. To that end, it would always be relevant to consider when the defendant first had notification of the claim. On the facts of the case, the judgment was set aside and the court exercised its discretion under s 33, as it was unlikely that the defendants were caused any appreciable prejudice and it was equitable to allow the claim to continue allowing for all of the circumstances of the case.

It has also been argued by defendants that the loss of the limitation defence itself, and the subsequent requirement to pay damages, is a prejudice which must be taken into account by the court when considering the exercise of the s 33 discretion. In *Cain v Francis; McKay v Hamlani* [2008] EWCA Civ 1451, both road traffic accident claims, the Court of Appeal considered the so-called 'windfall defence', which arises where the defendant has no defence other than one based on limitation due to the claimant's solicitors failing to issue proceedings on time. In each case, the defendant had admitted liability but, in the course of negotiating damages, the claimant's solicitors had missed the limitation deadline. In *Cain*, where there was a delay of just one day, the judge refused to exercise his discretion; in *McKay*, the delay was one year, but the judge exercised his discretion and allowed the case to proceed. In order to establish a consistency of approach, as opposed to a 'lottery for litigants', the Court of Appeal dealt with both cases together.

The Court of Appeal held that the defendant had a right to a fair opportunity to defend himself and had a complete procedural defence under s 11, which would remove the obligation for him to pay damages. However, fairness and justice meant that the obligation to pay damages should be removed only if the passage of time had significantly damaged the defendant's opportunity to defend himself. Parliament could not have intended the financial consequences for the defendant to be a consideration relevant to the exercise of discretion under s 33. The important factor is whether the defendant is able to defend himself, and therefore it would always be important to consider when the defendant was notified of the claim against him, and whether it was still possible for him to investigate the claim and gather evidence. This judgment has brought clarity to this area, and is likely to result in the court exercising its discretion under s 33 in more claims which were issued late but where the defendant's ability to defend himself is not prejudiced.

## 7.9 Dealing with limitation issues in practice

Failure to issue proceedings within the limitation period is a major source of negligence claims against solicitors. Although this chapter includes the law and procedure relevant to an application under s 33 to override the limitation period (see **7.8** above), prevention is better than cure. It is therefore essential that the claimant's solicitor establishes a routine of checking and rechecking the limitation period on the files for which he is responsible. There may also be many other files for which he is not responsible, but which may pass through his hands on a regular basis. Such files are often the source of limitation problems, as one solicitor may assume (wrongly) that the responsibility for checking limitation resides with someone else, and the date of limitation may go unnoticed. To avoid this, the solicitor should adopt a routine of checking for limitation on every file in which he is involved.

Needless to say, as the expiry of the limitation period provides the defendant with a significant, although not always watertight defence, those acting for defendants should always keep a watchful eye open for limitation issues.

### 7.9.1 Initial instructions

At the first interview, the claimant's solicitor should note the date of the cause of action and calculate the limitation period from this date. This can be verified by checking, for example, the relevant hospital A&E notes, the employer's accident report book, or police reports. If he is satisfied that there is sufficient time for him to investigate the matter and commence proceedings within the limitation period, he should mark the file with the expiry date and enter the date into the file management system, to ensure that limitation does not become a problem at a later stage.

If the limitation period has already expired, the solicitor will need to take account of this fact when carrying out the risk assessment. Where there appear to be no grounds for relying on a later date of knowledge or persuading the court to exercise its discretion under s 33, the client should be advised accordingly. It goes without saying that a solicitor must have the requisite knowledge to deal with the matter (Solicitors' Code of Conduct 2007, Rule 1.05). *Carlton v Fulchers (a Firm)* [1997] PNLR 337, CA, provides a valuable illustration as to how a solicitor can be found to be negligent due to a failure to be aware of limitation problems. In this case, even though the claimant did not consult the solicitor until after the three-year limitation period had expired, the solicitor was held liable due to his failure to advise of the possibility of an application under s 33.

Where the primary limitation period has expired and there are good arguments relating to later knowledge and/or s 33, the claimant's solicitor should issue proceedings without further delay. He may delay the service of the claim form and follow the procedure as set out in **7.9.2**.

In clinical negligence cases, where there is a possibility of public funding, further delays resulting from applying for such funding must be avoided, and therefore the solicitor should apply for emergency assistance from the Community Legal Service.

### 7.9.2 Protective proceedings

Where there is insufficient time to investigate the matter and comply with the relevant pre-action protocol before the limitation period expires, the claimant's solicitor should initiate protective proceedings in order to safeguard his client's position. The steps which should be taken are as follows:

(a) The claim form should be issued, which will stop the clock for limitation purposes, but should not be served upon the defendant. Under CPR, r 7.5(2), where it is to be served within the jurisdiction, it must be served within four months of being issued. This provides the claimant's solicitor with some time to investigate the matter and comply with the protocol. The particulars of claim must be served upon the defendant within 14 days after service of the claim form (CPR, r 7.4(1)(b)), but it too must be served within four months of the claim form being issued (CPR, r 7.4(2)).

(b) The claimant's solicitor should contact the defendant and notify him of the situation without delay. The date when the defendant first became aware of the claim or potential claim will be a relevant factor if the court is asked to consider whether the time limit should be disapplied under s 33.

(c) Both parties should then follow the relevant protocol. However, there may not be time to follow the protocol to the letter, eg there may not be time to allow the defendant three months to investigate the matter.

(d) Where time allowed for service of the claim form is about to expire, the claimant's solicitor should make an interim application to the court for an extension of the time limit relating to service (CPR, r 7.6). The application must be made in accordance with Part 23 and supported by evidence. It is vital that this application is made within the four months allowed for service of the claim form, as the powers of the court to grant an extension where the application is made after the expiry of this period are limited to when the court has been unable to serve the claim form, the claimant has taken all reasonable steps to serve it but has been unable to do so and, in either case, the application for the extension has been made promptly (CPR, r 7.6(3)).

(e) Where an application is made within the four-month time period, it is likely that the court will grant an extension of time for the service of the claim form. If so, it will also make directions in order to manage the case properly.

### 7.9.3 Commencing proceedings

Rule 16.4(a) of the CPR states that the particulars of claim should include a concise statement of the facts on which the claimant relies. It therefore follows that where a claim is issued outside the primary limitation period, the particulars of claim should, where relevant, include a statement that the claimant relies on a later date of knowledge, and the date should be specified.

It will be for the claimant to prove the later date of knowledge, and therefore this issue should be addressed in the witness statements of the claimant and any other witness who can give evidence on this point.

In practice, where there is a limitation problem and the parties have discussed this prior to commencement, the claimant's solicitor will deal with the limitation issue in the particulars of claim. However, if the matter has not been discussed before issue, some solicitors acting for claimants will not pre-empt a defence by raising the limitation problem in the particulars of claim, on the basis that it is not in their client's interests to do so. If the defendant is not aware of the existence of the rules relating to limitation, or does not notice that the limitation period has expired, he may admit the claim.

### 7.9.4 The defence

The defendant's solicitor should carefully check each particulars of claim for limitation problems. Where the claim form was issued outside the primary limitation period, he will need to address the issue in the defence. Where the claimant has relied on a later date of knowledge and the defendant seeks to rely on an earlier date of knowledge, whether actual or constructive, he should give details.

The defendant will have to prove any earlier date of knowledge he seeks to rely on. It is unlikely that he will be able to call witnesses of his own in this regard; rather, he will be obliged to extract the necessary information from the claimant and any other witness during cross-examination.

### 7.9.5 Dealing with limitation as a preliminary issue

In most cases, the limitation problem will be dealt with as a preliminary issue. The defendant should consider bringing the issue to a head either by applying for the claim to be stayed under CPR, r 3.1(f) or, in a clear case, by applying for summary judgment under CPR, r 24.2(a)(i). The claimant should respond by giving notice of his intention to ask the court to exercise its discretion to disapply the limitation period under s 33. Both parties should address the matter fully in the supporting witness statements. This will enable the court to consider the matter before trial.

If the defendant does not bring the matter to the court's attention by making an application, the claimant's solicitor should consider doing so by making an application under s 33.

Whilst the courts will normally seek to deal with limitation as a preliminary issue wherever feasible, there will be circumstances where it is not appropriate to do so. In the case of *J, K & P v Archbishop of Birmingham & Trustees of the Birmingham Archdiocese of the Roman Catholic Church* [2003] LTL, 21 August, which involved the alleged victims of child sexual abuse, the court held that it was not appropriate due to the large overlap of evidence and the additional stress on the victims having to give their evidence twice.

## 7.10 Further reading

McGee, *Limitation Periods* (Sweet & Maxwell).

## 7.11 Claimant's limitation checklist

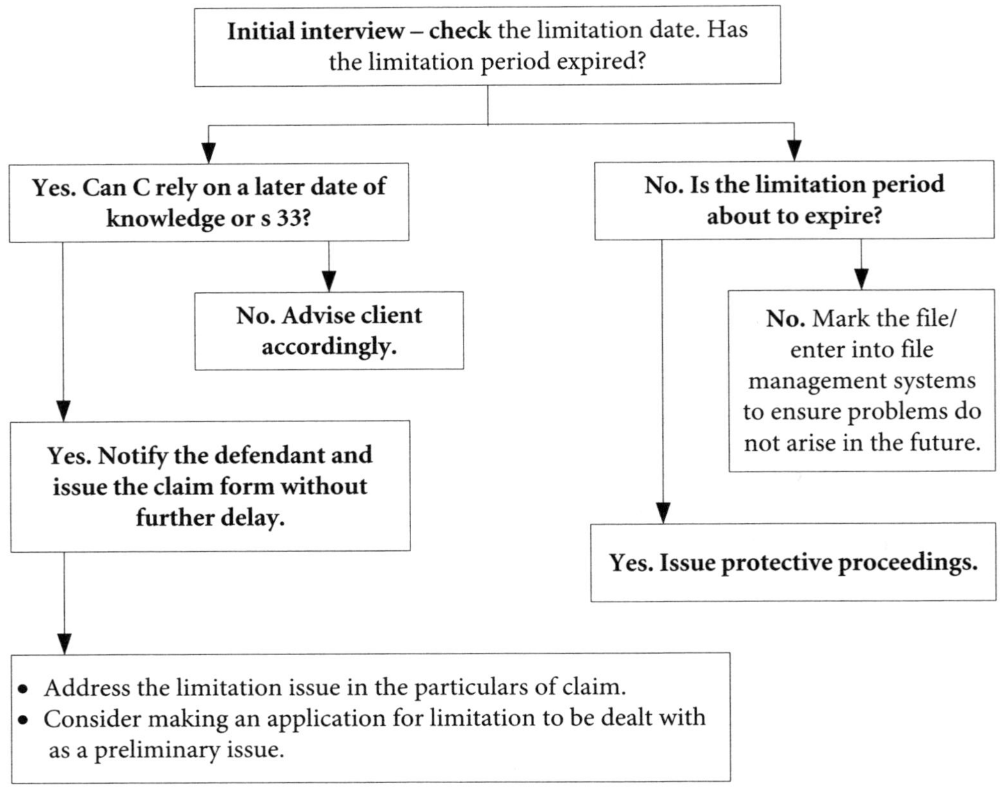

# Chapter 8
# The First Interview



## 8.1 Introduction

The first interview is the cornerstone of the solicitor/client relationship, and it is therefore worthwhile making the effort to get it right. The Law Society issued a Practice Note on initial interviews in May 2008, which contains useful guidance on this topic and can be obtained from The Law Society website. Reference should also be made to ***Skills for Lawyers***, which deals with how to conduct an interview. The interview will normally last at least an hour. The client should tell his own story, and the solicitor will often complete a long and detailed accident questionnaire, prior to drafting a proof of evidence. Detailed preparation at this stage will save a great deal of time later.

## 8.2 Funding

### 8.2.1 The first interview

#### 8.2.1.1 Free initial interviews

Many firms offer a free initial interview in order to persuade clients into their offices. Many people are wary of solicitors' charges, and are put off making claims accordingly. Some solicitors therefore offer free initial advice in which they will form a view as to the viability of a personal injury or clinical negligence claim, and advise clients about the various case-funding methods available.

#### 8.2.1.2 The growth of the claims management industry

There can be few people who have not, at some point, come across some form of advertising in respect of personal injury claims. The typical advertisement will contain an invitation to call a free-phone number and talk to an adviser about whether the caller has a viable claim. The caller is always assured that there will not be any obligation to pay for the advice received. The listener will doubtless be recompensed for his trouble by the grateful solicitor, who will ultimately have the privilege of taking on the caller's claim.

Undoubtedly this will be a 'free' service to the individual who has suffered injury. Usually (but not always) the solicitor will pay the claims manager for the service of having introduced the willing claimant. Thereafter the solicitor–client relationship will normally be based upon a conditional fee agreement (CFA, as to which see **9.2.2**).

The abolition of Legal Aid for personal injury claims, and the subsequent 'bonanza' for so-called 'claims farmers', has led in recent years to calls from some quarters (notably insurers) for greater regulation. There have been complaints about an alleged 'claims culture' developing, whereby individuals are encouraged to make a claim for personal injury merely on the off-chance that they might have a viable claim rather than out of any real need or desire to be compensated for their injury. It is often argued that mass advertising via the Internet and television has had the effect of bringing far greater numbers of claims forward, many of which are unlikely to succeed but nevertheless drain the insurer of resources due to the necessity to investigate the allegations made, thus driving up the cost of risk insurance.

Having created the necessary conditions for the growth of claims farmers in the first place, Parliament set about regulating the claims industry by passing the Compensation Act 2006, which received Royal Assent on 25 July 2006.

Part II of the Act establishes a framework for the regulation of the claims management industry. Essentially, all providers of claims management services (whether this is providing replacement vehicles, providing would-be claimants with access to solicitors' advice or providing vehicle repair following a non-fault accident) must either be authorised or exempt from such authorisation. It is unlawful to provide such regulated services without either authorisation or a relevant exemption.

The Regulator has powers under the Act to take action against persons suspected of providing regulated services without authorisation. If found guilty, the maximum penalty is two years' imprisonment, or a fine or both. There are also further sanctions against authorised persons suspected of breaching the regulations, or found guilty of unprofessional conduct. A finding of professional misconduct could lead the Regulator to vary, suspend or cancel a person's authorisation.

Once authorised, businesses have to comply with strict rules of conduct, including:

(a) a prohibition on cold calling in person;

(b) a prohibition on high-pressure selling;

(c) transparent contracts;

(d) disclosure of referral fees; and

(e) provision of a complaints procedure.

Under the current arrangements, the Secretary of State for Justice is the Regulator. A website provides guidance and information on the authorisation process and other aspects of regulation at http://www.justice.gov.uk.

### 8.2.2 Funding after the first interview

In order to comply with Rule 2.03 of the Solicitor's Code of Conduct 2007 (the Code), you must give the client the best information possible about the likely overall cost of a matter at the outset. This will mean going through all the available funding options, including the availability of public funding and insurance. The various methods of funding are discussed more fully in **Chapter 9**.

## 8.3 Urgent matters

If an urgent matter comes to light during the first interview, the solicitor should bear in mind the question of funding prior to making lengthy or expensive investigations on the client's behalf, and should consider making an application for emergency public funding if appropriate.

### 8.3.1 Limitation

Limitation is discussed in detail in **Chapter 7**. At the first interview in a personal injury or clinical negligence claim, it may become apparent that:

(a) the three-year primary limitation period is about to expire (see **7.2**). If so, the solicitor should consider issuing protective proceedings immediately (see **7.9.2**);

(b) the three-year primary limitation period has recently expired. If so, consideration should be given to issuing proceedings as soon as possible, including in the claim form or particulars of claim, a request for a direction that the limitation period should be disapplied (see **7.8**). Thereafter, the solicitor should inform the defendant without delay that proceedings have been issued, to minimise any claim by the defendant of prejudice due to the passage of time;

(c) there is a question as to the client's 'date of knowledge' of the injury complained of. The client should be questioned closely regarding the earliest date on which he realised he might have a cause of action, and how he came to that conclusion. The client's medical records should be obtained without delay in order to confirm the precise date of knowledge. Proceedings can then be issued as in point (b) above, and thereafter it can be argued that the limitation period has not yet expired because the client's date of knowledge of the injury is within the last three years. If this is not successful, an application should be made for the court to exercise its discretion and disapply the limitation period (see **7.8**).

Having established when the primary limitation period is due to expire, it is important that the time limit is recorded separately from the file in a diary system. The file itself may be similarly marked with the date on which limitation expires. This double recording of the primary limitation period is good practice, as negligence claims against solicitors in personal injury cases account for roughly 11% of claims on Solicitors' Liability. Failure to identify the correct limitation period is one of the most common pitfalls, and this can be avoided.

## 8.3.2 Photographs

In most personal injury cases, persons seeking advice following an accident will do so relatively soon after the accident occurs. If this is the case, a task, which is often overlooked, will be to secure photographic evidence.

### 8.3.2.1 The client

The client may attend the interview with an array of bruises and abrasions (soft tissue injuries). These will heal or fade relatively quickly, and an important piece of the claimant's evidence will be lost. The claimant's solicitor should therefore ensure that good colour photographs are taken of the client's injuries for subsequent disclosure. Such photographs will form very tangible evidence of the severity of the injuries sustained, when the case comes to be considered some months or years in the future. In cases where the client may suffer embarrassment at being photographed, or indeed in any case where a degree of sensitivity is needed, specialist medical photographers are available, for example at larger teaching hospitals.

### 8.3.2.2 The location of the accident

In road traffic cases, it is usually necessary to visit and take photographs of the location of the accident as soon as possible after the accident, because the layout of the road may change as time passes and/or the road may appear different depending on whether it is photographed in summer or in winter, especially if there are lots of trees or vegetation which could obscure a driver's view (see **10.9.3**).

Where accidents at work are concerned, it is good practice to obtain photographs of any machinery or equipment involved. Any delay may mean that the equipment involved is replaced and/or disposed of. Similarly, if the accident involves allegations of a defect in a floor surface, it would be helpful to obtain photographic evidence of that floor surface before it is corrected.

## 8.4 Advising the client

It is important for the solicitor not to lose sight of the fact that the client has come into his office seeking some meaningful advice, which he hopes will lead him to a decision as to whether he has an actionable case against some other party. The client therefore needs to have the best information available, in a form that he can understand, so that he can make an informed decision as to what to do next. It is best to set out the strengths and weaknesses of the case, based on what has been said by the client. The importance of the limitation period should be explained to the client if this is likely to be an issue. The solicitor should also explain to the client that it is for him to prove his case by evidence and that anything short of this is not enough. He should be informed of the basis of his case, and the level of proof needed by the court to prove it. The client should be left in no doubt that it is his case, to be proved by his evidence, and that he bears the risk that his case may fail. As such, he should think seriously prior to instructing his solicitor to issue proceedings. The solicitor should give an indication as to whether he believes that the case is likely to succeed, but he should make it clear that the assessment is based on the limited information available at this early stage. In any event, if the solicitor is considering taking the client's case but will be paid under a CFA, it will be necessary for the solicitor to conduct an assessment of risk at an early stage in order to decide whether or not to accept the client's instructions on that basis.

It may be that the solicitor advising the client will be required to produce to his superiors a report, from which his superiors will make a risk assessment in relation to whether or not the client should be accepted on a conditional fee basis. The risk assessment report may also consider such things as whether it is proposed that the client covers his own disbursements, or whether the firm is prepared to fund them on the client's behalf. The client is likely to press for an indication of the likely level of damages that may be recovered. Giving a firm indication based on inadequate information should be resisted. Instead, the solicitor should explain to the client why an assessment would be premature at this stage. The solicitor will not be in a position to assess the value of the claim until medical evidence dealing with diagnosis and prognosis has been obtained.

One reason for not giving a provisional indication of the likely level of damages is that the client may be found to have been contributorily negligent. This principle should be explained to the client, first to try to elicit whether the client has any reason to believe that it will be relevant to his claim and, secondly, to act as a warning to the client that it is likely that the opposition will try to allege that he was contributorily negligent.

The client should also be advised that he must prove every head (or type) of loss against his opponent. Although it is the case that the client is able to claim all he has lost as a direct result of the accident, he must also be in a position to prove every head of that loss to the court if he wishes to recover damages in respect of it. It should therefore be explained to the client that damages are made up of general damages (for pain, suffering and loss of amenity) and special damages (everything the client has had physically to pay for and other quantifiable losses as a direct result of the accident). For a detailed analysis of the subject of damages, see **Chapter 15**.

It will assist greatly, when it comes to proving his losses, if the client has kept a detailed record or account of his out-of-pocket expenses. To this end, the client should be advised at the first interview to keep all receipts for expenses incurred as a direct result of the accident, and that it is his responsibility to do so. Common examples are prescriptions, the cost of items lost or damaged beyond repair in the accident, and taxi fares to the out-patient or physiotherapy departments. Similarly, with respect to general damages for pain and suffering, although the client's distress may be keen at the first interview, by the time of trial his recollection may have dimmed, to the extent that he has forgotten many of the minor losses of function he suffered in the early stages of recovery from his injuries. The client should therefore be advised to keep a diary if he does not already do so, to record, for example, the fact that he is unable to sleep due to pain, or is unable to dress himself unaided or to do housework, and to record how long these disabilities last. Any number of tasks, either recreational or work-related, should be recorded so that they are not forgotten later when it comes to preparing the client's witness statement.

It is particularly important in clinical negligence cases that the client is made aware of the difficulties in pursuing the claim, and especially that he must establish not only a breach of duty, but also that the breach was causative of the damage that resulted (rather than the underlying illness or injury being the root cause of the loss). If the client is paying for the litigation privately, the high costs involved must be explained to him clearly. The solicitor should also explain the difficulty in giving a preliminary view on liability without first obtaining all the client's medical notes and at least one expert's views.

## 8.5 The client's proof of evidence

Client questionnaires are used frequently in personal injury work. The questionnaires are designed to elicit certain basic information about the client and the accident. Increasingly, law firms 'capture' these basic data about the client by keying the details into a case management system. This has the advantage that once 'captured', the data are available for use subsequently throughout the life of the claim.

The client's proof of evidence should not be confused with the client's witness statement. Although they are both statements taken from the client, they serve different functions. The proof is the 'rough copy', which may include irrelevant material and suspicions or 'versions' rather than facts provable by the client in court. The witness statement contains only those matters which the witness can prove, and is disclosed to the opposition at the relevant stage in the proceedings. The function of the proof is to obtain the fullest possible detail from the client, and only later to sift out what is strictly admissible as evidence. The proof can be taken at the end of the first interview when the client is still present, or from notes made at the time in conjunction with the questionnaire.

### 8.5.1 Contents of the proof

The proof should commence with the client's full name, address, date of birth and National Insurance number. It should state his occupation and whether he is married. If he was admitted to hospital, it should state his hospital number. The proof is intended for use by the client's solicitor and barrister, and, subsequently, in the preparation of the client's witness statement; as such, it should be the fullest possible statement from the client relating to the incident, the events immediately following the incident and its long-term effects. The client should begin his narrative at the earliest point in time that he feels to be relevant.

Following the client's personal details, the proof should next detail the date, time and location of the incident. It should then follow through chronologically and meticulously:

(a) the events leading up to the incident;
(b) the circumstances of the accident, including a clear explanation of the mechanics of the accident itself;
(c) what happened immediately after the incident;
(d) why the client feels that the incident was caused by the negligence of some other person;
(e) what medical treatment was given and injuries incurred; and
(f) how the client feels that the incident has affected his day-to-day life.

The solicitor should bear in mind that the proof will form the basis of the witness statement, and that, usually, the witness statement will be ordered to stand as the witness's evidence-in-chief at the trial. It is important, therefore, that the proof is detailed in its description of how the incident actually happened, and the effect the incident has had on the client's day-to-day life. All aspects of the client's life should therefore be considered in the proof. The following areas should always be covered, including an estimate in weeks or months of how long the incapacity affected the client's life, or confirmation that the incapacity is still continuing:

(a) Everyday tasks which he is unable to do for himself, eg dressing, bathing, housework, shopping, driving. This will be important if a claim is made for loss incurred in employing someone else to carry out these tasks.

(b) Recreational activities such as sports, hobbies, gardening, DIY in maintaining the home and the family car. The client's inability to participate in sports will have an effect on his loss of amenity claim for general damages. The client should also be asked whether he is a member of any sports team or club, and about any prizes or trophies he has won as further evidence of his level of commitment. The inability to carry out jobs of maintenance around the home will similarly affect his claim for loss of amenity. If the client gives evidence that DIY is a hobby, details should be obtained of any projects he has undertaken. This will also affect his special damages claim for the labour element of the cost of having to employ someone else to fulfil those tasks in the future.

(c) Whether and to what extent the injury has affected his sex life. This area of loss of amenity should always be broached with the client, as the stress of an accident can often bring about a degree of sexual dysfunction, even if the injury itself would not immediately suggest that such was the case.

(d) Specifically, whether the incident will affect the client's ability to continue with his employment, and the extent to which he is affected. It may be obvious that the client will never work again, or will be unable to work in his pre-incident position but will have to retrain, or that he intends to return to his pre-incident employment but is unsure whether he will cope. Details should also be obtained as to the client's position if he were to be made redundant, and the degree of difficulty he would have in obtaining similar employment elsewhere because of his injuries.

It is important that all of the above issues are considered and, if relevant, that they are covered in the proof in some detail, as there is little point in the client and/or his solicitor knowing the extent to which the incident has ruined the client's life, if this is not articulated sufficiently to the court. If a matter is not covered in the client's witness statement, the chances are the court will never hear of it; and if the court is not made aware of all relevant matters, the claimant's solicitor has not achieved one of his main aims, that of maximising the client's damages.

Before finishing the proof in personal injury cases, the client should always be asked whether he has had any pre-existing incident injury which may affect the current case.

The proof should always end with the client's signature and the date on which it was prepared so that, if the client dies prior to the conclusion of the case, the proof will still be of use evidentially.

### 8.5.2 Proofs in relation to different types of incident

The following types of incident will require the proof to cover certain areas in particular detail.

#### 8.5.2.1 Incidents at work

The nature of the work process that gave rise to the incident must be thoroughly understood from the outset if the case is to be dealt with properly. The client should be asked to explain:

(a) his job title;

(b) what that involves in the work process;

(c) the level of training or instruction received;

(d) the level of seniority he held;

(e) the level of supervision over him;

(f) whether he can recall any written or oral confirmation of his work duties;
(g) a description of his usual duties;
(h) what he was doing on the day in question that gave rise to the incident;
(i) whether anything out of the ordinary occurred that day;
(j) details of other similar incidents known to the claimant;
(k) any representations made by a trade union about the machine or system of work;
(l) any comments made at health and safety meetings;
(m) any witnesses to the incident or the unsafe practice.

**Example**

John is an instrument artificer employed to work at a chemical plant. Part of his duties is to check the temperature of certain chemicals stored in large tanks above ground on the site. On the day of the accident, John climbed to the top of a storage tank and removed the outer cover. Without warning, John was blown backwards by excess pressure in the tank, causing him to fall from the tank approximately 4 metres to the ground. Because the chemical was corrosive on contact with the skin, John suffered burns to his face and hands, as well as a damaged spine and broken left leg. John tells you that he has done the same task many times before without incident, but he believes that whoever last checked that particular tank failed adequately to secure the inner seal, so that when he next opened the outer seal the sudden change in pressure was like releasing a cork from a bottle. John tells you that he is usually accompanied by a fellow employee when doing these checks, as the company's safety policy requires this. On the day of the incident, his colleague had telephoned in sick, but the duty manager had not called in anyone else to take his place. John also tells you that the company used to have a nurse on site to deal with minor injuries, but when the last nurse ceased to be employed she was not replaced, John believes that this was because of the expense involved. John also believes that his burns would not be so severe if he had received first aid more quickly.

In the above example, if, when describing any part of his duties, John becomes unclear, he should be asked to explain it again, perhaps drawing a sketch to assist his narrative. It is important that there is no misunderstanding at this stage, as the solicitor will probably use this information as the basis for his statement of case. In addition, if the solicitor is unsure from the client's explanation precisely how the incident happened, it is also likely that a judge will be similarly confused. It is therefore vitally important that any ambiguity is resolved at this point. If ambiguity remains, facilities should be sought for a site inspection. Where the place of work is privately-owned property, and may be a dangerous environment for the visitor, the solicitor must always seek permission from the employer for a site inspection. The inspection can be carried out with the claimant's expert engineer if the accident involves a piece of machinery.

In the above example, it is necessary to include in the proof John's suspicions as to:

(a) the cause of the incident;
(b) disregard of safety policy; and
(c) his belief that the burns were worsened by delay in treatment.

All these matters will have to be checked, however, as the chemical engineer who inspects the plant may conclude that the incident had a completely different cause, possibly involving contributory negligence by John himself. It may be apparent to the engineer that the tank is fitted with a large pressure gauge that John should have checked prior to opening the tank. Similarly, the company safety policy may specify that rubber gloves and a full face mask must be worn when working with corrosive chemicals, and that the burn time for that particular chemical is less than 30 seconds, in which case having medical personnel on site would have made no difference to John's injuries.

The function of the proof is to form the basis of the witness statement. As such, the client's assertions must be checked thoroughly in order to decide whether they are provable and can be included in the statement.

#### 8.5.2.2 Road traffic incidents

When taking the proof in the case of a road incident, it is important first to have in mind the stretch of road in question. A large-scale map of the area in question is invaluable at this stage, as it will cut short any unproductive argument as to how or where, for example, the road bends. If the client has difficulty explaining how the incident happened, it can be useful to get him to draw a sketch of the relative position of the vehicles involved, or to use toy cars to illustrate what happened. Care should be taken to ensure that the client is entirely clear about the following matters:

(a) the direction in which he was travelling;
(b) the time of day;
(c) whether there was anyone else in the car with him;
(d) the weather conditions;
(e) the speed of travel;
(f) familiarity with the car;
(g) familiarity with the road;
(h) whether there were any witnesses;
(i) the make and registration numbers of all vehicles involved;
(j) who he believes to be responsible for the incident and why;
(k) what happened immediately after the incident;
(l) exactly what he said to anyone after the incident;
(m) exactly what anyone said to him, and whether anyone else heard what was said;
(n) whether the police were called and, if not, why not;
(o) if the police were called, which police force and the name of the officer attending;
(p) whether the client is aware of any pending prosecutions (eg, whether he was warned that he might be prosecuted, or that he might be needed as a witness in the prosecution of the other driver);
(q) whether he is comprehensively insured and the amount of excess he has to pay on his own insurance policy (his uninsured loss);
(r) whether he is the owner of the vehicle, and details of the owner if he is not.

If the client wrote anything down at the time of the incident, such as the name and address of the other driver(s), this should be retained. If he explains what happened, for example by referring to the offside and nearside of his vehicle, the solicitor should check that he understands what is meant by those terms. Clients may believe that they have to speak to their solicitor using words which they would not normally use in everyday speech, and consequently they may use words that they do not fully understand. For the avoidance of doubt, the solicitor should check with the client that when referring to a vehicle's 'offside' the client means the driver's side, and that 'nearside' refers to the side of the vehicle nearest the gutter.

In road traffic cases, it is vitally important to trace and interview witnesses as soon as possible. It is unlikely that the witnesses will be known to the client and they may prove difficult to trace if not contacted immediately, and in any event their memory of the events will fade quickly and will therefore be of less use evidentially. The question of whether there are any independent third party witnesses is of central importance, because the case will be much easier to prove if an independent witness can be found who is prepared to give evidence to a court that he saw the incident and believes that the cause of the incident was the fault of the other driver. If the client does not have any details of witnesses, the police accident report may have statements from witnesses whom the solicitor can contact. The police should be notified of all incidents involving personal injury, and will prepare a report on the incident including witness statements (see **Chapter 10**).

#### 8.5.2.3 Tripping/slipping incidents

Trips and slips make up a large proportion of incidents in the workplace, and the HSE has targeted this area in order to heighten awareness of the problem (see the HSE publication *Watch Your Step* (1985) and *Slips and Trips: Guidance for employers on identifying hazards and controlling risks* (May 1996)).

Tripping incidents occurring other than at the workplace are governed by s 41 of the Highways Act 1980, under which the highway authority (usually the local district council responsible for the area in which the fall or trip took place) has a duty to maintain the highway, which includes the pavements used by the public. It is for the claimant to show that the highway was not reasonably safe. Uneven paving stones or the sites of road improvements with poor temporary surfaces usually claim the most victims. Local authorities sometimes contract out such road works to independent contractors, in which case it may be advisable to sue both the contractor responsible for the safety of the site and the local authority which delegated the improvement work to them. If the client can show that the highway was not reasonably safe, the authority must show that it has taken such care as in all the circumstances was reasonably required to ensure that the highway was not dangerous.

Applying the above rule to the client's proof, it will be necessary to ask the client:

(a) the time of day;
(b) the weather conditions;
(c) whether he was in a hurry or was running at the time of the incident;
(d) whether he was carrying anything which obscured his view;
(e) whether there was a warning sign to take care and, if so, what the sign said;
(f) whether there were any witnesses;
(g) what sort of shoes the client was wearing; and
(h) the exact location of the incident.

It will then be necessary to procure photographs of the location without delay, as the local authority may act quickly to repair the relevant area as soon as it becomes aware of a possible claim, in order to show that it has taken such care as in all the circumstances was reasonably required.

#### 8.5.2.4 Clinical negligence claims

In a clinical negligence claim, the client is likely to be in a more confused or uncertain position than in a personal injury matter. While a client is normally able to explain, for example, what occurred during a road traffic incident, he may not understand the treatment and care he received from a medical practitioner. The terminology will be unfamiliar and, in the case of alleged negligence during hospital treatment, the client may not be able to recall or identify the doctors or nurses who treated him.

When obtaining a proof in a clinical negligence case, it is important that every detail is obtained, such as what exactly was said when the claimant attended at the hospital or when the client was asked to sign the consent form.

Unless the alleged negligent act arises out of an illness not previously suffered by the client, full details of any previous medical problems should be obtained. Other matters contained in the proof could be as follows:

(a) the symptoms which led the client to seek medical advice;
(b) the information given by the client to the doctor;
(c) any questions asked by the doctor (eg, where the client went to his GP complaining of headaches, whether the doctor asked the client if he had hit his head or whether the

client had been sick – questions which would lead a competent GP to suspect a severe head injury);

(d) whether the client was given details of a diagnosis at that time;

(e) what form of treatment was prescribed;

(f) whether the treatment was explained to the client, and whether he was warned of any potential risks and the likely consequences of not receiving treatment;

(g) the name of the doctor who treated the client and his status;

(h) whether the client was receiving treatment from different doctors;

(i) whether the client asked for a second opinion;

(j) whether any witnesses were present at the consultation;

(k) any previous medical problems which could have affected the client;

(l) whether the client has complained to the hospital/doctor;

(m) whether the client has received any reply or relevant correspondence;

(n) whether an apology has been received.

This should be followed by details of the injury in the normal fashion.

In certain cases, it can be useful to ask what prompted the client to contact a solicitor. In some cases, the client is advised by other medical professionals to seek legal advice as they believe that a mistake may have been made.

**Example**

A client injures his leg playing football and attends at the local A&E department. The department is busy and, although the client is sent for an x-ray, the house officer fails to spot the fracture and discharges the client immediately. The client is in considerable pain for a number of weeks and eventually visits his GP, who refers him back to the hospital for another x-ray. In such circumstances, the client may be told that in fact the leg is fractured and that it was missed when the client first attended. Such information is clearly of assistance in assessing liability.

## 8.6 Welfare benefits

It will be necessary to advise the client of the welfare benefits he may be entitled to receive because of the incident. It may be months or years before the claim is settled, and if the client is unfit for work, he may experience financial difficulties and feel pressured into accepting the first offer of compensation from the defendant. The solicitor should give the client general advice on the types of benefits that may be available to him to cover payment in respect of his inability to work, assistance with mobility, assistance with household tasks and even assistance with child care. It should be stressed that if only general guidance is given then the client should seek detailed advice from Jobcentre Plus (an agency of the Department for Work and Pensions (DWP)) or from the firm's welfare rights adviser, if the solicitor is not fully familiar with the current benefits available. Regulations relating to particular benefits change frequently, and up-to-date information on benefits can be obtained from Jobcentre Plus on free or low-cost telephone information lines. It should be stressed to the client that he must act quickly when seeking benefits, as it is not normally possible to back-date them and benefits may be lost due to delay. More information on benefits and how to claim them can be found at www.direct.gov.uk.

### 8.6.1 Eligibility for benefits

Clients who do not have an employer because they are self-employed or unemployed may claim employment and support allowance.

The client should be advised that, although he may qualify for benefits, if his claim is successful he will be subject to recoupment under the Social Security (Recovery of Benefits) Act 1997. This area is considered in detail in **Chapter 16.**

The client's eligibility for benefits will be assessed by the DWP. People who claim incapacity or disablement benefit are examined either by doctors who work for the DWP Medical Services, or by health service doctors who are paid a fee. The doctor tests whether the person claiming can perform a range of tasks, and reports his findings back to the DWP. The test the doctor applies when assessing people for incapacity benefit or severe disablement allowance is called the 'all work' test.

For the employment and support allowance, there is an assessment called the 'work capability assessment', which examines what the claimant can do, rather than what he cannot.

When considering eligibility for benefits, it is necessary to have regard to whether the receipt of compensation will take the claimant out of financial eligibility for means-tested benefits. In *Beattie v Secretary of State for Social Security* [2001] 1 WLR 1404, Charles Beattie was injured in a road traffic accident and rendered quadriplegic. He sued by his litigation friend and Court of Protection receiver, Stephen Beattie. The claimant appealed a decision of the Social Security Commissioner that he was not entitled to income support because payments 'falling to be treated as income' under a structured settlement took him beyond the limit on income for the purpose of claiming income support. This issue was appealed because guidance from the Public Trust Office suggested that, as long as the compensation was held on trust and payments were made on a discretionary basis and were not used to fund items that would normally be paid for using benefits, then those payments would not affect benefit entitlement. In *Beattie* the court ruled that the agreement, as part of the structured settlement, to make regular payments for a fixed number of years was in fact an annuity and was therefore 'capital treated as income' under reg 41(2) of the Income Support (General) Regulations 1987 (SI 1987/1967). The essential difference in this case is that the compensation was paid to the Court of Protection, which would hold the money for the benefit of the patient, rather than simply held on discretionary trust.

## 8.7 Rehabilitation, early intervention and medical treatment

It has long been recognised that a claimant's long-term prognosis can be dramatically improved by the intervention of rehabilitative treatment at the earliest possible opportunity. Research by insurers has found that the UK lags behind much of Europe and North America in terms of the ability to provide restorative care for injured claimants. The result of early intervention strategies in other countries is that they have a far better rate of return to work at an earlier stage than is able to be achieved in the UK. While it is recognised that the reasons for this are complex, insurers whose operations include much of Europe are starting to question why return to work rates are so poor in the UK.

The problem in the past has been that the claimant is not able to fund the treatment adequately until after his claim for damages for personal injuries is settled. Insurance companies are now recognising that early intervention in the form of extra sessions of physiotherapy, for example, can be in their own best interests as well as the claimant's if it assists the claimant to recover sufficiently to return to employment either earlier or at all. In the long term, insurers recognise that, if they fail to cooperate in paying for rehabilitative treatment in cases where liability is unlikely to be an issue, both they and the claimant will be the ultimate losers. The claimant will lose the opportunity of therapeutic medical treatment at the earliest opportunity and the insurer (if found liable) is likely to find an increased claim for future loss as the claimant is not fit to return to work.

To alleviate this problem, the pre-action protocol for use in personal injury claims includes (at Annex D) the revised code of practice on rehabilitation, early intervention and medical treatment. This has been drafted by insurers and lawyers with the aim of ensuring that both sides are aware of the rehabilitation issue and of their respective obligations under the code. The code places responsibilities on both claimants' solicitors and insurers to consider whether rehabilitation is appropriate, and places a duty on both to contact the other to raise the issue if either of them thinks that the claimant could benefit. The code is reproduced in full at **Appendix 2**.

Examples of such early treatment are: surgery, physiotherapy, counselling, occupational therapy and speech therapy. Examples may also include making adaptations to the claimant's home to make his life easier in the period prior to the settlement of the claim.

## 8.8 Conclusion

If the first interview is handled correctly, it should save the solicitor a great deal of time in the future. As personal injury litigation is 'front loaded', much of the essential work is covered during or shortly after the first interview. If essential matters have been missed, old ground will need to be covered again, which will lead to inevitable delay and upset for the client. If this is allowed to happen, the solicitor will have failed in one of his main objectives, that of avoiding delay, and thereby will allow the opposition to gain the advantage.

## 8.9 Further reading

*Slips and Trips: Guidance for employers on identifying hazards and controlling risks* (Stationery Office)

Statutory Sick Pay Manual for Employers

*Five Steps to Risk Assessment* (HSE Publications)

*A Guide to Risk Assessment Requirements* (HSE Publications)

Code of Best Practice on Rehabilitation, Early Intervention and Medical Treatment in Personal Injury Claims (BICMA).

www.justask.org.uk

www.direct.gov.uk

The Law Society Initial Interviews Practice Note, 15 May 2008

## 8.10 Overview of matters to be considered at the first interview

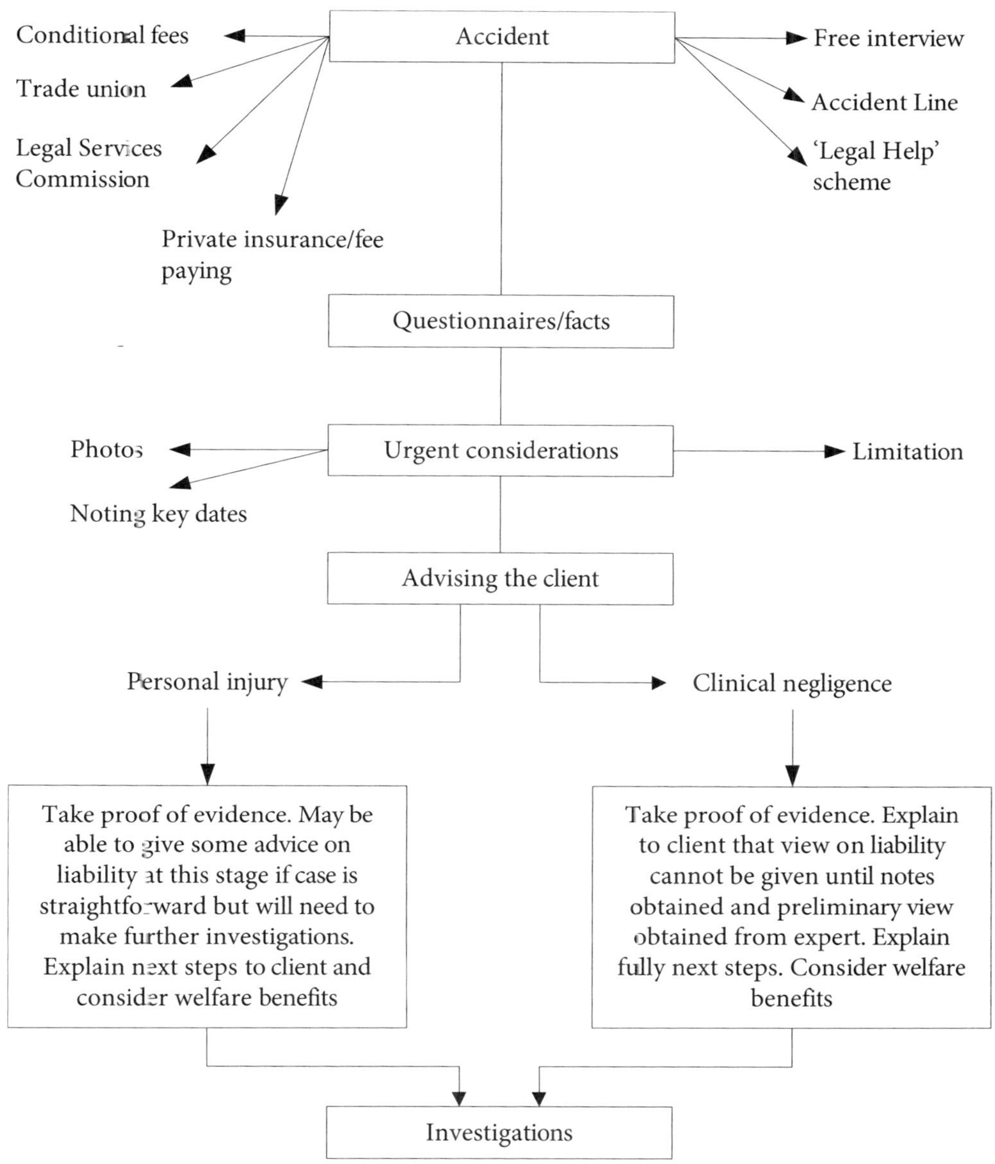

# Chapter 9
# Methods of Funding and Fixed Recoverable Costs



## 9.1 Introduction

The information that solicitors must give to clients about costs and methods of funding is now contained in the Solicitor's Code of Conduct 2007 ('the Code'). Rule 2.03 of the Code states that a solicitor should give the client the 'best information possible' about the likely overall cost of a matter, both at the outset and as the matter progresses. This involves discussing with the client the various methods by which he might pay his own solicitor's costs and also whether insurance might be available to pay the other party's costs in the event that the client loses.

As with all litigation, the successful party can expect to have his reasonable costs paid by the other side following a judgment or settlement in his favour. However, the amount of costs that can be recovered from the other side following a successful claim is now limited in some road traffic accident (RTA) claims following the introduction of a fixed recoverable costs scheme in Part 45 of the CPR. Part 45 also limits the level of success fee that can be claimed in RTA and employers' liability (EL) claims which are funded by a conditional fee agreement.

This chapter summarises the methods of funding available and sets out the main provisions of the fixed costs scheme in CPR Part 45 which apply to personal injury claims.

## 9.2 Methods of funding

### 9.2.1 Public funding

Public funding for personal injury and clinical negligence cases is becoming increasingly rare, but Rule 2.03(1)(d)(i) of the Code nevertheless requires solicitors to discuss whether the client may be eligible and should apply for public funding.

On 1 April 2000, the Government implemented ss 1–11 and 19–26 of the Access to Justice Act 1999. These are the key provisions which reformed the public funding of civil cases. The Legal Services Commission (LSC) was established and replaced the Legal Aid Board. It is responsible for the Community Legal Service (CLS), which handles funding in civil matters from that date. Schedule 2 to the Access to Justice Act 1999 generally excludes personal injury claims (other than clinical negligence claims) from CLS funding. The Community Legal Service (Scope) Regulations 2005 (SI 2005/2008), which came into effect on 25 July 2005, provide for the exclusion of all personal injury proceedings except clinical negligence and cases covered by the Lord Chancellor's Directions.

The CLS decides funding issues in accordance with the Funding Code published in October 1999. The Code has two parts: Part 1 defines the 'Levels of Service' which the CLS provides; Part 2 deals with the procedures for obtaining funding.

### 9.2.1.1 Funding in personal injury cases

Unlike clinical negligence cases, personal injury cases are normally outside the scope of CLS funding because they are suitable for conditional fee agreements (CFAs). 'Support funding', which was available in cases with a wider public interest, has been abolished with effect from 25 July 2005, although it can still apply in cases where support funding had already been granted before that date. In addition, The Lord Chancellor's Department has produced draft guidelines on the availability of 'exceptional funding', which is designed for use in specific cases, for example representation at inquests involving deaths in police or prison custody (see **9.2.1.3** below).

### 9.2.1.2 Funding in clinical negligence cases

Applications for Legal Representation for proceedings in clinical negligence cases are subject to the General Funding Code.

The scope of clinical negligence, as defined in the Funding Code, is:

(a) a claim for damages in respect of an alleged breach of duty of care or trespass to the person committed in the course of the provision of clinical or medical services (including dental or nursing services); or

(b) a claim for damages in respect of alleged professional negligence in the conduct of such a claim.

Only firms with a clinical negligence contract are eligible for CLS funding. Firms with a clinical negligence franchise are required to have a supervisor who is either a member of The Law Society's Clinical Negligence Panel or a member of Action Against Medical Accidents (AvMA) (an organisation which provides advice and support to people affected by medical accidents).

**Claims not exceeding £10,000**

If the likely value of the claim is not more than £10,000, Investigative Help may be refused if use of the NHS complaints procedure would be in the best interests of the client rather than pursuing litigation in the first instance. Although the LSC accepts that the NHS complaints procedure was never designed to replace recourse to the court system, nevertheless it wishes it to be recognised that in small value claims (between £5,000 and £10,000) it is much more cost-effective (of public funds) for the claimant to seek redress in the form of explanation and apology rather than compensation through the civil court system. In claims where the likely level of damages will not exceed £5,000, the Funding Code recommends that Investigative Help should be refused on the ground that the potential cost greatly outweighs the benefit to be achieved. However, there is a caveat that the damages cut-off will not apply to claims which have a significant wider public interest or are of overwhelming importance to the client (for example, claims involving the death of an infant).

If the claim is valued at less than £10,000, the solicitor will need to provide specific reasons as to why the complaints procedure is not the appropriate avenue of redress for the client. The Funding Code contains a number of examples of circumstances in which, it says, it would not be appropriate to refuse funding, which are as follows:

(a) the NHS complaints scheme is not available to the client, or clients being told a complaint may not be pursued;

(b) the claim has overwhelming importance to the client, for example, because it relates to infant death;

(c) there are problems with the NHS complaints scheme in the client's region, for example, there are unusually long delays in responding to complaints;

(d) proceedings must be issued as a matter of urgency, for example because of limitation; or

(e) it is clear the relationship between the client and NHS has broken down to such an extent that any prospect of the complaints procedure resolving the complaint is very remote.

**Investigative Help for clinical negligence claims**

Investigative Help will be granted only where the prospects of success on a claim are not clear and substantial work needs to be undertaken before the prospects of success can be determined accurately. Certificates limited to Investigative Help will be subject to a limitation that the certificate covers only the obtaining of medical notes and records, obtaining one medical report per specialism, complying with all steps under the clinical disputes pre-action protocol, considering relevant evidence with counsel or an external solicitor with higher court advocacy rights and experts if necessary, and thereafter obtaining counsel's opinion, up to and including settling proceedings if counsel so advises.

The cost of the above is nevertheless limited to £3,500 (including costs and disbursements but not VAT).

According to para 9.2.1 of the General Funding Code, the potential to obtain a CFA will not be a ground for refusal of Investigative Help in clinical negligence claims.

**Criteria for granting of Full Representation**

The Funding Code makes it clear that an application for Full Representation will be refused either if:

(a) prospects of success are unclear; or

(b) prospects of success are borderline (ie, not better than 50%); or

(c) prospects of success are poor (clearly less than 50%).

The cost–benefit criterion gives the minimum cost–benefit ratios for damages to costs in clinical negligence claims:

(a) 1:1 – for cases with 80% or more prospects of success, ie the likely damages must at least break even with and should exceed the likely cost in cases with very good prospects of success;

(b) 1.5:1 – for 60–80% prospects of success, ie the prospects of success are good, likely damages must exceed likely cost by at least 1.5;

(c) 2:1 – for cases with 50–60% prospects of success, ie the prospects of success are moderate, likely damages must be at least twice the likely costs.

These are the minimum cost–benefit ratios in the General Funding Code.

If the prospect of success and the cost–benefit criteria set out above are satisfied, the solicitor should make an application for Full Representation after the investigative stage. The certificate will then be issued, limited to all steps up to and including exchange of statements and reports and CPR Part 35 questioning of experts, and thereafter obtaining counsel's opinion or the opinion of an external solicitor with higher court advocacy rights.

In the event that the claimant wishes to proceed to full trial, the cost–benefit criteria above are reapplied to the case; if the criteria are satisfied then application can be made once again to amend the scope of the Full Representation certificate to cover the cost of trial.

### 9.2.1.3 'Exceptional funding'

Under s 6(8)(b) of the Access to Justice Act 1999, the Lord Chancellor has power to provide funding in cases which would normally be outside the scope of the scheme.

The exceptional funding provisions can be used to obtain funding for representation at an inquest. The Lord Chancellor's Guidance on Exceptional Funding states that in general cases, there will be a need to show either 'significant wider public interest', or 'overwhelming importance to the client'. Significant wider public interest is confined to cases where representation is likely to benefit the public by facilitating a real prospect of a change in the law or recommendations that will improve public safety. The 'overwhelming importance to the client' test will usually be a very difficult test to satisfy, and is reserved for cases such as deaths in custody and infant deaths. The test has been revised in relation to applications for representation at inquests, so that consideration is now given to whether funded representation will assist the coroner to investigate the case effectively and establish the facts.

Before requesting such funding, the LSC must be satisfied that the client is financially eligible for Legal Representation according to eligibility limits and that no alternative source of funding is available. The most likely level of funding to be granted is in the form of a one-off grant to cover only the advocacy and representation at the hearing itself, as the preparation work in advance of the inquest is already covered by Legal Help. The Guidance suggests that applications for exceptional funding should address the issues set out in the Lord Chancellor's Guidance. Applications should include a breakdown of the funding required, setting out hours claimed and rates charged. As funding is by way of a one-off grant, the Lord Chancellor may approve funding retrospectively if necessary.

### 9.2.2 Conditional fee agreements

The decline in public funding has led to a huge increase in CFAs. Under s 58 of the Courts and Legal Services Act 1990, a solicitor and client can agree that the client will have to pay his own solicitor's costs only in certain agreed circumstances or conditions, the condition usually being that the client wins his case (hence '*conditional* fee agreement').

On 1 November 2005, the Conditional Fee Agreements Regulations 2000 (as amended) and the Collective Conditional Fee Agreements Regulations 2000 (as amended) were repealed by the Conditional Fee Agreements (Revocation) Regulations 2005 (SI 2005/2305). The old 2000 Regulations continue to apply to CFAs entered into before 1 November 2005 but are not discussed here.

#### 9.2.2.1 Conditional fee agreements signed on or after 1 November 2005

A CFA is enforceable only if it meets the requirements of ss 58 and 58A of the Courts and Legal Services Act 1990, which provide that a CFA:

(a) must be in writing;
(b) must state the percentage success fee to be applied, which cannot exceed 100% of the solicitor's normal charges;
(c) may not be used in family and criminal proceedings.

When advising the client about costs in accordance with Rule 2.03 of the Code, Rule 2.03(2) states that in respect of a CFA the solicitor must explain the circumstances in which the client may be liable for his own costs (and when the solicitor would seek payment) and the client's right to an assessment of those costs.

The CFA must be in writing and be signed by the client and by the legal representative.

The Law Society's Conditional Fees Committee has prepared a model agreement for use in personal injury cases post-31 October 2005.

The Law Society's guide to CFAs recommends that the solicitor should read through the agreement with the client, emphasise its binding nature and check that the client understands the agreement fully. To this end, it is good practice for the solicitor to send The Law Society's leaflet, *Conditional Fees Explained*, to the client prior to the meeting. The leaflet includes a checklist of 'questions to ask your solicitor', and it is therefore essential for the solicitor to be prepared to answer these questions and to be able to explain those answers to the client.

#### 9.2.2.2 The success fee

If the claim is successful, the solicitor will normally expect to receive an enhanced fee to reflect his 'success'. The enhancement on the fee is a percentage increase of the solicitor's normal fee and not a percentage of damages. The percentage increase on the solicitor's fee is agreed in writing between the client and the solicitor prior to the litigation, and will take into account a number of factors discussed below (see **9.2.2.3**), including the likelihood of winning the case.

By way of example, consider *Burton v Kingsley* [2005] EWHC 1034 (QB). The claimants had sustained serious injuries and liability was uncertain. The claimants entered into a CFA with their solicitors with a success fee of 100%. The claimants argued that they were entitled to recover the 100% uplift. The defendants submitted that 10% to 20% was the appropriate figure. The court found that it had been reasonable for the claimants' solicitors to enter into the CFA. The court concluded that the solicitors' risk assessment was a fair reflection of the position in relation to the risk being undertaken by the claimants' solicitors *based on what they knew at that time*. It had been reasonable to recognise that there were uncertainties and difficulties with the case that gave rise to a significant element of risk. The instant case did not fall within the category of modest and straightforward claims. However, the 100% success fee specified by the claimants' solicitors was too high. The chances of success were higher than evens. The degree of risk was such that a reasonable figure would have been between 33% and 50%. Accordingly, a success fee of 50% under the CFA was allowed.

In *C v W* [2008] EWCA Civ 1459, the Court of Appeal reduced a 98% success fee to 20% on the basis that at the time the agreement was entered into the defendant had admitted liability and there was no indication of anything other than the defendant's negligence causing the accident.

#### 9.2.2.3 Risk assessment and CFAs

In order to decide:

(a) whether to take a potential claim on *at all* on a CFA basis; and

(b) once the decision has been made to accept the client's case on a CFA basis, what is the appropriate level of success fee to apply to the agreement,

it will be necessary for the claimant's solicitor to undertake assessment of the risk of the potential claim in every case.

The method of risk assessment adopted will differ from one firm to another, with some adopting paper-based systems while others utilise computer software to capture basic information and assist in speeding up the risk assessment process. Whichever method is used, the underlying principles are the same.

**Principles of risk assessment**

The *Oxford English Dictionary* defines 'risk' as: 'the chance or possibility of loss or bad consequence. If a solicitors' firm accepts a case on a 'no win no fee' basis, it exposes itself to the risk of loss in not getting paid for the work it has done on behalf of the client. However, this is only half of the equation. There is equally the chance of a successful outcome. So risk assessment can be seen as the process of balancing the risk of losing against the chance of winning. That is easy enough to say, but rather more difficult to quantify objectively in a way that gives predictable and workable results. Nevertheless, this is exactly what a personal injury practitioner has to do when deciding whether or not to take a case on a CFA basis.

**Practice of risk assessment**

In practice the skill of the personal injury practitioner will be in his ability to spot the factors relevant to risk and then go on to assess the severity of that risk. The majority of firms make use of a checklist for this purpose, which may be paper- or electronically based.

The factors relevant to risk (or hazards) will include anything that could harm the claim. The risk will be the percentage chance that the factor will actually occur.

Common risk factors will include:

(a) *The facts*: is the client a credible witness and are there any other witnesses who will confirm his version?

(b) *Liability*: will the client be able to show that there was a relevant duty of care and that this duty has been breached?

(c) *Causation*: will the client be able to show that the injuries sustained are causally linked to the accident?

(d) *Limitation*: are there any issues due to limitation of claims or delay (ie 'stale' evidence)?

(e) *The potential defendant*: is the opponent a 'viable' source of damages – does he carry insurance or have funds to meet a damages claim, and have insurance details been confirmed?

(f) *Loss and damage*: can the losses sustained be proved by way of medical and other forms of evidence?

The second stage in the risk assessment is to assess the chance of each of the above risk factors actually occurring and harming the viability of the case. To do this, each factor needs to be categorised or 'scored' in some way. This can be done either by giving each factor a percentage, or a score between 1 and 10, or more simply still, by assessing it as a high, medium or low risk.

Based on the result (or score) from the above assessment, a risk assessment co-ordinator (usually a partner in the firm) will judge whether to accept the case on a conditional fee basis and, if so, on what level of success fee. In the event that he is unable to do so, because of insufficient information being available, he will pass the file back to the case worker for further investigation, for example obtaining witness statements or contacting the police for clarification of key issues.

In the event that the claim is accepted on a CFA basis, it is essential to record the reasoning behind the decision and the reason for the success fee claimed, as this will be needed in the event that the claim is successful and costs are assessed at the close of the case.

### 9.2.2.4 Recovery of the success fee

If the client wins his case and the opponent is ordered to pay his costs, these may include the success fee to the extent that it is 'reasonable'.

According to CPR, r 44.3B:

(a) recovery of the success fee will not include recovery of any proportion of the success fee which relates to the cost to the solicitor of funding the case (ie, the costs to the firm of having payment of costs delayed);

(b) recovery of the success fee will not include recovery of any part of the success fee for any period during which that party was in breach of a rule, Practice Direction or court order concerning provision of information on funding arrangements (as to which see below);

(c) if the solicitor is required by the court or PD Costs supplementing CPR Parts 43 to 48 to disclose the reasons for setting a particular level of success fee and fails to do so, he may not recover the success fee.

Where part (or all) of the success fee is disallowed, the solicitor is not allowed to recover the remainder from his client unless the court orders otherwise.

### 9.2.2.5 After the event insurance

If a CFA client loses a case, he will not have to pay his own solicitor's costs but he may be liable to pay the other side's costs. The client's potential liability to pay the other side's costs and disbursements and his own disbursements can be insured against by what is often referred to as 'after the event' insurance (AEI). As the name suggests, AEI is taken out only once the need for the legal action has become apparent but before the proceedings have commenced. Here, the insurance is not against the risk of litigation but merely against the risk of having to pay the other side's costs and disbursements should the litigation fail, and can cover the cost of the party's own disbursements as well. This type of insurance can be obtained alongside a CFA, or on its own as insurance against liability for the other side's costs. If necessary, many AEI insurers will arrange a loan to the client to fund both the disbursements and the cost of the AEI premium. If he wins, the interest on the loan is not recoverable from his opponent but is usually deducted from the damages recovered.

As with success fees, the AEI premium for insuring against liability to pay the other side's costs and disbursements is recoverable from the loser provided it is reasonable.

**Staged AEI premiums**

Many AEI providers see staged premiums as the likely saviour of AEI insurance. The way this works is as follows: with traditional AEI insurance, the underwriter considers the level of risk of the claimant losing and sets a premium accordingly. In so doing he bears in mind that the majority of claims are settled either pre- or post-issue, but long before trial. Another big tranche of claims will fight on at least until directions are complied with (so that each side has had the benefit of full disclosure from the opposition) and will then settle before being set down for trial. Only a small number of claims will go on to trial. By staging premiums at these trigger points (pre-issue, on setting down for trial, commencement of trial) the insurer can set a lower premium earlier on (accurately reflecting the risk) and an appropriately larger premium only for those cases that do not settle at an early stage. Clearly, a claim which does not settle until trial has a much greater prospect of going to trial, and is therefore much more likely actually to fail on liability and land the insurer with a big bill for the other side's costs. Hence the nearer the claim is to trial, the higher the AEI premium should be.

In *Rogers v Merthyr Tydfil CBC* [2006] EWCA Civ 1134, the Court of Appeal considered whether a party who had an AEI policy with staged premiums should have warned its opponent of that fact and should have stated clearly at what stage the further payments were 'triggered'.

Mr Rogers had been provided with AEI cover by an insurance company in relation to a claim for damages against the local authority who had been found liable. Mr Roger's solicitor had chosen a policy with a three-stage premium as being the most appropriate for his client's needs. The local authority had objected to the high cost of the third-stage premium of £4,860 plus insurance premium tax, when compared to the agreed damages of £3,000. The judge had reduced the AEI premium payable to £900.

The Court of Appeal found that the fact that damages had been agreed at only £3,000 did not directly touch on the issue of whether the costs claimed were proportionate. Should the court conclude that it was necessary to incur the staged premium, it should be adjudged a proportionate expense. There was in principle no difference between a two-stage success fee, consistently endorsed by the courts, and a staged AEI premium. The financial risk to which an AEI provider was exposed inevitably rose as a case proceeded towards trial. While defendants could be liable to pay a higher premium if they took a case to trial and lost, the situation was no different from that facing them in relation to their liability to pay a higher success fee when claims were resolved against them 14 days before the trial date in cases covered by the arrangements for fixed recoverable success fees in Part 45 of the CPR (see **9.4.3**).

The Court went on to give some guidance as to advance notice to defendants of staged AEI premiums. In the future, a party who had an AEI policy with staged premiums should inform its opponent of that and should set out the triggers when the second or later stages would be reached. If issues arose about the size of a second or third stage premium, it would ordinarily suffice for a claimant's solicitor to write a brief note for the purposes of the costs assessment, explaining how he came to choose the particular AEI product for his client and whether the premium was block rated.

#### 9.2.2.6 Notifying the other side of a CFA or AEI cover

If the client enters in to a CFA or takes out AEI insurance before proceedings are issued, para 4 A of the Practice Direction on Pre- Action Protocols provides that he should inform the other potential parties that he has done so. This is likely to be done in the letter of claim.

Once proceedings are issued, Notice of Funding (Form N251) must be served with the claim form (or, if acting for a defendant, with the acknowledgement of service). Under CPR, r 44.3B, a party may not recover the success fee and/or AEI premium for any period in proceedings during which he failed to provide the required information.

There is no requirement to reveal the percentage increase specified as the success fee, or the amount of any AEI premium. All that is required is:

(a) the date on which the CFA was entered into;

(b) the date of any relevant insurance policy, the name and address of the insurer, and the policy number;

(c) where there is a staged AEI premium, the trigger points for the various stages (see *Rogers v Merthyr Tydfil CBC* at **9.2.2.5** above).

An example of a completed Form N251 appears at **Appendix 1.**

#### 9.2.2.7 Conditional fees and counsel

The Law Society model agreement at condition 6 specifies two ways of dealing with counsel's fees:

(a) The solicitor enters into a separate CFA with the barrister, in which case:
   (i) if the client wins the case, the barrister's basic fee will be recovered as a disbursement from the opponent. The solicitor will pay the barrister's 'uplift' agreed in the barrister's CFA, but will have regard to this expense when agreeing his own fee 'uplift' with the client;
   (ii) if the client loses the case, he will owe the barrister nothing.

(b) There is no CFA between the barrister and the solicitor, in which case:
   (i) if the client wins the case and has been paying the barrister's fees on account (ie, up front), there will be no extra success fee to pay, and the barrister's fees can be recovered from the opponent as before;
   (ii) if the client wins the case and has not been paying the barrister's fees on account, the solicitor will recover that disbursement from the opponent. Because of this greater outlay by the solicitor (and greater financial loss to the firm in the event that the client loses), the solicitor will charge an extra success fee in the event that the client wins;
   (iii) if the client loses the case and has not been paying the barrister's fees on account, the solicitor is liable to pay them, and will not be able to pass this loss on to the client.

### 9.2.3 Legal expenses insurance

The client may have legal expenses insurance (known as 'before the event' or 'BTE' insurance) as a part of either his home or motor insurance policy, or as an extra service from his credit card provider, or as an extra for which he has paid an additional premium. This is something that the client may either be unaware of or have forgotten, and it is therefore important that this is considered at the first interview.

Where the client has the benefit of a BTE insurance policy, the presumption is that he will use it rather than take out additional insurance in the form of an AEI policy. There is no need to enter in to a CFA because BTE insurance generally covers both sides' costs. However, the level and type of cover available under the BTE policy should be checked to make sure it is suitable. Many BTE policies have a limit of indemnity of £25,000, which may not be sufficient to cover the larger multi-track cases. If the cover is insufficient then it may well be reasonable to enter into a CFA and to take out AEI instead.

In *Sarwar v Alam* [2001] EWCA Civ 1401, [2001] 4 All ER 541, the claimant had taken out an AEI policy when there was the opportunity to benefit from an existing legal expense insurance policy or BTE insurance. In the costs-only proceedings, the issue was whether the AEI premium was recoverable. The Court of Appeal gave guidance that although a solicitor is not obliged to embark on a 'treasure hunt' in relation to pre-existing insurance, a solicitor should develop a practice of sending a standard letter requesting sight of:

(a) any relevant motor insurance policy;

(b) any household insurance policy;

(c) any stand-alone BTE insurance policy belonging to the client and/or any spouse or partner living in the same household, and, if possible, their driver (if they are an injured passenger), in advance of the first interview.

A decision then needs to be made about whether any legal expenses insurance policy is satisfactory. The Court emphasised that the decision related to small road traffic accident claims with a quantum of £5,000 or less and that enquiries should be proportionate. (See also *Kilby v Gawith* [2008] WLR (D) 163, below at **9.3.4**.)

As with union-funded work (see **9.2.5** below), the insurer may have nominated firms of solicitors who must be instructed to undertake the insured's claim. If the insured is free to instruct the solicitor of his choice, it is usual for the insurer to require the solicitor to report to it regularly on the progress of the case. In terms of confidentiality, it is essential for the solicitor to explain to the client at the outset that a term of the insurance is that the insurer has the right to receive reports on the viability of the case and whether or not it is worthwhile to continue with it. The progress of the case can be slowed down considerably by the obligation on the solicitor to report back to the insurer to seek approval (and therefore funding) to continue with the claim to the next stage.

### 9.2.4 Choice of solicitor under legal expense insurance policies

The Insurance Companies (Legal Expenses Insurance) Regulations 1990 (SI 1990/1159) give effect to European Directive 87/344. The Regulations cover, amongst other things, BTE insurance cover in respect of road traffic accidents. Regulation 6 of the 1990 Regulations specifies:

> **6. Freedom to choose a lawyer**
>
> (1) Where under a legal expenses insurance contract recourse is had to a lawyer … to defend, represent or serve the interests of the insured in any *enquiry or proceedings*, the insured shall be free to choose that lawyer (or other person). (emphasis added)

The interpretation given to the term 'enquiry or proceedings' will determine whether or not the insured person does have freedom to choose his lawyer. Some insurance companies providing legal expenses insurance (LEI) cover put a narrow interpretation on it, saying that only when there are actual court proceedings is there any freedom for the policy holder to choose. The insurer will often prefer to refer the insured's claim to its panel of solicitors only, effectively concentrating the bulk of claims to so-called 'panel firms'. Not all LEI providers operate panels of preferred solicitors but many do, citing quality assurance and consistency of claims handling as the rationale for insisting on operating panels to which to channel claims. Non-panel firms see this as damaging to their position, as they may be forced to advise clients that they should avail themselves of pre-existing LEI cover rather than take up the non-panel solicitors' offer to work on the basis of a CFA. The non-panel solicitors will often take the view that the wording of reg 6(1) of the 1990 Regulations should be given a wide interpretation, and 'enquiry or proceedings' will encompass the work undertaken at pre-issue stage under the pre-action protocol. Their justification for this is due to the 'front loading' of litigation, where much of the work and advice is, of necessity, conducted before the issue of proceedings.

A case which illustrates many of the points outlined above is *Chappell v De Bora's of Exeter* (SCCO, 2004). This is a Supreme Court Costs Office case in which the costs claim of a non-panel local firm of solicitors was allowed despite the existence of pre-existing LEI. The facts briefly are as follows. The claimant's claim was in respect of the personal injuries she suffered when she fell down some steps at the defendant's shop in Exeter. The claimant, who lived near Exeter, instructed solicitors in Exeter. They entered into a CFA with a success fee of 71%. They also arranged a policy of AEI and corresponded with DAS, the legal expenses insurers with whom the claimant had an existing BTE insurance policy. DAS said that, under the terms of her policy with them, the claimant was obliged to instruct solicitors who were on their panel for any work which had to be done before the issue of proceedings, although she was entitled to instruct the solicitors of her choice for the purpose of the proceedings themselves should proceedings be necessary. The claimant's solicitors (who were not on the DAS panel) undertook the usual pre-proceedings work, including sending the letter of claim, taking witness evidence and obtaining two medical reports. The defendant's solicitors eventually offered to settle the matter for £31,156 plus costs. This offer was accepted, but the issue of costs could not be agreed and, following detailed assessment, the defendant was given permission to appeal on the issue of whether it was reasonable for the claimant to enter into a CFA with a success fee and AEI with the solicitors of her choice, when BTE insurance was available but the claimant's chosen solicitors were not on the BTE insurers' panel.

The defendant's counsel submitted that the onus was on the claimant to show why it was reasonable, on the standard basis, that the more expensive route of proceedings under a CFA with AEI should have been adopted. He submitted that solicitors on the DAS panel up and down the country conducted very many cases no less serious and complex than the present case on a regular basis. He accepted what the Master of the Rolls had said in *Sarwar v Alam* (see **9.2.3 above**):

> In this case we are concerned only with a relatively small personal injury claim in a road traffic accident. We are not concerned with claims which look as if they will exceed about £5,000, and we are not concerned with any other type of BTE claim. We have no doubt that, if a claimant possesses pre-existing BTE cover which appears to be satisfactory for a claim of that size, then in the ordinary course of things that claimant should be referred to the relevant BTE insurers.

The claimant's counsel submitted that this was not a straightforward case and that the amount of the damages, in excess of £31,000, reflected those complexities. It had been reasonable for the claimant to go to solicitors in Exeter to handle her case rather than to solicitors in Bristol or Salisbury. He submitted that the costs which the district judge had allowed were proportionate in relation to a multi-track case of this nature. The judge concluded that it was reasonable in a case of this kind for the claimant to instruct the solicitors of her choice in Exeter rather than DAS panel solicitors, the nearest of whom would have been many miles away from where she lived. Accordingly, he dismissed the appeal in so far as it related to the claimant's choice of solicitor.

### 9.2.5 Trade unions

If the client has had an accident at work and belongs to a trade union, he may be entitled to receive free access to legal advice as part of his membership. This is something of which the client may not be aware initially, and the solicitor should therefore cover this point at the first interview.

If the client is entitled to advice through his union, the union may have its own legal department or nominated solicitors whom it always uses. If this is the case, the solicitor first consulted by the client is unlikely to be instructed, but should nevertheless advise the client to seek advice from his union on this point. The advantage to the client, if he is able to procure the support of union funding, is that, provided he has paid his membership fees to the union, he will have the full financial support of the union behind him. His solicitor will still have to convince the union as to the merits of the case, and will also be obliged to report on the case prior to proceeding with it. However, the claimant will not have to worry that part of his damages may be taken away to pay his legal expenses, as would be the case if he was funded either through public funding or via a CFA.

### 9.2.6 Private fee-paying clients

Some clients will have no alternative but to fund their cases privately, or may choose to do so in any event. In such circumstances the solicitor is obliged, under the Written Professional Standards, to explain to the client fully his liability for costs and disbursements. The solicitor should give the best information on costs that he can, including likely disbursements and the hourly rate that the solicitor proposes to charge (as to which see ***Legal Foundations***, Part II, Professional Conduct).

## 9.3 Recovery of costs – the fixed costs regime

### 9.3.1 Fixed costs for straightforward road traffic accident claims valued at less than £10,000

The CPR, r 45 provides for fixed (or 'predictable') costs to be recovered in respect of disputes which are settled prior to proceedings being issued in respect of road traffic accidents. The scheme applies to disputes where the total agreed value of damages exceeds £1,000 but does not exceed £10,000.

### 9.3.2 Calculation of fixed recoverable costs and disbursements

#### 9.3.2.1 Fixed costs

Part 45 includes detailed tables setting out how fixed costs are calculated and the level of success fee allowed, and specifies the only disbursements that will be allowed.

According to r 45.8, the only costs which are to be allowed are:

(a) fixed recoverable costs calculated in accordance with r 45.9;

(b) disbursements allowed in accordance with r 45.10; and

(c) a success fee allowed in accordance with r 45.11.

**Rule 45.9 – amount of fixed recoverable costs**

> (1) Subject to paragraphs (2) and (3), the amount of fixed recoverable costs is the total of—
>
> (a) £800;
>
> (b) 20% of the damages agreed up to £5,000; and
>
> (c) 15% of the damages agreed between £5,000 and £10,000.

For example, if agreed damages are £7,523, this would result in recoverable costs of £2,178.45, ie £800 + (20% of £5,000) + (15% of £2,523) = 2,178.45.

(2) Where the claimant—
  (a) lives or works in an area set out in the relevant practice direction; and
  (b) instructs a solicitor or firm of solicitors who practice in that area,
  the fixed recoverable costs shall include, in addition to the costs specified in paragraph (1), an amount equal to 12.5% of the costs allowable under that paragraph.

(3) Where appropriate, value added tax (VAT) may be recovered in addition to the amount of fixed recoverable costs and any reference in this Section to fixed recoverable costs is a reference to those costs net of any such VAT.

#### 9.3.2.2 Disbursements

Under r 45.10(2), the only allowable disbursements are:

(a) the cost of obtaining—
  (i) medical records,
  (ii) a medical report,
  (iii) a police report,
  (iv) an engineer's report, or
  (v) a search of the records of the Driver Vehicle Licensing Authority;

(b) the amount of an insurance premium; or, where a membership organisation undertakes to meet liabilities incurred to pay the costs of other parties to proceedings, a sum not exceeding such additional amount of costs as would be allowed under Section 30 in respect of provision made against the risk of having to meet such liabilities;

(c) where they are necessarily incurred by reason of one or more of the claimants being a child or patient as defined in Part 21—
  (i) fees payable for instructing counsel, or
  (ii) court fees payable on an application to the court;

(d) any other disbursement that has arisen due to a particular feature of the dispute.

### 9.3.3 Fixed success fees

In addition to the provisions relating to fixed costs in low value RTA cases, CPR Part 45 provides for fixed success fees in RTA and EL claims:

#### 9.3.3.1 Fixed percentage increase in road traffic accident claims

According to r 43.2(1)(l), 'percentage increase' means the percentage by which the amount of a legal representative's fee can be increased in accordance with a CFA which provides for a success fee.

**Percentage increase of solicitors' fees (r 45.16)**

The percentage increase which is to be allowed in relation to solicitors' fees in RTA claims is:

(a) 100% where the claim concludes at trial; or

(b) 12.5% where—
  (i) the claim concludes before a trial has commenced; or
  (ii) the dispute is settled before a claim is issued.

In *Lamont v Burton* [2007] EWCA Civ 429, the issue that arose on appeal was whether the 100% increase in r 45.16(a) is mandatory in all cases, or whether, as the defendant submitted, there is a discretion to vary it in cases where a Part 36 offer has been made but not accepted, and the claimant has failed to beat the Part 36 offer. The defendant argued that the claimant should only receive the uplift that would have been applicable at the latest point that the Part 36 offer could have been accepted. However, the Court rejected that argument and held that the claimant was entitled to a 100% success fee on his costs even though, had he accepted the offer when it was made, he would have received a success fee of only 12.5%.

**Percentage increase of counsel's fees (r 45.17)**

The percentage increase which is to be allowed in relation to counsel's fees is also fixed:

(a) 100% where the claim concludes at trial;

(b) if the claim has been allocated to the fast track—

  (i) 50% if the claim concludes 14 days or less before the date fixed for the commencement of the trial; or

  (ii) 12.5% if the claim concludes more than 14 days before the date fixed for the commencement of the trial or before any such date has been fixed;

(c) if the claim has been allocated to the multi-track—

  (i) 75% if the claim concludes 21 days or less before the date fixed for the commencement of the trial; or

  (ii) 12.5% if the claim concludes more than 21 days before the date fixed for the commencement of the trial or before any such date has been fixed;

(d) 12.5% where—

  (i) the claim has been issued but concludes before it has been allocated to a track; or

  (ii) in relation to costs-only proceedings, the dispute is settled before a claim is issued.

**Application for an alternative percentage increase where the fixed increase is 12.5% (r 45.18)**

A party may apply for a percentage increase greater or less than the fixed amount if the parties agree damages of an amount greater than £500,000, or the court awards damages of an amount greater than £500,000 disregarding contributory negligence. However, under r 45.19 there are costs penalties for a claimant who makes such an application and is awarded a success fee of 20% or less, and for a defendant applicant who fails to get the claimant's success fee reduced to less than 7.5%.

### 9.3.3.2 Fixed success fees in employers' liability claims

Part 45 of the CPR also provides for fixed success fees in EL claims. The regime is basically the same as in RTA claims (a two-stage success fee for solicitors, a three-stage success fee for counsel, and an opportunity to seek a lower or higher success fee in claims worth £500,000). However, fixed success fees are set at a higher level than those for RTA claims.

**Non-disease EL claims (r 45.21)**

The percentage increase which is to be allowed in relation to solicitors' fees in non-disease EL claims is:

(a) 100% where the claim concludes at trial; or

(b) 25% where—

  (i) the claim concludes before a trial has commenced; or

  (ii) the dispute is settled before a claim is issued

**Disease EL claims (r 45.23)**

In order to fall within the scope of r 45.23, the dispute must be between an employee (or his estate, if deceased) and his employer relating to a disease with which the employee is diagnosed. If it is alleged to have been contracted as a consequence of the employer's alleged breach of statutory or common law duties of care in the course of the employee's employment, and the claimant has entered into a funding arrangement such as a CFA or CFFA which provides for a success fee, then r 45.23 will apply.

In order to give some guidance as to the types of disease claim falling within this Part, the rule and its Practice Direction set out the types of claim covered (designated Type A, B or C, with a (non-exhaustive) list of each case type in the Practice Direction):

(a) 'Type A claim' means a claim relating to a disease or physical injury alleged to have been caused by exposure to asbestos;

(b) 'Type B claim' means a claim relating to—

  (i) a psychiatric injury alleged to have been caused by work-related psychological stress,

  (ii) a work-related upper limb disorder which is alleged to have been caused by physical stress or strain, excluding hand/arm vibration injuries; and

(c) 'Type C claim' means a claim relating to a disease not falling within either Type A or Type B.

The table reproduced below is taken from section 25B of the Practice Direction supplementing Part 45 and contains a non-exclusive list of diseases within Type A and Type B.

**Table 9.1 Diseases in Type A and Type B claims**

| ***Claim type*** | ***Description*** |
|---|---|
| A | Asbestosis |
| | Mesothelioma |
| | Bilateral Pleural Thickening |
| | Pleural Plaques |
| B | Repetitive Strain Injury/WRULD |
| | Carpal Tunnel Syndrome caused by Repetitive Strain Injury |
| | Occupational Stress |

**Percentage increase of solicitors' fees in EL disease claims**

The percentage increase which is to be allowed in relation to solicitors' fees is:

(a) if the claim concludes at trial – 100%;

(b) if the claim concludes before a trial has commenced, or the dispute is settled before a claim is issued—

  (i) Type A claims—

    (1) 30% if a membership organisation has undertaken to meet the claimant's liabilities for legal costs in accordance with s 30 of the Access to Justice Act 1999; and

    (2) 27.5% in any other case;

  (ii) Type B claims, 100%; and

  (iii) Type C claims—

    (1) 70% if a membership organisation has undertaken to meet the claimant's liabilities for legal costs in accordance with s 30 of the Access to Justice Act 1999; and

    (2) 62.5% in any other case.

### 9.3.4 The effect of the fixed costs regime and the indemnity principle

In *Butt v Nizami* [2006] EWHC 159 (QB), the court revisited the question of pre-existing BTE insurance, only this time the court took into account the fact that such road traffic claims are now governed by the predictive costs regime in any event. Like *Sarwar*, the challenge to costs recovery centred around the allegation that, before the signing of the CFAs, the claimants' solicitors failed to make appropriate enquiries about the availability of BTE insurance.

The claimants were the driver and passenger respectively of a car which had stopped at traffic lights. The car was struck from behind, and as a result both the claimants suffered whiplash injuries. The claimants entered into CFAs with their solicitors. The claims were settled before proceedings were begun, but costs could not be agreed. The defendant's insurers asserted that the CFAs did not comply with the Conditional Fee Agreements Regulations 2000; specifically that, before the signing of the CFAs, the claimants' solicitors failed to make appropriate enquiries about the availability of BTE insurance, the existence of which might invalidate the CFAs.

The defendant's insurers asserted that the indemnity principle precluded recovery in this type of claim, due to the fact that an unsuccessful party cannot be held liable to pay more to a successful party than the successful party is himself legally liable to pay. It was for this reason that (in June 2003) the law was changed so that 'costs to be paid to such representatives is not limited to what would have been payable by him to them if he had not been awarded costs' (Supreme Court Act 1981, s 51(2)). The amendment conferred the power to make rules of court which provided for the inter-party recovery of costs which would otherwise be precluded by the indemnity principle.

The defendant argued that the indemnity principle required that the costs claimed should be costs properly payable by the claimants to their solicitors, and that this presupposed valid and enforceable CFAs.

At first instance, Senior Costs Judge O'Hare ruled that entitlement to the fixed recoverable costs under r 45.9 of the CPR 1998 and the success fee under r 45.11 did not depend on the existence of a valid and enforceable CFA, but disbursements were still subject to assessment:

> The purpose of the Rules was to simplify the payment of costs in small cases, not to make it more complex. The fixed recoverable costs are just that; they are fixed. But they are payable by the defendant whether or not the claimant's solicitor's retainer is valid. An extra 12.5% is payable if the claimant and his solicitor entered into a CFA, whether that CFA is valid or not.

On appeal, Simon J was equally scathing of the approach taken by the defendant's insurers, sending a clear message that the courts have no appetite for such 'satellite litigation' and pointing out that such challenges had been shown to have a 'significantly detrimental effect on the efficient conduct of personal injury litigation and were inconsistent with the overriding objective of enabling the court to deal with cases justly'.

More recently, In *Kilby v Gawith* [2008] WLR (D) 163, the defendant disputed the claimant's entitlement to the success fee on the ground that she already had BTE insurance which would have enabled her solicitors to have conducted the claim without risk, that it was therefore unreasonable for her to have entered into a CFA with her solicitors which provided for a success fee, and that the court should therefore exercise its discretion under CPR, r 45.11(1) to disallow the fee. The Court of Appeal dismissed the appeal, holding that the court had no discretion under CPR, r 45.11(1) to disallow a successful claimant a success fee provided for in the CFA with her solicitors.

In light of the findings in this case, in RTA cases up to £10,000 it is clear that the indemnity principle has no application, because the basis for paying costs is the fixed costs regime and not the retainer between client and solicitor.

## 9.4 Conclusion

The removal of public funding from most personal injury claims and the increase in the use of CFAs have in recent years, led to a great deal of 'satellite litigation' in the courts, with numerous challenges being made to the enforceability of CFAs and the recoverability of AEI premiums. However, the revocation of the CFA Regulations 2000 and the introduction of fixed costs and success fees seem to have had the desired effect of reducing such technical challenges, and things appear to have settled down.

Costs in personal injury cases continue to be under scrutiny, and following Lord Justice Jackson's preliminary report on the review of costs in civil litigation, which was published in

May 2009, it is clear that changes are on the way. Lord Justice Jackson's final report following consultation is expected to be published in December 2009.

For the time being, although the majority of personal injury or clinical negligence claims are likely to be funded by way of a CFA (with AEI to provide protection in the event that a client loses), solicitors must ensure that they consider *all* available methods of funding with the client in order to comply with Rule 2.03 of the Code of Conduct. Whilst a failure to do so may not result in the CFA being unenforceable (unlike under the old 2000 CFA Regulations), it could result in a reduction in the amount of costs recoverable on assessment on the grounds of reasonableness, and could also result in a complaint and/or disciplinary action by the Solicitors Regulation Authority (SRA).

If a CFA is entered into, the solicitor must ensure that the other side is notified of that fact, together with details of any AEI premium taken out, if he is to be sure of recovering the success fee and premium on assessment.

## 9.5 Further reading

*Cook on Costs* ( Butterworths)

*The Legal Services Commission Manual* (Sweet & Maxwell)

www.lawsociety.org.uk

# Chapter 10
# Investigating the Claim and Preliminary Steps



## 10.1 Introduction

During the first interview, the claimant's solicitor will have taken a proof of evidence from his client, who may have been able to supply additional evidence, such as documents or photographs. In straightforward, low-value personal injury cases, the solicitor may now be in possession of sufficient information to enable him to send a letter of claim to the proposed defendant. However, in many personal injury cases, and in all occupational disease and illness and clinical negligence cases, the claimant's solicitor will need to conduct further investigations before the letter of claim can be sent. In all cases where liability is not accepted by the proposed defendant, full investigations must be made before proceedings are issued.

The defendant may contact his solicitor immediately after the incident which has given rise to the potential claim, but in many cases the defendant's solicitor will become involved only after the letter of claim has been received by the defendant or, particularly where insurers are involved, after proceedings have been issued. In any event, the defendant's solicitor must also make full investigations and, where a claim is to be defended, gather evidence in support of his client's case.

Solicitors acting for both parties should be keen to gather evidence quickly, while events are fresh in the minds of clients and witnesses, and before real and documentary evidence is repaired, misplaced or destroyed. In this chapter, the investigations that should be made will be outlined. This chapter will also deal with the procedural steps that must be taken before proceedings are issued. In this regard, the parties and their solicitors are guided by the relevant pre-action protocols (PAPs).

## 10.2 Pre-action Protocols

Solicitors dealing with personal injury and clinical negligence claims must be familiar with the PAPs relating to these claims and the associated Practice Direction. There are three separate protocols, and it is important to ensure that the correct one is consulted for each individual claim. The protocols are as follows:

(a) PAP for personal injury claims. This is the correct protocol to use for road traffic, tripping and slipping, and employer liability claims (except those resulting in disease or illness) with a value of less than £15,000, and which are therefore likely to be allocated to the fast track. However, in higher-value, multi-track cases, the court will expect the parties to be bound by the spirit of the PAP and to comply with it as far as possible. If one or both parties consider that the PAP is not appropriate to their case, the court will expect an explanation as to why it has not been followed. This PAP is set out in full in **Appendix 2**.

(b) PAP for disease and illness claims. This is the correct protocol to use for all personal injury claims where the injury takes the form of an illness or disease, eg mesothelioma, asthma or dermatitis, which arises through working in or occupying premises or using products. These claims are likely to be complex and therefore unsuitable for fast track procedures, even where the value is less than £15,000. This PAP is set out in full in **Appendix 3**. In April 2009, a Practice Direction was introduced, dealing with mesothelioma claims. The contents of the Practice Direction are beyond the scope of this book.

(c) PAP for the resolution of clinical disputes. This is the correct protocol to use where the claim relates to injuries resulting from healthcare and medical treatment. The PAP recognises that it is in the interests of everyone involved – patients, healthcare professionals and providers – that patients' concerns, complaints and claims are dealt with quickly, efficiently and professionally, and that the patient/clinician relationship is preserved if at all possible, not least because the patient may need further treatment. This PAP is set out in full in **Appendix 4**.

In addition to these protocols, there is a new Practice Direction on pre-action conduct ('PD Pre-action Conduct') which replaces the Practice Direction for pre-action protocols. This Practice Direction describes the conduct the court will normally expect of the prospective parties prior to the start of the proceedings.

Paragraph 4 sets out the court's expectation that the parties and those representing them will comply with this Practice Direction and any relevant PAP, and its requirement for a party to provide an explanation where there has been non-compliance. When considering non-compliance, the court will take into account whether the shortcomings are substantial or merely minor or technical, the proportionality of the steps compared to the size and importance of the matter, the urgency of the matter and the overall effect on the other party. In accordance with para 4.6, where there has been non-compliance, the court may impose any of the following sanctions:

(a) staying (that is suspending) the proceedings until steps which ought to have been taken have been taken;

(b) an order that the party at fault pays the costs, or part of the costs, of the other party or parties;

(c) an order that the party at fault pays those costs on an indemnity basis;

(d) if the party at fault is the claimant in whose favour an order for the payment of a sum of money is subsequently made, an order that the claimant is deprived of interest on all or part of that sum, and/or that interest is awarded at a lower rate than would otherwise have been awarded;

(e) if the party at fault is a defendant, and an order for the payment of a sum of money is subsequently made in favour of the claimant, an order that the defendant pay interest on all or part of that sum at a higher rate, not exceeding 10% above base rate, than would otherwise have been awarded.

The PAPs deal with such matters as the letter of claim and the defendant's response, but before the claimant's solicitor can think about writing the letter of claim, he will need to investigate the matter further and ensure that he has identified the correct defendant.

## 10.3 Identifying the defendant

In many cases, the identity of the defendant will be obvious. Nevertheless, this question should always be addressed by the claimant's solicitor, as matters are not always as straightforward as they seem. It is crucial to issue proceedings within the primary limitation period against the correct defendant. Generally, there is little point in pursuing a claim against a defendant unless he is insured, or has the means with which to pay the judgment sum.

### 10.3.1 Road traffic incidents and other highway claims

In a road traffic accident claim, it is necessary to establish not only the name of the driver of the vehicle and his insurance position, but also the name of the owner of the vehicle and of his insurer. Under the Fourth EU Motor Insurance Directive, it is a requirement that the insurer of a vehicle must be readily identifiable from the vehicle registration number. Therefore, when trying to trace the owner and insurer of a vehicle involved in a road traffic accident, if the claimant has taken down the registration of the other driver's vehicle, the solicitor should be able to trace the insurance details. The UK insurance industry has met this requirement by introducing the Motor Insurance Database (MID), which provides details of all vehicles and their associated insurance policies. Individual firms of solicitors can apply for a licence to operate the MID system, allowing them almost instant access to insurance details of third parties, accessed by means of the vehicle registration mark.

#### 10.3.1.1 Driving in the course of employment

Frequently, the driver may be using a vehicle owned and insured by his employer. In such cases, the claim would normally be issued against the employer (or vehicle operator in the case of commercial vehicles). If it is unclear whether or not the driver was acting within the course of employment, it is usual to sue both the driver and the employer. Similarly, if protective proceedings are necessary to avoid the claim being statute-barred under the LA 1980 (see **7.9.2**), and there is insufficient time to investigate the issue of vicarious liability properly, the claim should be issued against both driver and employer.

#### 10.3.1.2 Insured drivers – naming the insurer as defendant

Under reg 3 of the European Communities (Rights against Insurers) Regulations 2002 (SI 2002/3061), where a claimant has an action in tort against an insured person arising out of an accident, he has a direct right of action in the courts against the driver's insurer. This means that he can issue proceedings against the insurer alone, or in addition to the driver. How this is dealt with in practice varies. Some solicitors acting for claimants always issue proceedings directly against insurers where they are able to do so; some never do so. On a practical level, it is unlikely to make any measurable difference to how the proceedings are conducted or to the final outcome. Where a driver is insured, it will be the insurance company and its solicitors who will determine how the proceedings are conducted, and it will be the insurance company who will pay up, should liability be established, whether or not it is named as a defendant. Under the terms of the policy, the driver will be obliged to cooperate with the insurer in defending the matter, including giving evidence at trial if necessary, whether or not he is named as a defendant.

#### 10.3.1.3 Invalid insurance – Road Traffic Act 1988, ss 151 and 152

Sometimes, a situation will arise where a vehicle was covered by a policy of insurance at the time of the accident, but the policy did not cover the driver or the insurer has grounds to void the policy. The claimant should not be dissuaded from commencing proceeding against the driver on the grounds that he may be impecunious, as the insurance company will be obliged to pay out on the judgment to the claimant, provided the correct notice is given (see **3.3** and **12.3.4**).

#### 10.3.1.4 Uninsured drivers

Where the accident is caused by an uninsured driver, the claim should be issued against that individual. The claimant need not worry about whether or not the defendant driver has the financial means to satisfy the judgement as, provided the correct procedures are followed, the

Motor Insurers' Bureau (MIB) will settle the claim in accordance with the Uninsured Drivers Agreement 1999. This scheme is considered in **3.4**. It is not usual to name the MIB as defendant unless a ruling on the construction of the agreement itself is sought. However, in some instances, the MIB will apply to the court to be added as a defendant.

#### 10.3.1.5 Untraced drivers

Where the accident is caused by a 'hit and run' driver who cannot be traced, it will not be possible to commence court proceedings. Instead, an application should be made to the MIB on behalf of the injured party under the Untraced Drivers Agreement 2003. This scheme is considered in **3.4**.

#### 10.3.1.6 Highway authorities, statutory undertakers and other owners of the highway

Where there are indications that the actions or omissions of a highway authority, statutory undertaker or some other owner of the highway have caused or contributed to the claimant's accident, enquiries may be made of the local council in order to identify who that body is. Every council is obliged to keep and allow access to records detailing the ownership of highway land within its area (see **3.5.1**); and it will also have information about any activities of statutory undertakers on highway land, as the council operates a licensing system (see **3.5.2.4**). Whilst highway authorities and statutory undertakers will always have public liability insurance, other owners of the highway may not.

### 10.3.2 Employers' liability claims

If an incident occurs at work, notwithstanding that the incident was caused by another employee or someone acting as agent for the employer, provided that person was acting in the course of employment, it is usual to sue the employer only (see **4.4**). (Although the defendant will generally be the employer, a claim may also be made against the occupier of the premises, or against the person with control of the premises if different from the employer. This lies beyond the scope of this book.) All employers should have appropriate insurance, although a minority of rogue employers may not.

### 10.3.3 Cases involving negligence of doctors and medical staff

#### 10.3.3.1 Claims arising out of NHS hospital treatment

If the claim arises out of treatment in a hospital by an employee of the NHS, the relevant NHS Trust is named as the defendant. It is not appropriate to sue individual doctors or nurses in the direct employment of the Trust.

In order to identify the name and address of the relevant Trust, a search can be made on the NHS website (www.nhs.uk) by typing in the name of the hospital.

The National Health Service Litigation Authority (NHSLA) is responsible for handling all clinical negligence claims against NHS Trusts and their employees, who are indemnified under the Clinical Negligence Scheme for Trusts. The NHSLA has a panel of firms of solicitors to deal with such claims on its behalf (see **5.7**).

#### 10.3.3.2 General practitioners

General practitioners (GPs) are almost always self-employed, and they contract their services to the NHS. A GP is liable for his own acts and for the acts of his employees. General Practitioners often operate in partnerships, and in such cases, the claim may be issued against the individual GP concerned or against the partnership. General Practitioners will carry indemnity insurance from an organisation such as the Medical Defence Union or the Medical Protection Society.

#### 10.3.3.3 Private hospitals and clinics

If the claim arises out of treatment in a private hospital or clinic, the decision as to who should be named as the defendant will depend upon the basis of the claim. The doctors and some other healthcare providers will usually be independent contractors. Where it is their breach of duty which has led to the claim, the claim should be issued against them as individuals, as vicarious liability is not applicable. They will be indemnified by their own medical defence organisations.

The hospital or clinic will employ the staff who run and administer it, and this will usually include nursing staff. If the claim arises out of the actions of employees, the hospital or clinic should be named as defendant. It will carry its own insurance. The hospital or clinic will advise the claimant's solicitor as to the position of individuals who are employed or who otherwise use their premises.

#### 10.3.3.4 Private treatment from dentists

A dentist treating private patients is not under any statutory or professional requirement to have insurance cover in respect of professional negligence – although the majority are insured.

## 10.4 Clinical negligence claims – preliminary steps

The PAP for the resolution of clinical disputes assumes that the patient's medical records will be provided to him by the health care provider *before* the letter of claim is sent. It may also be necessary for the claimant's solicitor to instruct an expert to look at the records and advise as to liability and/or causation prior to the letter of claim.

### 10.4.1 Obtaining medical records

The claimant's solicitor should obtain a copy of his client's records from his GP and from the hospital where he was treated, in order to build up a full picture of his client's health prior to the incident and of the treatment he received. The GP's records should contain notes of symptoms, medication and treatment, referrals to hospital, reports back from hospital doctors and referrals to other professionals such as occupational therapists, physiotherapists or community nurses. The hospital records will contain details of the client's admission, his consents to treatment, x-rays, photographs, print-outs from monitoring equipment, nursing records and comments made by the doctors who were treating him.

The claimant's solicitor should ensure that he obtains all the notes, not just those which are supplied and marked relevant to the matter in hand, as background history may be highly relevant. In *Wickham v Dwyer* (1995) *Current Law Weekly*, 1 January, the court held that it was for the expert to determine whether or not there was any information of any irrelevance contained within the notes, and therefore it was fair to allow the solicitors and experts access to the full notes.

Until all records have been traced and disclosed, the solicitor will not be in a position to instruct an expert to review the evidence and form a view on liability and/or causation. Early and full disclosure is the key to successful clinical negligence litigation as, without this, it may be impossible for the claimant and his solicitor to know exactly what happened.

#### 10.4.1.1 Client's authority

The solicitor must obtain from his client a signed authority permitting the solicitor to make an application to the relevant doctor(s)/hospital for copies of the client's records. Although a short letter addressed to the solicitor and signed by the client will suffice, many practitioners use the form of consent for release of health records produced by The Law Society and the BMA.

The aim of the form is to demonstrate that the patient's *informed* consent to the release of the records has been obtained. It requires the solicitor to sign and confirm that he needs the records for a legitimate purpose, and it also makes it clear to the client that, in giving his consent, he understands that the defendant may also gain access to all of the client's health records.

### 10.4.1.2 Right of access to medical records

**Records of living individuals**

The Data Protection Act 1998 (DPA 1998) gives the right to living individuals to access their personal health records. For the purposes of the Act, 'records' may be handwritten or in a computerised form, and will include imaging records, such as x-rays, photographs and print-outs from monitoring equipment.

**Records of deceased individuals**

The Access to Health Records Act 1990 governs access to the health records of individuals who have died. Access may be requested only by a personal representative or a person who may have a claim arising out of the death.

### 10.4.1.3 Best practice guidance

In 2006, an agreement was made between The Law Society, APIL, the Association of British Insurers and the health sector that, *subject to the expert witnesses' view*, there is a rebuttable presumption that no patient records will be requested for claims below £10,000. This agreement was reached on the understanding that it is best practice to try to reduce the bureaucracy involved in lower-value claims. Consequently, practitioners should think about whether patient records are necessary in a particular case and not request them unless they *are* necessary. This guidance should not be taken as a bar to seeking records, and solicitors can seek records if they deem it necessary to do so. Patients can also request sight of their own records. This is best practice advice and does not amend the PAP for personal injury claims.

### 10.4.1.4 Procedure for obtaining access to medical records

At Annex B of the PAP for the resolution of clinical disputes, there is a Protocol for Obtaining Hospital Medical Records, which contains a specimen application form for use when making a request for copies of a client's medical records. Most healthcare providers have an application form which is based on that found in the PAP. The request should contain enough information to allow the data controller to identify the data subject (the individual) and to locate the information requested.

Where it is the solicitor who is making the request, the client's consent should be supplied. In addition, the solicitor would normally be expected to give an undertaking to be responsible for the reasonable charges incurred in supplying copies of the records to him. The maximum charge for supplying copies is £50, which is for copying and posting the records only and should not result in a profit for the record holder. No fee is chargeable where the request is for access merely to inspect the health records.

The DPA 1998 allows the record holder 40 days from the date of the request to supply the information requested, although the Department of Health's policy is to comply with the request promptly and, in any event, within 21 days.

### 10.4.1.5 The content of medical records

The following list summarises the type of information the solicitor might expect to be supplied to him in response to a request for records or notes. The exact contents of the records or notes will vary from case to case and the following list is not exhaustive, but it is intended as a general guideline to the type of information which the solicitor can expect to receive:

(a) *Admission details/record sheet.* These should give the date and the time of admission, the record number, the name of the ward and the name of the consultant in charge of the case.

(b) *In-patient notes.* These include casualty notes (where appropriate), personal details of the patient, a detailed history of the patient and of the initial examination, daily progress and record notes, discharge notes, a copy of the letter to the GP giving details of the patient's treatment and a general report to the GP.

(c) *Nursing records.* Nursing records are detailed notes made by nursing staff including temperature charts, vital signs, test results, results of all investigations carried out, and details of drugs prescribed and taken.

(d) *Letters of referral.* These include referrals from GPs, responses to GPs following consultation or complaint of a missed appointment, and comments on the patient's demeanour and attitude.

(e) *Records of x-rays.* These include other films taken. Copies of the x-rays and films themselves are not supplied automatically (only the record of the fact that the x-ray was carried out) and copies of the films will have to be obtained separately.

(f) *Anaesthetic details.* These are details of the examination of the patient prior to an operation, a record of the drugs administered during pre-medication and during the operation itself.

(g) *Patient consent forms.* These forms show what treatments the patient consented to have performed on him.

(h) *Internal enquiry reports.* Where an internal enquiry has been held and the dominant purpose of that enquiry was not in contemplation of litigation, the enquiry notes will be discoverable.

(i) *Obstetric cases.* The following documents should also be supplied:
   (i) progress of labour cards;
   (ii) cardiotachograph (CTG) traces showing foetal contractions;
   (iii) partogram (showing labour in chart form);
   (iv) ante-natal records;
   (v) neo-natal records;
   (vi) paediatric notes.

#### 10.4.1.6 General practitioner notes

Information kept by a GP may be in paper or electronic form. Records will include the doctor's own notes, and may include reports of any investigations requested by him, letters of referral to hospitals or consultants and any responses, letters from hospital regarding out-patient clinic attendances and treatment, and in-patient discharge summaries.

The GP's records will be relevant in many cases where there is no potential claim against the GP. In such cases, when making a request for records, the claimant's solicitor should inform the GP that he is not a potential claimant. In all cases, the GP should be asked to preserve the original records, so that they are not inadvertently destroyed or microfiched before the trial.

#### 10.4.1.7 Examining the records

The solicitor should ensure (as far as possible) that the notes or records supplied to him are complete and are in chronological order, which will show the pattern of the disease or problem and its treatment, and may also highlight missing documents or records. Where the claimant's solicitor suspects that a document or documents may be missing, or where documents have been badly copied or are otherwise illegible, he should raise the issue with the records holder, since an incomplete set of records may distort the overall picture and thus give a false impression of the claim. It may be necessary to make an appointment with the GP or hospital to inspect the original documents. It is also helpful for the solicitor to go through the records with the client to ensure that the treatment shown on the records accords with the client's recollection of what actually occurred. The records should be supplied to the solicitor and not direct to the expert, so that the solicitor has an opportunity to check them through before instructing the expert to prepare his report.

#### 10.4.1.8 The defendant Trust

Where the potential defendant is an NHS Trust or other member of the Clinical Negligence Scheme for Trusts, a request for medical records will prompt an initial inquiry by the Trust. Where this inquiry suggests that there has been a serious adverse event, or if there is a potential claim of a value of over £250,000, the Trust will notify the NHSLA, which may instruct solicitors from its panel to act on behalf of the Trust (see **5.7**). In such a case, the defendant will be legally represented from an early stage.

### 10.4.2 Instructing an expert on liability and/or causation

In clinical negligence cases, it will be necessary to instruct one or more medical experts to consider the claimant's medical records and provide an opinion on matters relating to breach of duty and causation. Frequently, it will be appropriate to do this before the letter of claim is sent. In due course, other medical experts will deal with issues relating to quantum. Expert evidence is dealt with in **Chapter 11**.

## 10.5 Employers' liability claims for disease and illness – preliminary steps

Disease and illness claims are very difficult to establish, particularly the so-called 'long-tail' claims, where the illness or disease manifests itself many years after exposure to the causative substance or working conditions (see **4.7**). It will not be possible for the claimant's solicitor to assess whether there is a claim with a reasonable chance of success until he has seen the medical notes held by his client's GP and has obtained his occupational records from the potential defendant, who will be either the claimant's current employer or a former employer. These notes will enable the claimant's solicitor to draw up a chronology of events and map the progress of the disease. He may need a medical expert to advise as to causation before the letter of claim is sent.

Records should be obtained from the GP as discussed in **10.4**.

### 10.5.1 Obtaining occupational records

In accordance with para 4 of the PAP for disease and illness claims (see **Appendix 3**), the claimant's solicitor should write to the potential defendant, the client's employer or former employer, requesting his occupational records, including health and personnel records, before the letter of claim is sent. The DPA 1998 applies. Sufficient information should be given in the letter of request to alert the potential defendant or his insurer to the fact that a potential disease claim is being investigated. A specimen letter and request form to be used for this purpose is set out at Annexes A and A1 of the Protocol.

Records should be provided within a maximum of 40 days of the request, free of charge. The Protocol suggests that as a matter of good practice, the potential defendant should also disclose any product data documents which the claimant has requested which may resolve a causation issue. Where documents are not provided within 40 days and no information is forthcoming from the defendant to explain the reasons for the delay, the claimant should apply to the court for an order for pre-action disclosure (see **10.9.2**).

The claimant's solicitor should also seek to obtain relevant occupational records held by other bodies or individuals who have employed the claimant in the past.

## 10.6 Preliminary notification of the claim

In many instances, the potential defendant will be aware of the possibility of a claim before the letter of claim is sent. Where this is not the case, the claimant's solicitor may wish to give the potential defendant early notification before he is in possession of sufficient information to enable him to send the letter of claim. In accordance with the para 2.6 of the PAP for personal injury claims, this will not start the clock ticking for the purposes of the time limit set for the defendant's response.

## 10.7 Letter of claim

### 10.7.1 Purpose

The letter of claim should be sent to the proposed defendant, although a copy should be also sent to the insurer, where known, in personal injury cases. The principal function of the letter of claim is to notify the defendant of the proposed claim and, where the insurer's details are not yet known, to request that a copy is forwarded to the insurer, thus ensuring that the insurer is involved at the earliest possible date.

### 10.7.2 When should it be sent?

#### 10.7.2.1 Personal injury claims

The PAP for personal injury claims states that the letter of claim should be sent 'immediately sufficient information is available to substantiate a realistic claim and before issues of quantum are addressed in detail' (para 3.1). The PAP for disease and illness claims has similar wording (para 6.1).

In practice, this means that before the letter of claim is sent, sufficient investigative work must be carried out in order to satisfy the claimant's solicitor that there is a reasonable prospect of the claim being successful. However, bearing in mind the overriding objective set out in r 1 of the CPR, particularly the issue of proportionality, and the fact that the defendant might admit liability, the claimant's solicitor does not need to investigate every part of his client's case before the letter of claim is sent to the defendant. At this stage, he should avoid expensive disbursements, such as those associated with instructing experts, if possible, although this will depend on the nature of each individual case.

In occupational disease and illness claims, the claimant's solicitor will need to obtain occupational and medical records, and obtain an expert's opinion on those records prior to the letter being sent (see **10.5**).

#### 10.7.2.2 Clinical negligence claims

The PAP for clinical negligence claims states that as soon as the patient and his adviser decide that there are grounds for a claim, the letter should be sent 'as soon as practicable'. It will not be possible for the claimant's solicitor to assess whether or not there are grounds for a claim until his client's medical records have been obtained and analysed by a medical expert. The letter of claim should be sent after the medical expert has confirmed that liability and causation can be established (see **10.4**).

### 10.7.3 What should it contain?

The precise wording contained in the three pre-action protocols differs, and therefore reference to the relevant protocol should be made in order to determine precisely what the letter of claim should contain in each type of case. The specimen letters of claim which are set out in the Appendices of each of the pre-action protocols are also useful. However, the following should be included:

(a) a clear summary of the facts on which the claim is based;

(b) the main allegations of negligence/breach of statutory duty (and an outline of the causal link where this is likely to be in dispute);

(c) an indication of the nature of all of the injuries that have been sustained, including current condition and prognosis where relevant; and

(d) an indication of other financial losses.

The letter should contain enough information to enable the defendant, his insurer or his solicitor to investigate the proposed claim and put a broad valuation on the claim. However, the claimant's solicitor should not attempt to quantify damages at this stage as, in most cases, he will not have investigated quantum in any detail.

The letter of claim does not have the same status as a statement of case and therefore the claimant will not be held to the content of the letter. Nevertheless, the claimant's solicitor should be as accurate as possible, in order to avoid credibility issues should the matter go to trial.

Depending upon the nature and circumstances of each individual case, the following matters may also be relevant:

(a) In person injury cases only, two copies of the letter should be sent to the defendant, and the letter should contain a request to the defendant to pass one copy on to his insurers. Where the insurer's details are already known, this will not be necessary and a copy of the letter should be forwarded directly to the insurers.

(b) In most clinical negligence claims, medical reports will have already been obtained from the proposed defendant; and in occupational disease and illness claims, occupational records and possibly product data information will have been obtained. However, where there may be further relevant information and in all other cases, the letter should contain a request for the early disclosure of relevant documents which the claimant anticipates are in the defendant's possession. Upon notifying the claimant of his denial of the claim, a defendant should disclose any documents he holds that are material to the issues. However, it is best practice for the claimant's solicitor to assist him by identifying in the letter of claim those which he believes are material (see **10.9.1**).

(c) Where the claimant has entered into a funding arrangement in relation to the proposed claim, ie a CFA or an AEI policy, details should be given in the letter of claim. In accordance with CPR, r 44.3B(1)(c), a party may not recover any additional liability (ie the success fee or insurance premium) for any period in the proceedings during which he failed to provide information about a funding arrangement. Notice is required to be given with the claim form on issue of proceedings (see **9.2.2.1** and **12.3.2**). However, it is recommended that this information be given at the earliest opportunity, as the sooner the opposition is on notice that there is an additional liability, the less likely it is that there will be a problem in recovering the additional liability at the conclusion of the proceedings. The letter should set out the date the CFA was entered into, but should not give details of the success fee, as this would give some indication to the defendant as to how the claimant's solicitors perceive the strength of the claim. Likewise, the letter should set out the date of the AEI policy, the policy number, and the name and address of the insurance company, but should not disclose the amount of the premium.

(d) In RTA cases where the claimant was treated in hospital, the letter of claim should set out the name and address of the hospital and his hospital number, where available.

(e) In occupational disease and illness claims and the more complex clinical negligence claims, the letter should include or enclose a chronology of events.

(f) In occupational disease and illness claims, particularly where the claimant had several employers and the disease has a long latency period, the letter should include or enclose details of the claimant's employment history.

(g) In EL claims, the letter should include a request for information relating to the claimant's earnings, for quantum purposes (see **10.5.1.1**).

(h) In a clinical negligence claim, the letter should refer to any documents, including medical records, which the claimant considers to be relevant and, if possible, enclose copies of those which are not already in the possession of the potential defendant.

(i) In an occupational disease or illness claim, the letter should refer to any relevant documents, including health records not already in the potential defendant's possession. Copies of these records should *not* be enclosed with the letter of claim. Instead, the defendant should be invited to nominate an insurance manager or a solicitor to whom the documents may be supplied upon receipt of the defendant's response.

(j) In the majority of cases, witness statements and the reports of experts would not be disclosed at this stage. However, where the claimant's solicitor feels that such evidence demonstrates a very strong case on liability, he may decide to disclose it with the letter of claim, as this may lead to an admission of liability by the defendant.

(k) The claimant's solicitor may make an offer to settle in the letter of claim, by setting out what his client would be willing to accept in full and final settlement of the matter. However, in many cases, a detailed investigation into quantum will not have been undertaken by the claimant's solicitor and therefore an offer should not be made.

## 10.8 Response to the letter of claim

### 10.8.1 Personal injury claims

In personal injury claims, including those relating to disease and illness, the defendant has 21 calendar days of the date of the posting of the letter of claim to send a preliminary response to the claimant. In this letter, the defendant should identify his insurer, if any, and highlight any significant omissions from the letter of claim. Any documents material to the issues (which are not privileged) should be enclosed.

The defendant has three months from the date of acknowledging the claim to investigate the matter and provide a substantive response. Where the claim is denied, reasons for the denial and any alternative versions of events should be set out. The individual pre-action protocols give further information as to what information should be included.

### 10.8.2 Clinical negligence claims

In clinical negligence claims, the defendant has less time to respond. The letter of claim must be acknowledged within 14 days of receipt and the person dealing with the matter should be identified. Where the claim is denied, full reasons for the denial should be provided within three months of the letter of claim. A template for the letter of response is at Annex C2 of the PAP for the resolution of clinical disputes (see **Appendix 4**).

As an internal matter, where the defendant is a member of the NHSLA's Clinical Negligence Scheme for Trusts, it must notify the NHSLA within 24 hours of receipt of a letter of claim. The NHSLA may appoint solicitors from its panel to deal with the potential claim at this stage, where the complexity of the issues and the likely value of the claim warrant it.

## 10.9 Acquiring evidence in respect of liability

Although the claimant's solicitor will have obtained sufficient evidence to justify the dispatch of the letter of claim, where the defendant denies liability, he will need to obtain further evidence in order to ensure that liability can be proved at trial, if need be.

### 10.9.1 Documents held by the defendant

The claimant's solicitor will have no difficulties in obtaining documents which are in the possession of his client, or documents to which the public have access. However, many of the documents which will give real insight into the causes of the accident will be in the possession of the proposed defendant.

The pre-action protocols are designed to encourage parties to have an open-handed approach to litigation, and this requires each party to allow the other to see relevant documents at an early stage. In clinical negligence claims and in occupational disease and illness claims, the relevant pre-action protocols envisage that the claimant will obtain medical records or occupational health records prior to the sending of the letter of claim (see **10.4** and **10.5**). In all other cases, where the defendant denies liability, he should enclose with his letter of reply copies of all documents in his possession which are material to the issues between the parties and which would be likely to be ordered to be disclosed by the court, either on an application for pre-action disclosure or on disclosure during proceedings. In clinical negligence and occupational disease and illness claims, the defendant should disclose any relevant documents he has not yet disclosed.

#### 10.9.1.1 Documents relevant to personal injury claims

Annex B to the PAP for personal injury claims contains lists of documents which are likely to be in the defendant's possession in various types of claim, and in the letter of claim the claimant's solicitor should set out which documents he requires, should liability not be admitted. However, Annex B does not provide an exhaustive list of what the defendant may have and there might be other relevant documents, including, for example, minutes of meetings, memorandums between in-house departments or individuals, and reports. With experience, the personal injury solicitor will obtain an understanding of the types of documents which might be available in certain circumstances, but the claimant's solicitor should always listen carefully to what his client and other witnesses have to say, as they may know of the existence of documentation without understanding its relevance.

It is important to remember that, for the purpose of disclosure, the term 'document' is not restricted to written documents but includes anything in which information of any description is recorded. It therefore includes audiotapes, videotapes, photographs and electronic documents such as e-mails. Footage from CCTV cameras is becoming increasingly available, and in workplace claims, it is possible that the employer had installed a CCTV camera in, for example, a factory, warehouse or supermarket, which has captured images of the accident.

#### 10.9.1.2 Documents relevant to employer liability claims

A list of documents which the defendant employer may be expected to have following an accident at work are set out in Annex B to the PAP for personal injury claims. However, the following documents may require an explanation:

(a) *The Accident Book*. Under the Reporting of Injuries, Diseases and Dangerous Occurrences Regulations 1995 (RIDDOR 1995) (SI 1995/3163), employers are required to keep an accident book of an approved type where details of all accidents that occur on the premises must be recorded. The claimant's solicitor should not only ask the employer for a copy of the relevant page from the accident book, but should also consider whether the book itself should be inspected for evidence of similar incidents in the past.

(b) *RIDDOR report to the HSE*. Employers are required to report certain classes of injury or disease sustained by people at work and specified dangerous occurrences. The RIDDOR 1995 require the responsible person (ie the safety officer/manager) to inform the HSE as soon as possible of the incident, and to follow it up with written confirmation within 10 days. The defendant should retain a copy of the report in its files.

    The reportable occurrences are:

    (i) the death of any person;

    (ii) any person suffering a specified major injury;

    (iii) any person not at work due to an injury resulting in evacuation of the person to a hospital for treatment;

(iv) any person not at work due to an injury sustained due to working at a hospital;

(v) where there has been a dangerous occurrence. Dangerous occurrences are listed in Sch 2 to RIDDOR 1995 and include such things as dangerous occurrences involving overhead electric lines, biological agents and radiation generators, as well as occurrences in mines, at quarries, on the railways and at off-shore installations.

### 10.9.2 Application for pre-action disclosure and inspection

Where the claimant's solicitor believes the proposed defendant has relevant documentation which he has not disclosed in compliance with the protocol, and he has failed to respond to written requests to do so, an application for disclosure prior to the start of proceedings should be made under s 33 of the Supreme Court Act 1981 or s 52 of the County Courts Act 1984. The application must be supported by appropriate evidence, and the procedure is the same in both the High Court and county court. Under r 31.16, the court may make an order for disclosure only where:

(a) the respondent is likely to be a party to subsequent proceedings;

(b) the applicant is also likely to be a party to the proceedings;

(c) if proceedings had started, the respondent's duty by way of standard disclosure, set out in rule 31.16, would extend to the documents or classes of documents of which the applicant seeks disclosure; and

(d) disclosure before proceedings have started is desirable in order to—

  (i) dispose fairly of the anticipated proceedings; or

  (ii) assist the dispute to be resolved without proceedings; or

  (iii) save costs.

An order under r 31.16 will specify the documents or class of documents which the respondent must disclose and require him, when making such disclosure, to specify any of those documents which he no longer has, or which he claims the right or duty to withhold from inspection. The order may also specify the time and place for disclosure and inspection to take place.

### 10.9.3 Documents held by third parties

Relevant documents may also be held by third parties. In some instances, for example where documents are held by the police or the HSE, the claimant's solicitor will generally be able to obtain copies, although he may be frustrated by the delay. Where documents contain the claimant's personal data, for example, occupational records held by someone other than the proposed defendant, he is entitled to see them under the DPA 1998.

In other cases, where a third party holds documents and it is under no statutory obligation to disclose them, the claimant's solicitor should make a polite request, offering to pay all the reasonable costs associated with providing access to or copies of the documents. If the third party refuses to cooperate, generally the claimant's solicitor cannot apply to the court for an order of disclosure and inspection until proceedings have commenced (see CPR, r 31.17). The court does have an equitable power to make a pre-action order for disclosure against third parties, but this will be exercised only in rare circumstances, a consideration of which lies beyond the scope of this book.

#### 10.9.3.1 Documents relevant to RTAs – the police accident report

In the case of a road traffic incident, it may be useful to obtain a copy of the police accident report (PAR), if one exists. The following should be borne in mind:

(a) The PAR will contain statements from the parties and a sketch plan, as well as the police officer's comments on the condition of the vehicles, the road surface, the weather conditions and details of any criminal proceedings that have been commenced as a result of the accident. It may also include photographs and witness statements. Some PARs contain more useful information than others and, bearing in mind that a fee will be payable, it may be advisable to ask what the PAR does contain before seeking to obtain a copy.

(b) In order to obtain a copy of the PAR, the solicitor should contact the accident records department at the police force headquarters for the area in which the accident occurred (not the police officer assigned to the case). The letter should include details of the date, time and place of the accident, the registration numbers of the vehicles and the full names of those involved.

(c) The PAR will not be released until the conclusion of any criminal investigation and proceedings. If the defendant is convicted of an offence which is relevant to the issue of negligence, it is likely that he (or more likely his insurers) will want to settle the proceedings, and therefore it will not be necessary to obtain a copy of the PAR.

(d) A fee is payable for the PAR. The amount of the fee varies, depending upon the relevant police force, the length of the report and the type of accident. For example, the Durham Constabulary charges £100 for a standard PAR relating to a slight injury and £150 for a standard report relating to a serious or fatal accident. The Essex Police charge £75 for a PAR of up to 30 pages, £120 for a PAR over 30 pages and £220 where the report relates to a fatal accident. The solicitor should ensure that funds are available to cover the fee.

(e) In addition to the PAR, there may also be a collision investigation report, particularly in the case of an accident involving serious injury or death. This report is much more extensive than the standard PAR and will usually contain a large number of photographs, which are numbered to cross-reference with the collision investigation report. This report may be obtained on payment of a further fee. The photographs will also be available only on payment of a fee.

(f) On payment of a further fee, the police officer who prepared the PAR may be interviewed, in the presence of a senior officer. (If the matter goes to trial, police officers will give evidence in civil proceedings, but they must be witness summonsed and a further fee will be payable.)

(g) If there is no PAR, it is still possible to obtain copies of police notebooks and witness statements on payment of a fee. Because reports may be destroyed (in some cases after as little as one year), a request for a report should be made promptly, notwithstanding that the report will not actually be released until the conclusion of criminal investigations.

### 10.9.3.2 Documents relevant to work-based claims – HSE reports

Health and Safety Executive reports are the equivalent of police reports in the field of industrial incidents. Generally, the same rules apply as with police reports, although, due to lack of resources, a report may only be available in the case of very serious injury or death.

The HSE officer responsible for the factory or workplace concerned should be approached with a request for a copy of his report. As with the PAR, the HSE report will not be available until after any criminal prosecution has been dealt with. If the HSE is unwilling to provide a copy of its report voluntarily, it may be necessary to wait until after proceedings have been commenced and then make an application for non-party disclosure.

The HSE will also have other relevant documentation, such as the RIDDOR and correspondence with the defendant regarding the incident. However, the defendant should have a copy of these documents in its own files and may possibly have a copy of the HSE report. All these documents should be disclosed to the claimant with other relevant documents it holds.

### 10.9.4 Real evidence

Real evidence is a material object, such as a piece of machinery, an article of personal protective clothing, etc, which is relevant to the issues of the case. Where it is practicable for the item to be produced at court, the claimant's solicitor should take appropriate steps to obtain the item, instruct an expert to examine it where necessary, and then put it into safe-keeping until it is required. If it is impracticable for an item (eg a large piece of machinery) to be produced at court, photographs should be taken.

#### 10.9.4.1 Application for preservation and inspection

Where the defendant refuses to allow the claimant to inspect relevant evidence which is in the possession of the defendant, or where the claimant fears that the defendant may destroy or otherwise tamper with the item, an application may be made to the court for an order to secure the preservation of evidence under s 7 of the Civil Procedure Act 1997. The application may be made by any person who is or is likely to become a party to any existing or proposed proceedings, and the order will enable that party:

(a) to carry out a search for or inspection of anything described in the order; and

(b) to make or obtain a copy, sample or other record of anything so described.

The application is made under r 25.5 of the CPR and must be supported by evidence to show the relevance of the item to the proceedings.

### 10.9.5 Photographs and sketch plans of the location of the accident

In road traffic cases, it is usually necessary to produce photographs and sketch plans of the location of the accident for two reasons. First, the layout of the road may change between the date of accident and the date of trial, and/or the road may appear different depending on whether it is photographed in summer or in winter, especially if there are lots of trees or vegetation which could obscure a driver's view. Secondly, it may be necessary to try to show the location from the perspective of the car drivers at the time. An aerial view or plan of a road junction will do nothing, for example, to prove to a court how badly the approach of a vehicle was obscured by trees and bushes or roadside property. The solicitor should not lose sight of the fact that he must be able to prove to the court what could or could not be seen from a particular vantage point. It is open to the court to visit the site of the accident, but this may not be practicable, and in any event, it would take an inordinate amount of time. The solicitor should always visit the site if possible, in order to get a feel for the case.

Police accident reports (see **10.9.3.1**) often contain good quality photographs which can be purchased on payment of an extra fee per print, and which may prove helpful in showing not only the severity and location of the damage to each vehicle, but also the final position on the road in which the vehicles were immediately following the accident. This evidence may assume significance at a later date, or may contradict the oral evidence of the witnesses. It is, however, important to read the PAR closely, as it will confirm whether or not the vehicles were moved from their original resting position prior to the taking of the photographs.

In road traffic cases, the photographer should mark on a plan the precise location from which each photograph was taken and the direction in which the camera was pointing.

Site visits in non-road traffic cases are no less important. For example, in a case where the client has tripped on a broken pavement, it is not uncommon for the local authority, upon receiving intimation of a possible claim, to send a team of operatives to mend the offending paving stone. It is therefore vitally important to secure good quality photographs of the pavement, etc as soon as possible, usually on the same day that the client is interviewed. Photographs must contain some indication of scale, and it is therefore necessary to place an item, such as a ruler, within the photograph.

In modern times, the availability of mobile telephones with inbuilt cameras means that claimants or their friends or family members may have taken relevant photographs of the site at or about the time of the accident. Whilst such photographs may have some use, particularly in low-value cases, it is not good practice to entrust the taking of photographs to the client, who may underestimate the importance of the task and forget about it until it is too late. Photographs taken by the client may be out of focus, underexposed or otherwise taken in a manner which will not help the client's case. A good example of this can be found in *Flynn v Leeds City Council*, 10 September 2004, where the claimant was injured when she tripped on the edge of an uneven paving stone. She claimed that the discrepancy between the heights of the paving stones was over an inch and that the pavement was therefore dangerous to pedestrians. Photographs of the paving stones, with the alleged discrepancy highlighted by the presence of a 50 pence piece and a ruler, had been taken by the claimant's partner, who happened to be a litigation solicitor. The defendant claimed that these photographs appeared to have been 'massaged slightly'. The judge did not feel that anything sinister was being suggested, but he accepted that the 50 pence piece appeared to be leaning at an angle and that there may have been some slight excavation of material between the paving stones. The claimant failed to prove that the discrepancy between the paving stones was a dangerous one and the judge found in favour of the defendant.

### 10.9.6 Evidence of criminal convictions

If the proposed defendant is charged with a criminal offence in relation to the incident which caused the injury to the claimant, ideally the claimant's solicitor should attend the proceedings to note the evidence. The date of the proceedings may be obtained from the police or the HSE, as appropriate.

Any resulting conviction of the defendant which is relevant to the issues in civil proceedings (ie relevant when seeking to prove or disprove negligence or breach of statutory duty) may be referred to in the civil proceedings (Civil Evidence Act 1968, s 11). In an RTA claim, for example, a conviction for speeding or dangerous driving arising out of the incident itself is a relevant conviction. However, a conviction for driving without insurance at the time of the accident, or a previous conviction for driving with excess alcohol in the blood, is not a relevant conviction, as it does not prove that the defendant was negligent at the time of the accident.

For the purposes of the civil proceedings, the defendant will be taken to have committed the offence 'unless the contrary is proved'. The defendant may seek to argue that he should not have been convicted, but if he does so, the burden of proving this on the balance of probabilities will pass to him. In most cases where there is a relevant conviction, the defendant will seek to settle the matter.

Where a claimant is convicted for failing to wear a safety belt or a safety helmet, the conviction is relevant to the issue of damages as it indicates contributory negligence.

Should the matter go to trial, the party seeking to rely on the conviction will need to produce a certificate from the convicting court in order to prove the conviction.

### 10.9.7 Evidence of lay witnesses

Witnesses should be contacted and interviewed by the claimant's solicitor as soon as possible. The defendant's solicitor, in the normal course of events, will be instructed at a later date than the claimant's solicitor, but he too should contact and interview witnesses without delay. Where a witness is not interviewed at an early stage, his memory of the events may fade or he may become untraceable. If the claimant was injured at work and the witness is a fellow employee of the claimant, he may be concerned about his employer's reaction and become increasingly reluctant to speak to the claimant's solicitor. Witnesses to road incidents are often initially enthusiastic, but later decide that they have little to gain and would rather not get involved. For this reason, the solicitor should not delay in contacting the witness and obtaining a proof of evidence, or at the very least a letter confirming what he saw and/or heard and that he is prepared to make a statement to that effect.

In a straightforward case, it may not be necessary to interview the witness. If his letter of response is sufficiently clear, a proof can be prepared from it and from any questionnaire he may also have been sent. A copy of the proof should be forwarded for approval and signature by the witness. This should be accompanied by a stamped addressed envelope and covering letter, requesting the witness to read the proof carefully and make any amendments or additions that he feels to be necessary before signing and dating the document for return in the envelope provided. The witness is a volunteer to the client's cause and should be thanked accordingly for the time and trouble he has taken on the client's behalf.

The proof of evidence, once converted into a formal witness statement and exchanged with the other side, will form the basis of the witness's evidence to be relied on at trial and will stand as his evidence-in-chief. Furthermore, the statement may have to be used at the trial under the Civil Evidence Act 1995 if the witness subsequently becomes unavailable. Consequently, it should contain all the relevant evidence the witness can give and, needless to say, it should be the truth. In accordance with r 22.1 of the CPR, the witness statement must conclude with a statement of truth, and this must be signed by the witness himself.

In an EL case, it may be advisable for the claimant's solicitor to obtain statements from individuals, such as shop stewards or co-workers, who, although they may not have seen the accident, may know of other similar accidents in the past, or be able to give background information on policy changes that may have taken place within the organisation. In road incident or tripping cases, people living or working adjacent to the location of the incident may be able to give useful information relating to similar incidents that have happened in the past, and even as to the identities of past claimants in similar incidents, or information on how long the defect has been in existence.

### 10.9.8 Expert evidence

Almost all cases will involve some expert evidence. There may be a requirement for non-medical experts, such as engineers or RTA reconstruction experts, but most experts will be from the medical field. In clinical injury cases, experts will be required in respect of liability, causation and quantum. In most personal injury cases, the evidence of a medical expert will relate to quantum rather than liability, although there will be some cases where a medical opinion in relation to causation will be required, for example where the claimant has suffered a disease or illness. Consequently, the claimant's solicitor will not normally seek to obtain a report from a medical expert until he is satisfied that the claimant has a strong case on liability, or liability has been admitted by the defendant. See **Chapter 11** for a detailed consideration of the role of experts.

## 10.10 Acquiring evidence in respect of quantum

### 10.10.1 Evidence of lost earnings

The client's loss of earnings is likely to form a significant part of his claim for special damages. See **Chapter 13** for a detailed consideration of this point.

#### 10.10.1.1 Obtaining details from employers

In an EL claim against the claimant's current employer, a request for details of the claimant's earnings should be set out in the letter of claim. In other cases, the claimant's solicitor should write to the client's employer to ask for details of earnings for 13 weeks prior to the incident and for a copy of the client's contract of employment. The loss of earnings details should be set out to show weekly earnings (both gross and net) so as to reveal a pattern over 13 weeks.

#### 10.10.1.2 Self-employed clients

Documentary evidence in the form of the client's previous year's trading accounts (or longer if appropriate) should be obtained if possible, together with other evidence of contracts or offers of work that had to be turned down as a result of the incident. The client's accountant, business associates and colleagues in the same area of work should be approached to assist in this.

#### 10.10.1.3 Unemployed clients

Even if the client is unemployed, evidence should be obtained of his last employer and of the likelihood of his obtaining suitable work which he could have undertaken but for the accident, as evidence of earning capacity. Colleagues in the same area of business and employment agencies should be approached for evidence of availability of work within the client's specialism and the level of possible earnings.

### 10.10.2 Evidence of other special damages

During the first interview with his client, the claimant's solicitor should ask him to keep details of any articles damaged in the accident, repair costs, private medical treatment, journeys to hospital, parking tickets, etc which have resulted from the accident, and to retain any relevant quotes, invoices, receipts or tickets. Where the defendant admits liability, or where the court finds in favour of the claimant, many of these items will be admitted by the defendant, provided evidence is produced.

### 10.10.3 Evidence of pain, suffering and loss of amenity

#### 10.10.3.1 Medical records

It may be necessary to obtain copies of the claimant's medical records from his GP and/or from a hospital where he was treated (see **10.4.1**) in order to prove the extent of the claimant's suffering and, if necessary, disprove that any pre-existing condition contributed to the injuries suffered by the claimant.

#### 10.10.3.2 Medical experts

Medical experts provide crucial evidence for the assessment of general damages for pain, suffering and loss of amenity. In a fairly straightforward case, one medical expert of an appropriate specialisation will be able to deal with all aspects of liability and quantum in his report. In more complex cases, such as where the claimant has suffered major brain trauma, several experts might be required, including, for example, a neurologist, a neuropsychologist, an occupational therapist, and an expert on the need for care and general support.

#### 10.10.3.3 Lay witnesses

The claimant's own testimony is important. During the first interview, the claimant's solicitor should ask his client to keep a pain diary. The claimant should set out the extent of his suffering and its effect on his life in his witness statement.

The evidence of members of the claimant's family, friends and work colleagues may also provide a valuable insight into the impact of the accident.

#### 10.10.3.4 Photographs

Photographs of the injuries immediately after the accident, during the various stages of recovery and as at the date of trial, where they are continuing, are also very useful.

## 10.11 Conclusion

The claimant's solicitor is obliged, under the overriding objective found in r 1 of the CPR and under the pre-action protocols, to be fully prepared before proceedings are commenced. Once proceedings have been issued, the court will actively manage the case and will require the parties to deal with each step of the proceedings in accordance with the timetable it lays down in the order for directions. Where a solicitor fails to prepare adequately prior to issue and consequently is unable to comply with the directions within the specified time limits, the court may impose cost penalties.

The essential element when gathering evidence at the preliminary stage is to act quickly. A failure to act on the client's instructions as soon as they are received can have disastrous consequences for the subsequent conduct of the litigation. In extreme cases, this may seriously prejudice the client's chances of success and can amount to negligence on the part of the solicitor.

## 10.12 Further reading

Middleton and Solomon, *Personal Injury Practice & Procedure* (Sweet & Maxwell)

# Chapter 11
# Instructing Experts



## 11.1 Introduction

In almost every personal injury or clinical negligence case, the claimant's solicitor will instruct at least one medical expert. Commonly, an expert will prepare a report on the claimant's injuries for quantum purposes, which is often referred to as a report on condition and prognosis. In clinical negligence and disease and illness claims, medical evidence will not only be required in order to assist the court in assessing damages, but will also be necessary in order to prove liability and/or causation. Indeed, the claimant's solicitor may be unable to understand precisely what happened to the claimant, and therefore advise him in relation to the claim, until such evidence has been obtained. In some personal injury cases, other types of experts, such as accident reconstruction experts or engineers, may be required for liability purposes.

The use of experts in civil trials is primarily governed by Part 35 of the CPR and the accompanying Practice Direction. Rule 35.1 states that expert evidence should be 'restricted to that which is reasonably required to resolve the proceedings', and solicitors should be mindful that the court's permission is required before a party may call an expert or put in evidence an expert's report (CPR, r 35.4(1)). In determining whether a party should be entitled to use an expert, the court will be governed by the overriding objective found in r 1 of the CPR, in particular, ensuring that the parties are on an equal footing, saving expense and dealing with case in ways which are proportionate.

In September 2005 the Civil Justice Council issued the Protocol for the Instruction of Experts to give evidence in civil courts, which replaces all previous codes of guidance for expert witnesses. The protocol gives clear guidance to experts and to those instructing them in the interpretation of and compliance with CPR Part 35 and PD 35. The protocol emphasises that the expert has an overriding duty to the court on matters within his expertise. It stresses that the expert's duty is to be independent, and offers a 'test' for independence as being: 'Would the expert express the same opinion if given the same instructions by an opposing party?' It sets out clear guidance on the matters to be covered in the instructions to experts, as well as guidance to experts on the contents of their report for litigation purposes. It stresses that a summary of conclusions is a mandatory requirement with full reasons in support. This should prove useful to instructing solicitors in ensuring that the quality of reports is all that it should be.

## 11.2 Who is an expert?

An expert is an individual with a high level of skill, knowledge and experience in a particular area which is outside the knowledge of the court. The expert will be permitted to give his opinion when the court would otherwise be unable properly to understand the factual evidence which has been placed before it and requires the expert's assistance in order to determine a matter of dispute between the parties. This evidence should be presented in a clear and concise way so that the court can use the information to reach its own conclusions.

The court is not obliged to accept the evidence of an expert. In *Armstrong and Another v First York Ltd* [2005] EWCA Civ 277, the Court of Appeal held that the trail judge had been entitled to reject the evidence of a forensic motor vehicle engineer who had been jointly instructed by the parties. The two claimants had allegedly sustained neck and spinal injuries when their car had been hit by a bus owned by the defendant. The expert's evidence was that there had been insufficient force generated by the impact to cause the injuries claimed. Although the trial judge found that the expert's evidence had been flawless, this could not be reconciled with his belief that the claimants were credible and honest witnesses. Consequently, he was entitled to find that there must have been a flaw in the expert's evidence, even though he had not been able to identify that flaw.

In *Stewart v Glaze* [2009] EWHC 704 (QB), the judge said that although the expert could be of considerable assistance, it was the primary factual evidence which was of the greatest importance, and that expert evidence should not be elevated into a fixed framework or formula against which the defendant's actions were to be judged rigidly with mathematical precision.

## 11.3 Areas of expertise

The number and variety of experts available to prepare reports are often surprising to those unfamiliar with this area. The following are examples of experts who provide reports.

### 11.3.1 Medical experts

Medical experts are usually required in order to assist the court in relation to the assessment of damages. In other words, they will report on the condition and prognosis of the claimant and the cost of living with the particular injury suffered by the claimant. In a simple, low-value case, a report from a general practitioner may be sufficient, but in a complex, high-value case, experts in several areas of medical expertise may be required. The types of medical experts who may assist in this regard are numerous, but may include doctors of various specialities, occupational therapists, behavioural therapists, speech therapists and physiotherapists.

In clinical negligence cases, it will be necessary to instruct an expert to advise in relation to liability and possibly causation. A consultant should be instructed with expertise in the same speciality as the doctor who is alleged to have been negligent.

A list of the most common areas of medical expertise can be found at **2.3**.

### 11.3.2 Other experts

In road traffic accidents, the following types of experts may be helpful in order to establish liability:

(a) accident investigators to reconstruct the events leading up to the road traffic accident;

(b) mechanical engineers to examine the vehicles involved in the accident, to identify damage or to investigate if any mechanical defects were present in the vehicle.

In employers' liability cases, the following types of experts may be helpful to establish liability:

(a) general consulting engineers to provide reports on machinery, systems of work, slipping accidents;

(b) mining engineers;

(c) ergonomics experts;

(d) bio-engineers;

(e) pharmacologists.

When dealing with quantum, in addition to doctors of the appropriate speciality, the following experts may be useful in relation to condition and prognosis and the costs of living with a particular injury:

(a) occupational therapists;

(b) behavioural therapists;

(c) speech therapists;

(d) physiotherapists;

(e) employment consultants;

When dealing with quantum, the following experts may be useful in relation to financial loss and the investment of damages:

(a) employment consultants;

(b) accountants;

(c) actuaries.

## 11.3.3 Specific experts

The following types of experts warrant further attention

### 11.3.3.1 Accident reconstruction experts

In more serious RTA claims, an accident reconstruction expert may be required. If the claimant's solicitor is instructed immediately following the accident, the accident reconstruction expert should be contacted without delay and requested to attend the scene of the accident in order to examine any skid marks, etc. It may also be appropriate for the expert to examine the vehicles involved in the accident, and the claimant's solicitor should take appropriate steps to ensure that the vehicles are not disposed of or repaired prior to the expert carrying out his examination. The evidence of tachographs will be particularly useful. The reconstruction expert will want to see the PAR and any associated reports prepared by the police, such as a police reconstruction report, and proofs of evidence from anyone involved in the accident or anyone who witnessed the accident. He will then be in a position to provide an opinion as to the cause of the accident.

### 11.3.3.2 Consulting engineers

Many personal injury claims involve machinery or systems of work (especially EL claims), and in such cases it may be thought appropriate for a consulting engineer to be instructed to prepare a report on the machinery involved or the system of work undertaken.

**Example**

A client is injured while driving a fork-lift truck and alleges that the steering wheel failed to respond while he was driving it. It is part of the client's case that the employer failed adequately to maintain the fork-lift truck. If the truck has not been modified prior to the solicitor being instructed, a consulting engineer may be instructed to examine the vehicle and its maintenance records. The solicitor will therefore obtain an expert's view as to whether the appropriate system of maintenance was adopted and attempt to identify the cause of the accident.

The expert will need to inspect the machinery, and the permission of the proposed defendants (who are normally the claimant's employers in such cases) is required. If this is not granted then it will be necessary to apply to court for an order for preservation and inspection (see **10.9.3.1**).

Where both parties are given permission to instruct their own experts, it is common for them to attend the scene of the accident at the same time in order to conduct a joint inspection. This has the advantage of saving costs and time, as the engineers can agree on measurements and technical details.

#### 11.3.3.3 Clinical case managers

In certain high-value/severe injury cases, a clinical case manager may be appointed to consider the claimant's appropriate care regime. In *Wright (by her litigation friend Karen Fay) v Kevin Sullivan* [2005] EWCA Civ 656, it was held that the clinical case manager would owe a duty to the claimant to work in his best interests and should not be jointly appointed. The evidence given by such a witness is evidence of fact and not expert opinion.

## 11.4 The expert's overriding duty to the court

As has been mentioned in **11.1** above, the Protocol for the Instruction of Experts emphasises the expert's overriding duty to the court. Paragraph 1 of PD 35 gives the following guidance as to the nature of that duty:

> 1.1 It is the duty of an expert to help the court on matters within his own expertise: rule 35.3(1). This duty is paramount and overrides any obligation to the person from whom the expert has received instructions or by whom he is paid: rule 35.3(2).
>
> 1.2 Expert evidence should be the independent product of the expert uninfluenced by the pressures of litigation.
>
> 1.3 An expert should assist the court by providing objective, unbiased opinion on matters within his expertise, and should not assume the role of an advocate.
>
> 1.4 An expert should consider all material facts, including those which might detract from his opinion.
>
> 1.5 An expert should make it clear:
>
> (a) when a question or issue falls outside his expertise; and
>
> (b) when he is not able to reach a definite opinion, for example because he has insufficient information.
>
> 1.6 If, after producing a report, an expert changes his view on any material matter, such change of view should be communicated to all the parties without delay, and when appropriate to the court.

The expert's report must contain a statement that he understands and has complied with his primary duty to the court.

The expert's fee should in no way depend upon the success of the party instructing him in the matter.

## 11.5 Case management and the use of experts

### 11.5.1 General principles

As mentioned in **11.1** above, a party will be allowed to use expert evidence only where it is reasonably required to resolve the proceedings and where permission has been given by the court. The following should be noted:

(a) Generally, permission will be sought in the allocation questionnaires and will be given in the directions made by the court for the management of the case (see **11.5.3**). The directions made on allocation will stipulate the field of expertise of the expert and, if already known, the name of the expert. If necessary, further directions relating to the use of experts may be given on listing or upon the application of a party.

(b) Usually, the claimant's solicitor will be obliged to instruct an expert before permission is given by the court for the use of that expert. In clinical negligence and disease and illness claims, it will be necessary for the claimant's solicitor to instruct an expert in order to advise in relation to liability and/or causation before the letter of claim is sent and, in almost all cases, a medical report will be attached to the particulars of claim. This is well understood by the court, and there is unlikely to be a problem in obtaining permission for the use of such an expert. Solicitors instructed by both claimants and defendants should give careful consideration as to whether it is necessary to instruct any other expert prior to permission being given. The court may decide that expert evidence is not required at all, or may determine that a single joint expert should be used. The client should be informed of the risks of instructing an expert before permission has been given, ie that he may not be permitted to use the expert's evidence and costs relating to that expert will not be recoverable even where the client is successful in the claim.

(c) At trial, expert evidence is to be given by means of a written report unless the court gives permission for the expert to give oral evidence. In fast track cases, permission will be given only if it is necessary in the interests of justice (CPR, r 35.5) and, if allowed, will be restricted to a maximum of one per party in no more than two specialist fields (CPR, 26.6(5)).

(d) A party will be entitled to use the report or call the expert at trial only if the report has been disclosed to the other parties to the action in accordance with CPR, r 35.13.

(e) The PAP for personal injury claims encourages the joint selection of experts, mostly medical experts for quantum purposes but also experts dealing with liability, where appropriate (PAP, para 2.14). In accordance with para 3.15, before a party instructs an expert, he must provide his opponent with a list of one or more experts whom he considers to be suitable for the case. In many cases, the claimant's solicitor will do this in the letter of claim and three names are usually supplied. The defendant then has 14 days within which to communicate any objections he has to any expert appearing on the list, and the claimant's solicitor is thereby able to select a mutually acceptable expert. The expert is instructed only by the claimant's solicitor (and in this respect, joint selection differs from joint instruction as envisaged by CPR, r 35.7 – see (f) below), but there is a presumption in fast track cases that the defendant will not be permitted to instruct his own expert in relation to that issue. The defendant is provided with a copy of the report and may send written questions to the expert, the answers to which must be sent by the expert directly to the defendant (PAP, para 3.21). Where the defendant objects to all the experts suggested by the claimant, he may instruct his own expert. However, if the matter proceeds, the court will consider whether the defendant acted reasonably in this regard.

(f) Where the parties wish to submit expert evidence on a particular issue, the court has the power, under CPR, 35.7, to direct that a single joint expert be used. See **11.5.2** below.

## 11.5.2 The single joint expert

In fast track cases, the court is likely to direct that a single joint expert be used unless there is good reason not to do so (PD 28, para 3.9(4)). Similar wording is used in PD 29, para 4.10(4) in relation to multi-track cases, but the insertion of the words 'on any appropriate issue' reflects the reality that there will be more issues in a multi-track case which will not be suitable for a single joint expert to determine. Single joint experts are more likely to be used to determine issues in relation to quantum than issues relating to liability or causation. In clinical negligence and illness and disease cases, it is recognised that single joint experts are less likely to be acceptable to the parties, and the pre-action protocols state that the courts are less prescriptive as to the use of experts in these types of claim.

Where the parties are unable to agree who the single joint expert should be, the court may select an expert from a list provided by the parties, or direct how the expert should be selected (CPR, 35.7(3)). In accordance with CPR, 35.8, where the use of a single joint expert is ordered, each party may give instructions to the expert and, where he does so, supply a copy of those instructions to the other side. Unless the court otherwise directs, the instructing parties are jointly and severably liable for the expert's fees and expenses.

### 11.5.3 Directions relating to the use of experts

In fast track cases, standard directions given on allocation in relation to expert evidence will order the use of the written report of a single joint expert or, where permission is given for the parties to use their own experts, order the disclosure of experts' reports by way of simultaneous exchange (usually within 14 weeks of allocation). Where the reports are not agreed, a discussion between the experts in accordance with CPR, r 35.12(1) and the preparation of a report under r 35.12(3) (PD 28, para 3.9) are required. In addition, the court may direct that a party put written questions to an expert instructed by another party or to a single joint expert about his report (CPR, r 35.6). Bearing in mind the tight timetable between allocation and trial (30 weeks), little time will be available for these steps.

Directions in multi-track cases are tailored to the requirements of each individual case and are likely to be more complex. Where the parties are permitted to use their own experts on any issue, typical directions will include:

(a) exchange of reports, either simultaneously or sequentially;

(b) the service of written questions to the experts and the service of answers;

(c) the agreement of expert reports where possible;

(d) where agreement is not possible, a without prejudice meetings between the experts in order to try to resolve the matters upon which they are unable to agree, and the subsequent filing of a report setting out the points upon which they agree and disagree;

(e) permission for the experts to give oral evidence at trial or that the reports shall stand as evidence.

The time allowed for each step outlined above will be dependent upon the complexities of the individual case and, in some cases, the availability of the experts themselves.

## 11.6 How to find an expert

It is vital that the solicitor responsible instructs the correct person to provide expert evidence in the case. Many firms will have their own in-house directory of experts, which should be referred to in the first instance. Frequently, other fee-earners will have inserted comments about the expert alongside the entry in the directory. Information such as how well the expert gave evidence in court, can be extremely useful. If an in-house directory of experts is not available or is inappropriate then other sources can be used.

The following sources may also be of use:

(a) The Association of Personal Injury Lawyers. This organisation provides information to members on appropriate experts.

(b) Action against Medical Accidents (AvMA)

(c) The Academy of Expert Witnesses.

(d) The Society of Expert Witnesses.

(e) Expert Witness Institute.

(f) The *New Law Journal* and *Solicitor's Journal* regularly issue expert witness supplements which carry advertisements from experts who are prepared to provide reports for the purposes of litigation.

(g) Many professional institutes also prepare a directory of expert witnesses.

(h) The Medico-Legal Society publishes reports which may reveal the name of a suitable expert.

### 11.6.1 The use of medical agencies

Increasingly, solicitors rely on medical agencies to source suitable experts to write reports. The rise in popularity of medical agencies has come about due to the growth of large personal injury practices which accept claims from clients anywhere in England and Wales. It is necessary to find a medical expert (or better still a choice of experts in the same specialism) who is sufficiently local to the home of the client. Without the assistance of a national agency to co-ordinate this search, this would represent something of a headache for the claimant's solicitor.

Medical agencies are able to provide a choice of experts local to the client, and they will send copies of the CVs of those experts direct to the solicitor, together with an indication of the waiting time for preparation of the report. Subject to the arrangement they have with the instructing solicitor, they may also attempt to agree the choice of expert with the defendant insurer direct, obtain the client's medical records, arrange the medical appointment for the client and forward the subsequent report direct to the solicitor. The agency will charge a fee for this service which, if reasonable, will be allowed as part of the disbursements incurred on the claim at assessment of costs stage.

In the case of *Woollard v Fowler* [2006] EWHC 90051 (Costs), 12 April 2006, the court held that it was entirely proper that a payment made by a solicitor to such an agency should be treated as a disbursement under the fixed costs regime in section II of Part 45 of the CPR 1998, and therefore as recoverable in full from the losing party.

The PAP for personal injury claims states that where a claimant wishes to use a medical agency, the defendant's prior consent should be sought and, if the defendant so requests, the medical agency should provide in advance the names of the doctors whom they are considering instructing (para 2.15).

## 11.7 Key qualities to look for in an expert

A number of key qualities must be looked for when selecting an expert:

(a) Is the individual appropriately qualified to deal with the matter and does he have the relevant practical experience in the area? If not, the court is unlikely to consider him to be an expert.

(b) Can the expert be regarded as impartial? In *Liverpool Roman Catholic Archdiocesan Trust v Goldberg* [2001] Lloyd's Rep PN 518, the evidence of an expert was disregarded due to his close relationship with the defendant.

(c) Is the expert usually instructed on behalf of defendants when you are instructed by a claimant, or vice versa? Although all experts have an overriding duty to the court and should give the same evidence in a particular case no matter who is instructing them, it is unwise to instruct an expert who has an impressive record of appearing against the type of client you are representing.

(d) Does the expert have sufficient time to deal with the case properly? A good expert will refuse instructions when he has insufficient time, but this will not always happen. Whether the case is a personal injury or clinical negligence claim, the expert will have to spend considerable time on the matter, either examining the papers or the claimant, or inspecting a vehicle, a piece of machinery or the scene of the accident.

(e) Can the expert provide a clear and comprehensive report?

(f) Does the expert have experience in litigation of this type? Does he prepare reports and attend at trial regularly to give evidence? Only a small percentage of cases proceed to trial, and thus an expert may claim to have been involved in, say, 200 cases but may have given evidence in only a few of them (especially as, in the fast track, expert evidence is normally given in written form). It cannot be assumed that the case will settle and, however good the written report might be, convincing oral testimony (where allowed by the court) and the ability to withstand tough cross-examination are essential. The expert's general reputation should be checked with his colleagues who practise in the same area.

## 11.8 Preliminary enquiries of the expert

Once a party has decided to instruct an expert in relation to any issue in a case and an appropriate expert has been identified, the solicitor should approach the expert with a number of preliminary enquiries, in order to establish whether he is willing and able to act in relation to the matter. Some health practitioners may be reluctant to provide reports for claimants in clinical negligence cases, and their views on this must be obtained. Even if the expert has been used by the solicitor before, it is good practice to send a preliminary letter to establish whether the proposed expert has any personal or professional connection with others who may be involved in the case, such as one of the parties, a health professional who is alleged to have been negligent or experts instructed by another party. Even though experts have an overriding duty to the court, it is preferable to avoid any possibility of bias or allegations of bias.

The preliminary letter to the expert might usefully cover the following matters:

(a) request confirmation that the expert deals with the appropriate speciality and has the necessary qualifications and experience;

(b) request confirmation that he is willing to accept instructions to provide a report and, where time is an important consideration, details of when the report will be available;

(c) request confirmation that the expert is prepared to carry out any necessary post-initial report work, such as attending conference with counsel and attending experts' meetings;

(d) request confirmation that he would be willing to provide oral evidence to support his written report, if required;

(e) inform the expert of the identity of the potential defendant and, in a clinical negligence claim, the name of any health professional who is alleged to have been negligent;

(f) obtain details of the expert's charging rate and/or to explain that the client has the benefit of public funding; and

(g) confirm on whose behalf the solicitor is acting (but without giving any view on liability).

(h) where the expert is a medical expert and relevant medical records have been obtained, confirm that this is the case (however, they must not be forwarded to the expert at this stage);

If the expert is prepared to act in response to an initial letter of enquiry then a full letter of instruction should be sent.

## 11.9 Letter of instruction

The nature of the letter of instruction to a medical expert will, of course, be determined by what it is the expert is required to do.

### 11.9.1 Medical experts in relation to quantum

Generally, in an RTA claim or an EL claim not involving illness or disease, the only medical expert instructed will be required to examine the claimant in order to provide a condition and prognosis report for quantum purposes. Medical experts will also be required for quantum purposes in clinical negligence and disease and illness claims. The specimen letter of instruction to a medical expert which is set out at Annex C to the PAP for personal injury claims (see **Appendix 2**) is suitable for this purpose.

It may be necessary to provide the expert with copies of the claimant's medical records where they relate to the injuries sustained and/or the treatment received by the claimant as a result of the defendant's negligence, or where there is a pre-existing condition which may have an impact on the assessment of damages. However, the claimant's solicitor should bear in mind the best practice guidance as set out in **10.4.1.3** and seek to obtain the claimant's medical records only where they are necessary, particularly where claims have a value of less than £10,000.

The heading of the letter should contain: the client's full name, address, date of birth, date of the accident, his telephone number and, if considered appropriate, details of the hospital where the client was treated. It is important that the letter of instruction makes it clear on whose behalf the solicitor is acting and whether the notice of appointment should be sent directly to the claimant or via his solicitor.

Where a defendant is given permission to instruct an expert to examine the claimant and provide a report on condition and prognosis, specific questions included in the letter of instruction may require the expert to comment, for example, on the reasonableness of the special damages claim, ie did the client reasonably need assistance with gardening and, if so, for how long?

## 11.9.2 Medical experts in relation to liability and causation

In clinical negligence and disease and illness claims, it will be necessary to instruct a medical expert of an appropriate speciality to advise in relation to liability and/or causation. These experts may not need to examine the claimant and their expert opinion will be primarily based on the claimant's medical records, copies of which should be enclosed. The letter of instruction may include the following matters:

(a) a chronology of the events/factual resumé to which the expert can refer. A concise overview of the events should be available for the expert to consider;

(b) a brief explanation of the relevant standard of care, with reference to the *Bolam* test as modified by *Bolitho* (see **5.3**). In the case of *Sharpe v Southend Health Authority* [1997] 8 Med LR 299, the Court of Appeal stated that an expert in a clinical negligence case should make it clear in his report whether the approach adopted by the defendant was in accordance with a responsible body of medical practitioners, even if he himself would have adopted a different approach. If it is not known that the expert is aware of this point, then this must also be mentioned in the letter of instruction;

(c) a reminder that it will be necessary to establish a causational link between the identified negligence and injury;

(d) an offer for the expert to meet the claimant if he so wishes. This may not be necessary but the facility should be made available;

(e) the date by which the report is needed;

(f) who is responsible for the fee;

he shld note if something important is missing. –

(g) a request that the expert consider whether all relevant notes have been disclosed and, if not, what further notes should be obtained;

(h) a request that the expert advise as to whether any other type of expert evidence is required in addition to his own;

(i) a request that the expert make reference to medical publications to support his case. The expert should be asked to refer to texts and authoritative works that were available at the time of the incident (see *Breeze v Ahmed* [2005] EWCA Civ 223);

(j) specific questions that the expert is required to answer;

(k) a reminder that the expert may be required to attend a conference with counsel at the appropriate time;

(l) a reminder as to how the doctor should structure the report.

The medical notes must not be sent to the expert without first being checked by the solicitor to ensure that they are complete and in order. Identical ring binders should be prepared, with copies of paginated medical notes included, in date order, indexed and divided into relevant sections. A ring binder of notes should be prepared for each expert, counsel and the solicitor.

## 11.10 The expert's report

Practice Direction 35, para 2.2 states that an expert's report must:

> (1) give details of the expert's qualifications;
>
> (2) give details of any literature or other material which the expert has relied on in making the report;
>
> (3) contain a statement setting out the substance of all facts and instructions given to the expert which are material to the opinions expressed in the report or upon which those opinions are based;
>
> (4) make clear which of the facts stated in the report are within the expert's own knowledge;
>
> (5) say who carried out any examination, measurement, test or experiment which the expert has used for the report, give the qualifications of that person, and say whether or not the test or experiment has been carried out under the expert's supervision;
>
> (6) where there is a range of opinion on the matters dealt with in the report –
>
> (a) summarise the range of opinion, and
>
> (b) give reasons for his own opinion;
>
> (7) contain a summary of the conclusions reached;
>
> (8) if the expert is not able to give his opinion without qualification, state the qualification; and
>
> (9) contain a statement that the expert understands his duty to the court, and has complied and will continue to comply with that duty.

In relation to the requirement for a statement of the substance of the instructions given to the expert, it should be noted that r 35.10(4) specifically states that the instructions are not privileged. However, the court will not normally allow cross-examination of the expert on the instructions, unless it believes the statement is inaccurate (see also *Lucas v Barking, Havering and Redbridge Hospitals NHS Trust* [2003] EWCA Civ 1102, [2003] All ER (D) 379 (Jul)).

Once an expert's report has been received, it should be read (and understood) by the solicitor and sent to the client for his approval. It should then be disclosed to the other party in accordance with the order for directions.

A specimen medical report can be found at **Appendix 1(7)**.

## 11.11 Conference with expert and counsel where expert instructed by one party

### 11.11.1 The initial conference prior to proceedings being issued

#### 11.11.1.1 Personal injury

An initial conference prior to proceedings being issued is not normally necessary in personal injury cases, but consideration should be given to this approach if the claimant is resistant to the solicitor's advice that the claim is likely to fail, or if the matter is unusually complicated.

#### 11.11.1.2 Clinical negligence and illness and disease claims

In clinical negligence and illness and disease cases, because the issues involved are likely to be complex, it may be appropriate to arrange a conference with the expert, counsel and the client after the initial medical report on liability and/or causation has been provided. This will provide an opportunity to examine all the issues in full, to test the expert's evidence and ensure that he is the appropriate person to be instructed, and to determine whether proceedings should be issued. An initial conference at this stage is also appropriate when the medical report is unfavourable and it appears that the claim should not proceed.

The conference also provides a valuable opportunity to satisfy the client that every possibility has been investigated, that he is not being sidelined by the legal process and that there is no medical conspiracy against him.

Consideration should be given to instructing counsel to produce a written advice following the conference, to ensure that all matters have been dealt with. During the conference, a detailed note should be taken of matters covered. This note should be sent to all the experts who attended the conference to confirm that it accurately records the views they expressed.

If the case is going to proceed, the next stage is the drafting of the letter of claim which is to be sent to the potential defendant.

### 11.11.2 Conference with counsel after proceedings issued

#### 11.11.2.1 Personal injury

In the vast majority of personal injury cases, proceedings will be issued without the need for a conference with counsel, and many low-value cases proceed to trial without such a conference. In more complex personal injury cases, the solicitor and counsel will want to be sure that the expert has studied all the papers sent to him, has understood the facts of the case, and that he has excellent communication skills. These and other matters can be assessed at a conference.

#### 11.11.2.2 Clinical negligence

In addition to the conference prior to the issue of proceedings in a clinical negligence case, it is common to have a further conference after the exchange of lay witness statements to check whether all the experts can still support the case. A further conference is normally arranged prior to the trial to review matters.

## 11.12 Conclusion

The role that the expert has in a personal injury or clinical negligence case is a significant one. The importance of the selection of the correct individual cannot be overestimated.

## 11.13 Further reading

Kemp and Kemp, *The Quantum of Damages* (Sweet & Maxwell)

Pre-action Protocol for Personal Injury Claims

Pre-action Protocol for the Resolution of Clinical Disputes

Protocol for the Instruction of Experts to Give Evidence in Civil Claims

## 11.14 Key points

| | |
|---|---|
| Expert evidence | Will be restricted to that which is necessary, and permission of the court is always required either to call an expert or to use an expert's report. |
| How to find an expert | In-house directory.<br>Recommendation.<br>Organisations: APIL/AvMA. |
| Qualities of an expert | Important to pick the correct expert – experience, time, cost and availability. |
| Who instructs? | Note: CPR 1998, Part 35. Joint instruction/selection – obligations under personal injury PAP. See example letter of instruction. |
| Clinical negligence | More complex. Report on liability, report on causation/report on quantum. Need to be of correct speciality and status. |
| CPR 1998 requirements | Reports need to contain certain specified points. See Part 35 and relevant PDs. |

# Chapter 12
# Commencement of Proceedings



## 12.1 Introduction

Where the defendant has denied liability, or where he has failed to respond within the time limits set out in the relevant pre-action protocol (see **10.2**), the claimant is entitled to commence proceedings by issuing and serving the claim form.

It is usually to the claimant's advantage to begin proceedings early for the following reasons:

(a) To avoid problems with the limitation period. In personal injury litigation, proceedings must normally be commenced within three years of the accident occurring (see **Chapter 7**). Ongoing negotiations with the proposed defendant/defendant's insurers do not have the automatic effect of extending the limitation period, and in any event, negotiations may continue after proceedings have been commenced.

(b) To avoid further delay in so-called 'long-tail' occupational disease and illness claims, and in some clinical negligence claims where claimants will be relying on a later date of knowledge in order to overcome limitation problems. Claimants may have suffered from poor health for many years, and it is important that their claims are progressed with expediency.

(c) To exert pressure on the defendant/defendant's insurers to act in relation to the claim. In personal injury cases, it will often precipitate the defendant's file moving from the insurance company claims department to the insurer's nominated solicitors, who may be more willing to negotiate.

(d) In practice, judgment usually carries entitlement to interest and costs. A settlement achieved prior to the commencement of proceedings does not carry such an entitlement (although the claimant's solicitor will always include in any such settlement an element in respect of interest and costs). After proceedings have been issued, if there is any argument by the defendant as to how much of the claimant's costs he should pay on settlement, the claimant's solicitor can have his costs assessed by the court.

(e) Commencing proceedings enables the claimant to apply to the court for an interim payment in the event that a voluntary payment cannot be negotiated.

## 12.2 Pre-issue checklist

Unless the limitation period is about to expire (in which case see **7.9.2**), proceedings should not be commenced until the claimant's solicitor is satisfied that:

(a) the period allowed by the relevant pre-action protocol for the defendant to respond to the letter of claim has expired and either the defendant has not responded or the defendant has denied liability;

(b) a full investigation of the matter has been conducted and the claimant's solicitor is in possession of all relevant evidence in relation to liability and quantum;

(c) a re-evaluation of the risk assessment has been carried out which takes into account the defendant's response to the letter of claim, the documents supplied by him and other evidence obtained following the dispatch of the letter of claim. Where the risk assessment indicates that the claim is unlikely to succeed, the claimant's solicitor should not issue proceedings but should try to settle the matter, if at all possible;

(d) the requirements of the relevant pre-action protocol have been complied with. In particular, an approach has been made to the proposed defendant with the aim of settling the matter without the need for litigation;

(e) the claimant's solicitor is ready to process the claim once proceedings have started, in accordance with the directions and the associated timetable which will be set out by the court on allocation. The court will actively manage the claim and, in fast track cases in particular, there will be limited time to prepare for each stage of the proceedings. The court will not be best pleased if the claimant's solicitor is unable to keep to the timetable due to inadequate preparation prior to issue;

(f) where the client has before the event insurance (BEI) or after the event insurance (AEI), the insurer has given permission for proceedings to be commenced;

(g) in clinical negligence claims which are being funded by the LSC from the Community Legal Services Fund (the CLSF), the certificate covers the issue of proceedings; and

(h) the claimant understands the situation and has given his instructions for the matter to proceed.

## 12.3 Matters to consider upon issue

Additional steps must be taken in certain circumstances before, at the time of, or shortly following the issue of proceedings. The claimant's solicitor needs to be suitably organised before proceedings are issued, as the consequences of failing to carry out the required steps may be severe.

### 12.3.1 Medical report and schedule of past and future loss and expense

A medical report and a schedule setting out past and future loss and expense should be served with the particulars of claim. Medical experts can be extremely busy and there may be a lengthy delay in obtaining an appointment for the claimant. Schedules in relation to substantial claims may be complex and cannot be put together overnight. Bearing in mind the fact that the particulars of claim must be served within 14 days of service of the claim form, the claimant's solicitor should be wary of issuing proceedings until these documents are available.

### 12.3.2 Notice of funding by CFA/AEI policy

When issuing proceedings in a case being funded by a conditional fee agreement (CFA) and/ or an AEI, regard must be had to the requirement to give notice that the matter is being funded in this way (see **9.2.2.7** and **10.7.3**). Where a claimant has entered into a CFA or has obtained an AEI policy prior to issue, he should file with the court and serve upon the defendant a Notice of Funding in Form N251 (see **Appendix 1(12)**). The Notice should set out the date the CFA was entered, the date the AEI policy was obtained, the policy number, and the name and address of the insurer. It should not reveal the amount of the success fee or insurance premium, as this would give the defendant insight into the claimant's solicitor's view of the strengths or otherwise of the claimant's case.

### 12.3.3 Notice of Legal Aid Certificate

In clinical negligence cases funded by the LSC from the CLAF (see **9.2.1.2**), where proceedings are issued and the claimant has not yet served notice of the issue of the certificate on the defendant, the claimant must now serve notice, in the prescribed form, and file a copy at court.

### 12.3.4 Notice in road traffic cases: Road Traffic Act 1988, ss 151 and 152

In RTA claims, where the claimant is entitled to require an insurance company to settle the judgment under s 151 of the Road Traffic Act 1988 (see **3.3.1** and **10.3.1.3**), the claimant must give the insurer notification of the claim under s 152, either before or within seven days of the commencement of the claim. It makes sense to give this notification as soon as possible, although some solicitors may chose to wait until commencement and then serve the notice on the insurers with a copy of the claim form and particulars of claim. There is no prescribed form for the notice.

### 12.3.5 Notice to MIB: Uninsured Drivers Agreement 1999

Where proceedings are being commenced against an uninsured driver and the claimant seeks to enforce the judgment against the MIB in accordance with the Uninsured Drivers Agreement 1999, the claimant must give the MIB notice in writing that he has commenced proceedings. This notice, together with the completed application form and documents in support, must be received by the MIB no later than 14 days after commencement of proceedings. Service must be either by facsimile transmission, or by registered or recorded delivery post to the MIB's registered office. (See **3.4.1.2**.)

## 12.4 Issuing proceedings

### 12.4.1 Where to issue

All tort proceedings can be issued in the county court. Proceedings which include a claim for damages for personal injury can be commenced in the High Court only where the total claim is worth at least £50,000 or, due to the complexity of the facts, legal issues, remedies or procedures involved or the importance of the outcome to the general public, the claimant believes it ought to be dealt with by a high court judge (CPR, PD 7, para 2). Article 5 of the High Court and County Courts Jurisdiction Order 1991 (SI 1991/724) states that this minimum value does not apply to proceedings in respect of an alleged breach of care committed in the course of the provision of clinical or medical services, which no doubt reflects the increased complexity of these types of cases and their importance to the general public.

Bearing in mind the possible costs consequences of starting a claim in the High Court which is subsequently transferred to the county court, it is perhaps advisable to commence personal injury claims and the more straightforward clinical negligence claims of a value of less than £50,000 in the county court. If a defence is filed, a request may be made in the allocation questionnaire for the matter to be transferred to the High Court should either party consider this to be appropriate (see **13.2.2**).

When calculating the value of the claim for commencement purposes, the claimant must disregard interest and costs, any possible counterclaim or finding of contributory negligence which may be made against him, and any recoupment of benefits by the Compensation Recovery Unit (CPR, r 16.3(6)).

The procedure for issuing proceedings is dealt with in ***Civil Litigation***.

### 12.4.2 Claim form – statements of value

In a claim for personal injuries, the claimant must state on the claim form whether the amount which he reasonably expects to recover in general damages for pain, suffering and loss of amenity is either not more than £1,000 or more than £1,000. This is to enable the court to allocate the claim to the correct track should a defence be filed (see **13.3**).

If a claim is to be issued in the High Court, it must state that the claimant reasonably expects to recover £50,000 or more; or must state that some other enactment provides that the claim may be commenced in the High Court and specify that enactment.

## 12.5 Particulars of claim

The particulars of claim must be contained in or served with the claim form, or be served on the defendant by the claimant within 14 days after service of the claim form. In any event, particulars of claim must be served on the defendant no later than the latest time for serving a claim form (ie, within four months after date of issue of the claim form).

It is vital that the particulars of claim are drafted carefully. They should set out the basis of the claim clearly, accurately and comprehensively. If they do not do this, the worst case scenario is that the claim will be struck out for failing to disclose reasonable grounds for bringing the claim (CPR, r 3.4(2)(a)) or summary judgment will be given against the claimant (CPR, r 24.2). At the very least, the claimant's solicitor will give an impression of sloppiness or incompetence.

### 12.5.1 Structure and content of the particulars of claim

The formalities set out in PD 5, para 2.2 and the main principles of drafting are discussed in ***Civil Litigation***. A suggested structure for particulars of claim in a personal injury case can be found at **12.15** below, and an example is included in the case study at **Appendix 1(10)**. Particulars of claim in clinical negligence cases and in more complex personal injury cases are generally drafted by counsel.

Rule 16.4 of the CPR and PD 16 deal with the contents of the particulars of claim. The particulars must include, *inter alia*:

(a) a concise statement of the facts on which the claimant relies. When drafting, it is useful to remember that the claimant will need to prove that the defendant owed him a duty of care and/or there was a statutory duty, that this duty was breached by the defendant, and that this caused injury and loss which was reasonably foreseeable. As far as is reasonably possible, the particulars should deal with these elements in separate, consecutively numbered paragraphs, with one allegation in each paragraph and in a chronological order.

   Although the CPR allow references to evidence and statutory provisions, the particulars should deal with the 'bare bones' of the claim, and it is therefore preferable not to include these details unless the information is specifically required. Four examples of where evidence or statutory provisions should be set out are as follows:

   (i) Where the claimant wishes to rely on the evidence of a medical expert, a medical report should be attached to the particulars (see (e) below).

   (ii) Where the claimant alleges breach of statutory duty, such as in an employer's liability case, the relevant statutory provisions should be set out.

(iii) Where the claimant relies on a criminal conviction of the defendant (see (b) below).

(iv) Where the claimant is seeking an order for provisional damages (see (g) below);

(b) where the claimant is relying on a relevant conviction of the defendant, the nature of the conviction, the date of conviction, and the name of the convicting court and the issue in the claim to which it relates;

(c) where the claimant is relying on a later date of knowledge for the purposes of limitation (see **Chapter** 7), details of the date of knowledge (PD 16, para 8.2);

(d) for the purposes of assessing damages, the claimant's date of birth and brief details of his injuries. The main points of the medical report can be summarised for this purpose but, especially in a high-value claim, it is important to ensure that all the relevant information is included, ie the immediate impact of the accident, the duration of any stay in hospital, the number and nature of any operations or other treatments, continuing pain and disability, the practical effects on the claimant's life, disability in the labour market, loss of congenial employment, etc;

(e) if the claimant wishes to rely on the evidence of a medical expert, a report detailing the injuries, which must be served with or attached to the particulars of claim;

(f) details of past and future expenses and losses, which should be provided in a schedule attached to the particulars;

(g) if the claimant is seeking provisional damages, a statement to that effect and his grounds for claiming them. Further guidance as to what must be set out is found in PD 16, para 4.4, namely:

(i) that the claimant is seeking the award under either s 32A of the Supreme Court Act 1981, or s 51 of the County Courts Act,

(ii) that there is a chance that at some future time he will develop some serious disease or suffer some serious deterioration in his physical or mental condition, and

(iii) the disease or type of deterioration in respect of which an application may be made at a future date;

(h) where the claim relates to a fatal accident, a statement by the claimant covering:

(i) the fact that it is brought under the FAA 1976;

(ii) the dependants on whose behalf the claim is made;

(iii) the date of birth of each dependant; and

(iv) details of the nature of the dependency claim.

The particulars of claim and the schedule of special damages must also contain a statement of truth, ie that the claimant (and if the claimant is acting as a litigation friend, the litigation friend) believes that the facts stated in the document are true. This may be signed by the claimant (or litigation friend), or by the solicitor on his behalf (CPR, r 22).

If the claimant seeks interest, a statement detailing the interest claimed must be included in the particulars of claim.

## 12.6 Service of proceedings

After the claim form has been issued, it must be served within four months after the date of issue. This may be extended, however, with leave of the court. If the claim form is to be served out of the jurisdiction, the period is six months.

See ***Civil Litigation*** for the rules governing the service of court documents.

## 12.7 Acknowledgement of service

The defendant may respond to the claim by:

(a) defending the claim; or
(b) admitting the claim; or
(c) acknowledging service of the claim form.

If the defendant makes no response to the claim, the claimant may enter default judgment.

Where the defendant is unable to file a defence in time, he may gain extra time by acknowledging service. The time for acknowledgement of service is 14 days from the service of the claim form, unless the claim form indicates that the particulars of claim are to follow separately, in which case the defendant does not have to acknowledge service until 14 days after service of those particulars of claim. The acknowledgement of service form must be signed by the defendant or his legal representative, and must include an address for service for the defendant which must be within the jurisdiction.

On receipt of such an acknowledgement of service, the court must notify the claimant in writing of this.

## 12.8 The defence

The defendant must file a defence within 14 days of service of the particulars of claim, or, if the defendant has filed an acknowledgement of service, within 28 days after service of the particulars of claim.

The parties may agree an extension of time for filing of the defence of up to 28 days. The defendant must give the court written notice of any such agreement.

### 12.8.1 Contents of the defence

The defence must deal with every allegation set out in the particulars of claim by admitting, denying or not admitting (neither admitting nor denying) each allegation. This will be an easier task if the particulars have dealt with one allegation per paragraph.

The following should also be noted.

(a) Where allegations are denied, the defendant must give reasons for that denial and, where relevant, give his own version of the facts. If the defendant disputes the claimant's statement of value, he must give reasons for doing so and, if possible, give his own estimate of value.
(b) The defence should make clear the defendant's version of the facts, in so far as it is different from that stated in the claim.
(c) Where the defendant wishes to rely on the fact that he took all reasonable care or on a statutory defence, such as s 58 of the Highways Act 1980, he should say so.
(d) Where the defendant claims that the claimant was himself negligent, and therefore contributed to the accident or increased the severity of his injuries, the particulars of the claimant's negligence should be set out in the defence.
(e) The defendant should give details of the expiry period of any limitation period on which he wishes to rely (PD 16, para 14.1).
(f) If the claimant has attached a medical report to his particulars of claim, the defendant should state whether he admits, denies or does not admit the matters contained in it, and give reasons for any matters he denies. For example, the defendant may claim that the claimant has failed to mitigate loss, that the injuries were not caused by the alleged negligence but rather by some pre-existing condition, or that the claimant has

fraudulently made or exaggerated the claim. If the defendant has obtained his own medical report on the claimant, he should attach it to the defence.

(g) If the claimant has attached a schedule of past and future expenses and losses to his particulars of claim, the defendant must include with his defence a counter-schedule stating which items he agrees, disputes, or neither agrees nor disputes but has no knowledge of. If items are disputed, an alternative figure must be supplied.

(h) The defence must contain a statement that the defendant, or, if the defendant is conducting proceedings with a litigation friend, the litigation friend, believes the facts stated in it are true. The statement of truth may be signed either by the defendant (or litigation friend), or by his legal adviser.

(i) Unless the defendant has already acknowledged service, the defendant must give an address for service which is within the jurisdiction.

## 12.9 The counterclaim

If a defendant wishes to make a counterclaim against a claimant, he should file his counterclaim with his defence (CPR, r 20.4). Provided the counterclaim is filed at the same time as the defence, the defendant will not need permission of the court to make the counterclaim. Generally, the counterclaim will form part of the same document as the defence and will follow on from the defence.

## 12.10 The reply to defence and defence to counterclaim

The claimant may file a reply to the defence, but if he does not do so, he will not be deemed to admit the matters raised in the defence. The reply must respond to any matters in the defence which have not been dealt with in the particulars of the claim, and must contain a statement of truth.

The claimant may file a reply and a certificate of reply when he files his allocation questionnaire (see **13.2**). If he does serve a reply, he must also serve it on all other parties.

Where there is a counterclaim and the claimant disputes the counterclaim, he must file a defence to it within the usual 14-day period. This will be way of a reply to the defence and a defence to the counterclaim. If the claimant does not file a defence to the counterclaim, the defendant will be entitled to enter judgment in respect of the counterclaim.

The particulars of claim, defence and reply are said to be the statements of case. No subsequent statements of case may be filed without the court's leave.

## 12.11 Amendment to statements of case

Sometimes, the claimant's solicitor may need to amend the particulars of claim. Where this arises before the particulars have been served on the defendant, the amendments may be made without the court's permission. On occasion, the defence may highlight a need for an amendment, for example the need to add a further defendant, or even to pursue a different defendant. Amendments may be made at any time after service, provided the defendant gives his written consent. Where consent is not forthcoming, the permission of the court must be sought (see CPR, rr 17 and 23).

In *Goode v Martin* [2001] EWCA Civ 1899, [2002] 1 WLR 1828, the claimant sought permission to amend her statement of claim after the expiry of the limitation period. The amendment consisted of a response to the defendant's version of events and no new facts were being introduced. The claimant also argued that if the amendment could not be allowed under a conventional approach to r 17.4, a less conventional approach should be adopted to comply with Article 6 of the European Convention on Human Rights.

The court found that because the claimant's new cause of action arose out of the same facts that were in issue in the original claim, she should be allowed to add to her claim the alternative plea proposed. The Court of Appeal agreed with the claimant that to prevent the claimant from putting her alternative case before the court would impose an impediment on her access to the court that would have to be justified. It was possible to interpret r 17.4 in such a way as to allow the claimant's amendment, and that should be done to comply with Article 6 of the Convention.

## 12.12 Additional claims (CPR 20.5)

In accordance with s 1(1) of the Civil Liability (Contribution) Act 1978, 'any person liable in respect of any damage suffered by another person may recover contribution from any other person liable in respect of the same damage (whether jointly with him or otherwise)'.

A solicitor acting for a defendant who wishes to claim an indemnity or a contribution from someone else in respect of the damages sought by the claimant, should take the appropriate steps to make that individual or body a party to the proceedings. This will enable the court to apportion blame and liability to pay damages, which it will do on a percentage basis. In order to bring another party into the proceedings, the claimant must comply with the procedure set out in CPR Part 20 and the accompanying Practice Direction. The aim of CPR Part 20 is to ensure that counterclaims and additional claims are managed in the most convenient and effective manner.

### 12.12.1 What are 'additional claims'?

Part 20 of the CPR deals with counterclaims, but it also gives rise to what are known as 'additional claims'. These are claims made by:

(a) a defendant who wishes to seek a contribution or an indemnity from a co-defendant. Once he has filed his acknowledgement of service or defence, the defendant may proceed with his additional claim against the co-defendant by filing a notice stating the nature and grounds of his claim and serving it upon the co-defendant. Provided he serves the notice with his defence, he will not require the court's permission. Otherwise, he must seek leave (CPR, r 20.6);

(b) a defendant who wishes to seek a contribution or an indemnity from someone who is not already a party to the proceedings (commonly known as 'third party proceedings'). The defendant must issue an additional claim and serve it on the third party, together with particulars of claim, the forms for defending and admitting the claim and acknowledging service, a copy of the statements of case which have been served in the main claim, and any other document the court directs. Provided the claim is issued before or at the same time as the defence is filed, the court's permission is not required. Otherwise, leave will be necessary (CPR, r 20.7);

(c) where an additional claim has been made against a third party, when that third party wishes to seek a contribution or an indemnity from someone else, whether or not already a party. Where a new party is introduced, the procedure is the same as in (b) above.

### 12.12.2 Obtaining permission to issue an additional claim

Where permission is required for an additional claim, an application notice must be filed and served. together with a copy of the proposed additional claim and a witness statement setting out the matters contained in PD 20, paras 2.1 to 2.3, namely:

(a) the stage the proceedings have reached;

(b) the nature of the additional claim to be made, or details of the question or issue which needs to be decided;

(c) a summary of the facts on which the additional claim in based;

(d) the name and address of the proposed additional party;

(e) where there has been a delay, an explanation for the delay. The court will be concerned to ensure that the late introduction of an additional party will not cause prejudice to any existing party; and

(f) a timetable of the proceedings to date.

### 12.12.3 Case management in relation to an additional claim

Where the defendant to an additional claim files a defence, a case management hearing will take place to enable the court to consider the future conduct of the proceedings. In accordance with PD 20, para 5.3, the court may treat the hearing as a summary judgment hearing, order that the Part 20 proceedings be dismissed and/or make appropriate directions.

### 12.12.4 Example of an additional claim

Carol was injured in a road traffic accident when her car was hit by a vehicle driven by Darren. Darren had failed to stop at a junction. Carol (the claimant) issued proceedings in negligence against Darren (the defendant). The day before the accident, Darren had taken his car to be serviced by Tyrone, who had fitted new brake pads. Darren alleges that when he tried to apply his brakes they failed to work, and this was the cause of the accident. Darren makes an additional claim against Tyrone (the third party). Tyrone alleges that the brakes failed because the brake pads he fitted to Darren's car, which were purchased from Fab-Brakes Limited, were defective. Tyrone makes an additional claim against Fab-Brakes Limited (the fourth party).

## 12.13 Group litigation

Engaging in group litigation is time-consuming, difficult and (therefore) costly. Group litigation results when there are a number of prospective claimants who have a common interest or common defendant arising out of a common incident. An example of group litigation is that brought by a number of families following the drowning of 51 passengers of the pleasure boat *Marchioness*, which sank after being hit by the dredger *Bowbelle* on the Thames in 1989.

The relevant rule of the CPR 1998 governing group litigation can be found at Part 19, with its accompanying PD 19B. Part 19 provides for the making of a group litigation order (GLO) at the request of the parties where there are, or are likely to be, a number of similar claims. The aim of the GLO is to 'steer' the group litigation by ensuring that the case is managed to suit the needs of multi-party litigation.

The GLO seeks to ensure that all cases that are eligible to join the group do so and are then all treated in like manner to ensure consistency of result. The GLO must include specific directions for the maintenance of a group register, specify the GLO issues, and appoint a particular court and particular judge to oversee the case management process. By giving one court/judge 'ownership' of the management process, the case can be more effectively managed than if all potential claimants were allowed to issue and deal with their case at any court of their choosing. The managing judge appointed to the group litigation will quickly amass specialist knowledge in relation to that particular group litigation, and will therefore be able to deal with matters as they arise more quickly and effectively.

The details of group litigation are beyond the scope of this book but recourse should be had, as a starting point, to PD 19B and to The Law Society's Multi-party Action Information Service.

## 12.14 Further reading

Curran, *Personal Injury Pleadings* (Sweet & Maxwell)

Bare, Copnall, Thorp and Axon, *APIL Model Pleadings and Applications* (Jordan Publishing)

## 12.15 Suggested structure of particulars of claim in personal injury case

Court inserts case number

**IN THE HIGH COURT OF JUSTICE ETC**

Parties

**PARTICULARS OF CLAIM**

- Describe parties to establish duty of care if necessary
- Succinctly describe what happened
- Allege breach of statutory duty/duty of care

**PARTICULARS OF BREACH OF STATUTORY DUTY**

Where relevant, set out the breaches with specific reference to the relevant statutory provisions. Be as comprehensive as possible.

**PARTICULARS OF NEGLIGENCE**

Set out what the defendant did or did not do which constitutes negligence. Be as specific as possible. Where you have set out breaches of statutory duty, state here 'The Claimant repeats the allegations of breach of statutory duty as allegations of negligence', then particularise negligence.

- Criminal conviction (if relevant) – nature of conviction, date of conviction, name of convicting court and the issue in the claim to which it relates
- Allege injury and loss caused

**PARTICULARS OF INJURY**

- Date of birth
- Summary of injuries, treatment and continuing effect on claimant
- Weakening in labour market (*Smith v Manchester*)
- Refer to attached medical report(s)

**PARTICULARS OF LOSS**

- Refer to attached schedule

- Claim for interest
- Remedies sought (the prayer)
  AND THE CLAIMANT SEEKS
- Statement of truth
- Ending

# Chapter 13
# Case Management and Interim Applications



## 13.1 Introduction

The court will actively manage cases in accordance with the overriding objective set out in r 1 of the CPR. This will take place during the 'interim stage', ie subsequent to the issue of the proceedings and prior to the trial. As far as the parties are concerned, the interim stage is taken up mainly with obtaining and then complying with the directions issued by the court, to ensure that the case is properly prepared for trial. In addition, circumstances may arise which require a party to make an interim application to the court. The following paragraphs deal with this stage as it relates to personal injury and clinical negligence claims. A detailed consideration of this area is given in ***Civil Litigation***.

## 13.2 Allocation questionnaire

Where a claim is defended, on receipt of the defence the court will serve each party with an allocation questionnaire. Each party must return the completed allocation questionnaire within 14 days, indicating which court they consider should deal with the matter and to which track the case should be allocated. The parties are encouraged by the CPR to agree directions, and where this happens, the claimant's solicitor should file a draft consent order for directions with the completed allocation questionnaire. If either of the parties fails to return the questionnaire or provides insufficient information in his statement of case or allocation questionnaire, the court may make an order for the party to provide further information or may hold an allocation hearing.

A specimen allocation questionnaire can be found at **Appendix 1(15)**.

### 13.2.1 Stay to allow settlement of case

A party returning his allocation questionnaire may request a stay of up to one month while the parties try to settle the case. Where all parties request a stay, or where the court, of its own initiative, considers such a stay would be appropriate, the court will direct a stay for one month. The court may also extend the period of the stay until such a date or such a period as it considers appropriate. If proceedings are settled during the stay, the claimant must inform the court.

### 13.2.2 Transfer of proceedings between courts

The court has the power to transfer cases between the High Court and the county courts and within district registries of the High Court (CPR, r 30.1). It may do so of its own volition, or upon application by a party to the proceedings. Where the matter has been commenced in the county court and a party believes that it is suitable for trial in the High Court or vice versa, it should set out its reasons in the allocation questionnaire (see **12.4.1**).

## 13.3 Allocation to track

In accordance with CPR, r 26.6, personal injury and clinical negligence claims are allocated to the appropriate track within a three-tier system largely in accordance with the value of the claim as a whole and the value of the claim for damages for 'personal injuries' suffered, ie that part of the damages which relates to pain, suffering and loss of amenity.

The *small claims track* is the normal track where:

(a) the value of the claim as a whole is not more than £5,000; and
(b) the value of any claim for damages for personal injuries is not more than £1,000.

The *fast track* is the normal track for any claim for which the small claims track is not the normal track and which has a value of:

(a) not more than £25,000 (for proceedings issued on or after 6 April 2009); and
(b) not more than £15,000 (for proceedings issued before 6 April 2009).

However, such a case will be allocated to the fast track only if the court considers that:

(a) the trial is likely to last for no longer than one day; and
(b) oral expert evidence at trial will be limited to one expert per party in relation to a maximum of two expert fields.

The *multi-track* is the normal track for any claim for which the small claims track or the fast track is not the normal track.

Once the court has allocated a claim to a track, it will notify all parties, and it will also serve them with copies of the allocation questionnaire provided by all other parties and a copy of any further information provided by a party about his case.

### 13.3.1 Factors taken into account

When allocating a case, the court may take into account the following factors (CPR, r 26.8(1)):

(a) the financial value of the claim (or amount in dispute if different);
(b) the nature of remedy sought;
(c) the likely complexity of the facts, law or evidence;
(d) the number of parties or likely parties;
(e) the value of any counterclaim or other claim and the complexity of any matters relating to it;
(f) the amount of oral evidence that may be required;
(g) the importance of the claim to persons who are not parties to the proceedings;
(h) the views expressed by the parties;
(i) the circumstances of the parties.

When assessing the value of the claim for the purposes of track allocation, the court will disregard any amounts not in dispute, interest, costs and any possible finding of contributory negligence which may be made against the claimant (CPR, r 26.8(2)).

If the statements of case are later amended and it becomes clear that the case has been allocated to an inappropriate track, the court may subsequently re-allocate a claim to a different track.

### 13.3.2 Transfer between tracks

When considering an application to re-allocate a case from one track to another, the court has an unfettered discretion under r 26.10 of the CPR (see *Maguire v Molin* [2002] EWCA Civ 1083, [2002] 4 All ER 325). In this case proceedings were issued with damages limited to £15,000. The claim was allocated to the fast track. Part way through the trial on liability the claimant's solicitors made an application to amend the statement of case to remove the £15,000 limit. The application was refused on the grounds that it had been made very late and that allowing it would disadvantage the defendant. On appeal, the Court of Appeal found that the judge at first instance had jurisdiction to allow the amendment and continue with the hearing of the issue of liability on the fast track. However, on the facts of the case the district judge reached the right decision in refusing to re-allocate the case.

The Court of Appeal gave the following guidance. Even though the value of a claim was important in determining where it should be held in the first place, so long as a claim remained in the fast track a district judge did have the right to hear it. A claim did not cease to be in the fast track simply because its value had been increased beyond £15,000. The amount by which the financial value of a claim exceeded the normal limit for a track as a result of an amendment was highly relevant. If the amount by which the limit had been exceeded had been small then it would not usually require re-allocation to the multi-track. However, if the amount were large then re-allocation would usually be necessary, even if that meant considerable delay to the litigation.

## 13.4 The small claims track

The small claims track has been specifically designed to enable individuals to pursue or defend a claim without the need to instruct solicitors. The Government considered raising the financial limits for small claims but, in July 2008, announced that it would not do so. A consideration of the procedure for these claims is beyond the scope of this book.

## 13.5 The fast track

When the court allocates a claim to the fast track, generally it will give standard directions for the management of the case, which will not be more than 30 weeks from allocation to trial. Usually a case management conference will not be necessary, although the parties should request such a hearing if the circumstances of the case make this desirable. Typical directions and the associated timetable in the fast track would be as follows:

| | |
|---|---|
| Disclosure | 4 weeks |
| Exchange of witness statements | 10 weeks |
| Exchange of experts' reports | 14 weeks |
| Pre-trial checklists, listing questionnaires sent out by court | 20 weeks |
| Pre-trial checklists, listing questionnaires filed by parties | 22 weeks |
| Trial | 30 weeks |

When giving directions relating to the trial, the court may fix a trial date but would more usually set a 'trial period', a three-week period within which the trial will take place.

The PAP for personal injury cases is specifically designed for fast track cases. The PAP for disease and illness claims acknowledges that these sort of claims are complex and frequently not suitable for fast track procedures, even where they fall within the fast track financial limits. Where clinical negligence claims are dealt with on the fast track, the PAPl applies.

## 13.6 The multi-track

Where the value of the claim is more than £25,000 (£15,000 if issued before 6 April 2009), or where other factors make it unsuitable for the fast track, the claim will be allocated to the multi-track. Claims will range from those which are just above the financial limit and which are fairly straightforward, to those of high value where the issues, evidence and law are extremely complex, and the court will adopt a flexible approach in order to manage the claim in accordance with its needs. When allocating a case to the multi-track, the court will either:

(a) use the information contained in the allocation questionnaires in order to give directions for case management and set a timetable; or

(b) fix a case management conference or a pre-trial review, or both, when it will hear from the parties and then give such directions relating to management of the case as it thinks fit.

Although, strictly speaking, the PAP for personal injury does do not apply to multi-track cases, the court will expect the parties to be bound by the spirit of the protocol, and will require an explanation where it has not been followed.

## 13.7 The case management conference and pre-trial review

Where the court decides that directions cannot be given without hearing directly from the parties, it may, at any time after the filing of the defence, fix a date for a case management conference and/or, after the return of the listing questionnaires, set a date for a pre-trial review (see **13.11**). Where a party is legally represented, any case management conference or pre-trial review called by the court must be attended by a legal representative who is familiar with the case and has the authority to take decisions regarding the management of the case. It is therefore important that the solicitors have obtained their client's instructions regarding all matters which are likely to be dealt with at the hearing. The court will expect the parties to be in a position to deal with all outstanding matters regarding the conduct of the case, and to reach an agreement regarding these matters wherever possible.

### 13.7.1 Case management in relation to an additional claim

Where the defendant to an additional claim (see **12.12**) files a defence, a case management hearing will take place to enable the court to consider the future conduct of the proceedings and give appropriate directions. It is obliged to ensure, in so far as it is practicable, that the original claim and all additional claims are managed together (CPR, r 20.13). In accordance with PD 20, para 5.3, at the hearing the court may:

(a) treat the hearing as a summary judgment hearing;

(b) order that the additional claim be dismissed;

(c) give directions about the way any claim, question or issue set out in or arising from the additional claim should be dealt with;

(d) give directions as to the part, if any, the additional defendant will take at the trial of the claim;

(e) give directions about the extent to which the additional defendant is to be bound by any judgment or decision to be made in the claim.

Paragraph 7 of PD 20 sets out how parties should be described in the proceedings when there are additional claims. In summary, the claimant and defendants in the original claim should be referred to as such, and additional parties should be referred to as 'Third Party' or 'Fourth Party', depending on the order in which they were joined to the proceedings.

## 13.8 Disclosure and inspection of documents

A party is not required to give more than standard disclosure unless the court otherwise orders (CPR Part 31).

Standard disclosure means that a party is required to disclose only:

(a) the documents on which he relies;

(b) the documents which could adversely affect his own case, adversely affect another's case or support another party's case; and

(c) all documents which he is required to disclose by any Practice Direction.

The court may dispense with or limit standard disclosure, and the parties can agree in writing to dispense with or limit any part of standard disclosure. The duty of standard disclosure continues throughout the proceedings, and if a document comes to a party's notice at any time, that party must immediately notify every other party. Privileged documents, however, should not be disclosed. See ***Civil Litigation***, for a detailed consideration of this area.

### 13.8.1 Procedure

Each party must make and serve a list of documents, which must identify the documents 'in a convenient order and manner as concisely as possible'. The list must indicate documents which are no longer in the parties' control and state what has happened to those documents.

The list must include a disclosure statement by the party:

(a) setting out the extent of the search made to locate the documents;

(b) certifying that he understands the duty of disclosure and that, to the best of his knowledge, he has carried out that duty.

### 13.8.2 Specific disclosure

Where a party believes that the other party has failed to carry out his duty of disclosure and inspection under CPR Part 31, he may apply for an order for specific disclosure under CPR, r 31.12. An order for specific disclosure can require a party to disclose specified documents or classes of documents, or carry out a search for specified documents and disclose any documents located as a result of that search.

An application for specific disclosure must be supported by evidence. The court will order specific disclosure only if necessary to dispose fairly of the claim or save costs.

For applications for an order for pre-action disclosure, see **10.9.2**.

## 13.9 The evidence of lay witnesses

As part of its management powers, the court will decide the issues on which it requires evidence, the nature of that evidence and the way in which the evidence should be placed before the court.

Facts should normally be proved at the trial by oral evidence of witnesses, and at any other hearing by the written evidence of witnesses. The court may allow a witness to give evidence by any means, which includes by means of a video link.

### 13.9.1 Procedure

According to CPR, r 32.4(1): 'A witness statement is a written statement signed by a person which contains the evidence which that person would be allowed to give orally.'

The court will normally give directions that each party serve the witness statements of the oral evidence on which he intends to rely at the trial. The directions usually envisage that simultaneous exchange will take place, but that court may give directions as to the order in which such witness statements are to be served and whether or not the statements are to be filed.

If a witness statement has been served and a party wishes to rely on that evidence at trial, the party must call the witness to give oral evidence unless the court otherwise orders.

### 13.9.2 Statements to stand as evidence-in-chief

Where a witness is called to give oral evidence, his statement shall stand as evidence-in-chief, unless the court orders otherwise.

The witness giving the oral evidence may amplify the witness statement, and give evidence in relation to new matters that have arisen since the statement was served. However, he may do this only if the court considers there is a good reason not to confine his evidence to the contents of the statement that has been served.

Evidence in proceedings other than at the trial should be by witness statement, unless the court or a particular Practice Direction otherwise directs.

### 13.9.3 Witness summary

Where a party is required to serve a witness statement and he is unable to obtain such a statement, for example because the witness refuses to communicate with the party's solicitor, he may apply to the court for permission to serve only a witness summary instead. This application should be made without notice. The witness summary is a summary of the evidence which would otherwise go into a witness statement, or, if the evidence is not known, matters about which the party serving the witness summary will question the witness.

Where a witness statement or a witness summary is not served, the party will not be able to call that witness to give oral evidence unless the court allows it.

## 13.10 Use of plans, photographs and models at trial

Where a party wishes to use evidence such as plans, photographs or models, or other evidence:

(a) which is not contained in a witness statement, affidavit or expert's report;

(b) which is not given orally at trial;

(c) which has already been disclosed in relation to hearsay evidence;

the party wishing to use the evidence must disclose his intention to do so not later than the latest date for serving witness statements (CPR, r 33.6).

If the evidence forms part of expert evidence, it must be disclosed when the expert's report is itself served on the other party. Having disclosed such evidence, the party must give every other party an opportunity to inspect it and agree its admission without further proof.

## 13.11 Expert evidence

The duties of experts in relation to court proceedings and the directions which the courts are likely to make are dealt with in r 35 of the CPR (see **Chapter 11** generally and **11.5** for case management and the use of experts).

## 13.12 Listing questionnaire

In accordance with the order for directions, the court will send each party a listing questionnaire to complete and return to the court by the date specified in the notice of allocation. The date specified for filing a listing questionnaire is not more than eight weeks before the trial date.

If a party fails to file a completed listing questionnaire within the time limit, or fails to give all of the information, or the court thinks it is necessary, the court may fix a listing hearing or give such other directions as it thinks appropriate.

On receipt of the parties' listing questionnaires, the court may decide to hold a pre-trial review, or cancel a pre-trial review if it has already decided to hold one, having regard to the circumstances of the case.

Using the information given in the listing questionnaires or at the pre-trial review or listing hearing, the court will set a timetable for the trial, including confirming or fixing the trial date and setting out any further steps that need to be taken by the parties prior to the trial.

The court will give each party at least three weeks' notice of the trial date. Only in exceptional circumstances will the notice period be shorter than this.

## 13.13 Variation of case management timetable

The parties may agree in writing to extend the dates for the carrying out of any steps set out in the directions subject to CPR, r 29.5. This states that if a party wishes to vary any of the dates which the court has fixed for:

(a) the case management conference;

(b) the pre-trial review;

(c) the return of listing questionnaires;

(d) the trial;

he may do so only with leave of the court. The parties should not agree to make any other variations to the timetable which would make it impossible for them to comply with the time limits set for the above steps.

## 13.14 Interim applications

Interim applications are applications which are made by either party between the issue of proceedings and trial. The general rules governing such applications are set out in CPR Part 23, but practitioners should be aware that some types of application are governed by specific rules. For a detailed consideration of interim applications, see ***Civil Litigation***. This text will deal with the following types of application:

(a) interim payments;

(b) specific disclosure – see **13.7.2** above; and

(c) specific disclosure against a non-party.

## 13.15 Interim payments

An interim payment is a payment made to the claimant, prior to the conclusion of the matter, in partial settlement of the claim. It is defined as 'a payment on account of any damages, debt or other sum (excluding costs) which that party may be held liable to pay to or for the benefit of another party to the proceedings if a final judgment or order of the court in the proceedings is given or made in favour of that other party' (Supreme Court Act 1981, s 32(5) and County Courts Act 1984, s 50(5)).

In a multi-track case where liability has been admitted or proven, or where the claimant can demonstrate a strong case on liability, an interim payment will assist in mitigating the effects of financial hardship caused by the often lengthy period between the accident and the determination of the claim. Interim payments are particularly important where the claimant has suffered catastrophic injuries or disablement and requires access to a substantial sum of money in order to pay for accommodation and/or a care regime.

An interim payment cannot be made in a small claims track case and, whilst not forbidden in a fast track case, will be rarely made due both to the value of the claim and to the relatively short period of time from issue of proceedings to trial.

Where the grounds for making an order are satisfied, the court has a discretionary power to order that the defendant make an interim payment under r 25.6 of the CPR. The order may specify that such payment be made by instalments, and more than one order may be made during the lifetime of a claim. Where the claimant is a child (see **19.3**) or a protected party, the payment will usually be made to the Court of Protection.

In accordance with CPR, r 25.9, where an interim payment has been made either voluntarily or pursuant to a court order, unless the defendant agrees, this shall not be disclosed to the trial judge until all questions of liability and quantum have been decided.

### 13.15.1 Grounds for making the order

In accordance with CPR, r 25.7(1), the court may order an interim payment only if:

(a) the defendant admits liability; or

(b) the claimant has a judgment for damages to be assessed; or

(c) if the matter were to proceed to trial, the claimant would obtain judgment for a substantial amount of money.

It is no longer the case that an order for an interim payment can only be made against an individual defendant who is insured, a public body or where liability will be met by the MIB. In all other cases, the court will take into account the defendant's ability to pay the interim payment before making an order.

In a claim where there are two or more defendants, the court may make an order for interim payment against any of them if it is satisfied that, if the claim went to trial, the claimant would obtain judgment for substantial damages against at least one of the defendants although it cannot determine which. It will do so only where all the defendants are either insured or they are a public body, or liability will be met by the MIB.

Although a claimant will normally set out in his application why the interim payment is required, he is not obliged to show that there is a *need* for the payment. In *Stringman v McCardle* [1994] 1 WLR 1653, Stuart-Smith LJ said: 'It should be noted that the plaintiff does not have to demonstrate any particular need over and above the general need that a plaintiff has to be paid his or her damages as soon as reasonably may be done.'

### 13.15.2 Procedure

Before making an application to the court for an interim payment, the claimant's solicitor should contact the defendant's solicitor and request that the defendant make a voluntary interim payment. The defendant may be amenable to such a request; if the payment is to fund treatment or rehabilitation costs, this may reduce the final award of damages and interest payments will be reduced. However, where the claimant is a child or protected party, the permission of the court is required before an interim payment is made (PD 25B, para 1.2).

A claimant may not seek an interim payment until after the time for acknowledging service has expired.

The application should be made using Form N244 and must be supported by evidence. Although the evidence may be set out on the application form itself, generally it will be set out in a witness statement. Paragraph 2.1 of PD25B states that the evidence must deal with the following:

(1) the sum of money sought by way of an interim payment,

(2) the items or matters in respect of which the interim payment is sought,

(3) the sum of money for which final judgment is likely to be given,

(4) the reasons for believing that the conditions set out in rule 25.7 are satisfied,

(5) any other relevant matters,

(6) in claims for personal injuries, details of special damages and past and future loss, and

(7) in a claim under the Fatal Accidents Act 1976, details of the person(s) on whose behalf the claim is made and the nature of the claim.

Paragraph 2.2 of PD 25B states that any documents in support of the application should be exhibited, including, in personal injuries claims, the medical report(s).

The application notice and witness statement in support must be served on the defendant (the respondent) at least 14 days before the return date for the application. If the defendant wishes to rely on a witness statement in response to the application, he must file and serve a copy of that witness statement at least seven days before the hearing; and if the claimant (the applicant) wishes to file a further witness statement in reply, he must do so at least three days before the hearing.

Where the claimant has been in receipt of recoverable benefits which will fall to be repaid by the defendant to the Compensation Recovery Unit (CRU) (see **Chapter 16**), the defendant should obtain a certificate of recoverable benefits and file this with the court.

### 13.15.3 The amount of the interim payment

When dealing with an application for an interim payment, the court will seek to avoid making an overpayment which may lead to the claimant having to repay money to the defendant (see **13.15.4**). In accordance with CPR, r 25.7(4) and (5), the amount of the interim payment must not exceed a reasonable proportion of the likely amount of the final judgment, taking into account contributory negligence and any relevant set-off or counterclaim.

Where there is a large discrepancy between what the claimant and the defendant believe will be ultimately awarded, the court will first look at the amount of special damages which have already accrued and the amount of special damages which will arise prior to the date of trial. There can be a large degree of certainty as to the likely amount of damages to be awarded in this respect. The court will then attempt to determine what the court is likely to award in respect of pain, suffering and loss of amenity, etc, and future loss of earnings and costs of care, which is much more speculative.

Defendants have sought to limit the size of interim payments by arguing:

(a) that allowing substantial interim payments to cover the cost of purchasing new accommodation and/or an expensive care regime, in circumstances where the defendant argues that the accommodation or care regime is excessive for the claimant's needs, distorts the 'level playing filed' against defendants. When quantum is ultimately considered by the court, it is considerably harder for the defendants to argue this point when the accommodation has already been purchased and the care regime is up and running, and where expert witnesses are able to give evidence as to how the claimant's needs are being met. In *Spillman v Bradfield Riding Centre* [2007] EWHC 89, the claimant, a minor, suffered serious head injuries when she was kicked by a horse at the defendant's riding school. The application for an interim payment to fund special care and to enable her parents to purchase a larger house, which they argued was necessary for her benefit, was rejected at first instance. At appeal, the defendant unsuccessfully argued that if the interim payment was ordered in the amount sought by the claimant, the head of damage would become self-fulfilling as, at the date of trial, the claimant would have benefitted from the accommodation and care to which the defendants argued she was not entitled;

(b) that allowing a substantial interim payment may prevent the court at trail from awarding periodical payments (see **15.5**) because there will be insufficient damages left to be paid. This argument is particularly relevant to cases where the claimant's life expectancy has been reduced significantly. Where it is likely that the final judgment would involve an order for periodical payments to be made, the court has to consider what is the 'likely amount' for the purposes of CPR, r 25.7(4). In *Braithwaite v Homerton University Hospitals Foundation Trust* [2008] EWHC 353 (QB), the court held that the amount of the final judgment was the capital sum plus a periodical sum payable during the life of the claimant. Consequently, the court must be confident that the amount of the proposed interim payment is not in excess of the capital sum ultimately awarded at trail.

There is no rule as to what constitutes a 'reasonable proportion', but decided cases appear to suggest that the courts will order a maximum of 75% of the likely final award of damages.

For guidance in cases where an interim payment is sought and where the final judgment is likely to include a periodical payment order, see the Court of Appeal's judgment in *Cobham Hire Services Ltd v Eeles* [2009] EWCA Civ 204.

It should be noted that where recoverable benefits have been received by the claimant, he will receive the interim payment net of the amount of the benefits. The defendant will pay an amount equal to the recoverable benefits to the CRU.

### 13.15.4 Repayment and variation

In accordance with r 25.8 of the CPR, where a defendant has made an interim payment either voluntarily or pursuant to an order, the court may order that all or part of that sum be repaid by the claimant, or that the defendant be reimbursed by another defendant.

In addition, where a defendant makes an interim payment which it transpires exceeds his liability under the final judgment, the court may award interest on the overpaid amount from the date the interim payment was made.

## 13.16 Specific disclosure of documents held by a third party

Once proceedings have been commenced, the court may make an order for specific disclosure of documents against a non-party under CPR, r 31.17(3), only where:

(a) the documents of which disclosure is sought are likely to support the case of the applicant or adversely affect the case of one or other of the parties to the proceedings; and

(b) disclosure is necessary to dispose fairly of the claim or save costs.

The application must be supported by appropriate evidence. An order under r 31.17 will specify the documents or class of documents which must be disclosed, and require the respondent to make disclosure or specify any of those documents which are no longer in his possession or for which he claims the right or duty to withhold from inspection. The order may specify a time and place for such disclosure and inspection.

## 13.17 Conclusion

The above statements in relation to the CPR 1998 are correct at time of writing. However, the CPR 1998 are subject to continuing amendment, and it is essential to check that the version of the Rules and Practice Directions being consulted is current. An up-to-date version can be found on the Ministry of Justice website.

## 13.18 Further reading

Ministry of Justice website – www.justice.gov.uk

*The Civil Court Practice* (the Green Book) (Butterworths)

*Civil Procedure* (the White Book) (Sweet & Maxwell)

# Chapter 14

# Negotiations, Alternative Dispute Resolution and Trial



## 14.1 Introduction

Over 90% of personal injury claims and many clinical negligence claims settle without trial. It is usually the case that the solicitor's skill in arguing his client's claim with the other side's representative, rather than his ability to argue the case at trial, will determine the level of damages. For this reason, the personal injury solicitor is more likely to become a skilled negotiator than a trial advocate.

In order to avoid a potential negligence claim, it is imperative that the claimant solicitor is absolutely sure that the client's medical prognosis is clear prior to proceeding to settle the claim, or to advising the client that it is appropriate to settle the claim. In this regard the solicitor will rely heavily on the medical report and the prognosis for recovery contained within it. It should be stressed to the client that the prognosis is only an estimate, and if the client does not feel that he has recovered then the solicitor cannot advise the client to settle his claim prematurely. It should be pointed out to the client that the compensation offered by the defendant is a 'once and for all payment', and he therefore cannot (normally) return at a future date to obtain further compensation if the prognosis for recovery should prove to be incorrect.

This chapter aims to summarise the main factors to take into account when negotiating, and considers other methods of alternative dispute resolution (ADR) which may be used in personal injury and clinical negligence cases. Inevitably there will be cases which are not capable of settlement and which must proceed to trial, in which case it is vital to prepare properly as a poorly presented case will not impress a judge. The steps that should be taken to prepare the case for trial are also explained below.

## 14.2 Professional conduct

As a matter of conduct, a solicitor does not have ostensible authority to settle a client's claim until after proceedings have been issued. It is imperative for the solicitor to seek the client's specific instructions prior to settling a claim. For example, even if the client instructs his solicitor that he can settle his claim as long as the client receives at least £1,000, the solicitor should, when negotiating with the defence, stipulate that any agreement is 'subject to his client's instructions'. In this way, if the client should change his mind (which he may do at any time), the solicitor will not have committed the client to the settlement irrevocably. A solicitor acting for the defendant must be careful not to exceed any authority he has been given to settle by his insurance client.

Negotiations should always be entered into on an expressly 'without prejudice' basis. When talking to an insurer in person or on the telephone, it is advisable for the solicitor to preface anything he says by stating expressly at the outset that the entire conversation is without prejudice to his client's claim.

## 14.3 Negotiating with insurance companies and defence solicitors

Claims can be settled by agreement being reached between the parties at any stage. The pre-action protocols encourage early disclosure of information to facilitate this. Claimant solicitors have in the past considered that defendant insurers will not make reasonable offers for settlement prior to issue of proceedings. For this reason, many claimant solicitors have tended to issue proceedings first and negotiate second. This strategy is not encouraged by the CPR 1998. The pre-action protocols require that attempts be made to settle disputes. For a detailed consideration of the protocols, see **Chapter 10**. If the claim is being funded by a CFA, there is also the further requirement to disclose to the insurer that the matter is being funded in this way and the identity of any AEI insurer; it is not necessary to give any further details. In particular, it is not required or desirable to disclose the level of the success fee, as this would give the insurer a good indication of how confident the claimant's solicitor was about winning the case at trial.

When negotiating with the defendant's insurer or its solicitor, a firm approach should be taken by the claimant's solicitor. He must be alert to the fact that the insurer is in business to make money for its shareholders, and its employees are employed to ensure that as little money as possible is paid out in damages. Therefore, the claimant's solicitor should not delay in issuing proceedings, after the pre-action protocol has been complied with if the defendant has failed or refused to make an acceptable response. Failure to do so is likely to be a failure to act in the best interests of the client.

## 14.4 Preparing for the negotiation

Prior to any negotiation, the solicitor should first familiarise himself with the file, noting specifically any matters likely to increase the level of damages, such as the risk of osteoarthritis or permanent scarring. There is a risk that the solicitor will fail to remember the file adequately because he may be running many very similar claims at any one time. When reviewing the file it is good practice to build up a profile of the severity of the injuries by reading the medical reports and client's statement. Matters relevant to each head of loss should be noted, so that the solicitor has a list of areas of loss without having to make reference to the specifics of the claim itself.

### Example

Client A is aged 56. She suffered injuries to her left shoulder and abrasions to both arms and legs when she tripped over a loose paving stone in her local high street. She is a keen gardener and likes to attend aerobics once a week, and enjoys walking her dog in the countryside near her home. Her husband took early retirement due to ill-health and is not able to assist her much, but he has been driving her to the doctor and to physiotherapy, and has been helping her bathe and dress herself. Day-to-day cleaning of the house and gardening has been undertaken by friends and relations.

The profile in such a case would be:

General damages claim:

(a) female aged 56, therefore likely to take some time for injuries to mend, danger of osteoarthritis revealed in medical report;

(b) report revealed split fracture to the clavicle (collar bone) together with a tear to the *latissimus dorsi* (muscle beneath the shoulder) and associated soft tissue damage;

(c) medical intervention involved substantial and uncomfortable strapping to render the injury immobile followed by light physiotherapy. Physiotherapy continued for 20 weeks;
(d) reasonably fit, unable to undertake pastimes such as aerobics and walking in countryside for X weeks.

Special damages:
(a) clothes and personal items lost or damaged in the accident;
(b) mileage claim for travel to and from hospital/physiotherapy;
(c) prescription charges;
(d) daily care necessary;
(e) husband unable to care on his own due to his own ill-health;
(f) cleaning of house and garden maintenance undertaken by others.

Having built up such a profile, the next stage is for the solicitor to become familiar with the likely level of damages to be awarded in such a claim. Such familiarity comes with experience. The method of approach to calculation of damages is considered in detail in **Chapter 15**.

In addition to reviewing quantum, the solicitor must ensure he has a good grasp of the facts of the accident and the evidence supporting the case on liability. The solicitor must undertake a thorough review of all pleadings, witness statements and other documents disclosed, and consideration should be given to possible arguments of contributory negligence.

The client should be aware that any form of litigation carries with it a certain amount of risk that the claim will fail because the evidence may not come up to proof at trial. Because of this 'litigation risk', it is likely that the defence solicitor will seek some reduction in damages because the claimant is being spared the upset and risk of failure at trial.

If acting for the defendant, the solicitor must obtain a certificate of recoverable benefit from the DWP before making any offer in settlement so that any relevant benefits can be taken into account.

## 14.5 Conducting the negotiation

The technique of negotiation is contained in ***Skills for Lawyers***. When conducting negotiations, it is worth bearing in mind the following:

(a) Settlement should not be entered into prematurely. If proceedings are never issued and the defendant's insurers make clear that they do not contest the case, argument will centre on quantum, and it will be fairly safe to negotiate. If, however, the matter is contested, it is unwise to negotiate prior to disclosure of each side's evidence. For this reason, many solicitors believe that settlement should not be contemplated prior to the exchange of witness evidence. Once the solicitor has considered the evidence, he can then assist the client to make an informed decision as to whether he should accept a settlement.

(b) The solicitor must never negotiate when unprepared. The file must be considered thoroughly prior to proceeding with negotiations. If the solicitor receives a surprise telephone call from a defendant insurer seeking a settlement, it is better for the solicitor to call back later, after having considered the case afresh.

(c) The defence should be invited to put forward its settlement figure with supporting argument as to why that figure is correct. Comments should be kept to a minimum and further negotiations postponed while the offer is considered. This is easiest to do if negotiating over the telephone, as negotiation can be cut short and re-established later with minimum difficulty. The telephone has the added advantage that the person making an offer cannot see the reaction of the recipient of the call, and will be unable to gauge how well or how badly the offer is received. The claimant's solicitor should never disclose his valuation of the claim first in negotiations, and should not reveal any figures until he believes the defendant is putting forward a realistic amount.

(d) The defence opening offer is unlikely to be the best it is prepared to come up with. All offers must, however, be put to the client. A solicitor has a duty to act in the best interests of his client, and this includes obtaining the best possible settlement figure.

(e) An offer by the defence to pay the claimant's costs to date should not sway the solicitor into advising his client to accept an offer. If the defence is offering to settle, it is effectively admitting (albeit without prejudice) that there is merit in the claim, and it would normally be obliged to pay the claimant's reasonable costs if the case went to trial.

(f) Often the solicitor has specific instructions to try to settle the case on the client's behalf. In such circumstances, he may seek confirmation that a settlement will be agreed as long as the client will receive at least £*x*. If this is the case, the solicitor must be careful not to jump at the first offer simply because it will secure for the client the minimum that he requires and will usually also secure payment of the solicitor's costs.

(g) Consideration of the defendant's offer should not be rushed. Any attempt to force an agreement quickly should be regarded as spurious. The defence would not have made an offer if it was happy to take the case to trial. Therefore, regardless of whether a time limit is placed on the offer, it is likely that unless fresh evidence comes to light strengthening the defence case, an offer once made will remain open. By making an offer at all the defence is saying that it would far rather pay than fight.

(h) When negotiating, defendant insurers will often offer to 'split the difference' if agreement cannot be reached on a particular head of loss. This is a favourite tactic that the claimant solicitor should consider carefully before accepting. On the face of it, it may appear to be a generous offer, bringing negotiations to a speedy conclusion. On closer scrutiny, it may be a ploy which results in the loss of a substantial portion of the client's legitimate expectation in a particular head of damages.

## 14.6 Negotiating in clinical negligence claims

When considering negotiation in the context of clinical negligence claims, the following additional points should be borne in mind.

(a) In many cases, the NHS complaints procedure will already have been put to use, and there may therefore be greater clarity as regards the issues of the claim.

(b) It is unlikely that any negotiations with a view to settlement will be made prior to full recourse to the clinical disputes PAP. Only after both sides have had access to full disclosure and expert opinion will it be possible for any meaningful negotiation to take place.

(c) In straightforward claims of low value, negotiating tactics as outlined above may be appropriate. In relation to more complex claims, it is more likely that there would be a meeting of the parties' solicitors, with or without experts, to try to narrow as many issues as possible. In appropriate cases, counsel for both sides may be asked to discuss the case informally to try to narrow areas in dispute.

## 14.7 Alternative dispute resolution

The use of ADR is likely to become more important in the resolution of disputes, as the overriding objective (stated in Part 1 of the CPR 1998) encourages its prompt use as a way of furthering the overriding objective and to aid prompt settlement. Most disputes are capable of resolution either by discussion and negotiation, or by trial on the issues. The rules encourage the use of alternatives to litigation as a first resort and of litigation as a last resort. ***Civil Litigation*** explains ADR in detail.

## 14.7.1 Different types of ADR

All of the methods of ADR are mechanisms which aim to bring the parties together to obtain a consensual agreement rather than a ruling which is forced upon them. The main types of ADR available today are as follows.

### 14.7.1.1 Mediation

In mediation, a neutral third party is chosen by the parties as their intermediary (mediator). The mediator is likely to meet the opposing parties separately to try to establish some common ground before finally bringing the parties together to try to reach an agreement.

### 14.7.1.2 Conciliation

Conciliation is a similar process to mediation. However, the conciliator is likely to take a more interventionist approach by taking a more central role. He will often consider the case as put forward by both sides, and then suggest terms of settlement which he feels to be most appropriate.

### 14.7.1.3 The mini-trial

The format and content of a mini-trial is much more like a trial. It will be chaired by a neutral mediator who will sit with a representative from each party.

## 14.7.2 Case management conference

At the case management conference/pre-trial review, the parties will be told to confirm whether the question of ADR has been considered and also to confirm, if it has not, why this is the case.

When considering the conduct of the parties, the judge is entitled to consider the parties' unreasonable refusal to use ADR, as this is central to the ethos of how to deal with disputes in accordance with Part 1 of the CPR 1998. Where ADR has been refused, or where a party has later failed to co-operate with ADR, the court is entitled to take that into account when considering what costs order to make, or whether to make any costs order at all.

## 14.7.3 ADR and personal injury claims

Use of the pre-action protocol will ensure that the parties are better able to obtain a greater depth of knowledge about the case against them than in the past. Full use of pre-action disclosure, and preliminary disclosure of key documents, will enable each side to obtain a far better view of the issues of the case in relation to liability, and will therefore allow them to make a far better and earlier assessment of their client's case.

At the stage where the parties complete their allocation questionnaire, they will be asked whether they would like their proceedings to be stayed while they try to settle the case by way of ADR.

Because the court is very likely to ask whether the parties are interested in attempting ADR, and whether the possibility of ADR has been discussed with the client prior to the case management conference, it follows that the solicitor will need to ask his client at an early stage whether he would be interested in pursuing the matter by way of ADR, and must explain to the client what this will entail.

In *Halsey v Milton Keynes General NHS Trust* [2004] EWCA Civ 576, the Trust refused to refer the matter to mediation as it was of the steadfast view that there had been no negligence and therefore referral to ADR would increase costs and delay. The claim was dismissed by the court. When the court came to consider the question of costs, it stated that when deciding whether a successful party had acted unreasonably in refusing to agree to ADR, the court should bear in mind the advantages of ADR over the court process and have regard to all of the circumstances of the particular case. The following factors were found to be of relevance:

(a) the nature of the dispute;
(b) the merits of the case;
(c) the extent to which other settlement methods had been attempted;
(d) whether the costs of ADR would be disproportionately high;
(e) whether any delay in setting up and attending the ADR would have been prejudicial;
(f) whether the ADR had a reasonable prospect of success.

### 14.7.4 The timing of ADR

It is likely that in complicated cases ADR will not be appropriate until such time as statements of case and disclosure of documents by both sides have been dealt with. Only then will ADR be a practical alternative to a trial. It is therefore likely that parties in cases which were initially felt to be unsuitable for ADR may find that ADR is a possibility once the case is at the case management conference stage.

### 14.7.5 Procedure following failed ADR

Where the parties have attempted ADR and this has failed to produce a settlement, the parties are likely to wish to fall back on their original court proceedings or intended court proceedings.

At this stage, if proceedings have already been issued, the solicitor for the claimant will need to apply promptly for further directions in the case so that the matter may proceed swiftly to trial.

However, although ADR may fail to produce a settlement, it may produce a degree of information about the other side's case which prior to ADR had not been clear. If this is so, it may be that an offer to settle or payment should be considered by either party or both parties.

### 14.7.6 ADR in clinical negligence cases

The *Legal Services Commission Manual* recommends the use of ADR techniques to resolve clinical negligence disputes. Guidance notes make the point that although most successful claims settle, they do so at a very late stage. Because many clinical negligence claims are very complex, lengthy and costly, a settlement reached earlier would have the effect of saving significant amounts of CLS funding. The NHSLA, which handles large clinical negligence claims, also encourages the use of ADR. The Clinical Disputes Forum has also produced a guide on the use of mediation in clinical negligence disputes.

The guidance aims to:

(a) ensure that the use of ADR is considered by clients and solicitors at key points in clinical negligence claims;
(b) require solicitors to report to their regional office at various stages in the litigation, explaining why ADR has not been pursued if appropriate;
(c) explain the approach regional offices should take in deciding whether to limit a certificate to work necessary to progress ADR;
(d) help the parties set up mediation.

#### 14.7.6.1 When should ADR be considered in clinical negligence claims?

The parties should keep the possibilities of ADR in mind at all times. However, at the outset of litigation ADR is not likely to be appropriate until the PAP for use in clinical negligence claims has been complied with, because the client and his solicitor are unlikely to have information available to enter into a fair settlement of the claim.

According to the *Legal Services Commission Manual*, once the clinical negligence PAP has been complied with, solicitors should consider with their clients the use of ADR at the following stages:

(a) prior to issue of proceedings;
(b) before and immediately after a case management conference;
(c) before and immediately after pre-trial review;
(d) whenever the other side offers ADR;
(e) whenever the new parties are specifically asked to consider ADR by the court or the LSC.

If at any of the above points it is decided by the client or solicitor not to pursue ADR, the reason for that decision should be recorded on the solicitor's file. Following on from this, where application is made by the solicitor for the certificate to be extended, the reason for not pursuing ADR must be reported to the regional office when submitting Form APP 8 for amendment of certificate.

#### 14.7.6.2 Cases where ADR may not be appropriate

The *Legal Services Commission Manual* gives the following specific guidance and examples of types of claims that may not be suitable for ADR:

(a) where essential basic information (such as relevant medical records, key expert evidence on liability and causation) is not available;
(b) where there is no clear prognosis for the condition of the client and time is needed to see how the client progresses before settlement can be considered;
(c) ADR is unnecessary as all parties are already negotiating effectively;
(d) proceedings need to be issued urgently in order for the claim to be within the relevant limitation period;
(e) the claim includes a future cost of care claim and information is needed as to quantum before any settlement can be discussed;
(f) the case is a 'test case' and requires a ruling from a court in order to lay down a precedent for future claims;
(g) ADR would not be a cost-effective way of dealing with the claim because there is no reason to believe that the claim will be resolved more quickly or cheaply by using it.

Although the LSC in its *Manual* states that it does not wish to impose ADR as a condition of funding, it does make it clear that it will consider limiting a certificate so that it only covers participation in ADR in the following circumstances:

(a) when it receives a report that ADR has been refused;
(b) where the opponent or the NHSLA suggests ADR has been unreasonably refused;
(c) where an application is made to extend the scope of a clinical negligence certificate to full representation or to cover the costs of a trial.

In any of the above cases, the regional office will consider the reason given for not pursuing ADR. In the guidance notes, the LSC states that the following reasons are not good reasons for refusing ADR:

(a) the client refuses ADR and still wishes to have his day in court;
(b) that there are important, outstanding facts or legal issues between the parties;
(c) the parties feel that their positions are so far apart that they cannot foresee settling;
(d) further information or exchange of evidence is required but this information is not sent forward to the client's case.

Once ADR has been attempted, the LSC will lift restrictions on the certificate if the ADR, having been attempted in good faith, breaks down.

In cases where ADR is not successful, the LSC expects both sides to be able to put forward their most realistic Part 36 offers as a result of having taken part in the ADR.

### 14.7.7 NHS complaints procedure

The complaints procedure (which is dealt with in detail in **Chapter 5**) is designed specifically to provide an explanation to patients in cases where they have felt sufficiently concerned about the healthcare received to make a complaint. The procedure is not designed or able to give compensation to patients. It is useful if the only or main issue at stake is for an explanation or an apology to be obtained, or simply to find more information to help the patient to come to terms with an event, or to help him decide whether he should take further action and, if so, what form this should take.

### 14.7.8 Mediation

Mediation may be appropriate in some cases where the parties agree. This may be seen as particularly useful when there are allegations of clinical negligence, as ADR will be conducted in private, and this is something which is likely to appeal to medical practitioners who may not wish the allegations to be made public and reportable, as would be the case if the matter were to proceed in open court to a trial.

## 14.8 Funding any settlement

In nearly all personal injury cases, there will not be a problem with the financing of any settlement, as the defendant will have been required to be insured in respect of the potential liability and a commercial insurer will normally meet any settlement.

In clinical negligence cases too, the defendant will normally not have a problem with the financing of any settlement but the administration of the settlement can be rather more complicated in certain cases. The NHSLA administers the Existing Liability Scheme and Clinical Negligence Scheme for Trusts (CNST). The CNST came into being as a result of concern over the financing of damages claims, and the object of the scheme is to protect NHS Trusts and improve the quality of risk management. The CNST is not an insurance scheme but a mutual fund.

The administration of any settlement is normally of little concern to claimant solicitors, but many practitioners become frustrated by the delays which can arise with insurance companies in personal injury cases and also the NHSLA, as they operate a system whereby certain levels of claims have to be given specific approval.

## 14.9 Court orders

It is good practice to obtain a court order formally stating the terms of the settlement. A settlement on behalf of a minor should always be contained in a court order (see **Chapter 19**). The court will charge a fee for sealing the consent order.

### 14.9.1 Advantages of obtaining a court order

The advantages of obtaining an order are:

(a) payment of interest and costs can be dealt with specifically;

(b) if the amount stated in the order is not paid, the order can be enforced in the same way as any other judgment;

(c) if costs cannot be agreed, they can be assessed by the court if there is provision in the order;

(d) if the client has CLS funding, he will need an order for CLS assessment.

The order should contain a provision that the claim be stayed rather than dismissed, and the stay should contain provision for a return to court in the event that the terms of the stay are not complied with.

### 14.9.2 Drawing up the consent order

The procedure for drawing up a consent order is:

(a) it must be drawn up in the agreed terms;

(b) it must be expressed as being 'by consent';

(c) it must be signed by solicitors or counsel for the parties;

(d) it must be presented to the court for entry and sealing.

An order takes effect from the date given, unless the court orders otherwise. An order for payment of money (including costs) must be complied with within 14 days, unless the order or any rule of the CPR specifies otherwise. When drafting a consent order, the guiding principle is that the order shows where the money is to come from to satisfy the order and where that money will go.

**Example**

In a case where a settlement is achieved by which the defendant agrees to pay £3,000 plus costs to be assessed if not agreed, the order should state:

(a) that the claim is stayed on payment of £3,000;

(b) that the £3,000 is to be paid by the defendant within a given timescale (usually 14 days);

(c) where the money is to go (in this case to the claimant). In a case involving a minor the money will usually be ordered to be invested by the court;

(d) who is to bear the costs. If this has been agreed, the figures should be stated with a time limit for payment. Usually, the provision will be for costs to be assessed if not agreed;

(e) whether CLS assessment is needed; and

(f) liberty to apply – which simply allows the parties to return to the court if there is subsequently a disagreement as to what the terms of the order mean or because the terms have not been complied with.

If there had been an interim payment in the above example, this should also be reflected in the terms of the order. The order should state that the amount agreed in full and final settlement takes into account the interim payment, specifying the amount and the date it was given, or the date of the court order so ordering it to be paid. An example of a consent order can be found at **Appendix 1**.

## 14.10 Part 36 offers

If negotiations do not result in a settlement, consideration should be given to making a Part 36 offer in order to place the opponent under some pressure as to costs. For a detailed discussion of Part 36 offers, refer to ***Civil Litigation***.

### 14.10.1 Form and content of a Part 36 offer – the basic requirements

An offer can be made using Form N242A or simply by letter.

Pursuant to CPR, r 36.2, to be a valid Part 36 offer it must:

(a) be in writing;

(b) state on its face that it is intended to have the consequences of Part 36;

(c) specify a period of not less than 21 days within which the defendant will be liable for the claimant's costs if the offer is accepted;

(d) state whether it relates to the whole of the claim or to part of it, or to an issue that arises in it; and if so, to which part or issue; and

(e) state whether it takes into account any counterclaim.

In addition to the above basic requirements, further information must be set out in the offer if the claim involves future pecuniary loss, provisional damages or the deduction of State benefits.

### 14.10.2 Special provisions applicable to Part 36 offers and personal injury claims for future pecuniary loss

It is possible to make an offer to settle a claim involving future pecuniary loss either by way of a lump sum, or by way of periodical payments or a combination of both (see **Chapter 15**). To be treated as a Part 36 offer with all the costs consequences that follow, the offer must explicitly set out the amounts which relate to the lump sum and periodical payments, and the duration of the periodical payments. If the offer is accepted, in addition to serving a notice of acceptance, the claimant must apply to the court for an order for an award of damages in the form of periodical payments. This must be done within seven days of the date of acceptance.

Rule 36.5 provides as follows:

> (3) A Part 36 offer may contain an offer to pay, or an offer to accept—
>
> (a) the whole or part of the damages for future pecuniary loss in the form of—
>
> (i) a lump sum; or
>
> (ii) periodical payments; or
>
> (iii) both a lump sum and periodical payments;
>
> (b) the whole or part of any other damages in the form of a lump sum.
>
> (4) A Part 36 offer to which this rule applies—
>
> (a) must state the amount of any offer to pay the whole or part of any damages in the form of a lump sum;
>
> (b) may state—
>
> (i) what part of the lump sum, if any, relates to damages for future pecuniary loss; and
>
> (ii) what part relates to other damages to be accepted in the form of a lump sum;
>
> (c) must state what part of the offer relates to damages for future pecuniary loss to be paid or accepted in the form of periodical payments and must specify—
>
> (i) the amount and duration of the periodical payments;
>
> (ii) the amount of any payments for substantial capital purchases and when they are to be made; and
>
> (iii) that each amount is to vary by reference to the retail prices index (or to some other named index, or that it is not to vary by reference to any index); and
>
> (d) must state either that any damages which take the form of periodical payments will be funded in a way which ensures that the continuity of payment is reasonably secure in accordance with section 2(4) of the Damages Act 1996 or how such damages are to be paid and how the continuity of their payment is to be secured.
>
> (5) Rule 36.4 applies to the extent that a Part 36 offer by a defendant under this rule includes an offer to pay all or part of any damages in the form of a lump sum.
>
> (6) Where the offeror makes a Part 36 offer to which this rule applies and which offers to pay or to accept damages in the form of both a lump sum and periodical payments, the offeree may only give notice of acceptance of the offer as a whole.
>
> (7) If the offeree accepts a Part 36 offer which includes payment of any part of the damages in the form of periodical payments, the claimant must, within 7 days of the date of acceptance, apply to the court for an order for an award of damages in the form of periodical payments under rule 41.8.

### 14.10.3 Special provisions applicable to Part 36 offers and provisional damages

If the claim is for provisional damages (see **Chapter 15**), an offer to settle must specify whether or not the offeror is offering to agree to the making of an award for provisional damages. If he is, the offer must state

(a) the damages offered;

(b) the conditions to trigger a further claim;

(c) the period within which such further claim may be made.

Once the offer is accepted, the claimant must, within seven days, apply to the court for an order.

Rule 36.6 provides:

> (1) An offeror may make a Part 36 offer in respect of a claim which includes a claim for provisional damages.
>
> (2) Where he does so, the Part 36 offer must specify whether or not the offeror is proposing that the settlement shall include an award of provisional damages.
>
> (3) Where the offeror is offering to agree to the making of an award of provisional damages the Part 36 offer must also state—
>
> (a) that the sum offered is in satisfaction of the claim for damages on the assumption that the injured person will not develop the disease or suffer the type of deterioration specified in the offer;
>
> (b) that the offer is subject to the condition that the claimant must make any claim for further damages within a limited period; and
>
> (c) what that period is.
>
> (4) Rule 36.4 applies to the extent that a Part 36 offer by a defendant includes an offer to agree to the making of an award of provisional damages.
>
> (5) If the offeree accepts the Part 36 offer, the claimant must, within 7 days of the date of acceptance, apply to the court for an order for an award of provisional damages under rule 41.2.

### 14.10.4 Compensation recovery and Part 36 offers – deduction of benefits

A Part 36 offer in a personal injury claim may state that the offer is made without regard to any liability for recoverable benefits, ie it is a net offer and the compensator will pay benefits in addition.

Alternatively, the offer should state that it is intended to include any deductible CRU benefits.

According to r 36.15, the offer must state:

(a) the amount of gross compensation before CRU benefits are offset;

(b) the name of any deductible benefit;

(c) the amount of any deductible benefit by which the gross amount is reduced; and

(d) the net amount after deduction.

Remember, when calculating what benefits can be offset, that specific benefits can be offset only against certain heads of claim and must not exceed the amount claimed under that head. Where it is agreed or alleged that the claimant was contributorily negligent, the damages from which benefits can be offset must be net of the deduction for contributory negligence.

For the purpose of establishing whether the claimant has failed to beat a Part 36 offer, the sums to be considered are those after deduction of the deductible benefits. In other words, the court will look at what sum the claimant was offered net of benefits and what sum he recovered net of benefits.

Where the claimant accepts a Part 36 offer out of time and the CRU repayment has increased, the court may direct that the additional benefits should be deducted from the net offer.

### 14.10.5 Keeping offers under review

Under r 36.9, an offer is accepted when written notice is served. An offeree may accept a Part 36 offer at any time, whether or not the offeree has subsequently made a different offer, unless the offeror has served notice of withdrawal (r 36.9(2)).

Parties must therefore retain a record of all Part 36 offers and keep them under review. If new evidence comes to light that means that a Part 36 offer made some time previously is now too high (or, if a claimant's offer, too low), it should be withdrawn in writing so that it is no longer capable of acceptance. A new Part 36 offer can be served at the same time as the notice to withdraw the previous offer.

## 14.11 Preparation for trial

### 14.11.1 Outstanding orders

Once it becomes apparent that the case will proceed to trial as no satisfactory Part 36 offer has been received, the claimant's solicitor should undertake a thorough stocktaking of the file to ensure that all directions or other orders of the court have been complied with. Any outstanding matters in the claimant's own file should be attended to without further delay, and any outstanding matters for the defendant to attend to should be chased by issuing an interim application for judgment in default of compliance with the direction/other order if necessary.

### 14.11.2 Experts

Experts' reports will usually have been exchanged in accordance with directions. Provision of joint experts and agreed expert evidence is dealt with in **Chapter 11**.

### 14.11.3 Use of counsel

The solicitor may not have instructed counsel before this stage if the claim has been straightforward. If the case has been complex, as is likely in a clinical negligence case, counsel will probably have been involved at an early stage, from drafting documents to advising on evidence. It is usual for the barrister who drafted the statements of case also to be briefed for the trial. As counsel will be handling the witnesses at trial, it may be thought to be appropriate to send the witness statements to counsel for approval before exchange to ensure that an important area concerning the conduct of the case at trial is not overlooked. It may be more cost-efficient to brief counsel for the trial than for the solicitor himself to attend. However, with trial on the fast track limited to one day, and with fixed costs of trial, it may be that many more solicitor-advocates will undertake the advocacy of this type of claim.

If the case involves complex elements, such as clinical negligence, catastrophic injuries, or difficult questions of fact or law, consideration should be given to whether it would be appropriate to instruct leading counsel; junior counsel will usually advise the solicitor if he thinks that this would be appropriate. The solicitor should advise the client accordingly of the extra cost involved and, if the client is CLS funded, seek authority from the CLS to instruct leading counsel. The client should also be advised that if leading counsel is instructed, and this is disallowed on assessment, the cost will ultimately be borne by the client in the form of the statutory charge on the client's damages.

### 14.11.4 Narrowing the issues

When preparing for trial the solicitor should ask himself, 'What do I have to prove?' A review should be made of the case file to ascertain areas of agreement which are no longer in issue. One useful device may be a list comprising two columns: the left-hand column listing the facts which have to be proved (eg, that the claimant was driving the car; that an accident occurred; the date of the accident; the place of the accident; an itemised list of the losses, etc); and the right-hand column indicating whether the fact is admitted by the opponent.

Admissions will normally be found in the statements of case or in open correspondence.

### 14.11.5 Schedule of special damages

Note that CPR, PD 22, para 1.4(3) requires that a statement of truth is included in a schedule or counter-schedule of expenses and losses, and in any amendments to such a schedule or counter-schedule, whether or not the schedule is contained in a statement of case.

The claimant's solicitor must check that the schedule of special damages is up to date, and if necessary, serve an updated schedule of special damages. Ideally, this should be the final schedule (although it may have to be revised again if there is a significant delay before the trial), the purpose of which is to identify the areas of agreement and disagreement between the parties. With this in mind, the following format could be usefully employed (the figures are merely for illustration):

| *Item of claim* | *Claimant's figure* | *Defendant's figure* | *Discrepancy* |
|---|---|---|---|
| Purchase of wheelchair | £350 | £350 | Nil |
| Loss of future earnings | £50,000 (multiplicand = £5,000, multiplier = 10) | £32,000 (multiplicand = £4,000, multiplier = 8) | £18,000 |

The defendant's solicitor should be sent the updated schedule of special damages, with a covering letter requesting that he agrees it or specifies the items he is not prepared to agree, and giving a time limit for the reply. It should be pointed out that if he fails to reply, the claimant's solicitors will have to issue a witness summons for any persons necessary to prove the amounts claimed, and the claimant will ask for the costs of this exercise be paid by the defendant in any event.

In clinical negligence claims, where special damages claims are likely to involve substantial amounts of money, it is more likely that the defence will seek to query items claimed as special damages. For this reason the directions will normally require that the defendant also provide a counter-schedule of special damages itemising the areas of disagreement.

### 14.11.6 Trial bundles

In both the High Court and the county court, bundles of documents upon which the parties intend to rely must be lodged within the appropriate time, for use by the trial judge.

The bundle must be paginated and indexed. The medical records must be complete and in good order to enable medical experts to study them easily. X-rays or scans included in the bundle should be clearly identified. Scans may be several feet long and should be professionally copied if possible. The index to the trial bundle is normally agreed with the defendant.

The quality of preparation of bundles varies enormously, and this can have serious implications for the client's case if preparation is not undertaken properly. Although there are rules governing the content of the bundles, there is very little guidance on how the documents should be presented. When preparing the bundle the aim should be to enable whoever is conducting the trial to turn to any document at any time with the minimum of fuss or delay, and that all others concerned with the case can do likewise. The more documents there are in the bundle, the more difficult this task becomes. In a straightforward road traffic claim, there will be few documents and, as such, the bundle should be relatively easy to prepare. In serious cases involving multiple injuries or in clinical negligence cases, however, the documents are likely to extend to many hundreds of pages. In such cases, it is even more important that the court is not hindered by trying to find documents that should be readily to hand. Poor preparation of the case will not impress the judge, neither will it go unnoticed. Documents will need to be split into a number of smaller bundles which are easier to handle. Using colour-coded lever arch files is often a good method, with a separate file for each class of document. As a matter of courtesy, if counsel has been instructed, the solicitor may wish to send the proposed index to the core bundle of documents to counsel in advance of the trial, so that counsel has the opportunity to ask for further items to be included if necessary.

### 14.11.7 Use of visual aids

Plans, photographs and models can be of enormous value at the trial as an aid to clarity, thereby shortening the length of the trial (avoiding long testimony of a witness) and saving costs. A judge may more readily understand the testimony of a witness if that witness is allowed to refer to a plan or photograph. Medical experts can often supply good quality colour diagrams, anatomical illustrations or models to make their testimony more comprehensible. In clinical negligence cases, it is worth the extra time and effort to find good visual aids. A judge is unlikely to have in-depth medical knowledge, and attempts to help the judge fully comprehend the circumstances giving rise to the alleged negligence are likely to be gratefully received.

Visual aids must be disclosed to the opponent in advance. No plan, photograph or model will be receivable in evidence at trial unless the party wishing to use the evidence discloses it no later than the latest date for serving witness statements.

A video-recording is more useful than photographs in the case of 'movement'. Two common examples are:

(a) a video-recording of an industrial process;

(b) a video-recording showing the difficulties of the claimant in coping with his injuries (a 'day in the life'). Although the claimant should call, in addition to his own evidence, members of his family or friends to give evidence as to how he manages with his injuries (evidence of his bodily and mental condition before and after the accident), a video film (eg, showing the medical assistance required, such as physiotherapy or even surgery) may illustrate the situation more graphically.

If the photographs or other visual aids are agreed, they are admissible in the absence of the maker. If the aids are not agreed, the maker must be called to prove their authenticity.

The solicitor should ensure at the trial that there are enough copies of photographs for the use of the judge, advocates and witnesses.

## 14.12 The trial

### 14.12.1 The morning of the trial

The solicitor should arrive early to ensure that he has time:

(a) to check with the clerk to the court that the court has the trial bundles, and place a bundle in the witness-box;

(b) to ensure that counsel has arrived and consider any last-minute questions he may have;

(c) to meet the client on his arrival and attempt to put him at his ease;

(d) to introduce counsel to the client (if they have not already met in conference);

(e) to ensure that an interview room is reserved for the pre-trial conference with counsel.

### 14.12.2 Advice to clients and witnesses

The case will often turn on how well or how badly the witnesses give their evidence, and how they are perceived by the judge. The client and other witnesses should be reminded that they will not be able to take their statements into the witness-box. The solicitor should run through the procedure to be adopted when giving oral evidence with the witnesses, as follows:

(a) explain the procedure on taking the oath, and whether the client wishes to affirm;

(b) remind the witness that all responses should be addressed to the judge regardless of who asked the question; and

(c) that the judge must be addressed in the appropriate manner; and

(d) go through the order in which the witnesses will be examined.

Each witness's statement will normally stand as evidence-in-chief, in which case the witness's evidence will move to being cross-examined almost immediately.

It is important to allay the client's fears about giving oral evidence. The solicitor should advise the client to speak slowly and directly to the judge, just as if there was no one else in the room. The judge will be writing notes, and therefore the witness should watch the judge's pen and resume speaking only when the judge has finished writing.

It is unlikely that the client and lay witnesses will have given evidence before. They should be advised that if they do not understand the question they should say so, and to take their evidence slowly, answer only the question put to them and not to engage in questioning opposing counsel or offer unsolicited opinions of their own. It is up to the solicitor to keep his witnesses in check and ensure that they do not embarrass the client or harm his case.

### 14.12.3 Conduct of the trial

Counsel (if instructed) will have the conduct of the trial, and the solicitor's function will be to sit behind counsel and take full notes of evidence. For the purpose of costing, a note should be made of the start time, any adjournments and the time the trial finishes. The questions asked by counsel should be noted, as well as the responses given, as counsel will not be able to make any notes himself while on his feet.

### 14.12.4 Order of evidence

Although evidence is usually given by the claimant first, followed by the defence, in clinical negligence cases all witnesses of fact may be called first, followed by witnesses giving evidence of opinion. This is because the facts themselves are often complex and it assists the judge greatly if the facts are laid out clearly by hearing evidence from the witnesses of fact for the claimant, followed directly by those of the defence. The object is to clarify the areas of disagreement so that experts can concentrate their efforts there, and shorten the length of trial. However, the parties must apply to the trial judge on the first day of the trial to use this procedure, as the order of evidence in the judge's court will be decided by the individual judge as a matter of discretion.

### 14.12.5 Judgment

The solicitor should take a careful note of the judgment delivered by the judge at the end of the case, as it may be crucial if the client decides to appeal.

Counsel must be made aware of any specific orders which may be necessary. In addition, counsel must be informed about any Part 36 offers which may have a bearing on costs.

The solicitor should also check the pre-trial orders to see if costs were reserved in any interim proceedings, and if so, that this is brought to the attention of the judge so that a costs order can be made in relation to that application.

The judgment should be fully explained to the client, which can be undertaken by counsel.

### 14.12.6 The order

Following trial in the county court, the court will draw up the order, which should be checked carefully to ensure that it reflects the judge's decision, as mistakes are sometimes made by the court staff.

## 14.13 Conclusion

Most cases settle, and taking a case to trial will be the exception rather than the rule in personal injury litigation. Nevertheless, every case must be approached from the standpoint that it will go to trial, and must be prepared accordingly. It is important to keep a case under review as the case progresses. In particular, any Part 36 offers should be kept under review and, if necessary, withdrawn if further evidence comes to light which alters your views of quantum and /or liability.

## 14.14 Further reading

*Civil Court Practice* (the Green Book) (Butterworths)

*Civil Procedure* (the White Book) (Sweet & Maxwell)

# Chapter 15
# The Quantification of Damages



## 15.1 Introduction

The aim of the claimant's solicitor is to establish liability against the defendant and to achieve the highest possible level of damages for his client (without falsifying or exaggerating the claim). The primary aim of the defendant's solicitor is to defeat the claimant's claim. However, if he cannot prevent his client being found liable for the claimant's injuries and loss, his fallback position is to minimise the level of damages his client is obliged to pay. It therefore follows that the task of valuing the claimant's losses is just as important to those representing defendants as it is to those representing claimants. Although the claimant and defendant will usually only be interested in the final amount of the award, the personal injury solicitor must fully understand the various heads of damages which the court can order, to ensure that he can achieve the best possible result for his client. However, even the most experienced personal injury lawyer will be able to quantify the damages only approximately, and therefore solicitors should take care to manage their client's expectations. It is a wise claimant's solicitor who gives his client a slightly lower assessment of the likely damages, and a wise defendant's solicitor who gives his client a slightly higher assessment.

In negligence, the aim of the award of damages is to restore the claimant to the position that he was in prior to the accident. Of course, it is impossible to take away the pain and suffering associated with a personal injury, particularly as, in many cases, there will be lasting physical and/or psychological disability. The award of monetary compensation is the only remedy available to the court and, particularly in cases of catastrophic injury, claimants and their families will cope better with the physical, mental, social and financial consequences of the injuries where appropriate monetary compensation is received.

In most cases, the claimant will receive a lump sum award in full and final settlement of his claim, which means he will not be able to return to court at a later date to seek additional compensation (see provisional damages and periodical payments at **15.4** and **15.5** below for exceptions to this rule). It is therefore important that the claimant's solicitor is thorough in his investigations to identify all losses. Where the case is determined at trial, damages are assessed as at the date of the trial (or, in 'split trials', at a later hearing), and therefore detailed and up-to-date evidence, such as an updated loss of earnings calculation and medical report, should be provided to the court. Most claims are settled through negotiation, but it is equally important for the claimant's solicitor to have detailed and up-to-date evidence available whenever quantum is discussed with the defendant's solicitor.

### 15.1.1 Heads of damage

The following heads of damage can be claimed in personal injury and clinical negligence cases:

(a) Special damages (also known as past pecuniary loss). These are the financial losses which the claimant has incurred prior to trial, and they are capable of fairly precise calculation.

(b) General damages. These are damages that cannot be calculated precisely and therefore require the application of certain formulaic approaches plus a little educated guesswork. They can be split into two categories:

   (i) Non-pecuniary loss. This is the element of the compensation award that does not reflect financial losses at all but rather reflects the claimant's pain, suffering and loss of amenity.

   (ii) Future pecuniary loss. Although this element of the compensation reflects financial losses, such as future loss of earnings or the cost of the care which the claimant will require, it cannot be calculated precisely as it is impossible to say with precision, for example, how long the claimant will live, what he would have earned had he not been injured or how much his care requirements will cost in future years.

Terminology may create problems for the unwary, as some practitioners use the term special damages' when referring to all items of pecuniary loss, both past and future, and the term 'general damages' is used routinely in case reporting to mean pain, suffering and loss of amenity only. It goes without saying that, when negotiating a settlement, solicitors must be precise about the nature of the damages to which they are referring. In this text, we shall give the terminology its traditional meaning as set out in (a) and (b) above.

The distinction between special damages and the two heads of general damages is significant not only in the method of calculation, but also with regard to the level of interest awarded by the court (see **15.6**).

## 15.2 Special damages – 'past pecuniary loss'

Special damages are the items of financial loss incurred by the claimant between the date of the accident and the date of trial which can be specifically calculated.

The main heads of special damages are:

(a) loss of earnings;
(b) clothing and personal effects;
(c) cost of medical care and expenses;
(d) cost of care and quasi-nursing services;
(e) cost of DIY, gardening and housework services;
(f) cost of aids and appliances;
(g) cost of alternative and/or adapted accommodation;
(h) transport costs.

In RTA cases, there may also be:

(i) cost of repairs to or replacement of the claimant's vehicle;
(j) vehicle recovery and storage charges;
(k) loss of use of a motor vehicle or hire of a substitute vehicle;
(l) loss of a no claims bonus and wasted road fund licence.

You should note that some of the above heads will also be relevant to any general damages claim for future pecuniary loss.

## 15.2.1 Loss of earnings up to the date of the trial

In most cases, there will be a claim for loss of earnings up to the date of trial. The claimant is entitled to recover his net loss of earnings, ie what he would have earned after tax, National Insurance and contractual pension payments.

In many cases, where the claimant was in regular employment, it will be reasonably straightforward to determine precisely how much the claimant has lost. In other cases, the calculation will not be so precise. For example, where the claimant's pre-accident wages varied markedly from week to week, or where there has been a fairly lengthy period of time between the accident and trial and the claimant argues that he would have been promoted to a more lucrative position had he still been working.

### 15.2.1.1 Calculating loss of earnings

The starting point in the calculation is to determine the claimant's average net wage for the period immediately prior to the accident. The common approach is to obtain, from the claimant's wage slips or bank statements or from his employer, details of his earnings for the 13-week period prior to the accident. Where that 13-week period is not representative of the claimant's average pre-accident wage, a longer period, for example six months, should be considered. Whatever period is looked at, appropriate adjustments should be made to take account of any overtime, bonus payments, benefits such as company cars or commission that the claimant would have earned had he been at work. Further adjustments should be made to take account of any pay increase, promotion, or further benefits which the claimant would have obtained during the period from the date of the action to trial.

In some cases, such as where the claimant had obtained a job immediately prior to the accident and a clear pattern of pre-accident wages cannot be provided, or where there has been a lengthy period between the date of the accident and the assessment of damages, it may be useful to obtain details of a comparative earner. This involves identifying someone who was in a similar post and earning a similar salary to the claimant immediately prior to the accident, and determining what his earnings pattern had been and, where appropriate, tracking his career progression and salary increases during the period up to trial. Clearly, it would be most useful if the comparative earner is employed by the claimant's employer, but where this is not possible, a comparative earner from a similar business or organisation can be used.

Some claimants have more complex employment histories, such as where they worked on short-term contracts or were self-employed. In such circumstances, more detailed enquiries must be made in order to provide evidence of income lost before the trial. Self-employed claimants should be asked to supply copies of their accounts and/or tax returns for the year prior to the accident, or a longer period if one year's figures are not representative. This information may be difficult to obtain, leaving scope for those representing defendants to argue that losses have been exaggerated. It may be necessary to obtain a report from an accountant (the term 'forensic accountant' is often used for those who specialise in this area).

In an attempt to establish details of how much the claimant would have earned between the accident and trial in cases where an erratic employment history is presented, reference can be made to the Annual Survey of Hours and Earnings produced by the Office for National Statistics, which is a statistical analysis of earnings throughout the country. The Survey can provide details of average earnings for particular industries or occupations on a national or regional basis, and can be useful in attempting to persuade the defendant to accept that the claimant would have received a particular wage.

It is possible for an accident victim who was, prior to the accident, receiving earnings from a lawful source but failing to pay tax or National Insurance, to bring a claim for past and future loss of earnings (although adjustments will have to be made to the past and future loss of earnings calculation) (see *Newman v Marshall and Dunlop Tyres Ltd* [2001] LTL, 19 June and *Duller v South East Lincs Engineers* [1981] CLY 585).

Very few employees receive no income whatsoever while absent from work, and so the calculation of the claimant's lost earnings is not simply a case of multiplying the net weekly loss by the number of weeks' absence. Such an approach would place the claimant in a better financial position than he would have been in had the accident not occurred. A detailed examination of what income the claimant received while absent from work is required, as certain types of income have to be credited in calculating the net loss figure.

### 15.2.1.2 Items which must be accounted for in the calculation

The following are the most common items which must be accounted for in the net loss of earnings figure (for both past and future loss of earnings calculations), ie these amounts must be deducted from the net salary in order to calculate the total loss of earnings:

(a) *Tax refunds received due to absence from work as a result of the accident.* A claimant who is an employee will generally pay income tax on the Pay As You Earn (PAYE) system. To a certain extent this system is a payment of tax in advance, as it assumes that the claimant's earnings will continue throughout the whole of the forthcoming year. In the event of the claimant's absence from work, he may then have paid too much tax. In this case, the claimant may receive a tax rebate via his employer. An amount equivalent to the whole of the rebate has to be given credit for in the calculation of wage loss (*Hartley v Sandholme Iron Co Ltd* [1975] QB 600). Occasionally, instead of a 'cash-in-hand' tax rebate, the claimant may receive a tax credit against future tax liability, so that on his return to work he pays no tax for a period (a 'tax holiday'). A sum equivalent to this tax credit also has to be given credit for in the calculation of the wage loss (*Brayson v Wilmot-Breedon* [1976] CLY 682).

(b) *Sums paid to the claimant by his employer.* Whether sums equivalent to such payments fall to be deducted from the damages depends on the basis of the payment and the identity of the tortfeasor.

The following are the most common situations:

(i) The sum is paid under a legal obligation (eg, under the claimant's contract of employment) and is not refundable by the claimant to his employer. An amount equivalent to the whole of the payment should be deducted from the damages.

(ii) The sum is paid under a legal obligation (eg, under the contract of employment) and must be repaid by the claimant to his employer out of any damages the claimant receives from the defendant. Such a payment is effectively a loan and, as such, is not deducted when assessing the damages.

(iii) The sum is paid *ex gratia* by the employer who is not the tortfeasor. Such a payment is effectively a 'charitable' payment and is not to be deducted when assessing the damages (*Cunningham v Harrison* [1973] 3 All ER 463).

(iv) The sum is paid *ex gratia* by the employer who is the tortfeasor. An amount equivalent to the whole of the payment may (in certain circumstances) be deducted from the damages (*Hussain v New Taplow Paper Mills Ltd* [1988] AC 514).

(v) The claimant receives statutory sick pay (SSP) from his employer. This is not a recoverable benefit to the DWP (see **Chapter 16**), and therefore an amount equivalent to the whole payment should be deducted (the contract of employment may need to be examined in case the employer is entitled to claw back the SSP in some way). See also *Palfrey v Greater London Council* [1985] ICR 437.

(c) *Any saving to an injured person attributable to his maintenance wholly or partly at public expense.* This would apply where the claimant was, for example, admitted into an NHS hospital, a nursing home or other institution. The savings must be calculated and set off against any claim for income lost as a result of the injuries (Administration of Justice Act 1982, s 5). In practice, this deduction is overlooked because in most cases the sums saved are *de minimis*. (While in hospital the claimant will generally have to meet the same household expenses such as rent, mortgage and council tax; any saving will usually be only in regard to the cost of food. This saving is then so small as to be ignored.)

(d) *Redundancy payments*. An equivalent amount is to be deducted in full from the damages calculation when redundancy occurs as a result of the injury caused by the accident (*Colledge v Bass Mitchells & Butlers* [1988] 1 All ER 536).

(e) *Benefits outside the ambit of the Social Security (Recovery of Benefits) Act 1997*. A sum equivalent to certain benefits received by the claimant as a result of the accident will deducted from the judgment sum or negotiated settlement by the defendant and paid directly to the Compensation Recovery Unit (see **Chapter 16**). However, when calculating the award, benefits which are not subject to offsetting are potentially deductible. In *Clenshaw v Tanner* [2002] EWCA Civ 1848, the Court of Appeal held that as the claimant was not required to reimburse the local authority for receipt of housing benefit, if he was allowed to recover for loss of earnings in full, he would be overcompensated to the extent of the housing benefit. Consequently, the housing benefit payments were deducted from the loss of earnings award. It therefore follows that, potentially, other benefits, such as council tax benefit, child tax credit, working tax credit, motability payments, etc are deductible.

### 15.2.1.3 Items which are not accounted for

The following items are the most common payments to be left out of account in assessing an award for loss of past (and future) earnings:

(a) *State retirement pension*. The State retirement pension is ignored in assessing an award for loss of past and future earnings (*Hewson v Downs* [1970] 1 QB 73).

(b) *Pensions received*. The general rule is that if the claimant receives a pension, this cannot be set against the claim for loss of earnings. However, if there is a separate claim for loss of pension rights, for example since the claimant is unable to work he will receive less pension in the future, any pension he does receive may be offset against the claim for loss of pension rights (*Parry v Cleaver* [1970] AC 1; *Smoker v London Fire and Civil Defence Authority* [1991] 2 All ER 449; *Longden v British Coal Corporation* [1997] 3 WLR 1336; see also **13.3.6**).

(c) *Insurance moneys*. Where a claimant has taken out an insurance policy specifically to cover him against the risk of sustaining personal injuries, or where such cover is an incidental' benefit to other types of insurance, such as motor insurance, he may receive a payment as a result of injuries caused by the defendant's negligence. In such cases, the payment is usually a fixed sum according to the type of injury; for example, in the event of a loss of a specified limb, the insurance company will pay the insured the sum of £5,000.

The claimant need not give credit for moneys received under such a policy against the damages payable by the defendant, provided he paid for or contributed to the policy premiums. The justification is that the defendant should not benefit from the fact that the claimant had the foresight to take out the cover and pay the premium (*Bradburn v Great Western Railway Co* (1874) LR 10 Exch 1; *McCamley v Cammell Laird Shipbuilders Ltd* [1990] 1 All ER 854). Where the claimant does not pay for or contribute to the policy, as where the employer sets up a non-contributory group personal accident insurance policy, credit must be given (see *Pirelli v Gaca* [2004] EWCA Civ 373).

In cases where credit does not have to be given to the defendant, the terms of the insurance policy should be checked carefully. There will often be a provision (particularly in motor insurance) which obliges a policyholder to reimburse the insurance company for any sum it paid to him under the policy in respect of a loss for which he receives compensation from a third party. In such a case, the claimant will not receive any financial benefit from commencing proceedings, but the insurance company may insist on commencing and conducting proceedings in his name.

(d) *Charitable payments.* If money is received by the claimant as a charitable payment (even if it is on an informal basis such as the proceeds of a collection taken among his friends) then the claimant is not required to give credit for such payment against the damages received. The justification is that as a matter of policy, people should not be discouraged from making such payments to the victims of accidents. However, the exact circumstances and sources of the *ex gratia* payment must be considered. In *Williams v BOC Gases Ltd* [2000] PIQR Q253, the Court of Appeal held that where an employer (who was the tortfeasor) made an *ex gratia* payment on termination of the claimant's employment on the basis that it was to be treated as an advance against any damages that might be awarded in respect of any claim the claimant had against the employer, credit had to be given for that amount in a subsequent personal injury claim.

### 15.2.2 Clothing and personal effects

Where the claimant has been injured as a result of an accident, there may be damage to items of clothing and other personal effects, such as mobile telephones, laptop computers, watches, etc. Where such items are damaged beyond repair, the claimant is entitled to claim their pre-accident value, and appropriate documentary evidence (such as receipts or valuations) should be provided. Solicitors acting for defendants will be keen to ensure that items have not been overvalued by the claimant and that discounts are given in respect of items which were not brand-new at the time of the accident. This type of loss does not arise in clinical negligence cases.

### 15.2.3 Cost of medical care and expenses

The claimant is entitled to recover all medical expenses reasonably incurred as a result of the defendant's breach of duty, for example prescriptions, over-the-counter drugs, and private medical care and treatment. However, where the claimant has been treated as an in-patient, only the cost of the medical care may be claimed; he cannot claim for the 'hotel' element included in the cost of staying in hospital, for example the proportion of the fees that relate to the provision of meals, heating and lighting (*Lim Poh Choo v Camden and Islington Area Health Authority* [1979] 2 All ER 910).

Treatment may be in relation to essential matters (such as a colostomy), non-emergency, non-life threatening matters (such as dealing with bed sores), or incidental treatments (such as IVF, required, for example, where a claimant is unable to father a child naturally due to a spinal cord injury). The courts will allow the costs of numerous types of therapeutic care, such as psychiatric assistance, physiotherapy and occupational therapy, and may allow the cost of alternative medical treatments, such as acupuncture. The availability of free NHS treatment is ignored (Law Reform (Personal Injuries) Act 1948, s 2(4); see also *Eagle v Chambers* [2004] EWCA Civ 1033), although a claimant cannot be treated free under the NHS and then claim for private treatment.

In cases where there are long waiting lists under the NHS, if the claimant does not himself raise the matter, the claimant's solicitor should suggest that the client undergo private medical treatment in an attempt to speed the recovery period. Indeed, where the claimant has a strong case on liability, the defendant's solicitors may well suggest this, as prompt treatment may reduce the level of damages ultimately payable by the defendant. Reference should be made to the Rehabilitation Code (Annex D to the PAP for personal injury claims; see **Appendix 2**), which requires the parties to co-operate in order to assess and provide for the claimant's rehabilitation needs.

**Example**

A 10-year-old girl is injured and has to undergo major abdominal surgery at the local hospital, which leaves her with a large surgical incision. As part of her general damages award she will claim for pain and suffering relating to the scarring. It is also likely that she will claim that she will suffer psychological problems in relation to the embarrassment of wearing swimming costumes throughout her teenage years and perhaps in later life. In such a case, the claimant should undergo specialist plastic surgery in an attempt to reduce the significance of the scarring and the potential psychological problems, which, in turn, will reduce the level of damages that the defendant will pay.

Future private medical care may also be claimed as part of the future pecuniary loss head of general damages (see **15.3.5**), provided it is reasonably likely to be incurred.

## 15.2.4 Cost of care and quasi-nursing services

In cases where the claimant is seriously injured, the cost of providing care and quasi-nursing services may form a substantial part of both the special damages claim for past pecuniary losses and the general damages claim for future pecuniary losses (see **15.3.5**). The cost of such services may also form part of the special damages claim where injuries have been less severe. In most cases, at least some of the care will have been provided gratuitously, by a member of the claimant's family or a close friend. As with medical care and expenses, the claimant is under no obligation to use care services provided by the NHS.

### 15.2.4.1 Professional care

Where care services are provided on a commercial basis, they can be recovered from the defendant provided they are reasonable in amount and are reasonably incurred as a result of the injuries. The claimant will bear the burden of proving that he needed or will need the level of care provided.

### 15.2.4.2 Gratuitous care

In relation to gratuitous care, the carer is unable to make a claim against the defendant due to the general principle that a third party cannot claim in respect of losses he has incurred as a result of the claimant's injuries. However, the claimant may recover the value of care services provided to him on a gratuitous basis, so long as such services were rendered necessary by the negligence of the defendant. In other words, the care provided must be over and above that which the claimant would have normally received from the carer. So, for example, where a mother is severely injured and her child slightly injured in a road traffic accident as a result of the defendant's negligence, it is not possible for the child to claim damages for the care element from the defendant, as the mother would normally provide such care. The appropriate course is for the mother to include, as part of her damages claim, the costs of the care of the child which she can no longer provide herself (see *Buckley v Farrow and Buckley* [1997] PIQR Q78).

The value of gratuitous services may be claimed by the claimant irrespective of whether the third party has been put to actual expense in providing those services, for example by incurring loss of earnings, and it is unnecessary for there to be any agreement between the claimant and the third party as to reimbursement for the services.

Initially, courts were reluctant to award damages for the cost of gratuitous care except in the most serious cases. However, in *Giambrone & Others v JMC Holidays Ltd (formerly t/a Sunworld Holidays Ltd)* [2004] EWCA Civ 158, holiday makers who had developed gastro-enteritis at the defendant's hotel, which persisted for more than 14 days, were able to recover for gratuitous care provided by family members once they had returned home. The Court of Appeal rejected the defendant's argument that an award for the value of such services should be made only in serious cases or where the claimant could point to a demonstrable financial expense in providing the necessary care. Consequently, claimants' solicitors should always include a claim for gratuitous care when it has been provided.

As has already been said, the claim for the value of the services is made by the claimant, not by the third party, as it is the claimant's loss (his need for the services) which is being compensated. However, although it is the claimant who obtains the award for the value of the services, the damages are held by him in trust for the carer. Therefore, where the carer is also the defendant (eg, where a wife is injured as a result of her husband's negligent driving and the husband provides quasi-nursing services to her), the claimant cannot recover the value of those services from the defendant/carer, as the claimant would have to repay the damages to the defendant/carer (*Hunt v Severs* [1994] 2 All ER 385, HL).

#### 15.2.4.3 The valuation of gratuitous care

In the case of professional services, the claimant is entitled to the reasonable fee payable for those services; but in the case of gratuitous care where no fee is incurred, the valuation may be more problematical. Each case will be assessed on its own facts.

Where the relative or spouse has given up work in order to look after the claimant, and has thereby incurred loss of earnings, the lost earnings will be recoverable, provided they were reasonably incurred.

Where there is no loss of income by the third party, the court will normally take account of what it would cost to employ professional help. In this regard, there has been a recent tendency to favour the standard hourly rate paid at spinal point 8 of the National Joint Council for Local Government Services table. This rate, currently £6.75 per hour, which represents the earnings of home care workers, may be weighted to take account of location and also whether care is provided during the night or in extremely difficult circumstances. (See *Massey v Tameside & Glossop Acute Services NHS Trust* [2007] EWHC 317 (QB), where the court found that the flat rate at spinal point 8 did not adequately recompense a mother who provided particularly demanding services during the night and at weekends to her claimant son.) In addition, the court will normally apply a discount of somewhere between 20 and 30%, to reflect the absence of tax and National Insurance deductions, travelling costs to and from work, the profit element associated with commercial care services and the fact that professional carers might be more efficient.

If the claimant seeks a rate in excess of the commercial rate, he has the onus of proving the higher value (*Rialas v Mitchell* (1984) *The Times,* 17 July, where the claimant justified care at home which was approximately twice the cost of care in an institution) (see also *Fitzgerald v Ford* [1996] PIQR Q72).

### 15.2.5 Cost of DIY, gardening and housework services

The claimant is entitled to recover from the defendant the reasonable costs of obtaining DIY, gardening and housework services which he used to provide for himself but has been unable to do as a result of the accident. The services may be provided commercially or gratuitously, and there may be a claim for past loss under special damages and/or a general damages claim for future loss.

### 15.2.6 Costs of aids and appliances

The claimant may require specific aids or equipment to enable him to cope better with his disabilities. Such items will result in one-off payments, and where this expense has been incurred before the trial, it will form part of the claim for special damages. However, such items may be required at regular intervals after trial and throughout the claimant's life, and therefore the replacement cost must be included within any future loss calculation.

The types of aids and appliances which a claimant may require are too numerous to list here, but the following are a few examples:

(a) adaptations to the family car to allow the claimant to drive;

(b) wheelchairs (defendants may argue that these can be provided free by the State, in which case claimant's solicitors should argue that these would not be suitable);
(c) special beds;
(d) incontinence pads;
(e) odour control in the house due to incontinence;
(f) hoists, to assist in moving the claimant in and out of bed;
(g) tilting chairs;
(h) exercise equipment, such as stationary cycles;
(i) therapy balls, to help with mobility.

### 15.2.7 Cost of alternative accommodation and/or adaptations

Where a disabled claimant is living at home, it is possible that the accommodation he had prior to the accident is no longer suitable. It may require alterations and adaptations, such as the installation of ramps for a wheelchair or a hoist for access to the bath, alterations to the internal layout of the premises to facilitate access to bedrooms and bathrooms, or the creation of extra storage space to accommodate wheelchairs and other aids or appliances. It may be necessary to create accommodation for a resident nurse or carer. Where such alterations and adaptations do not add value to the accommodation, the cost may be recovered in full from the defendant. If the expense has been incurred prior to trial, it will form part of the special damages calculation. If not, it will form part of the future loss calculation.

Some alterations, such as an extension, may be expensive, but they will add value to the accommodation and, in such cases, the added value must be accounted for in the claim for damages

In some circumstances, the claimant's existing home may be incapable of adaptation and it is not unreasonable for him to move to more suitable accommodation. Provided that accommodation is reasonable for his needs, he will be entitled to purchase a home which is more expensive than his previous one. Clearly, the claimant will incur expenses in the move which are recoverable from the defendant. However, if he were entitled to recover from the defendant the purchase price of the more expensive new property less the proceeds from the sale of his previous home, he would be overcompensated. He would benefit from a more expensive house than perhaps he would otherwise have been able to buy, and the capital value of the property would remain intact on his death and represent a windfall to his estate.

In such circumstances, the solution developed by the courts is to say that the loss is not a straightforward capital loss, ie the cost of buying a larger house less the proceeds from the sale of the previous house, but rather the loss of the net income which that capital sum would have earned had it been invested. This lost income is not calculated by reference to a normal commercial rate of interest but in accordance with the rate set by the Court of Appeal in *Roberts v Johnstone* [1988] 3 WLR 1247. The rate of 2.5% per annum represents the real rate of return on a risk-free investment.

The loss to the claimant is calculated as follows:

- Past loss: extra capital outlay x 2.5% (rate of return) x number of years of loss
- Future loss: extra capital outlay x 2.5% x whole life multiplier (obtained from the Ogden tables)
- In either case, add any cost of conversion less any enhancement value

**Example**

The claimant, Abdul, was 39 at the time of the accident and has, as a result of catastrophic injuries, been confined to a wheelchair. Prior to the accident, he had lived in a third-floor flat, which was wholly unsuitable for his needs following the accident. Consequently, a year before the trial, he sold his former flat for £200,000 and moved to a bungalow, which he purchased for £300,000. The bungalow was more or less suitable for his needs, but a number of adaptations were required, including alterations to the bathroom and the installation of a ramp to the front door, which cost a further £15,000. In addition, an extension was built, costing £55,000, in order to accommodate a full-time carer. The extension has added £60,000 to the value of the bungalow. The other adaptations have not altered the valuation in any way.

| | | |
|---|---|---|
| Cost of replacement accommodation: | £300,000 | |
| LESS: value of current house: | £200,000 | |
| Capital difference | £100,000 | |
| @2.5% of £100,000 | £2,500 | |
| Past loss - £2,500 x 1 | | **£2,500** |
| Future loss - Multiplier (Table 1, Pecuniary loss of life, male; aged 39 at trial) = 26.15 | | |
| £2,500 x 26.15 | | **£65,375** |
| ADD conversion costs | | **£70,000** |
| | | **£135,375** |
| LESS increase in value | | **£60,000** |
| Future loss | | £75,375 |
| Total loss claimable: | | £77,875 |

## 15.2.8 Travelling costs

The claimant is entitled to claim reasonable travelling costs, whether by private car or other transport, such as buses, trains and taxis, which have arisen as a result of the accident. The costs of travelling to hospitals, doctors, physiotherapists, etc are all claimable, but the costs of travelling to a medical expert for the purposes of the litigation are not, as these should be claimed as legal costs rather than damages.

Where the claimant uses his own vehicle, there is usually a dispute between the parties regarding the reasonable amount payable for mileage. Claimants may seek to rely on the amount the Revenue allows employees to claim for business mileage before tax is charged – currently 40p per mile for up to 10,000 miles per year and 25p per mile for any additional miles – or the rate paid by the LSC – currently 45p per mile. The defendant may seek to rely on figures based on running costs, such as those provided by the AA and the RAC. For example, the 2009/10 AA rates for petrol vehicles range from 17.49p to 26.20p, depending on the purchase price of the car when (see www.theaa.com).

In many cases, family members and friends will incur additional travelling expenses, for example by visiting the claimant whilst he is in hospital. The claimant is able to claim such expenses as part of his loss (because he has a need for the visit), but it will be necessary to prove that they were reasonably incurred as a result of his injuries. Consequently, only those expenses which exceed what the family member or friend would have ordinarily spent on visiting the claimant can be recovered.

**Example**

The claimant, Peter, lived with his girlfriend, Sally, prior to the accident. Ordinarily, Sally would not have incurred any expense in seeing him, so all travelling expenses associated with visiting him in hospital can be claimed. On the other hand, if she had lived several miles away from Peter, a claim could be made only in respect of the costs which were over and above the normal travelling costs. If the hospital is further away than Peter's house, or she visits him more frequently than she would have otherwise done, a claim should be made for the additional expense.

Where there is a claim for future travelling costs, these can be calculated by means of a multiplicand and multiplier (see **15.3.5**). A claim for parking charges should also be made where appropriate.

### 15.2.9 Repairs to or replacement of the claimant's vehicle; recovery and storage costs

Where the claimant's vehicle is damaged beyond repair, he is entitled to claim its pre-accident value, less any salvage price obtained. Where the vehicle has been repaired, he is entitled to the reasonable costs of the repairs. The claimant will also be able to claim any reasonable costs incurred in recovering the vehicle from the accident site and storage costs prior to repair or disposal. As the claimant is under an obligation to mitigate his losses, he should not allow his vehicle to languish in storage facilities for too long or he may find he is unable to recover all of the associated charges.

### 15.2.10 Loss of use of a motor vehicle or hire of substitute vehicle

Where the claimant's vehicle is damaged and is off the road for a number of weeks while being repaired, the claimant may claim damages for the 'loss of use' of his vehicle. A weekly amount should be claimed, and this will reflect the level of inconvenience and hardship incurred by the claimant's having to rely on other means of transport. Special damages claims for loss of use of a motor vehicle have decreased in recent years, as the claimant is more likely to hire a substitute vehicle and claim the associated costs. However, such claims are still relevant where the claimant is no longer able to drive, and in such cases there might also be a general damages claim for the future loss of use of a motor vehicle.

Although it is clear that car hire charges incurred while the claimant's vehicle is being repaired can be claimed, the claimant must show that he has acted reasonably. The defendant should challenge the claim where the claimant has hired a more expensive type of vehicle than that involved in the accident, or has continued to hire a vehicle after his own vehicle has been repaired. Also, if the hire car is hired at the more expensive daily rate rather than at the cheaper weekly rate, then the defendant should argue that only the weekly rate should be recovered, although the claimant may be able to show a good reason for using the daily rate (see *Usher v Crowder* [1994] CLY 1494).

In certain circumstances, the claimant may use a vehicle supplied by a 'credit hire' company, but for any such agreement to be enforceable, it must comply with the Consumer Credit Act 1974 (or be exempt), and the amount recoverable should be the 'market rate' (*Dimond v Lovell* [2000] 2 WLR 1121).

Where a claim for hire charges is made, generally, a claim for loss of use will not be made as the claimant has not been without a vehicle.

### 15.2.11 No-claims bonus and wasted road fund licence

Under the terms of an insurance policy, a no-claims bonus (NCB) will entitle the policyholder to a discount on his annual premiums where he has not made any claims under the policy for a specified period. Where there is a NCB of five years or more, the policyholder may be entitled to a discount of as much as 60% to 75% and, as premiums are becoming increasingly expensive, the loss of the NCB may represent a significant monetary loss to the claimant. The claimant will lose the NCB where, as a result of his being involved in an accident, the insurance company has to make payments to either the claimant or a third party under the terms of the policy, and is unable to recoup such losses from anyone else. As it is a NCB and not a no-fault bonus, it is immaterial whether the claimant was at fault or not. Where the claimant has lost his NCB, or is at risk of doing so, the loss should be included in the claim for damages. If, ultimately, the claimant's insurer is able to recover all its losses from the defendant (or more usually the defendant's insurer), the NCB will not be lost and the defendant's solicitor should ensure that the claim for the NCB is withdrawn.

The claimant is entitled to claim for any wasted road fund licence, although he is expected to mitigate his loss by obtaining a refund for any full months remaining on the licence.

### 15.2.12 Evidence of items of special damages

It is for the claimant to prove all items of special damages, and details should be set out in the appropriate witness statement(s). Where damaged items are capable of repair or services are required, the claimant should obtain two or three estimates in order to demonstrate that the costs incurred are reasonable. A decision to use a more expensive service provider should be explained in full. The claimant should be reminded at the outset of the case that he should retain documentary evidence (such as receipts, estimates and valuations) wherever possible. Defendants' solicitors should challenge items that cannot be supported by appropriate evidence. Where there is no documentary evidence, it is open to the claimant to attempt to prove the loss by his own oral testimony at trial, but see *Hughes v Addis* [2000] LTL, 23 March, where the Court of Appeal upheld the judge's decision not to allow petrol costs where no receipts were supplied.

## 15.3 General damages

General damages are those which are not capable of precise mathematical calculation. They may be divided into:

(a) pain, suffering and loss of amenity (sometimes known as non-pecuniary loss); and

(b) financial losses incurred from the date of trial (or date of assessment of damages) for as long as court deems the losses will continue into the future (sometimes know as future pecuniary loss).

The main heads of general damages are:

(a) pain, suffering and loss of amenity;

(b) handicap in the labour market;

(c) loss of congenial employment;

(d) future loss of earnings;

(e) future cost of medical expenses and care/non-medical care and aids and appliances;

(f) lost pension.

### 15.3.1 Pain, suffering and loss of amenity

Awards of damages under this head are designed to compensate the claimant for the pain and suffering attributable to any physical injury and psychological illness caused by the defendant's actions, from the moment of the accident to the date of trial, when damages are assessed, and, where appropriate, future pain and suffering.

The award is made on the basis of a subjective test, ie a consideration of the pain and suffering of this particular claimant. If there is no evidence that the claimant actually experienced pain, such as where he has never regained consciousness following an accident, then no award will be made.

#### 15.3.1.1 Damages for loss of amenity

Strictly speaking, there is a separate head of damages known as 'loss of amenity', but compensation for this loss is usually included with compensation for pain and suffering. This element is designed to compensate the claimant for the loss of enjoyment of life which has resulted from the accident. Examples under this head include interference with the claimant's sex life, or the loss or impairment of his enjoyment of holidays, sports, hobbies and other pursuits.

The award for loss of amenity is based on an objective test (in contrast to pain and suffering), and thus may be awarded irrespective of whether the claimant is personally aware of his loss, for example if he is unconscious (*West v Shephard* [1964] AC 326).

Although the test is primarily objective, it does have subjective overtones in so far as the court will have regard to the claimant's former lifestyle. This may be particularly pertinent where the claimant was formerly a very active person (eg a keen sportsman) and can no longer pursue his sport. Although his pain and suffering may be the same as that of another person with a similar disability, his loss of amenity may be greater and, as such, the total award for pain and suffering and loss of amenity may be greater.

Damages for loss of congenial employment (see **15.3.4**) may also be argued under this head, but increasingly, the courts are making separate reference to these types of damages.

### 15.3.1.2 Quantification of damages for pain, suffering and loss of amenity

There is no minimum award which must be made for pain, suffering and loss of amenity (however, only exceptionally would an injury not be worth, for example, £500 or £750); neither is there any maximum.

The award is incapable of precise mathematical calculation. The solicitor's first step is to examine the claimant's witness statement and the medical report in order to identify details of the following:

(a) The claimant's life prior to the accident. This will be relevant to the loss of amenity claim.
(b) The pain and suffering associated with the accident itself and the immediate aftermath. What were the injuries? How did the claimant react? Was he taken to hospital by ambulance?
(c) Any periods of time the claimant was in hospital, and the number and nature of any operations or other medical procedures he had to undergo.
(d) The short-term/long-term prognosis. Will the claimant recover in full? If not, what will his continuing pain/disabilities be, and how long will they continue?
(e) Is there a risk of any future degeneration (eg, osteoporosis)?
(f) What has been/will be the effect of the injuries on the claimant's lifestyle?

In attempting to value the claim, courts will refer to the awards made in comparable cases, so the solicitor's next step is to carry out the relevant research. As no two cases are exactly alike (for example, there may be differences in relation to the sex and age of the claimant, the injuries suffered and the effect on the claimant's life), this is not as straightforward as it might appear.

A useful starting point is the Judicial Studies Board's *Guidelines for the Assessment of General Damages in Personal Injury Cases*, which are commonly used by personal injury lawyers and judges to obtain a ball-park figure for the claimant's injuries. (An on-line version of the 8th edition of the *Guidelines* can be found on Lawtel Personal Injury.) The *Guidelines* are based on an analysis of previous judgments and provide an easy reference to broad categories of injuries, such as head injuries, psychiatric damages, injuries affecting the senses, injuries to internal organs, etc. These categories are further divided, so, for example, the section on orthopaedic injuries is divided into neck injuries, back injuries, shoulder injuries, etc. Finally, each of these sub-categories is divided into severe, serious, moderate and minor classifications, with an indication of what each of these types of injuries are worth. You should not base your assessment of the claimant's losses solely on the *Guidelines* but rather should make reference to specific comparable cases. The importance of comparable cases was stressed by the Court of

Appeal in *Dureau v Evans* [1996] PIQR Q18, when it commented on the limited assistance provided by the *Guidelines* in relation to claimants who have suffered multiple injuries. Similarly, in *Reed v Sunderland Health Authority* (1998) *The Times*, 16 October, it was held that while the *Guidelines* were an important source of information, they did not have the force of law, and the Court of Appeal is unlikely to overturn a decision if the *Guidelines* are not followed precisely (see *Davis v Inman* [1999] PIQR Q26).

Traditionally, solicitors looking for comparable cases would use specialist sources, such as:

(a) Kemp and Kemp, *The Quantum of Damages* (Sweet & Maxwell);

(b) *Butterworths Personal Injury Service*;

(c) *Personal Injuries and Quantum Reports* (Sweet & Maxwell);

(d) *Current Law* (Sweet & Maxwell);

(e) *Personal and Medical Injuries Law Letter* (IBC).

However, increasingly, solicitors are using on-line services, such as Butterworth's PI or Lawtel (which includes access to Kemp and Kemp), to identify comparable cases.

Once a comparable case has been found, the relevant figure is that relating to pain, suffering and loss of amenity. Remember the difficulties associated with terminology. Frequently, the case reports will helpfully set out a figure for pain, suffering and loss of amenity, but sometimes they will refer to 'general damages'. If it is clear from the facts of the case that there are no future losses, or alternatively a figure for future losses appears, it is safe to assume that the term 'general damages' is the award for pain, suffering and loss of amenity. If it is unsafe to make such an assumption, further investigations will need to be made.

There will be differences between the claimant's situation and the circumstances of the claimants in the comparable case so, once the relevant figure in the comparable case has been identified, adjustments will need to be made in order to take account of the following matters:

(a) *Sex* – for example, scarring (especially scars on the face) on a female claimant carries a higher award than for a male claimant (see Judicial Studies Board *Guidelines*).

(b) *Age of the victim* – in cases of permanent disability, younger victims tend to get more compensation than older victims as the young will suffer longer. On the other hand, some injuries will have a more severe impact on an older claimant than on a younger one.

(c) *Loss of amenity* – this is heavily influenced by whether the victim had a previously active lifestyle.

(d) *Limb injuries* – injuries to dominant limbs attract higher awards than injuries to non-dominant limbs.

(e) *Inflation* – previous awards must be inflated to present-day values. The inflation table in Kemp and Kemp, *The Quantum of Damages*, can be used for that purpose although on-line sources, such as the one on Lawtel PI, provide both original and inflated figures in their quantum reports. Lawtel also has an on-line calculator which is very easy to use.

(f) *Uplift* – in the case of *Heil v Rankin and Another* [2000] 2 WLR 1173, the Court of Appeal considered the level of damages for pain and suffering, concluded that they were too low, and stated that there should be staged increases for all future cases where the value of awards for pain and suffering was in excess of £10,000. Consequently, when seeking to rely on a pre-March 2000 case in excess of £10,000, a conversion table (such as that found in *Quantum* 2/2000, 18 April 2000 (Sweet & Maxwell)), must be used to update the award, which will then need to be inflated to present-day values. The inflated figures provided in Lawtel's quantum reports take account of *Heil v Rankin*, and their on-line calculator will do this automatically, where relevant. The 5th edition of the *Guidelines* also takes the increases into account.

When carrying out the research relating to a client who has sustained multiple injuries, it is extremely unlikely that a comparable case will be found. The accepted approach is to identify the most serious injury, find a comparable award for that injury and then take account of awards made for the other injuries. It will not normally be appropriate simply to bolt the separate awards together, as the court will seek to compensate the claimant for the totality of his pain and suffering, and some discount will be required in recognition of this.

#### 15.3.1.3 Damages where there are pre-existing injuries or conditions

One of the arguments that the defendant may use to bar or limit recovery of loss for pain and suffering is that the whole or part of the claimant's injuries or disabilities is due to a pre-existing condition.

The egg-shell skull rule, which states that the defendant 'must take the victim as he finds him', means that a defendant will not escape liability in situations where the claimant had pre-existing injuries which made him more vulnerable to further injury. However, it does not mean that the defendant will be liable for the full extent of any injuries or disabilities suffered by the claimant. Rather, the defendant will be liable for the full extent of *the aggravation or exacerbation* of the claimant's pre-existing conditions. Where the defendant is able to show that the claimant would eventually have suffered similar symptoms in any event, damages will be restricted to those arising during the acceleration period, ie the period of time by which the symptoms have been brought forward by reason of the defendant's negligence.

**Example**

Samantha suffered from a degenerative condition of the spine prior to her involvement in a RTA caused by the defendant's negligence. The defendant argues that this condition would eventually have generated the symptoms of which Samantha is now complaining, and that his actions have merely accelerated her disabilities. The defendant is able to prove that, but for his actions, her symptoms would have developed in five years time in any event. The court will apply the 'acceleration period' approach and the defendant will be liable only for a five-year period for injury, loss and damage.

#### 15.3.1.4 Evidence

Although the medical evidence will be the primary matter to which the court will have regard in determining the award for pain, suffering and loss of amenity, the claimant will also give evidence of his injuries at trial. It is important that details are contained within the client's witness statement. It is surprising how many clients forget the exact details of the difficulties they had immediately post-accident or post-operation, and it is good practice for the claimant's solicitor to suggest that a diary is kept by the client, detailing the pain and practical difficulties that were suffered. It may also be helpful to obtain evidence from others, such as the claimant's spouse and family members, or his employer, as to the effect of the injuries on the claimant.

### 15.3.2 Handicap in the labour market

The purpose of this award is to compensate the claimant for the potential difficulties he may face in obtaining another job, should he lose his current job, as a result of his injuries. For the court to award such damages, the claimant should have suffered a 'weakening' of his competitive position in the open labour market. In practice, this is referred to as a *Smith v Manchester* claim (see *Smith v Manchester Corporation* (1974) 17 KIR 1).

In deciding whether this type of award is appropriate, the court will:

(a) consider whether there is a 'substantial' or 'real' risk that the claimant will lose his present job at some time before the estimated end of his working life; and if there is

(b) assess and quantify the present value of the loss which the claimant will suffer if that risk materialises. In doing so, the court will have regard to the degree of risk, the time when it is likely to materialise and the factors, both favourable and unfavourable, which may affect the claimant's chance of getting another job at all or an equally well-paid job.

When seeking to establish whether there is a risk that the claimant will lose his job, the courts have given the words 'substantial' or 'real' a liberal interpretation, so that what is required to be shown is that the risk is 'real' rather than 'speculative'. The risk might lie in the nature of the injuries themselves, which might make it impossible for the claimant to continue in that line of work. If this is the case, the matter should be addressed in the medical report, and the claimant may also give evidence in his witness statement. Alternatively, the risk might lie in matters that have nothing to do with the injuries, such as business restructuring. The client's trade union will have details of any redundancies that have been made by the employer in recent years, and it may also be able to provide information about the employer's future plans, of which the client may not have been aware. If the client does not belong to a trade union, evidence should be obtained from the client's workmates or managers. (If the defendant is the claimant's employer, such information should be obtained from the defendant's insurers or solicitor.) The solicitor representing the defendant must obtain clear evidence concerning the claimant's job security in an attempt to refute the *Smith v Manchester* claim.

Once the first test has been satisfied, the court will attempt to quantify the risk and calculate the appropriate damages. The court has to anticipate what would be the claimant's chances of getting an equally well-paid job if he was forced onto the labour market. This head of damages is notoriously hard to quantify as the court will consider each individual case on its own facts, but a common approach is to award between zero to two years' net loss of earnings as at the date of trial. However, the Court of Appeal in *Foster v Tyne and Wear County Council* [1986] 1 All ER 567 stated that there was no 'conventional' figure for damages under this head, and awarded a sum equivalent to four years' net salary.

Examples of cases where a *Smith v Manchester* award may be considered appropriate include the following:

(a) The claimant has returned to work after the accident and thus he has no continuing loss of earnings claim. However, there is a risk that he will lose his job in the future and will have difficulty in obtaining a job as well paid due to his injuries. A *Smith v Manchester* award will be claimed.

(b) The claimant has returned to work and is earning, say, 20% less than he did prior to the accident. As a result, he will have a continuing partial loss of earnings claim that could be calculated by using the multiplier/multiplicand approach (see **15.3.3**). In addition, the court is satisfied that he will lose his job and will have difficulty in obtaining another equally well-paid job due to his injuries. A *Smith v Manchester* award will be claimed.

(c) The claimant is still absent from work at the time of the trial as a result of the injuries suffered in the accident, but he expects to return to his job in a few years when he has recovered further. The medical evidence suggests that, should he lose his job, he may still have problems in obtaining equally well-paid work due to his injuries. In these circumstances, a *Smith v Manchester* award will be claimed.

This type of award is not normally appropriate where the claimant will never be able to return to work, as he will be compensated by his claim for future lost earnings. However, the number of cases where the claimant is unable to work at all in the future will be small.

A *Smith v Manchester* award should normally be claimed in the particulars of claim (*Chan Wai Tong v Li Ping Sum* [1985] AC 446). However, the Court of Appeal, in *Thorn v Powergen* [1997] PIQR Q71, upheld a decision allowing a *Smith v Manchester* award in a case where it had not been claimed specifically but was found by the trial judge to be implied due to the nature of the injuries revealed by the medical evidence.

Evidence must be obtained concerning the claimant's future job prospects, including any skills he possesses (eg, a labourer of 50 years of age with no qualifications will find it difficult to retrain if he loses his job), the prospects of the industry in which the claimant works and any unusual local problems that may be relevant to the claimant. It may be necessary to instruct an employment consultant to provide information about these matters, or to obtain relevant information from other sources, for example the Annual Survey of Hours and Earnings. The expert would consider the client's injuries and personal qualifications, and analyse employment statistics and local press advertisements in order to report on the severity of the handicap on the labour market. In other cases, the trial judge will be aware of the employment situation in his area and be able to formulate the appropriate award.

Any evidence relating to handicap on the labour market claim must be included within the medical report and the witness statements for exchange.

### 15.3.3 Loss of congenial employment

The concept of compensating the claimant for a loss of job satisfaction has been accepted by the courts for some time. In *Morris v Johnson Matthey & Co Ltd* (1967) 112 SJ 32, a precious metal worker, aged 52, sustained a serious injury to his left hand, which left him incapable of continuing his craft. His employers found him alternative employment as a storeman, which he described as 'at times rather boring'. Edmund-Davies LJ stated:

> the joy of the craftsman in his craft is beyond price. But the court has to give some monetary value to the loss of craft. The court should give consideration to the fact that a craftsman had to replace his craft with humdrum work.

Traditionally, the award was incorporated within the award for pain, suffering and loss of amenity, but it is now well established that the court will normally make a separate award under this heading. Generally, those who received such awards were deprived of jobs which have a vocational element or where a period of training is required, such as firemen, nurses, members of the armed forces, dancers, actors, and craftsmen such as carpenters. Those employed in repetitive manual work, such as factory workers, are unlikely to be able to convince a court that they found their job rewarding. However, claimants' solicitors should listen carefully to what their clients have to say on this point, as courts will judge each case on its facts. In *McCrae v (1) Chase International Express Ltd (2) Justin Smith* [2003] LTL, 14 March, the Court of Appeal overturned an award made to a motor-cycle courier on the basis that it was not satisfied with the evidence in support of the claim, but said that that an award might otherwise have been appropriate. In *Lane v The Personal Representatives of Deborah Lake (Deceased)* [2007] All ER (D) 258, the defendant tried to argue that this award should be reserved for policemen, firemen, etc, but this was rejected by the judge on the basis that such an award 'should be confined to those who truly have suffered a loss under this head and not be awarded merely by reference to the type of employment nor automatically as an extra'.

Awards tend to be in the range of £5,000 to £10,000. In *Willbye (by her mother and next friend) v Gibbons* [2003] EWCA Civ 372, the Court of Appeal reduced an award of £15,000 which had been made to a girl who had been 12 years old at the time of the accident and who had wanted to become a nursery nurse. It said that it was important to keep this head of damages in proportion and reduced the award to £5,000. Nevertheless, higher awards will be made in appropriate circumstances. The highest award so far was made in *Appleton v Medhat Mohammed El Safty* [2007] EWHC 631 (QB), to a footballer who had been playing for West Bromwich Albion before clinical negligence cut short his career. The Court of Appeal found the facts of this case to be exceptional and awarded £25,000.

Any evidence relating to a loss of congenial employment claim must be included within the witness statements for exchange. In particular, the claimant must give full details of the nature of his previous employment, any training or qualifications required, his career progression, etc, so that the loss of job satisfaction can be proved.

### 15.3.4 Future loss of earnings

Damages for loss of earnings after the date of trial will be assessed as general damages. The court will need to determine what the claimant would have earned, had he not been injured, up to the time he would have ordinarily retired or for a specified period, if he is expected to recover sufficiently to be able to work in the future. Even the most straightforward case will require the court to tackle uncertainty, and the more complex the case, the more 'crystal ball gazing' will be required.

Under the conventional method of calculating future loss of earnings, a lump sum award will be calculated using a multiplier and a multiplicand. The object is to assess the amount of money which can be invested today which will represent a fund which should last for precisely the period of the lost earnings. In other words, the capital sum is invested, the claimant periodically draws out from the fund what he would have earned throughout the period of loss, and the fund gradually decreases until it is exhausted at the very end of the period of loss. That is, at least, the theory.

#### 15.3.4.1 The multiplicand

The multiplicand is the figure which represents the claimant's annual loss, so where a claimant is not able to work at all, it will be the net annual earnings that he would have received had he not been injured. Where the claimant is able to work but will earn less than his pre-accident salary, the multiplicand is the difference between the two net annual earnings. The items to be included or ignored in the calculation of the multiplicand are the same as for pre-trial earnings, as identified at **15.2.1**.

#### 15.3.4.2 The multiplier

The multiplier is based on the period of likely future loss. This will depend on the facts of the case. For example, in the case of a male claimant who will never work again, the period of loss will normally extend until his likely retirement age (normally 60 or 65). The period of loss is taken from the date of trial, as pre-trial losses will be claimed as special damages.

The period of loss is then converted into a multiplier. Following the House of Lords' decision in the joint appeals of *Page v Sheerness Steel Co Ltd; Wells v Wells; Thomas v Brighton Health Authority* [1998] 3 WLR 329, it can now be assumed that the starting point when attempting to identify the multiplier is to use the Government's actuarial tables (the Ogden Tables; see **Appendix 5**).

The multipliers in Tables 1 to 26 are based on mortality rates for the United Kingdom, with different tables for males and females, and a discount to take account of accelerated receipt (ie the claimant will receive a lump sum which he can invest).

In order to find the appropriate multiplier, the solicitor will;

(a) identify the correct table from Tables 3 to 14 by using the claimant's sex and anticipated retirement age had it not been for the accident;
(b) find the claimant's age at the date of trial along the left-hand vertical column;
(c) find the correct discount rate along the top horizontal line. In 2001, the Lord Chancellor set the 'discount rate' that should be referred to when using the Ogden Tables at 2.5%. This represents the real rate of return (ie, after tax and making allowance for inflation) calculated over the appropriate period of time. Although there should be no argument about the applicable rate, it is open to the courts under s 1(2) of the Damages Act 1996 to adopt a different rate if there are exceptional circumstances;
(d) identify the appropriate multiplier, which can be found where the relevant vertical and horizontal columns meet;

don't do in exam but say it will be done.



(e) consider whether further discounts are appropriate to take account of other 'risks and vicissitudes of life', such as the possibility that there would be periods when the claimant would not have been earning due to ill-health or loss of employment. The factors which are to be taken into account are as follows:

  (i) whether the claimant was employed or not at the time of the accident. Employed includes being self-employed or being on a government training scheme,

  (ii) whether the claimant was disabled or not at the time of the accident. A claimant is disabled if he has either a progressive illness or an illness which has lasted or is expected to last for over a year, satisfies the Disability Discrimination Act definition that the impact of the disability substantially limits his ability to carry out normal day-to-day activities *and* his condition affects either the kind or the amount of work he can do,

  (iii) the claimant's level of educational attainment at the time of the accident. There are three levels: degree or equivalent and higher, GCSE grades A to C up to A levels and equivalent, and below GCSE grade C or CSE grade 1 or no qualifications.

  Section B of the Ogden Tables gives further information regarding these discounts and how they should be applied (see **Appendix 5**).

### 15.3.4.3 The calculation

In order to determine the amount for future loss of earnings, the multiplicand is multiplied by the amended multiplier.

> **Example**
>
> Simon was 43 when the accident occurred and 45 at trial. He was employed as a labourer prior to the accident, earning £20,000 per annum. He was not disabled, had no qualifications and was due to retire 65.
>
> (a) As he is male and his retirement age is 65, the correct table is Table 9;
>
> (b) Using his age at trial, 45, and the 2.5% rate of return, a multiplier of 15.19 is identified.
>
> (c) Account for risks other than mortality, ie for Simon being employed, not disabled and having no qualifications. Table A is the correct table as Simon is male, would have retired at 65, and was not disabled. Identify the correct age bracket on the left hand side (45–49) and, across the top, identify the correct column. This is the third column (headed O), as he was employed but without qualifications. The correct discount figure is 0.86.
>
> (d) The amended multiplier is 15.19 x 0.86 = 13.06
>
> (e) The future loss of earnings 13.06 x £20,000 = £261,200

### 15.3.4.4 Career progression and loss of earnings

In cases where the period of loss will continue for many years into the future, it is particularly important to ensure that account is taken of likely periodic changes to the claimant's income. The claimant will want to point to anticipated career progressions where, for example, he was a junior doctor, a trainee solicitor or a junior officer in the armed forces. In such cases, the court will either

(a) determine an average multiplicand, based upon the likely earnings throughout the period of loss, which will then be applied to the full period of the loss; or

(b) use stepped multiplicands for each stage of the claimant's career. Generally, this will result in a lower multiplicand at the beginning and possibly at the very end of the period of loss, with one or more higher multiplicands to represent the likely career progression that would have been followed.

In *Collett v Smith and Middlesborough Football & Athletics Company (1986) Ltd* [2008] EWHC 1962 (QB), the court was required to assess damages in relation to a young man whose promising football career had been cut short, at the age of 18, as a result of a negligent tackle.

In assessing damages for future loss of earnings at £3,854,328, the court was obliged to make decisions on such issues as the level at which he would have played football and at what remuneration, how long he would have played for, whether his career would have otherwise have been cut short by injury and whether he would have gone on to work as a coach or manager.

The amount of 'crystal ball gazing' which the court will of necessity have to undertake in this exercise is increased in cases where the claimant was a child at the time of the accident. If the child is old enough to have attended school, taken a few exams and shown some interest in one career or another, it might be possible to anticipate a likely career progression. With a younger child, this will be much more difficult. The court will take into account the following evidence, where available:

(a) the nature of the employment of the claimant's parents and siblings;
(b) any qualifications obtained so far;
(c) evidence from the claimant's former teachers, club leaders, sports trainers, etc regarding the claimant's abilities and personality;
(d) neuropsychological evidence of the claimant's pre-accident IQ;
(e) the claimant's own evidence and personality, as demonstrated in the witness-box.

#### 15.3.4.5 Evidence

The importance of expert evidence in such a case is vital. Medical evidence can provide an indication as to what work the claimant will be capable of undertaking, both at present and in the future. This, together with evidence of the claimant's employment prospects, will assist the court in determining what will happen to the claimant in the future, which, while often appearing unsatisfactory to many clients, is usually the approach that the court will take.

### 15.3.5 Future cost of medical expenses, care and quasi-nursing services, and aids and appliances

In cases of catastrophic injury, it is possible that the claim for the cost of future care and quasi-nursing services will exceed the claim for future loss of earnings. This is because the need for care will often continue beyond the claimant's normal retirement age, plus the fact that specialist care is extremely expensive. It must be remembered that the cost and type of care may change in the future. For example, a severely injured child's costs of care will increase as he becomes older because it is unlikely that his parents will be able to look after him when they are elderly and, as such, increased professional help will be required.

The calculation for the future cost of care is carried out in the same way as set out in **15.3.4**. However, when identifying the multiplier, the correct table will be either Table 1 or Table 2, depending upon whether the claimant is male or female. In addition, following the House of Lords' decision in *Page v Sheerness Steel Co Ltd; Wells v Wells; Thomas v Brighton Health Authority* (see **15.3.4.2**), it is not appropriate to discount whole life multipliers.

The cost of medical expenses and aids and appliances may also be dealt with using a multiplier from Tables 1 or 2 and a multiplicand where a continuing need can be demonstrated. For example, the claimant may include the cost of a wheelchair as part of his special damages claim. That wheelchair will not last the claimant for the rest of his life, and therefore the replacement cost will need to be annualised. So, where the cost of a wheelchair is £1,000 and it would have a life span of five years, the multiplicand would be £200. Generally, the annual cost of items relevant to the same period of loss are added together to produce one multiplier.

Alternatively, the claimant may require an operation which will not need to be repeated, or an appliance which will not need to be replaced. In such cases, a one-off payment should be included in the claim.

### 15.3.6 Loss of pension

In more serious cases, where the claimant does not return to work or returns on a lower wage, consideration must be given to a claim for lost pension. The claimant's pension is normally based upon his period of service with the company and the salary that he would have earned at retirement age. Reference should be made to specialist texts on this subject.

## 15.4 Provisional damages

### 15.4.1 The problem which provisional damages are intended to solve

When the court awards damages or the parties agree a settlement, it will be on the basis of a full and final settlement of the claim. Consequently, the normal rule is that the claimant is unable to return to court to ask for a further award to be made, even where his condition has seriously deteriorated.

This being the case, the claimant's solicitor should ensure that the claimant is properly compensated, by ensuring that expert medical evidence deals with any deterioration that is likely to arise in the future. Where the court is satisfied that the claimant is more than 50% likely to suffer a specified deterioration in his condition, the court will award damages on the basis that the deterioration *will* occur and a provisional damages order is not appropriate. The problem lies in cases where the deterioration, although possible, is less than probable.

**Example**

Fred is injured. At the time of the trial he has no loss of sight, but there is a 10% possibility that in the future he will lose the sight in one eye. Bearing in mind that quantum for pain and suffering and loss of amenity for the total loss of sight in one eye is approximately £30,000, how does the judge award damages to Fred?

If the judge awards £3,000 (10% of £30,000) and Fred does lose the sight in his eye in the future, Fred will be under-compensated by £27,000 but cannot return to court for more damages. If Fred does not lose the sight in his eye in the future, Fred is unjustly enriched by £3,000 and the defendant cannot recover the excess damages.

Provisional damages are aimed at solving the above problem by providing an exception to the basic rule. In certain limited circumstances the claimant can be compensated for his injuries with the proviso that if a specific condition occurs in the future, he will be allowed to return to court so that further damages can be awarded.

### 15.4.2 The statutory provisions

Rule 41.2 of the CPR states that the court may make an order for provisional damages, provided the claim is included in the particulars of claim and the court is satisfied that s 32A of the Supreme Court Act 1981 or s 51 of the County Courts Act 1984 applies.

In accordance with s 32A of the Supreme Court Act 1981, an order for provisional damages can be made where there is

> a chance that at some definite or indefinite time in the future the injured person will, as a result of the act or omission which gave rise to the cause of action, develop some serious disease or suffer some serious deterioration in his physical or mental condition.

A similar provision is found in s 51 of the County Courts Act 1984.

If the court considers that there is a suitable case for provisional damages (see CPR Part 41 and PD 41), it will:

(a) assess damages on the assumption that the injured person will not develop the disease or suffer the deterioration in his condition;

(b) identify the disease or deterioration that has been disregarded;

(c) stipulate a period (which may be indefinite) during which the claimant may return to court for further damages if he develops the disease or suffers the deterioration;

(d) make an order that relevant documents are to be kept by the court.

If the claimant subsequently suffers the specified disease or deterioration within the specified time frame, he may apply to the court for further damages. The order will set out with precision the circumstances which must arise before the claimant is allowed to return to court, as it will wish to avoid a situation where there is a subsequent dispute as to whether the proper circumstances had arisen.

#### 15.4.2.1 'Chance'

The expression 'chance' is not defined in the legislation. It clearly indicates something less than a probability, ie less than 50% likelihood, and in *Curi v Colina* [1998] EWCA Civ 1326, the Court of Appeal said there had to be a 'possibility but no more than a possibility'. However, it must be measurable rather than merely fanciful (*Willson v Ministry of Defence* [1991] 1 All ER 638, where it was held that the possibility that the claimant would incur further injury from a fall as a result of an ankle injury was not evidence of 'serious deterioration' as it might not ever happen).

In order to be measurable, the chance should be expressed in terms of a percentage figure. The courts have been prepared to make an order for provisional damages where the likelihood of deterioration has been expressed in terms of single figure percentages, but each case will depend on its own facts. If there is doubt as to whether the case is appropriate for a provisional damages claim then advice from a solicitor or barrister with expertise in this area should be sought.

#### 15.4.2.2 'Serious deterioration'

'Serious deterioration' is not defined in the legislation. In *Willson*, it was held that 'serious deterioration' meant:

(a) a clear and severable risk of deterioration (not merely the natural progression of the injury); and

(b) something beyond ordinary deterioration.

On the facts of *Willson*, the court held that the chance of arthritis was merely a natural progression of the injury and was not a suitable case for provisional damages. The most common examples of conditions in which provisional damages have been awarded in practice are where there is the chance of the claimant suffering from epilepsy, or from a disease such as cancer or asbestosis as a result of exposure to a dangerous substance.

### 15.4.3 Procedural approach

The claim for provisional damages must be included in the particulars of claim, and if the possibility of provisional damages emerges after these documents have been served, the documents must be amended. Part 16 of the CPR 1998 and the accompanying Practice Direction set out the necessary information which must be included.

The court will be slow to make an order for provisional damages, on the basis that finality is better for all parties. Evidence is therefore very important, and the medical report should address the issues with precision. In particular, it should set out the nature of the deterioration, the chance of deterioration by means of a percentage figure and an anticipated time frame.

The only basis for an award of provisional damages is a court order. Any application by consent for an award of provisional damages should follow the procedure set out in Part 23 of the CPR 1998.

If the specified disease or deterioration occurs within the specified period, the claimant must give at least 28 days' written notice to the defendant of his intention to apply for further damages.

It is possible to apply to extend the period of time for claiming further damages, and a medical report should be filed in support of such an application. Such an application must be made within the original time limit.

### 15.4.4 The claimant's and defendant's perspectives

Even where the claimant's claim falls within the realm of provisional damages, the claimant may not want to pursue this option, preferring instead that the claim is satisfied once and for all by the award of a lump sum. The defendant will also usually prefer the matter to be dealt with by one lump sum award, and will therefore be prepared to negotiate an additional amount to take account of the risk of deterioration in an attempt to persuade the claimant to abandon his claim for provisional damages.

The claimant's solicitor must advise his client of the implications of each option, preferably in writing, and obtain his instructions, again preferably in writing. The claimant must appreciate that if he chooses to accept a lump sum in full and final settlement, he will not be able to return to court to ask for additional compensation should his condition deteriorate, no matter how serious the deterioration is. Alternatively, if the court makes an order for provisional damages, he will be able to return to court only if the specified deterioration occurs within the specified time limit.

Solicitors must ensure that they preserve their own files for the appropriate length of time.

### 15.4.5 Provisional damages and the Fatal Accidents Act 1976

Section 3 of the Damages Act 1996 allows an application to the court under the FAA 1976 where a person is awarded provisional damages and subsequently dies.

### 15.4.6 Provisional damages and Part 36 of the CPR

Where there is a claim for provisional damages and the defendant makes a Part 36 offer, the offer notice must specify whether or not the settlement includes the making of a provisional damages award (see **14.10.3**).

## 15.5 Periodical payments

### 15.5.1 The problems which periodical payments are intended to solve

The assessment of damages, particularly in relation to future pecuniary loss, depends upon matters which are uncertain and unpredictable. Consequently, a lump sum payment may result in the following:

(a) over-compensation, leading to unfairness to the defendant. A claimant may die early and his beneficiaries be unjustly enriched;

(b) under-compensation, leading to a lack of financial security for the claimant. Where a claimant will be dependent on care for many years, the money may run out;

(c) a lack of prudence on the part of the claimant or his family. Few have experience of managing large sums of money, and inappropriate spending or unwise investment may dissipate the fund;

(d) a lack of flexibility. The general rule is that the claimant cannot return to court if his condition deteriorates (unless there is an order for provisional damages, see **15.4** above).

These problems will be less severe where the court orders periodical payments to be made. Here, the court will assess the annual needs of the claimant in order to calculate the amount of the periodic payments; the payments rise in accordance with inflation and are paid, free of tax, to the end of claimant's life. In addition, the management and administration involved in the investment of damages is transferred from the claimant to the defendant, but as the payments must be secure, the continuity of the payments is guaranteed.

### 15.5.2 The statutory provisions

#### 15.5.2.1 The court's power to make an order for periodical payments

Under s 2 of the Damages Act 1996 (as amended by s 100 of the Courts Act 2003), where an order for damages includes an amount for future pecuniary loss in respect of personal injury, the court must consider whether an order for periodical payments is appropriate. Where there is a claim for damages in respect of future pecuniary loss, such as the future loss of earnings or the future costs of care, the court can order that the damages wholly or partly take the form of periodical payments, and it can do so without obtaining the consent of the parties.

The court can make an order for periodic payments in respect of other damages, such as past pecuniary loss and pain, suffering and loss of amenity, only where both parties consent (s 2(2)).

Under s 2(3), the court can make such an order only where it is satisfied that the continuity of payment is reasonably secure. Section 2(4) states that a payment is 'reasonably secure' where:

(a) it is protected by a guarantee given under s 6 of or the Schedule to the Act;

(b) it is protected by a scheme under s 213 of the Financial Services and Markets Act 2000; or

(c) the source of payment is a government or health service body.

Where none of the above applies, a defendant may be able to prove that payment is reasonably secure by purchasing a life annuity for the claimant's benefit, which would be protected by the Financial Services Compensation Scheme or by some other means.

#### 15.5.2.2 The order

Under CPR, r 41.8(1), where the court awards damages in the form of periodical payments, it must specify:

> (a) the annual amount awarded, how each payment is to be made during the year and at what intervals;
>
> (b) the amount awarded for future—
>
> (i) loss of earnings and other income; and
>
> (ii) care and medical costs and other recurring or capital costs;
>
> (c) that the claimant's annual future pecuniary losses, as assessed by the court, are to be paid for the duration of the claimant's life, or such other period as the court orders; and
>
> (d) that the amount of the payments shall vary annually by reference to the retail prices index, unless the court orders otherwise under section 2(9) of the 1996 Act.

#### 15.5.2.3 Indexation

Under s 2(8) of the Damages Act 1996, the payments will rise by reference to the Retail Price Index (RPI), although s 2(9) allows for s 2(8) to be disapplied. There has been much controversy as to whether the RPI is the appropriate index as it is based on prices, which historically have not risen as sharply as wages. In the provision of care services, it has been wages that have been driving the cost up, and it is therefore argued that the Aggregate Annual Survey of Hours and Earnings (ASHE 6115) is the appropriate index to use. In *Tameside and Glossop Acute Services NHS Trust v Thompstone* [2008] EWCA Civ 5, the Court of Appeal settled this debate by endorsing the use of ASHE 6115.

#### 15.5.2.4 Variation

In accordance with the Damages (Variation of Periodical Payments) Order 2005 (SI 2005/ 841), where the court is satisfied that, at some time in the future, the claimant will:

(a) as a result of the act or omission which gave rise to the cause of action, develop some serious disease or suffer some serious deterioration; or

(b) enjoy some significant improvement in his physical or mental condition, where that condition had been adversely affected as a result of that act or omission;

the court can include in an order for periodical payments an order that they may be varied. The consent of the parties is not required. The wording is similar to that used for provisional damages (see **15.4**), and it is thought that the courts will apply the same strict criteria before including a provision for variation in a periodical payments order.

### 15.5.3 Procedural approach

In accordance with CPR, r 41.5, the party should address whether or not it considers periodical payments to be appropriate in its statement of case and set out the particulars of the circumstances it relies on. If a statement of case does not address the matter at all, or does not set out sufficient particulars, the court may order the party to rectify the situation.

The power to make an order for periodical payments must be exercised in accordance with CPR, r 41.7, which states that when considering whether to make such an order, the court must have regard to 'all the circumstances of the case and in particular the form of award which best meets the claimant's needs, having regard to the factors set out in the practice direction'. The relevant Practice Direction, PD 41B, para 1, states that these factors include:

> (1) the scale of the annual payments taking into account any deductions for contributory negligence;
>
> (2) the form of the award preferred by the claimant including
>
> (a) the reasons for the claimant's preference; and
>
> (b) the nature of any financial advice received by the claimant when considering the form of the award; and
>
> (3) the form of the award preferred by the defendant including the reasons for the defendant's preference.

Although the court must have regard to the wishes of the parties, ultimately it must decide what order best meets the claimant's needs, and this may not necessarily coincide with what the claimant prefers. The claimant's solicitor must instruct an independent financial adviser to report on the form of order which he considers is in the best interests of the claimant. However, in the *Tameside* case (see **15.5.2.3**), the Court of Appeal stated that it was able to have regard to the defendant's preferences without the need for the defendant to call evidence on this point. It went on to say that only in rare cases would it be appropriate for the defendant to call expert evidence in order to seek to demonstrate that the form of order preferred by the claimant would not best meet his needs.

### 15.5.4 The claimant's and defendant's perspectives

Generally speaking, claimants are not keen on the idea of periodical payments, preferring all damages to be paid as a lump sum. This gives them more control over their finances, and may be particularly important to the claimant who is keen to provide for his family in the event of his death. Defendants differ in their approach, and some may be deterred by the need to manage the fund on behalf of the claimant. However, where cases involve large claims for the cost of future care, defendants will usually prefer periodical payments, because they will assist with cash-flow and will prevent large over-payments where the claimant dies early.

## 15.6 Interest

A claim for interest should be included in the court proceedings. In the majority of personal injury cases, the court will award interest (simple, not compound) in addition to the basic damages. The purpose of an interest award is to compensate the claimant for having to wait to receive his compensation. Interest in a personal injury claim is generally awarded in accordance with the following guidelines:

(a) Special damages carry interest at half the short-term investment/special account rate from the date of the accident to the date of trial. On 1 February 2009, the special account rate was reduced from 6% to 3% per annum, and it was further reduced to 1.5% per annum on 1 June 2009. In *Roberts v Johnstone* [1989] QB 878, it was held that damages for unpaid past services of care and attendance should be awarded in a similar manner to any other items of special damages.

    It should also be noted that following the case of *Wadley v Surrey County Council* (2000) *The Times*, 7 April, the House of Lords confirmed that when calculating interest on special damages, the court should disregard deductible State benefits; interest is claimed on the gross amount (see **Chapter 12**).

(b) Damages for pain and suffering and loss of amenities carry interest from date of service of proceedings to the date of trial at 2% per annum, following the case of *Felmai Lawrence v Chief Constable of Staffordshire* (2000) *The Times*, 25 July.

(c) Damages for future losses carry no interest (as, by definition, the losses have not yet been incurred).

(d) General damages for a handicap on the labour market carry no interest.

It should be noted that these are general guidelines, but the court does have a discretion to depart from them in exceptional cases. In Kemp and Kemp, *The Quantum of Damages*, it is argued that while the general approach for special damages stated above is appropriate for regular losses between the accident and trial (eg, weekly wage loss), it is not satisfactory where the claimant had incurred a large, one-off item of expenditure shortly after the accident. In such circumstances, he would be under-compensated by the application of the normal interest rule, and therefore, it is argued, interest should be awarded at the full rate on such items.

Interest is awarded to mitigate the effects of delay. However, if the delay is the fault of the claimant, this may be a 'special reason' not to award full interest (*Birkett v Hayes* [1982] 2 All ER 70). This point was raised in the case of *Beahan v Stoneham* [2001] LTL, 16 May, where an appeal from an assessment of damages in a claim for personal injuries was allowed in part where the trial judge failed to reduce interest on damages. The matter concerned a case where there was a significant delay in proceeding with the claim (see also *Spittle v Bunney* [1988] 1 WLR 847). The court held that the judiciary should be more ready to mark their disapproval of delay in this matter.

### 15.6.1 Calculation of interest

The calculation of interest on general damages should not present any problem. However, the calculation of interest on special damages can be more difficult. Traditionally, solicitors used the Nelson–Jones table, which is printed annually in the *Law Society's Gazette*. However, on-line calculators are quicker and easier to use.

The inclusion of interest on the settlement of a case must not be forgotten by the claimant's solicitor.

## 15.7 The schedule of past and future loss and expense

In accordance with PD 16, para 4.2, the claimant must attach to his particulars of claim a schedule setting out details of any past and future expenses and losses (see **12.5.1** and

**Appendix 1(11)**). Where the defendant disputes the information contained in the schedule, he should serve a counter-schedule. Both the schedule and the counter-schedule should be revised for the trial.

## 15.8 Further reading

The text provides a basic introduction to this complex topic and further reference should be made to Kemp and Kemp, *The Quantum of Damages* (Sweet & Maxwell). The Ogden Tables (6th edn) can be found at www.gad.gov.uk.

# Chapter 16
# Recovery of Benefits and NHS Charges



## 16.1 Introduction

Where a claimant has received State benefits as a result of an accident or disease and is subsequently awarded compensation, the Department for Work and Pensions (DWP) will seek to recover those benefits from the defendant (or his insurer) via a system operated by the Compensation Recovery Unit (CRU). The CRU is also responsible for collecting from a defendant the cost of any NHS treatment that a claimant has received following an accident. The purpose of this chapter is to explain how these systems of recovery operate and how they may affect a compensation payment.

## 16.2 Recovery of benefits – key features of the system

The legislation on the recovery scheme is predominantly contained in the Social Security (Recovery of Benefits) Act 1997 ('the 1997 Act'). The key features of the scheme are as follows:

(a) No person should be compensated twice in respect of the same accident or disease.

(b) A defendant cannot make a compensation payment (other than an exempt payment) without first applying to the CRU for a Certificate of Recoverable Benefits. The defendant (or 'compensator') must pay to the DWP an amount equal to the total amount of the recoverable benefits on the certificate when he pays compensation to the claimant.

(c) In some circumstances it may be possible for the compensator to deduct some or all of the amount he has had to repay to the DWP from the compensation award (a practice known as 'offsetting'; see **16.4**).

(d) The compensator is responsible for repayment of *all* relevant benefits paid to the injured person, regardless of whether he is able to offset the full amount out of that person's damages.

The main regulations relevant to the scheme are found in the Social Security (Recovery of Benefits) Regulations 1997 (SI 1997/2205), as amended by paras 148–152 of Sch 7 to the Social Security Act 1998.

## 16.3 Key definitions

There are several key definitions in the 1997 Act:

### 16.3.1 The meaning of 'compensation payment'

A compensation payment is a payment made by a person (whether on his own behalf or not) to or in respect of any other person in consequence of any accident, injury or disease suffered by the other (s 1 of the 1997 Act). This is a very wide definition and is designed to cover payments made by the defendant or his insurer.

### 16.3.2 The meaning of 'compensator'

The compensator means the person, company or agent who is paying the compensation, usually an insurance company, on behalf of the insured.

### 16.3.3 The meaning of 'recoverable benefit'

A recoverable benefit is any listed benefit which has been or is likely to be paid in respect of an accident, injury or disease (s 1 of the 1997 Act).

'Recoverable benefits' are listed in Sch 2 to the 1997 Act and are reproduced at **12.7**.

### 16.3.4 The meaning of 'relevant period'

Recovery of benefits can occur only in respect of losses during what the 1997 Act terms 'the relevant period'.

The relevant period begins on:

(a) the day following an accident or injury; or

(b) in the case of a disease, the date on which a listed benefit was first claimed in consequence of the disease.

The relevant period ends on:

(a) the day a compensation payment is made in final discharge of a claim; or

(b) the date five years after the relevant period begins, whichever comes first.

## 16.4 Compensation subject to offsetting

### 16.4.1 Heads of damage subject to offsetting

Offsetting is allowed only against specified areas of loss. The three specified areas subject to offsetting are:

(a) compensation for loss of earnings;

(b) compensation for cost of care; and

(c) compensation for loss of mobility.

Scope for offsetting is further limited by the fact that it is only allowed on a 'like-for-like' basis (see below at **16.4.2**).

Therefore, the overall effect of the legislation is that:

(a) it allows offsetting only against certain items of special damage; and

(b) it ensures that general damages for pain suffering and loss of amenity, loss of congenial employment, handicap on the labour market and all future losses are protected from offsetting.

## 16.4.2 'Like-for-like' offsetting

Having established that only special damages can be the subject of offsetting, Sch 2 to the 1997 Act further safeguards special damages as it allows only 'like-for-like' offsetting. This means that only benefits which closely correspond to the relevant head of loss can be set against damages awarded in respect of that head of loss, as set out in **Table 16.1** below. For example, you will see that attendance allowance can be recouped only from compensation for cost of care, and not from compensation for loss of earnings.

**Example**

A claimant agrees to accept compensation totalling £100,000 which is broken down as follows: £40,000 for pain, suffering and loss of amenity (PSLA), £30,000 for loss of earnings, and £30,000 for the cost of care.

The Certificate of Recoverable Benefit shows that the claimant has received incapacity benefit totalling £5,000, income support totalling £10,000 and attendance allowance amounting to £10,000.

The compensator (the defendant's insurer) may not offset any of the benefits against the PSLA element of the award, but may offset the incapacity benefit and income support against the loss of earnings award. He therefore deducts a total of £15,000 from the loss of earnings sum, leaving £15,000 to be paid to the claimant.

Similarly the compensator may offset the £10,000 attendance allowance against the damages for cost of care, leaving £20,000 to be paid to the claimant.

The claimant has settled his claim for £100,000 but following offsetting he receives £75,000 (he has already received the remaining £25,000 in benefits so double compensation is avoided).

In addition to paying the claimant £75,000, the compensator must now pay £25,000 to the DWP, representing the amount of recoverable benefits.

If compensation for cost of care is less than the amount actually paid out in listed benefits during the relevant period, the claimant will receive nothing in respect of that head of loss; *however*, any excess in benefits for cost of care which has not so far been offset, cannot be offset against any other head of compensation. In this instance, the burden of paying off the excess falls on the compensator (usually the insurance company) and will be refunded to the DWP, so that the State will always achieve 100% recovery, the only question being how much will be out of compensation, and how much will be paid by the compensator.

**Table 16.1 Like-for-like offsetting**

| *Head of compensation* | *Benefit** |
|---|---|
| 1. Compensation for earnings lost during relevant period | Disability working allowance<br>Disablement pension payable under s 103 of the Social Security Contributions and Benefits Act 1992<br>Employment and support allowance<br>Incapacity benefit<br>Income support<br>Invalidity pension and allowance<br>Jobseeker's allowance<br>Reduced earnings allowance<br>Severe disablement allowance<br>Sickness benefit<br>Statutory sick pay before 6 April 1994<br>Unemployability supplement<br>Unemployment benefit |

| *Head of compensation* | *Benefit** |
|---|---|
| 2. Compensation for cost of care incurred during the relevant period | Attendance allowance<br>Care component of disability living allowance<br>Disablement pension increase payable under s 104 or s 105 of the 1992 Act |
| 3. Compensation for loss of mobility during the relevant period | Mobility allowance<br>Mobility component of disability living allowance |

(* The names of the various benefits have changed over the years. For example, from October 2008, incapacity benefit and income support are replaced by employment and support allowance. However, there are still claims involving certain of these benefits despite their no longer being available.)

The DWP Leaflet Z1 provides further details of damages that do and do not fall within Sch 2 (see also case law such as *Clenshaw v Tanner* [2002] EWHC 184 (QB), dealing with housing benefit, and *Lowther v Chatwin* [2003] EWCA Civ 729), and see also *Eagle v Chambers* [2004] EWCA Civ 1033 concerning benefits and the claimant's duty to mitigate.

*Note*: References to incapacity benefit, invalidity pension and allowance, severe disablement allowance, sickness benefit and unemployment benefit also include any income support paid with each of those benefits.

Any reference to statutory sick pay:

(a) includes only 80% of payments made between 6 April 1991 and 5 April 1994; and

(b) does not include payments made on or after 6 April 1994.

In the case of *Griffiths and Others v British Coal Corporation and the Department of Trade and Industry* [2001] 1 WLR 1493, it was held that an award of interest on damages for past loss of earnings fell within the expression 'compensation for earnings lost' in Sch 2 to the 1997 Act and was therefore subject to reduction on account of payments by the defendant to the DWP. In the same case, it was also held that any compensation for services in the nature of care, gratuitously rendered, fell within the term 'compensation for cost of care incurred during the relevant period', and allowed the defendant to set off the benefits paid against the damages.

## 16.5 Contributory negligence

Since 'compensation payment' is defined as the sum falling to be paid to the claimant, it follows that the relevant sum from which benefits can be deducted is that which is paid to the claimant after any deduction for the claimant's contributory negligence. However, the compensator remains liable to pay the full amount of any benefits listed on the certificate regardless of contributory negligence (*Williams v Devon County Council* [2003] EWCA Civ 365). This may have the result after trial that the compensator has to pay a total sum in excess of that which the court has awarded by way of damages.

### Example

Assume that on a full liability basis the claimant's damages are valued at £10,000 for pain, suffering and loss of amenity (PSLA) and £10,000 for loss of earnings (LE), and that the certificate of recoverable benefit shows that he has received £7,500 in incapacity benefit.

If the claimant is 25% contributorily negligent, the calculation is as follows:

Total damages awarded £15,000 (£7,500 PSLA plus £7,500 LE)

Benefits deducted £7,500 (from LE award)

Defendant pays claimant £7,500

Defendant repays benefits to DWP £7,500

> If the Claimant is 50% contributorily negligent, the calculation is as follows:
> Total damages awarded £10,000 (£5,000 PSLA plus £5,000 LE)
> Benefits deducted £5,000 (from LE award)
> Defendant pays claimant £5,000
> Defendant repays benefits to DWP £7,500
> In this second calculation, as a result of the finding of 50% contributory negligence, the amount of recoverable benefits now exceeds the sum awarded for the relevant head of damage (LE) against which they can be deducted. However, the defendant must still repay the full amount of benefits to the DWP.

## 16.6 Procedure

### 16.6.1 Notifying the DWP

(a) Section 4 of the 1997 Act requires the compensator to inform the DWP not later than 14 days after receiving the claim.

The notification is made on Form CRU 1 which is sent to the DWP. The information required by the compensator to complete Form CRU 1 includes:

(i) the full name and address of the claimant;

(ii) (if known) the date of birth and National Insurance number of that person;

(iii) the date of the accident or injury (or in the case of disease, the date of diagnosis);

(iv) the nature of the accident, injury or disease (as alleged by the claimant);

(v) (if known) the name and address of the claimant's employer and his payroll number at the relevant time.

(b) On receipt of Form CRU 1, the CRU will send Form CRU 4 to the defendant. This has a two-fold function:

(i) it acknowledges receipt of the notification of claim; and

(ii) the compensator should retain it safely on the file as it will be needed later to obtain the certificate of recoverable benefit (ie, the details of the benefit paid or to be paid to the claimant).

(c) The claim then progresses to the settlement stage.

(d) When ready to make an offer of compensation, the compensator submits Form CRU 4 to obtain a certificate of recoverable benefit.

(e) The CRU acknowledges receipt of Form CRU 4 (within 14 days).

(f) The CRU sends the certificate of recoverable benefit to the compensator. A copy will also be sent to the claimant's solicitor. The compensator will then settle the compensation claim and pay the relevant amount to the DWP within 14 days of the settlement.

Despite the requirement that the DWP be informed of the claim within 14 days of notification of the claim, this is sometimes overlooked by insurance companies. If proceedings are issued and the insurer instructs solicitors, Form CRU 1 should be completed immediately, if this has not already been done. In such circumstances, it may be appropriate for the address of the compensator given on Form CRU 1 to be care of the solicitors, to ensure that the certificate of recoverable benefit is forwarded to the solicitors, who are likely to make the compensation payment to the claimant.

When the matter is lodged with the DWP, the claimant's solicitor will be notified and a Form CRU 4R will also be sent to the claimant's representative, which can be used to obtain benefit information (the claimant's solicitor can also obtain benefit details by writing to the DWP). It is important that, prior to negotiating any settlement or accepting any payment into court, the claimant himself examines the benefit details to ensure that they are correct. It is therefore essential to send a copy of the CRU certificate to the client.

### 16.6.2 The Certificate of Recoverable Benefit

The provision central to the whole system is that no compensation is to be paid until the defendant has obtained a 'Certificate of Recoverable Benefit'. If compensation is paid without obtaining a certificate, the DWP can still take steps against the defendant to recover the benefits.

The defendant obtains the certificate by completing and returning Form CRU 4 to the CRU. The defendant must ensure that all the information required by Forms CRU 1 and CRU 4 is given, after which the CRU will acknowledge the form in writing and send a certificate to the defendant and a copy to the claimant.

The certificate details:

(a) the amount of relevant benefits paid or likely to be paid by a specified date;

(b) the details of any continuing benefit; and

(c) the amount to be recouped in the event of a compensation payment being made.

An example of a Certificate of Recoverable Benefit can be found at **Appendix 1**.

## 16.7 Exempt payments

Schedule 1, Pt 1 to the 1997 Act and reg 2 of the Social Security (Recovery of Benefits) Regulations 1997, list the payments which are exempt from offsetting under the Act. These include payments by or under the following:

(a) the FAA 1976;

(b) Criminal Injuries Compensation Authority payments;

(c) vaccine damage payments;

(d) the Macfarlane Trust (established partly under funds from the Secretary of State to the Haemophilia Society) and the Eileen Trust;

(e) British Coal, in accordance with the NCB Pneumoconiosis Compensation Scheme;

(f) cases of hearing loss, where the loss is less than 50db in one or both ears;

(g) the National Health Service (Injury Benefits) Regulations 1974 (SI 1974/1547) and subsequent amendments;

(h) criminal court compensation orders, s 35 of the Powers of Criminal Courts Act 1973;

(i) certain trust funds (in particular 'disaster funds', where more than half of the fund is raised by public subscription);

(j) certain private insurance contracts between the victim and his insurer entered into before the contract;

(k) any redundancy payment already accounted for in the assessment of damages;

(l) any amount which is referable to costs;

(m) any contractual amount paid to an employee by an employer in respect of incapacity for work (eg, occupational sick pay);

(n) any small payment, as defined in Pt II of Sch 1 to the Social Security (Recovery of Benefits) Act 1997. There are currently no small payment exceptions.

## 16.8 Multiple defendants ('compensators')

In certain cases, the claimant will sue two or more defendants, and as such, all defendants are jointly and severally liable to reimburse the CRU. However, in practice, it is usual for a sharing agreement to be made as between defendants, whereby the defendants reach an agreement as to how they are to pay the claimant and the CRU.

## 16.9 Clinical negligence

The rules relating to the recovery of benefit apply to clinical negligence claims. Due to their complexity, especially with regard to causation, the CRU has set up a specialist group to deal with the claims, and makes a special request that compensators inform the CRU about clinical negligence claims as soon as the pre-action correspondence is received.

## 16.10 Part 36 offers

A party who wishes to make a Part 36 offer must first apply for a Certificate of Recoverable Benefit (see **16.6.2**) from the CRU.

Rule 36.15(3) requires a defendant who makes an offer to state whether or not the offer is intended to include any deductible benefits.

Rule 36.15(6) requires the offer to state:

(a) the amount of the gross compensation;

(b) the name and amount of any deductible benefit by which that gross amount is reduced; and

(c) the net amount paid in after the reduction.

Although Part 36 does not spell it out, guidance from case law suggests that the offer should therefore particularise the various heads of damage and indicate the amount of benefits to be deducted against each head (*Williams v Devon County Council* [2003] EWCA Civ 365).

## 16.11 Interim payments

It should be noted that if an interim payment is made, the compensator is liable to repay any relevant recoverable benefits at that stage. Therefore a Certificate of Recoverable Benefit (see **16.6.2**) should be obtained before any voluntary payment or hearing of an application for an interim payment takes place.

## 16.12 Appeals system

An appeal may be made:

(a) on the ground that any amount, rate or period in the Certificate of Recoverable Benefits is incorrect;

(b) against the calculations in the Certificate of Recoverable Benefits relating to benefits not paid in consequence of accident, injury or disease.

An appeal can be made only after final settlement of the compensation claim and payment of the recoverable benefits has been made. The basic time limit for the appeal is one month from the date on which the compensator makes the full payment of recoverable benefits; it is dealt with by an independent tribunal administered by the Appeals Service.

An appeal can be made by:

(a) the person who applied for the certificate, ie, the compensator; or

(b) the injured person whose compensation payment has been reduced.

There is a less formal procedure that can be adopted, known as a 'review'. This can be requested at any time, and as a result the CRU will look at the matter again and clear the benefits that are listed as recoverable.

## 16.13 Recovery of NHS charges

The CRU operates a similar recovery scheme on behalf of the Government in respect of the cost of NHS treatment given as a result of an accident. Initially the scheme applied only to road traffic accidents, but this was expanded to include all types of accident as from 29 January 2007. The main details of the scheme are as follows.

### 16.13.1 Key features of the scheme

The legislation is contained in the Road Traffic (NHS Charges) Act 1999 ('the 1999 Act') and the Health and Social Care (Community Health and Standards) Act 2003 ('the 2003 Act'). The purpose of this legislation is to provide a national administration system, the aim of which is to ensure that costs of treatment are, in fact, recovered in as many cases as is possible.

The 1999 Act allows for recovery of NHS treatment charges as a result of a road traffic accident which occurs on or after 5 April 1999. This includes MIB cases. It allows for NHS charges to be calculated according to a tariff. The tariff allows for:

(a) a set fee for patients treated in A&E departments or out-patient clinics (the fee will be the same regardless of the number of out-patient appointments);

(b) a daily rate for patients admitted to hospital.

Part 3 of the 2003 Act makes provision for an expanded scheme to recover the costs of providing treatment to an injured person where that person has made a successful personal injury compensation claim against a third party. This allows recovery of NHS hospital costs in all cases where personal injury compensation is paid, not just following road traffic accidents, but also, for example, following accidents at work. It applies to all accidents which occur on or after 29 January 2007.

The expanded scheme builds on the existing scheme introduced by the 1999 Act. In addition, the 2003 Act allows the recovery of NHS ambulance service costs for the first time. The scheme applies to injuries only; diseases are excluded from the scheme, unless the disease in question has been contracted as a direct result of an injury that falls within the scope of the scheme. Costs of treatment given by general practitioners in the primary care setting are also not included in the scheme.

### 16.13.2 Procedure

In many ways, the NHS costs recovery scheme mirrors the benefit recovery scheme considered above. However, unlike the benefit recovery scheme, the NHS costs recovery scheme will not affect the amount of damages recovered by the claimant, and if the injury occurs on or after 29 January 2007, the 2003 Act makes provision to take into account contributory negligence.

The procedure to follow is as follows:

(a) The compensator will apply to the CRU in the usual way by completing Form CRU 1, and must ensure that the form contains the name and address of the hospital where treatment was provided.

(b) The CRU will send Form CRU 4 to the compensator to acknowledge receipt of Form CRU 1.

(c) The case progresses to the settlement stage.

(d) When ready to make an offer to the claimant, the compensator submits Form CRU 4.

(e) The CRU will provide a Certificate of NHS Charges at the same time as the Certificate of Recoverable Benefit. The Certificate of NHS Charges will specify the name of the NHS Trust or Health Board where the treatment took place, the number of days' admission, the appropriate NHS treatment and ambulance charges.

(f) The compensator must pay to the DWP the amount shown on the Certificate of NHS Charges within 14 days of making the compensation payment.

The appeal and review procedures for NHS costs recovery are designed to mirror the appeal and review provisions governing benefit recovery under the Social Security (Recovery of Benefits) Act 1997, as to which, see **16.12** above.

## 16.14 Conclusion

Solicitors should exercise care when dealing with this area, to ensure that it is clear whether any offer put forward is net or gross of benefits, and that the benefit figures are correct. In *Hilton International v Martin-Smith* [2001] LTL, 12 February, it was held that where a party made an error of judgment (in this case, in relation to the amount stated on the Certificate of Recoverable Benefits), it did not follow that the court would permit that party to escape its consequences. Similarly, solicitors acting for defendants also need to ensure that benefits listed as recoverable benefits are as a consequence of the accident (see *Eagle Star Insurance v Department of Social Development (Northern Ireland)* (only persuasive) (2001) NICE, 12 February). See also *Williams v Devon County Council* [2003] EWCA Civ 365, [2003] All ER (D) 255 (Mar), concerning details to be included on a notice of payment into court and details of the benefits to be included; and *Bruce v Genesis Fast Food Ltd* [2003] EWHC 788, concerning whether defendants are entitled to take the benefit of any reduction in recoverable benefits when an appeal takes place.

## 16.15 Further reading

DWP/CRU Leaflet Z1, *A Recovery of Benefits Guide for Companies and Solicitors – Procedures for Liaison with the Compensation Recovery Unit*

Kemp and Kemp, *The Quantum of Damages* (Sweet & Maxwell)

## 16.16 Overview of recovery of benefits

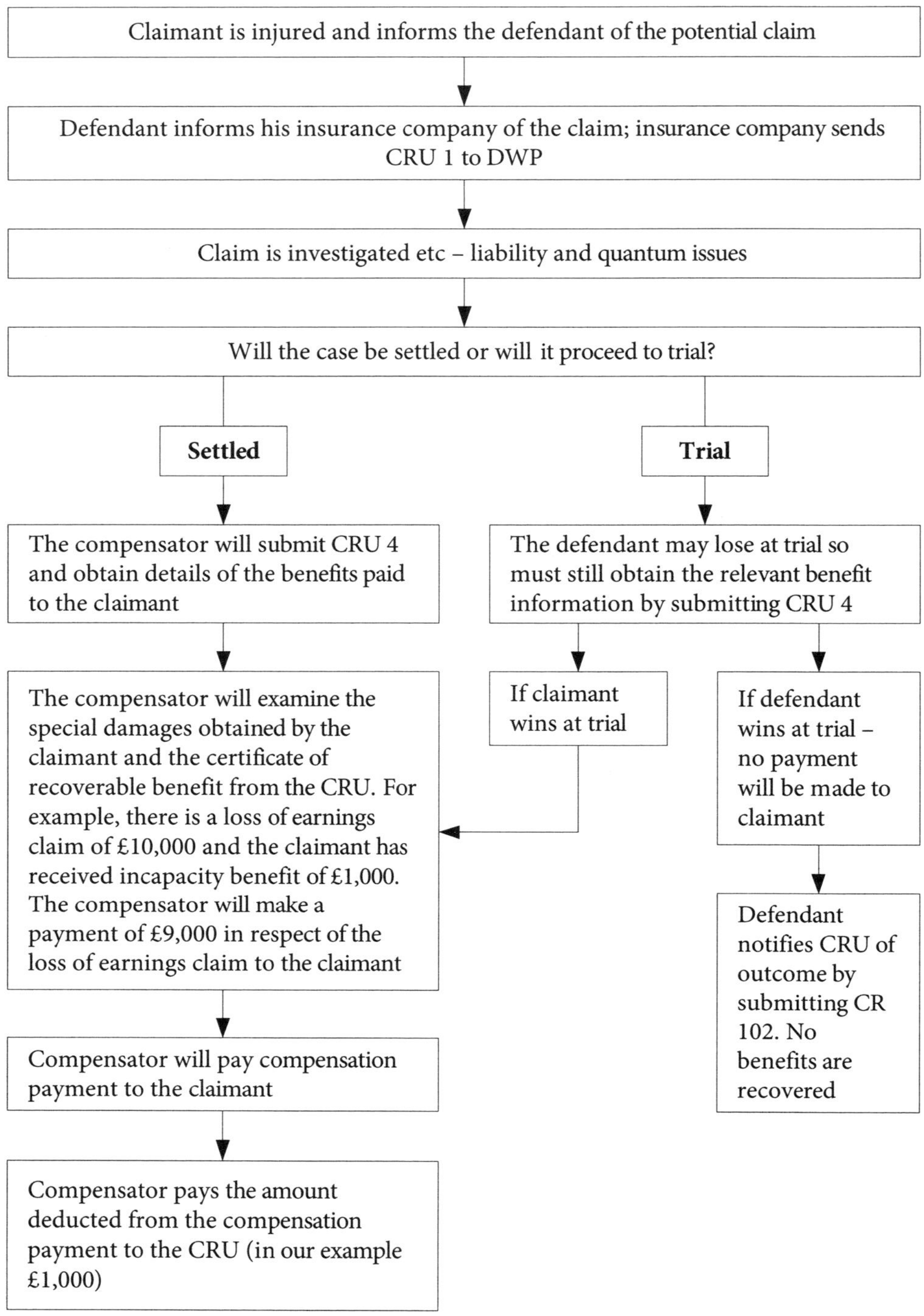

# Chapter 17
# Post-death Investigations



## 17.1 Introduction

The personal injury/clinical negligence solicitor must, on occasion, advise either the family of an accident victim who has died, or the person who it is claimed is responsible for the death. There are two main processes in which the solicitor may become involved:

(a) the coroner's inquest; and

(b) a criminal prosecution for:

    (i) manslaughter (corporate or individual);

    (ii) death by dangerous or careless driving; or

    (iii) offences under the HSWA 1974.

Although each process has its own purpose, post-death investigations offer an important opportunity to gain evidence on liability for the civil claim.

## 17.2 The coroner's court

If acting for the claimant, the solicitor is likely to be instructed by a relative who may be upset and in a state of complete despair. The relative may also be looking to identify the person responsible for the death. It is important that the solicitor explains the post-death process thoroughly to the client, who, although he may recognise the phrases 'coroner's court' and 'inquest', may not understand the purpose of the process.

While the claimant's solicitor may wish to use the inquest to examine the evidence surrounding the accident and to obtain full details of the circumstances leading to the death, the coroner is concerned only with how the death occurred (see **17.2.6**), and this should be made clear to the client.

Prior to advising a client on this area, reference must be made to the Coroners Act 1988 and the Coroners Rules 1984 (SI 1984/552). (See also **17.2.10**, where the impact of Article 2 of the European Convention on Human Rights (ECHR) is considered.)

If acting for the defendant, the solicitor is likely to have been instructed by the defendant's insurance company, or, in the case of clinical negligence, by the hospital or defence union. In these circumstances, the solicitor's aim is:

(a) to protect the interests of the client (eg, by making sure he does not incriminate himself); and

(b) to obtain as much evidence as possible relating to the issue of liability.

A fatal accident which leads to an inquest is one of the occasions where a defendant's solicitor is instructed close to the time of the accident. He can therefore obtain details of any potential claims so that the insurance company can establish a reserve in its accounts for any potential liability.

Normally, the coroner will formally open the inquest and then immediately adjourn for enquiries to be made. The inquest will take place at the coroner's court (if the district has a specific court), or in the magistrates' court, council offices or at another public building. The inquest will be held in public unless matters of national security are being considered.

## 17.2.1 Personnel involved at an inquest

### 17.2.1.1 The coroner

The coroner is responsible for the inquest procedure, and although appointed by the local government body responsible for the area where the coroner sits, he is an independent judicial officer. A number of coroners are qualified both as doctors and (normally) as barristers, although this is not a strict requirement of obtaining the post. Those who are legally qualified only, normally have significant knowledge of medical matters.

In certain cases, the coroner may sit with an 'assessor', who is a person with specialist knowledge of the matters being considered, for example a consultant anaesthetist in a case where a patient died due to an airway not being maintained. However, the assessor must remain under the control of the coroner and cannot give expert evidence (see *R v Surrey Coroner, ex p Wright* [1997] 2 WLR 16).

### 17.2.1.2 The coroner's officer

The coroner will be assisted by the coroner's officer, who is usually a serving or ex-police officer and will often be the first person with whom the personal injury solicitor will communicate about the case. The coroner's officer will obtain evidence relating to the accident, or liaise with the police if they are carrying out investigations. His role is important to the solicitor, as he can provide information regarding the investigations which are being carried out and details of the incident, and may provide details of any witnesses the coroner intends to call.

The coroner's officer will notify the relevant parties and/or their solicitors of the inquest date. In certain specified circumstances, the deceased's trade union and the HSE will also be notified.

### 17.2.1.3 The deputy coroner

A coroner will appoint a deputy coroner, who will normally stand in when the coroner is absent. Provided specific requirements for allowing a deputy to act are fulfilled, the deputy has all the powers of the coroner.

## 17.2.2 Circumstances which lead to an inquest

The circumstances in which a coroner will become involved in a death are set down in s 8(1) of the Coroners Act 1988.

If the coroner is informed that a dead body is within his jurisdiction (it is the fact that there is a body in his jurisdiction and not where the death occurred that is important), the coroner will hold an inquest as soon as practicable, where it is reasonable to suspect that a person has died:

(a) a violent or unnatural death; or
(b) a sudden death of which the cause is unknown; or
(c) in prison; or
(d) in such place or such circumstances as to require an inquest in pursuance of any Act.

Normally, the police, the GP or the hospital will contact the coroner's officer and inform the coroner of the death. However, there is a wider duty to report the matter (see below) and, on occasions, the relatives of the deceased will contact the coroner's officer if they believe that there has been an act of clinical negligence.

In addition to the criteria set down in s 8(1), there is an obligation on a GP to inform the Registrar of Births and Deaths of the death, stating the cause of the death, if the GP was treating the 'last illness', or on the hospital doctor if a patient dies undergoing surgery.

Once the coroner has been informed of the death, the coroner's officer will make preliminary enquiries, and the coroner may then require a post-mortem examination to be made.

### 17.2.2.1 Post-mortem examinations

Although no absolute obligation is placed upon the coroner, usually he will request that a post-mortem takes place (see *R v HM Coroner for Greater Manchester Northern District, ex p Worch and Another* [1988] QB 513). Care should be taken to ensure that if the death occurred in hospital, the pathologist is not connected with the hospital where the death occurred. There are detailed provisions contained in the Coroners Rules 1984, r 6 on this point. The claimant's solicitor must make strong representations on this matter if there is any possibility of a clinical negligence claim, and in certain circumstances (if the first report is unsatisfactory) consideration should be given to carrying out a second post-mortem.

Consideration should be given to making a request that blood and tissue samples taken at the post-mortem are preserved, as they may provide important information.

Section 21(3) of the Coroners Act 1988 provides:

> Where a person states upon oath before the coroner that in his belief the death of the deceased was caused partly by or entirely by the improper or negligent treatment of a medical practitioner or other person, that medical practitioner or other person shall not be allowed to perform or assist at the post-mortem examination of the deceased.

The coroner must inform the relatives of the deceased, the GP and the hospital (if the deceased died in hospital) of the arrangements for the post-mortem. These are normally referred to as the 'interested parties' and can be represented at the post-mortem by a doctor. The coroner can, in his discretion, also allow any other person to attend at the post-mortem (Coroners Rules 1984, r 7(4)).

The post-mortem report is vital evidence, and an immediate request should be made to the coroner for a copy (but see **17.2.5**). The report may contain evidence which will assist in establishing civil liability. For example, if the death resulted from a road traffic accident, the pathologist will give a detailed description of the injuries, and photographs will be taken of the body. The pathologist's investigations in respect of this may be vital in indicating the events which occurred prior to the accident, for example whether the deceased was wearing a seat-belt. In fatal accident at work cases, the pathologist's report may also be of use in identifying whether the cause of the death resulted from exposure to dangerous materials at work, such as coal dust or asbestos. While the Coroners Rules 1984, r 57(1) makes provision for a copy of the post-mortem report to be provided to 'interested parties', it is unclear if the right relates to any request prior to the inquest, but many coroners do provide a copy of the post-mortem prior to the inquest.

If acting for the defendant, the post-mortem may reveal whether there are any intervening illnesses from which the deceased may have died. This may then be used in negotiations, in an attempt to reduce the multiplier in the future loss calculation (see **15.7**). In addition, in a road traffic case, it is important to check the blood alcohol levels to see if the deceased had been drinking at the time of the accident. Such evidence can provide important arguments regarding liability and quantum.

### 17.2.3 The criteria for an inquest

As noted at **17.2.2** above, the coroner will hold an inquest only if the criteria in s 8(1) of the Coroners Act 1988 are satisfied. The personal injury/clinical negligence solicitor will be concerned only with the first two criteria.

The first limb of s 8(1) requires that there must have been a 'violent or unnatural death'. What exactly is meant by this term?

(a) A violent death is normally regarded as one where an injury has occurred, and will normally be apparent. For example, when a factory operative falls into machinery and dies.

(b) An unnatural death is not legally defined and it will be a question for the coroner to decide. Certain coroners believe that the phrase should be given its 'ordinary meaning'.

    The coroner decides whether the death is natural or unnatural at his discretion, and this decision may need to be challenged. For example, in *R v Poplar Coroner, ex p Thomas* [1993] 2 WLR 547, a woman died following an asthma attack after there had been a considerable delay in an ambulance reaching her. There was evidence that if she had reached hospital earlier, she might have survived. Was this an unnatural death? The Court of Appeal overturned the decision of the Divisional Court that it was an unnatural death and stated that 'unnatural' was an ordinary word the meaning of which should be left to the coroner (unless his decision was unreasonable). If a solicitor believes that the death was unnatural, the coroner's officer must be contacted immediately and informed of the solicitor's interest. See also *R v Inner London North Coroner, ex p Touche* [2001] 3 WLR 148 and *R v HM Coroner for Avon, ex p Smith* (1998) 162 JP 403.

The second limb of s 8(1) requires that there must have been a sudden death of which the cause is unknown. In the context of a personal injury claim, this is less likely to be a significant cause, but it may be appropriate in certain circumstances.

If the coroner refuses to call an inquest, the following options may be considered:

(a) to make an application to the Divisional Court of the High Court;

(b) to make an application for judicial review.

### 17.2.4 Funding representation at the inquest

It may be possible for a solicitor (with an appropriate contract) to provide assistance under the Legal Help scheme for the initial preparations for an inquest. A solicitor may not represent the family at the inquest under the scheme using this method of funding. However, on 1 November 2001, the Lord Chancellor published *Revised Guidance on Applications for Exceptional Funding*, and this brings representation at certain inquests within the scope of CLS funding (see *R ((1) Challender and (2) Morris) v Legal Services Commission* [2004] EWHC 925; and see the Community Legal Service (Financial) (Amendment No 2) Regulations 2003 (SI 2003/2838)). In exceptional cases, the Secretary of State for Constitutional Affairs has power under s 6(8)(b) of the Access to Justice Act 1999 to provide funding on an individual basis to cover advocacy and representation at an inquest. Consideration should be given to this option where the matter has a 'significant wider public interest' or 'overwhelming importance to the client'.

All possible alternative sources of finance should be considered (eg, in a fatal road traffic accident, the deceased's legal expense insurance may cover the cost of representation for the estate). Immediate enquiries must be made in respect of any claim on any insurance policy and, if appropriate, prior authorisation should be obtained from the insurer. Enquiries should also be made as to whether a trade union will fund representation at the inquest, or whether any *pro bono* service may be able to provide assistance.

Interestingly, in the case of *King (Administratrix of the Estate of Robert Gadd deceased) v Milton Keynes General NHS Trust* [2004] LTL, 4 June, it was held that when assessing the costs of civil proceedings the court did have jurisdiction to award the costs of attending at an inquest if the material purpose was to obtain information or evidence for use in civil proceedings. Similarly, in *Stewart and Hubbard v Medway NHS Trust* [2004] LTL, 20 September, the cost of counsel attending an inquest in a clinical negligence case was held to be recoverable. More recently, in *Roach v Home Office* [2009] EWHC 312 (QB), it was held that the costs of attendance at an inquest by both solicitor and counsel were recoverable as costs incidental to subsequent civil proceedings.

If there is a possibility of a clinical negligence claim being brought, any doctor who is required to give evidence will be represented by the NHSLA solicitors or his defence union. Similarly, in a personal injury case, if a civil claim is likely to follow as a result of the death, the employers (eg, in a factory accident) or the driver of the other vehicle (in a road traffic accident) will be represented by solicitors instructed by their respective insurers.

### 17.2.5 Preparation for the hearing

Only the coroner can decide which documents should be placed before the court. This makes preparation for the inquest difficult for the solicitor, as he may have little idea of what evidence will be called. The coroner's officer may be able to assist informally, and he should be contacted to see what view the coroner may be taking in respect of the evidence. The coroner may decide to release documents before the inquest, and a request should be made in each case.

In the case of *R (Bentley) v HM Coroner for Avon* [2001] EWHC 170 (Admin), [2001] LTL, 23 March, it was held that, on the facts, the request for advance disclosure was reasonable, and since straightforward disclosure was requested by a party who would, in the end, be entitled to see it, the document should be disclosed. The court has emphasised that while there was no requirement for advance disclosure in the Coroners Rules, there was a requirement of natural justice and fairness.

In certain complicated matters, the coroner may be willing to hold a 'pre-inquest review' to allow the parties and the coroner to consider matters prior to the actual inquest. The coroner may summarise the evidence that he proposes to call and give the parties the opportunity to suggest any other witnesses that they may wish to call.

Normally, statements have been taken from the proposed witnesses by the coroner's officer or police, and it can be of considerable advantage if these can be obtained beforehand. At the hearing of the inquest, further evidence or information can become available. If such information leads the solicitor to believe that he cannot represent his client adequately, he should request an adjournment.

In an attempt to overcome the above difficulties, prior to the hearing detailed enquiries must be made of such bodies as the police, trade union or HSE, which may be able to provide general background information. The more information that is obtained prior to the hearing the better.

In a clinical negligence case, the deceased's medical records should be obtained (see *Stobart v Nottingham Health Authority* [1992] 3 Med LR 284). Once received, they should be placed in an ordered, paginated file, and legible copies made. If the solicitor is instructed by an insurance company on behalf of the deceased's estate, in-depth research should be carried out into the nature of the illness, the usual treatment which is prescribed for the illness, and the usual consequences of and recovery time for the illness. This research will include relevant medical literature, and copies should be taken of any appropriate material. Medical school libraries are generally very helpful with this form of research, and can provide assistance and copying facilities. Research may reveal whether the treatment fell below the level which can be expected and required of the medical staff.

In addition, a solicitor may seek assistance from an expert who can advise him on how to examine any medical experts giving evidence on behalf of the doctor. Informed examination will test a witness's evidence, and may be useful if civil proceedings are later issued. It is important for the claimant's solicitor to make such detailed preparation, because solicitors acting for a doctor will be experienced in this field and have access to a wide range of sources, including many experts.

### 17.2.6 Procedure at the inquest

The inquest is formally opened without any significant evidence being given, and the formalities are carried out by the coroner sitting alone (who, for example, will take initial evidence, evidence of identification of the body, issue an order for disposal of the body and adjourn until a more suitable time). Evidence will be called concerning the death at the resumed full hearing, with legal representatives for both sides attending. If appropriate, a jury (see **17.2.6.1**) will also be in attendance at that time.

The coroner will not proceed with the inquest until the relevant authority has been contacted (see Coroners Rules 1984, r 26(3), eg in the case of industrial diseases) or after certain criminal proceedings have been brought (eg, in the case of death by dangerous driving). In the latter case, the claimant's solicitor should attend the criminal proceedings and take notes of the trial (see below), as useful evidence may be obtained which can assist in identifying any civil liability for the death.

The majority of evidence at the resumed inquest will usually be given orally by witnesses on oath, but the coroner has power to admit documentary evidence if he believes that the evidence is unlikely to be disputed. However, it is possible to object to such a decision, and a solicitor should do this where he believes that a witness should be called to answer questions (see also *R (Bentley) v HM Coroner for Avon* [2001] EWHC 170 (Admin), [2001] LTL, 23 March).

The actual order of calling the witnesses lies entirely within the discretion of the coroner. However, the pathologist may be the first substantive witness to give evidence (see *R v HM Coroner for Kent (Maidstone District), ex p Johnstone* (1994) 158 JP 1115). When the pathologist gives evidence, he will undoubtedly use medical language, and it is important that the solicitor is able to understand the evidence which is given. Thus, research should be carried out prior to the inquest, so as to become familiar with the potential medical terms that may be used. The solicitor should not be afraid to ask the doctor to explain himself in full.

The coroner will normally then examine each witness so that the evidence is heard in the same order as the events leading to the death occurred. The solicitor should make careful notes, as these witnesses may need to be contacted in relation to a potential civil claim. If the witness does not give evidence in accordance with his previous written statement to the coroner, and the interested party is not aware of this, then the coroner must deal with this point (see *R v HM Coroner for Inner London North District, ex p Cohen* (1994) 158 JP 644, DC). Once the coroner has dealt with the witness, each interested party (or their legal representatives) will be allowed to question him. A witness is examined by his own representative last (r 21).

#### 17.2.6.1 Juries

A jury will be used at the coroner's court if the death:

(a) occurred in prison;

(b) occurred while the deceased was in police custody, or resulted from injury caused by a police officer in the execution of his duty;

(c) was caused by an accident, poisoning or disease, notice of which is required to be given under any Act to a government department or to any inspector or other officer of a government department, or to an inspector appointed under s 19 of the Health and Safety at Work, etc Act 1974 (see *R (Aineto) v HM Coroner for Brighton and Hove* [2003] LTL, 21 July);

(d) occurred in circumstances the continuance or possible reoccurrence of which is prejudicial to the health and safety of the public or any section of the public.

A personal injury solicitor is most likely to be involved in cases coming within heads (c) and (d) above.

The jury will consist of between seven and 11 people.

#### 17.2.6.2 Witnesses

The coroner is the only person who has the power to call witnesses (the interested parties cannot), but if a solicitor believes that a particular witness should be called, representation can be made to the coroner (see *R (Nicholls) v Coroner for the City of Liverpool* [2001] EWHC 922 (Admin), where an application for judicial review was successful where the coroner's reasons for not allowing a medical expert requested by the deceased's family could not be sustained). Enquiries need to be made of the coroner's officer (prior to the hearing) as to which witnesses the coroner intends to call.

Persons entitled to examine witnesses at an inquest are as follows:

(a) the parent, child, spouse or any personal representative of the deceased;

(b) any beneficiary under a policy of insurance issued on the life of the deceased;

(c) the insurer who issued such a policy of insurance;

(d) any person whose act or omission, or that of his agent or servant, may, in the opinion of the coroner, have caused, or contributed to, the death of the deceased;

(e) any person appointed by a trade union to which the deceased belonged at the time of his death, if the death of the deceased may have been caused by an injury received in the course of his employment or by an industrial disease;

(f) an inspector appointed by, or a representative of, an enforcing authority, or any person appointed by a government department to attend the inquest;

(g) the chief officer of police;

(h) any other person who, in the opinion of the coroner, is a properly interested person.

The Coroners Rules 1984 provide that the above persons can examine witnesses either in person, or through counsel or solicitors. In *R v Portsmouth City Coroner, ex p Keane* (1993) 153 JP 658, the coroner refused leave to a brother of the deceased to examine certain witnesses through counsel on the basis that the brother was not a properly interested person within r 20(2) of Coroners Rules 1984. It was held that the coroner was entitled by use of his discretion to come to that decision.

The questioning of witnesses at the inquest can be a difficult matter as the strict purpose of the inquest is limited to finding:

(a) who the deceased was;

(b) how, when and where the deceased came by his death (see **17.2.10**);

(c) the particulars required by the Registration Acts to be registered concerning the death.

aim not to apportion blame though verdicts may imply

The Divisional Court has repeatedly reaffirmed that these are the only matters with which the coroner's court is concerned, and the coroner will wish to concentrate on these fundamental points. However, there can be no doubt that many solicitors attend the inquest with a slightly wider agenda, that of trying to identify who was liable for the death and to examine the evidence surrounding the case. Much will depend upon the individual coroner as to the types of questions which are allowed, but the coroner will always limit questions concerned with civil liability.

To prevent the inquest apportioning blame, the Coroners Rules 1984, r 22 specifically provides that a witness is not obliged to answer any questions tending to incriminate himself. The witness may be called to the witness-box and asked merely to give his name and address. On occasion, no further questions will be put to him. However, practice varies widely on this point, and in *R v Lincolnshire Coroner, ex p Hay* (1999) 163 JP 666, it was held that the privilege against self-incrimination did not give the witness complete immunity against further questioning. The privilege against self-incrimination is against criminal proceedings (and not civil proceedings), and this should be borne in mind when the coroner is deciding if the witness is entitled to claim self-incrimination. The solicitor may have to remind the coroner about this point. If the coroner allows the witness to be questioned, it is for the witness's representative to make the objection if a question is put which might lead to self-incrimination. If the witness answers the question, he will waive the privilege.

In certain cases, it is desirable for a witness's identity to be protected, as in the case of *R v Newcastle-upon-Tyne Coroner, ex p A* (1998) 162 JP 387, where a police officer was allowed to give evidence from behind a screen. (See also *R (A and Another) v Inner South London Coroner* (2004) *The Times*, 12 July and 11 November; and *Family of Derek Bennett v (1) HM Coroner and (2) Commissioner of Police for the Metropolis* [2004] EWCA Civ 1439.)

### 17.2.6.3 Summation

If a jury are present, the coroner will sum up the evidence to the jury after the witnesses have given evidence and will direct the jury on points of law. In *R v HM Coroner for Inner London South District, ex p Douglas-Williams* (1998) 162 JP 751, it was held that, in complex cases, it would be good practice for the coroner to prepare a written statement of matters which the law requires in relation to possible verdicts. If such a policy is followed, a solicitor should request to inspect the statement prior to summing up. The jury may wish to make other comments outside their terms of reference (normally with the motive of trying to prevent another death occurring), but the coroner will not allow this.

If no jury are present, the coroner normally sums up by means of a revision of the evidence and states his conclusions.

### 17.2.6.4 Reports to prevent future deaths

Rule 43 of the Coroners Rules 1984 allows a coroner to announce at the inquest that he is reporting the matter in writing to a person or organisation where the coroner believes that action should be taken to prevent future deaths.

### 17.2.6.5 Verdicts

If a jury are present, they will retire to consider their verdict. No communication is permitted with the jury once they have retired. A majority verdict is allowed where the minority is not more than two. The coroner may accept a majority verdict, but is not bound to do so (see *R (Dawson and Others) v HM Coroner for East Riding and Kingston-upon-Hull Coroners District* [2001] EWHC 352 (Admin) – a coroner need not leave all possible verdicts to a jury).

A document called an 'inquisition' is completed by the coroner at the end of the inquest, which is signed by the coroner and jury members who concur with it. The form requires five matters to be dealt with:

(a) the name of the deceased;
(b) the injury or disease causing death;
(c) the time, place and circumstances at or in which the injury was sustained;

(d) the conclusion of the jury/coroner as to the death; and
(e) the particulars under the Registration Acts.

(The above vary depending on the particular type of case – see the Coroners Rules 1984, Sch 2, Form 22.)

The standard inquisition form gives a comprehensive list of suggested verdicts, of which the most significant in personal injury/clinical negligence cases are:

(a) industrial disease (this is given no defined meaning);
(b) want of attention at birth;
(c) accident/misadventure (the courts have taken the view that any distinction between the two words is undesirable);
(d) unlawful killing;
(e) open verdict;
(f) suicide;
(g) natural causes;
(h) neglect.

(The notes to Form 22 have no binding effect whatsoever and are merely advisory.)

The following points should be noted in relation to possible verdicts:

(a) Accident/accidental death. Even if such a verdict is given, it does not mean that a civil case cannot be brought.
(b) An open verdict. This means simply that there is insufficient evidence to reach a conclusion.
(c) Neglect. This is a controversial verdict. Following the case of *R v Surrey Coroner, ex p Wright* [1997] 2 WLR 16, it appears that a coroner cannot return a verdict of 'lack of care', but the term 'neglect' may be used to describe a situation where there has been a period of neglect which resulted in the death. In this context, neglect means continuous, or at least 'non-transient', neglect (see also *R v HM Coroner for North Humberside and Scunthorpe, ex p Jamieson* [1995] QB 1, CA). This verdict does not necessarily mean that negligence can be established, as it does not necessarily mean that the three elements of negligence required to be proved in a civil court can be established (see also *R v HM Coroner for Swansea and Gower, ex p Tristram* (2000) 164 JP 191; *R v HM Coroner for Coventry, ex p Chief Constable of Staffordshire Constabulary* [2000] LTL, 28 September; and *R (Amin) v Secretary of State for the Home Department; R (Middleton) v Secretary of State for the Home Department* [2002] EWCA Civ 390, [2002] 3 WLR 505 – concerning Article 2 of the ECHR and returning a verdict of neglect).

   Some commentators state that neglect can rarely, if ever, be a verdict on its own. Rather, it is ancillary to any verdict where there is a link between the relevant conduct and the cause of death. In *R (S) v HM Coroner for Inner West London* [2001] EWHC 105 (Admin), (2001) 61 BMLR 222, a fresh inquest was allowed due to the fact that the coroner had not left a verdict incorporating an element of neglect to the jury (see also *R v Coroner for Western Somerset, ex p Middleton* [2004] UKHL 10; *R v HM Coroner for West Yorkshire, ex p Sacker* [2004] UKHL 11; *R (Mumford) v HM Coroner for Reading and Secretary of State for the Home Department* [2002] EWHC 2184 (Admin)).

   Following *Middleton* (above), it is arguable that the term 'neglect' should be avoided. Certain coroners now, where appropriate, provide narrative verdicts that comment on the factual issues and thus avoid the need for short phrases.
(d) Suicide or unlawful killing. The standard of proof required for a suicide or unlawful killing verdict to be returned is that of 'beyond reasonable doubt'. See *R (on the application of Neil Sharman) v HM Coroner for Inner London* [2005] EWHC 857,

concerning the returning of a verdict of unlawful killing; and *R (on the application of Anderson and Others) v HM Coroner for Inner North Greater London* [2004] EWHC 2729.

All other verdicts require a burden of proof based on the balance of probabilities.

In *R (O'Connor) v HM Coroner for the District of Avon* [2009] EWHC 854 (Admin), it was held that a coroner's verdict of unlawful killing predicated a finding equivalent to that required for a conviction of at least manslaughter in a criminal trial, and that insanity, if properly raised in the evidence, had to be disproved to the criminal standard to sustain a verdict of unlawful killing.

The Divisional Court (and the Coroners Rules 1984 themselves) have made it clear that the coroner's court does not decide the responsibility for the death. Therefore, verdicts in the coroner's court are framed so as not to identify any individual as being responsible (see also *R v HM Coroner for Derby and South Derbyshire, ex p John Henry Hart Jnr* (2000) 164 JP 429 and *R v Director of Public Prosecutions, ex p Manning and Another* [2000] 3 WLR 463).

#### 17.2.6.6 Transcripts

At the conclusion of the inquest, the coroner's officer will collect any documents or copy statements which were used during the hearing. A copy of the transcript of the case can be obtained on payment of a fee. (See also *R (on the application of the Ministry of Defence) v Wiltshire and Swindon Coroner* [2005] EWHC 889.)

### 17.2.7 Representing the family

The inquest can be difficult for lay persons to understand. Lay persons will be unfamiliar with the role of the coroner and may expect that the purpose of the inquest is not to establish how the deceased died but to establish fault. Because of potential problems with lack of advance disclosure of evidence, the family of the deceased may not be aware what evidence will be given and may be upset by the evidence disclosed at the inquest.

The procedure that the coroner will follow during the inquest must be explained to the family of the deceased. It will be necessary to discuss the evidence with them and, in particular, to discuss the verdict. The verdict should be explained thoroughly, and the deceased's family should be reminded that the purpose of the inquest and the verdict is not to apportion blame but to establish by what means the deceased came by his death.

### 17.2.8 Representing the potential defendant

#### 17.2.8.1 Clinical negligence cases

**Requesting records and taking statements**

The solicitor for the health authority or NHS Trust should obtain all relevant records, and obtain statements from any medical and nursing staff who have been called by the coroner to give evidence at the inquest.

The solicitor should help the staff by reviewing their statements prior to submission to the coroner. He should ensure that the statements contain only relevant facts and do not offer any opinion which the witness is not competent to give. For example, a house officer should not give an opinion on whether specific parts of the treatment contributed to the death but should restrict his statement to the facts alone.

If it appears from the statements that disciplinary action might be taken against a member of the medical staff (eg, because a mistake in treatment has been made), that person should be advised to seek his own representation from his defence organisation as his interests will conflict with those of the hospital.

The solicitor should advise the medical and nursing staff that the original records will be available at the inquest, and that they are permitted to refer to these.

**Purpose, form and limits of inquest**

The solicitor should advise the medical and nursing staff about the purpose and form of an inquest, and encourage an attitude of openness and co-operation at the inquest.

**Expert evidence**

The solicitor may consider obtaining a specialist opinion on the issues arising at the inquest from a hospital consultant (but not from a consultant who is directly involved in the case).

#### 17.2.8.2 Personal injury cases

In a personal injury case, as soon as the solicitor is instructed, he will make contact with the insured and attempt to investigate the matter further. This will normally involve attending at the insured's premises, if the accident was work-based, or at the scene of the accident with the insured, in the case of a road traffic accident. The defendant's solicitor will be under strict instructions from the insurer to formulate a view on liability and attempt to find out as much as possible about the deceased, so that some idea can be obtained about quantum. In a road traffic accident, the inquest will provide early access to the police investigation report (which may have involved a partial reconstruction), and useful information, such as whether a seat-belt was worn, may become apparent. In the case of an industrial accident, the solicitor investigating the case will normally be concerned with the system of work used or the employment history of the deceased. This may be particularly useful in asbestosis claims, where it may become apparent that the deceased's main exposure to asbestos was during his employment with another employer.

### 17.2.9 Publicity at the inquest

There is often publicity attached to inquests. Reporters may request an interview with the key witnesses and, in particular, the family. The appropriate advice to witnesses is at the discretion of the solicitors acting for the parties. Usually, the solicitor representing the hospital or doctors will decline to say anything to the press, to avoid saying anything amounting to an admission in subsequent proceedings, or which may be upsetting to the family. The solicitor should also advise the doctors and nursing staff not to make any comments to the media. In some cases, it may be appropriate, from a public relations point of view, for the hospital to issue a brief statement offering sympathy to the family following the death of the deceased.

If the family wishes to express its anger in a more public forum, the press is usually happy to provide this opportunity. If there are any concerns to which the inquest gave rise, these could be expressed to the press. It is important, however, that the family's solicitor does not get carried away on the tide of emotion and risk slandering any of the individuals concerned.

### 17.2.10 The impact of the Human Rights Act 1998

In the cases of *R v HM Coroner for Western Somerset, ex p Middleton* [2004] UKHL 10 and *R v Coroner for West Yorkshire, ex p Sacker* [2004] UKHL 11, the House of Lords examined the relationship between Article 2 of the ECHR (the 'right to life') and the role of inquests, where the deceased dies while under the control of the State or as a consequence of the actions of a State agent. Although full reference to the cases must be made, the following points should be noted:

(a) Acts or omissions may be recorded, but expressions that suggest civil liability, in particular 'neglect' or 'carelessness', should be avoided.

(b) There are some cases where short verdicts in the traditional form did not enable the inquest jury to express their conclusion on the central issues in the case, and this did not meet the requirements of the Convention. Where a short-form verdict was not satisfactory, it would be for the coroner to decide how best to elicit the jury's conclusion.

(c) The rules for conducting inquests enacted by Parliament should be respected, save for the interpretation of 'how' in the phrase 'how, when and where the deceased came by his death' in r 36 of the Coroners Rules 1984. The phrase should be interpreted in the broad sense, meaning 'by what means and in what circumstances', rather than simply as 'by what means'.

Other recent cases relating to Article 2 of the ECHR include *R ((1) Challender and (2) Morris) v Legal Services Commission* [2004] EWHC 925, concerning a refusal of funding by the LSC; *R ((1) A and (2) B) v HM Coroner for Inner South District of Greater London* [2004] EWHC 1592 (Admin), concerning a coroner's refusal to grant anonymity to two police officers; and *Re McKerr* [2004] UKHL 12, where the duty to investigate an unlawful killing under Article 2 did not arise in domestic law in respect of deaths before 2 October 2000 when the Human Rights Act 1998 came into force. See also *R (Wilson) v Secretary of State for the Home Department* [2004] EWHC 2462 and *Pearson v HM Coroner for Inner London North* [2005] EWHC 833.

Coroners are clearly having regard to Article 2 in their day-to-day work. However, such cases as *Plymouth City Council v HM Coroner for Devon (defendant) and the Secretary of State for Education and Skills* [2005] FLR 1279 illustrate that there can be difficulties in the interpretation of the Article 2 requirements. In *Plymouth City Council* the coroner decided to hold a 'broad inquest' (by including certain statutory child protection agencies) in relation to a child's death, but it was held on judicial review that the investigation duty under Article 2 had not been activated and there was no need for a broad inquest. See also *Goodson v HM Coroner for Bedfordshire and Luton* [2004] EWHC 2931, in relation to when the State's procedural obligation under Article 2 is invoked.

### 17.2.11 Coroners and Justice Bill

A draft Coroners Bill was originally published on 12 June 2006 and was followed by a lengthy period of consultation. At the beginning of 2009 the Government placed the Coroners and Justice Bill before Parliament, and it is currently making its way through the House of Lords.

#### 17.2.11.1 Background

Pressure for reform of the coroner system manifested itself following a series of high-profile disasters such as Hillsborough in 1989, where the coroner's verdict at the inquest into the deaths of the 96 victims was simply 'accidental death', which meant that no one has ever properly been held to account. In the 1990s coroners came under further, intense public scrutiny for their actions. For example, there were many concerns raised over the coroner in the *Marchioness* disaster, who ordered the hands of the victims to be cut off for identification purposes. Then there was the Shipman case, where the faking of patients' death certificates brought home the shortcomings of the death certification process.

The proposed changes in the new Bill stem from a series of inquiries into the coroner system led by Dame Janet Smith, and from the 2003 Home Office *Report of the Fundamental Review of Death Certification*. These identified a court process that was fragmented, localised and out of step with the modern world.

#### 17.2.11.2 Proposals for reform

The Bill provides six key reforms to the death investigation system of coroners:

(a) Bereaved people will be able to contribute to coroners' investigations to a greater extent. They will be able to bring their concerns to the attention of the coroner even where a death certificate has been issued. A coroners' charter will set out the service bereaved people can expect.

(b) National leadership will be introduced with the appointment of a Chief Coroner, together with guidance and support from an advisory Coronial Council (see further below). The Chief Coroner will be accountable to Government. Coroners will continue to be appointed and funded by local councils, and served by coroners' officers drawn from the local police or local authority.

(c) There will be fewer coroners, who will become full-time, and current boundaries will be reshaped to create a smaller number of coroner jurisdictions.

(d) Coroners will have new powers, aimed at modernising the investigation and inquest processes to ensure better investigations and inquests.

(e) Investigations of treasure finds will be dealt with by a new national treasure coroner, enabling other area coroners to concentrate on their core activity (ie enquiries into unnatural deaths).

(f) Coroners will have better medical support and advice at both local and national level.

In limited circumstances (eg, suicide and child deaths), coroners will have a discretion to complete investigations without holding public inquests, if they consider that no public interest is served by doing so. The inquest will be concluded by a written report equivalent to a public inquest. This is to address the concern of grieving families, who feel the unnecessary intrusion of the media at a time of intense personal grief

It is proposed that the Chief Coroner will be given powers to audit and inspect individual coroners' performance, including implementation of the Coroners' Charter. Powers to hear appeals will also be put in the hands of the Chief Coroner (replacing the current system of judicial review, which is seen as slow and expensive).

The Chief Coroner will also oversee the training of coroners. He will be supported by a national Coronial Council, with provision for lay and voluntary group membership. It is proposed that the legally qualified coroners (ie those without a medical background) will receive national medical support through a new Chief Medical Adviser.

Full details of the Bill, the Draft Charter for Bereaved People and the responses to the consultation can be found on the Ministry of Justice website: www.justice.gov.uk. Although the consultation period has now ended, it is not clear when the new legislation will be brought into force. The Government has simply stated that the Bill will be introduced in Parliament 'as soon as parliamentary time allows'. The Bill is expected to receive the Royal Assent in 2010.

## 17.3 Criminal prosecutions

Where an accident results in a fatality, a criminal prosecution of those thought to be responsible will often follow. The procedure adopted in the magistrates' courts and Crown Court for such a prosecution is dealt with in **Criminal Litigation**.

If such a prosecution occurs, the claimant's solicitor should attend at court to obtain details of the circumstances of the accident and take notes of the evidence. If a conviction is obtained, this will be very useful for the civil proceedings, and in these circumstances the relevant insurance company will often settle any claim.

Many insurance policies provide for the cost of defending such criminal charges, and the insurance company will nominate solicitors to act on the insured's behalf. The defendant's insurers will use the proceedings to establish a view on civil, as well as criminal liability

### 17.3.1 Criminal prosecution following a fatal road traffic accident

On 18 August 2008, the Road Traffic Act 2006 (RTA 2006) introduced three new offences to add to the existing offence of causing death by dangerous driving under the Road Traffic Act 1988 (RTA 1988). The four offences which may be prosecuted now following a fatal road traffic accident are as follows:

(a) *Causing death by dangerous driving* (RTA 1988, s 1). Under s 2 of the RTA 1988, a person is to be regarded as driving dangerously if the standard of driving falls 'far below what would be expected of a competent and careful driver and it would be obvious to a competent and careful driver that driving in that way would be dangerous'. The Sentencing Guidelines Council has issued a definitive guideline on sentencing ('the Guideline') which gives examples of driving behaviour likely to result in this charge. They include aggressive driving, racing or competitive driving, speeding, and using a hand-held mobile phone when the driver was avoidably and dangerously distracted by that use.

The maximum penalty in the Crown Court is 14 years' imprisonment with a minimum disqualification of two years.

(b) *Causing death by careless driving* when under the influence of drink or drugs, or having failed without reasonable excuse either to provide a specimen for analysis or to permit the analysis of a blood sample (RTA 1988, s 3A).

According to s 3ZA of the RTA 1988, careless driving is driving that 'falls below what would be expected of a competent and careful driver'. In comparison with dangerous driving, the level of culpability in the actual manner of driving is lower, but that culpability is increased by the fact that the driver has driven after consuming drugs or alcohol.

The maximum penalty in the Crown Court is 14 years' imprisonment with a minimum disqualification of two years.

(c) *Causing death by careless or inconsiderate driving* (RTA 1988, s 2B). Careless driving is described in (b) above. Under s 3ZA of the RTA 1988, a person is to be regarded as driving without reasonable consideration for other persons, 'only if those persons are inconvenienced by his driving'. Examples of careless driving given in the Guideline include overtaking on the inside, emerging from a side road into the path of another vehicle, and tuning a car radio. Examples of inconsiderate driving include flashing of lights to force drivers in front to give way and driving with undipped headlights.

The maximum penalty for this offence is five years' imprisonment with a minimum of 12 months' disqualification.

(d) *Causing death by driving: unlicensed, disqualified or uninsured drivers* (RTA 1988, s 3ZB). This charge is likely to be prosecuted alongside one of the more serious offences outlined in (a) to (c) above, and is self-explanatory. It carries a maximum penalty of two years' imprisonment with a minimum disqualification of 12 months.

### 17.3.2 Criminal prosecution following an accident at work

Following a fatal accident at work, the HSE may bring a prosecution under the HSWA 1974 (see **4.9**). It is also possible for an individual (such as a director of a company) to be prosecuted for gross negligence manslaughter.

Where the evidence indicates that a serious criminal offence other than a health and safety offence may have been committed, the HSE is required to liaise with the CPS in deciding whether to prosecute. Health and safety offences are usually prosecuted by the HSE, or by the local authority responsible for enforcement. The CPS may also prosecute health and safety offences, but usually does so only when prosecuting other serious criminal offences, such as manslaughter, arising out of the same circumstances.

There is also the possibility that the CPS could now bring a prosecution against an employer for corporate manslaughter under the Corporate Manslaughter and Corporate Homicide Act 2007, which is discussed in more detail below (see **17.3.4**).

### 17.3.3 Criminal prosecution following clinical negligence

The CPS may bring a prosecution for manslaughter against an individual (such as a doctor or nurse) following a clinical negligence incident which results in the death of a patient. Such a charge will be on the basis that the breach of duty committed was so great as to constitute gross negligence and therefore merits criminal sanctions rather than a duty to just compensate the victim (see *R v Adomako* [1995] 1 AC 171).

Over the years, a number of doctors have been convicted of manslaughter by gross negligence. In 2003, two senior house officers were so convicted following the death of a man who had been placed in their post-operative care. Following a routine knee operation at Southampton University Hospital, the patient contracted an infection and subsequently died of toxic shock syndrome. The doctors had failed to deal with the clear signs of serious illness, take appropriate blood samples, administer antibiotics or consult senior colleagues. Their appeal against a suspended sentence of 18 months each was dismissed by the Court of Appeal (*R v Misra; R v Srivastava* [2004] EWCA Crim 2375).

Following their conviction, the CPS also instigated criminal proceedings against the NHS Trust (*R v Southampton University Hospitals NHS Trust* [2006] EWCA Crim 2971) for its failure to discharge its duty under s 3 of the HSWA 1974. This section requires an employer to conduct his undertakings in such a way as to ensure, so far is reasonably practical, that persons not in his employment and who may be affected (in this instance a patient) are not exposed to risks to their health and safety. The Trust had failed to provide enough junior doctors in the Trauma and Orthopaedic Department, and had failed to implement systems for the adequate supervision of staff by consultants. The Trust pleaded guilty, and the initial fine of £100,000 was reduced on appeal to £40,000 on the grounds that the judge had not taken account of the early guilty plea and that the public would suffer as a result of a large fine.

It is also now possible that an NHS Trust or health authority could be prosecuted for corporate manslaughter (see **17.3.4** below).

### 17.3.4 The Corporate Manslaughter and Corporate Homicide Act 2007

#### 17.3.4.1 The background

The Corporate Manslaughter and Corporate Homicide Act 2007 (CMCHA 2007) came into force on 6 August 2008 in response to problems applying the existing offence of manslaughter by gross negligence to organisations rather than to individuals. The main problem under existing criminal law is that, in order for a company or other organisation to be guilty of gross negligence manslaughter, it is necessary for a senior individual (the 'controlling mind'), who can be said to embody the company, to be guilty of the offence. This is sometimes referred to as the 'identification doctrine'.

The matter was examined in *Attorney-General's Reference (No 2 of 1999)* [2000] 2 Cr App R 207, which concerned a train collision at Southall in 1997 in which seven passengers died and 151 were injured. Great Western Trains was prosecuted for manslaughter on the basis that it had allowed the train to be operated with two important safety devices switched off, as a result of which the driver of the train had failed to notice a warning signal. The company was acquitted as there was no human being with whom the company could be identified. On a reference by the Attorney-General, the Court of Appeal stated that the identification doctrine remained the only basis in common law for corporate liability in gross negligence manslaughter.

As a result of the identification doctrine there have been very few successful prosecutions for corporate manslaughter. The only successful prosecutions have been of small, owner-managed companies, where it was not difficult to pinpoint a senior individual who effectively ran the company, such as in *Kite and Others* (1994) *Independent*, 9 December, where four teenagers drowned while canoeing during an adventure holiday.

The failures of the law led to a sustained campaign for reform, which finally resulted in the offence of corporate manslaughter being introduced by the CMCHA 2007. The new offence is intended to work in conjunction with other forms of accountability, such as gross negligence manslaughter for individuals and other health and safety legislation.

The first case under the CMCHA 2007 has been listed for trial in February 2010. The company charged, Cotswold Geotechnical Holdings Ltd, is alleged to have caused the death of an employee who was crushed to death in 2008 when the sides of an excavated pit collapsed while he was collecting soil samples. A director of the company has also been charged with common law manslaughter and an offence under s 37 of the HSWA 1974.

### 17.3.4.2 The offence

Section 1 of the CMCHA 2007 states:

> (1) An organisation to which this section applies is guilty of an offence if the way in which its activities are managed or organised —
>
> (a) causes a person's death; and
>
> (b) amounts to a gross breach of a relevant duty of care owed by the organisation to the deceased.
>
> (2) An organisation is guilty of an offence ... only if the way in which its activities are managed or organised by its senior management is a substantial element in the breach referred to in subsection (1).

To prove the offence, therefore, the CPS must prove:

(a) the defendant is a qualifying *organisation*;

(b) the organisation *causes* a person's death;

(c) there was a *relevant duty of care* owed by the organisation to the deceased;

(d) there was a *gross breach* of that duty; and

(e) a substantial element of that breach was in the way those activities were managed or organised *by senior management*; and

(f) that the defendant does not fall within one of the *exemptions* for prosecution under the Act.

Therefore the court will have to consider how the fatal activity was managed, or organised, throughout the organisation, including any systems and processes for managing safety and how these were operated in practice. A substantial part of the failure within the organisation must have been at a senior level.

**Meaning of 'organisation'**

Section 1(2) states the offence applies to the following bodies:

(a) a corporation;

(b) a department or other body listed in Sch 1;

(c) a police force; and

(d) a partnership, or trade union or employer's association that is an employer.

Crown immunity has been a long-established legal doctrine that means that Crown bodies (such as government departments) cannot be prosecuted. Section 11(1) now allows prosecutions under the Act to apply to such bodies. Schedule 1 sets out a list of government departments to which the offence applies.

The Act will also apply to a wide range of statutory public bodies which are not part of the Crown, including local authorities and NHS bodies.

**Causation**

It will not be necessary for the management failure to have been the sole cause of death. The prosecution will need to show that 'but for' the management failure (including the substantial element attributable to senior management), the death would not have occurred. The law does not, however, recognise very remote causes, and in some circumstances the existence of an intervening event may mean that the management failure is not considered to have caused the death.

**Relevant duty of care**

Section 2(1) requires that the relevant duty of care is to be one that is owed under the law of negligence. The Act does not create new duties in addition to those already owed in the civil law of negligence.

The duty must be a relevant one for the offence. Relevant duties are set out in s 2(1) of the Act and include:

(a) employer and occupier duties;

(b) duties owed in connection with:

  (i) supplying goods and services (whether or not for consideration),

  (ii) construction and maintenance work (note that simply because there is a statutory duty to perform an act, this does not create a relevant duty of care; thus although a highways authority has a duty to maintain and repair roads (HA 1980, s 41), the failure to do so does not give rise to a duty of care to a motorist in negligence. However a negligent repair would do so),

  (iii) other activities on a commercial basis, and

  (iv) using or keeping plant, vehicles or other things.

**Gross breach**

Once a relevant duty of care has been established, any breach must fall far below what could reasonably be expected of the organisation in the circumstances (s 1(4)(b)).

This is a matter for the jury to decide, and s 8 sets out factors for the jury to consider. Section 8(2) states that the jury *must* consider whether health and safety legislation was breached and, if so:

(a) how serious the breach was (s 8(2)(a)); and

(b) how much of a risk of death it posed (s 8(2)(b)).

**Meaning of 'senior management'**

The term 'senior management' is defined in s 1(4) to mean those persons who play a *significant* role in the management of the whole of, or a *substantial* part of, the organisation's activities. This covers both those in the direct chain of management and those in, for example, strategic or regulatory compliance roles.

Neither 'significant' nor 'substantial' is defined, but the former is likely to be limited to those whose involvement is influential, and will not include those who simply carry out the activity.

Whether the activity in question is itself a 'substantial' part of the company's activities will be of great importance in determining if the offence applies, especially where a company has multiple businesses or is a national organisation with regional managers. The test of senior management is wider than the former 'controlling mind', which effectively restricted the offence to actions of directors. A regional manager would probably count, but this may itself depend on the number of regions, the number of higher tiers of management, the diversity of the organisation's activities and his own job description.

**Exemptions**

Corporate manslaughter will not apply to certain public and government functions where there exist wider questions of public policy. So, for example, the Act exempts the military, the police and the emergency services when conducting certain activities, including dealing with emergencies, terrorism and violent disorder.

#### 17.3.4.3 Punishment for corporate manslaughter

The court has a range of sentencing options following a conviction for corporate manslaughter:

(a) *Unlimited fine*. The Sentencing Guidelines Council is currently working on a guideline to support the new offence. The Sentencing Advisory Panel has suggested that a conviction under CMCHA 2007 should result in a fine significantly greater than under the HSWA 1974, which should have a starting point of 5% of annual turnover.

(b) *Remedial orders*. The court can make a remedial order, requiring the organisation to address the cause of the fatal injury.

The Ministry of Justice Guidance suggests that

> ... the courts will impose a remedial order in relatively rare circumstances since the relevant regulator will have been involved in the case from the outset and will have been able to use their existing enforcement powers to address any dangerous practices long before a case comes to court. Nevertheless, this power enables the judge to impose an order if it still appears necessary.

Any organisation that fails to take the action set out in the order can be prosecuted for failure to do so. An unlimited fine can be imposed on conviction.

(c) *Publicity orders* (s 10). On conviction the court may make a publicity order which requires the organisation to publicise the fact that it has been convicted of the offence. Note that if a company fails to comply with either a publicity order, it commits an offence punishable with a fine.

## 17.4 Conclusion

Inquests and criminal prosecutions are important processes which can be used to gather evidence at an early stage, and the outcome of a criminal prosecution can be extremely influential in establishing liability in a civil claim for compensation. From a personal injury solicitor's point of view this can be very demanding work, as the client is likely to make considerable demands of the solicitor both professionally and emotionally.

## 17.5 Further reading and information

Matthews, *Jervis on Coroners* (Sweet & Maxwell) and the cumulative supplement

Advice may be obtained from the organisation 'Inquest', which can be contacted at Alexandra National House, 330 Seven Sisters Road, Finsbury Park, London N4 2PJ.

Ministry of Justice, 'Guidance for Coroners on Changes to Rule 43: Coroner reports to prevent future deaths'

www.sentencing-guidelines.gov.uk

www.justice.gov.uk

www.CPS.gov.uk

## 17.6 Investigating fatal accidents

Criminal prosecution
(a) Health and Safety at Work, etc Act 1974
(b) Manslaughter
(c) Road Traffic Act 1988
(d) Corporate manslaughter

↓

Conviction may be relied on as evidence of negligence in later civil claim

Coroner's inquest

↓

Coroner involved if Coroners Act 1988, s 8(1) applies, including:
(a) violent or unnatural death;
(b) sudden death of which cause unknown;
(c) death in prison

↓

Purpose of inquest:
(a) who deceased was;
(b) show, when and where the deceased came by his death;
(c) particulars required by the Registration Acts

↓

Other matters:
Post-mortem
Obtain evidence/medical notes
Contact coroner's office
Explain role of inquest to client

↓

Verdict:
Purpose *not* to express blame

# Chapter 18

# Introduction to Fatal Accident Claims — Procedure and Quantification



## 18.1 Introduction

This chapter sets out the basic principles involved in assessing damages in personal injury and clinical negligence cases where the victim has died before trial.

There are two main causes of action in such circumstances:

(a) the Law Reform (Miscellaneous Provisions) Act 1934 (LR(MP)A 1934), which allows a claim for the benefit of the deceased's estate; and

(b) the Fatal Accidents Act 1976 (FAA 1976), which allows a claim for the benefit of the dependants and those entitled to an award of bereavement damages.

It will be assumed that the death occurred on or after 1 January 1983, as the above Acts were amended substantially relating to deaths after that date. While the Acts provide two separate causes of action, they are commonly brought together.

In certain cases, specific statutes provide for recompense for the deceased's family, such as the Carriage by Air Act 1961 in cases of death arising out of civil aviation accidents. These are not dealt with in this text.

## 18.2 Cause of action

The LR(MP)A 1934 provides (for the benefit of the deceased's estate) for the continuation of the cause of action to which the deceased was entitled the instant before he died (LR(MP)A 1934, s 1(2)). It does not create a separate cause of action.

The FAA 1976 does create a separate cause of action for the dependants (and those entitled to the award of bereavement damages), but it is based on the pre-condition that the deceased, had he lived, would have been able to sue successfully (FAA 1976, s 1).

Three things follow from this, namely:

(a) if the deceased had no cause of action then the estate and the dependants have no cause of action;

(b) any defence that could have been used against the deceased can be used against the estate and the dependants;

(c) if the deceased was contributorily negligent then the damages of the estate and the dependants are reduced accordingly.

> **Example 1**
>
> Tom is driving his car when it collides with a car driven by Sharon. Tom dies as a result of his injuries. He is survived by his widow, Elaine, and his son, Christopher. The accident is entirely the fault of Tom. As a result, neither Tom's estate, nor Elaine or Christopher has any right of action against Sharon.

> **Example 2**
>
> Lucy is killed in an accident at work. She is survived by her husband, Michael, and daughter, Patricia. Lucy and her employers are equally to blame for the accident. Although Lucy's estate, Michael and Patricia may claim against the employers, the damages awarded to each will be reduced by 50%.

In the case of *Jameson and Another v Central Electricity Generating Board and Another* [2000] AC 455, the House of Lords held that in a case where the second co-defendant had paid a compensation payment to the injured person when he was still alive (on a less than full liability basis), this did prevent the dependants bringing a claim under FAA 1976 against the first co-defendant (who was a concurrent tortfeasor) and did amount to a settlement of claim.

Pleadings may be amended to plead a fatal accident claim if the deceased dies during the course of proceedings which were commenced in his name when he was alive. However, once judgment is given or a claim is settled by a living claimant, there can be no subsequent claim by dependants. If there is a possibility that a claimant might die of his injuries during the course of proceedings, a claim for provisional damages should be made (see **15.4**). Section 3 of the Damages Act 1996 makes it clear that a provisional damages award does not bar a claim under the FAA 1976, although the award will be taken into account in assessing damages payable to the dependants under the 1976 Act.

## 18.3 The appointment of personal representatives

Fatal accident claims are normally representative actions. This means that the personal representative normally brings a claim simultaneously on behalf of the estate under the LR(MP)A 1934 and on behalf of the dependants under the FAA 1976. The grant of probate or letters of administration should therefore be obtained before the claim is commenced.

## 18.4 Damages under the Law Reform (Miscellaneous Provisions) Act 1934

Generally, the damages awarded to the estate under the LR(MP)A 1934 are based on the losses for which the deceased could have claimed at the instant before he died. In essence, the estate inherits the deceased's right to sue in respect of the death. Any head of damages that is duplicated between the LR(MP)A 1934 and the FAA 1976 is recoverable only once.

The following heads of damages may be appropriate.

### 18.4.1 Pain, suffering and loss of amenity

There must be evidence that there was suffering. This will mean, in practice, that there must be a period of survival. If there is no significant period of survival (ie in the case of instantaneous death) an award will not be made. In *Hicks v Wright* [1992] 2 All ER 65, no damages under this head were awarded to victims of the Hillsborough disaster for the short period of terror and pain they experienced before death (see **6.2**). However, if there is a significant period of survival and, during that period, the victim becomes aware of impending death, the award for pain and suffering will be increased.

The amount of the award for pain, suffering and loss of amenity will depend upon the actual level of pain and the length of time over which the pain was experienced. For example, in *Robertson v Lestrange* [1985] 1 All ER 950, an award of £150 ( the equivalent of about £350 at today's values) was made for four days' pain and suffering between injury and death. In *Fallon v Beaumont*, 16 December 1993, CC (Leeds), a 22-year-old man was involved in a high-speed road accident, during which the car in which he was a passenger exploded and burst into flames. He was trapped in the burning car until the emergency services arrived, and was conscious throughout. He died 30 days later. He would have had significant insight into the gravity of his situation and an award of £10,000 ( the equivalent of about £15,000 at today's values) was made for pain and suffering.

### 18.4.2 Loss of income

The estate is entitled to claim the lost net earnings of the deceased from the time of the accident until death, calculated in the same way as for a living claimant (see **15.2.1**). No claim can be made for loss of income in respect of any period after that person's death (LR(MP)A 1934, s 1(2)(a)(ii), as amended by the Administration of Justice Act 1982).

### 18.4.3 Funeral expenses

Funeral expenses are specifically provided for in s 1(2)(c) of the LR(MP)A 1934. The expenses may be claimed provided they are:

(a) reasonable; and

(b) incurred by the estate.

What is 'reasonable' will depend on the individual circumstances of the case, including the social standing and racial origin of the deceased. In *Gammell v Wilson* [1982] AC 27, the court drew a distinction between the cost of the funeral service and a headstone (which was allowed), and the cost of a wake and a memorial to the deceased (which was not allowed).

If the expenses are incurred by a dependant of the deceased rather than by the deceased's estate, the dependant may claim the expenses as part of the fatal accidents claim.

On a practical note, it is important to obtain receipts in order to prove all the expenses incurred. Many insurers are amenable to making an immediate interim payment in relation to the funeral expenses, in order to relieve the dependents of some of the immediate expenses and to prevent interest accruing on those expenses.

### 18.4.4 Value of services rendered by third parties

Services rendered by third parties may include, for example: nursing services rendered by a relative to the deceased up to the time of death; expenses incurred by a third party in assisting in bringing the deceased's body home from abroad; or the costs incurred by relatives in visiting the hospital. The quantum is the proper and reasonable cost of supplying the need. (For the general principles involved, see **Chapter 15**.)

### 18.4.5 Other losses

Other losses may include, for example, damage to chattels, such as the car the deceased was driving at the time of the incident, or the clothing which he was wearing.

### 18.4.6 Distribution of damages

Damages under the LR(MP)A 1934 pass to the deceased's estate, and from there to the deceased's beneficiaries according to the deceased's will or the rules of intestacy.

Damages under the LR(MP)A 1934 are, in appropriate cases (eg, where there was a long interval between the accident and the death, and the deceased had been in receipt of recoverable benefits), subject to the Social Security (Recovery of Benefits) Act 1997 (see **Chapter 16**), but are not subject to any other losses or gains to the estate, such as the receipt of insurance money (LR(MP)A 1934, s 1(2)).

### 18.4.7 Conclusion

In the case of instantaneous death, damages under the LR(MP)A 1934 will normally be limited to damages for funeral expenses and damage to chattels. Where there is a period of survival, the damages may be more extensive but will normally still be severely curtailed by the inability of the estate to claim the lost future income of the deceased.

## 18.5 Damages under the Fatal Accidents Act 1976

In general terms, there are three possible heads of damages, namely:

(a) a dependency claim for the financial losses suffered by the dependants of the deceased;
(b) an award of bereavement damages; and
(c) a claim for the funeral expenses, if paid by the dependants.

### 18.5.1 Loss of dependency

To succeed in a dependency claim, the claimant

(a) must be a dependant as defined by the FAA 1976; and
(b) must have had a reasonable expectation of financial benefit from the deceased.

#### 18.5.1.1 The statutory meaning of 'dependant'

'Dependant' is defined in s 1(3) of the FAA 1976 as follows:

> (a) the wife or husband or former wife or husband of the deceased;
> (aa) the civil partner or former civil partner of the deceased;
> (b) any person who:
> (i) was living with the deceased in the same household immediately before the date of the death; and
> (ii) had been living with the deceased in the same household for at least two years before that date; and
> (iii) was living during the whole of that period as the husband or wife or civil partner of the deceased;
> (c) any parent or other ascendant of the deceased;
> (d) any person who was treated by the deceased as his parent;
> (e) any child or other descendant of the deceased;
> (f) any person (not being a child of the deceased) who, in the case of any marriage to which the deceased was at any time a party, was treated by the deceased as a child of the family in relation to that marriage;
> (fa) any person (not being a child of the deceased) who, in the case of any civil partnership in which the deceased was at any time a civil partner, was treated by the deceased as a child of the family in relation to that civil partnership;
> (g) any person who is, or is the issue of, a brother, sister, uncle or aunt of the deceased.

The requirement to come within the statutory definition of 'dependant' has resulted in adverse judicial comment (see *Shepherd v Post Office* (1995) *The Times*, 15 June), and the introduction of the cohabitee as a possible claimant ((b) above) by the Administration of Justice Act 1982 was controversial.

In *Fretwell v Willi Betz*, 8 March 2001, the definition of a 'dependant' was challenged, by virtue of the Human Rights Act 1998. The case was settled without any admission as regards the claimant's status as a 'dependant' (the argument concerned a child of the girlfriend who was living with the deceased prior to the accident), but it does illustrate the possibility of using the Human Rights Act 1998 to challenge the narrow statutory definition of a 'dependant' (see also *Ogur v Turkey* (2001) 31 EHRR 912).

The requirement to have been living together for two years prior to the death should be noted, and evidence should be obtained on this point if it is anticipated that the defendant will challenge this (see *Kotke v Saffarini* [2005] EWCA Civ 221). The FAA 1976 contains a provision that the cohabitee's lack of enforceable right to support is to be taken into account (FAA 1976, s 3(4)). This may mean that a cohabitee will receive less compensation than a lawful spouse, as the court may use a lower multiplier in determining the dependency claim. For example, a multiplier of 13 was used for a cohabiting couple, instead of 15 which would have been used if they were married.

#### 18.5.1.2 Further provisions with regard to the meaning of 'dependant'

Section 1(4) of the FAA 1976 (as amended by the Administration of Justice Act 1982) provides:

> ... former wife or husband ... includes a reference to a person whose marriage to the deceased has been annulled or declared void as well as a person whose marriage to the deceased has been dissolved.

Section 1(5) of the FAA 1976 (as amended by the Administration of Justice Act 1982) provides:

> (a) any relationship by affinity shall be treated as a relationship by consanguinity, any relationship of the half blood as a relationship of the whole blood, and the stepchild of any person as his child;
>
> (b) an illegitimate person shall be treated as the legitimate child of his mother and reputed father.

Thus, for example, the stepbrother of the deceased is treated as his true brother; the uncle of a wife is treated as the husband's uncle.

The Adoption Act 1976 provides that, generally, an adopted child is treated as the natural child of the adopters.

#### 18.5.1.3 Identifying the dependants

It is important to identify all prospective dependants, as s 2(3) of the FAA 1976 provides that 'not more than one action shall lie' and, as a result, only one claim will be brought. A defendant is entitled to full particulars of all those on whose behalf the claim is being brought. In practice, the particulars of the dependants are set out in the court documentation and generally include details of:

(a) the age of the dependants;

(b) their relationship with the deceased;

(c) the nature of the dependency (eg, the dependant was a minor son wholly supported by the deceased father who was the family breadwinner and who had good promotion prospects).

In the case of *Cachia v Faluyi* [2001] EWCA Civ 998, [2001] 1 WLR 1966, the Court of Appeal held that it was possible to interpret s 2(3) of the FAA 1976 under the ECHR, so as to prevent a dependent child's claim from becoming statute-barred for limitation purposes.

On occasions, the defendants will argue that a claimant is not a true 'dependant' under the FAA 1976, and this is often resolved by the court ordering a trial of the point as a preliminary issue.

#### 18.5.1.4 The requirement of 'financial loss'

It is not sufficient that the claimant merely satisfies the statutory meaning of 'dependant'. It must be shown in addition that there is a reasonable likelihood that the claimant has or will suffer financial loss as a result of the death of the deceased. In the case of *Thomas v Kwik Save*

*Stores Ltd* (2000) *The Times*, 27 June, the Court of Appeal reaffirmed the principle that, when awarding damages under the FAA 1976, the court was concerned with the financial loss and not the emotional dependency of the claimant on the deceased.

In many cases, the dependants will have a clear and immediate financial loss. For example, where a husband was maintaining his wife and children before his death, the fact that they will suffer financial loss as a result of the husband's death is obvious. In addition to the loss of the deceased's earnings, consideration should be given to whether the dependents have lost any fringe benefits to which he was entitled, such as a company car.

The loss may still be regarded as 'financial' even if there was no expenditure by the deceased, provided the support can be quantified in monetary terms (eg, where the deceased's elderly mother was allowed to live rent-free in the deceased's house before his death, the mother would be able to claim a quantifiable financial loss). If the deceased regularly did DIY, gardening or other jobs around the house, the dependants can claim for the loss of those gratuitous services. In *Crabtree v Wilson* [1993] PIQR Q24 the court valued the deceased's work around the home at £1,500 per annum.

In the case of *Cox v Hockenhull* [1999] 3 All ER 577, the Court of Appeal held that the important point in assessing the dependency was to identify the loss the claimant has suffered as a result of a death. In that case, the deceased's income had been certain State benefits which she and her husband had relied upon. The Court allowed the husband's claim for dependency on the basis that he was dependent on certain benefits that had been received prior to the death and which he no longer obtained after his wife was killed in a road traffic accident.

#### 18.5.1.5 The loss must be as a result of a personal family relationship with the deceased

If the loss to the dependant is, in reality, a loss attributable to a business relationship with the deceased, the claim for loss of dependency will fail (*Burgess v Florence Nightingale Hospital for Gentlewomen* [1955] 1 QB 349).

> **Example**
>
> Tom is killed in a car accident as a result of the negligent driving of Keith. Tom is survived by his widow, Sally, and his 6-month-old son, Brian. Tom was the sole financial support of Sally and Brian. Tom worked in business with his brother, Joe. As a result of Tom's death, the business fails and Joe suffers heavy financial losses. Tom's married sister, Edwina, is very upset at the news of her brother's death.
>
> Sally and Brian may claim as defined dependants who suffer financial losses as a result of a family relationship with Tom.
>
> Joe cannot claim because, although he is a defined dependant, his financial losses are as a result of a business relationship with Tom.
>
> Edwina cannot claim because, although she is a defined dependant, she has suffered no financial losses (merely grief and sorrow).

### 18.5.2 Assessing loss of dependency – the traditional method

The award for loss of dependency is ascertained by a multiplicand and multiplier system. The multiplicand is the net annual loss of the dependants; the multiplier is based on the number of years' loss of dependency (ie, the length of time that the claimant would have been dependent on the deceased).

#### 18.5.2.1 The multiplicand – the net annual loss to the dependants

**The deceased wage earner**

The starting point is to calculate the amount of the deceased's earnings and deduct the estimated amount representing the sum that would have been spent by the deceased on his own personal and living expenses. The remaining balance will be the dependency multiplicand.

The deceased's net annual earnings must be calculated as at the date of the trial (*Cookson v Knowles* [1979] AC 556). No allowance is made for inflation (*Auty v National Coal Board* [1985] 1 All ER 930), but the deceased's future earning capacity (eg, as result of promotion) must be taken into account. For example, a trainee doctor may have been earning a relatively modest income at the date of death, but his earnings would clearly have increased substantially on qualifying and again on becoming a consultant. Evidence will be needed in support of this, and the best evidence may be from a comparative employee or employees who have gone, or who are going through, the same career structure as the deceased would have done. This evidence could be obtained, for example, from the deceased's trade union or employer.

Conversely there may be evidence of likely loss of earning capacity, for example because of redundancy.

**Calculating the dependency figure**

There are two approaches that the courts have considered:

(a) The 'old' system for calculating the dependency figure is to add up all the financial benefits received by the dependants from the deceased. It is necessary to produce a list of the items which contributed to the annual value of dependency and for the claimant to provide documentary evidence, bills, etc for the year prior to the death. A proportion is then deducted for the deceased's own expenses. For example, the following items have been considered: How much housekeeping money was paid to the wife? How much was spent on the deceased's food? How much was spent on the food for the rest of the family? Who paid how much for the children's shoes, etc? This type of calculation is very difficult and in practice is rarely attempted.

(b) The customary modern practice, which was established in the case of *Harris v Empress Motors* [1983] 3 All ER 561, is to deduct a percentage from the net income figure to represent what the deceased would have spent exclusively on himself. Conventional percentages are adopted. Where the family unit was husband and wife, the usual figure is one-third. Where the family unit was husband, wife and children, the usual figure is one-quarter. However, it is important to note that each case must be judged on its own facts. The court is willing to depart from the conventional figures where there is evidence that they are inappropriate (*Owen v Martin* [1992] PIQR Q151), for example where the deceased was particularly frugal or a spendthrift. In such circumstances, less or more than the conventional figure should be deducted (see also *Coward v Comex Houlder Diving Ltd*, 18 July 1988, CA and *Dhaliwal v Personal Representatives of Hunt (Deceased)* [1995] PIQR Q56, CA).

Furthermore, it is quite possible that different multiplicands may have to be selected according to different times in the period of dependency. Had he lived, the deceased's financial affairs would not have remained constant throughout his life. Similarly, therefore, the multiplicand will not remain constant either. For example, in the case of a husband with wife and children, 75% of the husband's earnings may be the appropriate initial multiplicand while his children are likely to be dependent. However, from the point where the children can be expected to become independent the multiplicand may be merely two-thirds of the husband's earnings (see also *Coward v Comex Houlder Diving Ltd*, above).

Frequently, both husband and wife would have been earning at the time of death, and in such circumstances the approach adopted is to calculate the dependency as two-thirds or three-quarters (as the case may be) of the total joint net income, less the continuing earnings of the surviving spouse .

**Example**

Mike and Susan both earn £50,000 pa net. They have no children. Mike dies in an accident at work. Two-thirds of their joint income is approximately £66,600 (£100,000 x 66%), but Susan's earnings of £50,000 must be deducted to calculate her dependency claim. Susan's annual loss of dependency is therefore £16,000.

**Services rendered by the deceased**

The deceased may have been contributing to the support of the family not only in terms of a percentage of his earnings, but also by rendering services to the family free of charge. Examples of such services include:

(a) DIY jobs (eg, painting the house annually);

(b) vegetable gardening (therefore saving on grocery bills);

(c) nursing services to a sick member of the family;

(d) contributions to childcare.

On the deceased's death, such free services will be lost. The family will have to pay for the services (eg, by employing a decorator) and thus incur a loss. The value of these services can add considerably to the multiplicand. Evidence must be obtained, for example by quotations from the appropriate source.

In *Beesley v New Century Group Ltd* [2008] EWHC 3033 (QB), the claimant's husband had died from malignant mesothelioma as a result of his employment with the defendant company. The court made an award of damages for loss of 'intangible benefits' in respect of the extra value to be attached to help such as domestic services provided by a husband. The court held that there were considerable advantages in having jobs around the house and garden done by a husband in his own time and at his own convenience, rather than having to employ a professional. Accordingly, it awarded the claimant £2,000. See also *Manning v King's College Hospital NHS Trust* [2008] EWHC 3008 (QB), in which similar sums were awarded to the husband and children of the deceased for the loss of personal attention of a wife and mother, 'in recognition that what is lost goes beyond the material'.

**The deceased non-wage earner**

Where the deceased was a wage earner, the valuation of the multiplicand in the dependency claim is predominantly based on a proportion of the deceased's earnings (see above). This is so whether the deceased was male or female (eg, whether husband, father, wife or mother). It is not uncommon, however, that the deceased was not in paid employment. In this case, the value of the services rendered to the family becomes the vital issue. For example, if the deceased was the wife and mother of the family, and was not a wage earner at the date of her death, the services rendered by her to the family might be quantified in the terms of employing a housekeeper to provide the same services. In *Regan v Williamson* [1976] 1 WLR 305, Watkins J said that in this context 'the word "services" [has] been too narrowly construed. It should at least include an acknowledgement that a wife and mother does not work to set hours, and, still less, to rule'. Accordingly, a value in excess of a housekeeper was awarded in that case. In *Mehmet v Perry* [1977] 2 All ER 529, the claimant widower, on the death of his wife, reasonably gave up his job in order to look after his young children. The starting point for the value of the services of the deceased wife was taken as the husband's loss of earnings.

**Claims by parents, if children unmarried**

A claim can be made by a parent (who is often unemployed or ill) who was dependent on the support from his unmarried child. When the court considers this type of case, it will have regard to the fact that the child may have married and the financial assistance provided by the child may have ceased.

### 18.5.2.2 The multiplier – the period of loss

Having calculated the multiplicand, the other side of the equation is to calculate the number of years' loss of dependency.

**Commencement of period of loss**

The starting point for the number of years' loss is the date of death (not the date of trial: *Graham v Dodds* [1983] 2 All ER 953; *White v ESAB Group (UK) Ltd* [2002] All ER (D) 02 (Jan) and *ATM v MS* (2002) *The Times*, 3 July). However, see the 6th edition of the Ogden Tables for further commentary on this point.

**End of the period of loss**

In the case of a deceased wage earner, prima facie the number of years' loss will extend to the end of the deceased's working life (ie, usually up to what would have been the deceased's retiring age). Direct evidence should be called on this point. It must be remembered that certain items of loss, such as the claim for the cost of DIY, may extend beyond retirement age, as the deceased would not necessarily have stopped doing DIY when he retired from work.

However, each case will turn upon its own facts, and the period of dependency may end before or after what would have been the normal date of the deceased's retirement. For example, where the deceased was a professional person, he might have been expected to work and support his dependants beyond normal retirement age. Equally, if the deceased would have enjoyed a pension, it may be argued that he would have continued to provide for his dependants beyond normal retirement age (although evidence would be needed to substantiate this: *Auty v National Coal Board* [1985] 1 All ER 930; see **Chapter 15**).

Conversely, the period of dependency may stop before what would have been the normally expected retirement age of the deceased. For example, if the deceased was already in a poor state of health, he may not have been expected to work until normal retirement age, and the financial support for the dependants would therefore have ended earlier. Similarly, if the dependant himself is in a poor state of health and has a short life-expectancy, the period of dependency will be shorter.

**Effect of likely divorce or remarriage**

Where there is a claim by a widow as dependant, the likelihood that the marriage would have ended in divorce may be taken into account in assessing the period of dependency. In *Owen v Martin* [1992] PIQR Q151, the judge adopted a multiplier of 15, but the Court of Appeal reduced this to 11 on the basis that the widow's attitude towards her marriage vows, as shown by her personal history, led the court to believe that the marriage might not have lasted the whole of the natural life of the deceased. The court should take this approach only provided there is some evidence of likelihood of divorce (*Wheatley v Cunningham* [1992] PIQR Q100). See also *D and D v Donald* [2001] PIQR Q44, concerning an extra-marital affair. In *O'Loughlin v Cape Distribution Ltd* [2001] EWCA Civ 178, [2001] JPIL 191, the court confirmed that there was no prescribed method by which damages for loss of dependency had to be identified. The key factor was showing economic loss. However, the widow's prospects of remarriage or actual remarriage are to be ignored (FAA 1976, s 3(3)). Therefore, the period of the widow's dependency on her deceased husband is calculated without regard to the fact that she is or may be financially supported by a new husband.

**Conversion of the period of loss to a multiplier**

Once the number of years' loss of dependency has been ascertained, this is then converted to a multiplier using the Ogden Tables (see **Chapter 15**) .

### 18.5.2.3 The multiplication

Having established the appropriate multiplicand and the overall multiplier, one method of calculating the award for loss of dependency is as follows:

(a) Pre-trial losses – calculate the actual number of years' loss from the date of death until the trial and apply to the multiplicand (or multiplicands).The resulting amount(s) will be treated as special damages and will attract interest.

(b) Future losses – deduct the number of pre-trial years from the overall multiplier and apply the balance of the multiplier to the multiplicand (or multiplicands).

**Example**

Tom Brown is killed in a road traffic accident. At the time of his death, Tom was 30 years old. Tom has left a widow, Lucy, aged 29, and twin boys, Mark and James, aged 9. Tom was a DIY enthusiast, and performed many decorating and maintenance tasks in the family home. The value of the services to the family was £750 per year. Prior to the accident, Tom was in good health and was expected to work until he was 65. His net annual earnings at trial have been calculated as £10,000. The case comes to trial three years after the accident.

A simplified schedule of loss for the above example is set out below:

Tom Brown's date of birthJanuary 1977

Date of accident/death1 January 2007

Date of schedule/trial1 January 2010

| | |
|---|---|
| 1. BEREAVEMENT DAMAGES | £11,800 |
| 2. FUNERAL EXPENSES | £1,390 |
| 3. PAST LOSSES | |
| Past loss of earnings to date of schedule | |
| Net pre-accident wage £10,000 pa | |
| Reduction for deceased's own needs: 25% so initial multiplicand = £7,500 | |
| 1 January 2007 to 1 January 2010 (3 years) 3 x £7,500 = £ 22,500 | |
| Other services to family per annum (eg, gardening, housework, DIY) | |
| 3 × £750 = £2,250 | |
| TOTAL PAST LOSS OF DEPENDENCY | £24,750 |
| 4. FUTURE LOSSES | |
| Future loss of dependency – earnings | |
| Annual rate of £7,500 | |
| Multiplier based on Tom Brown retiring at 65 = 19.78 (22.78 – 3) | |
| £7,500 x 19.78 = £148,350 | |
| Future non-financial dependency – gardening, DIY etc | |
| Annual rate of £750 | |
| Multiplier of 26.05 (29.05 – 3) | |
| £750 x 26.05 = £19,537.50 | |
| TOTAL FUTURE LOSS OF DEPENDENCY | £167,887.50 |
| SUMMARY | |
| Pre-trial loss | £24,750 |
| Future loss | £167,887.50 |
| Bereavement damages | £11,800 |
| Funeral expenses | £1,390 |
| TOTAL | £205,827.50 |

In addition, interest is claimed on the pre-trial loss to the date of trial at half the short-term rate, and on bereavement damages and funeral expanses at the full short-term investment account rate.

The significant factors in the calculation are as follows:

(a) The length of loss of earnings dependency is likely to be based on Tom's age of 30 and his retirement age of 65, that is a period of 35 years. This is likely to produce an overall multiplier of 22.78 using table 9 of the Ogden Tables (see **Appendix 5**).

(b) There is a separate multiplicand based on the value of the services. The length of this dependency would be longer than the earnings dependency, on the assumption that Tom would have continued to provide these services throughout his lifetime Using table 1 of the Ogden Tables this produces a multiplier of 29.05.

(c) In practice the multipliers may be further reduced to take account of contingencies other than mortality (see **Chapter 15**).

(d) Three years have elapsed from the date of death to the date of this schedule. These three years must be deducted from the overall multipliers which are calculated from the date of death (not the date of trial as in straightforward personal injury cases). Losses in this period are treated as special damages and will attract interest.

(e) The calculation may be split into various sub-calculations to reflect, for example, that for the first nine years after the accident (but for his death) Tom would have been supporting a wife and children (therefore he might have been expected to spend one-quarter of his net earnings on his own maintenance), but for the remaining 26 years of his working life (after the children became independent) he would have been supporting only a wife (and therefore he might be expected to spend one-third of his net earnings on his own maintenance). Another reason for splitting the calculation may be to reflect any increased earnings because of promotion.

The above example is given merely to illustrate the general principles of quantifying a claim. It will be appreciated that, in practice, it will be rare that a person's working and family life can be predicted with such certainty, and other methods of calculating the loss of dependency (eg, nil discount tables issued by the Government's Actuary's Department) have been advocated.

It should also be remembered that different multipliers must be applied to items that would not have ceased at the age of 65. Detailed instructions need to be obtained from the client on this point In practice, therefore, the facts of a particular case are usually such as to defy precise mathematical calculation. The assessment of dependency damages is a difficult matter, and the court has to anticipate what would have occurred in the future. To assist the court, as much evidence as possible should be obtained.

## 18.5.3 Apportionment of the dependency

Whenever there is more than one dependant under the FAA 1976, the court must apportion the damages between them. Where a claim is made by a surviving spouse and child, the court's approach is often to assess the claim for dependency of the widow alone, and then to apportion a small amount ('pocket money') to the child. This approach may be justified on the basis that

(a) the surviving spouse will be expected to provide for the child out of her damages;

(b) compared to the surviving spouse, the period of dependency of the child will often be short (ending probably between the ages of 16 to 21 depending on whether the child is expected to go on to higher education); and

(c) it avoids repeated applications to the court for the release of invested funds for the benefit of the child.

However, the court is keen to protect the child's interest, and this approach may not be followed in every case. For example, if the surviving spouse is a known spendthrift and cannot be trusted to provide for the child, the court may assess the claims of the surviving spouse and child separately (see *H and Another v S* [2002] EWCA Civ 792, [2003] QB 965, concerning the protection of any damages for child dependants).

Where the claim involves a minor dependant (or any other protected party), the court's approval of any settlement should be sought, as it will be necessary to satisfy the court that the child's interests are protected.

### 18.5.4 Bereavement

#### 18.5.4.1 The claimants

The claim for bereavement is open only to a limited class (not just 'dependants' generally: see **18.5.1.1**). The possible claimants are:

(a) the spouse of the deceased; or

(b) the parents of a legitimate unmarried deceased minor;

(c) the mother of an illegitimate unmarried deceased minor.

It should be noted that a cohabitee is excluded from the definition, despite the fact that a cohabitee can pursue a dependency claim, as noted above. Furthermore, a child is not entitled to the award of bereavement on the death of his parent; and in a case where both parents can claim, the damages are divided equally between them (FAA 1976, s 1A(4)). However, in *Navaei v Navaei*, 6 January 1995, the mother was negligent, and this resulted in the death of her daughter. The father claimed all of the bereavement damages and stated that they should not be shared with the mother. He argued that if he were to be paid only half of the damages, the mother/tortfeasor would be benefiting contrary to public policy. The court held that in bringing a claim under the FAA 1976, a claimant is under a duty to act on behalf of all dependants and the father was allowed only half the damages.

In the case of *Griffiths and Others v British Coal Corporation* (QBD, 23 February 1998), it was held that the FAA 1976 did not require an apportionment of damages for bereavement where there were two causes of death (in this case, smoking and exposure to mine dust), and therefore the claimant recovered the full statutory sum.

The claim for the bereavement award by parents depends on the deceased being a minor at the date of death, not at the date of the accident (*Doleman v Deakin* (1990) *The Times*, 30 January).

#### 18.5.4.2 The amount of the bereavement award

The award is a fixed amount of £11,800 in respect of causes of action arising on or after 1 January 2008. Many people have criticised the level of award. In certain cases, especially those with a media interest, defendants have offered a figure higher than the statutory minimum, so as to avoid allegations by the press that they have undervalued a life. Once entitlement is established, defendants are often amenable to paying this part of the claim early by way of an interim payment.

### 18.5.5 Funeral expenses

Funeral expenses can be claimed if reasonable and paid by a dependant (FAA 1976, s 3(5)). The question of reasonableness will be a decision on the facts of each case. Reference should be made to previous case law in circumstances where the client puts forward an unusual claim, so as to determine whether the court will regard the claim as reasonable or otherwise.

If the funeral expenses are paid by the estate then they are claimed as part of a LR(MP)A 1934 claim (see **18.4.3**). Clearly, funeral expenses cannot be claimed under both the LR(MP)A 1934 and the FAA 1976.

### 18.5.6 Disregarding benefits

Section 4 of the FAA 1976 provides:

> In assessing damages in respect of a person's death in an action under this Act, benefits which have accrued or will or may accrue to any person from his estate or otherwise as a result of his death shall be disregarded.

For example, if a dependant receives insurance money as a result of the deceased's death, the dependant does not have to give credit for that money against the FAA 1976 damages.

Similarly, if damages awarded to the estate under a LR(MP)A 1934 claim end up in the hands of a dependant by reason of the deceased's will or rules of intestacy, those damages do not necessarily reduce any FAA 1976 damages which may be awarded to that dependant.

See also *H and Another v S* [2002] EWCA Civ 792, [2003] QB 965, concerning support now being given by a surviving parent who was unlikely to have supported the children if the death had not occurred.

### 18.5.7 Recoupment and offsetting of benefits

Any payment made in consequence of a claim under the FAA 1976 is not subject to recoupment under the Social Security (Recovery of Benefits) Act 1997 (see **Chapter 16**).

## 18.6 Interest

Interest on the bereavement damages may be awarded at the full short-term investment rate (*Sharman v Sheppard* [1989] CLY 1190) from the date of death.

The pecuniary losses to the date of the trial, including funeral expenses, are treated as special damages in a fatal injury claim, and therefore are often awarded interest at half the short-term investment rate, although it is arguable that interest can be awarded at the full rate in certain circumstances (see **15.6**). Future pecuniary loss attracts no interest.

## 18.7 Pension loss

Investigations should be made as to whether there will be a reduced pension fund available to the deceased's dependants due to the early death, and this should be included within the claim if appropriate (see also **15.3.6**).

## 18.8 Establishing the case

A fatal accident case will be dealt with in essentially the same way as any other personal injury or clinical negligence claim. Evidence is needed to establish liability and the highest level of damages. The claimant's solicitor must remember to obtain a signed proof of evidence or statement from a client as soon as possible in every case, as this will be of considerable assistance if the client dies either due to the injuries sustained in the accident or otherwise. If the solicitor has failed to take this precaution he will make proving the case more difficult. Under the Civil Evidence Act 1995, the client's statement or proof can now be put before the court, and it should be regarded by the court as important evidence.

It should also be remembered that the inquest and/or any criminal prosecution will be an important source of information (see **Chapter 17**), and as much information as possible should be obtained.

## 18.9 Conduct

To avoid conflicts of interest arising, it is good practice to ensure that none of the dependants who could be to blame in whole or part for the accident that resulted in the death are appointed as personal representatives.

The conduct of a fatal accident claim clearly requires sympathy and diplomacy on the part of the solicitor. There are frequently conflicts of personality between the dependants and personal representatives, and this is compounded by the fact that only one claim can be brought in respect of the fatal accident. If, after the fatal accident, it comes to light that the deceased had more than one dependent family, it can be anticipated that any interviews with the deceased's wife may be difficult!

## 18.10 Conclusion

Acting on behalf of the relatives in a fatal accident claim requires the personal injury/clinical negligence solicitor to have tact, sympathy and a detailed understanding of the law involved. It should be appreciated that each case will be dealt with on its own facts, and only broad principles have been established by the case law in this area. In fatal accident cases the court is required to anticipate what would have occurred in the future, which will be different in every case.

## 18.11 Further reading

Kemp and Kemp, *The Quantum of Damages* (Sweet & Maxwell)

# Chapter 19
# Criminal Injuries Compensation Authority



## 19.1 The Criminal Injuries Compensation Scheme 2008

Those who have suffered injury as a result of violence are often dissuaded from commencing proceedings against the perpetrators of that violence, because the latter are unlikely to have the financial means to settle the judgment sum. However, victims of crimes of violence who have suffered injuries can apply for compensation from the Criminal Injuries Compensation Authority (CICA). The Criminal Injuries Compensation Scheme 2008 ('the Scheme') deals with applications received on or after 3 November 2008. This Scheme, and its predecessor the 2001 Scheme can be viewed on the CICA website at www.cica.gov.uk. The application forms and the Guide to the 2008 Compensation Scheme ('the Guide'), which is essential reading if a claim is to be made, are also available on the website.

In order to be eligible to make an application, an applicant must show that he has suffered a personal injury (ie a physical (including fatal) injury, a mental injury or disease), in Great Britain, as a result of:

(a) a crime of violence (including arson, fire-raising or an act of poisoning). There is no definition of a 'crime of violence' and CICA and the courts have shied away from specifying which criminal offences would be included. Nevertheless, it is safe to assume that crimes involving a physical attack would give rise to an application;

(b) an offence of trespass on a railway. This allows applications from train drivers who suffer physical or psychological injuries as a result of suicides, attempted suicides or other acts of trespass on railway lines; or

(c) the apprehension or attempted apprehension of an offender or a suspected offender, the prevention or attempted prevention of an offence, or the giving of help to any constable who is engaged in any such activity.

It is not necessary for the assailant to have been convicted of an offence in connection with the injury (para 10), and in some cases, the applicant will not know the identity of the offender.

Two exclusions should be noted:

(a) Victims of accidents arising from motoring offences are not entitled to apply under the Scheme unless the vehicle was used as a weapon, as where it is deliberately driven at the victim (para 11).

(b) Where the victim and assailant were living in the same household as members of the same family at the time of the offence, compensation will be paid only if the assailant has been prosecuted in connection with the offence (or the claims officer is satisfied that there were practical, technical or other good reasons why a prosecution was not brought) and, where the violence involved adults, the victim and assailant had stopped living in the same household before the application was made and are unlikely to live together in the future.

## 19.2 Procedure

It is important to note that the CICA will not meet any legal costs associated with making a claim under the Scheme (para 19). Consequently, a solicitor who is asked by a client to deal with an application on his behalf must make this clear to him. It may be appropriate to direct the client to the independent charity Victim Support, which provides free assistance and advice to victims of crime, and which will assist those wishing to apply under the Scheme to complete the necessary forms.

An application for compensation under the Scheme must be received by the CICA within two years of the date of the relevant incident (para 18). There is no automatic extension in relation to applications by children or those with a mental disability. However, in all cases, there is a discretionary power to extend the time period where it is practicable for the application to be considered and it would not have been reasonable to expect the applicant to have made the application within the two-year period.

The correct application form must be completed, as different forms are supplied for use in personal injury and fatal accident claims. (The consideration of fatal accident claims under the Scheme falls outside the ambit of this book.) By signing the application form, the applicant gives his consent to the CICA to obtain relevant records relating to the incident, the injuries, and the applicant's earnings and benefits entitlement. A claims officer will be assigned to the claim. He will need to be satisfied, on the balance of probabilities, that the applicant suffered injury as a result of a crime of violence etc. He will obtain reports from the police, doctors and hospitals, and may require the applicant to attend an independent medical examination (in which case, the CICA will cover the costs). However, the applicant can and should provide any other evidence he has at his disposal.

## 19.3 Compensation calculation

Compensation is based on a tariff award for the injuries suffered and, where relevant, compensation for lost earnings and/or special expenses. The minimum award that can be made is £1,000 and the maximum award that may be made in respect of one injury is £500,000. It is important to note that this is the maximum that can be awarded:

(a) before any deductions are made (see **19.4**);

(b) in respect of any one injury, so that where several people are applying for compensation following the death of a victim of a crime of violence, the total amount they can receive cannot exceed £500,000.

### 19.3.1 The tariff award

In order to calculate the amount due under the tariff award, the claims officer will consult the list of fixed levels of compensation, which is set out in the Scheme under the heading 'Tariff of Injuries'. This list sets out descriptions of over 400 different types of injuries and, in relation to each one, specifies both the level of seriousness – by means of a figure from 1 (being the least serious) to 25 – and the associated tariff. A Level 1 injury is valued at £1,000 and a Level 25 injury is valued at £250,000. Compensation is not payable under the Scheme for injuries that are not serious enough to amount to a Level 1 injury, unless there are at least three minor injuries that can be grouped together to form the Level 1 injury, known as 'minor multiple injuries' (see Note 12 of the Scheme).

Instructions as to how to use the list is set out in para 27. In order to calculate the total tariff award, the three most serious injuries must be identified and the associated tariffs added together as follows:

(a) 100% of the tariff for the highest rated injury; plus, where relevant

(b) 30% of the tariff for the second highest injury; plus, where relevant

(c) 15% of the tariff for the third highest injury.

No compensation is payable in respect of any additional injuries.

### 19.3.2 Compensation for lost earnings

Where an applicant is entitled to a tariff payment, he may also be entitled to be compensated for lost earnings or loss of earnings capacity. No such compensation is payable for the first 28 weeks of loss. After the first 28 weeks, compensation may be payable for as long as the claims officer determines, subject to the maximum award of £500,000.

Compensation for past loss of earnings is calculated in a manner which is similar to that used by the courts (para 31), and compensation for future loss of earnings, calculated by means of a multiplicand and a multiplier, is also akin to the manner used by the courts (para 32). However, the relevant multipliers are found in the scheme itself (see Note 3 of the Scheme) rather than in the Ogden Tables, and are identified by the number of years of loss, rather than by the applicant's age at the date of the incident. The number of years loss is calculated from the date of the application to the date when the applicant is expected to return to work, or such other period as the case worker determines. If the applicant's injuries are such that he will never return to work, the anticipated date of retirement will be used. It should also be noted that credit must be given for pension payments and DSS benefits.

### 19.3.3 Compensation for special expenses

Compensation may be paid for special expenses from the date of the injury, but only where the applicant has lost earnings or earnings capacity for longer than 28 days. What amounts to special expenses is set out in paras 35 and 36 of the Scheme and includes:

(a) the cost of medical treatment which cannot reasonably be provided by the NHS;

(b) the cost of care provided in a residential establishment, or provided gratuitously by a friend or relative at home; and

(c) the cost of necessary adaptations to the applicant's home and/or aids and appliances.

Compensation is calculated by means of a multiplicand and a multipler, as with the loss of earnings calculation.

## 19.4 Withholding or reduction of award

The Scheme is funded by the Government on the basis that the public are sympathetic to innocent victims of crime and wish to see them supported. Consequently, compensation may be refused or discounted in respect of applications by those who may be seen as morally undeserving of support. In addition, the Scheme must be protected from fraudulent claims and applicants should not be permitted to be over-compensated.

Compensation may be withheld or reduced in the following circumstances:

(a) where the applicant has failed to report the incident to the police, or has thereafter failed to co-operate with the police or with the CICA (para 13(a)–(c)). Generally, the applicant must make a formal report to the police immediately following the incident, and this must be done by the applicant in person, unless his injuries prevent him from doing so. Co-operation with the police includes making a statement, attending identity procedures and giving evidence in court, if required. Co-operation with the CICA includes supplying complete and truthful information, and attending independent medical examinations, if required;

(b) where the applicant behaved inappropriately either before, or during or after the incident (paras 13(d) and 14). This will include where the applicant's consumption of alcohol or illegal drugs contributed to the incident, where he voluntarily took part in a fight, where he threw the first punch, or where his use of abusive language or gestures led to the incident;

(c) where the applicant has unspent criminal convictions (para 13(e). A conviction leading to a prison sentence of 30 months or more can never be spent. The claims officer has a discretion as to how the conviction will effect the award, but will base his decision on a system of penalty points which is set out in the Guide. Generally, the more recent the conviction and the more serious the penalty, the greater the discount will be;

(d) where the applicant has received State benefits or insurance payouts in respect of the injury (para 45), or compensation from either a civil or a criminal court (para 48).

## 19.5 Example

Last year, Jacob was attacked in Birmingham city centre as he made his way home from work. He was punched to the ground and kicked repeatedly by assailants who have not been identified. He suffered a depressed fracture of the skull, for which he required surgery, his jaw was dislocated and a front tooth was knocked out. The tooth has been replaced, but his other injuries are continuing to cause him significant difficulties. In addition, he has lost his sense of smell. Jacob was unable to work for 40 weeks, but he has now returned to his previous job as a shop assistant. His salary throughout the period when he was unable to work would have been £250 per week, but Jacob received only statutory sick pay of £79.15 per week during this period.

Tariff for injuries: depressed fracture of skull requiring operation = £6,600 (Level 11); dislocated jaw causing continuing significant disability = £5,500 (Level 10); loss of one front tooth = £3,300 (Level 7); total loss of smell = £11,000 (Level 13). Only the three most serious injuries may be considered.

Calculation: 100% of £11,000 (loss of smell) = £11,000; 30% of £6,600 (fractured skull) = £1,980; 15% of £5,500 (dislocated jaw) = £825.

Total for injury = £13,805.

Lost salary: Nothing for first 28 weeks. Thereafter, 12 weeks at £250 per week (£3,000) less statutory sick pay of £79.15 for the 12 weeks (£949.80) = £2,050.20.

Total payment: £13,805 + £2,050.20 = £15,855.20.

# Chapter 20
# Claims on Behalf of Children



## 20.1 Introduction

Rule 21 of the CPR deals with special provisions relating to children and protected parties, ie those who lack capacity to conduct proceedings. Many of these provisions apply equally to children and protected parties but a detailed consideration of those rules relating to protected parties only is beyond the ambit of this book.

In civil law, a child is a person who is not yet 18 years old. Under that age, a child is termed 'a person under a disability' (although this term is not used in the CPR 1998). While under a disability the limitation period does not run against the child (see **Chapter 6**), but during that time the child cannot normally bring proceedings in his own name. The solutions therefore are either:

(a) to wait until the child reaches the age of 18; or

(b) during his minority to bring proceedings through a 'litigation friend' (usually a parent).

It is important to ensure that there is no conflict of interest between the child and the person who is bringing the claim on the child's behalf. For example, if a child is injured in a road traffic accident while a passenger in a car being driven by his father, it would be sensible to appoint the child's mother as litigation friend (rather than the father) as the father may eventually be a defendant in the proceedings.

## 20.2 Court's approval of settlements

Rule 21.10 of the CPR states that no settlement involving a child (including the acceptance of money paid into court and a claim in a fatal accident case where there is a child dependant) is valid without the court's approval. This approval is necessary to ensure that the claim is not settled for less than it is worth and that the award is invested appropriately or, where there are future pecuniary losses, periodical payments are considered. Moreover, if such approval to a settlement is not obtained, a child claimant may, upon reaching 18, issue proceedings against the defendant or, alternatively, issue proceedings against the litigation friend for negligently dealing with his claim.

If an agreement is made between the parties prior to proceedings being issued and the sole purpose of issuing proceedings is to obtain the court's approval, the solicitor must follow the procedure set out in Part 8 of the CPR, and a specific request must be included with the claim form for approval of the settlement. In addition, a draft consent order must be provided to the court using Practice Form N292.

### 20.2.1 The approval hearing

The aim of the hearing is to ensure that the settlement agreed is a reasonable one and is in the child's best interests. At the hearing, the court will wish to have made available a number of documents, including the following:

(a) the child's birth certificate (certainly details of the child's age);

(b) where proceedings have been commenced, the statements of case and other documents already on the court file;

(c) evidence on liability (information as to whether liability is in dispute or the extent to which the defendant admits liability) and documents such as the PAR, inquest report and details of any prosecutions brought;

(d) an up-to-date calculation of past and future losses (with supporting documentation);

(e) an up-to-date medical report or reports;

(f) the litigation friend's certificate of suitability;

(g) the litigation friend's approval of the settlement;

(h) an interest calculation to date;

(i) Court Funds Office Form 320 (request for investment);

(j) a copy of an opinion on the merits of the agreed settlement given to counsel or a solicitor (while the case is a simple one).

Full details of the court's requirements are set out in Part 21 of the CPR and the accompanying Practice Direction.

### 20.2.2 The order

If the proposed settlement is approved, the court will give directions as to the investment of the damages. In the case of *Beatham v Carlisle Hospitals NHS Trust* (1999) *The Times*, 20 May, it was held that the court's approval of a settlement on behalf of a child or a protected person should normally be given in public.

It should be noted that the court has an obligation to consider making an order for periodical payments where there are future pecuniary losses (see **15.5**).

# Appendices

# Appendix 1
# Employers' Liability Case Study

## INTRODUCTION

The following case study is illustrative of the low-value personal injury cases which form the bulk of the personal injury lawyer's caseload. The documentation charts the basic procedural steps, from instruction, through commencement of proceedings, to settlement. It does not cover all eventualities and not all documents which would be relevant to the case have been provided. The claim proceeds as follows:

- The claimant, Neil Worthing, instructs a firm of solicitors, Goodlaw, in relation to an injury he has suffered whilst in the employment of Guildshire Engineering Limited. A proof of evidence is taken (**Document 1**). The matter is funded by means of a CFA backed up by an AEI policy.
- A letter of claim is sent (**Document 2**).
- Guildshire Engineering Limited is covered by BTE insurance. The insurer instructs Winter Wood & Co, to act on its behalf. A letter of denial is sent (**Document 3**) together with relevant documents, including the accident report (**Document 4**) and the RIDDOR report (**Document 5**).
- In accordance with the PAP for personal injury claims, the claimant's solicitors write to the defendant's solicitors with the aim of appointing a jointly selected medical expert (**Document 6**). They provide three names.
- The defendant does not raise any objection to those named, one is instructed and a medical report is obtained (**Document 7**).
- Following receipt of the medical report, the assistant solicitor acting for the claimant conducts research into what the claimant would be entitled to in respect of general damages for pain, suffering and loss of amenity, and he sends a memo to his principal solicitor setting out his findings (**Document 8**).
- A claim form is issued (**Document 9**) and served with the particulars of claim (**Document 10**), the Schedule of Past and Future Expenses and Losses (**Document 11**), the medical report and the funding notice (**Document 12**).
- The defendant's solicitors notify the Compensation Recovery Unit (CRU) of the claim by means of Form CRU 1 (**Document 13**).
- The defence is filed (**Document 14**).
- Allocation questionnaires are completed by both sides (**Document 15**).
- The case is allocated to the fast track and directions are given (**Document 16**).
- Following disclosure of witness statements, solicitors for the parties discuss a possible settlement, and the claimant subsequently indicates to his solicitors that he wants to settle. The defendant's solicitors have already obtained a CRU certificate of repayable benefits (CRU100) for this purpose, which shows that there are no recoverable benefits. The CRU also sends a copy of CRU100 to the claimant's solicitors (**Document 17**). The assistant solicitor acting for the claimant sends a memo to his principal (**Document 18**).
- The defendant's solicitors send a Part 36 offer letter to the claimant's solicitors (**Document 19**). The assistant solicitor acting for the claimant consults his client and contacts the defendant's solicitors, asking them for an improved offer. He notes this in a memo to his principal (**Document 20**).
- The claimant's solicitors write to the defendant's solicitors accepting the updated offer (**Document 21**) and enclosing a draft consent order (**Document 22**).

# DOCUMENT 1 - PROOF OF EVIDENCE

I, Neil Matthew Worthing, of 22 Elstead House, Griffin Road, Christlethorpe, Guildshire GU48 1XX will say:

1. My date of birth is 14 December 1986 and I am 21 years old. My National Insurance number is WK987999X. I am single and I have lived in rented accommodation at the above address since 9 June 2007.
2. I am currently a full-time student at Queen Margaret's College, Guildshire, where I am studying law. This is the final year of my degree course. Throughout my years of study, I have taken temporary jobs during the summer breaks in order to help fund my studies.
3. In June 2008, after the end of term, I was able to get a temporary contract with Guildshire Engineering Limited (GEL) at their factory at 77 Blizzard Lane, Christlethorpe, Guildshire, GU59 2YZ. They manufacture metal tools for industrial use. I was to work on their production line as a process engineer. The contract was to run for 10 weeks from Monday 9 June to Friday 15 August.
4. When I arrived at the factory on 9 June, I was shown where I was to work by the foreman, Tony Benson. He gave me a short demonstration on how to use the machinery, gave me some written health and safety information, and told me that the Health and Safety Representative would talk to me when he came back from holiday the following Monday. Everything went very well the first week until the last day.
5. On Friday 13 June 2008, at about 2.30pm, Tony asked me to help Jerry Packman, another process engineer, to move several boxes of widgets from one part of the factory to another. We were to use two metal trolleys, which had handles on each end, to transport the boxes. He told us the boxes were heavy, so we were to move each box between us and keep our backs straight when we were doing it. He said we were to put only four boxes on each trolley. Jerry was mucking about when Tony was talking to us, and Tony told him to listen and behave himself. Jerry is great fun and a bit of a practical joker, but he seems to be in trouble quite a lot.
6. We stacked the first trolley with four boxes and then I pushed it about three feet further forward. The boxes were heavy so it took considerable effort on my part to move the trolley. Jerry then moved the second trolley to about a foot behind the first one, and we stacked that with four boxes. There was only one box left, so we decided to put this box on the second trolley. Once the fifth box was loaded, Jerry tried to move the trolley, but it wouldn't budge at all. It looked quite funny as Jerry is quite small and skinny. I was standing to the side of the first trolley with my left hand on the handle. I told Jerry to stop being such a weed and to push harder. Suddenly, the trolley he was pushing shot forward and the thumb of my left hand was caught between the handles of the two trolleys. It was excruciatingly painful.
7. I immediately went to see the first aider, Alison Jacobs, who examined my thumb and said she thought it might be broken. My hand was already swelling up, and I was in great pain and very distressed. As I am left handed, I was worried about being able to write. Also I was concerned about my ability to play the piano, which is my great passion. I perform as a pianist in the restaurant at the Swan Lake Hotel on Tuesday, Thursday, and Friday evenings from 7pm to 11pm, for which I am paid £40 each Tuesday and Thursday evening and £50 each Friday evening.
8. As I was unable to drive, Alison Jacobs drove me to the A&E department at Guildshire Hospital. By the time we arrived, the pain and swelling in my thumb had increased. My left thumb was x-rayed, which confirmed that it had been fractured. A plaster cast was applied to my thumb up to my elbow and I was given a sling. I wore this plaster for two weeks and then a splint for a further two weeks.

9. Obviously I could not go to work. On Wednesday 18 June, I received a call from Tony Benson. He sounded quite cross. He said that the accident had been due to me mucking about with Jerry and that I hadn't carried out his instructions. He said that he would send me two weeks' wages, which was more than generous and that my services were no longer needed.

10. A few days later, I received a cheque from GEL for two weeks' wages, £480. Because of the injury, I was incapable of working for about four weeks, but when I had recovered enough to work, I was unable to find another job for what remained of the summer break. In addition, I lost money due to being unable to play the piano at the Swan Lake Hotel for a period of eight weeks. Luckily, they took me back once I was able to play again. I did not claim benefits as I did not think I would be entitled to any.

11. I was unable to cook or clean, or do anything much after the accident. Consequently, my mother came and stayed with me for two weeks to look after me. She doesn't work, so she didn't lose any money, but it was very inconvenient for her and quite embarrassing for me.

12. I had a course of five physiotherapy treatments at Guildshire Hospital. I incurred travelling expenses attending these physiotherapy treatments. I travelled in my own car to the hospital, which is a round trip of 10 miles from my flat.

13. I was then advised to continue with a course of exercises at home. I still do these exercises on a daily basis as I still have restricted movement in my thumb. It continues to give me pain, especially in cold weather, or if I knock or catch it accidentally. Sometimes, it locks when I am trying to grip with my left hand. I can play the piano, but it does hurt towards the end of the four-hour period when I am playing at the hotel. It also hurts when I have been writing for a while, which obviously I have to do at college.

14. Jerry rang me a few weeks after the accident to apologise and to ask how I was. He told me that he had never received any information or training regarding stacking boxes or moving trolleys, and that GEL had recently had foam placed over the metal handles of all the trolleys in the factory.

Signed *Neil Worthing* 2 September 2008

## DOCUMENT 2 – LETTER OF CLAIM

**Goodlaw Solicitors**

Fox Chambers, Maidstone, Kent, MH1 4XJ

DX 3214 GUILDSHIRE; Tel: 01483 606060; Fax: 01483 606099

Guildford Engineering Limited
77 Blizzard Lane,
Guildford,
Surrey
GU59 2YZ

Our ref : BB/WORTH/08/426
Date: 15 September 2008

Dear Sirs,

**OUR CLIENT: Mr Neil Worthing**
**ADDRESS: 22 Elstead House, Griffin Road, Guildford, GU48 1XX**
**ACCIDENT DATE: 13 June 2008**
**WORKS NUMBER: GEL 4520**

We are instructed by Mr Worthing to claim damages for injuries he sustained in an accident at work that occurred on 13 June 2008 at your factory at the above address.

Kindly confirm the identity of your insurers. Please note that the insurers will need to see this letter as soon as possible, and it may affect your insurance cover and/or the conduct of any subsequent legal proceedings if you do not send this letter to them.

The circumstances of the accident are:

Our client and another of your employees, Mr Packman, were transporting boxes of widgets from one part of the factory to another on two metal trolleys. Mr Packman pushed his trolley with force and our client suffered injuries when his thumb was trapped between the handles of the two trolleys.

The reason why we are alleging fault is:

The accident was caused by the negligence of you, your servants or agents and/or was in breach of your statutory duty to our client because you:

1. failed to make a proper risk assessment in relation to the moving of the trolleys contrary to reg 3(1) of the Management of the Health and Safety at Work Regulations 1999 (the 'Management Regulations') and reg 4(1)(b)(i) of the Manual Handling Operations Regulations 1992 (the 'Manual Handling Regulations');
2. failed to provide information to your employees on health and safety risks and protective measures contrary to reg 10 of the Management Regulations and reg 8 of the Provision and Use of Work Equipment Regulations 1998 (the 'Work Equipment Regulations');
3. failed to provide adequate health and safety training to your employees contrary to reg 13 of the Management Regulations and reg 9 of the Work Equipment Regulations;
4. failed to ensure the suitability of the trolleys for the purpose for which they were provided contrary to reg 4 of the Work Equipment Regulations. It is our understanding

that, since the accident, you have improved the suitability of the trolleys by putting foam on the metal handles;

5. failed to ensure that your employees received proper information and training on how to handle loads correctly in the process of moving loaded trolleys contrary to reg 4(1)(b)(ii) of the Manual Handling Regulations;
6. failed to take appropriate steps to reduce the risk of injury to our client arising out of undertaking the operation set out above to the lowest practicable level contrary to reg 4(1)(b)(ii) of the Manual Handling Regulations;
7. failed to provide competent fellow workers. Our client informs us that Mr Packman was well known to his colleagues and to you as a practical joker. It was as a direct result of Mr Packman's inappropriate behaviour that the injury to our client arose.

The above matters should not be taken as a comprehensive list of allegations of fault. We reserve the right to include any further allegations of fault as are appropriate once we have received a substantive response to this letter and when any further necessary investigations which may be required have been concluded.

Injuries and losses.

As a result of your negligence/breach of statutory duty our client has suffered personal injuries which consist of a fractured thumb. He lost 8 weeks' salary from his employment with you and 8 weeks' salary from his work as a professional piano player at the Swan Lake Hotel. He has also incurred miscellaneous expenses relating to travelling to hospital for physiotherapy and the provision of care gratuitously provided by his mother for a two-week period immediately following the accident.

Disclosure of documents.

Unless liability is admitted in full we expect you to disclose all relevant documents in accordance with the protocol. At this stage of our enquiries we consider that the documents contained in the standard disclosure list for workplace claims and sections A, B and D of that list to apply. Please confirm that the originals of all relevant documents will be preserved.

Should you fail to provide the disclosure requested above, in so far as that it is required by the protocol, please be aware that we will make the appropriate application to the court to ensure disclosure is complied with. Should this be necessary, we reserve the right to draw the contents of this letter to the attention of the court in relation to the question of costs.

Details of earnings.

We understand that our client had been working for you for only four and a half days when the accident had happened, that he had entered into a contract with you that he would work for a total of 10 weeks and that he has been paid for two weeks' work. Could you please confirm that this is the case and provide details of:

(1) the agreed weekly gross and net earnings for the 10-week period;
(2) any other financial benefits he would have been entitled to had he not been injured, for example, loss of overtime, shift allowance, bonus, commission and pension or other benefits; and
(3) any sick pay paid to our client during his absence from work, including company sick pay, statutory sick pay and tax refunds. If any payments of company sick pay have been made, please state whether these are refundable or not.

Alternative Dispute Resolution (ADR).

Our client would prefer to try to resolve this matter without the need for litigation. We consider the appropriate method of ADR to be negotiation. We hope that you will comply with your obligations under the pre-action protocol. If you fail to do so, we reserve the right to refer the court to the contents of this letter when seeking orders on case management that may be necessary due to your failure to negotiate.

Funding.

Please note that we are acting for our client under a conditional fee agreement dated 2 September 2008 which provides for a success fee. Our client also has the benefit of an insurance policy issued by Taskers Insurance Limited and dated 2 September 2008. The insurer's address is High Pavement Road, Christlethorpe, Guildshire GU77 4BY. The policy number is ABC454321.

Timetable of pre-action protocol.

We consider that this letter commences the timetable applicable under the pre-action protocol for personal injury claims. We therefore request acknowledgement of this letter from you or your insurers by 8 October 2008 and a decision on liability by 8 January 2009 at the latest. A copy of this letter is enclosed for your insurers.

We look forward to hearing from you or your insurers in response to this letter of claim in accordance with the pre-action protocol.

Yours faithfully

Goodlaw Solicitors

## DOCUMENT 3 – LETTER OF DENIAL

**Winter Wood & Co Solicitors**

Rembrandt House,
Lee Lane, Brampton
Guildshire, GU7 8TU
DX 26438 GUILDSHIRE
Tel: 01483 432143
Fax: 01483 432156

Goodlaw Solicitors
DX 3214 GUILDSHIRE

Our ref: NG/GELTD/08/A48
Your ref: BB/WORTH/08/426
Date: 10/11/2008

Dear Sirs

**YOUR CLIENT: Mr Neil Worthing**
**OUR CLIENT: Guildshire Engineering Limited**
**ACCIDENT DATE: 13 June 2008**

We act for Guildshire Engineering Limited in relation to the above mentioned matter and refer to your letter of 15 September 2008.

Our client disputes liability in this matter.

Although it is accepted that Mr Worthing did suffer an injury on 13 June at our client's premises, the causes of the accident are disputed.

- Our client carried out risk assessments as required by Regulation 3 of the Management of Health and Safety at Work Regulations in relation to all activities conducted in their premises. A copy of the pre and post-accident risk assessments are attached. You will note that trolleys are dealt with in paragraph 14.10 of both documents and that no specific risks are identified. There are no risks associated with pushing a trolley provided the person doing the pushing behaves sensibly. It is our client's contention that Mr Worthing was not behaving sensibly at the time of the accident.
- Mr Worthing was provided with appropriate health and safety information and training, both generally and in relation to manual handling. The foreman, Mr Benson, gave him written information on all relevant matters on the first day of Mr Worthing's employment with our client and he also gave specific instructions as to how the boxes of widgets should be moved. In particular he told Mr Worthing that no more than four boxes should be placed on a trolley at one time, which your client chose to ignore. Mr Benson did not give instructions or training on how to push the trolley as this is a matter of common sense.
- The trolleys were, at the time of the alleged accident, suitable in every respect for their intended purpose. Whilst it is true that our client has since placed foam on the handles of the trolleys, this in no way an acceptance that they were previously unsuitable. These adaptations had been discussed prior to the alleged accident not due to safety issues but because the handles are thin and uncomfortable to push. It is unreasonable to suggest that all hard surfaces in a factory should be covered in foam.
- Our client strongly disputes the allegations that it failed to provide competent fellow workers. Our client provides training to each individual employee in accordance with its legal obligations and insists on the highest levels of behaviour and discipline from its staff. It is our understanding that the extra box of widgets was placed on the trolley at

Mr Worthing's suggestion and that it was his inappropriate behaviour which caused his injury.

In addition to the risk assessment mentioned above, we enclose the following documents:

- Copy of your client's contract of employment. Please note the requirement for employees to read the health and safety information and the standards of behaviour required by all employees at all times.
- Copies of all health and safety documents supplied to your client
- Accident book entry
- First aider report
- RIDDOR report to the HSE
- Earnings information

There are not further relevant documents to disclose.

Mr Worthing was dismissed by our client due to his unreasonable behaviour.

This was an unfortunate accident for which we have every sympathy with your client. Nevertheless, we have no offers to make to settle this matter as we do not consider that our client was either negligent or in breach of statutory duty.

Please note that, should you wish to continue with this matter, we are instructed to accept service of proceedings on our client's behalf.

Yours faithfully,

Winter Wood & Co

# DOCUMENT 4 – ACCIDENT REPORT

M62 Report Number (consecutive)

M62 Report Number (consecutive)

## Accident Record

**1 About the person who had the accident**

Name NEIL MATTHEW WORTHING

Address 22 ELSTEAD HOUSE, GRIFFIN ROAD, CHRISTLETHORPE

GUILDSHIRE Postcode GU48 1XX

Occupation PROCESS ENGINEER

**2 About you, the individual filling in this record**

If you did not have the accident write your address and occupation.

Name ALISON JACOBS

Address

Postcode

Occupation SECRETARY & FIRST AIDER

**3 Details of the accident** (Continue on the back of this form if you need to)

When it happened. Date 13 / 06 / 08 Time 2.45pm (approx).

Where it happened. State location. Factory Floor

How did the accident happen? Give the cause if possible. Mr Worthing & another process engineer were using trolleys to transport components from one part of the factory to another when his thumb became trapped between two handles of the two trolleys.

If the person who had the accident suffered an injury, give details Crushed left thumb – fractured.

Sign the record and date it.

Sign Alison Jacobs. Date 13 / 06 / 08

**4 For the employer only**

Complete this box if the accident is reportable under the Reporting of Injuries, Diseases and Dangerous Occurrences Regulations 1995 (RIDDOR).

How was it reported? Form sent by e-mail.

Sign Alison Jacobs. Date 19 / 06 / 08

# DOCUMENT 5 – RIDDOR

HSE Health & Safety Executive

*Health and Safety at Work etc Act 1974* ?

*The Reporting of Injuries, Diseases and Dangerous Occurrences Regulations 1995*

Click here for report guidance

## Report of an injury or dangerous occurrence

**Filling in this form**

This form must be filled in by an employer or other responsible person.

## Part A

### About you

1 What is your full name?

Adam Oliver Kilbride

2 What is your job title?

Works Manager

3 What is your telephone number?

01483 454545

### About your organisation

4 What is the name of your organisation?

Guildshire Engineering Limited

5 What is its address and postcode?

77 Blizzard Lane, Christlethorpe, Guildshire, GU59 2YZ

6 What type of work does the organisation do?

Manufacture of industrial tools

## Part B

### About the incident

1 On what date did the incident happen?

13/06/2008

2 At what time did the incident happen?
(Please use the 24-hour clock eg 0600)

14:45

3 Did the incident happen at the above address?

Yes ☑ Go to question 4

No ☐ Where did the incident happen?

☐ elsewhere in your organisation – give the name, address and postcode

☐ at someone else's premises – give the name, address and postcode

☐ in a public place – give details of where it happened

If you do not know the postcode, what is the name of the local authority?

4 In which department, or where on the premises, did the incident happen?

Factory floor

F2508 (05.00)

## Part C

### About the injured person

If you are reporting a dangerous occurrence, go to Part F. If more than one person was injured in the same incident, please attach the details asked for in Part C and Part D for each injured person.

1 What is their full name?

Neil Matthew Worthing

2 What is their home address and postcode?

22 Elstead House, Griffin Road, Christlethorpe, Guildshire, GU48 1XX

3 What is their home phone number?

07777 888444

4 How old are they?

21

5 Are they

☑ male?

☐ female?

6 What is their job title?

Process engineer

7 Was the injured person (tick only one box)

☑ one of your employees?

☐ on a training scheme? Give details:

☐ on work experience?

☐ employed by someone else? Give details of the employer:

☐ self-employed and at work?

☐ a member of the public?

## Part D

### About the injury

1 What was the injury? (eg fracture, laceration)

fracture

2 What part of the body was injured?

left thumb

Next Page

3 Was the injury (tick the one box that applies)

- ☐ a fatality?
- ☐ a major injury or condition? (see accompanying notes)
- ☐ an injury to an employee or self-employed person which prevented them doing their normal work for more than 3 days?
- ☐ an injury to a member of the public which meant they had to be taken from the scene of the accident to a hospital for treatment?

4 Did the injured person (tick all the boxes that apply)

- ☐ become unconscious?
- ☐ need resuscitation?
- ☐ remain in hospital for more than 24 hours?
- ☐ none of the above.

# Part E

## About the kind of accident

Please tick the one box that best describes what happened, then go to Part G.

- ☐ Contact with moving machinery or material being machined
- ☐ Hit by a moving, flying or falling object
- ☐ Hit by a moving vehicle
- ☐ Hit something fixed or stationary

- ☐ Injured while handling, lifting or carrying
- ☐ Slipped, tripped or fell on the same level
- ☐ Fell from a height

How high was the fall?

metres

- ☐ Trapped by something collapsing

- ☐ Drowned or asphyxiated
- ☐ Exposed to, or in contact with, a harmful substance
- ☐ Exposed to fire
- ☐ Exposed to an explosion

- ☐ Contact with electricity or an electrical discharge
- ☐ Injured by an animal
- ☐ Physically assaulted by a person

- ☐ Another kind of accident (describe it in Part G)

# Part F

## Dangerous occurrences

Enter the number of the dangerous occurrence you are reporting. (The numbers are given in the Regulations and in the notes which accompany this form)

# Part G

## Describing what happened

Give as much detail as you can. For instance

- the name of any substance involved
- the name and type of any machine involved
- the events that led to the incident
- the part played by any people.

If it was a personal injury, give details of what the person was doing. Describe any action that has since been taken to prevent a similar incident. Use a separate piece of paper if you need to.

Mr Worthing was a temporary member of staff. He states that he and a co-worker, Jarry Packman, were transporting boxes of metal parts across the factory floor using two trolleys when his thumb was crushed between the metal handles of the two trolleys.

It is believed that some horseplay was involved. Mr Packman has been given a written warning regarding his behaviour and Mr Worthing is no longer employed by this company.

# Part H

## Your signature

Signature

Adam Kilbride

Date

19/06/2008

If returning by post/fax, please ensure this form is signed, alternatively, if returning by E-Mail, please type your name in the signature box

**Where to send the form**

Incident Contact Centre, Caerphilly Business Centre, Caerphilly Business Park, Caerphilly, CF83 3GG.
or email to riddor@natbrit.com or fax to 0845 300 99 24

Continue

**For official use**

Client number | Location number | Event number | ☐ INV REP ☐ Y ☐ N

# DOCUMENT 6 – LETTER PROPOSING MEDICAL EXPERT

***Goodlaw Solicitors***

Fox Chambers, Maidstone, Kent, MH1 4XJ

DX 3214 GUILDSHIRE; Tel: 01483 606060; Fax: 01483 606099

Winter Wood & Co Solicitors
DX 26438 GUILDSHIRE

Our ref: BB/WORTH/08/426
Your ref: NG/GELTD/08/A48
Date: 19 November 2008

Dear Sirs,

OUR CLIENT: Mr Neil Worthing
YOUR CLIENT: Guildshire Engineering Limited
ACCIDENT DATE: 13 June 2008

Thank you for your letter dated 10 November.

In accordance with the pre-action protocol, we write to inform you of our intention to instruct one of the following consultant orthopaedic surgeons to examine our client and prepare a report for these proceedings:

1. Mr G D Cookson, MB ChB, FRCS (Tr & Orth), Crown House, Victoria Drive, Sandford, Storeshire, SS56 6YP.
2. Mr R B Alimi, MB ChB, FRCS (Orth), BSc (Hons), Hampton Hospital, Hampton, Hillshire HS1 89P.
3. Mrs F Field, MB ChB, FRCS (Orth) FRCS (Ed), The Shambles, Greenway, Heston, Scarshire SS35 1QW.

If you have any objections to any of the above, please let us know before 8 December.

Yours faithfully,

Goodlaw Solicitors

# DOCUMENT 7 – MEDICAL REPORT

**Mr G D Cookson MB ChB, FRCS (Tr & Orth),**
Consultant Orthopaedic Surgeon
Crown House, Victoria Drive, Sandford, Storeshire, SS56 6YP
Tel: 01354 787878; Fax: 01358 675675

Our ref: GDC/09/23/WORTHING
Your ref: B3/WORTH/08/426
14 January 2009

This Medical Report is addressed to the Court

1. **Qualifications**

1.1 I am a consultant Orthopaedic and Trauma Surgeon with over 35 years' experience in this field. I became a consultant in 1978. My full CV is attached to this report.

2. **Instructions**

2.1 This medical report was produced on the instructions of Goodlaw Solicitors set out in their letter dated 5 December 2008. I was requested to examine their client, Mr Neil Worthing, who had been injured in an accident at work. The injury was said to be a fracture of the left thumb.

2.2 I interviewed and examined Mr Worthing at Crown House on 16 January 2009. I was also provided with photocopies of his medical records from his GP and from the A&E Department at Guildshire Hospital.

3. **History**

3.1 Mr Worthing is a 22-year-old law student. He is single and lives in rented accommodation with other students. He is left handed.

3.2 Last summer, he was working at a factory owned by Guildshire Engineering Limited on a temporary basis. On 13 June 2008, He was moving boxes of metal components, when his thumb was trapped between the metal handles of two trolleys. He said that the trolleys had been pushed together with some force.

3.3 Immediately after the accident, he was seen by the First Aider at the workplace, who examined his hand and took him to the A&E department at Guildshire Hospital. An examination and x-ray revealed a fracture of the left thumb and, on the advice of the on-call orthopaedic registrar, a POP was applied to the thumb up to the elbow. He was advised to take painkillers and was discharged with a sling. He had difficulty sleeping for the first week and took Nurofen tablets regularly for the first two weeks. He returned to the Fracture Clinic at Guildshire Hospital two weeks after the accident when the plaster was changed to a thumb spika. He was then bandaged for a further two weeks. Mr Worthing subsequently underwent a course of 5 physiotherapy treatments at the hospital.

3.4 Mr Worthing tells me he was unable to work for one month, by which time he had lost his temporary position at the factory. He was unable to find alternative employment for the remainder of the summer vacation. He was unable to play the piano to the standard required by the hotel for a period of 8 weeks.

4. **Previous medical history**

Mr Worthing is a fit and healthy young man. There is nothing in his medical records which could have any bearing at all on the current injury.

5. **Present condition**

Mr Worthing told me that he is still experiencing pain across the back of the metacarpo-phalangeal joint of his left thumb and that the joint often felt stiff. He said that it would sometimes lock, especially if he was holding objects tightly, and on occasions he would drop them. Writing or playing the piano for long periods of time would cause pain and discomfort. Mr Worthing has to do both of these activities on a regular basis as he is a student and plays the piano at a hotel several evenings a week on a commercial basis. He can drive without difficulty. His sleep is not disturbed unless he has been playing the piano at the hotel. On those occasions, he sometimes has to take pain killers in order to get a good night's sleep.

6. **On examination**

The left thumb was not swollen, bruised or discoloured. However, there was light tenderness over the dorsal aspect of the MCP joint. Ligaments and tendons to the thumb appeared to be intact. Resisted movements of the MCP and IP joints of the thumb were possible without pain. He felt, however, that he could not bend the left thumb as well as the right thumb. The grip and pinch grip of the left hand appeared to be normal.

7. **Diagnosis and opinion**

7.1 Undisplaced avulsion fracture base of proximal phalanx radial side left thumb with bruising to IP joint.

7.2 In my opinion, an injury of this nature would have prevented Mr Worthing from working for one month following the accident and from playing the piano competently for a period of two months following the accident.

7.3 Mr Worthing appears to have made a good but not complete recovery from the injury. There appears to be some slight stiffness of the MCP joint of the left thumb with tenderness over the dorsal aspect but resisted movements are pain free. Gripping appears to cause some pain and discomfort, the thumb occasionally 'locks' and he sometimes drops objects.

7.4 On a balance of probabilities, I believe that his symptoms will gradually settle over a period of 18 months from the accident. He will not develop osteoarthritic changes in his left thumb, IP or MCP joints as a result of the injury sustained on 13 June 2008 and his ability to work and pursue leisure activities will not be disadvantaged as a result of these injuries 18 months post-accident.

8. **Declaration**

8.1 I understand that my overriding duty is to the court, both in preparing reports and in giving oral evidence.

8.2 I have set out in my report what I understand from those instructing me to be the questions in respect of which my opinion as an expert is required.

8.3 I have done my best, in preparing this report, to be accurate and complete. I have mentioned all matters which I regard as relevant to the opinions I have expressed. All of the matters on which I have expressed an opinion lie within my field of expertise.

8.4 I have drawn to the attention of the court all matters, of which I am aware, which might adversely affect my opinion.

8.5 Wherever I have no personal knowledge, I have indicated the source of factual information.

8.6 I have not included anything in this report which has been suggested to me by anyone, including the lawyers instructing me, without forming my own independent view of the matter.

8.7 Where, in my view, there is a range of reasonable opinion, I have indicated the extent of that range in the report.

8.8 At the time of signing the report I consider it to be complete and accurate. I will notify those instructing me if, for any reason, I subsequently consider that the report requires any correction or qualification.

8.9 I understand that this report will be the evidence that I will give under oath, subject to any correction or qualification I may make before swearing to its veracity.

8.10 I have attached to this report a summary of my instructions. [not reproduced]

I believe that the facts I have stated in the report are true and that the opinions I have expressed are correct.

Signed *G D Cookson* Dated 14/01/09

# DOCUMENT 8 – MEMORANDUM RE DAMAGES

*From:* Ravinder Omar, Assistant Solicitor, Goodlaw

*Sent:* 23/01/09

*To:* Belinda Braithwaite, Principal Solicitor, Goodlaw

*Subject:* Neil Worthing case – general damages

Hi Belinda,

I have now had the chance to read through the medical report provided by Mr Cookson and, as you have requested, I have researched the general damages position.

I suggest the injury falls within heading (y) Severe Dislocation of the Thumb, indicating an award of between £2,300 to £4,000. However, the Defendant may argue it falls within heading (z) Minor Injuries to the Thumb – a fracture which has recovered in six months except for residual stiffness and some discomfort. Suggest we argue client's injury is more serious than this – pain from writing/playing the piano and still dropping things.

I looked up similar injuries in Kemp and on Lawtel PI but there isn't really anything that is completely on a par with the client's injuries:

- Pearson v Snax 24 Ltd [2006] – older lady dislocated middle joint of right thumb, also a laceration. Looks as if right hand is dominant hand (though it doesn't say!). This seems to be a more serious injury as she was left with constant stiffness, a loss of grip and 50% flexion of the interphalangeal joint – injury permanent and she had also suffered from minor arthritis. PSLA £4,500 (£4,996.15 RPI).
- Jones v Manchester City Council [2004] – lady – soft tissue strain to dominant right thumb. Satisfactory recovery after 18 months but permanent minor loss of function with intermittent swelling and aching, slight loss of grip strength. Injury less serious than Mr W's but some permanent loss of function. PSLA £3,500 (£4,063 RPI).
- Lawrence v Scott Ltd [1998] – older male – crush injury to dominant thumb, fracture of terminal phalanx of thumb – similar sort of injury. No significant pain after 6 months, permanent slight deformity, minor scarring, continuing cold intolerance. Couldn't do DIY for 10 weeks or swimming for 6 mths. PSLA £2,500 (£3,393 RPI).
- Moore v Johnstone [1987] – older male fractured interphalangeal joint of non-dominant thumb. Left with slight loss of grip in left hand. Small amount of discomfort experienced when practising hobby or archery. Difficulty in picking up small components and operating certain types of lathes. Non-dominant thumb and similar type of injury but also covers concussion to head. PSLA £2,300 (£5,065 RPI).

Suggest we aim for top end of heading (y) – £4,000. Do you agree?

Ravi

# DOCUMENT 9 – CLAIM FORM

## Claim Form

| In the | GUILDSHIRE COUNTY COURT |
|---|---|
| | *for court use only* |
| Claim No. | GU 09 123 |
| Issue date | 06 February 2009 |

SEAL

Claimant

Mr Neil Matthew Worthing
22 Elstead House
Griffin Road
Christlethorpe
Guildshire
GU48 1XX

Defendant(s)

Guildshire Engineering Limited
77 Blizzard Lane
Christlethorpe
Guildshire
GU59 2YZ

Brief details of claim

The Claimant claims damages for personal injuries suffered and losses and expenses incurred as a result of an accident which occurred on 13th June 2008 whilst he was in the employment of the Defendant at its factory at 77 Blizzard Lane Christlethorpe Guildshire as a result of the Defendant's negligence and/or breach of statutory duty.

Value

I expect to recover more than £5,000 but not more than £15,000.

**Defendant's name and address**

Guildshire Engineering Limited
77 Blizzard Lane
Christlethorpe
Guildshire
GU59 2YZ

| | £ |
|---|---|
| Amount claimed | |
| Court fee | £360 |
| Solicitor's costs | to be assessed |
| Total amount | |

The court office at Guildshire County Court, Law Courts Road, Christlethorpe, Guildshire GU88 6YV

is open between 10 am and 4 pm Monday to Friday. When corresponding with the court, please address forms or letters to the Court Manager and quote the claim number.

**N1** Claim form (CPR Part 7) (01.02) *Printed on behalf of The Court Service*

| Claim No. | |
|---|---|

Does, or will, your claim include any issues under the Human Rights Act 1998? ☐ Yes ☑ No

Particulars of Claim (attached)(~~to follow~~)

Statement of Truth
*(~~I believe~~)(The Claimant believes) that the facts stated in these particulars of claim are true.
* I am duly authorised by the claimant to sign this statement

Full name Ravinder Omar

Name of claimant's solicitor's firm Goodlaw Solicitors

signed Ravinder Omar position or office held Assistant Solicitor

*(~~Claimant~~)(~~Litigation friend~~)(Claimant's solicitor) (if signing on behalf of firm or company)

*delete as appropriate*

Goodlaw Solicitors
4 College Road
Christlethorpe
Guildshire GU1 4DZ

DX 3214 GUILDSHIRE
Tel: 01483 606060
Fax: 01483 606099

**Claimant's or claimant's solicitor's address to which documents or payments should be sent if different from overleaf including (if appropriate) details of DX, fax or e-mail.**

# DOCUMENT 10 – PARTICULARS OF CLAIM

Claim No: GU 09 123

IN THE GUILDSHIRE COUNTY COURT

BETWEEN

MR NEIL MATTHEW WORTHING — Claimant

and

GUILDSHIRE ENGINEERING LIMITED — Defendant

## PARTICULARS OF CLAIM

1. The Defendant is a manufacturer of industrial tools. At all material times, the Claimant was employed by the Defendants as a process engineer at their factory at 77 Blizzard Lane, Guildshire, Surrey GU59 2YZ.
2. On 13 June 2008, at approximately 2.45pm, whilst acting in the course of his employment, the Claimant and a co-worker, Mr Jeremy Packman, were in the process of moving boxes of widgets from one part of the factory to another. They were transporting the boxes on two trolleys both of which had metal handles on each side. The Claimant was standing at the side of the first trolley, with his left hand on the handle, when the second trolley was pushed forward by Mr Packman with force, causing it to slam into the first trolley. The Claimant's left thumb was trapped between the handles of the two trolleys.
3. At all times, the provisions of the Management of Health and Safety at Work Regulations 1999 ('the Management Regulations'), the Manual Handling Operations Regulations 1992 (the 'Manual Handling Regulations') and the Provision and Use of Work Equipment Regulations 1998 ('the Work Equipment Regulations') applied.
4. The accident was caused or contributed to by the negligence and/or breach of statutory duty of the Defendant, its servants or agents acting in the course of their employment.

PARTICULARS OF BREACH OF STATUTORY DUTY

The Defendant, its servants or agents, were in breach of its statutory duty in that they:

(a) failed to make a suitable and sufficient assessment of the risks to health and safety of their employees in relation to the moving of the trolleys, contrary to reg 3(1) of the Management Regulations and reg 4(1)(b)(i) of the Manual Handling Regulations;

(b) failed to provide information to the Claimant and/or Mr Packman on health and safety risks and protective measures that should be adopted, contrary to reg 10 of the Management Regulations, and, specifically, failed to provide information and instruction in the use of equipment, namely the trolleys, contrary to reg 8 of the Work Equipment Regulations;

(c) failed to provide adequate health and safety training to the Claimant and/or Mr Packman contrary to reg 13 of the Management Regulations, and, specifically, failed to provide adequate training in the use of equipment contrary to reg 9 of the Work Equipment Regulations;

(d) failed to ensure the suitability of work equipment for the purpose for which it was provided contrary to reg 4 of the Work Equipment Regulations;

(e) failed to ensure that the Claimant and/or Mr Packman received proper information and training on how to handle loads correctly in the process of moving loaded trolleys contrary to reg 4(1)(b)(ii) of the Manual Handling Regulations;

(f) failed to take appropriate steps to reduce the risk of injury to the Claimant arising out of undertaking the operation set out above to the lowest practicable level contrary to reg 4(1)(b)(ii) of the Manual Handling Regulations.

PARTICULARS OF NEGLIGENCE

The Claimant repeats the allegations of breach of statutory duty as allegations of negligence and further alleges the Defendant was negligent in that it:

(a) failed to provide a safe system of work in that the Claimant was not given adequate information, instruction and training in relation to manual handling and health and safety matters;

(b) failed to provide safe or adequate plant in that the trolleys were not reasonably safe;

(c) failed to provide the Claimant with competent fellow workers. The Defendant was aware that Mr Packman was prone to practical jokes and horseplay within the workplace;

(d) exposed the Claimant to a foreseeable risk of injury.

5. By reason of the matters aforesaid the Claimant has suffered pain and injury and sustained loss and damage.

PARTICULARS OF INJURY

The Claimant, who was born on 14 December 1986, suffered a fracture to his left thumb. He has made a good but not complete recovery and continues to suffer from some joint stiffness and tenderness. It is anticipated that he will make a full recovery within 18 months of the accident. Further details of the Claimant's injuries and prognosis are provided in the attached medical report of Mr G D Cookson, Consultant Orthopaedic Surgeon.

PARTICULARS OF PAST AND FUTURE EXPENSES AND LOSSES

See Schedule attached.

6. The Claimant claims interest on damages pursuant to Section 69 of the County Courts Act 1984 at a rate to be assessed by the Judge.

AND the Claimant seeks:

(a) Damages; and

(b) Interest pursuant to paragraph 6.

DATED this 6th day of February 2009 SIGNED *Goodlaws Solicitors*

STATEMENT OF TRUTH

I believe that the facts stated in these Particulars of Claim are true.

Signed: *Neil Worthing*

Full name: Neil Matthew Worthing, Claimant

The Claimant's solicitors are Goodlaw Solicitors of 4 College Road, Christlethorpe, Guildshire, GU1 4DZ, where they will accept service of proceedings on behalf of the Claimant.

To: the Defendant
To: the Court Manager

## DOCUMENT 11 – SCHEDULE OF LOSS

Claim No: GU 09 123

IN THE GUILDSHIRE COUNTY COURT

BETWEEN

| | |
|---|---|
| MR NEIL MATTHEW WORTHING | Claimant |
| and | |
| GUILDSHIRE ENGINEERING LIMITED | Defendant |

### SCHEDULE OF PAST AND FUTURE EXPENSES AND LOSSES

| | | | |
|---|---|---|---|
| Loss of earnings | | | |
| Guildshire Engineering Ltd | | | |
| Pre-accident weekly net wage = £240 | | | |
| 9 weeks @ £240 | | £2,160 | |
| Less received from employers | £240 | | |
| Net loss of earnings | | £1,920 | |
| Swan Lake Hotel | | | |
| Pre-accident weekly net wage = £130 | | | |
| 8 weeks @ £130 | | £1,040 | |
| Total net loss of earnings | | | £2,960 |
| Travelling expenses | | | |
| Journeys to and from hospital/outpatients | | | |
| 5 x trips (10 miles @ 40p per mile £4 per trip) | £20 | | |
| Car parking 5 x £2 | £10 | | |
| Journey to and from consultation with Mr. Cookson for the purposes of these proceedings | £30 | | |
| Total | | | £60 |
| Cost of care | | | |
| 4 hours per day for 14 days @ £7 per hour | | | £392 |
| TOTAL | | | £3,412 |

STATEMENT OF TRUTH

I believe the facts stated in this schedule are true

Signed: *Neil Worthing*

Dated this 6th day of February 2009

# DOCUMENT 12 – FUNDING NOTICE

## Notice of funding of case or claim

Notice of funding by means of a conditional fee agreement, insurance policy or undertaking given by a prescribed body should be given to the court and all other parties to the case:

- on commencement of proceedings
- on filing an acknowledgment of service, defence or other first document; and
- at any later time that such an arrangement is entered into, changed or terminated.

| | |
|---|---|
| **In the** GUILDSHIRE COUNTY COURT | |
| The court office is open between 10 am and 4 pm Monday to Friday. When writing to the court, please address forms or letters to the Court Manager and quote the claim number. | |
| **Claim No.** | GU 09 1234 |
| **Claimant** (include Ref.) | Mr Neil Matthew Worthing<br>BB/WORTH/08/426 |
| **Defendant** (include Ref.) | Guildshire Engineering Limited<br>NG/GELTD/08/A48 |

**Take notice that** in respect of

☑ all claims herein

☐ the following claims

☐ the case of *(specify name of party)*

[is now][was] being funded by:

*(Please tick those boxes which apply)*

☑ a conditional fee agreement

**Dated** 2 September 2008

which provides for a success fee

☑ an insurance policy issued on

**Date** 2 September 2008 **Policy no.** XYZ/200000400

**Name and address of insurer**
Taskers Insurance Ltd.
High Pavement Road
Christlethorpe
Guildshire GU77 4BY

☐ an undertaking given on

**Date**

by

**Name of prescribed body**

in the following terms

The funding of the case has now changed:

☐ the above funding has now ceased

☐ the conditional fee agreement has been terminated

☐ a conditional fee agreement

**Dated**

which provides for a success fee has been entered into;

☐ an insurance policy

**Date**

has been cancelled

☐ an insurance policy has been issued on

**Date** **Policy no.**

**Name and address of insurer**

☐ an undertaking given on

**Date**

has been terminated

☐ an undertaking has been given on

**Date**

**Name of prescribed body**

in the following terms

**Signed**

Solicitor for the (claimant) (defendant)
(Part 20 defendant) (respondent) (appellant)

**Dated** 6 February 2009

**N251** Notice of funding of case or claim (06.04) *The Court Service Publications Branch*

# DOCUMENT 13 – FORM CRU 1

**DWP** Department for Work and Pensions

**Notification of a claim for compensation**
PLEASE USE CAPITALS WHEN COMPLETING THIS FORM
ALL PARTS SHOULD BE COMPLETED UNLESS STATED OTHERWISE

## Injured Person's details

Sex *Select* F *for female,* M *for male* M

National Insurance Number: WK987999X

Date of Birth: 14/12/1986 — *Office use Enter V or NV*

Surname: WORTHING

Date of Death: — *Office use: Enter V or NV*

First Forename: NEIL

Other Forename: MATTHEW

Any other known surname(s) eg. *Maiden name*:

Address: 22 ELSTEAD HOUSE, GRIFFIN ROAD, CHRISTLETHORPE, GUILDSHIRE

Title: MR

Postcode: GU48 1XX

## Reason for claim as alleged by the Injured Person

**If accident or alleged clinical negligence:**

Date of accident/incident: 13/062008

Full description of injuries resulting from the accident (state Left or Right where appropriate) and condition/reason for which compensation is claimed.

FRACTURED LEFT THUMB ARISING FROM ACCIDENT AT WORK

**If disease:**

Name of disease – if compensation is also being claimed for condition(s) prior to disease being diagnosed, give those details as well

*Office use: Disease code*

## Type of Liability

E for Employer
P for Public
M for Motor
C for Clinical Negligence
O for Other

E

## Compensator details

Name of compensator or compensator's representative: WINTER WOOD & CO, SOLICITORS

On behalf of: (Enter name of compensator if representative's details given opposite): BRIGHT INSURANCE CO. LTD.

Your reference: NG/GELTD/08/A48

DX address or postal address: DX 26438 GUILDSHIRE

Name of Insured or Policy Holder: GUILDSHIRE ENGINEERING LIMITED

Telephone: 01483 432143

Postcode:

Fax: 01483 432156

## Injured Person's Representative Details

| | |
|---|---|
| **Name of representative** | **Reference** |
| GOODLAW SOLICITORS | BB/WORTH/08/426 |
| **DX address or postal address** | **Telephone** |
| DX 3214 GUILDSHIRE | 01483 606060 |
| | **Fax** |
| | 01483 606099 |
| **Postcode** | |
| | |

## Hospital details

**All incidents on or after 29.01.07**
**Road Traffic Accidents only before 29.01.07**

**If the incident is on or after 29.01.07 and the compensator is the same as the Trust, or in Scotland the NHS Board who provided treatment, do not provide own hospital details.**

**Did the injured person receive NHS treatment because of the incident?** Yes☒ No☐

Give details of the hospital(s) or trust(s) the Injured Person attended or was admitted to in order of attendance

| **Name & Address of hospital (1)** | **Name & Address of hospital (2)** |
|---|---|
| GUILDSHIRE HOSPITAL | |
| **Address** | **Address** |
| RUTLAND ROAD,<br>CHRISTLETHORPE,<br>GUILDSHIRE | |
| **Postcode** GU20 2PY | **Postcode** |

**<u>For Road Traffic accidents before 29.01.07: -</u> If you are claiming exemption from recovery of NHS Charges on the grounds of nil requirement to carry compulsory insurance, (section 144, Road Traffic Act 1988) state category of exemption here:**

## Employment details

***Only complete in disease cases or if date of accident is before 06.04.1994***

**Did the Injured Person work for an employer at the time of the accident OR Was the Injured Person absent from work prior to 06.04.1994 as a result of the disease/condition(s) for which compensation has been claimed?** Yes☐ No☐

**If Yes, please give name and address of employer(s) and employee payroll number, if known, on a separate sheet and attach it to this CRU1. If this is an Employer Liability claim you must also provide details of any SSP paid when you request a Certificate of Recoverable Benefits.**

## What to do now

**Send this form to :-** Compensation Recovery Unit
Durham House
Washington
Tyne & Wear
NE38 7SF

DX68560
Washington 4
Tel: <u>Contacts</u>
Fax. 0191 2252324
Date:............

Alternatively you can email this form to: <u>cru1@dwp.gsi.gov.uk</u>

| | | | | | | | | |
|---|---|---|---|---|---|---|---|---|
| *OFFICE USE* | **STB** | | **IS** | | **AA** | | **DWA** | |
| **Benefit Offices** | **DISB** | | **JSA** | | | | **DLA** | |

**Scrutinized by:.......................................** **CRU Ref:.........................**

# DOCUMENT 14 – DEFENCE

Claim No: GU 09 123

IN THE GUILDSHIRE COUNTY COURT

BETWEEN

| | |
|---|---|
| MR NEIL MATTHEW WORTHING | Claimant |
| and | |
| GUILDSHIRE ENGINEERING LIMITED | Defendant |

DEFENCE

1. Paragraph 1 of the Particulars of Claim is admitted.
2. It is admitted that the Claimant suffered an accidental injury on 13 June 2008 at the Defendants premises but no other admissions are made in relation to the allegations set out in paragraph 2.
3. Paragraph 3 is admitted.
4. It is denied that the Defendant its servant or agent was negligent or in breach of statutory duty as alleged in paragraph 4 or at all.
5. All relevant regulations were complied with. In particular:
   (a) a suitable and sufficient risk assessment was carried out;
   (b) adequate health and safety information and training was provided to the Claimant and to Mr Packman regarding manual handling and stacking the trolleys. The Defendant will argue that how to push a trolley is a matter of common sense and specific training in this respect is not required;
   (c) the trolleys were suitable for the purpose for which they were provided;
   (d) the Claimant was instructed to put no more than four boxes on the trolleys.

   Consequently, all appropriate steps were taken to reduce the risk of injury to the Claimant. The Defendant will rely upon the defence of reasonable practicability.
6. If, which is not admitted, the Claimant's thumb became trapped between the handles of the trolleys as alleged and this was caused wholly or partly by any inappropriate behaviour on the part of Mr Packman, which is denied, Mr Packman was acting contrary to instructions given to him by the Defendant and was therefore not acting in the course of his employment.
7. If, which is not admitted, ·the Claimant's thumb became trapped between the handles of the trolleys as alleged, the accident was wholly caused or alternatively materially contributed to by his own negligence.

<u>PARTICULARS OF NEGLIGENCE</u>

The Claimant:

(a) stacked the second trolley with five boxes instead of four as instructed;

(b) engaged in horseplay with Mr Packman and encouraged him to behave irresponsibly;

(c) failed to exercise reasonable care for his own safety.

8. Paragraph 5 is not admitted. The Defendant makes no admissions in relation to the matters set out in the medical report of Mr Cookson and reserves the right to question him and/or obtain its own medical evidence.
9. No admissions are made in relation to the Schedule of Past and Future Expenses and Losses and the defendant puts the Claimant to strict proof of the items claimed.
10. Accordingly, it is denied the Claimant is entitled to the relief claimed at paragraph 6 or at all.

DATED this 18th day of February 2009 SIGNED *Winter Wood & Co*

STATEMENT OF TRUTH

The Defendant believes that the facts stated in this Defence are true.

I am duly authorised by the Defendant to sign this statement.

Full name: Jacob Hudson

Signed: *J Hudson* Position held: Managing Director

The Defendant's solicitors are Winter Wood & Co, Rembrandt House, Lee Lane, Brampton, Guildshire, GU7 8TU where they will accept service of proceedings on behalf of the Defendant.

To: The Claimant
To: The Court Manager

# DOCUMENT 15 – ALLOCATION QUESTIONNAIRE

## Allocation questionnaire

To be completed by, or on behalf of,

Mr. Neil Matthew Worthing

who is ~~[1st][2nd][3rd]~~[ ][Claimant]~~[Defendant]~~ ~~[Part 20 claimant]~~ in this claim

| | |
|---|---|
| Name of court | GUILDSHIRE COUNTY COURT |
| Claim No. | GU 09 123 |
| Last date for filing with court office | 6th March 2009 |

Please read the notes on page six before completing the questionnaire.

You should note the date by which it must be returned and the name of the court it should be returned to since this may be different from the court where the proceedings were issued.

If you have settled this claim (or if you settle it on a future date) and do not need to have it heard or tried, you must let the court know immediately.

Have you sent a copy of this completed form to the other party(ies)? ☑ Yes ☐ No

## A Settlement

Under the Civil Procedure Rules parties should make every effort to settle their case before the hearing. This could be by discussion or negotiation (such as a roundtable meeting or settlement conference) or by a more formal process such as mediation. The court will want to know what steps have been taken. Settling the case early can save costs, including court hearing fees.

**For legal representatives only**

I confirm that I have explained to my client the need to try to settle; the options available; and the possibility of costs sanctions if they refuse to try to settle. ☑

**For all**

Your answers to these questions may be considered by the court when it deals with the questions of costs: see Civil Procedure Rules Part 44.3 (4).

1. Given that the rules require you to try to settle the claim before the hearing, do you want to attempt to settle at this stage? ☐ Yes ☑ No
2. If Yes, do you want a one month stay? ☐ Yes ☑ No
3. Would you like the court to arrange a mediation appointment? ☐ Yes ☑ No
   (A fee will be payable to the mediation provider appointed by the National Mediation Helpline.)
4. If you answered 'No' to question 1, please state below the reasons why you consider it inappropriate to try to settle the claim at this stage.

Reasons:

Attempts to settle were made pre-issue but were unssuccessful. There is no possibility of settlement at this stage but both parties will consider the matter following the exchange of documents/evidence.

 

## B Location of trial

Is there any reason why your claim needs to be heard at a particular court? ☑ Yes ☐ No

If Yes, say which court and why?

The Guildshire County Court as it is local to both parties.

## C Pre-action protocols

You are expected to comply with the relevant pre-action protocol.

Have you done so? ☑ Yes ☐ No

If No, explain why?

## D Case management information

What amount of the claim is in dispute? £7,412.00

### Applications

Have you made any application(s) in this claim? ☐ Yes ☑ No

If Yes what for? (e.g. summary judgment, add another party) For hearing on

### Witnesses

So far as you know at this stage, what witnesses of fact do you intend to call at the trial or final hearing including, if appropriate, yourself?

| Witness name | Witness to which facts |
|---|---|
| Mr Neil Worthing - claimant | The lack of information / training he received; the accident; the injury and associated losses and expenses. |

## Experts

Do you wish to use expert evidence at the trial or final hearing? ☑ Yes ☐ No

Have you already copied any experts' report(s) to the other party(ies)? ☐ None yet obtained ☑ Yes ☐ No

Do you consider the case suitable for a single joint expert in any field? ☐ Yes ☑ No

Please list any single joint experts you propose to use and any other experts you wish to rely on. Identify single joint experts with the initials 'SJ' after their name(s).

| Expert's name | Field of expertise (eg. orthopaedic surgeon, surveyor, engineer) |
|---|---|
| Mr G D Cookson (jointly selected) | Consultant Orthopaedic Surgeon |

Do you want your expert(s) to give evidence orally at the trial or final hearing? ☐ Yes ☑ No

If Yes, give the reasons why you think oral evidence is necessary:

## Track

Which track do you consider is most suitable for your claim? Tick one box

☐ small claims track
☑ fast track
☐ multi-track

If you have indicated a track which would not be the normal track for the claim, please give brief reasons for your choice

## E Trial or final hearing

How long do you estimate the trial or final hearing will take?

| days | 3 hours | minutes |
|---|---|---|

Are there any days when you, an expert or an essential witness will not be able to attend court for the trial or final hearing? ☐ Yes ☑ No

If Yes, please give details

| Name | Dates not available |
|---|---|
| | |

## F Proposed directions *(Parties should agree directions wherever possible)*

Have you attached a list of the directions you think appropriate for the management of the claim? ☑ Yes ☐ No

If Yes, have they been agreed with the other party(ies)? ☑ Yes ☐ No

## G Costs

*Do **not** complete this section if you have suggested your case is suitable for the small claims track **or** you have suggested one of the other tracks and you do not have a solicitor acting for you.*

What is your estimate of your costs incurred to date? £2,250.00

What do you estimate your overall costs are likely to be? £4,750.00

In substantial cases these questions should be answered in compliance with CPR Part 43

## H Fee

Have you attached the fee for filing this allocation questionnaire? ☑ Yes ☐ No

An allocation fee is payable if your claim or counterclaim exceeds £1,500.

Additional fees will be payable at further stages of the court process.

## I Other information

Have you attached documents to this questionnaire? ☑ Yes ☐ No

Have you sent these documents to the other party(ies)? ☑ Yes ☐ No

If Yes, when did they receive them? 27th February 2009

Do you intend to make any applications in the immediate future? ☐ Yes ☑ No

If Yes, what for?

In the space below, set out any other information you consider will help the judge to manage the claim.

Signed *Goodlaw Solicitors* Date 03/03/09

[~~Counsel~~] [Solicitor] [for the][~~1st~~][~~2nd~~][~~3rd~~][ ]
[Claimant] [D~~efendant~~] ~~[Part 20 claimant]~~

Please enter your name, reference number and full postal address including (if appropriate) details of telephone, DX, fax or e-mail

| | | |
|---|---|---|
| Goodlaw Solicitors, 4 College Road, Christlethorpe,Guildshire, GU1 4DZ. | If applicable | |
| | Telephone no. | 01483 606060 |
| | Fax no. | 01483 606099 |
| | DX no. | DX3214 GUILDSHIRE |
| Postcode | Your ref. | BB/WORTH/08/426 |

| | |
|---|---|
| E-mail | b.braith@goodlaw.co.uk |

# DOCUMENT 16 – NOTICE OF ALLOCATION TO FAST TRACK AND DIRECTIONS

Notice of Allocation to
The Fast Track

To: the Claimant's
Solictor

Goodlaw Solicitors
4 College Road
Christlethorpe
Guildshire
GU1 4DZ

| In the | GUILDSHIRE County Court |
|---|---|
| Claim Number | GU 09 123 |
| Claimant (including ref) | Mr Neil Matthew Worthing |
| Defendant (including ref) | Guildshire Engineering Limited |
| Date | 22/04/09 |

DISTRICT JUDGE BILLINGHURST has considered the statements of case and allocation questionnaires filed, and allocated the claim to **the fast track**.

1. This case is allocated to the fast track
2. (a) Standard disclosure by lists between the parties by 4:00pm on the 25 May 2009 and CPR 31.21 shall apply in the event of default.
   (b) Inspection of documents by 4:00pm on the 8 June 2009
3. (a) Statements of witnesses as to fact to be exchanged by 4:00pm on the 6 July 2009
   (b) Witness statements shall stand as evidence in chief.
   (c) Evidence shall not be permitted at trial from a witness whose evidence has not been served in accordance with this order.
4. (a) The Claimant is permitted to rely on the written report of Mr G D Cookson.
   (b) The Defendant shall raise any questions of the said expert in writing by 4:00pm on the 20 July 2009 which shall be responded to by 4:00pm on the 17 August 2009.
5. (a) The Claimant shall serve an updated schedule of damages by 4:00pm on the 24 August 2009 and the Defendant shall serve any counter schedule by 4:00pm on the 31 August 2009 both incorporating an estimate of the general range of damages.
   (b) Within 7 days of the exchange of schedules the parties shall communicate and shall agree subject to liability the range of general damages and the extent to which the general damages are agreed and shall agree a case summary setting out the extent of agreement and of disagreement giving reasons for the disagreement.
6. The parties shall file a Listing Questionnaire by 4:00pm on the 28 September 2009 together with the case summary directed at 5(b) above.
7. (a) The matter be listed for trial before a District Judge in a 3 week trial window commencing the 2 November 2009 with an estimated length of hearing of 3 hours.
   (b) The Claimant shall lodge the trial bundle by no later than 5 days prior to the date of trial.
8. Non-compliance with any of these directions may result in sanctions including the striking out of a Claim or Defence.

Dated 22 April 2009

Notes:

- You and the other party, or parties, may agree to extend the time periods given in the directions **except**
  - where a rule, practice direction or court order requires a party to comply with a direction within a specified time **and** specifies the consequences of failing to comply;
  - where an extension of time will affect the date given for returning the pre-trial checklist or the date of the trial or trial period.
- If you do not comply with these directions, any other party to the claim will be entitled to apply to the court for an order that your statement of case (claim or defence) be struck out.
- Leaflets explaining more about what happens when your case is allocated to the fast track are available from the court office, **or online at** www.hmcourts-service.gov.uk/cms/infoabout.htm.

---

The court office at GUILDSHIRE County Court is open between 10am and 4pm Monday to Friday. When corresponding with the court, please address forms or letters to the Court Manager and quote the claim number. Tel: 01483 123123 Fax: 01483 123345.

N154 Notice of Allocation to the Fast Track

# DOCUMENT 17 – CRU CERTIFICATE

**DWP** Department for Work and Pensions

CRU
DX68560
Washington 4

Compensation Recovery Unit
Durham House
Washington
Tyne & Wear
NE38 7SF

Tel.: 0191-2252377
Fax.: 0191-2252366
Typetalk:-18001019122 52377

Our Ref: NLB – 416

Your Ref: BB/WORTH/08/426

Date : 03/07/2009

---

Below is a copy of the Certificate of Recoverable Benefits sent to Winter Wood & Co.

**Please note: This is for information only – no payment is required from you**

**CRU101**

---

***Certificate of Recoverable Benefits***

Date of issue: 03/07/2009

Your ref: NG/GELTD/08/A48

Our ref: NBL – 416

Injured person: NEIL M WORTHING

This certificate shows the amount due to the Department for Work and Pensions (DWP), as a result of an accident or injury which occurred on 13/06/2008 to the person named above and is issued in response to your request for a Certificate of Recoverable Benefits which was received on 02/07/2009.

The amount due is NIL. No recoverable benefits have been paid.

This Certificate is valid until 04/01/2010.

Authorized by S Peters Compensation Recovery Unit
On behalf of the Secretary of State

Issue No. 19988776 **CRU100**

## DOCUMENT 18 – MEMORANDUM RE OFFER

From: Ravinder Omar, Assistant Solicitor, Goodlaw

Sent: 09/07/09

To: Belinda Braithwaite, Principal Solicitor, Goodlaw

Subject: Neil Worthing case – settlement

Hi Belinda

Just to let you know that the witness statements came in last week. Jerry Packman, the guy who was loading the trolleys with Mr W, confirms that it was Mr W who suggested putting the extra box onto the second trolley. He also says that it was Mr W who started messing about with the trolleys, that Mr W pushed his trolley at Mr P's trolley first and then stood about laughing as Mr P tried to push his trolley. That's when the accident happened. In addition, contrary to what he told our client, he is now saying that he did have H&S/manual handling training.

I discussed this with Rosie Smith at Winter Wood on Friday. I said that they couldn't avoid liability. Just handing over H&S info to Mr W isn't sufficient instruction and training, particularly as he has never worked in a factory before. They haven't got any evidence to back up their statement that the foam on the handles was sorted out before the accident and Mr Packman was messing about too. She more or less said she agreed and that she would be talking to her client about making a Part 36 offer on a 25% contrib. basis. She said that she had already obtained a certificate from the CRU and that there are no repayable benefits. (There are NHS charges of £457, which relate to the treatment our client received at hospital, but the defendant has to pay that.)

She was unhappy about our claim for gratuitous care, saying that the number of hours claimed and the amount per hour are unreasonable. She didn't like our mileage rates either but I don't think they'll quibble over a few pounds.

I couldn't get hold of Mr W until this morning. He admitted that Mr P's account was accurate. He is keen to settle and understands that the defendant will want to knock a bit off for contributory negligence. I told him we would wait and see what they offered and then we would talk again.

What do you think?

Ravi

# DOCUMENT 19 – PART 36 OFFER LETTER

## Winter Wood & Co Solicitors

Rembrandt House,
Lee Lane, Brampton
Guildshire, GU7 8TU
DX 26438 GUILDSHIRE
Tel: 01483 432143
Fax: 01483 432156

Goodlaw Solicitors
DX 3214 GUILDSHIRE

Our ref: NG/GELTD/08/A48
Your ref: BB/WORTH/08/426

Date: 10 July 2009

Dear Sirs

**YOUR CLIENT: Mr Neil Worthing**
**OUR CLIENT: Guildshire Engineering Limited**
**ACCIDENT DATE: 13 June 2008**
**PART 36 OFFER – without prejudice save as to costs**

We are instructed by our client to put forward the following offer which is made without prejudice save as to costs pursuant to Part 36 of the Civil Procedure Rules 1998:

1. Our client agrees to pay your client the sum of £4,750 inclusive of interest in full and final settlement of all claims your client has or may have against our client in this matter.
2. Our client agrees in addition to pay your client's reasonable costs, including costs that have been incurred up to 21 days after the date you receive this letter, as agreed or, if not agreed within 14 days, to be assessed by detailed assessment.
3. This offer is open for acceptance for 21 days from the date you receive this letter.

We await hearing from you.

Yours faithfully,

Winter Wood & Co

# DOCUMENT 20 – MEMORANDUM RE PART 36 OFFER

*From:* Ravinder Omar, Assistant Solicitor Goodlaw

*Sent:* 14/07/2009

*To:* Belinda Braithwaite, Principal Solicitor, Goodlaw

*Subject:* Neil Worthing

Hi Belinda

I telephoned Mr W to inform him of the offer. I talked him through the options and advised him that I thought it was reasonable but perhaps a little on the low side. We agreed that I would speak to the defendant's solicitors to see if I can get them to improve their offer but if not, he wanted to accept their offer.

I then spoke to Saul Edozie at Winter Wood & Co. His offer was based on generals of £3,000 and 25% contributory negligence. He also wanted a reduction in our claim for gratuitous care. After some negotiation he agreed to increase the offer to £5,250 which I accepted on Mr W's behalf. I will send a consent order to finalise the matter.

I rang Mr W to tell him the good news – he is delighted!

Ravi

# DOCUMENT 21 – ACCEPTANCE LETTER

*Goodlaw Solicitors*

Fox Chambers, Maidstone, Kent, MH1 4XJ

DX 3214 GUILDSHIRE; Tel: 01483 606060; Fax: 01483 606099

Winter Wood & Co Solicitors
DX 26438 GUILDSHIRE
Your ref: NG/GELTD/08/A48

Our ref : BB/WORTH/08/426
Date: 15 July 2009

Dear Sirs,

**OUR CLIENT: Mr Neil Worthing**
**ADDRESS: 22 Elstead House, Griffin Road, Guildford, GU48 1XX**
**ACCIDENT DATE: 13 June 2008**

Further to our telephone conversation with Mr Edozie we confirm that our client is prepared to accept your offer of £5,250 in full and final settlement of his claim plus our costs to be assessed if not agreed. Please sign and return the enclosed consent order which we will then file at court.

Yours faithfully

Goodlaw Solicitors

# DOCUMENT 22 – DRAFT CONSENT ORDER

Claim No: GU 09 123

IN THE GUILDSHIRE COUNTY COURT

BETWEEN

MR NEIL MATTHEW WORTHING — Claimant

and

GUILDSHIRE ENGINEERING LIMITED — Defendant

**CONSENT ORDER**

Upon the parties agreeing to settle this matter

AND BY CONSENT

IT IS ORDERED THAT

1. The Defendant pay the Claimant the sum of £5,250 by 4pm on Friday 31 July 2009;
2. Upon payment, claim GU 09 123 be stayed;
3. The Defendant pay the Claimant's costs of this matter to be assessed on the standard basis if not agreed.
4. Liberty to apply.

| | |
|---|---|
| We consent to the terms of this order. | We consent to the terms of this order. |
| **Goodlaw Solicitors** | **Winter Wood & Co Solicitors** |
| Dated 16 July 2009 | Dated 16 July 2009 |

# Appendix 2
# Pre-action Protocol for Personal Injury Claims

## Contents



## 1 Introduction

1.1 Lord Woolf in his final Access to Justice Report of July 1996 recommended the development of pre-action protocols:

> To build on and increase the benefits of early but well informed settlement which genuinely satisfy both parties to dispute.

1.2 The aims of pre-action protocols are:

- more pre-action contact between the parties
- better and earlier exchange of information
- better pre-action investigation by both sides
- to put the parties in a position where they may be able to settle cases fairly and early without litigation
- to enable proceedings to run to the court's timetable and efficiently, if litigation does become necessary
- to promote the provision of medical or rehabilitation treatment (not just in high value cases) to address the needs of the claimant

1.3 The concept of protocols is relevant to a range of initiatives for good litigation and pre-litigation practice, especially:

- predictability in the time needed for steps pre-proceedings
- standardisation of relevant information, including documents to be disclosed.

1.4 The Courts will be able to treat the standards set in protocols as the normal reasonable approach to pre-action conduct. If proceedings are issued, it will be for the court to decide whether non-compliance with a protocol should merit adverse consequences. Guidance on the court's likely approach will be given from time to time in practice directions.

1.5 If the court has to consider the question of compliance after proceedings have begun, it will not be concerned with minor infringements, e.g. failure by a short period to provide relevant information. One minor breach will not exempt the 'innocent' party from following the protocol. The court will look at the effect of non-compliance on the other party when deciding whether to impose sanctions.

## 2 Notes of Guidance

2.1 The protocol has been kept deliberately simple to promote ease of use and general acceptability. The notes of guidance which follows relate particularly to issues which arose during the piloting of the protocol.

**Scope of the protocol**

2.2 This protocol is intended to apply to all claims which include a claim for personal injury (except those claims covered by the Clinical Disputes and Disease and Illness Protocols) and to the entirety of those claims: not only to the personal injury element of a claim which also includes, for instance, property damage.

2.3 This protocol is primarily designed for those road traffic, tripping and slipping and accident at work cases which include an element of personal injury with a value of less than £15,000 which are likely to be allocated to the fast track. This is because time will be of the essence, after proceedings are issued, especially for the defendant, if a case is to be ready for trial within 30 weeks of allocation. Also, proportionality of work and costs to the value of what is in dispute is particularly important in lower value claims. For some claims within the value 'scope' of the fast track some flexibility in the timescale of the protocol may be necessary, see also paragraph 3.8.

2.4 However, the 'cards on the table' approach advocated by the protocol is equally appropriate to higher value claims. The spirit, if not the letter of the protocol, should still be followed for multi-track type claims. In accordance with the sense of the civil justice reforms, the court will expect to see the spirit of reasonable pre-action behaviour applied in all cases, regardless of the existence of a specific protocol. In particular with regard to personal injury cases worth more than £15,000, with a view to avoiding the necessity of proceedings parties are expected to comply with the protocol as far as possible e.g. in respect of letters before action, exchanging information and documents and agreeing experts.

2.5 The timetable and the arrangements for disclosing documents and obtaining expert evidence may need to be varied to suit the circumstances of the case. Where one or both parties consider the detail of the protocol is not appropriate to the case, and proceedings are subsequently issued, the court will expect an explanation as to why the protocol has not been followed, or has been varied.

**Early notification**

2.6 The claimant's legal representative may wish to notify the defendant and/or his insurer as soon as they know a claim is likely to be made, but before they are able to send a detailed letter of claim, particularly for instance, when the defendant has no or limited knowledge of the incident giving rise to the claim or where the claimant is incurring significant expenditure as a result of the accident which he hopes the defendant might pay for, in whole or in part. If the claimant's representative chooses to do this, it will not start the timetable for responding.

**The letter of claim**

2.7 The specimen letter of claim at Annex A will usually be sent to the individual defendant. In practice, he/she may have no personal financial interest in the financial outcome of the claim/dispute because he/she is insured. Court imposed sanctions for non-compliance with the protocol may be ineffective against an insured. This is why the protocol emphasises the importance of passing the letter of claim to the insurer and the possibility that the insurance cover might be affected. If an insurer receives the letter of claim only after some delay by the insured, it would not be unreasonable for the insurer to ask the claimant for additional time to respond.

2.8 In road traffic cases, the letter of claim should always contain the name and address of the hospital where the claimant was treated and, where available, the claimant's hospital reference number.

2.9 The priority at letter of claim stage is for the claimant to provide sufficient information for the defendant to assess liability. Sufficient information should also be provided to enable the defendant to estimate the likely size of the claim.

2.10 Once the claimant has sent the letter of claim no further investigation on liability should normally be carried out until a response is received from the defendant indicating whether liability is disputed.

**Reasons for early issue**

2.11 The protocol recommends that a defendant be given three months to investigate and respond to a claim before proceedings are issued. This may not always be possible, particularly where a claimant only consults a solicitor close to the end of any relevant limitation period. In these circumstances, the claimant's solicitor should give as much notice of the intention to issue proceedings as is practicable and the parties should consider whether the court might be invited to extend time for service of the claimant's supporting documents and for service of any defence, or alternatively, to stay the proceedings while the recommended steps in the protocol are followed.

**Status of letters of claim and response**

2.12 Letters of claim and response are not intended to have the same status as a statement of case in proceedings. Matters may come to light as a result of investigation after the letter of claim has been sent, or after the defendant has responded, particularly if disclosure of documents takes place outside the recommended three-month period. These circumstances could mean that the 'pleaded' case of one or both parties is presented slightly differently than in the letter of claim and response. It would not be consistent with the spirit of the protocol for a party to 'take a point' on this in the proceedings, provided that there was no obvious intention by the party who changed their position to mislead the other party.

**Disclosure of documents**

2.13 The aim of the early disclosure of documents by the defendant is not to encourage 'fishing expeditions' by the claimant, but to promote an early exchange of relevant information to help in clarifying or resolving issues in dispute. The claimant's solicitor can assist by identifying in the letter of claim or in a subsequent letter the particular categories of documents which they consider are relevant.

**Experts**

2.14 The protocol encourages joint selection of, and access to, experts. The report produced is not a joint report for the purposes of CPR Part 35. Most frequently this will apply to the medical expert, but on occasions also to liability experts, e.g. engineers. The protocol promotes the practice of the claimant obtaining a medical report, disclosing it to the defendant who then asks questions and/or agrees it and does not obtain his own report. The Protocol provides for nomination of the expert by the claimant in personal injury claims because of the early stage of the proceedings and the particular nature of such claims. If proceedings have to be issued, a medical report must be attached to these proceedings. However, if necessary after proceedings have commenced and with the permission of the court, the parties may obtain further expert reports. It would be for the court to decide whether the costs of more than one expert's report should be recoverable.

2.15 Some solicitors choose to obtain medical reports through medical agencies, rather than directly from a specific doctor or hospital. The defendant's prior consent to the action should be sought and, if the defendant so requests, the agency should be asked to provide in advance the names of the doctor(s) whom they are considering instructing.

**Alternative dispute resolution**

2.16 The parties should consider whether some form of alternative dispute resolution procedure would be more suitable than litigation, and if so, endeavour to agree which form to adopt. Both the Claimant and Defendant may be required by the Court to provide evidence that alternative means of resolving their dispute were considered. The Courts take the view that litigation should be a last resort, and that claims should not be issued prematurely when a settlement is still actively being explored. Parties are warned that if the protocol is not followed (including this paragraph) then the Court must have regard to such conduct when determining costs.

2.17 It is not practicable in this protocol to address in detail how the parties might decide which method to adopt to resolve their particular dispute. However, summarised below are some of the options for resolving disputes without litigation:

- Discussion and negotiation.
- Early neutral evaluation by an independent third party (for example, a lawyer experienced in the field of personal injury or an individual experienced in the subject matter of the claim).
- Mediation – a form of facilitated negotiation assisted by an independent neutral party.

2.18 The Legal Services Commission has published a booklet on 'Alternatives to Court', CLS Direct Information Leaflet 23 (www.clsdirect.org.uk/legalhelp/leaflet23.jsp), which lists a number of organisations that provide alternative dispute resolution services.

2.19 *It is expressly recognised that no party can or should be forced to mediate or enter into any form of ADR.*

## 3 The protocol

**Letter of claim**

3.1 The claimant shall send to the proposed defendant two copies of a letter of claim, immediately sufficient information is available to substantiate a realistic claim and before issues of quantum are addressed in detail. One copy of the letter is for the defendant, the second for passing on to his insurers.

3.2 The letter shall contain **a clear summary of the facts** on which the claim is based together with an indication of the **nature of any injuries** suffered and of **any financial loss incurred**. In cases of road traffic accidents, the letter should provide the name and address of the hospital where treatment has been obtained and the claimant's hospital reference number. Where the case is funded by a conditional fee agreement (or collective conditional fee agreement), notification should be given of the existence of the agreement and where appropriate, that there is a success fee and/or insurance premium, although not the level of the success fee or premium.

3.3 Solicitors are recommended to use a **standard format** for such a letter – an example is at Annex A: this can be amended to suit the particular case.

3.4 The letter should ask for **details of the insurer** and that a copy should be sent by the proposed defendant to the insurer where appropriate. If the insurer is known, a copy shall be sent directly to the insurer. Details of the claimant's National Insurance number and date of birth should be supplied to the defendant's insurer once the defendant has responded to the letter of claim and confirmed the identity of the insurer. This information should not be supplied in the letter of claim.

3.5 **Sufficient information** should be given in order to enable the defendant's insurer/solicitor to commence investigations and at least put a broad valuation on the 'risk'.

3.6 The **defendant should reply within 21 calendar days** of the date of posting of the letter identifying the insurer (if any) and, if necessary, identifying specifically any significant omissions from the letter of claim. If there has been no reply by the defendant or insurer within 21 days, the claimant will be entitled to issue proceedings.

3.7 The **defendant**('s insurers) will have a **maximum of three months** from the date of acknowledgment of the claim **to investigate**. No later than the end of that period the defendant (insurer) shall reply, stating whether liability is denied and, if so, giving reasons for their denial of liability including any alternative version of events relied upon.

3.8 Where the accident occurred outside England and Wales and/or where the defendant is outside the jurisdiction, the time periods of 21 days and three months should normally be extended up to 42 days and six months.

3.9 Where **liability is admitted**, the presumption is that the defendant will be bound by this admission for all claims with a total value of up to £15,000. Where the claimant's investigation indicates that the value of the claim has increased to more than £15,000 since the letter of claim, the claimant should notify the defendant as soon as possible.

**Documents**

3.10 If the **defendant denies liability**, he should enclose with the letter of reply, **documents** in his possession which are **material to the issues** between the parties, and which would be likely to be ordered to be disclosed by the court, either on an application for pre-action disclosure, or on disclosure during proceedings.

3.11 Attached at Annex B are **specimen**, but non-exhaustive, **lists** of documents likely to be material in different types of claim. Where the claimant's investigation of the case is well advanced, the letter of claim could indicate which classes of documents are considered relevant for early disclosure. Alternatively these could be identified at a later stage.

3.12 Where the defendant admits primary liability, but alleges contributory negligence by the claimant, the defendant should give reasons supporting those allegations and disclose those documents from Annex B which are relevant to the issues in dispute. The claimant should respond to the allegations of contributory negligence before proceedings are issued.

3.13 No charge will be made for providing copy documents under the Protocol.

**Special damages**

3.14 The claimant will send to the defendant as soon as practicable a Schedule of Special Damages with supporting documents, particularly where the defendant has admitted liability.

**Experts**

3.15 Before any party instructs an expert he should give the other party a list of the **name**(s) of **one or more experts** in the relevant speciality whom he considers are suitable to instruct.

3.16 Where a medical expert is to be instructed the claimant's solicitor will organise access to relevant medical records – see specimen letter of instruction at Annex C.

3.17 **Within 14 days** the other party may indicate **an objection** to one or more of the named experts. The first party should then instruct a mutually acceptable expert (which is not the same as a joint expert). It must be emphasised that if the Claimant nominates an expert in the original letter of claim, the defendant has 14 days to object to one or more of the named experts after expiration of the period of 21 days within which he has to reply to the letter of claim, as set out in paragraph 3.6.

3.18 If the second party objects to all the listed experts, the parties may then instruct **experts of their own choice**. It would be for the court to decide subsequently, if proceedings are issued, whether either party had acted unreasonably.

3.19 If the **second party does not object to an expert nominated**, he shall not be entitled to rely on his own expert evidence within that particular speciality unless:

(a) the first party agrees,

(b) the court so directs, or

(c) the first party's expert report has been amended and the first party is not prepared to disclose the original report.

3.20 **Either party may send to an agreed expert written questions** on the report, relevant to the issues, via the first party's solicitors. The expert should send answers to the questions separately and directly to each party.

3.21 The cost of a report from an agreed expert will usually be paid by the instructing first party: the costs of the expert replying to questions will usually be borne by the party which asks the questions.

## 4 Rehabilitation

4.1 The claimant or the defendant or both shall consider as early as possible whether the claimant has reasonable needs that could be met by rehabilitation treatment or other measures.

4.2 The parties shall consider, in such cases, how those needs might be addressed. The Rehabilitation Code (which is attached at Annex D) may be helpful in considering how to identify the claimant's needs and how to address the cost of providing for those needs.

4.3 The time limit set out in paragraph 3.7 of this Protocol shall not be shortened, except by consent to allow these issues to be addressed.

4.4 The provision of any report obtained for the purposes of assessment of provision of a party's rehabilitation needs shall not be used in any litigation arising out of the accident, the subject of the claim, save by consent and shall in any event be exempt from the provisions of paragraphs 3.15 to 3.21 inclusive of this protocol.

## 5 Resolution of issues

5.1 Where the defendant admits liability in whole or in part, before proceedings are issued, any medical reports obtained under this protocol on which a party relies should be disclosed to the other party. The claimant should delay issuing proceedings for 21 days from disclosure of the report (unless such delay would cause his claim to become time-barred), to enable the parties to consider whether the claim is capable of settlement.

5.2 The Civil Procedure Rules Part 36 permit claimants and defendants to make offers to settle pre-proceedings. Parties should always consider before issuing if it is appropriate to make Part 36 Offer. If such an offer is made, the party making the offer must always supply sufficient evidence and/or information to enable the offer to be properly considered.

5.3 Where the defendant has admitted liability, the claimant should send to the defendant schedules of special damages and loss at least 21 days before proceedings are issued (unless that would cause the claimant's claim to become time-barred).

## ANNEX A

### Letter of claim

To

Defendant

Dear Sirs

**Re: Claimant's full name**
**Claimant's full address**
**Claimant's Clock or Works Number**
**Claimant's Employer (name and address)**

We are instructed by the above named to claim damages in connection with an ***accident at work/road traffic accident/tripping accident*** on day of ***(year)*** at ***(place of accident which must be sufficiently detailed to establish location)***

Please confirm the identity of your insurers. Please note that the insurers will need to see this letter as soon as possible and it may affect your insurance cover and/or the conduct of any subsequent legal proceedings if you do not send this letter to them.

The circumstances of the accident are:
**(brief outline)**

The reason why we are alleging fault is:
***(simple explanation e.g. defective machine, broken ground)***

A description of our clients' injuries is as follows:
***(brief outline)***

***(In cases of road traffic accidents)***

Our client (state hospital reference number) received treatment for the injuries at name and address of hospital).

*Our client is still suffering from the effects of his/her injury. We invite you to participate with us in addressing his/her immediate needs by use of rehabilitation.*

He is employed as ***(occupation)*** and has had the following time off work ***(dates of absence)***. His approximate weekly income is (insert if known).

***If you are our client's employers, please provide us with the usual earnings details which will enable us to calculate his financial loss.***

***We are obtaining a police report and will let you have a copy of the same upon your undertaking to meet half the fee.***

We have also sent a letter of claim to ***(name and address)*** and a copy of that letter is attached. We understand their insurers are ***(name, address and claims number if known)***.

At this stage of our enquiries we would expect the documents contained in parts ***(insert appropriate parts of standard disclosure list)*** to be relevant to this action.

*Please note that we have entered into a conditional fee agreement with our client dated in relation to this claim which provides for a success fee within the meaning of section 58(2) of the Courts and Legal Services Act 1990. Our client has taken out an insurance policy with [name of insurance company] of [address of insurance company] to which section 29 of the Access Justice Act 1999 applies. The policy number is and the policy is dated . Where the funding arrangement is an insurance policy, the party must state the name and address of the insurer, the policy number and the date of the policy, and must identify the claim or claims to which it relates (including Part 20 claims if any).*

A copy of this letter is attached for you to send to your insurers. Finally we expect an acknowledgment of this letter within 21 days by yourselves or your insurers.

Yours faithfully

## ANNEX B

## Pre-action personal injury protocol standard disclosure lists

### RTA Cases

**Section A**

In all cases where liability is at issue—

(i) Documents identifying nature, extent and location of damage to defendant's vehicle where there is any dispute about point of impact.

(ii) MOT certificate where relevant.

(iii) Maintenance records where vehicle defect is alleged or it is alleged by defendant that there was an unforeseen defect which caused or contributed to the accident.

**Section B**

Accident involving commercial vehicle as defendant—

(i) Tachograph charts or entry from individual control book.

(ii) Maintenance and repair records required for operators' licence where vehicle defect is alleged or it is alleged by defendant that there was an unforeseen defect which caused or contributed to the accident.

**Section C**

Cases against local authorities where highway design defect is alleged.

(i) Documents produced to comply with Section 39 of the Road Traffic Act 1988 in respect of the duty designed to promote road safety to include studies into road accidents in the relevant area and documents relating to measures recommended to prevent accidents in the relevant area.

### Highway tripping claims

Documents from Highway Authority for a period of 12 months prior to the accident—

(i) Records of inspection for the relevant stretch of highway.

(ii) Maintenance records including records of independent contractors working in relevant area.

(iii) Records of the minutes of Highway Authority meetings where maintenance or repair policy has been discussed or decided.

(iv) Records of complaints about the state of highways.

(v) Records of other accidents which have occurred on the relevant stretch of highway.

### Workplace claims

(i) Accident book entry.

(ii) First aider report.

(iii) Surgery record.

(iv) Foreman/supervisor accident report.

(v) Safety representatives accident report.

(vi) RIDDOR (Reporting of Injuries, Diseases and Dangerous Occurrences Regulations) report to HSE.

(vii) Other communications between defendants and HSE.

(viii) Minutes of Health and Safety Committee meeting(s) where accident/matter considered.

(ix) Report to DSS.

(x) Documents listed above relative to any previous accident/matter identified by the claimant and relied upon as proof of negligence.

(xi) Earnings information where defendant is employer.

Documents produced to comply with requirements of the Management of Health and Safety at Work Regulations 1992—

(i) Pre-accident Risk Assessment required by Regulation 3.

(ii) Post-accident Re-Assessment required by Regulation 3.

(iii) Accident Investigation Report prepared in implementing the requirements of Regulations 4, 6 and 9.

(iv) Health Surveillance Records in appropriate cases required by Regulation 5.

(v) Information provided to employees under Regulation 8.

(vi) Documents relating to the employees health and safety training required by Regulation 11.

## Workplace claims – disclosure where specific regulations apply

### Section A – Workplace (Health Safety and Welfare) Regulations 1992

(i) Repair and maintenance records required by Regulation 5.

(ii) Housekeeping records to comply with the requirements of Regulation 9.

(iii) Hazard warning signs or notices to comply with Regulation 17 (Traffic Routes).

### Section B – Provision and Use of Work Equipment Regulations 1998

(i) Manufacturers' specifications and instructions in respect of relevant work equipment establishing its suitability to comply with Regulation 5.

(ii) Maintenance log/maintenance records required to comply with Regulation 6.

(iii) Documents providing information and instructions to employees to comply with Regulation 8.

(iv) Documents provided to the employee in respect of training for use to comply with Regulation 9.

(v) Any notice, sign or document relied upon as a defence to alleged breaches of Regulations 14 to 18 dealing with controls and control systems.

(vi) Instruction/training documents issued to comply with the requirements of regulation 22 insofar as it deals with maintenance operations where the machinery is not shut down.

(vii) Copies of markings required to comply with Regulation 23.

(viii) Copies of warnings required to comply with Regulation 24.

### Section C – Personal Protective Equipment at Work Regulations 1992

(i) Documents relating to the assessment of the Personal Protective Equipment to comply with Regulation 6.

(ii) Documents relating to the maintenance and replacement of Personal Protective Equipment to comply with Regulation 7.

(iii) Record of maintenance procedures for Personal Protective Equipment to comply with Regulation 7.

(iv) Records of tests and examinations of Personal Protective Equipment to comply with Regulation 7.

(v) Documents providing information, instruction and training in relation to the Personal Protective Equipment to comply with Regulation 9.

(vi) Instructions for use of Personal Protective Equipment to include the manufacturers' instructions to comply with Regulation 10.

### Section D – Manual Handling Operations Regulations 1992

(i) Manual Handling Risk Assessment carried out to comply with the requirements of Regulation 4(1)(b)(i).

(ii) Re-assessment carried out post-accident to comply with requirements of Regulation 4(1)(b)(i).

(iii) Documents showing the information provided to the employee to give general indications related to the load and precise indications on the weight of the load and the heaviest side of the load if the centre of gravity was not positioned centrally to comply with Regulation 4(1)(b)(iii).

(iv) Documents relating to training in respect of manual handling operations and training records.

### Section E – Health and Safety (Display Screen Equipment) Regulations 1992

(i) Analysis of work stations to assess and reduce risks carried out to comply with the requirements of Regulation 2.

(ii) Re-assessment of analysis of work stations to assess and reduce risks following development of symptoms by the claimant.

(iii) Documents detailing the provision of training including training records to comply with the requirements of Regulation 6.

(iv) Documents providing information to employees to comply with the requirements of Regulation 7.

### Section F – Control of Substances Hazardous to Health Regulations 1999

(i) Risk assessment carried out to comply with the requirements of Regulation 6.

(ii) Reviewed risk assessment carried out to comply with the requirements of Regulation 6.

(iii) Copy labels from containers used for storage handling and disposal of carcinogenics to comply with the requirements of Regulation 7(2A)(h).

(iv) Warning signs identifying designation of areas and installations which may be contaminated by carcinogenics to comply with the requirements of Regulation 7(2A)(h).

(v) Documents relating to the assessment of the Personal Protective Equipment to comply with Regulation 7(3A).

(vi) Documents relating to the maintenance and replacement of Personal Protective Equipment to comply with Regulation 7(3A).

(vii) Record of maintenance procedures for Personal Protective Equipment to comply with Regulation 7(3A).

(viii) Records of tests and examinations of Personal Protective Equipment to comply with Regulation 7(3A).

(ix) Documents providing information, instruction and training in relation to the Personal Protective Equipment to comply with Regulation 7(3A).

(x) Instructions for use of Personal Protective Equipment to include the manufacturers' instructions to comply with Regulation 7(3A).

(xi) Air monitoring records for substances assigned a maximum exposure limit or occupational exposure standard to comply with the requirements of Regulation 7.

(xii) Maintenance examination and test of control measures records to comply with Regulation 9.

(xiii) Monitoring records to comply with the requirements of Regulation 10.

(xiv) Health surveillance records to comply with the requirements of Regulation 11.

(xv) Documents detailing information, instruction and training including training records for employees to comply with the requirements of Regulation 12.

(xvi) Labels and Health and Safety data sheets supplied to the employers to comply with the CHIP Regulations.

### Section G – Construction (Design and Management) (Amendment) Regulations 2000

(i) Notification of a project form (HSE F10) to comply with the requirements of Regulation 7.

(ii) Health and Safety Plan to comply with requirements of Regulation 15.

(iii) Health and Safety file to comply with the requirements of Regulations 12 and 14.

(iv) Information and training records provided to comply with the requirements of Regulation 17.

(v) Records of advice from and views of persons at work to comply with the requirements of Regulation 18.

### Section H – Pressure Systems and Transportable Gas Containers Regulations 1989

(i) Information and specimen markings provided to comply with the requirements of Regulation 5.

(ii) Written statements specifying the safe operating limits of a system to comply with the requirements of Regulation 7.

(iii) Copy of the written scheme of examination required to comply with the requirements of Regulation 8.

(iv) Examination records required to comply with the requirements of Regulation 9.

(v) Instructions provided for the use of operator to comply with Regulation 11.

(vi) Records kept to comply with the requirements of Regulation 13.

(vii) Records kept to comply with the requirements of Regulation 22.

### Section I - Lifting Operations and Lifting Equipment Regulations 1998

(i) Record kept to comply with the requirements of Regulation 6.

### Section J – The Noise at Work Regulations 1989

(i) Any risk assessment records required to comply with the requirements of Regulations 4 and 5.

(ii) Manufacturers' literature in respect of all ear protection made available to claimant to comply with the requirements of Regulation 8.

(iii) All documents provided to the employee for the provision of information to comply with Regulation 11.

### Section K – Construction (Head Protection) Regulations 1989

(i) Pre-accident assessment of head protection required to comply with Regulation 3(4).

(ii) Post-accident re-assessment required to comply with Regulation 3(5).

### Section L – The Construction (General Provisions) Regulations 1961

(i) Report prepared following inspections and examinations of excavations etc. to comply with the requirements of Regulation 9.

### Section M – Gas Containers Regulations 1989

(i) Information and specimen markings provided to comply with the requirements of Regulation 5.

(ii) Written statements specifying the safe operating limits of a system to comply with the requirements of Regulation 7.

(iii) Copy of the written scheme of examination required to comply with the requirements of Regulation 8.

(iv) Examination records required to comply with the requirements of Regulation 9.

(v) Instructions provided for the use of operator to comply with Regulation 11.

## ANNEX C

### Letter of Instruction to Medical Expert

Dear Sir,

Re: ***(Name and Address)***

D.O.B. –

Telephone No. –

Date of Accident –

We are acting for the above named in connection with injuries received in an accident which occurred on the above date. The main injuries appear to have been ***(main injuries)***.

We should be obliged if you would examine our Client and let us have a full and detailed report dealing with any relevant pre-accident medical history, the injuries sustained, treatment received and present condition, dealing in particular with the capacity for work and giving a prognosis.

It is central to our assessment of the extent of our Client's injuries to establish the extent and duration of any continuing disability. Accordingly, in the prognosis section we would ask you to specifically comment on any areas of continuing complaint or disability or impact on daily living. If there is such continuing disability you should comment upon the level of suffering or inconvenience caused and, if you are able, give your view as to when or if the complaint or disability is likely to resolve.

Please send our Client an appointment direct for this purpose. Should you be able to offer a cancellation appointment please contact our Client direct. We confirm we will be responsible for your reasonable fees.

*We are obtaining the notes and records from our Client's GP and Hospitals attended and will forward them to you when they are to hand/or please request the GP and Hospital records direct and advise that any invoice for the provision of these records should be forwarded to us.*

In order to comply with Court Rules we would be grateful if you would insert above your signature a statement that the contents are true to the best of your knowledge and belief.

In order to avoid further correspondence we can confirm that on the evidence we have there is no reason to suspect we may be pursuing a claim against the hospital or its staff.

We look forward to receiving your report within _______ weeks. If you will not be able to prepare your report within this period please telephone us upon receipt of these instructions.

When acknowledging these instructions it would assist if you could give an estimate as to the likely time scale for the provision of your report and also an indication as to your fee.

Yours faithfully

# ANNEX D

## The Rehabilitation Code

### (Code of Best Practice on Rehabilitation, Early Intervention and Medical Treatment in Personal Injury Claims)

The main aim of this Code, first introduced in 1999, is to promote the use of rehabilitation and early intervention in the claims process so that the injured person makes the best and quickest possible medical, social and psychological recovery. This objective applies whatever the severity of the injury sustained by the claimant. The Code provides a framework supported by all the main associations for insurers and personal injury lawyers in the UK, but is neither compulsory nor the only way to approach rehabilitation. The objectives of the Rehabilitation Code will be met whenever the parties co-operate to assess and then provide for the claimant's rehabilitation needs.

### 1. Introduction

1.1 It is recognised that, in many claims for damages for personal injuries, the claimant's current medical situation, and/or the long-term prognosis, may be improved by appropriate medical treatment, including surgery, being given at the earliest practicable opportunity, rather than waiting until the claim has been settled. Similarly, claims may involve a need for non-medical treatment, such as physiotherapy, counselling, occupational therapy, speech therapy and so forth ('rehabilitation'): again, there is a benefit in these services being provided as early as practicable.

1.2 It is also recognised that (predominantly in cases of serious injury) the claimant's quality of life can be immediately improved by undertaking some basic home adaptations and/or by the provision of aids and equipment and/or appropriate medical treatment as soon as these are needed ('early intervention'), rather than when the claim is finally settled.

1.3 It is further recognised that, where these medical or other issues have been dealt with, there may be employment issues that can be addressed for the benefit of the claimant, to enable the claimant to keep his/her existing job, to obtain alternative suitable employment with the same employer or to retrain for new employment. Again, if these needs are addressed at the proper time, the claimant's quality of life and long-term prospects may be greatly improved.

1.4 Solicitors acting for claimants understand that, taking all these matters into account, they can achieve more for the claimant – by making rehabilitation available – than just the payment of compensation. The insurance industry realises that great benefit may be had in considering making funds available for these purposes.

1.5 The aim of this Rehabilitation Code is therefore to ensure that the claimant's solicitor and the insurer (and the insurer's solicitor or handling agent) both actively consider the use of rehabilitation services and the benefits of an early assessment of the claimant's needs. The further aim is that both should treat the possibility of improving the claimant's quality of life and their present and long-term physical and mental well-being as issues equally as important as the payment of just, full and proper compensation.

1.6 The report mentioned in section 6 of the Code focuses on the early assessment of the claimant's needs in terms of treatment and/or rehabilitation. The assessment report is not intended to determine the claimant's long-term needs for care or medical treatment, other than by way of general indication and comment.

### 2. The Claimant's Solicitor's Duty

2.1 It shall be the duty of every claimant's solicitor to consider, from the earliest practicable stage, and in consultation with the claimant and/or the claimant's family, whether it is likely or possible that early intervention, rehabilitation or medical treatment would improve their present and/or long-term physical or mental well-being. This duty is ongoing throughout the life of the case but is of most importance in the early stages.

2.2 It shall be the duty of a claimant's solicitor to consider, with the claimant and/or the claimant's family, whether there is an immediate need for aids, adaptations or other matters that would seek to alleviate problems caused by disability, and then to communicate with the insurer as soon as practicable about any rehabilitation needs, with a view to putting this Code into effect.

2.3 It shall not be the responsibility of the solicitor to decide on the need for treatment or rehabilitation or to arrange such matters without appropriate medical consultation. Such medical consultation should involve the claimant and/or the claimant's family, the claimant's primary care physician and, where appropriate, any other medical practitioner currently treating the claimant.

2.4 Nothing in this Code shall in any way affect the obligations placed on a claimant's solicitor by the Pre-Action Protocol for Personal Injury Claims ('the Protocol'). However, it must be appreciated that very early communication with the insurer will enable the matters dealt with here to be addressed more effectively.

2.5 It must be recognised that the insurer will need to receive from the claimant's solicitor sufficient information for the insurer to make a proper decision about the need for intervention, rehabilitation or treatment. To this extent, the claimant's solicitor must comply with the requirements of the Protocol to provide the insurer with full and adequate details of the injuries sustained by the claimant, the nature and extent of any, or any likely, continuing disability and any suggestions that may already have been made concerning rehabilitation and/or early intervention. There is no requirement under the Protocol, or this Code, for the claimant's solicitor to have obtained a full medical report. It is recognised that many cases will be identified for consideration under this Code before medical evidence has actually been commissioned.

### 3. The Insurer

3.1 It shall be the duty of the insurer to consider, from the earliest practicable stage in any appropriate case, whether it is likely that the claimant will benefit in the immediate, medium or longer term from further medical treatment, rehabilitation or early intervention. This duty is ongoing throughout the life of the case but is of most importance in the early stages.

3.2 If the insurer considers that a particular claim might be suitable for intervention, rehabilitation or treatment, the insurer will communicate this to the claimant's solicitor as soon as practicable.

3.3 On receipt of such communication, the claimant's solicitor will immediately discuss these issues with the claimant and/or the claimant's family pursuant to his duty as set out above and, where appropriate, will seek advice from the claimant's treating physicians/surgeons.

3.4 Nothing in this or any other Code of Practice shall in any way modify the obligations of the insurer under the Protocol to investigate claims rapidly and in any event within three months (except where time is extended by the claimant's solicitor) from the date of the formal claim letter. It is recognised that, although the rehabilitation assessment can be done even where liability investigations are outstanding, it is essential that such investigations proceed with the appropriate speed.

### 4. Assessment

4.1 Unless the need for intervention, rehabilitation or treatment has already been identified by medical reports obtained and disclosed by either side, the need for and extent of such intervention, rehabilitation or treatment will be considered by means of an independent assessment.

4.2 'Independent assessment' in this context means that the assessment will be carried out by either:

a. One or more of the treating physicians/surgeons, or

b. By an agency suitably qualified and/or experienced in such matters, which is financially and managerially independent of the claimant's solicitor's firm and the insurers dealing with the claim.

4.3 It is essential that the process of assessment and recommendation be carried out by those who have an appropriate qualification (to include physiotherapists, occupational therapists, psychologists, psychotherapists and so forth). It would be inappropriate for assessments to be done by someone who does not have a medical or other appropriate qualification. Those doing the assessments should not only have an appropriate qualification but should have experience in treating the type of disability from which the individual claimant suffers.

## 5. The Assessment Process

5.1 Where possible, the agency to be instructed to provide the assessment should be agreed between the claimant's solicitor and the insurer. The instruction letter will be sent by the claimant's solicitor to the medical agency and a copy of the instruction letter will be sent to the insurer.

5.2 The medical agency will be asked to interview the claimant at home (or in hospital, if the claimant is still in hospital, with a subsequent visit to the claimant's home) and will be asked to produce a report, which covers the following headings:

1. The injuries sustained by the claimant
2. The claimant's present medical condition (medical conditions that do not arise from the accident should also be noted where relevant to the overall picture of the claimant's needs)
3. The claimant's domestic circumstances (including mobility, accommodation and employment), where relevant
4. The injuries/disability in respect of which early intervention or early rehabilitation is suggested
5. The type of intervention or treatment envisaged
6. The likely cost
7. The likely short/medium-term benefit to the claimant

5.3 The report will not deal with diagnostic criteria, causation issues or long-term care requirements.

## 6. The Assessment Report

6.1 The reporting agency will, on completion of the report, send copies to both the instructing solicitor and the insurer simultaneously. Both parties will have the right to raise queries on the report, disclosing such correspondence to the other party.

6.2 It is recognised that for this independent assessment report to be of benefit to the parties, it should be prepared and used wholly outside the litigation process. Neither side can therefore rely on its contents in any subsequent litigation. With that strict proviso, to be confirmed in writing by the individual solicitor and insurer if required, the report shall be disclosed to both parties.

6.3 The report, any correspondence relating to it and any notes created by the assessing agency will be covered by legal privilege and will not under any circumstances be disclosed in any legal proceedings. Any notes or documents created in connection with the assessment process will not be disclosed in any litigation, and any person involved in the preparation of the report or involved in the assessment process shall not be a compellable witness at court.

6.4 The provision in paragraph 6.3 above as to treating the report, etc. as outside the litigation process is limited to the assessment report and any notes relating to it. Once the parties have agreed, following an assessment report, that a particular regime of rehabilitation or treatment should be put in place, the case management of that regime falls outside this Code and paragraph 6.3 does not therefore apply. Any notes and reports created during the subsequent case management will be governed by the usual principles relating to disclosure of documents and medical records relating to the claimant.

6.5 The insurer will pay for the report within 28 days of receipt.

6.6 The need for any further or subsequent assessment shall be agreed between the claimant's solicitor and the insurer. The provisions of this Code shall apply to such assessments.

## 7. Recommendations

7.1 When the assessment report is disclosed to the insurer, the insurer will be under a duty to consider the recommendations made and the extent to which funds will be made available to implement all or some of the recommendations. The insurer will not be required to pay for intervention or treatment that is unreasonable in nature, content or cost. The claimant will be under no obligation to undergo intervention, medical investigation or treatment that is unreasonable in all the circumstances of the case.

7.2 Any funds made available shall be treated as an interim payment on account of damages. However, if the funds are provided to enable specific intervention, rehabilitation or treatment to occur, the insurers warrant that they will not, in any legal proceedings connected with the claim, dispute the reasonableness of that treatment nor the agreed cost, provided of course that the claimant has had the recommended treatment.

# Appendix 3
## Pre-action Protocol for Disease and Illness Claims

### Contents



**Annexes**



### 1 Introduction

1.1 Lord Woolf in his final Access to Justice Report of July 1996 recommended the development of protocols: 'To build on and increase the benefits of early but well informed settlement which genuinely satisfy both parties to dispute.'

1.2 The aims of these protocols are:

- more contact between the parties
- better and earlier exchange of information
- better investigation by both sides
- to put the parties in a position where they may be able to settle cases fairly and early without litigation
- to enable proceedings to run to the court's timetable and efficiently, if litigation does become necessary.

1.3 The concept of protocols is relevant to a range of initiatives for good claims practice, especially:

- predictability in the time needed for steps to be taken
- standardisation of relevant information, including documents to be disclosed.

1.4 The Courts will be able to treat the standards set in protocols as the normal reasonable approach. If proceedings are issued, it will be for the court to decide whether non-compliance with a protocol should merit adverse consequences. Guidance on the court's likely approach will be given from time to time in practice directions.

1.5 If the court has to consider the question of compliance after proceedings have begun, it will not be concerned with minor infringements, eg, failure by a short period to provide relevant information. One minor breach will not exempt the 'innocent' party from following the protocol. The court will look at the effect of non-compliance on the other party when deciding whether to impose sanctions.

## 2 NOTES OF GUIDANCE

### Scope of the protocol

2.1 This protocol is intended to apply to all personal injury claims where the injury is not as the result of an accident but takes the form of an illness or disease.

2.2 This protocol covers disease claims which are likely to be complex and frequently not suitable for fast-track procedures even though they may fall within fast track limits. Disease for the purpose of this protocol primarily covers any illness physical or psychological, any disorder, ailment, affliction, complaint, malady, or derangement other than a physical or psychological injury solely caused by an accident or other similar single event.

2.3 This protocol is not limited to diseases occurring in the workplace but will embrace diseases occurring in other situations for example through occupation of premises or the use of products. It is not intended to cover those cases, which are dealt with as a 'group' or 'class' action.

2.4 The 'cards on the table' approach advocated by the personal injury protocol is equally appropriate to disease claims. The spirit of that protocol, and of the clinical negligence protocol is followed here, in accordance with the sense of the civil justice reforms.

2.5 The timetable and the arrangements for disclosing documents and obtaining expert evidence may need to be varied to suit the circumstances of the case. If a party considers the detail of the protocol to be inappropriate they should communicate their reasons to all of the parties at that stage. If proceedings are subsequently issued, the court will expect an explanation as to why the protocol has not been followed, or has been varied. In a terminal disease claim with short life expectancy, for instance for a claimant who has a disease such as mesothelioma, the time scale of the protocol is likely to be too long. In such a claim, the claimant may not be able to follow the protocol and the defendant would be expected to treat the claim with urgency.

## 3 THE AIMS OF THE PROTOCOL

3.1 The ***general*** aims of the protocol are –

- to resolve as many disputes as possible without litigation;
- where a claim cannot be resolved to identify the relevant issues which remain in dispute.

3.2 The specific objectives are –

#### Openness

- to encourage early communication of the perceived problem between the parties or their insurers;
- to encourage employees to voice any concerns or worries about possible work related illness as soon as practicable;
- to encourage employers to develop systems of early reporting and investigation of suspected occupational health problems and to provide full and prompt explanations to concerned employees or former employees;
- to apply such principles to perceived problems outside the employer/ employee relationship, for example occupiers of premises or land and producers of products;
- to ensure that sufficient information is disclosed by both parties to enable each to understand the other's perspective and case, and to encourage early resolution;

### Timeliness

- to provide an early opportunity for employers (past or present) or their insurers to identify cases where an investigation is required and to carry out that investigation promptly;
- to encourage employers (past or present) or other defendants to involve and identify their insurers at an early stage;
- to ensure that all relevant records including health and personnel records are provided to employees (past or present) or their appointed representatives promptly on request, by any employer (past or present) or their insurers. This should be complied with to a realistic timetable;
- to ensure that relevant records which are in the claimant's possession are made available to the employers or their insurers by claimants or their advisers at an appropriate stage;
- to proceed on a reasonable timetable where a resolution is not achievable to lay the ground to enable litigation to proceed at a reasonable and proportionate cost, and to limit the matters in contention;
- to communicate promptly where any of the requested information is not available or does not exist;
- to discourage the prolonged pursuit of unmeritorious claims and the prolonged defence of meritorious claims.
- To encourage all parties, at the earliest possible stage, to disclose voluntarily any additional documents which will assist in resolving any issue.

## 4 THE PROTOCOL

This protocol is not a comprehensive code governing all the steps in disease claims. Rather it attempts to set out **a code of good practice** which parties should follow.

### Obtaining occupational records including health records

4.1 In appropriate cases, a **potential claimant** may request Occupational Records including Health Records and Personnel Records before sending a Letter of Claim.

4.2 Any request for records by the **potential claimant** or his adviser should **provide sufficient information** to alert the **potential defendant** or his insurer where a possible disease claim is being investigated; Annex A1 provides a suggested form for this purpose for use in cases arising from employment. Similar forms can be prepared and used in other situations.

4.3 The copy records should be provided **within a maximum of 40 days** of the request at no cost. Although these will primarily be occupational records, it will be good practice for a **potential defendant** to disclose product data documents identified by a **potential claimant** at this stage which may resolve a causation issue.

4.4 In the rare circumstances that the **potential defendant** or his insurer is in difficulty in providing information quickly details should be given of what is being done to resolve it with a reasonable time estimate for doing so.

4.5 If the **potential defendant** or his insurer fails to provide the records including health records within 40 days and fails to comply with paragraph 4.4 above, the **potential claimant** or his adviser may then apply to the court for an **order for pre-action disclosure**. The Civil Procedure Rules make pre-action applications to the court easier. The court also has the power to impose costs sanctions for unreasonable delay in providing records.

## 5 COMMUNICATION

5.1 If either the **potential claimant** or his adviser considers **additional records are required from a third party**, such as records from previous employers or general practitioner records, in the first instance these should be requested by the **potential claimant** or their advisers. Third party record holders would be expected to co-operate. The Civil Procedure Rules enable parties to apply to the court for pre-action disclosure by third parties.

5.2 As soon as the records have been received and analysed, the **potential claimant** or his adviser should consider whether a claim should be made. General practitioner records will normally be obtained before a decision is reached.

5.3 If a decision is made not to proceed further at this stage against a party identified as a **potential defendant**, the **potential claimant** or his adviser should notify that **potential defendant** as soon as practicable.

## 6 LETTER OF CLAIM

6.1 Where a decision is made to make a claim, the claimant shall send to the proposed defendant two copies of a letter of claim, as soon as sufficient information is available to substantiate a realistic claim and before issues of quantum are addressed in detail. One copy is for the defendants, the second for passing on to his insurers.

6.2 This letter shall contain a **clear summary of the facts** on which the claim is based, including details of the illness alleged, and the **main allegations of fault**. It shall also give details of present condition and prognosis. The **financial loss** incurred by the claimant should be outlined. Where the case is funded by a conditional fee agreement, notification should be given of the existence of the agreement and where appropriate, that there is a success fee and insurance premium, although not the level of the success fee or premium.

6.3 Solicitors are recommended to use a **standard format** for such a letter – an example is at Annex B: this can be amended to suit the particular case, for example, if the client has rehabilitation needs these can also be detailed in the letter.

6.4 A **chronology** of the relevant events (e.g. dates or periods of exposure) should be provided. In the case of alleged occupational disease an appropriate employment history should also be provided, particularly if the claimant has been employed by a number of different employers and the illness in question has a long latency period.

6.5 The letter of claim should identify any **relevant documents**, including health records not already in the defendant's possession e.g. any relevant general practitioner records. These will need to be disclosed in confidence to the nominated insurance manager or solicitor representing the defendant following receipt of their letter of acknowledgement. Where the action is brought under the Law Reform Act 1934 or the Fatal Accidents Act 1976 then **relevant documents** will normally include copies of the death certificate, the post mortem report, the inquest depositions and if obtained by that date the grant of probate or letters of administration.

6.6 The letter of claim should indicate whether a claim is also being made against any **other potential defendant** and identify any known insurer involved.

6.7 Sufficient information should be given to enable the defendant's insurer/ solicitor to commence **investigations** and at least to put a broad valuation on the 'risk'.

6.8 It is not a requirement for the claimant to provide **medical evidence** with the letter of claim, but the claimant may choose to do so in very many cases.

6.9 **Letters of claim and response** are not intended to have the same **status** as a statement of case in proceedings. Matters may come to light as a result of investigation after the letter of claim has been sent, or after the defendant has responded, particularly if disclosure of documents takes place outside the recommended three-month period. These circumstances could mean that the 'pleaded' case of one or both parties is presented slightly differently than in the letter of claim or response. It would not be consistent with the spirit of the protocol for a party to 'take a point' on this in the proceedings, provided that there was no obvious intention by the party who changed their position to mislead the other party.

6.10 **Proceedings should not be issued until after three months from the date of acknowledgement** (see paragraph 7), unless there is a limitation problem and/or the claimant's position needs to be protected by early issue. (See paragraph 2.5)

## 7 THE RESPONSE

7.1 The defendant should **send an acknowledgement within 21 calendar days** of the date of posting of the letter of claim, identifying the liability insurer (if any) who will be dealing with the matter and, if necessary, identifying specifically any significant omissions from the Letter of Claim. If there has been no acknowledgement by the defendant or insurer within 21 days, the claimant will be entitled to issue proceedings.

7.2 The identity of all relevant insurers, if more than one, should be notified to the claimant by the insurer identified in the acknowledgement letter, within one calendar month of the date of that acknowledgement.

7.3 The defendant or his representative should, **within three months of the date of the acknowledgement letter**, provide a **reasoned answer**: –

- if the **claim is admitted**, they should say so in clear terms;
- if only **part of the claim is admitted** they should make clear which issues of fault and/or causation and/or limitation are admitted and which remain in issue and why;
- if the **claim is not admitted in full**, they should explain why and should, **for example**, include comments on the employment status of the claimant, (including job description(s) and details of the department(s) where the claimant worked), the allegations of fault, causation and of limitation, and if a synopsis or chronology of relevant events has been provided and is disputed, their version of those events;
- if the **claim is not admitted in full**, the defendant should enclose with his letter of reply **documents** in his possession which are **material to the issues** between the parties and which would be likely to be ordered to be disclosed by the court, either on an application for pre-action disclosure, or on disclosure during proceedings. Reference can be made to the documents annexed to the personal injury protocol.
- where more than one defendant receives a letter of claim, the timetable will be activated for each defendant by the date on the letter of claim addressed to them. If any defendant wishes to extend the timetable because the number of defendants will cause complications, they should seek agreement to a different timetable as soon as possible.

7.4 If the parties reach agreement on liability and/or causation, but time is needed to resolve other issues including the value of the claim, they should aim to agree a reasonable period.

7.5 Where it is not practicable for the defendant to complete his investigations within 3 months, the defendant should indicate the difficulties and outline the further time needed. Any request for an extension of time should be made, with reasons, as soon as the defendant becomes aware that an extension is needed and normally before the 3 month period has expired. Such an extension of time should be agreed in circumstances where reasonable justification has been shown. Lapse of many years since the circumstances giving rise to the claim does not, by itself, constitute reasonable justification for further time.

7.6 Where the relevant negligence occurred outside England and Wales and/or where the defendant is outside the jurisdiction, the time periods of 21 days and three months should normally be extended up to 42 days and six months.

## 8 SPECIAL DAMAGES

8.1 The claimant will send to the defendant as soon as practicable a Schedule of Special Damages with supporting documents, particularly where the defendant has admitted liability.

## 9 EXPERTS

9.1 In disease claims expert opinions will usually be needed:

- on knowledge, fault and causation;
- on condition and prognosis;
- to assist in valuing aspects of the claim.

9.2 The civil justice reforms and the Civil Procedure Rules encourage economy in the use of experts and a less adversarial expert culture. It is recognised that in disease claims, the parties and their advisers will require flexibility in their approach to expert evidence. Decisions on whether experts might be instructed jointly, and on whether reports might be disclosed sequentially or by exchange, should rest with the parties and their advisers. Sharing expert evidence may be appropriate on various issues including those relating to the value of the claim. However, this protocol does not attempt to be prescriptive on issues in relation to expert evidence.

9.3 Obtaining expert evidence will often be an expensive step and may take time, especially in specialised areas where there are limited numbers of suitable experts. Claimants, defendants and their advisers, will therefore need to consider carefully how best to obtain any necessary expert help quickly and cost-effectively.

9.4 The protocol recognises that a flexible approach must be adopted in the obtaining of medical reports in claims of this type. There will be very many occasions where the claimant will need to obtain a medical report before writing the letter of claim. In such cases the defendant will be entitled to obtain their own medical report. In some other instances it may be more appropriate to send the letter of claim before the medical report is obtained. Defendants will usually need to see a medical report before they can reach a view on causation.

9.5 Where the parties agree the nomination of a single expert is appropriate, before any party instructs an expert he should give the other party a list of the **name**(s) of **one or more experts** in the relevant speciality whom he considers are suitable to instruct. The parties are encouraged to agree the instruction of a single expert to deal with discrete areas such as cost of care.

9.6 **Within 14 days** the other party may indicate **an objection** to one or more of the named experts. The first party should then instruct a mutually acceptable expert. If the Claimant nominates an expert in the original letter of claim, the 14 days is in addition to the 21 days in paragraph 7.1.

9.7 If the second party objects to all the listed experts, the parties may then instruct **experts of their own choice**. It would be for the court to decide subsequently, if proceedings are issued, whether either party had acted unreasonably.

9.8 If the **second party does not object to an expert nominated**, he shall not be entitled to rely on his own expert evidence within that particular speciality unless:

(a) the first party agrees,

(b) the court so directs, or

(c) the first party's expert report has been amended and the first party is not prepared to disclose the original report.

9.9 **Either party may send to an agreed expert written questions** on the report, relevant to the issues, via the first party's solicitors. The expert should send answers to the questions separately and directly to each party.

9.10 The cost of a report from an agreed expert will usually be paid by the instructing first party: the costs of the expert replying to questions will usually be borne by the party which asks the questions.

9.11 Where the defendant admits liability in whole or in part, before proceedings are issued, any medical report obtained under this protocol which **the claimant** relies upon, should be disclosed to the other party.

9.12 Where the defendant admits liability in whole or in part before proceedings are issued, any medical report obtained under this protocol which **the defendant** relies upon, should be disclosed to the claimant.

## 10 RESOLUTION OF ISSUES

10.1 The Civil Procedure Rules Part 36 enable claimants and defendants to make formal offers to settle before proceedings are started. Parties should consider making such an offer, since to do so often leads to settlement. If such an offer is made, the party making the offer must always supply sufficient evidence and/or information to enable the offer to be properly considered.

10.2 Where a claim is not resolved when the protocol has been followed, the parties might wish to carry out a 'stocktake' of the issues in dispute, and the evidence that the court is likely to need to decide those issues, before proceedings are started.

10.3 Prior to proceedings it will be usual for all parties to disclose those expert reports relating to liability and causation upon which they propose to rely.

10.4 The claimant should delay issuing proceedings for 21 days from disclosure of reports to enable the parties to consider whether the claim is capable of settlement.

10.5 Where the defendant is insured and the pre-action steps have been conducted by the insurer, the insurer would normally be expected to nominate solicitors to act in the proceedings and the claimant's solicitor is recommended to invite the insurer to nominate solicitors to act in the proceedings and to do so 7–14 days before the intended issue date.

## 11 LIMITATION

11.1 If by reason of complying with any part of this protocol a claimant's claim may be time-barred under any provision of the Limitation Act 1980, or any other legislation which imposes a time limit for bringing an action, the claimant may commence proceedings without complying with this protocol. In such circumstances, a claimant who commences proceedings without complying with all, or any part, of this protocol may apply to the court on notice for directions as to the timetable and form of procedure to be adopted, at the same time as he requests the court to issue proceedings. The court will consider whether to order a stay of the whole or part of the proceedings pending compliance with this protocol.

## ANNEX A

### Letter requesting occupational records including health records

Dear Sirs,

We are acting on behalf of the above-named who has developed the following ***(insert disease).*** We are investigating whether this disease may have been caused: -

- **during the course of his employment with you / name of employer if different**
- **whilst at your premises at (address)**
- **as a result of your product (name)**

We are writing this in accordance with the Protocol for Disease and Illness Claims

We seek the following records:-

***(Insert details eg, personnel / occupational health)***

Please note your insurers may require you to advise them of this request.

We enclose a request form and expect to receive the records within 40 days.

If you are not able to comply with this request within this time, please advise us of the reason.

Yours faithfully

## ANNEX A1

### Application on behalf of a potential claimant for use where a disease claim is being investigated

This should be completed as fully as possible

Company

Name

And

Address

| | | |
|---|---|---|
| 1 a) | Full name of claimant (including previous surnames) | |
| b) | Address now | |
| c) | Address at date of termination of employment, if different | |
| d) | Date of birth (and death, if applicable) | |
| e) | National Insurance number, if available | |
| 2 | Department(s) where claimant worked | |
| 3 | This application is made because the claimant is considering | |
| a) | a claim against you as detailed in para 4 | YES/NO |
| b) | Pursuing an action against someone else | YES/NO |

| | | |
|---|---|---|
| 4 | If the answer to Q3(a) is 'Yes' details of | |
| | a) the likely nature of the claim, eg dermatitis | |
| | b) grounds for the claim, eg exposure to chemical | |
| | c) approximate dates of the events involved | |
| 5 | If the answer to Q3(b) is 'Yes' insert | |
| | a) the names of the proposed defendants | |
| | b) have legal proceedings been started? | YES/NO |
| | c) if appropriate, details of the claim and action number | |
| 6 | Any other relevant information or documents requested | |
| | Signature of Solicitor | |
| | Name | |
| | Address | |
| | Ref. | |
| | Telephone Number | |
| | Fax number | |

I authorise you to disclose all of your records relating to me/the claimant to my solicitor and to your legal and insurance representatives.

Signature of Claimant

Signature of personal representative where claimant has died

## ANNEX B

### Template for letter of claim

To: Defendant

Dear Sirs

**Re: Claimant's full name**
**Claimant's full address**
**Claimant's National Insurance Number**
**Claimant's Date of Birth**
**Claimant's Clock or Works Number**
**Claimant's Employer *(name and address)***

We are instructed by the above named to claim damages in connection with a claim for: - ***Specify occupational disease***

We are writing this letter in accordance with the pre-action protocol for disease and illness claims.

Please confirm the identity of your insurers. Please note that your insurers will need to see this letter as soon as possible and it may affect your insurance cover if you do not send this to them.

The Claimant was employed by you ***(if the claim arises out of public or occupiers' liability give appropriate details)*** as ***job description*** from ***date*** to ***date.*** During the relevant period of his employment he worked:
***description of precisely where the Claimant worked and what he did to include a description of any machines used and details of any exposure to noise or substances***

The circumstances leading to the development of this condition are as follows:
***Give chronology of events***

The reason why we are alleging fault is:
***Details should be given of contemporary and comparable employees who have suffered from similar problems if known; any protective equipment provided; complaints; the supervisors concerned, if known.***

Our client's employment history is attached.

***We have also made a claim against:***
***Insert details***
***Their insurers' details are:***
***Insert if known***

We have the following documents in support of our client's claim and will disclose these in confidence to your nominated insurance manager or solicitor when we receive their acknowledgement letter.
***eg, Occupational health notes; GP notes***

***We have obtained a medical report from (name) and will disclose this when we receive your acknowledgement of this letter.***
***(This is optional at this stage)***

From the information we presently have:

*(i)* the Claimant first became aware of symptoms on ***(insert approximate date)***

*(ii)* the Claimant first received medical advice about those symptoms on ***(insert date) (give details of advice given if appropriate)***

*(iii)* the Claimant first believed that those symptoms might be due to exposure leading to this claim on ***(insert approximate date)***

A description of our client's condition is as follows:
***This should be sufficiently detailed to allow the Defendant to put a broad value on the claim***

He has the following time off work:
***Insert dates***

He is presently employed as a ***job description*** and his average net weekly income is **£**

***If you are our client's employers, please provide us with the usual earnings details, which will enable us to calculate his financial loss.***

***Please note that we have entered into a conditional fee agreement with our client dated in relation to this claim which provides for a success fee within the meaning of section 58(2) of***

***the Courts and Legal Services Act 1990. Our client has taken out an insurance policy dated with (name of insurance company) to which section 29 of the Access to Justice Act 1999 applies in respect of this claim.***

A copy of this letter is attached for you to send to your insurers. Finally we expect an acknowledgement of this letter within 21 days by yourselves or your insurers.

Yours faithfully

# Appendix 4

# Pre-action Protocol for the Resolution of Clinical Disputes

## Contents



## Executive Summary

1 The Clinical Disputes Forum is a multi-disciplinary body which was formed in 1997, as a result of Lord Woolf's 'Access to Justice' inquiry. One of the aims of the Forum is to find less adversarial and more cost effective ways of resolving disputes about healthcare and medical treatment. The names and addresses of the Chairman and Secretary of the Forum can be found at Annex E.

2 This protocol is the Forum's first major initiative. It has been drawn up carefully, including extensive consultations with most of the key stakeholders in the medico-legal system.

3 The protocol—

- encourages a climate of openness when something has 'gone wrong' with a patient's treatment or the patient is dissatisfied with that treatment and/or the outcome. This reflects the new and developing requirements for clinical governance within healthcare;
- provides **general guidance** on how this more open culture might be achieved when disputes arise;
- recommends **a timed sequence** of steps for patients and healthcare providers, and their advisers, to follow when a dispute arises. This should facilitate and speed up exchanging relevant information and increase the prospects that disputes can be resolved without resort to legal action.

4 This protocol has been prepared by a working party of the Clinical Disputes Forum. It has the support of the Lord Chancellor's Department, the Department of Health and NHS Executive, the Law Society, the Legal Aid Board and many other key organisations.

## 1 Why this Protocol?

### Mistrust in healthcare disputes

1.1 The number of complaints and claims against hospitals, GPs, dentists and private healthcare providers is growing as patients become more prepared to question the treatment they are given, to seek explanations of what happened, and to seek appropriate redress. Patients may require further treatment, an apology, assurances about future action, or compensation. These trends are unlikely to change. The Patients' Charter encourages patients to have high expectations, and a revised NHS Complaints Procedure was implemented in 1996. The civil justice reforms and new Rules of Court should make litigation quicker, more user friendly and less expensive.

1.2 It is clearly in the interests of patients, healthcare professionals and providers that patients' concerns, complaints and claims arising from their treatment are resolved as quickly, efficiently and professionally as possible. A climate of mistrust and lack of openness can seriously damage the patient/clinician relationship, unnecessarily prolong disputes (especially litigation), and reduce the resources available for treating patients. It may also cause additional work for, and lower the morale of, healthcare professionals.

1.3 At present there is often mistrust by both sides. This can mean that patients fail to raise their concerns with the healthcare provider as early as possible. Sometimes patients may pursue a complaint or claim which has little merit, due to a lack of sufficient information and understanding. It can also mean that patients become reluctant, once advice has been taken on a potential claim, to disclose sufficient information to enable the provider to investigate that claim efficiently and, where appropriate, resolve it.

1.4 On the side of the healthcare provider this mistrust can be shown in a reluctance to be honest with patients, a failure to provide prompt clear explanations, especially of adverse outcomes (whether or not there may have been negligence) and a tendency to 'close ranks' once a claim is made.

### What needs to change

1.5 If that mistrust is to be removed, and a more co-operative culture is to develop—

- healthcare professionals and providers need to adopt a constructive approach to complaints and claims. They should accept that concerned patients are entitled to an explanation and an apology, if warranted, and to appropriate redress in the event of negligence. An overly defensive approach is not in the long-term interest of their main goal: patient care;
- patients should recognise that unintended and/or unfortunate consequences of medical treatment can only be rectified if they are brought to the attention of the healthcare provider as soon as possible.

1.6 A protocol which sets out 'ground rules' for the handling of disputes at their early stages should, if it is to be subscribed to, and followed—

- encourage greater openness between the parties;
- encourage parties to find the most appropriate way of resolving the particular dispute;
- reduce delay and costs;
- reduce the need for litigation.

### Why this protocol now?

1.7 Lord Woolf in his Access to Justice Report in July 1996, concluded that major causes of costs and delay in medical negligence litigation occur at the pre-action stage. He recommended that patients and their advisers, and healthcare providers, should work more closely together to try to resolve disputes co-operatively, rather than proceed to litigation. He specifically recommended a pre-action protocol for medical negligence cases.

1.8 A fuller summary of Lord Woolf's recommendations is at Annex D.

### Where the protocol fits in

1.9 Protocols serve the needs of litigation and pre-litigation practice, especially—

- predictability in the time needed for steps pre-proceedings;
- standardisation of relevant information, including records and documents to be disclosed.

1.10 Building upon Lord Woolf's recommendations, the Lord Chancellor's Department is now promoting the adoption of protocols in specific areas, including medical negligence.

1.11 It is recognised that contexts differ significantly. For example, patients tend to have an ongoing relationship with a GP, more so than with a hospital; clinical staff in the National Health Service are often employees, while those in the private sector may be contractors; providing records quickly may be relatively easy for GPs and dentists, but can be a complicated procedure in a large multi-department hospital. The protocol which follows is intended to be sufficiently broadly based, and flexible, to apply to all aspects of the health service: primary and secondary; public and private sectors.

### Enforcement of the protocol and sanctions

1.12 The civil justice reforms will be implemented in April 1999. One new set of Court Rules and procedures is replacing the existing rules for both the High Court and county courts. This and the personal injury protocol are being published with the Rules, Practice Directions and key court forms. The courts will be able to treat the standards set in protocols as the normal reasonable approach to pre-action conduct.

1.13 If proceedings are issued it will be for the court to decide whether non-compliance with a protocol should merit sanctions. Guidance on the court's likely approach will be given from time to time in practice directions.

1.14 If the court has to consider the question of compliance after proceedings have begun it will not be concerned with minor infringements, eg, failure by a short period to provide relevant information. One minor breach will not entitle the 'innocent' party to abandon following the protocol. The court will look at the effect of non-compliance on the other party when deciding whether to impose sanctions.

## 2 The aims of the Protocol

2.1 The **general** aims of the protocol are—

- to maintain/restore the patient/healthcare provider relationship;
- to resolve as many disputes as possible without litigation.

2.2 The **specific** objectives are—

### Openness

- to encourage early communication of the perceived problem between patients and healthcare providers;
- to encourage patients to voice any concerns or dissatisfaction with their treatment as soon as practicable;
- to encourage healthcare providers to develop systems of early reporting and investigation for serious adverse treatment outcomes and to provide full and prompt explanations to dissatisfied patients;
- to ensure that sufficient information is disclosed by both parties to enable each to understand the other's perspective and case, and to encourage early resolution.

### Timeliness

- to provide an early opportunity for healthcare providers to identify cases where an investigation is required and to carry out that investigation promptly;
- to encourage primary and private healthcare providers to involve their defence organisations or insurers at an early stage;

- to ensure that all relevant medical records are provided to patients or their appointed representatives on request, to a realistic timetable by any healthcare provider;
- to ensure that relevant records which are not in healthcare providers' possession are made available to them by patients and their advisers at an appropriate stage;
- where a resolution is not achievable to lay the ground to enable litigation to proceed on a reasonable timetable, at a reasonable and proportionate cost and to limit the matters in contention;
- to discourage the prolonged pursuit of unmeritorious claims and the prolonged defence of meritorious claims.

### Awareness of options

- to ensure that patients and healthcare providers are made aware of the available options to pursue and resolve disputes and what each might involve.

2.3 This protocol does not attempt to be prescriptive about a number of related clinical governance issues which will have a bearing on healthcare providers' ability to meet the standards within the protocol. Good clinical governance requires the following to be considered—

(a) **Clinical risk management:** the protocol does not provide any detailed guidance to healthcare providers on clinical risk management or the adoption of risk management systems and procedures. This must be a matter for the NHS Executive, the National Health Service Litigation Authority, individual trusts and providers, including GPs, dentists and the private sector. However, effective co-ordinated, focused clinical risk management strategies and procedures can help in managing risk and in the early identification and investigation of adverse outcomes.

(b) **Adverse outcome reporting:** the protocol does not provide any detailed guidance on which adverse outcomes should trigger an investigation. However, healthcare providers should have in place procedures for such investigations, including recording of statements of key witnesses. These procedures should also cover when and how to inform patients that an adverse outcome has occurred.

(c) **The professional's duty to report:** the protocol does not recommend changes to the codes of conduct of professionals in healthcare, or attempt to impose a specific duty on those professionals to report known adverse outcomes or untoward incidents. Lord Woolf in his final report suggested that the professional bodies might consider this. The General Medical Council is preparing guidance to doctors about their duty to report adverse incidents and to co-operate with inquiries.

## 3 The Protocol

3.1 This protocol is not a comprehensive code governing all the steps in clinical disputes. Rather it attempts to set out **a code of good practice** which parties should follow when litigation might be a possibility.

3.2 The **commitments** section of the protocol summarises the guiding principles which healthcare providers and patients and their advisers are invited to endorse when dealing with patient dissatisfaction with treatment and its outcome, and with potential complaints and claims.

3.3 The **steps** section sets out in a more prescriptive form, a recommended sequence of actions to be followed if litigation is a prospect.

### Good practice commitments

3.4 **Healthcare providers** should—

(i) ensure that **key staff**, including claims and litigation managers, are appropriately trained and have some knowledge of healthcare law, and of complaints procedures and civil litigation practice and procedure;

(ii) develop an approach to **clinical governance** that ensures that clinical practice is delivered to commonly accepted standards and that this is routinely monitored through a system of clinical audit and clinical risk management (particularly adverse outcome investigation);

(iii) set up **adverse outcome reporting systems** in all specialties to record and investigate unexpected serious adverse outcomes as soon as possible. Such systems can enable evidence to be gathered quickly, which makes it easier to provide an accurate explanation of what happened and to defend or settle any subsequent claims;

(iv) use the results of **adverse incidents and complaints positively** as a guide to how to improve services to patients in the future;

(v) ensure **that patients receive clear and comprehensible information** in an accessible form about how to raise their concerns or complaints;

(vi) establish **efficient and effective systems of recording and storing patient records,** notes, diagnostic reports and x-rays, and to retain these in accordance with Department of Health guidance (currently for a minimum of eight years in the case of adults, and all obstetric and paediatric notes for children until they reach the age of 25);

(vii) **advise patients** of a serious adverse outcome and provide on request to the patient or the patient's representative an oral or written explanation of what happened, information on further steps open to the patient, including where appropriate an offer of future treatment to rectify the problem, an apology, changes in procedure which will benefit patients and/or compensation.

3.5 **Patients and their advisers** should—

(i) **report any concerns and dissatisfaction** to the healthcare provider as soon as is reasonable to enable that provider to offer clinical advice where possible, to advise the patient if anything has gone wrong and take appropriate action;

(ii) consider the **full range of options** available following an adverse outcome with which a patient is dissatisfied, including a request for an explanation, a meeting, a complaint, and other appropriate dispute resolution methods (including mediation) and negotiation, not only litigation;

(iii) **inform the healthcare provider when the patient is satisfied** that the matter has been concluded: legal advisers should notify the provider when they are no longer acting for the patient, particularly if proceedings have not started.

## Protocol steps

3.6 The steps of this protocol which follow have been kept deliberately simple. An illustration of the likely sequence of events in a number of healthcare situations is at Annex A.

## Obtaining the health records

3.7 Any request for records by the **patient** or their adviser should—

- **provide sufficient information** to alert the healthcare provider where an adverse outcome has been serious or had serious consequences;
- be as **specific as possible** about the records which are required.

3.8 Requests for copies of the patient's clinical records should be made using the Law Society and Department of Health approved **standard forms** (enclosed at Annex B), adapted as necessary.

3.9 The copy records should be provided **within 40 days** of the request and for a cost not exceeding the charges permissible under the Access to Health Records Act 1990 (currently a maximum of £10 plus photocopying and postage).[1]

3.10 In the rare circumstances that the healthcare provider is in difficulty in complying with the request within 40 days, the **problem should be explained** quickly and details given of what is being done to resolve it.

3.11 It will not be practicable for healthcare providers to investigate in detail each case when records are requested. But healthcare providers should **adopt a policy on which cases will be investigated** (see paragraph 3.5 on clinical governance and adverse outcome reporting).

3.12 If the healthcare provider fails to provide the health records within 40 days, the patient or their adviser can then apply to the court for an **order for pre-action disclosure.** The new Civil Procedure Rules should make pre-action applications to the court easier. The court will also have the power to impose costs sanctions for unreasonable delay in providing records.

3.13 If either the patient or the healthcare provider considers **additional health records are required from a third party,** in the first instance these should be requested by or through the patient. Third party healthcare providers are expected to co-operate. The Civil Procedure Rules will enable patients and healthcare providers to apply to the court for pre-action disclosure by third parties.

### Letter of claim

3.14 Annex C1 to this protocol provides **a template for the recommended contents of a letter of claim:** the level of detail will need to be varied to suit the particular circumstances.

3.15 If, following the receipt and analysis of the records, and the receipt of any further advice (including from experts if necessary – see Section 4), the patient/adviser decides that there are grounds for a claim, they should then send, as soon as practicable, to the healthcare provider/potential defendant, a **letter of claim.**

3.16 This letter should contain a **clear summary of the facts** on which the claim is based, including the alleged adverse outcome, and the **main allegations of negligence.** It should also describe the **patient's injuries,** and present condition and prognosis. The **financial loss** incurred by the plaintiff should be outlined with an indication of the heads of damage to be claimed and the scale of the loss, unless this is impracticable.

3.17 In more complex cases a **chronology** of the relevant events should be provided, particularly if the patient has been treated by a number of different healthcare providers.

3.18 The letter of claim **should refer to any relevant documents,** including health records, and if possible enclose copies of any of those which will not already be in the potential defendant's possession, eg any relevant general practitioner records if the plaintiff's claim is against a hospital.

3.19 **Sufficient information** must be given to enable the healthcare provider defendant to **commence investigations** and to put an initial valuation on the claim.

3.20 Letters of claim are **not** intended to have the same formal status as a pleading, nor should any sanctions necessarily apply if the letter of claim and any subsequent statement of claim in the proceedings differ.

3.21 **Proceedings should not be issued until after three months from the letter of claim,** unless there is a limitation problem and/or the patient's position needs to be protected by early issue.

---

1. Note that the relevant legislation is now the Data Protection Act 1998, and the relevant fee is £50 plus copying charges and postage.

3.22 The patient or their adviser may want to make an **offer to settle** the claim at this early stage by putting forward an amount of compensation which would be satisfactory (possibly including any costs incurred to date). If an offer to settle is made, generally this should be supported by a medical report which deals with the injuries, condition and prognosis, and by a schedule of loss and supporting documentation. The level of detail necessary will depend on the value of the claim. Medical reports may not be necessary where there is no significant continuing injury, and a detailed schedule may not be necessary in a low value case. The Civil Procedure Rules are expected to set out the legal and procedural requirements for making offers to settle.

### The response

3.23 Attached at Annex C2 is a template for the suggested contents of the **letter of response.**

3.24 The healthcare provider should **acknowledge** the letter of claim **within 14 days of receipt** and should identify who will be dealing with the matter.

3.25 The healthcare provider should, **within three months** of the letter of claim, provide a **reasoned answer**—

- if the **claim is admitted** the healthcare provider should say so in clear terms;
- if only **part of the claim is admitted** the healthcare provider should make clear which issues of breach of duty and/or causation are admitted and which are denied and why;
- if it is intended that any **admissions will be binding;**
- if the claim is denied, this should include specific comments on the allegations of negligence, and if a synopsis or chronology of relevant events has been provided and is disputed, the healthcare provider's version of those events;
- where additional documents are relied upon, eg an internal protocol, copies should be provided.

3.26 If the patient has made an offer to settle, the healthcare provider should **respond to that offer** in the response letter, preferably with reasons. The provider may make its own offer to settle at this stage, either as a counter-offer to the patient's, or of its own accord, but should accompany any offer by any supporting medical evidence, and/or by any other evidence in relation to the value of the claim which is in the healthcare provider's possession.

3.27 If the parties reach agreement on liability, but time is needed to resolve the value of the claim, they should aim to agree a reasonable period.

## 4 Experts

4.1 In clinical negligence disputes expert opinions may be needed—

- on breach of duty and causation;
- on the patient's condition and prognosis;
- to assist in valuing aspects of the claim.

4.2 The civil justice reforms and the new Civil Procedure Rules will encourage economy in the use of experts and a less adversarial expert culture. It is recognised that in clinical negligence disputes, the parties and their advisers will require flexibility in their approach to expert evidence. Decisions on whether experts might be instructed jointly, and on whether reports might be disclosed sequentially or by exchange, should rest with the parties and their advisers. Sharing expert evidence may be appropriate on issues relating to the value of the claim. However, this protocol does not attempt to be prescriptive on issues in relation to expert evidence.

4.3 Obtaining expert evidence will often be an expensive step and may take time, especially in specialised areas of medicine where there are limited numbers of suitable experts. Patients and healthcare providers, and their advisers, will therefore need to consider carefully how best to obtain any necessary expert help quickly and cost-effectively. Assistance with locating a suitable expert is available from a number of sources.

## 5 Alternative Dispute Resolution

5.1 The parties should consider whether some form of alternative dispute resolution procedure would be more suitable than litigation, and if so, endeavour to agree which form to adopt. Both the Claimant and Defendant may be required by the Court to provide evidence that alternative means of resolving their dispute were considered. The Courts take the view that litigation should be a last resort, and that claims should not be issued prematurely when a settlement is still actively being explored. Parties are warned that if the protocol is not followed (including this paragraph) then the Court must have regard to such conduct when determining costs.

5.2 It is not practicable in this protocol to address in detail how the parties might decide which method to adopt to resolve their particular dispute. However, summarised below are some of the options for resolving disputes without litigation:

- Discussion and negotiation. Parties should bear in mind that carefully planned face-to-face meetings may be particularly helpful in exploring further treatment for the patient, in reaching understandings about what happened, and on both parties' positions, in narrowing the issues in dispute and, if the timing is right, in helping to settle the whole matter especially if the patient wants an apology, explanation, or assurances about how other patients will be affected.
- Early neutral evaluation by an independent third party (for example, a lawyer experienced in the field of clinical negligence or an individual experienced in the subject matter of the claim).
- Mediation – a form of facilitated negotiation assisted by an independent neutral party. The Clinical Disputes Forum has published a Guide to Mediation which will assist – available on the Clinical Disputes Forum website at www.clinicaldisputesforum.org.uk.
- The **NHS Complaints Procedure** is designed to provide patients with an explanation of what happened and an apology if appropriate. It is not designed to provide compensation for cases of negligence. However, patients might choose to use the procedure if their only, or main, goal is to obtain an explanation, or to obtain more information to help them decide what other action might be appropriate.

5.3 The Legal Services Commission has published a booklet on 'Alternatives to Court', CLS Direct Information Leaflet 23 (www.clsdirect.org.uk/legalhelp/leaflet23.jsp), which lists a number of organisations that provide alternative dispute resolution services.

5.4 *It is expressly recognised that no party can or should be forced to mediate or enter into any form of ADR.*

## ANNEX A

### Illustrative Flowchart

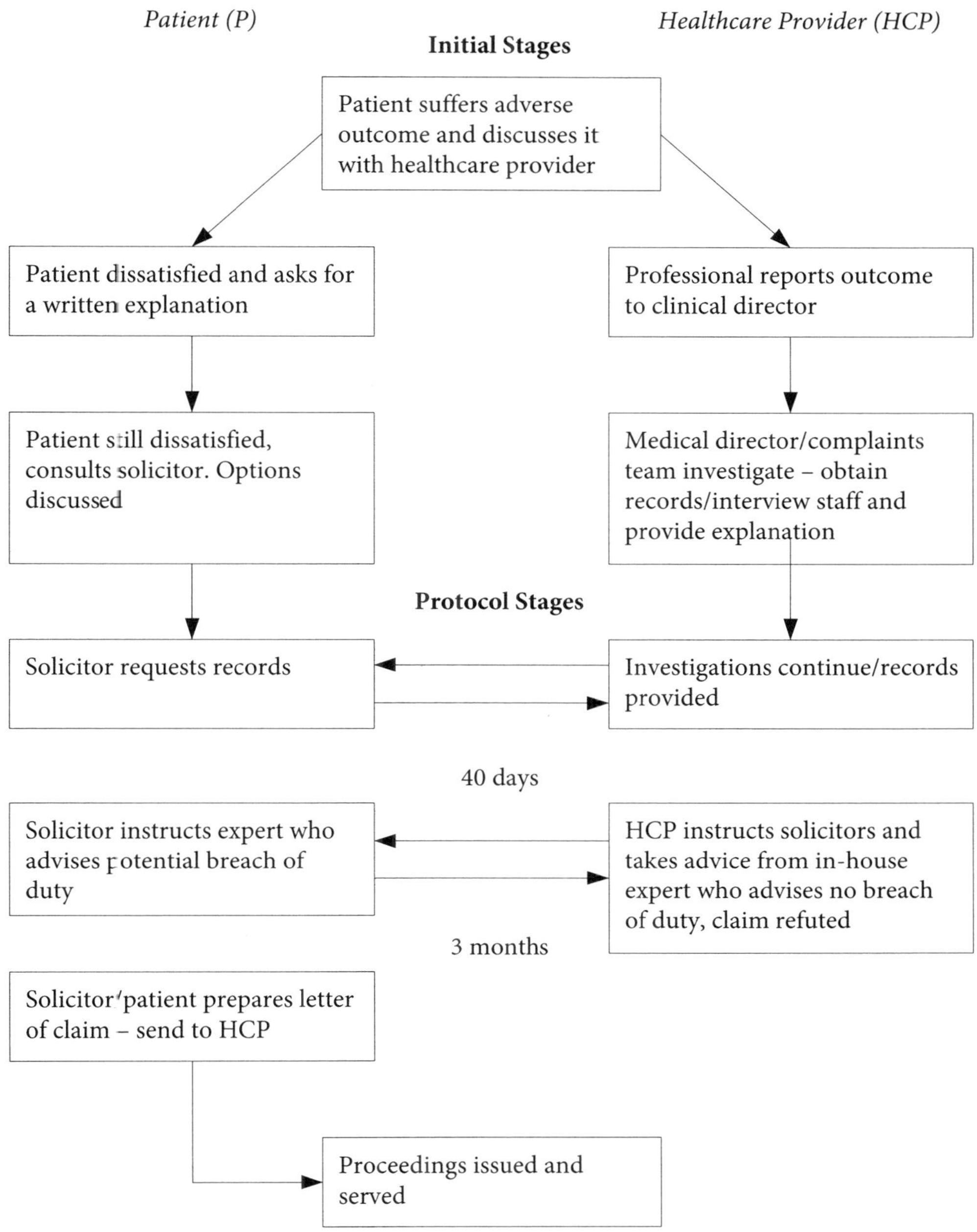

## ANNEX B

## Medical Negligence and Personal Injury Claims

## Protocol for Obtaining Hospital Medical Records

## (Revised Edition (June 1998); Civil Litigation Committee, The Law Society)

## Application on Behalf of a Patient for Hospital Medical Records for Use When Court Proceedings are Contemplated

### Purpose of the forms

This application form and response forms have been prepared by a working party of the Law Society's Civil Litigation Committee and approved by the Department of Health for use in NHS and Trust hospitals.

The purpose of the forms is to standardise and streamline the disclosure of medical records to a patient's solicitors, who are investigating pursuing a personal injury claim against a third party, or a medical negligence claim against the hospital to which the application is addressed and/or other hospitals or general practitioners.

### Use of the forms

Use of the forms is entirely voluntary and does not prejudice any party's right under the Access to Health Records Act 1990, the Data Protection Act 1984, or ss 33 and 34 of the Supreme Court Act 1981. However, it is the Department of Health policy that patients be permitted to see what has been written about them, and that healthcare providers should make arrangements to allow patients to see all their records, not only those covered by the Access to Health Records Act 1990. The aim of the forms is to save time and costs for all concerned for the benefit of the patient and the hospital and in the interests of justice. Use of the forms should make it unnecessary in most cases for there to be exchanges of letters or other enquiries. If there is any unusual matter not covered by the form, the patient's solicitor may write a separate letter at the outset.

### Charges for records

The Access to Health Records Act 1990 prescribes a maximum fee of £10. Photocopying and postage costs can be charged in addition. No other charges may be made.

The NHS Executive guidance makes it clear to healthcare providers that 'it is a perfectly proper use' of the 1990 Act to request records in that framework for the purpose of potential or actual litigation, whether against a third party or against the hospital or trust.

The 1990 Act does not permit differential rates of charges to be levied if the application is made by the patient, or by a solicitor on his or her behalf, or whether the response to the application is made by the healthcare provider directly (the medical records manager or a claims manager) or by a solicitor.

The NHS Executive guidance recommends that the same practice should be followed with regard to charges when the records are provided under a voluntary agreement as under the 1990 Act, except that in those circumstances the £10 access fee will not be appropriate.

The NHS Executive also advises—

- that the cost of photocopying may include 'the cost of staff time in making copies' and the costs of running the copier (but not costs of locating and sifting records);

- that the common practice of setting a standard rate for an application or charging an administration fee is not acceptable because there will be cases when this fails to comply with the 1990 Act.

### Records: what might be included

X-rays and test results form part of the patient's records. Additional charges for copying x-rays are permissible. If there are large numbers of x-rays, the records officer should check with the patient/solicitor before arranging copying.

Reports on an 'adverse incident' and reports on the patient made for risk management and audit purposes may form part of the records and be disclosable: the exception will be any specific record or report made solely or mainly in connection with an actual or potential claim.

### Records: quality standards

When copying records healthcare providers should ensure—

1 All documents are legible, and complete, if necessary by photocopying at less than 100% size.

2 Documents larger than A4 in the original, eg ITU charts, should be reproduced in A3, or reduced to A4 where this retains readability.

3 Documents are only copied on one side of paper, unless the original is two sided.

4 Documents should not be unnecessarily shuffled or bound and holes should not be made in the copied papers.

### Enquiries/further information

Any enquiries about the forms should be made initially to the solicitors making the request. Comments on the use and content of the forms should be made to the Secretary, Civil Litigation Committee, The Law Society, 113 Chancery Lane, London WC2A 1PL, telephone (020) 7320 5739, or to the NHS Management Executive, Quarry House, Quarry Hill, Leeds LS2 7UE.

The Law Society

May 1998

## Application on Behalf of a Patient for Hospital Medical Records for Use when Court Proceedings are Contemplated

This should be completed as fully as possible

| | | |
|---|---|---|
| Insert Hospital Name and Address | **TO: Medical Records Officer** | **Hospital** |

| | | |
|---|---|---|
| 1<br>(a) | Full name of patient (including previous surnames) | |
| (b) | Address now | |
| (c) | Address at start of treatment | |
| (d) | Date of birth (and death, if applicable) | |
| (e) | Hospital ref no if available | |
| (f) | N.I. number, if available | |
| 2 | This application is made because the patient is considering | |
| (a) | a claim against your hospital as detailed in para 7 overleaf | YES/NO |
| (b) | pursuing an action against someone else | YES/NO |
| 3 | Department(s) where treatment was received | |
| 4 | Name(s) of consultant(s) at your hospital in charge of the treatment | |
| 5 | Whether treatment at your hospital was private or NHS, wholly or in part | |
| 6 | A description of the treatment received, with approximate dates | |
| 7 | If the answer to Q2(a) is 'Yes' details of | |
| | (a) the likely nature of the claim | |
| | (b) grounds for the claim | |
| | (c) approximate dates of the events involved | |
| 8 | If the answer to Q2(b) is 'Yes' insert | |
| | (a) the names of the proposed defendants | |
| | (b) whether legal proceedings yet begun | YES/NO |
| | (c) if appropriate, details of the claim and action number | |
| 9 | We confirm we will pay reasonable copying charges | |
| 10 | We request prior details of | |
| | (a) photocopying and administration charges for medical records | YES/NO |
| | (b) number of and cost of copying x-ray and scan films | YES/NO |
| 11 | Any other relevant information, particular requirements, or any particular documents *not* required (eg copies of computerised records) | |
| | Signature of Solicitor | |
| | Name | |
| | Address | |
| | Ref | |
| | Telephone number | |

| | | |
|---|---|---|
| | Fax number | |
| | | *Please print name beneath each signature. Signature by child over 12 but under 18 years also requires signature by parent* |

Signature of patient

Signature of parent or next friend if appropriate

Signature of personal representative where patient has died

## First Response to Application for Hospital Records

| | | |
|---|---|---|
| NAME OF PATIENT<br>Our ref<br>Your ref | | |
| 1 | Date of receipt of patient's application | |
| 2 | We intend that copy medical records will be dispatched within 6 weeks of that date | YES/NO |
| 3 | We require pre-payment of photocopying charges | YES/NO |
| 4 | If estimate of photocopying charges requested or pre-payment required the amount will be | £ /notified to you |
| 5 | The cost of x-ray and scan films will be | £ /notified to you |
| 6 | If there is any problem, we shall write to you within those 6 weeks | YES/NO |
| 7 | Any other information | |
| | Please address further correspondence to | |
| | Signed | |
| | Direct telephone number | |
| | Direct fax number | |
| | Dated | |

## Second Response Enclosing Patient's Hospital Medical Records

Address

Our Ref
Your Ref

| | | |
|---|---|---|
| 1 | NAME OF PATIENT:<br>We confirm that the enclosed copy medical records are all those within the control of the hospital, relevant to the application which you have made to the best of our knowledge and belief, subject to paras 2–5 below | YES/NO |
| 2 | Details of any other documents which have not yet been located | |
| 3 | Date by when it is expected that these will be supplied | |
| 4 | Details of any records which we are not producing | |
| 5 | The reasons for not doing so | |
| 6 | An invoice for copying and administration charges is attached | YES/NO |
| | Signed | |
| | Date | |

## ANNEX C

## Templates for Letters of Claim and Response

### C1 Letter of claim

**Essential Contents**

1 **Client's name, address, date of birth, etc**

2 **Dates of allegedly negligent treatment**

3 **Events giving rise to the claim:**

- an outline of what happened, including details of other relevant treatments to the client by other healthcare providers.

4 **Allegation of negligence and causal link with injuries:**

- an outline of the allegations or a more detailed list in a complex case;
- an outline of the causal link between allegations and the injuries complained of.

5 **The client's injuries, condition and future prognosis**

6 **Request for clinical records (if not previously provided)**

- use the Law Society form if appropriate or adapt;
- specify the records required;
- if other records are held by other providers, and may be relevant, say so;
- state what investigations have been carried out to date, eg information from client and witnesses, any complaint and the outcome, if any clinical records have been seen or expert's advice obtained.

7 **The likely value of the claim**

- an outline of the main heads of damage, or, in straightforward cases, the details of loss.

**Optional information**

What investigations have been carried out
An offer to settle without supporting evidence

Suggestions for obtaining expert evidence
Suggestions for meetings, negotiations, discussion or mediation

**Possible enclosures**

Chronology
Clinical records request form and client's authorisation
Expert report(s)
Schedules of loss and supporting evidence

### C2 Letter of response

**Essential Contents**

1 Provide **requested records** and invoice for copying:
- explain if records are incomplete or extensive records are held and ask for further instructions;
- request additional records from third parties.

2 **Comments on events and/or chronology:**
- if events are disputed or the healthcare provider has further information or documents on which they wish to rely, these should be provided, eg internal protocol;
- details of any further information needed from the patient or a third party should be provided.

3 **If breach of duty and causation are accepted:**
- suggestions might be made for resolving the claim and/or requests for further information;
- a response should be made to any offer to settle.

4 **If breach of duty and/or causation are denied:**
- a bare denial will not be sufficient. If the healthcare provider has other explanations for what happened, these should be given at least in outline;
- suggestions might be made for the next steps, eg further investigations, obtaining expert evidence, meetings/negotiations or mediation, or an invitation to issue proceedings.

**Optional Matters**

An offer to settle if the patient has not made one, or a counter offer to the patient's with supporting evidence

**Possible Enclosures**

Clinical records
Annotated chronology
Expert reports

## ANNEX D

## Lord Woolf's Recommendations

1 Lord Woolf in his Access to Justice Report in July 1996, following a detailed review of the problems of medical negligence claims, identified that one of the major sources of **costs and delay** is **at the pre-litigation stage** because—

(a) Inadequate incident reporting and record keeping in hospitals, and mobility of staff, make it difficult to establish facts, often several years after the event.

(b) Claimants must incur the cost of an expert in order to establish whether they have a viable claim.

(c) There is often a long delay before a claim is made.

(d) Defendants do not have sufficient resources to carry out a full investigation of every incident, and do not consider it worthwhile to start an investigation as soon as they receive a request for records, because many cases do not proceed beyond that stage.

(e) Patients often give the defendant little or no notice of a firm intention to pursue a claim. Consequently, many incidents are not investigated by the defendants until after proceedings have started.

(f) Doctors and other clinical staff are traditionally reluctant to admit negligence or apologise to, or negotiate with, claimants for fear of damage to their professional reputations or career prospects.

2 Lord Woolf acknowledged that under the present arrangements **healthcare providers,** faced with possible medical negligence claims, have a number of **practical problems** to contend with—

(a) Difficulties of finding patients' records and tracing former staff, which can be exacerbated by late notification and by the health-care provider's own failure to identify adverse incidents.

(b) The healthcare provider may have only treated the patient for a limited time or for a specific complaint: the patient's previous history may be relevant but the records may be in the possession of one of several other healthcare providers.

(c) The large number of potential claims do not proceed beyond the stage of a request for medical records, or an explanation; and that it is difficult for healthcare providers to investigate fully every case whenever a patient asks to see the records.

## ANNEX E

### How to Contact the Forum

### The Clinical Disputes Forum

Chairman

Dr Alastair Scotland
Medical Director and Chief Officer
National Clinical Assessment Authority
9th Floor, Market Towers
London
SW8 5NQ
Telephone: (020) 7273 0850

Secretary

Sarah Leigh
c/o Margaret Dangoor
3 Clydesdale Gardens
Richmond
Surrey TW10 5EG
Telephone: (020) 8408 1012

# Appendix 5
# Actuarial Tables – Extracts

## SECTION B: CONTINGENCIES OTHER THAN MORTALITY

26. As stated in paragraph 19, the tables for loss of earnings (Tables 3 to 14) take no account of risks other than mortality. This section shows how the multipliers in these tables may be reduced to take account of these risks.

27. Tables of factors to be applied to the existing multipliers were first introduced in the Second Edition of the Ogden Tables. These factors were based on work commissioned by the Institute of Actuaries and carried out by Professor S Haberman and Mrs D S F Bloomfield (*Work time lost to sickness, unemployment and stoppages: measurement and application* (1990), Journal of the Institute of Actuaries 117, 533-595). Although there was some debate within the actuarial profession about the details of the work, and in particular about the scope for developing it further, the findings were broadly accepted and were adopted by the Government Actuary and the other actuaries who were members of the Working Party when the Second Edition of the Tables was published and have remained unchanged in later editions.

28. Some related work has more recently been published by Lewis, McNabb and Wass (*Methods of calculating damages for loss of future earnings*, Journal of Personal Injury Law, 2002 Number 2). Since the publication of the Fifth Edition of the Ogden Tables, the Ogden Working Party has been involved in further research into the impact of contingencies other than mortality carried out by Professor Richard Verrall, Professor Steven Haberman and Mr Zoltan Butt of City University, London and, in a separate exercise, by Dr Victoria Wass of Cardiff University. Their findings have been combined to produce the tables of factors given in this section.

29. The Haberman and Bloomfield paper relied on data from the Labour Force Surveys for 1973, 1977, 1981 and 1985 and English Life Tables No. 14 (1980-82). The Labour Force Survey (LFS) was originally designed to produce a periodic cross-sectional snapshot of the working age population and collects information on an extensive range of socio-economic and labour force characteristics. Since the winter of 1992/3, the LFS has been carried out on a quarterly basis, with respondents being included in the survey over 5 successive quarters. The research of Professor Verrall *et al* and Dr Wass has used data from the Labour Force Surveys conducted from 1998 to 2003 to estimate the probabilities of movement of males and females between different states of economic activity, dependent on age, sex, employment activity and level of disability. These probabilities permit the calculation of the expected periods in employment until retirement age, dependent on the initial starting state of economic activity, disability and educational attainment. These can then be discounted at the same discount rate that is used for obtaining the relevant multiplier from Tables 3 to 14, in order to give a multiplier which takes into account only those periods the claimant would be expected, on average, to be in work. These discounted working life expectancy multipliers can be compared to those obtained assuming the person remained in work throughout, to obtain reduction factors which give the expected proportion of time to retirement age which will be spent in employment.

30. The factors described in subsequent paragraphs are for use in calculating loss of earnings up to retirement age. The research work did not investigate the impact of contingencies other than mortality on the value of future pension rights. Some reduction to the multiplier for loss of pension would often be appropriate when a reduction is being applied for loss of earnings. This may be a smaller reduction than in the case of loss of earnings because the ill-health contingency (as opposed to the unemployment contingency) may give rise to significant ill-health retirement pension rights. A bigger reduction may be necessary in cases where there is significant doubt whether pension rights would have continued to accrue (to the extent not already allowed for in the post-retirement multiplier) or in cases where there may be doubt over the ability of the pension fund to pay promised benefits. In the case of a defined contribution pension scheme, loss of pension rights may be allowed for simply by increasing the future earnings loss (adjusted for contingencies other than mortality) by the percentage of earnings which the employer contributions to the scheme represent.

31. The methodology proposed in paragraphs 33 to 42 describes one method for dealing with contingencies other than mortality, which replaces that set out in earlier editions of the Ogden Tables. If this methodology is followed, in many cases it will be appropriate to increase or reduce the discount in the tables to take account of the nature of a particular claimant's disabilities. It should be noted that the methodology does not take into account the pre-accident employment history. The methodology also provides for the possibility of valuing more appropriately the possible mitigation of loss of earnings in cases where the claimant is employed after the accident or is considered capable of being employed. This will in many cases enable a more accurate assessment to be made of the mitigation of loss. However, there may be some cases where the *Smith v. Manchester Corporation* or *Blamire* approach remains applicable or otherwise where a precise mathematical approach is inapplicable.

32. The suggestions which follow are intended as a 'ready reckoner' which provides an initial adjustment to the multipliers according to the employment status, disability status and educational attainment of the claimant when calculating awards for loss of earnings and for any mitigation of this loss in respect of potential future post-injury earnings. Such a ready reckoner cannot take into account all circumstances and it may be appropriate to argue for higher or lower adjustments in particular cases. In particular, it can be difficult to place a value on the possible mitigating income when considering the potential range of disabilities and their effect on post-injury work capability, even within the interpretation of disability set out in paragraph 35. However, the methodology does offer a framework for consideration of a range of possible figures with the maximum being effectively provided by the post-injury multiplier assuming the

claimant was not disabled and the minimum being the case where there is no realistic prospect of post-injury employment.

**The deduction for contingencies other than mortality**

33. Under the proposed new method, multipliers for loss of earnings obtained from Tables 3 to 14 are multiplied by factors to allow for the risk of periods of non-employment and absence from the workforce because of sickness.

34. The new research by Professor Verrall *et al* and Dr Wass referred to in paragraphs 28 and 29 demonstrated that the key issues affecting a person's future working life are employment status, disability status and educational attainment.

35. The definitions of employed/not employed, disabled/not disabled and educational attainment used in this analysis and which should be used for determining which factors to apply to the multipliers to allow for contingencies other than mortality are as follows:

| | |
|---|---|
| Employed | Those who at the time of the accident are employed, self-employed or on a government training scheme. |
| Not employed | All others (including those temporarily out of work, full-time students and unpaid family workers). |
| Disabled | A person is classified as being disabled if all three of the following conditions in relation to the ill-health or disability are met:<br>(i) has either a progressive illness or an illness which has lasted or is expected to last for over a year,<br>(ii) satisfies the Disability Discrimination Act definition that the impact of the disability substantially limits the person's ability to carry out normal day-to-day activities<br>**and**<br>their condition affects either the kind **or** the amount of paid work they can do. |
| Not disabled | All others. |

Normal day-to-day activities are those which are carried out by most people on a daily basis, and we are interested in disabilities/health problems which have a substantial adverse effect on the respondent's ability to carry out these activities.

There are several ways in which a disability or health problem may affect the respondent's day-to-day activities:

***Mobility*** - for example, unable to travel short journeys as a passenger in a car, unable to walk other than at a slow pace or with jerky movements, difficulty in negotiating stairs, unable to use one or more forms of public transport, unable to go out of doors unaccompanied.

***Manual dexterity*** - for example, loss of functioning in one or both hands, inability to use a knife or fork at the same time, or difficulty in pressing buttons on a keyboard.

***Physical co-ordination*** - for example, the inability to feed or dress oneself, or to pour liquid from one vessel to another except with unusual slowness or concentration.

***Problems with bowel/bladder control*** - for example, frequent or regular loss of control of the bladder or bowel. Occasional bedwetting is not considered a disability.

***Ability to lift, carry or otherwise move everyday objects (for example, books, kettles, light furniture)*** - for example, inability to pick up a weight with one hand but not the other, or to carry a tray steadily.

***Speech*** - for example, unable to communicate (clearly) orally with others, taking significantly longer to say things. A minor stutter, difficulty in speaking in front of an audience, or inability to speak a foreign language would not be considered impairments.

***Hearing*** - for example, not being able to hear without the use of a hearing aid, the inability to understand speech under normal conditions or over the telephone.

***Eyesight*** - for example, while wearing spectacles or contact lenses - being unable to pass the standard driving eyesight test, total inability to distinguish colours (excluding ordinary red/green colour blindness), or inability to read newsprint.

***Memory or ability to concentrate, learn or understand*** - for example, intermittent loss of consciousness or confused behaviour, inability to remember names of family or friends unable to write a cheque without assistance, or an inability to follow a recipe.

***Perception of risk of physical danger*** - for example, reckless behaviour putting oneself or others at risk, mobility to cross the road safely. This excludes (significant) fear of heights or underestimating risk of dangerous hobbies.

Three levels of educational attainment are defined for the purposes of the tables as follows:

D Degree or equivalent or higher.

GE-A GCSE grades A to C up to A levels or equivalents.

O Below GCSE grade C or CSE grade 1 or equivalent or no qualifications.

The following table gives a more detailed breakdown of the allocation of various types of educational qualification to each of the three categories above and are based on the allocations used in the research by Professor Verrall *et al* and Dr Wass.

**Categories of highest educational attainment**

| **D**<br>**Degree or equivalent or higher** | **GE-A**<br>**GCSE grades A to C up to A levels or equivalent** | **O**<br>**Below GCSE grade C or CSE grade 1 or equivalent or no qualifications** |
|---|---|---|
| Any degree (first or higher) | A or AS level or equivalent | CSE below grade 1 |
| Other higher education qualification below degree level | O level, GCSE grade A-C or equivalent | GCSE below grade C |
| Diploma in higher education | | |
| NVQ level 4 or 5 | NVQ level 2 or 3 | NVQ level 1 or equivalent |
| HNC/HND, BTEC higher, etc | BTEC/SCOTVEC first or general diploma | BTEC first or general certificate |
| | OND/ONC, BTEC/SCOTVEC national | SCOTVEC modules or equivalent |
| RSA higher diploma | RSA diploma, advanced diploma or certificate | RSA other |
| Teaching<br>Nursing, etc | GNVQ intermediate or advanced | GNVQ/GVSQ foundation level |
| | City and Guilds craft or advanced craft | City and Guilds other |
| | SCE higher or equivalent Trade apprenticeship | YT/ YTP certificate |
| | Scottish 6th year certificate (CSYS) | Other qualifications |
| | | No qualification |
| | | Don't know |

*Note: 'educational attainment" is used here as a proxy for skill level, so that those in professional occupations such as law accountancy, nursing, etc who do not have a degree ought to be treated as if they do have one.*

36. The research also considered the extent to which a person's future working life expectancy is affected by individual circumstances such as occupation and industrial sector, geographical region and education. The researchers concluded that the most significant consideration was the highest level of education achieved by the claimant and that, if this was allowed for, the effect of the other factors was relatively small. As a result, the Working Party decided to propose adjustment factors which allow for employment status, disability status and educational attainment only. This is a change

from previous editions of the Ogden Tables where adjustments were made for types of occupation and for geographical region.

37. A separate assessment is made for (a) the value of earnings the claimant would have received if the injury had not been suffered and (b) the value of the claimant's earnings (if any) taking account of the injuries sustained. The risk of non-employment is significantly higher post-injury due to the impairment. The loss is arrived at by deducting (b) from (a).

38. In order to calculate the value of the earnings the claimant would have received if the injury had not been suffered, the claimant's employment status and the disability status need to be determined as at the date of the accident (or the onset of the medical condition) giving rise to the claim, so that the correct table can be applied. For the calculation of future loss of earnings (based on actual pre-accident earnings and also future employment prospects), Tables A and C should be used for claimants who were not disabled at the time of the accident, and Tables B and D should be used for those with a pre-existing disability. In all of these tables the three left-hand columns are for those who were employed at the time of the accident and the three right-hand columns are for those who were not.

39. In order to calculate the value of the actual earnings that a claimant is likely to receive in the future (i.e. after settlement or trial), the employment status and the disability status need to be determined as at the date of settlement or trial. For claimants with a work-affecting disability at that point in time, Tables B and D should be used. The three left-hand columns will apply in respect of claimants actually in employment at date of settlement or trial and the three right-hand columns will apply in respect of those who remain non-employed at that point in time.

40. The factors in Tables A to D allow for the interruption of employment for bringing up children and caring for other dependants.

41. In the case of those aged under 16 at the date of the accident, the relevant factor from the tables would be chosen on the basis of the level of education the child would have been expected to have attained, had the injury not occurred, together with an assessment as to whether the child would have become employed or not. The relevant factor for age 16 would be chosen using the assessed employment status and educational status likely to be ultimately attained, discounted by the appropriate factor from Table 27 for the number of years from the age at the date of trial to age 16.

42. Tables A to D include factors up to age 54 only. For older ages the reduction factors increase towards 1 at retirement age for those who are employed and fall towards 0 for those who are not employed. However, where the claimant is older than 54, it is anticipated that the likely future course of employment status will be particularly dependent on individual circumstances, so that the use of factors based on averages would not be appropriate. Hence reduction factors are not provided for these older ages.

**Table A**
**Loss of Earnings to Pension Age 65 (Males – Not disabled)**

| Age at date of trial | Employed | | | Not employed | | |
|---|---|---|---|---|---|---|
| | D | GE-A | O | D | GE-A | O |
| 16-19 | 0.90 | 0.90 | 0.85 | 0.85 | 0.85 | 0.82 |
| 20-24 | 0.92 | 0.92 | 0.87 | 0.89 | 0.88 | 0.83 |
| 25-29 | 0.93 | 0.92 | 0.89 | 0.89 | 0.88 | 0.82 |
| 30-34 | 0.92 | 0.91 | 0.89 | 0.87 | 0.86 | 0.81 |
| 35-39 | 0.90 | 0.90 | 0.89 | 0.85 | 0.84 | 0.80 |
| 40-44 | 0.88 | 0.88 | 0.88 | 0.82 | 0.81 | 0.78 |
| 45-49 | 0.86 | 0.86 | 0.86 | 0.77 | 0.77 | 0.74 |
| 50 | 0.83 | 0.83 | 0.83 | 0.72 | 0.72 | 0.70 |
| 51 | 0.82 | 0.82 | 0.82 | 0.70 | 0.70 | 0.68 |
| 52 | 0.81 | 0.81 | 0.81 | 0.67 | 0.67 | 0.66 |
| 53 | 0.80 | 0.80 | 0.80 | 0.63 | 0.63 | 0.63 |
| 54 | 0.79 | 0.79 | 0.79 | 0.59 | 0.59 | 0.59 |

**Table B**
**Loss of Earnings to Pension Age 65 (Males – Disabled)**

| Age at date of trial | Employed D | Employed GE-A | Employed O | Not employed D | Not employed GE-A | Not employed O |
|---|---|---|---|---|---|---|
| 16-19 | 0.61 | 0.55 | 0.32 | 0.61 | 0.49 | 0.25 |
| 20-24 | 0.61 | 0.55 | 0.38 | 0.53 | 0.46 | 0.24 |
| 25-29 | 0.60 | 0.54 | 0.42 | 0.48 | 0.41 | 0.24 |
| 30-34 | 0.59 | 0.52 | 0.40 | 0.43 | 0.34 | 0.23 |
| 35-39 | 0.58 | 0.48 | 0.39 | 0.38 | 0.28 | 0.20 |
| 40-44 | 0.57 | 0.48 | 0.39 | 0.33 | 0.23 | 0.15 |
| 45-49 | 0.55 | 0.48 | 0.39 | 0.26 | 0.20 | 0.11 |
| 50 | 0.53 | 0.49 | 0.40 | 0.24 | 0.18 | 0.10 |
| 51 | 0.53 | 0.49 | 0.41 | 0.23 | 0.17 | 0.09 |
| 52 | 0.54 | 0.49 | 0.41 | 0.22 | 0.16 | 0.08 |
| 53 | 0.54 | 0.49 | 0.42 | 0.21 | 0.15 | 0.07 |
| 54 | 0.54 | 0.50 | 0.43 | 0.20 | 0.14 | 0.06 |

**Table C**
**Loss of Earnings to Pension Age 60 (Females – Not disabled)**

| Age at date of trial | Employed D | Employed GE-A | Employed O | Not employed D | Not employed GE-A | Not employed O |
|---|---|---|---|---|---|---|
| 16-19 | 0.87 | 0.81 | 0.64 | 0.84 | 0.77 | 0.59 |
| 20-24 | 0.89 | 0.82 | 0.68 | 0.84 | 0.76 | 0.60 |
| 25-29 | 0.89 | 0.84 | 0.72 | 0.83 | 0.75 | 0.61 |
| 30-34 | 0.89 | 0.85 | 0.75 | 0.81 | 0.75 | 0.63 |
| 35-39 | 0.89 | 0.86 | 0.78 | 0.80 | 0.74 | 0.63 |
| 40-44 | 0.89 | 0.86 | 0.80 | 0.78 | 0.72 | 0.60 |
| 45-49 | 0.87 | 0.85 | 0.81 | 0.72 | 0.64 | 0.52 |
| 50 | 0.86 | 0.84 | 0.81 | 0.64 | 0.55 | 0.43 |
| 51 | 0.85 | 0.84 | 0.81 | 0.60 | 0.51 | 0.40 |
| 52 | 0.84 | 0.84 | 0.81 | 0.56 | 0.46 | 0.36 |
| 53 | 0.83 | 0.83 | 0.81 | 0.50 | 0.41 | 0.32 |
| 54 | 0.83 | 0.83 | 0.82 | 0.44 | 0.35 | 0.27 |

**Table D**
**Loss of Earnings to Pension Age 60 (Females – Disabled)**

| Age at date of trial | Employed | | | Not employed | | |
|---|---|---|---|---|---|---|
| | D | GE-A | O | D | GE-A | O |
| 16-19 | 0.65 | 0.43 | 0.25 | 0.58 | 0.35 | 0.19 |
| 20-24 | 0.64 | 0.44 | 0.25 | 0.58 | 0.33 | 0.17 |
| 25-29 | 0.63 | 0.45 | 0.25 | 0.50 | 0.32 | 0.16 |
| 30-34 | 0.62 | 0.46 | 0.30 | 0.44 | 0.31 | 0.15 |
| 35-39 | 0.61 | 0.48 | 0.34 | 0.42 | 0.28 | 0.14 |
| 40-44 | 0.60 | 0.51 | 0.38 | 0.38 | 0.23 | 0.13 |
| 45-49 | 0.60 | 0.54 | 0.42 | 0.28 | 0.18 | 0.11 |
| 50 | 0.60 | 0.56 | 0.47 | 0.23 | 0.15 | 0.10 |
| 51 | 0.61 | 0.58 | 0.49 | 0.21 | 0.14 | 0.09 |
| 52 | 0.61 | 0.60 | 0.51 | 0.20 | 0.13 | 0.08 |
| 53 | 0.62 | 0.62 | 0.54 | 0.18 | 0.11 | 0.07 |
| 54 | 0.63 | 0.66 | 0.57 | 0.16 | 0.09 | 0.06 |

**Different pension ages**

43. The factors in the preceding tables assume retirement at age 65 for males and age 60 for females. It is not possible to calculate expected working life times assuming alternative retirement ages from the LFS data, since the employment data in the LFS are collected only for the working population, assumed aged between 16 and 64 for males and between 16 and 59 for females. Where the retirement age is different from age 65 for males or age 60 for females, it is suggested that this should be ignored and the reduction factor and the adjustments thereto be taken from the above tables for the age of the claimant as at the date of trial with no adjustment, i.e. assume that the retirement age is age 65 for males and age 60 for females. However, if the retirement age is close to the age at the date of trial, then it may be more appropriate to take into account the circumstances of the individual case.

44. It should be noted that the reduction factors in Tables A, B, C and D are based on data for the period 1998 to 2003. Whilst the reduction factors and adjustments allow for the age-specific probabilities of moving into, or out of, employment over future working life time, based on data for the period 1998-2003, the methodology assumes that these probabilities remain constant over time; there is no allowance for changes in these age-specific probabilities beyond this period. It is also assumed that there will be no change in disability status or educational achievement after the date of the accident. Future changes in the probabilities of moving into, and out of, employment are especially difficult to predict with any certainty. It is the intention that the factors should be reassessed from time to time as new data become available.

**Table 1 Multipliers for pecuniary loss for life (males)** cost of care rest of life

| Age at date of trial | Multiplier calculated with allowance for projected mortality from the 2004-based population projections and rate of return of 0.0% | 0.5% | 1.0% | 1.5% | 2.0% | 2.5% | 3.0% | 3.5% | 4.0% | 4.5% | 5.0% | Age at date of trial |
|---|---|---|---|---|---|---|---|---|---|---|---|---|
| 0 | 86.63 | 69.86 | 57.39 | 47.98 | 40.76 | 35.15 | 30.72 | 27.17 | 24.28 | 21.91 | 19.94 | 0 |
| 1 | 85.96 | 69.49 | 57.21 | 47.91 | 40.76 | 35.19 | 30.77 | 27.24 | 24.36 | 21.99 | 20.01 | 1 |
| 2 | 84.86 | 68.78 | 56.74 | 47.60 | 40.55 | 35.05 | 30.68 | 27.17 | 24.32 | 21.96 | 19.99 | 2 |
| 3 | 83.76 | 68.05 | 56.26 | 47.28 | 40.34 | 34.90 | 30.58 | 27.10 | 24.27 | 21.93 | 19.97 | 3 |
| 4 | 82.65 | 67.32 | 55.77 | 46.95 | 40.12 | 34.75 | 30.48 | 27.03 | 24.22 | 21.89 | 19.94 | 4 |
| 5 | 81.53 | 66.58 | 55.27 | 46.61 | 39.89 | 34.59 | 30.37 | 26.95 | 24.16 | 21.85 | 19.91 | 5 |
| 6 | 80.42 | 65.83 | 54.77 | 46.27 | 39.65 | 34.43 | 30.25 | 26.87 | 24.10 | 21.81 | 19.88 | 6 |
| 7 | 79.30 | 65.08 | 54.26 | 45.92 | 39.41 | 34.26 | 30.13 | 26.79 | 24.04 | 21.76 | 19.85 | 7 |
| 8 | 78.18 | 64.32 | 53.74 | 45.56 | 39.16 | 34.08 | 30.01 | 26.70 | 23.98 | 21.71 | 19.81 | 8 |
| 9 | 77.06 | 63.56 | 53.22 | 45.20 | 38.91 | 33.91 | 29.88 | 26.61 | 23.91 | 21.66 | 19.78 | 9 |
| 10 | 75.95 | 62.79 | 52.69 | 44.83 | 38.65 | 33.72 | 29.75 | 26.51 | 23.84 | 21.61 | 19.74 | 10 |
| 11 | 74.83 | 62.02 | 52.16 | 44.46 | 38.39 | 33.53 | 29.61 | 26.41 | 23.77 | 21.56 | 19.70 | 11 |
| 12 | 73.71 | 61.25 | 51.62 | 44.08 | 38.11 | 33.34 | 29.47 | 26.31 | 23.69 | 21.50 | 19.65 | 12 |
| 13 | 72.59 | 60.47 | 51.07 | 43.69 | 37.84 | 33.14 | 29.33 | 26.20 | 23.61 | 21.44 | 19.61 | 13 |
| 14 | 71.48 | 59.69 | 50.52 | 43.30 | 37.56 | 32.93 | 29.18 | 26.09 | 23.52 | 21.38 | 19.56 | 14 |
| 15 | 70.36 | 58.90 | 49.96 | 42.90 | 37.27 | 32.72 | 29.02 | 25.97 | 23.44 | 21.31 | 19.51 | 15 |
| 16 | 69.25 | 58.12 | 49.40 | 42.50 | 36.97 | 32.51 | 28.86 | 25.85 | 23.35 | 21.24 | 19.45 | 16 |
| 17 | 68.[illegible]4 | 57.33 | 48.83 | 42.09 | 36.68 | 32.29 | 28.70 | 25.73 | 23.26 | 21.17 | 19.40 | 17 |
| 18 | 67.04 | 56.55 | 48.27 | 41.68 | 36.38 | 32.07 | 28.54 | 25.61 | 23.16 | 21.10 | 19.34 | 18 |
| 19 | 65.95 | 55.77 | 47.71 | 41.27 | 36.08 | 31.85 | 28.37 | 25.49 | 23.07 | 21.03 | 19.29 | 19 |
| 20 | 64.87 | 54.99 | 47.14 | 40.86 | 35.78 | 31.63 | 28.21 | 25.36 | 22.98 | 20.96 | 19.23 | 20 |
| 21 | 63.79 | 54.21 | 46.58 | 40.44 | 35.47 | 31.40 | 28.04 | 25.23 | 22.88 | 20.88 | 19.17 | 21 |
| 22 | 62.71 | 53.42 | 46.00 | 40.02 | 35.16 | 31.16 | 27.86 | 25.10 | 22.77 | 20.80 | 19.11 | 22 |
| 23 | 61.63 | 52.63 | 45.42 | 39.59 | 34.83 | 30.92 | 27.68 | 24.96 | 22.67 | 20.72 | 19.05 | 23 |
| 24 | 60.55 | 51.84 | 44.83 | 39.15 | 34.51 | 30.67 | 27.49 | 24.81 | 22.55 | 20.63 | 18.98 | 24 |
| 25 | 59.47 | 51.03 | 44.23 | 38.70 | 34.17 | 30.42 | 27.29 | 24.66 | 22.44 | 20.54 | 18.90 | 25 |
| 26 | 58.38 | 50.23 | 43.63 | 38.25 | 33.82 | 30.15 | 27.09 | 24.50 | 22.31 | 20.44 | 18.83 | 26 |
| 27 | 57.31 | 49.42 | 43.03 | 37.79 | 33.47 | 29.89 | 26.88 | 24.34 | 22.19 | 20.34 | 18.75 | 27 |
| 28 | 56.24 | 48.62 | 42.42 | 37.33 | 33.12 | 29.61 | 26.67 | 24.18 | 22.06 | 20.24 | 18.67 | 28 |
| 29 | 55.17 | 47.82 | 41.81 | 36.86 | 32.76 | 29.33 | 26.45 | 24.01 | 21.92 | 20.13 | 18.58 | 29 |
| 30 | 54.10 | 47.00 | 41.19 | 36.39 | 32.39 | 29.05 | 26.23 | 23.83 | 21.78 | 20.02 | 18.49 | 30 |
| 31 | 53.03 | 46.19 | 40.56 | 35.90 | 32.02 | 28.75 | 26.00 | 23.65 | 21.64 | 19.90 | 18.40 | 31 |
| 32 | 51.97 | 45.37 | 39.93 | 35.41 | 31.64 | 28.46 | 25.76 | 23.46 | 21.48 | 19.78 | 18.30 | 32 |
| 33 | 50.91 | 44.55 | 39.30 | 34.92 | 31.25 | 28.15 | 25.52 | 23.26 | 21.33 | 19.65 | 18.19 | 33 |
| 34 | 49.85 | 43.73 | 38.66 | 34.42 | 30.85 | 27.83 | 25.27 | 23.06 | 21.17 | 19.52 | 18.08 | 34 |
| 35 | 48.78 | 42.90 | 38.01 | 33.91 | 30.45 | 27.51 | 25.01 | 22.86 | 21.00 | 19.38 | 17.97 | 35 |
| 36 | 47.73 | 42.08 | 37.36 | 33.39 | 30.04 | 27.18 | 24.74 | 22.64 | 20.82 | 19.24 | 17.85 | 36 |
| 37 | 46.67 | 41.24 | 36.70 | 32.87 | 29.62 | 26.85 | 24.47 | 22.42 | 20.64 | 19.09 | 17.73 | 37 |
| 38 | 45.62 | 40.41 | 36.04 | 32.34 | 29.19 | 26.50 | 24.19 | 22.19 | 20.45 | 18.93 | 17.60 | 38 |
| 39 | 44.56 | 39.57 | 35.37 | 31.80 | 28.76 | 26.15 | 23.90 | 21.95 | 20.26 | 18.77 | 17.46 | 39 |
| 40 | 43.52 | 38.74 | 34.70 | 31.26 | 28.32 | 25.79 | 23.61 | 21.71 | 20.05 | 18.60 | 17.32 | 40 |
| 41 | 42.48 | 37.90 | 34.02 | 30.71 | 27.87 | 25.42 | 23.30 | 21.46 | 19.84 | 18.43 | 17.17 | 41 |
| 42 | 41.44 | 37.06 | 33.34 | 30.15 | 27.41 | 25.05 | 22.99 | 21.20 | 19.63 | 18.24 | 17.02 | 42 |
| 43 | 40.40 | 36.22 | 32.65 | 29.59 | 26.95 | 24.67 | 22.68 | 20.93 | 19.41 | 18.06 | 16.86 | 43 |
| 44 | 39.37 | 35.38 | 31.97 | 29.03 | 26.49 | 24.28 | 22.35 | 20.66 | 19.18 | 17.86 | 16.69 | 44 |
| 45 | 38.35 | 34.55 | 31.28 | 28.46 | 26.01 | 23.88 | 22.02 | 20.38 | 18.94 | 17.66 | 16.52 | 45 |
| 46 | 37.34 | 33.71 | 30.59 | 27.89 | 25.54 | 23.49 | 21.69 | 20.10 | 18.70 | 17.46 | 16.35 | 46 |
| 47 | 36.34 | 32.89 | 29.90 | 27.32 | 25.06 | 23.08 | 21.35 | 19.81 | 18.45 | 17.25 | 16.17 | 47 |
| 48 | 35.34 | 32.06 | 29.22 | 26.74 | 24.58 | 22.68 | 21.00 | 19.52 | 18.20 | 17.03 | 15.98 | 48 |
| 49 | 34.37 | 31.25 | 28.54 | 26.17 | 24.09 | 22.27 | 20.65 | 19.22 | 17.95 | 16.81 | 15.79 | 49 |
| 50 | 33.40 | 30.44 | 27.86 | 25.60 | 23.61 | 21.86 | 20.30 | 18.92 | 17.69 | 16.59 | 15.60 | 50 |
| 51 | 32.44 | 29.63 | 27.18 | 25.02 | 23.12 | 21.44 | 19.95 | 18.62 | 17.43 | 16.36 | 15.40 | 51 |
| 52 | 31.49 | 28.84 | 26.50 | 24.45 | 22.63 | 21.02 | 19.58 | 18.30 | 17.16 | 16.12 | 15.19 | 52 |
| 53 | 30.55 | 28.04 | 25.82 | 23.87 | 22.13 | 20.59 | 19.21 | 17.98 | 16.88 | 15.88 | 14.98 | 53 |
| 54 | 29.61 | 27.23 | 25.13 | 23.28 | 21.62 | 20.15 | 18.83 | 17.65 | 16.59 | 15.63 | 14.76 | 54 |
| 55 | 28.66 | 26.42 | 24.44 | 22.67 | 21.10 | 19.70 | 18.44 | 17.31 | 16.29 | 15.36 | 14.52 | 55 |
| 56 | 27.71 | 25.60 | 23.73 | 22.06 | 20.57 | 19.23 | 18.03 | 16.95 | 15.97 | 15.08 | 14.28 | 56 |
| 57 | 26.76 | 24.78 | 23.02 | 21.44 | 20.03 | 18.76 | 17.62 | 16.58 | 15.65 | 14.79 | 14.02 | 57 |
| 58 | 25.82 | 23.96 | 22.31 | 20.82 | 19.48 | 18.28 | 17.19 | 16.21 | 15.31 | 14.50 | 13.75 | 58 |
| 59 | 24.89 | 23.15 | 21.59 | 20.19 | 18.93 | 17.79 | 16.76 | 15.82 | 14.97 | 14.19 | 13.48 | 59 |
| 60 | 23.97 | 22.35 | 20.89 | 19.57 | 18.38 | 17.30 | 16.33 | 15.44 | 14.62 | 13.88 | 13.20 | 60 |
| 61 | 23.08 | 21.56 | 20.19 | 18.96 | 17.84 | 16.82 | 15.90 | 15.05 | 14.28 | 13.57 | 12.92 | 61 |
| 62 | 22.20 | 20.79 | 19.51 | 18.35 | 17.30 | 16.34 | 15.47 | 14.67 | 13.93 | 13.26 | 12.64 | 62 |
| 63 | 21.34 | 20.03 | 18.83 | 17.75 | 16.76 | 15.86 | 15.03 | 14.28 | 13.58 | 12.94 | 12.36 | 63 |
| 64 | 20.50 | 19.27 | 18.16 | 17.15 | 16.22 | 15.37 | 14.60 | 13.88 | 13.23 | 12.62 | 12.06 | 64 |
| 65 | 19.66 | 18.52 | 17.49 | 16.54 | 15.68 | 14.88 | 14.16 | 13.48 | 12.86 | 12.29 | 11.76 | 65 |
| 66 | 18.82 | 17.77 | 16.81 | 15.94 | 15.13 | 14.39 | 13.70 | 13.07 | 12.49 | 11.95 | 11.45 | 66 |
| 67 | 17.99 | 17.02 | 16.14 | 15.32 | 14.57 | 13.88 | 13.24 | 12.65 | 12.11 | 11.60 | 11.13 | 67 |
| 68 | 17.16 | 16.27 | 15.45 | 14.70 | 14.01 | 13.36 | 12.77 | 12.22 | 11.71 | 11.23 | 10.79 | 68 |
| 69 | 16.33 | 15.51 | 14.76 | 14.07 | 13.43 | 12.84 | 12.29 | 11.77 | 11.30 | 10.85 | 10.44 | 69 |

*continued*

**Table 1 Multipliers for pecuniary loss for life (males)** ***continued***

| Age at date of trial | Multiplier calculated with allowance for projected mortality from the 2004-based population projections and rate of return of | | | | | | | | | | | Age at date of trial |
|---|---|---|---|---|---|---|---|---|---|---|---|---|
| | 0.0% | 0.5% | 1.0% | 1.5% | 2.0% | 2.5% | 3.0% | 3.5% | 4.0% | 4.5% | 5.0% | |
| 70 | 15.50 | 14.75 | 14.07 | 13.43 | 12.85 | 12.30 | 11.79 | 11.32 | 10.87 | 10.46 | 10.08 | 70 |
| 71 | 14.67 | 14.00 | 13.38 | 12.80 | 12.26 | 11.76 | 11.29 | 10.85 | 10.44 | 10.06 | 9.70 | 71 |
| 72 | 13.86 | 13.25 | 12.69 | 12.16 | 11.67 | 11.21 | 10.78 | 10.38 | 10.00 | 9.65 | 9.32 | 72 |
| 73 | 13.07 | 12.52 | 12.01 | 11.53 | 11.09 | 10.67 | 10.28 | 9.91 | 9.56 | 9.24 | 8.94 | 73 |
| 74 | 12.31 | 11.81 | 11.35 | 10.92 | 10.51 | 10.13 | 9.78 | 9.44 | 9.13 | 8.83 | 8.55 | 74 |
| 75 | 11.57 | 11.13 | 10.71 | 10.32 | 9.95 | 9.61 | 9.29 | 8.98 | 8.70 | 8.42 | 8.17 | 75 |
| 76 | 10.86 | 10.47 | 10.09 | 9.74 | 9.41 | 9.10 | 8.81 | 8.53 | 8.27 | 8.03 | 7.79 | 76 |
| 77 | 10.19 | 9.84 | 9.50 | 9.19 | 8.89 | 8.61 | 8.35 | 8.10 | 7.86 | 7.64 | 7.42 | 77 |
| 78 | 9.55 | 9.24 | 8.94 | 8.66 | 8.39 | 8.14 | 7.90 | 7.68 | 7.46 | 7.26 | 7.06 | 78 |
| 79 | 8.95 | 8.67 | 8.40 | 8.15 | 7.91 | 7.69 | 7.47 | 7.27 | 7.08 | 6.89 | 6.71 | 79 |
| 80 | 8.38 | 8.13 | 7.89 | 7.67 | 7.45 | 7.25 | 7.06 | 6.88 | 6.70 | 6.53 | 6.38 | 80 |
| 81 | 7.83 | 7.61 | 7.40 | 7.20 | 7.01 | 6.83 | 6.66 | 6.49 | 6.34 | 6.19 | 6.04 | 81 |
| 82 | 7.31 | 7.12 | 6.93 | 6.75 | 6.58 | 6.42 | 6.27 | 6.12 | 5.98 | 5.85 | 5.72 | 82 |
| 83 | 6.81 | 6.64 | 6.47 | 6.32 | 6.17 | 6.02 | 5.89 | 5.75 | 5.63 | 5.51 | 5.39 | 83 |
| 84 | 6.32 | 6.17 | 6.03 | 5.89 | 5.76 | 5.63 | 5.51 | 5.39 | 5.28 | 5.17 | 5.07 | 84 |
| 85 | 5.87 | 5.73 | 5.61 | 5.49 | 5.37 | 5.26 | 5.15 | 5.05 | 4.95 | 4.85 | 4.76 | 85 |
| 86 | 5.44 | 5.33 | 5.22 | 5.11 | 5.01 | 4.91 | 4.81 | 4.72 | 4.64 | 4.55 | 4.47 | 86 |
| 87 | 5.05 | 4.95 | 4.85 | 4.76 | 4.67 | 4.58 | 4.50 | 4.42 | 4.34 | 4.27 | 4.19 | 87 |
| 88 | 4.68 | 4.60 | 4.51 | 4.43 | 4.35 | 4.27 | 4.20 | 4.13 | 4.06 | 4.00 | 3.93 | 88 |
| 89 | 4.35 | 4.28 | 4.20 | 4.13 | 4.06 | 4.00 | 3.93 | 3.87 | 3.81 | 3.75 | 3.69 | 89 |
| 90 | 4.05 | 3.99 | 3.92 | 3.86 | 3.80 | 3.74 | 3.68 | 3.63 | 3.57 | 3.52 | 3.47 | 90 |
| 91 | 3.76 | 3.71 | 3.65 | 3.59 | 3.54 | 3.49 | 3.44 | 3.39 | 3.34 | 3.30 | 3.25 | 91 |
| 92 | 3.49 | 3.44 | 3.39 | 3.34 | 3.30 | 3.25 | 3.21 | 3.16 | 3.12 | 3.08 | 3.04 | 92 |
| 93 | 3.26 | 3.21 | 3.17 | 3.12 | 3.08 | 3.04 | 3.00 | 2.96 | 2.93 | 2.89 | 2.86 | 93 |
| 94 | 3.06 | 3.02 | 2.98 | 2.94 | 2.91 | 2.87 | 2.83 | 2.80 | 2.77 | 2.73 | 2.70 | 94 |
| 95 | 2.88 | 2.85 | 2.81 | 2.78 | 2.75 | 2.71 | 2.68 | 2.65 | 2.62 | 2.59 | 2.56 | 95 |
| 96 | 2.71 | 2.68 | 2.65 | 2.62 | 2.59 | 2.56 | 2.53 | 2.51 | 2.48 | 2.45 | 2.43 | 96 |
| 97 | 2.55 | 2.52 | 2.49 | 2.46 | 2.44 | 2.41 | 2.39 | 2.36 | 2.34 | 2.32 | 2.29 | 97 |
| 98 | 2.38 | 2.36 | 2.33 | 2.31 | 2.29 | 2.26 | 2.24 | 2.22 | 2.20 | 2.18 | 2.16 | 98 |
| 99 | 2.22 | 2.20 | 2.18 | 2.15 | 2.13 | 2.12 | 2.10 | 2.08 | 2.06 | 2.04 | 2.02 | 99 |
| 100 | 2.06 | 2.04 | 2.02 | 2.01 | 1.99 | 1.97 | 1.95 | 1.94 | 1.92 | 1.90 | 1.89 | 100 |

**Table 2 Multipliers for pecuniary loss for life (females)** cost of care rest of life

| Age at date of trial | Multiplier calculated with allowance for projected mortality from the 2004-based population projections and rate of return of | | | | | | | | | | | Age at date of trial |
|---|---|---|---|---|---|---|---|---|---|---|---|---|
| | 0.0% | 0.5% | 1.0% | 1.5% | 2.0% | 2.5% | 3.0% | 3.5% | 4.0% | 4.5% | 5.0% | |
| 0 | 90.15 | 72.21 | 58.98 | 49.06 | 41.51 | 35.67 | 31.09 | 27.43 | 24.48 | 22.06 | 20.05 | 0 |
| 1 | 89.44 | 71.83 | 58.79 | 48.99 | 41.50 | 35.70 | 31.14 | 27.50 | 24.55 | 22.13 | 20.11 | 1 |
| 2 | 88.36 | 71.13 | 58.34 | 48.70 | 41.32 | 35.58 | 31.06 | 27.44 | 24.51 | 22.10 | 20.10 | 2 |
| 3 | 87.27 | 70.43 | 57.88 | 48.40 | 41.12 | 35.45 | 30.97 | 27.38 | 24.47 | 22.08 | 20.08 | 3 |
| 4 | 86.17 | 69.72 | 57.42 | 48.09 | 40.92 | 35.32 | 30.88 | 27.32 | 24.43 | 22.05 | 20.06 | 4 |
| 5 | 85.07 | 69.00 | 56.95 | 47.78 | 40.71 | 35.18 | 30.79 | 27.26 | 24.38 | 22.01 | 20.04 | 5 |
| 6 | 83.97 | 68.28 | 56.47 | 47.46 | 40.49 | 35.03 | 30.69 | 27.19 | 24.34 | 21.98 | 20.01 | 6 |
| 7 | 82.87 | 67.55 | 55.99 | 47.14 | 40.28 | 34.88 | 30.59 | 27.12 | 24.29 | 21.95 | 19.99 | 7 |
| 8 | 81.77 | 66.82 | 55.50 | 46.81 | 40.05 | 34.73 | 30.48 | 27.04 | 24.23 | 21.91 | 19.96 | 8 |
| 9 | 80.67 | 66.08 | 55.00 | 46.47 | 39.82 | 34.57 | 30.37 | 26.97 | 24.18 | 21.87 | 19.93 | 9 |
| 10 | 79.57 | 65.34 | 54.50 | 46.13 | 39.59 | 34.41 | 30.26 | 26.89 | 24.12 | 21.83 | 19.90 | 10 |
| 11 | 78.47 | 64.60 | 53.99 | 45.78 | 39.35 | 34.24 | 30.14 | 26.80 | 24.06 | 21.79 | 19.87 | 11 |
| 12 | 77.36 | 63.85 | 53.48 | 45.43 | 39.10 | 34.07 | 30.02 | 26.72 | 24.00 | 21.74 | 19.84 | 12 |
| 13 | 76.26 | 63.10 | 52.96 | 45.07 | 38.85 | 33.89 | 29.89 | 26.63 | 23.94 | 21.69 | 19.80 | 13 |
| 14 | 75.16 | 62.34 | 52.44 | 44.71 | 38.60 | 33.71 | 29.76 | 26.53 | 23.87 | 21.64 | 19.77 | 14 |
| 15 | 74.06 | 61.58 | 51.91 | 44.34 | 38.34 | 33.53 | 29.63 | 26.44 | 23.80 | 21.59 | 19.73 | 15 |
| 16 | 72.97 | 60.82 | 51.38 | 43.97 | 38.07 | 33.34 | 29.49 | 26.34 | 23.73 | 21.54 | 19.69 | 16 |
| 17 | 71.88 | 60.06 | 50.85 | 43.59 | 37.80 | 33.15 | 29.36 | 26.24 | 23.65 | 21.48 | 19.65 | 17 |
| 18 | 70.79 | 59.30 | 50.31 | 43.21 | 37.53 | 32.95 | 29.21 | 26.14 | 23.57 | 21.43 | 19.60 | 18 |
| 19 | 69.70 | 58.53 | 49.77 | 42.82 | 37.25 | 32.75 | 29.07 | 26.03 | 23.50 | 21.37 | 19.56 | 19 |
| 20 | 68.61 | 57.76 | 49.22 | 42.42 | 36.97 | 32.54 | 28.91 | 25.92 | 23.41 | 21.30 | 19.51 | 20 |
| 21 | 67.52 | 56.98 | 48.66 | 42.02 | 36.68 | 32.33 | 28.76 | 25.80 | 23.33 | 21.24 | 19.46 | 21 |
| 22 | 66.43 | 56.20 | 48.10 | 41.62 | 36.38 | 32.11 | 28.60 | 25.68 | 23.23 | 21.17 | 19.41 | 22 |
| 23 | 65.34 | 55.42 | 47.53 | 41.20 | 36.08 | 31.89 | 28.43 | 25.55 | 23.14 | 21.10 | 19.36 | 23 |
| 24 | 64.25 | 54.63 | 46.96 | 40.78 | 35.77 | 31.66 | 28.26 | 25.42 | 23.04 | 21.02 | 19.30 | 24 |
| 25 | 63.16 | 53.84 | 46.38 | 40.36 | 35.45 | 31.42 | 28.08 | 25.29 | 22.94 | 20.94 | 19.24 | 25 |
| 26 | 62.08 | 53.05 | 45.79 | 39.92 | 35.13 | 31.18 | 27.90 | 25.15 | 22.83 | 20.86 | 19.17 | 26 |
| 27 | 60.99 | 52.25 | 45.20 | 39.48 | 34.80 | 30.93 | 27.71 | 25.01 | 22.72 | 20.78 | 19.10 | 27 |
| 28 | 59.91 | 51.45 | 44.61 | 39.04 | 34.46 | 30.67 | 27.51 | 24.86 | 22.61 | 20.69 | 19.03 | 28 |
| 29 | 58.83 | 50.64 | 44.01 | 38.58 | 34.12 | 30.41 | 27.31 | 24.70 | 22.49 | 20.59 | 18.96 | 29 |
| 30 | 57.74 | 49.83 | 43.40 | 38.12 | 33.77 | 30.15 | 27.11 | 24.54 | 22.36 | 20.49 | 18.88 | 30 |
| 31 | 56.56 | 49.02 | 42.78 | 37.66 | 33.41 | 29.87 | 26.89 | 24.38 | 22.23 | 20.39 | 18.80 | 31 |
| 32 | 55.58 | 48.20 | 42.16 | 37.18 | 33.05 | 29.59 | 26.68 | 24.21 | 22.10 | 20.28 | 18.71 | 32 |
| 33 | 54.50 | 47.38 | 41.54 | 36.70 | 32.68 | 29.30 | 26.45 | 24.03 | 21.96 | 20.17 | 18.63 | 33 |
| 34 | 53.43 | 46.56 | 40.91 | 36.22 | 32.30 | 29.01 | 26.22 | 23.85 | 21.81 | 20.06 | 18.53 | 34 |
| 35 | 52.35 | 45.74 | 40.27 | 35.73 | 31.92 | 28.71 | 25.98 | 23.66 | 21.66 | 19.93 | 18.43 | 35 |
| 36 | 51.28 | 44.91 | 39.63 | 35.22 | 31.52 | 28.40 | 25.74 | 23.46 | 21.50 | 19.81 | 18.33 | 36 |
| 37 | 50.21 | 44.08 | 38.98 | 34.72 | 31.13 | 28.08 | 25.49 | 23.26 | 21.34 | 19.67 | 18.22 | 37 |
| 38 | 49.14 | 43.25 | 38.33 | 34.20 | 30.72 | 27.76 | 25.23 | 23.05 | 21.17 | 19.54 | 18.11 | 38 |
| 39 | 48.07 | 42.41 | 37.67 | 33.68 | 30.30 | 27.43 | 24.96 | 22.84 | 21.00 | 19.39 | 17.99 | 39 |
| 40 | 47.01 | 41.58 | 37.01 | 33.16 | 29.89 | 27.09 | 24.69 | 22.61 | 20.82 | 19.25 | 17.87 | 40 |
| 41 | 45.95 | 40.74 | 36.35 | 32.63 | 29.46 | 26.74 | 24.41 | 22.39 | 20.63 | 19.09 | 17.74 | 41 |
| 42 | 44.90 | 39.90 | 35.68 | 32.09 | 29.02 | 26.39 | 24.12 | 22.15 | 20.44 | 18.93 | 17.61 | 42 |
| 43 | 43.85 | 39.06 | 35.00 | 31.55 | 28.59 | 26.04 | 23.83 | 21.91 | 20.24 | 18.77 | 17.47 | 43 |
| 44 | 42.80 | 38.22 | 34.33 | 31.00 | 28.14 | 25.67 | 23.53 | 21.66 | 20.03 | 18.59 | 17.33 | 44 |
| 45 | 41.77 | 37.39 | 33.65 | 30.45 | 27.69 | 25.30 | 23.23 | 21.41 | 19.82 | 18.42 | 17.18 | 45 |
| 46 | 40.74 | 36.55 | 32.97 | 29.90 | 27.24 | 24.93 | 22.92 | 21.15 | 19.61 | 18.24 | 17.03 | 46 |
| 47 | 39.71 | 35.72 | 32.29 | 29.34 | 26.77 | 24.55 | 22.60 | 20.89 | 19.38 | 18.05 | 16.87 | 47 |
| 48 | 38.70 | 34.89 | 31.61 | 28.77 | 26.31 | 24.16 | 22.28 | 20.62 | 19.16 | 17.86 | 16.70 | 48 |
| 49 | 37.69 | 34.06 | 30.93 | 28.21 | 25.84 | 23.77 | 21.95 | 20.34 | 18.92 | 17.66 | 16.53 | 49 |
| 50 | 36.69 | 33.23 | 30.24 | 27.64 | 25.36 | 23.37 | 21.61 | 20.06 | 18.68 | 17.46 | 16.36 | 50 |
| 51 | 35.69 | 32.41 | 29.56 | 27.07 | 24.88 | 22.96 | 21.27 | 19.77 | 18.44 | 17.25 | 16.18 | 51 |
| 52 | 34.70 | 31.59 | 28.87 | 26.49 | 24.40 | 22.55 | 20.92 | 19.47 | 18.18 | 17.03 | 15.99 | 52 |
| 53 | 33.71 | 30.76 | 28.17 | 25.90 | 23.90 | 22.13 | 20.56 | 19.17 | 17.92 | 16.80 | 15.80 | 53 |
| 54 | 32.73 | 29.93 | 27.47 | 25.31 | 23.39 | 21.70 | 20.19 | 18.85 | 17.64 | 16.56 | 15.59 | 54 |
| 55 | 31.74 | 29.09 | 26.76 | 24.70 | 22.88 | 21.26 | 19.81 | 18.52 | 17.36 | 16.32 | 15.38 | 55 |
| 56 | 30.75 | 28.25 | 26.05 | 24.09 | 22.36 | 20.81 | 19.42 | 18.18 | 17.07 | 16.06 | 15.15 | 56 |
| 57 | 29.77 | 27.42 | 25.33 | 23.48 | 21.82 | 20.35 | 19.03 | 17.84 | 16.77 | 15.80 | 14.92 | 57 |
| 58 | 28.80 | 26.58 | 24.61 | 22.86 | 21.29 | 19.88 | 18.62 | 17.48 | 16.46 | 15.52 | 14.68 | 58 |
| 59 | 27.83 | 25.75 | 23.89 | 22.23 | 20.75 | 19.41 | 18.21 | 17.12 | 16.14 | 15.24 | 14.43 | 59 |
| 60 | 26.88 | 24.93 | 23.18 | 21.61 | 20.20 | 18.94 | 17.79 | 16.76 | 15.81 | 14.96 | 14.18 | 60 |
| 61 | 25.94 | 24.11 | 22.47 | 20.99 | 19.66 | 18.46 | 17.37 | 16.38 | 15.49 | 14.67 | 13.92 | 61 |
| 62 | 25.02 | 23.30 | 21.76 | 20.37 | 19.11 | 17.98 | 16.95 | 16.01 | 15.15 | 14.37 | 13.65 | 62 |
| 63 | 24.10 | 22.49 | 21.05 | 19.75 | 18.56 | 17.49 | 16.51 | 15.62 | 14.81 | 14.06 | 13.38 | 63 |
| 64 | 23.18 | 21.69 | 20.34 | 19.12 | 18.01 | 17.00 | 16.07 | 15.23 | 14.46 | 13.75 | 13.10 | 64 |
| 65 | 22.28 | 20.89 | 19.63 | 18.49 | 17.45 | 16.50 | 15.63 | 14.83 | 14.10 | 13.42 | 12.80 | 65 |
| 66 | 21.38 | 20.09 | 18.92 | 17.85 | 16.88 | 15.99 | 15.17 | 14.42 | 13.73 | 13.09 | 12.50 | 66 |
| 67 | 20.48 | 19.29 | 18.20 | 17.21 | 16.30 | 15.47 | 14.70 | 13.99 | 13.34 | 12.74 | 12.18 | 67 |
| 68 | 19.58 | 18.48 | 17.47 | 16.55 | 15.71 | 14.93 | 14.22 | 13.55 | 12.94 | 12.38 | 11.85 | 68 |
| 69 | 18.66 | 17.66 | 16.73 | 15.88 | 15.10 | 14.38 | 13.71 | 13.10 | 12.52 | 11.99 | 11.50 | 69 |

*continued*

**Table 2 Multipliers for pecuniary loss for life (females) *continued***

| Age at date of trial | Multiplier calculated with allowance for projected mortality from the 2004-based population projections and rate of return of | | | | | | | | | | | Age at date of trial |
|---|---|---|---|---|---|---|---|---|---|---|---|---|
| | 0.0% | 0.5% | 1.0% | 1.5% | 2.0% | 2.5% | 3.0% | 3.5% | 4.0% | 4.5% | 5.0% | |
| 70 | 17.74 | 16.82 | 15.97 | 15.19 | 14.47 | 13.81 | 13.19 | 12.62 | 12.09 | 11.59 | 11.13 | 70 |
| 71 | 16.82 | 15.98 | 15.21 | 14.50 | 13.84 | 13.22 | 12.65 | 12.13 | 11.63 | 11.17 | 10.74 | 71 |
| 72 | 15.90 | 15.14 | 14.44 | 13.79 | 13.19 | 12.63 | 12.11 | 11.62 | 11.17 | 10.74 | 10.34 | 72 |
| 73 | 14.99 | 14.31 | 13.67 | 13.09 | 12.54 | 12.03 | 11.55 | 11.11 | 10.69 | 10.30 | 9.93 | 73 |
| 74 | 14.10 | 13.49 | 12.92 | 12.39 | 11.89 | 11.43 | 11.00 | 10.59 | 10.21 | 9.85 | 9.51 | 74 |
| 75 | 13.24 | 12.69 | 12.18 | 11.71 | 11.26 | 10.84 | 10.45 | 10.08 | 9.73 | 9.40 | 9.10 | 75 |
| 76 | 12.42 | 11.93 | 11.47 | 11.05 | 10.64 | 10.27 | 9.91 | 9.58 | 9.26 | 8.96 | 8.68 | 76 |
| 77 | 11.64 | 11.20 | 10.79 | 10.41 | 10.05 | 9.71 | 9.39 | 9.09 | 8.80 | 8.53 | 8.28 | 77 |
| 78 | 10.89 | 10.51 | 10.14 | 9.80 | 9.48 | 9.17 | 8.88 | 8.61 | 8.35 | 8.11 | 7.88 | 78 |
| 79 | 10.19 | 9.84 | 9.52 | 9.21 | 8.93 | 8.65 | 8.39 | 8.15 | 7.92 | 7.70 | 7.48 | 79 |
| 80 | 9.51 | 9.21 | 8.92 | 8.65 | 8.39 | 8.15 | 7.92 | 7.70 | 7.49 | 7.29 | 7.10 | 80 |
| 81 | 8.87 | 8.60 | 8.35 | 8.11 | 7.88 | 7.66 | 7.46 | 7.26 | 7.07 | 6.89 | 6.72 | 81 |
| 82 | 8.26 | 8.02 | 7.80 | 7.58 | 7.38 | 7.19 | 7.01 | 6.83 | 6.66 | 6.50 | 6.35 | 82 |
| 83 | 7.67 | 7.46 | 7.27 | 7.08 | 6.90 | 6.73 | 6.57 | 6.41 | 6.26 | 6.12 | 5.98 | 83 |
| 84 | 7.10 | 6.92 | 6.75 | 6.59 | 6.43 | 6.28 | 6.14 | 6.00 | 5.87 | 5.74 | 5.62 | 84 |
| 85 | 6.57 | 6.41 | 6.26 | 6.12 | 5.98 | 5.85 | 5.73 | 5.60 | 5.49 | 5.38 | 5.27 | 85 |
| 86 | 6.07 | 5.93 | 5.80 | 5.68 | 5.56 | 5.44 | 5.33 | 5.23 | 5.12 | 5.02 | 4.93 | 86 |
| 87 | 5.60 | 5.48 | 5.37 | 5.26 | 5.16 | 5.06 | 4.96 | 4.86 | 4.77 | 4.69 | 4.60 | 87 |
| 88 | 5.17 | 5.06 | 4.97 | 4.87 | 4.78 | 4.69 | 4.61 | 4.53 | 4.45 | 4.37 | 4.30 | 88 |
| 89 | 4.77 | 4.68 | 4.60 | 4.51 | 4.43 | 4.36 | 4.28 | 4.21 | 4.14 | 4.08 | 4.01 | 89 |
| 90 | 4.41 | 4.33 | 4.26 | 4.19 | 4.12 | 4.05 | 3.99 | 3.92 | 3.86 | 3.80 | 3.75 | 90 |
| 91 | 4.08 | 4.01 | 3.95 | 3.89 | 3.83 | 3.77 | 3.71 | 3.66 | 3.60 | 3.55 | 3.50 | 91 |
| 92 | 3.79 | 3.73 | 3.67 | 3.61 | 3.56 | 3.51 | 3.46 | 3.41 | 3.36 | 3.32 | 3.27 | 92 |
| 93 | 3.53 | 3.47 | 3.42 | 3.38 | 3.33 | 3.28 | 3.24 | 3.20 | 3.15 | 3.11 | 3.07 | 93 |
| 94 | 3.30 | 3.25 | 3.21 | 3.17 | 3.12 | 3.08 | 3.04 | 3.00 | 2.97 | 2.93 | 2.90 | 94 |
| 95 | 3.08 | 3.04 | 3.01 | 2.97 | 2.93 | 2.89 | 2.86 | 2.82 | 2.79 | 2.76 | 2.73 | 95 |
| 96 | 2.89 | 2.85 | 2.82 | 2.78 | 2.75 | 2.72 | 2.69 | 2.66 | 2.63 | 2.60 | 2.57 | 96 |
| 97 | 2.70 | 2.67 | 2.64 | 2.61 | 2.58 | 2.55 | 2.53 | 2.50 | 2.47 | 2.45 | 2.42 | 97 |
| 98 | 2.53 | 2.50 | 2.48 | 2.45 | 2.42 | 2.40 | 2.37 | 2.35 | 2.33 | 2.30 | 2.28 | 98 |
| 99 | 2.37 | 2.34 | 2.32 | 2.30 | 2.27 | 2.25 | 2.23 | 2.21 | 2.19 | 2.17 | 2.15 | 99 |
| 100 | 2.21 | 2.19 | 2.17 | 2.15 | 2.13 | 2.11 | 2.09 | 2.07 | 2.05 | 2.03 | 2.02 | 100 |

**Table 7 Multipliers for loss of earnings to pension age 60 (males)**

| Age at date of trial | Multiplier calculated with allowance for projected mortality from the 2004-based population projections and rate of return of | | | | | | | | | | | Age at date of trial |
|---|---|---|---|---|---|---|---|---|---|---|---|---|
| | 0.0% | 0.5% | 1.0% | 1.5% | 2.0% | 2.5% | 3.0% | 3.5% | 4.0% | 4.5% | 5.0% | |
| 16 | 43.07 | 38.71 | 34.96 | 31.70 | 28.87 | 26.41 | 24.25 | 22.35 | 20.68 | 19.20 | 17.89 | 16 |
| 17 | 42.07 | 37.90 | 34.30 | 31.17 | 28.44 | 26.05 | 23.96 | 22.12 | 20.49 | 19.04 | 17.76 | 17 |
| 18 | 41.07 | 37.10 | 33.64 | 30.63 | 28.00 | 25.70 | 23.67 | 21.88 | 20.29 | 18.88 | 17.63 | 18 |
| 19 | 40.08 | 36.29 | 32.98 | 30.10 | 27.56 | 25.34 | 23.37 | 21.63 | 20.09 | 18.72 | 17.49 | 19 |
| 20 | 39.10 | 35.48 | 32.32 | 29.55 | 27.12 | 24.97 | 23.07 | 21.38 | 19.88 | 18.55 | 17.35 | 20 |
| 21 | 38.11 | 34.67 | 31.65 | 29.00 | 26.66 | 24.59 | 22.76 | 21.12 | 19.67 | 18.37 | 17.20 | 21 |
| 22 | 37.12 | 33.85 | 30.98 | 28.44 | 26.19 | 24.20 | 22.43 | 20.85 | 19.44 | 18.18 | 17.04 | 22 |
| 23 | 36.14 | 33.03 | 30.29 | 27.87 | 25.72 | 23.81 | 22.10 | 20.58 | 19.21 | 17.98 | 16.88 | 23 |
| 24 | 35.15 | 32.21 | 29.60 | 27.29 | 25.23 | 23.40 | 21.76 | 20.29 | 18.97 | 17.78 | 16.71 | 24 |
| 25 | 34.16 | 31.38 | 28.91 | 26.70 | 24.74 | 22.98 | 21.41 | 19.99 | 18.72 | 17.56 | 16.52 | 25 |
| 26 | 33.18 | 30.55 | 28.20 | 26.11 | 24.23 | 22.55 | 21.04 | 19.68 | 18.45 | 17.34 | 16.33 | 26 |
| 27 | 32.19 | 29.71 | 27.49 | 25.50 | 23.72 | 22.12 | 20.67 | 19.36 | 18.18 | 17.11 | 16.13 | 27 |
| 28 | 31.21 | 28.87 | 26.78 | 24.89 | 23.20 | 21.67 | 20.29 | 19.04 | 17.90 | 16.87 | 15.93 | 28 |
| 29 | 30.23 | 28.03 | 26.05 | 24.27 | 22.67 | 21.21 | 19.89 | 18.70 | 17.61 | 16.61 | 15.71 | 29 |
| 30 | 29.24 | 27.18 | 25.33 | 23.65 | 22.12 | 20.74 | 19.49 | 18.35 | 17.30 | 16.35 | 15.48 | 30 |
| 31 | 28.26 | 26.33 | 24.59 | 23.01 | 21.57 | 20.26 | 19.07 | 17.98 | 16.99 | 16.08 | 15.24 | 31 |
| 32 | 27.28 | 25.48 | 23.85 | 22.36 | 21.01 | 19.77 | 18.64 | 17.61 | 16.66 | 15.79 | 14.99 | 32 |
| 33 | 26.30 | 24.63 | 23.10 | 21.71 | 20.43 | 19.27 | 18.20 | 17.22 | 16.32 | 15.49 | 14.72 | 33 |
| 34 | 25.32 | 23.77 | 22.34 | 21.04 | 19.85 | 18.76 | 17.75 | 16.82 | 15.97 | 15.18 | 14.45 | 34 |
| 35 | 24.34 | 22.90 | 21.58 | 20.37 | 19.26 | 18.23 | 17.28 | 16.41 | 15.60 | 14.85 | 14.16 | 35 |
| 36 | 23.36 | 22.03 | 20.81 | 19.69 | 18.65 | 17.69 | 16.80 | 15.98 | 15.22 | 14.51 | 13.86 | 36 |
| 37 | 22.39 | 21.16 | 20.04 | 18.99 | 18.03 | 17.14 | 16.31 | 15.54 | 14.82 | 14.16 | 13.54 | 37 |
| 38 | 21.41 | 20.29 | 19.25 | 18.29 | 17.40 | 16.57 | 15.80 | 15.08 | 14.41 | 13.79 | 13.21 | 38 |
| 39 | 20.43 | 19.41 | 18.46 | 17.58 | 16.76 | 15.99 | 15.28 | 14.61 | 13.99 | 13.40 | 12.86 | 39 |
| 40 | 19.45 | 18.53 | 17.66 | 16.85 | 16.10 | 15.40 | 14.74 | 14.12 | 13.54 | 13.00 | 12.49 | 40 |
| 41 | 18.48 | 17.64 | 16.86 | 16.12 | 15.43 | 14.79 | 14.18 | 13.62 | 13.08 | 12.58 | 12.11 | 41 |
| 42 | 17.50 | 16.75 | 16.04 | 15.38 | 14.75 | 14.17 | 13.62 | 13.10 | 12.61 | 12.14 | 11.71 | 42 |
| 43 | 16.53 | 15.86 | 15.22 | 14.63 | 14.06 | 13.53 | 13.03 | 12.56 | 12.11 | 11.69 | 11.29 | 43 |
| 44 | 15.56 | 14.96 | 14.40 | 13.86 | 13.36 | 12.88 | 12.43 | 12.00 | 11.60 | 11.21 | 10.85 | 44 |
| 45 | 14.59 | 14.06 | 13.56 | 13.09 | 12.64 | 12.22 | 11.81 | 11.43 | 11.06 | 10.72 | 10.39 | 45 |
| 46 | 13.62 | 13.16 | 12.72 | 12.31 | 11.91 | 11.54 | 11.18 | 10.84 | 10.51 | 10.20 | 9.90 | 46 |
| 47 | 12.65 | 12.26 | 11.88 | 11.52 | 11.17 | 10.84 | 10.53 | 10.23 | 9.94 | 9.66 | 9.40 | 47 |
| 48 | 11.69 | 11.35 | 11.02 | 10.71 | 10.42 | 10.13 | 9.86 | 9.60 | 9.34 | 9.10 | 8.87 | 48 |
| 49 | 10.72 | 10.44 | 10.16 | 9.90 | 9.65 | 9.40 | 9.17 | 8.95 | 8.73 | 8.52 | 8.32 | 49 |
| 50 | 9.76 | 9.52 | 9.30 | 9.08 | 8.86 | 8.66 | 8.46 | 8.27 | 8.09 | 7.91 | 7.74 | 50 |
| 51 | 8.80 | 8.61 | 8.42 | 8.24 | 8.07 | 7.90 | 7.73 | 7.58 | 7.42 | 7.28 | 7.13 | 51 |
| 52 | 7.83 | 7.68 | 7.53 | 7.39 | 7.25 | 7.11 | 6.98 | 6.86 | 6.73 | 6.61 | 6.50 | 52 |
| 53 | 6.87 | 6.75 | 6.63 | 6.52 | 6.41 | 6.31 | 6.21 | 6.11 | 6.01 | 5.92 | 5.82 | 53 |
| 54 | 5.90 | 5.81 | 5.72 | 5.64 | 5.56 | 5.48 | 5.41 | 5.33 | 5.26 | 5.19 | 5.12 | 54 |
| 55 | 4.92 | 4.86 | 4.80 | 4.75 | 4.69 | 4.63 | 4.58 | 4.53 | 4.47 | 4.42 | 4.37 | 55 |
| 56 | 3.95 | 3.91 | 3.87 | 3.83 | 3.80 | 3.76 | 3.72 | 3.69 | 3.65 | 3.62 | 3.59 | 56 |
| 57 | 2.97 | 2.95 | 2.92 | 2.90 | 2.88 | 2.86 | 2.84 | 2.82 | 2.80 | 2.78 | 2.76 | 57 |
| 58 | 1.98 | 1.97 | 1.96 | 1.96 | 1.95 | 1.94 | 1.93 | 1.92 | 1.91 | 1.90 | 1.89 | 58 |
| 59 | 1.00 | 0.99 | 0.99 | 0.99 | 0.99 | 0.98 | 0.98 | 0.98 | 0.98 | 0.97 | 0.97 | 59 |

all other tables - loss of earnings up to retirement age.

already take account of mortality etc.
courts can vary to review employability, disabilities, stability + so forth.
pg 225 (e)

**Table 8 Multipliers for loss of earnings to pension age 60 (females)**

| Age at date of trial | Multiplier calculated with allowance for projected mortality from the 2004-based population projections and rate of return of | | | | | | | | | | | Age at date of trial |
|---|---|---|---|---|---|---|---|---|---|---|---|---|
| | 0.0% | 0.5% | 1.0% | 1.5% | 2.0% | 2.5% | 3.0% | 3.5% | 4.0% | 4.5% | 5.0% | |
| 16 | 43.49 | 39.07 | 35.26 | 31.97 | 29.10 | 26.60 | 24.42 | 22.50 | 20.81 | 19.32 | 17.99 | 16 |
| 17 | 42.49 | 38.27 | 34.62 | 31.44 | 28.68 | 26.26 | 24.14 | 22.27 | 20.63 | 19.16 | 17.87 | 17 |
| 18 | 41.50 | 37.46 | 33.96 | 30.91 | 28.24 | 25.91 | 23.85 | 22.04 | 20.43 | 19.01 | 17.74 | 18 |
| 19 | 40.50 | 36.65 | 33.30 | 30.37 | 27.80 | 25.55 | 23.56 | 21.80 | 20.23 | 18.84 | 17.60 | 19 |
| 20 | 39.51 | 35.84 | 32.63 | 29.82 | 27.35 | 25.18 | 23.25 | 21.55 | 20.03 | 18.67 | 17.46 | 20 |
| 21 | 38.51 | 35.02 | 31.96 | 29.27 | 26.89 | 24.80 | 22.94 | 21.29 | 19.81 | 18.49 | 17.31 | 21 |
| 22 | 37.51 | 34.20 | 31.28 | 28.70 | 26.43 | 24.41 | 22.62 | 21.02 | 19.59 | 18.31 | 17.16 | 22 |
| 23 | 36.52 | 33.37 | 30.59 | 28.13 | 25.95 | 24.01 | 22.28 | 20.74 | 19.35 | 18.11 | 16.99 | 23 |
| 24 | 35.52 | 32.54 | 29.89 | 27.55 | 25.46 | 23.60 | 21.94 | 20.45 | 19.11 | 17.91 | 16.82 | 24 |
| 25 | 34.53 | 31.70 | 29.19 | 26.96 | 24.96 | 23.18 | 21.59 | 20.15 | 18.86 | 17.69 | 16.64 | 25 |
| 26 | 33.53 | 30.86 | 28.48 | 26.36 | 24.46 | 22.75 | 21.22 | 19.84 | 18.60 | 17.47 | 16.45 | 26 |
| 27 | 32.54 | 30.02 | 27.77 | 25.75 | 23.94 | 22.31 | 20.85 | 19.52 | 18.33 | 17.24 | 16.25 | 27 |
| 28 | 31.54 | 29.17 | 27.04 | 25.13 | 23.42 | 21.86 | 20.46 | 19.19 | 18.04 | 17.00 | 16.04 | 28 |
| 29 | 30.55 | 28.32 | 26.32 | 24.51 | 22.88 | 21.40 | 20.07 | 18.85 | 17.75 | 16.74 | 15.83 | 29 |
| 30 | 29.56 | 27.47 | 25.58 | 23.87 | 22.33 | 20.93 | 19.66 | 18.50 | 17.44 | 16.48 | 15.60 | 30 |
| 31 | 28.56 | 26.61 | 24.84 | 23.23 | 21.77 | 20.45 | 19.24 | 18.14 | 17.13 | 16.20 | 15.36 | 31 |
| 32 | 27.57 | 25.74 | 24.09 | 22.58 | 21.21 | 19.95 | 18.81 | 17.76 | 16.80 | 15.92 | 15.10 | 32 |
| 33 | 26.58 | 24.88 | 23.33 | 21.92 | 20.63 | 19.45 | 18.36 | 17.37 | 16.46 | 15.61 | 14.84 | 33 |
| 34 | 25.59 | 24.01 | 22.57 | 21.25 | 20.04 | 18.93 | 17.91 | 16.97 | 16.10 | 15.30 | 14.56 | 34 |
| 35 | 24.60 | 23.14 | 21.80 | 20.57 | 19.44 | 18.39 | 17.44 | 16.55 | 15.73 | 14.97 | 14.27 | 35 |
| 36 | 23.61 | 22.26 | 21.02 | 19.88 | 18.82 | 17.85 | 16.95 | 16.12 | 15.35 | 14.63 | 13.97 | 36 |
| 37 | 22.62 | 21.38 | 20.23 | 19.18 | 18.20 | 17.29 | 16.45 | 15.67 | 14.95 | 14.28 | 13.65 | 37 |
| 38 | 21.63 | 20.49 | 19.44 | 18.47 | 17.56 | 16.72 | 15.94 | 15.21 | 14.53 | 13.90 | 13.31 | 38 |
| 39 | 20.64 | 19.60 | 18.64 | 17.75 | 16.91 | 16.14 | 15.41 | 14.74 | 14.11 | 13.51 | 12.96 | 39 |
| 40 | 19.65 | 18.71 | 17.83 | 17.02 | 16.25 | 15.54 | 14.87 | 14.24 | 13.66 | 13.11 | 12.59 | 40 |
| 41 | 18.67 | 17.81 | 17.02 | 16.27 | 15.58 | 14.92 | 14.31 | 13.74 | 13.20 | 12.69 | 12.21 | 41 |
| 42 | 17.68 | 16.92 | 16.20 | 15.52 | 14.89 | 14.30 | 13.74 | 13.21 | 12.71 | 12.25 | 11.80 | 42 |
| 43 | 16.70 | 16.01 | 15.37 | 14.77 | 14.19 | 13.66 | 13.15 | 12.67 | 12.22 | 11.79 | 11.38 | 43 |
| 44 | 15.71 | 15.11 | 14.54 | 14.00 | 13.48 | 13.00 | 12.54 | 12.11 | 11.70 | 11.31 | 10.94 | 44 |
| 45 | 14.73 | 14.20 | 13.69 | 13.22 | 12.76 | 12.33 | 11.92 | 11.53 | 11.16 | 10.81 | 10.48 | 45 |
| 46 | 13.76 | 13.29 | 12.85 | 12.43 | 12.02 | 11.64 | 11.28 | 10.93 | 10.60 | 10.29 | 9.99 | 46 |
| 47 | 12.78 | 12.37 | 11.99 | 11.62 | 11.27 | 10.94 | 10.62 | 10.32 | 10.03 | 9.75 | 9.48 | 47 |
| 48 | 11.80 | 11.46 | 11.13 | 10.81 | 10.51 | 10.22 | 9.94 | 9.68 | 9.43 | 9.18 | 8.95 | 48 |
| 49 | 10.82 | 10.53 | 10.25 | 9.99 | 9.73 | 9.48 | 9.25 | 9.02 | 8.80 | 8.59 | 8.39 | 49 |
| 50 | 9.85 | 9.61 | 9.37 | 9.15 | 8.94 | 8.73 | 8.53 | 8.34 | 8.15 | 7.97 | 7.80 | 50 |
| 51 | 8.87 | 8.67 | 8.49 | 8.30 | 8.13 | 7.96 | 7.79 | 7.63 | 7.48 | 7.33 | 7.19 | 51 |
| 52 | 7.89 | 7.74 | 7.59 | 7.44 | 7.30 | 7.16 | 7.03 | 6.90 | 6.78 | 6.66 | 6.54 | 52 |
| 53 | 6.91 | 6.79 | 6.68 | 6.56 | 6.46 | 6.35 | 6.25 | 6.15 | 6.05 | 5.95 | 5.86 | 53 |
| 54 | 5.93 | 5.84 | 5.76 | 5.67 | 5.59 | 5.51 | 5.44 | 5.36 | 5.29 | 5.22 | 5.14 | 54 |
| 55 | 4.95 | 4.89 | 4.83 | 4.77 | 4.71 | 4.66 | 4.60 | 4.55 | 4.50 | 4.44 | 4.39 | 55 |
| 56 | 3.96 | 3.93 | 3.89 | 3.85 | 3.81 | 3.78 | 3.74 | 3.70 | 3.67 | 3.64 | 3.60 | 56 |
| 57 | 2.98 | 2.96 | 2.93 | 2.91 | 2.89 | 2.87 | 2.85 | 2.83 | 2.81 | 2.79 | 2.77 | 57 |
| 58 | 1.99 | 1.98 | 1.97 | 1.96 | 1.95 | 1.94 | 1.93 | 1.92 | 1.91 | 1.90 | 1.90 | 58 |
| 59 | 1.00 | 0.99 | 0.99 | 0.99 | 0.99 | 0.99 | 0.98 | 0.98 | 0.98 | 0.98 | 0.97 | 59 |

**Table 9 Multipliers for loss of earnings to pension age 65 (males)**

| Age at date of trial | 0.0% | 0.5% | 1.0% | 1.5% | 2.0% | 2.5% | 3.0% | 3.5% | 4.0% | 4.5% | 5.0% | Age at date of trial |
|---|---|---|---|---|---|---|---|---|---|---|---|---|
| | Multiplier calculated with allowance for projected mortality from the 2004-based population projections and rate of return of | | | | | | | | | | | |
| 16 | 47.63 | 42.33 | 37.83 | 33.99 | 30.69 | 27.86 | 25.40 | 23.27 | 21.42 | 19.79 | 18.36 | 16 |
| 17 | 46.62 | 41.54 | 37.20 | 33.49 | 30.29 | 27.54 | 25.15 | 23.07 | 21.25 | 19.66 | 18.26 | 17 |
| 18 | 45.63 | 40.75 | 36.57 | 32.98 | 29.89 | 27.22 | 24.89 | 22.86 | 21.09 | 19.53 | 18.15 | 18 |
| 19 | 44.64 | 39.96 | 35.94 | 32.48 | 29.49 | 26.89 | 24.63 | 22.66 | 20.92 | 19.39 | 18.04 | 19 |
| 20 | 43.65 | 39.16 | 35.31 | 31.97 | 29.08 | 26.56 | 24.37 | 22.44 | 20.74 | 19.25 | 17.92 | 20 |
| 21 | 42.66 | 38.37 | 34.66 | 31.45 | 28.66 | 26.23 | 24.09 | 22.22 | 20.56 | 19.10 | 17.80 | 21 |
| 22 | 41.67 | 37.57 | 34.02 | 30.93 | 28.24 | 25.88 | 23.81 | 21.99 | 20.37 | 18.95 | 17.67 | 22 |
| 23 | 40.69 | 36.77 | 33.36 | 30.40 | 27.80 | 25.52 | 23.52 | 21.75 | 20.18 | 18.78 | 17.54 | 23 |
| 24 | 39.70 | 35.96 | 32.70 | 29.86 | 27.36 | 25.16 | 23.22 | 21.50 | 19.97 | 18.62 | 17.40 | 24 |
| 25 | 38.71 | 35.15 | 32.04 | 29.31 | 26.90 | 24.78 | 22.91 | 21.24 | 19.76 | 18.44 | 17.25 | 25 |
| 26 | 37.72 | 34.33 | 31.36 | 28.75 | 26.44 | 24.40 | 22.59 | 20.98 | 19.54 | 18.25 | 17.10 | 26 |
| 27 | 36.73 | 33.51 | 30.68 | 28.18 | 25.97 | 24.01 | 22.26 | 20.71 | 19.31 | 18.06 | 16.94 | 27 |
| 28 | 35.75 | 32.69 | 30.00 | 27.61 | 25.49 | 23.61 | 21.93 | 20.42 | 19.08 | 17.86 | 16.77 | 28 |
| 29 | 34.76 | 31.87 | 29.31 | 27.03 | 25.01 | 23.20 | 21.58 | 20.13 | 18.83 | 17.66 | 16.60 | 29 |
| 30 | 33.78 | 31.04 | 28.61 | 26.45 | 24.51 | 22.78 | 21.23 | 19.83 | 18.57 | 17.44 | 16.41 | 30 |
| 31 | 32.80 | 30.21 | 27.91 | 25.85 | 24.01 | 22.35 | 20.86 | 19.52 | 18.31 | 17.21 | 16.22 | 31 |
| 32 | 31.82 | 29.38 | 27.20 | 25.25 | 23.49 | 21.91 | 20.49 | 19.20 | 18.04 | 16.98 | 16.02 | 32 |
| 33 | 30.84 | 28.54 | 26.49 | 24.63 | 22.97 | 21.46 | 20.10 | 18.87 | 17.75 | 16.73 | 15.80 | 33 |
| 34 | 29.86 | 27.70 | 25.76 | 24.01 | 22.43 | 21.00 | 19.71 | 18.53 | 17.45 | 16.48 | 15.58 | 34 |
| 35 | 28.88 | 26.86 | 25.04 | 23.39 | 21.89 | 20.53 | 19.30 | 18.17 | 17.15 | 16.21 | 15.35 | 35 |
| 36 | 27.90 | 26.01 | 24.30 | 22.75 | 21.34 | 20.05 | 18.88 | 17.81 | 16.83 | 15.93 | 15.11 | 36 |
| 37 | 26.93 | 25.16 | 23.56 | 22.10 | 20.77 | 19.56 | 18.45 | 17.43 | 16.50 | 15.64 | 14.85 | 37 |
| 38 | 25.95 | 24.31 | 22.81 | 21.45 | 20.20 | 19.05 | 18.00 | 17.04 | 16.16 | 15.34 | 14.59 | 38 |
| 39 | 24.98 | 23.45 | 22.06 | 20.78 | 19.61 | 18.54 | 17.55 | 16.64 | 15.80 | 15.02 | 14.31 | 39 |
| 40 | 24.00 | 22.59 | 21.30 | 20.11 | 19.02 | 18.01 | 17.08 | 16.22 | 15.43 | 14.70 | 14.01 | 40 |
| 41 | 23.03 | 21.73 | 20.53 | 19.43 | 18.41 | 17.47 | 16.60 | 15.79 | 15.05 | 14.35 | 13.71 | 41 |
| 42 | 22.06 | 20.86 | 19.76 | 18.74 | 17.79 | 16.92 | 16.10 | 15.35 | 14.65 | 14.00 | 13.39 | 42 |
| 43 | 21.09 | 19.99 | 18.98 | 18.04 | 17.16 | 16.35 | 15.60 | 14.89 | 14.24 | 13.62 | 13.05 | 43 |
| 44 | 20.12 | 19.12 | 18.19 | 17.33 | 16.52 | 15.77 | 15.07 | 14.42 | 13.81 | 13.24 | 12.70 | 44 |
| 45 | 19.16 | 18.25 | 17.40 | 16.61 | 15.88 | 15.19 | 14.54 | 13.94 | 13.37 | 12.84 | 12.34 | 45 |
| 46 | 18.20 | 17.38 | 16.61 | 15.89 | 15.22 | 14.58 | 13.99 | 13.44 | 12.91 | 12.42 | 11.96 | 46 |
| 47 | 17.24 | 16.50 | 15.81 | 15.16 | 14.55 | 13.97 | 13.43 | 12.92 | 12.44 | 11.99 | 11.56 | 47 |
| 48 | 16.29 | 15.63 | 15.00 | 14.42 | 13.87 | 13.35 | 12.86 | 12.39 | 11.95 | 11.54 | 11.15 | 48 |
| 49 | 15.33 | 14.75 | 14.20 | 13.67 | 13.18 | 12.71 | 12.27 | 11.85 | 11.45 | 11.07 | 10.71 | 49 |
| 50 | 14.39 | 13.87 | 13.38 | 12.92 | 12.48 | 12.06 | 11.66 | 11.29 | 10.93 | 10.59 | 10.26 | 50 |
| 51 | 13.44 | 12.99 | 12.56 | 12.15 | 11.76 | 11.40 | 11.04 | 10.71 | 10.39 | 10.08 | 9.79 | 51 |
| 52 | 12.49 | 12.10 | 11.73 | 11.38 | 11.04 | 10.71 | 10.41 | 10.11 | 9.83 | 9.56 | 9.30 | 52 |
| 53 | 11.55 | 11.21 | 10.89 | 10.59 | 10.30 | 10.02 | 9.75 | 9.49 | 9.24 | 9.01 | 8.78 | 53 |
| 54 | 10.60 | 10.32 | 10.05 | 9.79 | 9.54 | 9.30 | 9.07 | 8.85 | 8.63 | 8.43 | 8.23 | 54 |
| 55 | 9.65 | 9.41 | 9.19 | 8.97 | 8.76 | 8.56 | 8.37 | 8.18 | 8.00 | 7.83 | 7.66 | 55 |
| 56 | 8.69 | 8.50 | 8.32 | 8.14 | 7.97 | 7.81 | 7.65 | 7.49 | 7.34 | 7.20 | 7.06 | 56 |
| 57 | 7.74 | 7.59 | 7.44 | 7.30 | 7.16 | 7.03 | 6.90 | 6.78 | 6.66 | 6.54 | 6.42 | 57 |
| 58 | 6.78 | 6.67 | 6.56 | 6.45 | 6.34 | 6.24 | 6.14 | 6.04 | 5.94 | 5.85 | 5.76 | 58 |
| 59 | 5.83 | 5.74 | 5.66 | 5.58 | 5.50 | 5.42 | 5.35 | 5.27 | 5.20 | 5.13 | 5.06 | 59 |
| 60 | 4.87 | 4.81 | 4.75 | 4.70 | 4.64 | 4.59 | 4.53 | 4.48 | 4.43 | 4.38 | 4.33 | 60 |
| 61 | 3.91 | 3.87 | 3.84 | 3.80 | 3.76 | 3.73 | 3.69 | 3.66 | 3.62 | 3.59 | 3.56 | 61 |
| 62 | 2.95 | 2.93 | 2.90 | 2.88 | 2.86 | 2.84 | 2.82 | 2.80 | 2.78 | 2.76 | 2.74 | 62 |
| 63 | 1.98 | 1.97 | 1.96 | 1.95 | 1.94 | 1.93 | 1.92 | 1.91 | 1.90 | 1.89 | 1.88 | 63 |
| 64 | 0.99 | 0.99 | 0.99 | 0.99 | 0.98 | 0.98 | 0.98 | 0.98 | 0.97 | 0.97 | 0.97 | 64 |

**Table 10 Multipliers for loss of earnings to pension age 65 (females)**

| Age at date of trial | Multiplier calculated with allowance for projected mortality from the 2004-based population projections and rate of return of | | | | | | | | | | | Age at date of trial |
|---|---|---|---|---|---|---|---|---|---|---|---|---|
| | 0.0% | 0.5% | 1.0% | 1.5% | 2.0% | 2.5% | 3.0% | 3.5% | 4.0% | 4.5% | 5.0% | |
| 16 | 48.22 | 42.83 | 38.24 | 34.34 | 30.99 | 28.11 | 25.62 | 23.46 | 21.58 | 19.93 | 18.48 | 16 |
| 17 | 47.22 | 42.04 | 37.62 | 33.84 | 30.60 | 27.80 | 25.37 | 23.26 | 21.42 | 19.80 | 18.38 | 17 |
| 18 | 46.22 | 41.25 | 37.00 | 33.35 | 30.20 | 27.48 | 25.12 | 23.06 | 21.26 | 19.68 | 18.28 | 18 |
| 19 | 45.23 | 40.46 | 36.37 | 32.84 | 29.80 | 27.16 | 24.86 | 22.86 | 21.09 | 19.54 | 18.17 | 19 |
| 20 | 44.23 | 39.66 | 35.73 | 32.33 | 29.39 | 26.83 | 24.60 | 22.64 | 20.92 | 19.40 | 18.06 | 20 |
| 21 | 43.23 | 38.86 | 35.08 | 31.81 | 28.97 | 26.49 | 24.32 | 22.42 | 20.74 | 19.26 | 17.94 | 21 |
| 22 | 42.23 | 38.05 | 34.43 | 31.29 | 28.54 | 26.15 | 24.04 | 22.19 | 20.55 | 19.10 | 17.81 | 22 |
| 23 | 41.24 | 37.24 | 33.77 | 30.75 | 28.11 | 25.79 | 23.75 | 21.95 | 20.36 | 18.94 | 17.68 | 23 |
| 24 | 40.24 | 36.43 | 33.11 | 30.21 | 27.66 | 25.43 | 23.45 | 21.71 | 20.16 | 18.78 | 17.54 | 24 |
| 25 | 39.24 | 35.61 | 32.44 | 29.66 | 27.21 | 25.05 | 23.14 | 21.45 | 19.95 | 18.60 | 17.40 | 25 |
| 26 | 38.25 | 34.79 | 31.76 | 29.10 | 26.75 | 24.67 | 22.83 | 21.19 | 19.73 | 18.42 | 17.25 | 26 |
| 27 | 37.25 | 33.97 | 31.08 | 28.53 | 26.28 | 24.28 | 22.50 | 20.92 | 19.50 | 18.23 | 17.09 | 27 |
| 28 | 36.25 | 33.14 | 30.39 | 27.95 | 25.80 | 23.88 | 22.16 | 20.63 | 19.26 | 18.03 | 16.92 | 28 |
| 29 | 35.26 | 32.31 | 29.69 | 27.37 | 25.31 | 23.46 | 21.82 | 20.34 | 19.02 | 17.82 | 16.75 | 29 |
| 30 | 34.26 | 31.47 | 28.99 | 26.78 | 24.81 | 23.04 | 21.46 | 20.04 | 18.76 | 17.61 | 16.56 | 30 |
| 31 | 33.27 | 30.63 | 28.28 | 26.18 | 24.30 | 22.61 | 21.10 | 19.73 | 18.50 | 17.38 | 16.37 | 31 |
| 32 | 32.28 | 29.79 | 27.56 | 25.57 | 23.78 | 22.17 | 20.72 | 19.41 | 18.22 | 17.15 | 16.17 | 32 |
| 33 | 31.28 | 28.94 | 26.84 | 24.95 | 23.25 | 21.72 | 20.33 | 19.08 | 17.94 | 16.90 | 15.96 | 33 |
| 34 | 30.29 | 28.09 | 26.11 | 24.33 | 22.71 | 21.26 | 19.93 | 18.73 | 17.64 | 16.65 | 15.74 | 34 |
| 35 | 29.30 | 27.24 | 25.38 | 23.69 | 22.17 | 20.78 | 19.52 | 18.38 | 17.33 | 16.38 | 15.51 | 35 |
| 36 | 28.31 | 26.38 | 24.63 | 23.05 | 21.61 | 20.30 | 19.10 | 18.01 | 17.01 | 16.10 | 15.26 | 36 |
| 37 | 27.32 | 25.52 | 23.88 | 22.39 | 21.04 | 19.80 | 18.67 | 17.63 | 16.68 | 15.81 | 15.01 | 37 |
| 38 | 26.33 | 24.66 | 23.13 | 21.73 | 20.46 | 19.29 | 18.22 | 17.24 | 16.34 | 15.51 | 14.74 | 38 |
| 39 | 25.34 | 23.79 | 22.36 | 21.06 | 19.87 | 18.77 | 17.76 | 16.84 | 15.98 | 15.19 | 14.46 | 39 |
| 40 | 24.36 | 22.92 | 21.60 | 20.38 | 19.27 | 18.24 | 17.29 | 16.42 | 15.61 | 14.86 | 14.17 | 40 |
| 41 | 23.37 | 22.04 | 20.82 | 19.69 | 18.66 | 17.70 | 16.81 | 15.99 | 15.23 | 14.52 | 13.86 | 41 |
| 42 | 22.39 | 21.17 | 20.04 | 19.00 | 18.03 | 17.14 | 16.31 | 15.54 | 14.83 | 14.16 | 13.54 | 42 |
| 43 | 21.41 | 20.29 | 19.25 | 18.29 | 17.40 | 16.57 | 15.80 | 15.08 | 14.41 | 13.79 | 13.21 | 43 |
| 44 | 20.43 | 19.41 | 18.46 | 17.58 | 16.76 | 15.99 | 15.28 | 14.61 | 13.99 | 13.40 | 12.86 | 44 |
| 45 | 19.45 | 18.53 | 17.66 | 16.85 | 16.10 | 15.40 | 14.74 | 14.12 | 13.54 | 13.00 | 12.49 | 45 |
| 46 | 18.48 | 17.64 | 16.86 | 16.12 | 15.43 | 14.79 | 14.19 | 13.62 | 13.08 | 12.58 | 12.11 | 46 |
| 47 | 17.51 | 16.75 | 16.05 | 15.38 | 14.76 | 14.17 | 13.62 | 13.10 | 12.61 | 12.15 | 11.71 | 47 |
| 48 | 16.54 | 15.86 | 15.23 | 14.63 | 14.07 | 13.54 | 13.04 | 12.56 | 12.11 | 11.69 | 11.29 | 48 |
| 49 | 15.57 | 14.97 | 14.41 | 13.87 | 13.37 | 12.89 | 12.44 | 12.01 | 11.60 | 11.22 | 10.85 | 49 |
| 50 | 14.60 | 14.07 | 13.57 | 13.10 | 12.65 | 12.23 | 11.82 | 11.44 | 11.07 | 10.73 | 10.39 | 50 |
| 51 | 13.64 | 13.17 | 12.74 | 12.32 | 11.93 | 11.55 | 11.19 | 10.85 | 10.52 | 10.21 | 9.91 | 51 |
| 52 | 12.67 | 12.27 | 11.89 | 11.53 | 11.18 | 10.85 | 10.54 | 10.24 | 9.95 | 9.67 | 9.41 | 52 |
| 53 | 11.70 | 11.36 | 11.04 | 10.73 | 10.43 | 10.14 | 9.87 | 9.61 | 9.35 | 9.11 | 8.88 | 53 |
| 54 | 10.73 | 10.45 | 10.17 | 9.91 | 9.66 | 9.41 | 9.18 | 8.95 | 8.74 | 8.53 | 8.33 | 54 |
| 55 | 9.77 | 9.53 | 9.30 | 9.08 | 8.87 | 8.66 | 8.47 | 8.28 | 8.09 | 7.92 | 7.74 | 55 |
| 56 | 8.80 | 8.61 | 8.42 | 8.24 | 8.06 | 7.90 | 7.73 | 7.58 | 7.42 | 7.28 | 7.13 | 56 |
| 57 | 7.83 | 7.68 | 7.53 | 7.38 | 7.25 | 7.11 | 6.98 | 6.85 | 6.73 | 6.61 | 6.49 | 57 |
| 58 | 6.86 | 6.74 | 6.63 | 6.52 | 6.41 | 6.30 | 6.20 | 6.10 | 6.01 | 5.91 | 5.82 | 58 |
| 59 | 5.89 | 5.80 | 5.72 | 5.64 | 5.56 | 5.48 | 5.40 | 5.33 | 5.25 | 5.18 | 5.11 | 59 |
| 60 | 4.92 | 4.86 | 4.80 | 4.74 | 4.68 | 4.63 | 4.57 | 4.52 | 4.47 | 4.42 | 4.37 | 60 |
| 61 | 3.94 | 3.91 | 3.87 | 3.83 | 3.79 | 3.76 | 3.72 | 3.69 | 3.65 | 3.62 | 3.59 | 61 |
| 62 | 2.97 | 2.94 | 2.92 | 2.90 | 2.88 | 2.86 | 2.84 | 2.82 | 2.80 | 2.78 | 2.76 | 62 |
| 63 | 1.98 | 1.97 | 1.96 | 1.96 | 1.95 | 1.94 | 1.93 | 1.92 | 1.91 | 1.90 | 1.89 | 63 |
| 64 | 1.00 | 0.99 | 0.99 | 0.99 | 0.99 | 0.98 | 0.98 | 0.98 | 0.98 | 0.97 | 0.97 | 64 |

# Index